Contents

Donald Judd Interviews

Foreword
Rainer Judd

Judd Foundation stewards the work of Donald Judd: physical, in the form of his art, architecture, and furniture; and intellectual, in his thinking and writing. This is manifest in the holdings of the Judd Foundation Archives.

Judd constituted the physical work of the Foundation in the preservation of his permanently installed spaces in Marfa, Texas, and New York. The Foundation is committed to processing and publishing our archival records and creating new tools to enable research and understanding of Judd's work. A recent culmination of this work was *Donald Judd Writings*, the most comprehensive collection of Judd's writing to date, published in 2016. This companion volume, *Donald Judd Interviews*, allows us to hear Judd speak about his work in the company of contemporaries, articulating his position in relation to others and heightening our sense of his individual ideas and interests.

We are grateful to many individuals and organizations for their support in the production of this title, and we would like to thank editors Flavin Judd and Caitlin Murray of Judd Foundation. We are indebted to the interviewers and participants whose thoughtful questions and statements occasioned Judd's responses. And we thank David Zwirner Books, our publishing partner, for their dedication to the project and for recognizing the importance of these interviews.

Introduction
Caitlin Murray

Donald Judd wrote in 1986, "I leapt into this world an empiricist."
He also, as he emphasized a few years later, was "skeptical of the
accumulated judgment and the long and superior view." Deeply
concerned with the falsification of history, he took to writing
and talking as corrective measures. Spanning the artist's career,
Donald Judd Interviews, though diverse in content and style, dem-
onstrates the consistency of Judd's thinking and the importance
he placed on speaking clearly, precisely, and without assumption about the qualities of his own work and the work of others. As Amy Goldin noted in the preface to a 1967 conversation
with Judd, "He is always careful to present his ideas as personal
observations and private preferences. Yet everything he said was
remarkably serious and unwhimsical – intellectually he is not at
all playful or self-indulgent. His reluctance to interpret his artistic judgments as binding anyone else to his conclusions, I finally
decided, is a matter of principle."

Talking – giving interviews, participating in symposia, lec-
turing, appearing in films and on television – served as a way
for Judd to defend his work. Yet his participation in such activities was not undertaken without a great deal of doubt and de-
liberation. As Judd said in a 1968 interview with Lucy R. Lippard,
"Apropos of interviews, I do all the talking, and nobody else sits
down and thinks about the work, and I'm sort of beginning to
resent explaining it myself." A decade later, when asked by a student from Marfa Junior High School, "Why don't you like people interviewing you?" Judd replied, "I think that the person
looking at the work should think about it and figure it out for
themselves and not ask me, 'Why?' Because I'm doing it, and
that's enough, I think." Judd's reluctance to provide simple explanations for complex ideas was anathema to the conventional
interview, which often relies on the transformation of thoughts
into quickly distilled statements. When asked by Mark di Suvero
during a 1967 panel discussion to provide a general explanation
of his own work, Judd responded, "What you want is a simple
explanation. Obviously, nobody can give that or paraphrase. So

that's why I don't want to answer." Throughout this volume, Judd refuses to yield simple explanations, instead providing measured and thoughtful answers to art historians, critics, curators, journalists, eighth-grade reporters, and artists alike. As a companion to *Donald Judd Writings*, an extensive selection of his published and unpublished writings compiled by Judd Foundation in 2016, *Donald Judd Interviews* extends our understanding of Judd's thinking on art, architecture, politics, and the environment, grounding these thoughts in concrete discussions of the pragmatic concerns of making and exhibiting work.

This volume presents a significant and varied selection of conversations with Judd from 1964 through 1993, many of which are being published for the first time. These conversations were produced in and for a wide range of formats, such as panel discussions, one-on-one interviews, symposia, television episodes, newspaper and magazine articles, films, and radio programs. The material is arranged chronologically; when a previously published conversation yielded two possible dates by which it could be indexed – the date of its initial spoken encounter (known for some, but not all, previously published material) and the date of its first publication – we have used the former. Introductions, which provide contextual information about Judd's activities at the time, accompany each text. Though this information does not always directly relate to the conversation it precedes, the intention is that it will help situate the interview in the overall shape of Judd's life and work.

The breadth of the selected interviews is the result of research in dozens of archives and repositories and also reflects the deep holdings of the Judd Foundation Archives. All attempts were made to work from audio or video documentation, although for many published articles, this material was no longer extant. The Judd Foundation Archives include published and unpublished writings by Judd; correspondence; interview and panel transcripts; photographs; moving image and audio material; drawings; exhibition and work files; and publications. Without this archive, *Donald Judd Writings* and *Donald Judd Interviews* would not have been possible.

Due to the immense quantity of material from which to select, not all interviews and discussions in which Judd participated are included in this volume. Many of the conversations within have been edited for clarity, with an effort made to maintain them in their whole when possible. All have been adjusted for consistency in spelling, punctuation, and style.

For their knowledge and expertise, we thank Barbara Castelli, Jamie Dearing, Julie Finch, Rutger Fuchs, Hans Haacke, John Jerome, Tim Johnson, Jack Macrae, Susanne Maurer, David Tompkins, and Kit Schluter.

For their tireless work on this project, we owe an enormous debt of gratitude to Richard Griggs, Ellie Meyer, Andrea Walsh, Katherine Stephens, Michael Dyer, Doro Globus, Lucas Zwirner, Jules Thomson, Anne Wehr, Anna Drozda, and Clare Fentress, as well as to Adrian Kohn for his incredible help in tracking down many previously unknown interviews.

During his lifetime, Judd compiled four major collections of his writings; a new collection, *Donald Judd Writings*, edited by Flavin Judd and Caitlin Murray, was compiled by Judd Foundation in 2016. In lieu of repeating lengthy citations within this volume, these collections are referred to by their titles only.

Donald Judd: Complete Writings 1959–1975
Includes the majority of Judd's gallery reviews, written as work for hire, as well as book reviews, articles, letters to the editor, reports, statements, and essays.

First published in 1975 in Halifax, Nova Scotia, by The Press of the Nova Scotia College of Art and Design and New York University Press and reprinted in 2005. Reprinted in 2015 by Judd Foundation.

Donald Judd: Complete Writings 1975–1986
Includes eighteen essays, many unpublished. All of these essays are included in *Donald Judd Writings*.

First published in 1987 in Eindhoven, The Netherlands, by the Van Abbemuseum.

Donald Judd: Architektur
Includes thirty-seven essays in German and English. A selection of these essays is included in *Donald Judd Writings*.

First published in 1989 in Münster, Germany, by the Westfälischer Kunstverein.

Donald Judd: Écrits 1963–1990
Includes thirty-six essays in French only. All of these essays are included in *Donald Judd Writings*.

First published in 1991 in Paris by Daniel Lelong éditeur.

Donald Judd Writings
Includes a comprehensive selection of essays, reviews, statements, letters, and previously unpublished notes that spans from 1958 to 1993.

First published in 2016 in New York by Judd Foundation and David Zwirner Books and reprinted in 2017.

Guide to Locations

302 and 304 East Twenty-Seventh Street: In 1953, Judd moved from the home of his parents, Roy and Effie Judd, in Westwood, New Jersey, to New York City, and subsequently to a railroad apartment on the first floor of 302 East Twenty-Seventh Street. He later moved to a second-floor railroad apartment at 304 East Twenty-Seventh Street.

326 East Eighty-Fifth Street: From August 1958 until August 1960, Judd lived at 326 East Eighty-Fifth Street, on New York's Upper East Side.

53 East Nineteenth Street: In August 1960, Judd moved to a loft on the top floor of 53 East Nineteenth Street, in New York's Flat-iron District, an address at which he lived and worked for nine years. In June 1962, he began renting the building's second-floor loft as well, which he used as a studio.

Eichholteren: Eichholteren is a former hotel located on Lake Lucerne near Küssnacht am Rigi, Switzerland. Judd used it as a residence and studio beginning in 1987. He began renovation of the original 1943 structure in 1989, working step by step, from the top story to the bottom, until 1993, when the project was completed. Judd did not own the building and it was sold shortly after his death in 1994.

Hafenstrasse: Judd used Hafenstrasse, a former brewery named after the road on which it was located, as a residence and studio in Cologne in the early 1990s.

In 1978, Judd partnered with Dia Art Foundation, who purchased Fort D. A. Russell and the Wool and Mohair Building in downtown Marfa, Texas, for the permanent installation of Judd's work and that of his contemporaries. After a separation with Dia in 1986, Judd realized this project as the Chinati Foundation/La Fundación Chinati and opened it to the public that same year. In addition to his own pieces, work by Ingólfur Arnarsson, John Chamberlain, Dan Flavin, Roni Horn, Ilya Kabakov, Richard Long, Claes Oldenburg and Coosje van Bruggen, and David Rabinowitch was permanently installed at Chinati. Following Judd's death in 1994, the foundation added permanent installations by Carl Andre, Robert Irwin, and John Wesley. In addition to the buildings below, Chinati also includes a number of former army barracks, some of which were converted by Judd into spaces for art. See Judd's "Statement for the Chinati Foundation/ La Fundación Chinati" (1987) in *Donald Judd Writings*, 484–89.

Arena: The Arena, a large former military gymnasium and equestrian facility located on the original grounds of Fort D. A. Russell, was reworked by Judd as a space for art and living.

Artillery Sheds: These two former artillery sheds located on the original grounds of Fort D. A. Russell were reworked by Judd to permanently house his 100 untitled works in mill aluminum (1982–86). See "Artillery Sheds" (1989) in *Donald Judd: Architektur*, 68–74.

Chamberlain Building: The Chamberlain Building, the former Wool and Mohair Building in downtown Marfa, houses the permanent installation of twenty-two of John Chamberlain's sculptures in painted and chromium-plated steel dating from 1972 to 1983. The building was architecturally adapted by Judd and the work installed by Chamberlain and Judd. See "Chamberlain Building" (1989) in *Donald Judd: Architektur*, 75–79.

In 1977, Judd established the idea of Judd Foundation, an organization founded to preserve his art, living and working spaces, libraries, and archives in New York and Marfa. See "Judd Foundation" (1977) in *Donald Judd Writings*, 284–86.

101 Spring Street: Judd purchased this five-story cast-iron building, located at the corner of Spring and Mercer Streets in the SoHo neighborhood of New York, in November 1968. He used the building as a home and studio beginning in July 1969. See "101 Spring Street" (1989) in *Donald Judd Writings*, 584–87.

La Mansana de Chinati: In 1973, Judd purchased the first three-quarters of this complex of buildings located in downtown Marfa. Referred to informally as "the Block," it encompasses a full city block and includes two large hangars where Judd installed his art. He acquired the rest of the Block, which includes a two-story house that served as his Marfa residence, in 1974. In addition, he built an office, bathrooms, a pool, an outdoor artwork, gardens, greenhouses, a chicken coop, a pergola, and a shed. See "La Mansana de Chinati" (1989) in *Donald Judd Writings*, 588–91.

Architecture Studio: Judd purchased the former Marfa National Bank building, located on Highland Avenue in downtown Marfa, in 1989. He renovated this building over a six-month period to create a space to work on architecture and design. The building contains early paintings and drawings by Judd, as well as furniture he designed and plans for architectural projects, which are installed throughout its two stories and more than fifteen rooms. Judd placed furniture and paintings by twentieth-century designers and artists in the Architecture Studio, including work by Alvar Aalto, Josef Albers, Ludwig Mies van der Rohe, Gerrit Rietveld, and Theo van Doesburg.

Cobb House and Whyte Building: Judd purchased these buildings on Oak Street in downtown Marfa in 1989 and renovated them for the installation of his paintings. The Cobb House includes paintings from 1956 to 1958; the Whyte Building contains paintings from 1960 to 1962.

Architecture Office: In January 1990, Judd purchased the Glascock building, located on Highland Avenue in downtown Marfa. The 1907 building was originally a store and later housed various commercial businesses. Judd renovated the street level of this two-story structure for use as his Architecture Office. The building contains furniture and prototypes designed by Judd, as well as plans and models of his architectural projects, including the Peter Merian Haus and Eichholteren.

Art Studio: In 1990, Judd purchased a former Safeway grocery store located on Oak Street in downtown Marfa. He converted this building into a studio, with long worktables and shelving for prototypes, material samples, and artworks in a variety of states.

Porter House: In 1990, Judd purchased the Porter House, located on Columbia Street in Marfa, and turned it into a space specially dedicated to writing. It was originally built by the family of the writer Katherine Anne Porter.

Ranch Office: In 1991, Judd purchased the Ranch Office, a former general store, located on Highland Avenue in downtown Marfa. Judd renovated the ground floor to house his wall reliefs and floor works, along with maps of his ranches south of Marfa.

Print Building: In 1991, Judd purchased the Print Building – previously home to a bank, a post office, and the Crews Hotel, located on Highland Avenue in downtown Marfa – with the intention of installing twenty-eight rooms on the top floor with the complete collection of his prints spanning from 1951 to 1994, which he had earlier set aside for such a display. He installed two large works in anodized aluminum on the ground floor from his exhibition at the Staatliche Kunsthalle Baden-Baden, Germany (August 27–October 15, 1989). Today, the building houses Judd Foundation offices, a conservation studio, and the Judd Foundation Archives.

Ayala de Chinati

Two ranches comprise Ayala de Chinati, Judd's 33,000-acre ranch south of Marfa, near the US-Mexico border. Judd purchased this land overlooking the Rio Grande beginning in 1976, along with its ranch houses: Casa Morales, Casa Perez, and Las Casas. See "Ayala de Chinati" (1989) in *Donald Judd Writings*, 592–94.

Casa Morales: Casa Morales, a two-bedroom rock house with a *tiendita* – a pantry and utility space – and a rock tank, was originally constructed in the 1920s. It is located at the base of the Chinati Mountains.

Casa Perez: Casa Perez is an adobe house built in the early 1900s, with structures for shade, bathing, and storage. It is located on the former Morales Ranch and was previously the main house of a goat ranch.

Las Casas: Las Casas ranch has two houses, a studio, a bunkhouse, lava rock corrals, and concentric circles of stone for a garden and tank.

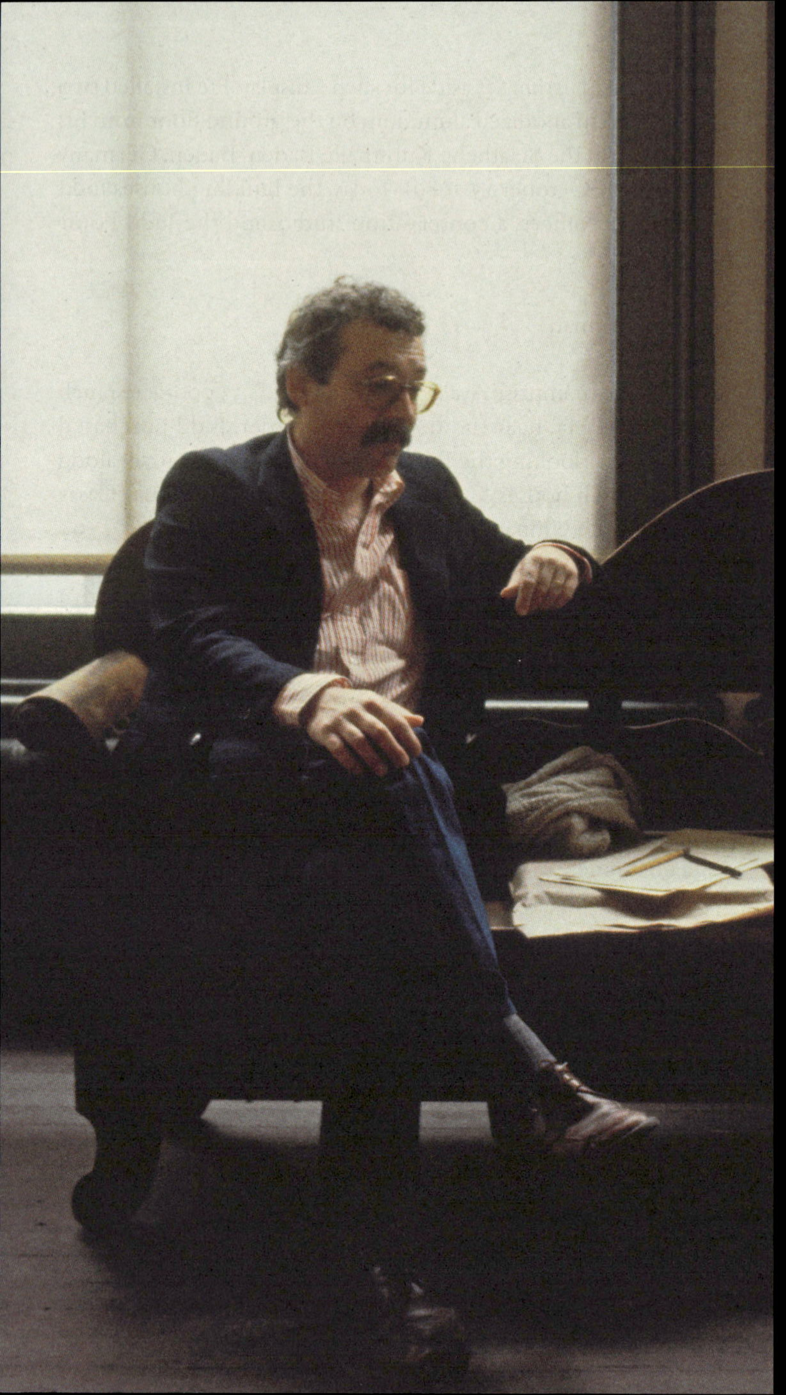

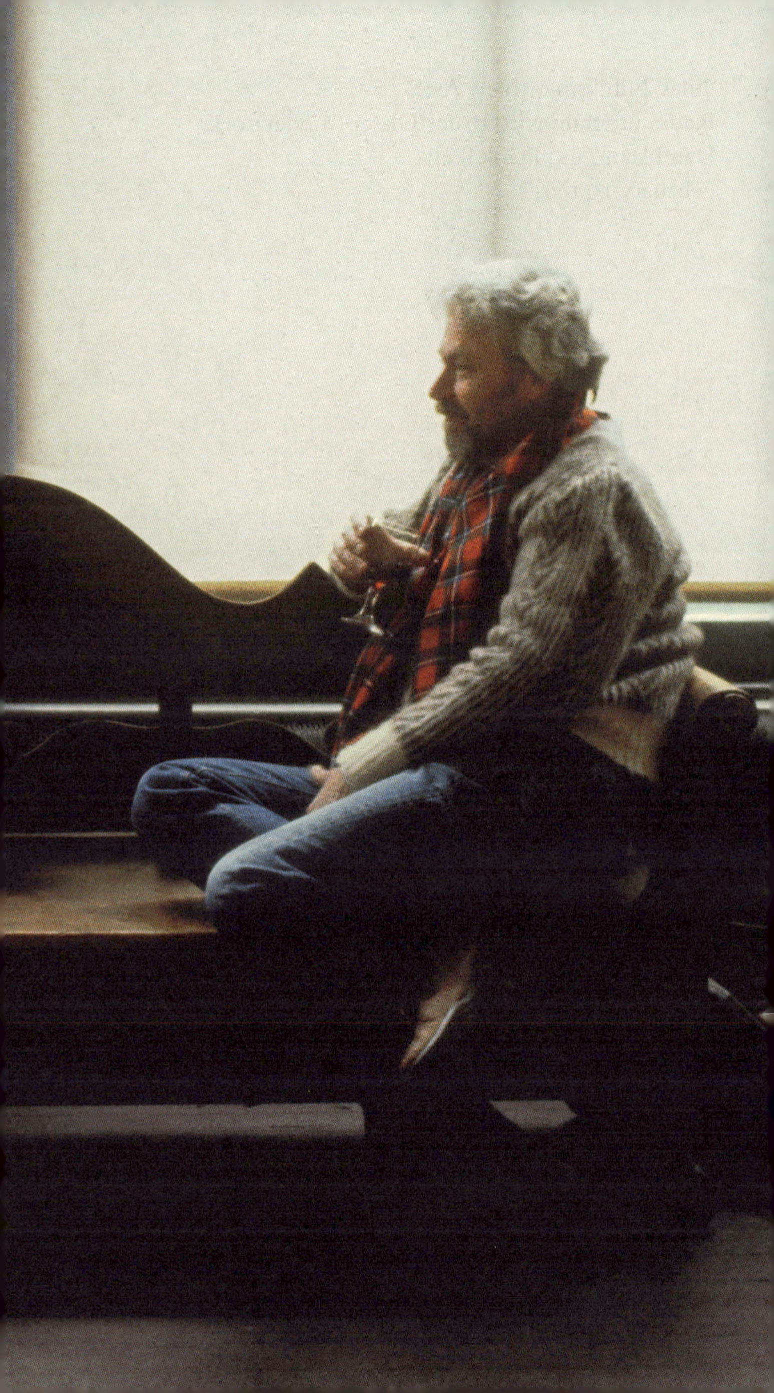

"New Nihilism or New Art?"
Radio program with Bruce Glaser (moderator),
Dan Flavin, and Frank Stella
February 15, 1964

"New Nihilism or New Art?" was one in a series of radio programs involving artists of the 1960s hosted and produced by art historian Bruce Glaser for WBAI-FM,
New York. Shortly before this interview was conducted, Judd had his first solo
exhibition to include work in three dimensions: *Don Judd*, at Richard Bellamy's
Green Gallery, New York (December 17, 1963–January 11, 1964).

Judd and Dan Flavin became friends in 1962. They first exhibited together
a year later, when their work was included in *New Work: Part I* at Green Gallery
(January 8–February 2, 1963). Judd also exhibited with Frank Stella for the first
time that same year, at Green Gallery's *Contemporary American Group Show [New
Work Part III]* (May–June 15, 1963). Works by both Flavin and Stella were later installed by Judd at 101 Spring Street and La Mansana de Chinati/The Block.

After airing on WBAI-FM, this interview was edited by art critic Lucy R. Lippard
for publication in *ARTnews*, at which point Flavin's contributions were removed
at his request. The full discussion, including Flavin's remarks, is printed here with
permission from the Estate of Dan Flavin.

BG [Bruce Glaser] Recently we've been hearing a lot of talk about the evolution of a new abstraction, which as yet hasn't been given any name. Some of this work has been seen around in exhibitions, such as at the Sidney Janis Gallery, in a show that's entitled *The Classic Spirit in 20th Century Art*.[1] This suggests that the evolution of this abstraction perhaps goes back to the early years of the twentieth century, and that you can find precedents for it in Malevich and Mondrian, and perhaps other constructivists or neoplasticists. Our guests tonight, Dan Flavin, Don Judd, and Frank Stella, seem to come under this category of the so-called classic spirit. I'm not sure if the term is accurate, but for want of another term, perhaps we can use that temporarily. Other terms have been applied to your kind of work; I understand that there has been an editorial letter that appeared in a magazine just recently that referred to this time, while all this work is going on, as "the time of the white surface."[2] And there are two other exhibitions that have been put on to illuminate some points about this style of art: an exhibition at the Wadsworth Atheneum, in Connecticut, and the Jewish Museum, here in New York, which recently closed an exhibition entitled *Black and White*.[3] The show up in Hartford was called *Black, White and Grey*.[4]

To give a simple description of this work, the morphology of it may be loosely categorized as extremely simple, sometimes with a colored surface of one hue, and when there is a design it's often symmetrical, or repeated, or both, but it's exceedingly spare. To many people, these works seem to offer a minimal plastic effect. Now, some of the older generation of American painters who have been an inspiration for the younger painters who work in this direction are Josef Albers, Barnett Newman, and Ad Reinhardt. Other artists who do this sort of thing, if you will, that you do are Ellsworth Kelly and Paul Brach, Nassos Daphnis, and many others.

I thought I'd simply start off by reading to you and asking for your comments on an editorial from the recent issue of *Art Voices* magazine. The editorial from the January 1964 issue says very simply, "A point of saturation has been reached in abstract painting, so that a simplification – in some cases, oversimplification – of patterns seems to be emerging. From tachism to action painting, from this to that, abstract art appears to be in quest of greater peace of mind and is tending towards a more serene interpretation of inner impulses. We have, indeed, recently come across virgin surfaces [*laughter*], reduced to the utmost simplicity, in fact to almost nothing; huge plains, harmonious spaces, painted in subtle shades such as pale gray, off-white, purple, yellow, blue, as if we were arriving in modern painting at an era to be known as 'the time of the white surface,' a restful trend that… considerably complicates the task of the critics." In any case, this editorial goes on, and it has a very strong exhortation to somebody – to the government, to civic centers, to communities, to newspapers, to leading citizens – that somebody ought to do something about it, and it concludes with the line, "We believe something ought to be done about it, soon, and by all concerned."[5]

I was just wondering what your reaction is to this exhortation and to this description of your work – Frank, do you have some ideas about this?

FS [Frank Stella] There's a lot you can say, but "do something about it" – I don't know what they mean there. People like Brian O'Doherty – everyone's been pointing and saying, "Oh, look, there's something going around."[6] And when they say "do something about it," what they mean by that is, "Put it in a museum show where you have them all together so that we know what it is."

BG I have the feeling that perhaps they're searching for some kind of explanation.

FS They want to categorize it, and also the obvious sort of public and critical complaint is that it's hard to talk about because there's not enough there to talk about. That seems to be the thing that bothers them the most. I think that what we do, the kind of art that they're talking about – I can't tell whether they want to really basically criticize it or whether they actually want to see what it is. I mean, O'Doherty says, "Well, we should have a show of this," and they say the public should see it and something like that, and they want to make it, I think, into a movement so that they can oppose it to something. Like, you would have pop art, and then if you could get a good name for this movement, it would really stick, and then you could have this other "new abstraction," which would make everybody happy.

BG   Do you think that's what the purpose of these shows at Hartford and at the Jewish Museum and at the Janis Gallery is?

FS   Yeah, basically it's to show that something else is going on, something new, and they kind of want to crystallize it in some way, categorize it, basically. It seems to be a pretty basic instinct for the art-world mechanism. I mean, people like Sam Wagstaff and Sidney Janis are certainly the barometers that are sort of always late.[7]

BG   Are you suggesting, Frank, that the kind of thing you do and the kind of thing that Dan and Don do is simply very traditional and it doesn't auger a new trend in abstraction?

FS   No, I don't think that. The thing that everyone said about what's going on is that there's always been a trend toward simpler painting, and it was bound to happen in one way or another.

BG   When you say "always," do you mean the twentieth century, or another time?

FS   I think that whenever painting gets complicated, say abstract expressionism, surrealism, you always get immediately, or adjacent to it, someone who's not painting complicated painting, someone who is trying to simplify. But you get that all the time.

BG   You're suggesting a kind of counterbalance to a more complex movement, but this Janis show seems to point out that all through the twentieth century there was this very simple kind of painting.

FS   That's right, but in that show, it seems to me that when you get to the so-called — as everybody said — meat of the show, the younger generation, it's not continuous. I mean, I don't know. When I first showed, [Robert] Coates in *The New Yorker* said, "Oh, how sad it is to find somebody so young right back where Mondrian was thirty years ago."[8] [*Laughter*] And I didn't really feel that way.

BG   In other words, you feel that there's no connection between you and Mondrian?

FS   I think that there are obvious connections. I mean, you're always related to something. Obviously, I'm related to the more geometric or simpler painting, but the motivation doesn't seem to have anything to do with European geometric painting. The obvious comparison, I think, with my work would be with [Victor] Vasarely, and I can't think of anything I like less.

BG   Why do you compare yourself with Vasarely, Frank? You don't deal with optical illusions or anything like that, do you?

FS   Well, it has less illusionism than Vasarely, say, but still there's that whole group of Vasarely, Vasarely's son, and [François] Morellet — I can't think of the name, but they have that group that they have [Groupe de Recherche d'Art Visuel], and they actually painted, before I did, all the patterns before I did, all the basic designs that are in my painting.[9] Not the way I did it, but you can find the schemes of what are actually the sketches I make for my own paintings; they have been painted in France by Vasarely and that group over the last seven or eight years. I didn't even know about it, but that's the kind of thing that's there. But, I mean, in spite of the fact that they used those ideas, those basic schemes, it still doesn't really have anything to do with it.

BG   Well, how do you feel about that – if someone has painted your paintings several years before you, and they've discarded it, or they haven't made much of it?

FS   Well, it just seems funny. It seems like a curio. I find all that European geometric painting – sort of that post–[Max] Bill school – a kind of curiosity.[10] It's very dreary. [*Laughter*]

DJ   [Donald Judd] There's an enormous break between that work and Frank's work or other present work in the United States, because Vasarely is a continuous development from what was going on in the '30s – in fact, he was doing it in the '30s. It has a small scale and a great deal of composition and qualities that European geometric painting of the '20s and '30s had. I think that there is an enormous break, despite the similarity in the patterns or anything. The scale itself is just one thing to pin down.

FS   The other thing is that they [European geometric painters] really strive for a thing that they call relationships and I call relational painting. The whole scheme of their idea is balance – you would do something in one corner, and you balance it with something in the other corner. Now, you said they characterize the "new painting" as being symmetrical very often, like Ken Noland will put things in the center, and I'll use a symmetrical pattern and stuff like that, but we use the symmetrical thing in a really different way. It's like it's nonrelational. In the newer American painting, whatever we want to call it, say Noland or myself, they strive to get the thing in the middle and symmetrical, but it's just to get a kind of force, just to get the thing on the canvas, in the middle of the canvas, and the balance factor isn't very important. It's not trying to jockey everything around.

BG   What do you mean that they want to get "the thing" on the canvas? What is "the thing"?

FS   I guess you'd have to describe it as the image, either the image or the scheme, whatever it is that they're really interested in. Ken would use concentric circles; he wants to get them in the middle because it's the easiest way to get them there, you know, rather than putting them off to the side. And he wants them there in the front, sort of on the surface of the canvas or up front. If you're that much involved with the surface of anything, the symmetrical thing is the most natural thing to do. Because as soon as you get into any kind of asymmetrical placement, you get into a terrible kind of fussiness, which I think is the one thing that most of the painters now want to avoid. That sort of fussy choice. It becomes sort of arch. When you're always making these delicate balances, it seems to present too many problems.

BG   Do you, Dan, find a relationship in your work to what Frank is talking about in reference to his work?

DF   [Dan Flavin] Well, yes and no. One thing that I'd like to say is that I don't look upon my work as a distinct reaction to abstract expressionism. I look at it as a proposal which digs into ground which stood long before the turgid painting reiterated itself. I have, in the context of my own work, proposed other things that were simple – other propositions. Which, in a sense, might have been more clearly a reaction to, say, de Kooning. I think that what I do now doesn't relate in that way, and I don't feel it that way. I feel it as a proposal. I don't look on asymmetrical-symmetrical difference as being fussy against the straight or something like that. I think I can live with either, when the situation presents itself. In fact, I was thinking about using the fluorescent tubes the way I do – they always seem to me to maintain their own distinction while working with each; they keep their own distinction in the group. Each tube exists of itself as an equal entity in the whole, so it almost looks as if it works against symmetry and asymmetry. I've been thinking about this more and more lately – that they are independent of each other. Although they can appear to be related. For instance, I can use all white tubes, and yet there are different whites, you know; there are four or five whites.

BG   Actually, the problems that you deal with, of course, don't necessarily require that you consider the problems of symmetry or asymmetry. In other words, you are working in another realm, or it would seem to me you are working with another kind of vocabulary, so to speak.

DF   Yes, but it can appear to be the old stuff, or the old fussy stuff, if you will. [*Laughter*]

FS   Yeah, but it's pretty hard. Of the work of yours that I've seen, it seems that the major force in your work comes toward the obvious thing that they've talked about, the simplification, and it tends to be symmetrical. It seems to me, like, how can you avoid it? Basically, when you take a box situation, you've sort of forced yourself into a symmetrical situation. The chances of you making a box that's an outlandishly long rectangle are very slim. It's going to tend to be more square, given the thing that you use.

DF   I think what you're talking about, though – I've had that experience. That's through.

FS   Well, I would say that the boxes were symmetrical, and that the thing of putting the long fluorescent light on the wall at an angle – the idea of the balance in there strikes me as something like some of the Kandinsky things with the long poles.[11] That kind of thing floating in space. That kind of angle.

DF   Yeah, I'd have to think about that. [*Laughter*]

BG   I've heard one statement – somebody said that they find symmetry extraordinarily sensuous. This came from an artist who works more in your vein. And on the other hand, I've heard some people say, or generally the comment is, that symmetry is very austere. I was wondering what your intentions are in either case. That is, if you use symmetry, say either Frank or Don, because I guess maybe in your two cases it maybe applies more – do you think you're trying to create a sensuous effect or an austere effect? Do you think this is relevant to the operation of the surface of your work? Don? [*Laughter*]

DJ   No, I don't think it has to be either one. I'm interested in spareness, but I don't think it has any connection to symmetry.

FS   Actually, your work – well, from what I've seen, it's really symmetrical. The only piece I can think of that deals with any kind of asymmetry is that one box, which is sort of square with the plane cut out [image 1]. That's not really symmetrical, though, in a way. It's not consistently symmetrical.

DJ   But I don't have any ideas as to symmetry or lack of it. I think they're symmetrical because, as you indicated, I wanted to get rid of any compositional effects, and the obvious way to do it is to be symmetrical. Now, if you cannot have any composition and still be asymmetrical, which you certainly can, I think, then you may as well do that, too. I don't intend to do symmetrical work forever, anyway.

BG   Why is it that you want to avoid these so-called compositional effects, Don?

DJ   Well, it has all the structures, values, feelings, and everything of the whole European tradition, which suits me fine if that's down the drain. You pointed out that the Vasarely painting in the Janis show, while it has optical effects within the squares, they're never enough. And he has at least three or four squares, one slanted, or tilted, rather, inside each other, and this is all arranged, which is about five times more composition and juggling than he needs, if you take it into –

BG   In other words, it's too busy?

DJ   – the terms of somebody like [Larry] Poons or something. But this [Vasarely's] composition has the effect of the type of order and the quality that old European painting had, which I find pretty objectionable.

BG   There seem to be several other characteristics that accompany this prevalence of symmetry in these paintings. As can be inferred from the things that we've said, there seems to be a very finished look in all of this work. There's a complete negation of the painterly approach that I think characterizes the majority of twentieth-century painting. Writers have written that twentieth-century painting has been mainly concerned with emphasizing the artist's presence in the work – in other words, that you felt there was this unfinished quality there, and you felt that you could experience or feel that you could relive the experience of the artist painting the picture. And all this seems to be denied in your work too. In fact, it has very clearly an industrial look. I'm wondering about that.

FS   I think you can characterize it very simply. The thing that's disappearing very quickly is the artist's tools – the traditional artist's brush, and maybe even the artist's oil paints. I think all of us three – maybe, Dan, you use oil paint on some of those, but it's mostly commercial paint that all three of us use.

DF   It takes on the look, anyhow.

FS   And also, generally, you tend toward larger brushes. In a way, abstract expressionism started with de Kooning seeing the house painter's brush and the house painter's technique.

BG   Pollock's use of commercial paint.

FS   Aluminum paint and stuff like that. I think that what happened gradually, at least for me – what happened was that when I first started painting, I would see Pollock and de Kooning, and sort of New York School abstract expressionism, and the one thing that they all had which I didn't have was art school. In other words, they were brought up on drawing, and basically they all ended up painting or drawing with the brush, and they got away from smaller brushes. In an attempt to free themselves, they got involved in commercial paints and house-painting brushes, but still it was basically drawing with the brush or drawing with the paint, which I think characterizes almost all of twentieth-century painting, up until now anyway. It seemed to me that the way my painting kept going, that was less and less necessary. In fact, the one thing that I wasn't going to do – I wasn't going to draw with the brush.

BG   What induced this conclusion that it wasn't necessary anymore? That you didn't need to execute the painting in the kind of –

FS   Well, it seems to me that what happens is that when you're painting – well, when you have a brush, and you've actually got paint on the brush, and you ask yourself why you're doing whatever it is that you're doing, what inflection you're actually going to make with the brush and with the paint that's on the end of the brush, it's all, like, the obvious thing: it's handwriting or inflection or something like that. And I found that I just didn't have anything to say in those terms. I didn't want to make variations. I didn't want to record a path. I didn't want to do any of those things. I wanted basically to get the paint down. A wise guy, or whatever you want to call him, who used to make fun of my paintings said – and he didn't like abstract expressionism, anyway, but he wasn't a painter – he said, "Well, they would be good paintings if they could only keep the paint as good as it is in the can." [*Laughter*] And that's what I tried to do.

BG   Actually, what you're implying is that you're really making – Don has at least implied this, and Frank has;

Dan hasn't — you're trying to make a break with traditional painting. Dan says that he's trying to make a proposal and he's not trying to destroy painting. But it seems to me that what Frank and Don are doing is trying to destroy painting.

FS   Well, it's just that you can't go back. It's not a question of destroying anything. I mean, if something's used up, something's done, something's over with, what's the point of you being involved in it?

DJ   Root, hog, or die.[12] [*Laughter*]

BG   In other words, are you suggesting that there are no more problems that exist in painting that a painter can work with?

FS   Well, we're working with it, it seems to me. We have a set of problems that are ours; it seems to us, at least, that we have problems. [*Laughter*]

DF   I mean, one indication of this kind of work is Morris Louis's instant masterpieces, you know, where as soon as they appear, everybody looks at them and says they're masterpieces. Because the terminology is so clearly abroad, in a sense. It's almost like it was expected.

FS   Louis is a really — it's hard to go into him, because he's a really interesting case. There's someone who in every sense — all his instincts were abstract expressionist, and he was terribly involved with all that.

DF   That's what I'm hinting at, I think.

FS   And when I went to his opening at French & Company, I was, like, the only one there for about twenty minutes or so.[13] Nobody looked at those paintings. [Nicholas] Marsicano had an opening, and that was the thing to do. They wouldn't even go look at the paintings when they showed at French & Company, literally. And they were dismissed as thin, and they still are. [*Laughter*] But anyway, those paintings are tied in, but he felt that he had to move, too, in a way.

DF   I wanted to say two things, which is off the track in a sense.

The thing is, first of all, my work becomes more and more an industrial object in the way I accept the fluorescent light for itself, you see. It is an industrial object, it's just a reiteration of it or a disorientation of it. So, I just wanted to put that in. The other thing that I think is important to talk about – I think Don has a sense of this – is the painting as object, as a physical object. I think that Frank is the farthest from that of us.

BG What do you mean by that, "farthest"?

DF Well, let's find out. [*Laughter*]

FS Any painting is an object. I mean, the argument that I always had or that you always get into with people who want the old values in painting, essentially all the humanistic values, is that they always find on the canvas – if you pin them down, there's always something there more than the paint on the canvas. In other words, Alexander Eliot or the general public or any kind of really felt opinion has it that there is always something there more than what's actually there.[14] Certainly, my paintings are based on the fact that only what's there is there, and that makes it an object, because it really is an object. I think that anyone who actually does it or gets involved enough in it finally has to face up to the objectness of whatever it is that he's doing. He's making a thing.

BG Are you saying you want to assert the painting as an object, or the construction as an object – that you want it to be felt as a three-dimensional presence rather than as a composition?

FS No, actually, that's the one thing I don't want. I think all of that should be taken for granted. Basically, I think that the discussion of the thing as object is, in a sense, ridiculous. The painting is a painting. The thing that I would like to see is if the thing is either lean enough, accurate enough, or right enough, you would just be able to look at it. All I want anyone to get out of my paintings or all I ever get out of them is the fact that you can see it all without any confusion. In that sense, what you see is what you see.

BG   Yes, but that doesn't leave too much, though, after that, does it?

FS   Well, I don't know what else there is. If you can really get a visual sensation that is pleasurable, or worth looking at, or enjoyable or something, or if it really does something to what you see –

BG   But some would claim, as I had said at the very beginning, that the plastic effect, so to speak, is minimal. That is, you're just giving us a symmetrical grouping of lines, and you're just giving us one color and stripes. One would assume that a nineteenth-century landscape painting offers more for contemplation than your painting does, simply because it's more complicated, if for no other reason.

DJ   I don't think it is more complicated, actually.

BG   You don't.

DJ   No.

FS   No, because you see, what you're saying essentially is that it's more complicated because there are two things working: you have the deep space, and then you have the actual way it's painted. In other words, you have the painterly application, you have paint applied in such a way that you can see how that's done, and then you can read how the figures work and what kind of depth there is. Well, if you look closely enough at all – let's get off my painting for a little bit; take Ken Noland's, for example, which is even simpler, just a few stains on a ground – if you want to look hard enough, if you want to wait around long enough, you want to look at the depth and the problems there, you get just as much problematic space, just as much space that you can actually get involved in looking at, and there's just as much involvement, if you want it. It's a little more simplified, but technically you can worry and wonder how he painted it the way he did. Some of them are extremely complicated. The way he would have to tip the canvas, or the way he would have to drip the canvas in order to get it to do those things – the technical problems would be just as complex. I mean, you can get just as involved if you really wanted to make the effort. A lot of the things about the Old Master and nineteenth-century painting is talking about the glazes, what he mixed, how he did this, so they're supposedly complicated.

DJ   It's got a great reputation for being profound and universal and all that, and it isn't necessarily.

FS   But I don't know how to get around the part that you just want to make something that's interesting to look at, I guess. Worth looking at, that's all. Basically, I want it to be so that you can't get around the fact that it's supposed to be entirely visual.

BG   In other words, you want to completely destroy any reference to illusionism.

FS   Well, I don't want to destroy anything, I mean, I just want to say that it's worth doing, to make something for the eyes – that there's something there to look at.

BG   But then there comes another problem. If you make so many canvases like one another, how much can the eye be stimulated by so much repetition? That is, one canvas after another looking like the next one.

FS   That's really a relative problem, because obviously it strikes different people different ways. Also, I find, say, Milton Resnick, for example, as repetitive as I am, if not more. The change in any given artist's work, picture to picture, isn't that great. I mean, take the Pollock show. In the Pollock show, you have a big span of years; you could break it down to three or four things.[15] Any given period, any given interest of the artist when he's working on a particular interest or problem, whatever it is, the paintings tend to be a lot alike. I think that it's really hard to find any artist that isn't like that. It seems to me a natural thing rather than unnatural. Also, obviously, you object to some kinds of painting. Everyone finds some things more boring than others, and it obviously works in visual schemes.

BG   Did you want to make some comment?

DJ   Yeah, I wanted to say something about the painterly thing. I think it certainly involves relationships between what's outside, nature or a figure or something, and the artist actually painting that thing and his particular feelings at the time, and I think that this is certainly just one area of feeling and no larger an area of feeling than any other. And I, for one, am not interested in it in my own work, and I can't do anything with it, I don't think. I think it's been fully exploited, and it's probably false for a lot of reasons, and I don't see why it should be made exclusively art.

BG   In other words, are you suggesting that there should be an art without feeling, or am I reading you wrong?

DJ   No, you're reading me wrong. Because I say this is one kind of feeling — this painterly feeling, which —

BG   Well, how would you characterize the painterly feeling in your work? If it's not austere and if it's not finished, what are you striving for?

DJ   Yeah [*laughter*], you can't paraphrase. You have to call it something. You're better at talking around it than I am.

BG   Well, okay. If you can talk around it —

DJ   Well, it's certainly more austere, somewhat, but that's a very loose word.

FS   One of the things that I would say characterizes your work — it's easier to talk about someone else's work and trying to keep it involved with that painterly business — is that if we take "painterly" now to simply mean abstract expressionism, to make it easier, they were obviously involved in what they were doing as they were doing it. And now, obviously, the thing that Don does, and I guess what I do, is that a lot of the effort is always directed toward the end. We really believe that we can find the end and that they will be finished. They always felt that it was very problematical when the painting was finished. Certainly, I think that we'd more readily accept the idea that our painting is finished and say, "Well, either it's a failure or not," rather than say, "Well, maybe it's not really finished," or something like that.

BG   This brings up another very important problem. What you're saying is that the painting is almost conceptualized in the mind before it's actually made. In other words, you can devise a diagram in your mind and actually put it on canvas. But I'm wondering whether – and this is the question – whether it's just not adequate enough to simply verbalize this image and give it to the public rather than giving them your paintings.

FS   Well, a simple thing is that a diagram is not a painting. That's as simple as that. I can make a painting from a diagram, but can you, or can the public? In other words, it just remains a diagram if that's all I do, or if it's a verbalization, it just remains a verbalization. Clement Greenberg talks about the ideas or the possibilities for painting – I think it's in "After Abstract Expressionism" or something like that – and that he allows a blank canvas to be an idea for painting, and that it might not be a good idea for painting, but that it's certainly a valid idea for painting.[16] And I mean, Yves Klein did the empty gallery. He sold air. That was a conceptualized art, I guess.[17] [*Laughter*]

BG   It has gone in some instances to reductio ad absurdum.

FS   Not absurd enough, though. [*Laughter*]

DJ   But even if you can plan the thing completely ahead of time, you still don't know what it looks like until it's right there, you see. You may be totally wrong once you go to all the trouble of building the thing.

FS   Yeah, and also that's what you want to do. You actually want to see the thing. I mean, that's the thing that motivates you to do it, is to see what it's going to look like.

DJ   You can think about it forever in all sorts of varieties, and they're nothing until you really do it.

BG   Yes, but the problem then is, say I go to an exhibition of such work. It doesn't matter to me, it seems, if I never see these paintings again, as long as I carry the image around in my mind.

FS   I mean, come on, you couldn't carry it more than ten seconds.

DJ   No, you can't have any impression of –

FS   I can think of the Pollock painting that I saw the other day or something that I liked, but I can't really remember it that well. There are supposedly the people with photo memories, but I don't know what those are like. You can't carry it very far.

BG   I was wondering about another term that seems to be relevant to this discussion also. I've read quite a few reviews and heard some reviewers talk about "presence" in a work. In fact, I heard one reviewer recently who said that presence is something that tells you that a work is great even when you're not looking at it. In other words, you can feel it from behind you, even if you've got your back turned to the painting. Even if you've never looked at the painting, you just know that you're in the presence of a great work of art. I was just wondering about this – do any of you have any idea about what constitutes presence?

DJ   It means the work is very good and interesting. That's about all it means.

FS   It means you like it and you'd like to think about it some more, and you're able to – I mean, you'd rather think about it than something else.

BG   Would any of you say that it's a fact that you're aware of, or something that you strive for, while you're making a painting?

FS   I don't think you can. It's like suicide. That would mean constantly comparing yourself with something, like saying, "Am I really as good as Titian?" every time you pick up a brush and a bucket. [*Laughter*]

BG   I have this feeling that this word "presence" is more frequently applied to paintings of this so-called new classic spirit than it is to more traditional paintings.

FS   What do you mean, Poons's optical stuff?

BG   Yes, paintings such as yours and Don's and Dan's. I have the feeling that people talk about presence in the face of those works more than they do in the presence of regular works. In other words, do you think that it's because there's so little that you can say in terms of verbalization before your works?

DJ   So little that *they* can say.

BG   Yeah, so little that critics can say, that's what I mean.

DJ   They'll figure it out in due time. [*Laughter*]

BG   Or do you think that your work generally has more presence than traditional works of art, or what?

FS   It's pretty awful. You can't say that your work has more of this or that than somebody else's work unless you want to say that. But I don't know, I mean, it's a kind of — the thing about "presence" is that it goes back to what we said before; it's about what you like. And people will talk about "strong" paintings, "tough" paintings — those are more popular. The abstract expressionists will use that instead of "presence" when they want to talk about something really good. De Kooning and Al Held paint "tough" paintings, and we would have to paint paintings with "presence," I guess. But I think it's sort of terminology. That's just another way to describe it.

DJ   Another way of saying you're very impressed by them. I'd like to get rid of the word "classic," though, while we're at it.

FS   Yes, let's get rid of that.

DJ   Because it has nothing to do with what any of us are doing.

DF   Or, you might say it's after the fact.

DJ   Other people in the Janis show —

FS   I don't think it had to do with anybody in that show either. What did they care? Who in that show cared about "classic" art?

BG   I think that the catalogue for that show simply defined "classic" as something that was not "romantic."

DJ   That's not very good either. What's romantic? Is Pollock —

BG   I think that one might conclude from that show that — you get the feeling that anything that had a hard edge or a very tight, taught line or used geometric shapes might be considered classic. And, since your work does have that, do you think —

DJ   It would certainly give Poussin a pain in the neck to hear that. [*Laughter*]

BG   In other words, you think it's all right to call Poussin classic, but —

DJ   Well, he asked for it.

BG   Yeah, I see, but you didn't.

DJ   And I don't think that it should be — it implies that abstract expressionism is romantic, which is not accurate for it, either. Anyway, the two terms belong in the beginning of the last century. They're better off there. [*Laughter*]

FS   Give it back to [Max Jakob] Friedländer or whatever.[18]

BG   I have the feeling that so many of these terms are just simply picked up by people who are putting on exhibitions because they have the vaguest resemblance to modern work, but nobody has really attempted to develop some kind of new terminology or new vocabulary to deal with the problems that these paintings deal with.

FS   On the one hand, I think that the paintings that we are trying to do are a little bit different, but on the other hand, it seems that they're still dealing basically with the problems that painting or making art always has. They're pretty much the same old problems. I don't see why everyone feels so desperately in need of a new terminology, and I don't see what there is in our work – I hope I can speak for the others – that really needs a new terminology to either explain it or to evaluate it. It seems to me it's art, or it wants to be art, or it asks to be considered as art, and therefore the terms we have for discussing art are probably good enough. I don't see that it necessarily needs new ones. You could say that the terms that have been used so far to discuss and evaluate art are pretty grim; you could make a very good case for that. But nonetheless, I think there's nothing necessary in the work now, the newer work now, nothing specifically in our work that asks for new terms, any more than any other art.

DF   I've always felt that in my own work that there is a distinct physical element. I think, Don, we talked about this one time up to four o'clock in the morning, if I remember. I think that it has to be called up. I think it concerns him very much, even more than it does me. We were talking about the weight of Frank's canvases – the cutout part. This is all to call attention to this quality, I think.

FS   Well, you two make objects. It's that simple. So they are either objects, sculpture, or something like that. But the reason I make the canvas deeper than ordinarily is – I didn't do it for any reason, it began accidentally, if you want to call it that. I turned one-by-threes on edge to make a quick frame and to butt-end them when I first started stretching canvases. And then I liked what that did. When you stand directly in front of the painting, it gives just enough depth to hold it off the wall. You're just conscious of a sort of shadow, just enough that actually it emphasizes the surface. In other words, it makes it more like a painting and less like an object, so that again, it simply emphasizes the surface quality.

BG   It's very curious; I've heard several artists have referred to your paintings as sculptural in form because of that thickness. It's very interesting that you say this, that this was simply an accidental feature.

DJ   Well, I thought of Frank's aluminum ones as slabs, in a way.[19] They seemed objects, in a way, to me.

DF   You can think of the difference, say, from Rothko. He hinted that he was going to add a certain weight to the stretcher. I think I get that feeling, you know, that the painting goes around the corner.

FS   Yeah, right, well, I think he did paint around the edge, but I don't. [*Laughter*]

DF   Yeah, well, we had to get it out because it means something.

FS   Yeah, I don't paint around the edge. A lot of people – Sven Lukin, in the show at Janis, paints around the edge too, but he's much more object than painting than I am. See, that's real.

BG   But his painting is also in relief, too, in a sense.

FS   Right, right, it is relief.

DF   Well, that's what's been suggested.

DJ   I think Frank's flat surface, too, made it seem more like an object, that was pretty rare. I think it was a first. [*Laughter*]

BG   But what about this problem of sentimentality in painting? I've heard often, or you've been quoted, Frank, as saying that you want to get the sentimentality out of painting. Or at least I seem to have read something like that in Sam Wagstaff's article in *ARTnews* about the show in Hartford.[20]

FS   He even says "nineteenth century" in that. I hope I didn't really say that. [*Laughter*] But it doesn't matter. I think what I said is that I didn't think it was necessary. And I didn't then and I don't now think it's necessary to make art objects or make paintings that will interest people in the sense that they can keep going back to explore a certain kind of painterly detail. Like – I hate to keep using Milton Resnick, but he's such a nice example. [*Laughter*] One could, if one wanted to, stand in front of any one of Milton Resnick's paintings for a long time, and walk back and forth in front of it, and inspect the depths of the pigment and the inflections and all the painterly brushwork for hours. But I wouldn't particularly want to do that, and I also wouldn't ask anyone to do that kind of thing in front of my painting. And I guess, to go further, I would like to prohibit them from doing that in front of my painting. So, that's why I make the paintings the way they are, more or less.

BG   Maybe this is searching too much, but why would you like to prohibit someone from doing such a thing?

FS   Basically, I guess it's a criticism of other painters. I just use Resnick to make it simple. In a sense, I feel that you shouldn't, you know – after a while, you're just sort of mutilating the paint. I don't feel like the paint ever did anything to deserve that. If you have some feeling about either color, or maybe direction, or line, or something like that, I think you can state it. You can either state it or make it. More simply than that, I don't think you have to – I've never gone in for the kind of art which is kneading material and sort of grinding it up. That seems destructive to me; it makes me very nervous. I find that attitude basically destructive rather than constructive.

BG   In other words, you seem to suggest that you are after, most of you are after, an economy of means, rather than trying to avoid sentimentality. That would be perhaps a more accurate way of phrasing it?

FS   Yes, but there's something awful about that "economy of means." I don't know why, but I really resent that almost instantly. I don't go out of my way to be economical in any way.

DJ   You've got all those lines. [*Laughter*]

DF   Yeah, that's what you have discussed before – irreducibility. As far as I'm concerned, it's irrelevant to me. It's no concern, and I don't want you to pin my ears back on that either, because I'm thirty years old and I have a lot to do. I hope.

FS   It seems to me that you're motivated by – it's hard to explain what exactly it is you're motivated by, but I don't think people are motivated by reduction. It would be nice if we were, but actually, you want to make something, and then you go about it in a way that seems best.

DJ   You're reducing the things that people earlier thought were essential to art – that's what you're getting rid of, but that's only incidental.

FS   Yeah, you want to get rid of things, too, that you think get you in trouble. It seems to me that the more you paint, or as you keep painting or doing things, you find things are getting in your way a lot, and those are the things that you try to get out of the way. You might be spilling a lot of a particular blue paint all over something, and it's because there's something wrong with that particular paint, and then you don't use that, or you find a better thinner, or you work in those kinds of ways, or you get better ways, or you get better nails. There's a lot of striving for better materials, I'm afraid. I don't know how good that is.

BG   There's just one more question that I'm bothered by. Several of you made the point that you certainly want to create some effect of enjoyment in your work. I think that Frank specifically made that comment – that you want people to come and look at your paintings and enjoy them. And you don't want to be bothered with a lot of complex effects of color and depth and illusionism or what have you, but the fact is that right now the majority of people who come before your works or come before your canvases seem to have some trouble in this regard, and they don't get this enjoyment that you seem to be very simply presenting to them. That is, they are still stunned and taken aback by the utter simplicity of it. Do you think that this is just because they have not come up to the point where they can comprehend these works, or they are just simply behind the artist again, the way it is throughout the whole history of art, or what?

FS   Maybe that's the quality of simplicity. When somebody hits the ball out of the park, say [Mickey] Mantle or someone like that, everyone is stunned for a minute because it's very simple. He just knocks it right out of the park, and that usually does it.

DF   What I've been noticing is the difference between Frank's attitude and mine. Bob Rosenblum said to me recently that I had destroyed painting for him.[21] Well, I'm just getting a real sense of this. I don't communicate that much with Frank, and I can see I've done it for myself unconsciously. I don't think in the terms in which he's thinking at all, and it's a surprise to me that I had considered myself a painter, in a sense, but I can see the difference. That's good.

FS   What are some of the differences?

DF   Oh, geez, you know — a consciousness of the way paint works. What you don't want to do with it. What you've seen done with it. I don't even think about it, in a sense. Very rarely. I don't think about that at all now. I think more like an arrangement of sticks, of color sticks — if that. It's more and more an object for me.

FS   How do you — well, I won't say "rationalize" — how do you deal with structural things or compositional things? For example, we're all left with that. That's what I wanted to say, part of the point I wanted to say about the terms. The problems aren't any different. I mean, for us, still basically all of us — well, I have to compose a picture, and if you make an object, you have to organize it or structure it. All I'm saying is that, finally, I don't think our work is that radical in any sense. I don't think between the three of us that you can find any structure, any compositional element, or any really new structural element. I don't know if that exists. It's like the idea of a color that you haven't seen before. Is there something that's, say, not a diagonal? Or not a straight line? Or not a compositional element that you can describe?

BG   So, Don, even your efforts to get away from European
     painting and its traditional compositional effects are some-
     what limited, because you're still going to be using some
     of the same devices that they used.

DJ   No, I don't think so.

BG   You don't think so.

DJ   No. I'm totally uninterested in European painting. I think
     it's over with.

FS   Yeah, but how can you say that you don't use any of the
     traditional devices?

DJ   You can use a diagonal, but no one there ever used as direct
     a diagonal as, say, Louis did. There's no such bare diagonal
     in all the history of European painting, that's one of his –

DF   Except *White on White*.[22]

DJ   Well, yeah, I'm not talking about twentieth-century things,
     but –

FS   All the Kandinsky. Look at those. Even the mechanical
     ones. They're sort of awful, but they have some pretty
     radical diagonals and stuff. Of course, they're always
     balanced.

DJ   When you make a diagonal clear across the whole thing
     as the main thing, in the main thing, it's very different.

FS   Right, but nonetheless, the idea of the diagonal has been
     around for a long time.

DJ   Yeah, well, actually, that's true; and there's always going
     to be something in one's work that's been around a long
     time, but the fact that, for example, now the structural ar-
     rangement isn't even that important is rather new. It's ob-
     viously very important to Vasarely, but really all I'm in-
     terested in is having a thing interesting to me in a lump. I
     don't think there's any way you can juggle a structure that
     would make it more interesting in parts.

BG   Don, I'm wondering – are you concerned with getting
     away from European painting because it's European, or
     because it's European painting?

DJ   No, because I'm uninterested in the quality of it. I think it belongs to another period. I'm not just promoting American painting, especially because there are Europeans who are doing this, too. I think Yves Klein, to some extent, comes out of European painting.

BG   Meyer Schapiro once said that there might be an analogy between, say, a Barnett Newman with a field of one color and one simple stripe down the middle and a mosaic field of some Byzantine church, where you might find a completely gold field and then a simple vertical form of the Madonna.[23] So perhaps, even here, we have some indication of a kind of precedent for twentieth-century painting. You have utter simplicity, a great big field that's just enjoyed for the sake of itself, and then the vertical division in the most symmetrical and obvious way.

DJ   Yeah, well, a lot of things look alike, but they aren't necessarily very much alike.

FS   Like, the whole idea is so complex – well, not so complex, but the idea of a field – what you mean by a field in a painting is a pretty difficult idea. In terms of a mosaic, a field can never have anything to do with, say, a field like you would get in a Morris Louis or something like that. The whole idea of saturated –

DJ   There's no field like that in a Newman, like there would be in a plain gold field, because Newman's doing something with his field.

FS   Yeah, it's in the canvas and all that, and it really does work differently.

DF   I didn't answer Frank, I think. In fact, I don't think I can right now. One thing is that I was trying to write a letter to Bob Rosenblum about what I was thinking about, and I found out what I was saying, in fact, was that I was trying to drop composition. And I don't see how I can do it right now. [*Laughter*]

FS   That's the kind of thing you get into with so-called really advanced painting, for example – dropping composition. That would be terrifically avant-garde; that's a really good idea. But the question is, how do you do it?

DF That's right, yeah, well –

BG That goes even beyond illuminating nothing on the canvas.

FS Actually, the best article I ever read about pure painting and all that was that thing that Elaine de Kooning wrote in *ARTnews* years ago, "Pure Paints a Picture."[24] I don't know if any of you saw that.

DF I was too young to read that, I guess.

DJ Yeah, I saw that.

FS That was really fantastic. Well, the way it ended was very pure, and he lived in a stainless-steel white loft or something like that. He was very meticulous and he gave up painting and brushes and all that and he had a syringe which he loaded with a colorless, odorless fluid, which he injected into clear, odorless styrene. That was how he created his art objects, by injecting colorless fluid into a colorless material.

DJ That makes Yves Klein a pretty radical artist.

FS Well, Yves Klein was no doubt a radical artist, but a bad artist, or he didn't do anything very interesting. But why is Yves Klein sort of not radical? It seems to me kind of interesting. I don't know. I have one of his paintings, which I sort of like in a way, but there's something about him that's not radical. I mean, what's not radical about the idea of selling air? It doesn't seem very interesting.

DJ No, it's not very interesting to me. One thing I want to do with art is to be able to see it, as you said. It is something you look at.

BG Well, it seems that you all end on a happy note. You ultimately affirm some kind of plastic value. You must see the work of art.

FS If my paintings work or get going, I do lose sight of the fact that it's canvas, even though I know it's a painting on canvas, and I just do *see* it, in a way. I don't get terribly hung up over the canvas. In other words, if the thing is going on the canvas strong enough, if the paint and the design or whatever it is, the visual action taking place there is strong enough, I don't get a very strong sense of the material quality of the canvas. That sort of disappears. But I don't like things that stress the material quality. A lot of times I don't like – even though I like the paintings a lot, say Ken's paintings or something – sometimes those big canvases with all the bare canvas kind of get me down a little bit, because there's just so much canvas. The physical quality of the cotton duck, it sort of gets in the way.

This discussion was sourced from an audio recording. The original recording is in the Pacifica Radio Archive (Los Angeles), Tape #BB 3394. An undated archival transcript is in the Lucy R. Lippard papers, 1930s–2010, bulk 1960s–1990, Archives of American Art, Smithsonian Institution, Washington, DC.

First published: Dan Flavin, Donald Judd, and Frank Stella, "New Nihilism or New Art?," interview by Bruce Glaser (recorded February 15, 1964), WBAI, New York, March 24, 1964; reprinted (excerpts): Bruce Glaser, "Questions to Stella and Judd," ed. Lucy R. Lippard, *ARTnews*, September 1966, 55–61; Bruce Glaser, "Questions to Stella and Judd," ed. Lucy R. Lippard, in *Minimal Art: A Critical Anthology*, ed. Gregory Battcock (New York: E. P. Dutton, 1968), 148–64.

1   *The Classic Spirit in 20th Century Art*, Sidney Janis Gallery, New York, February 4–29, 1964. The opening line of *The New York Times*'s review of the exhibition reads, "The first thing to say is that it is one of the year's important exhibitions. After that one can start arguing about it. There's going to be plenty of argument." Brian O'Doherty, "Art: 'The Classic Spirit,'" *The New York Times*, February 4, 1964, 66. Among the artists who exhibited were Josef Albers, Richard Anuszkiewicz, Ilya Bolotowsky, John Chamberlain, Nassos Daphnis, Stuart Davis, El Lissitzky, Kazimir Malevich, Piet Mondrian, Amédée Ozenfant, Larry Poons, Frank Stella, and Victor Vasarely. Judd included the catalogue for this exhibition in his library in Marfa, Texas.

2   "We have, indeed, recently come across virgin surfaces, reduced to the utmost simplicity, in fact to almost nothing … as if we were arriving in modern painting at an era to be known as 'the time of the white surfaces.'" St. Evremond, editorial, *Art Voices*, January 1964, 3.

3   *Black and White*, Jewish Museum, New York, December 12, 1963–February 5, 1964.

4   *Black, White and Grey*, Wadsworth Atheneum, Hartford, Connecticut, January 9–February 9, 1964. See Judd's review of *Black, White and Grey* in *Donald Judd: Complete Writings 1959–1975*, 117–19.

5   St. Evremond, editorial, 3.

6   Brian O'Doherty (1928–) is an Irish art critic, writer, and artist. He was a critic for *The New York Times* in the mid-1960s; see note 1 for O'Doherty's review of *The Classic Spirit in 20th Century Art*.

7   Samuel Wagstaff, Jr. (1921–1987), was an American curator and collector. Wagstaff organized *Black, White and Grey* at the Wadsworth Atheneum, where he was the curator from 1961 to 1968.

8   "It is discouraging to find Frank Stella, who specializes in rectangular arrangements of white pin stripes on a black ground, right back where Mondrian was thirty years ago." Robert Coates, "The Art Galleries," *The New Yorker*, January 2, 1960, 61.

9   Victor Vasarely (1906–1997) is considered the founder of op art. Groupe de Recherche d'Art Visuel (1960–68) was a Paris-based collaborative group of artists whose work often involved kinetic and optical effects. Julio Le Parc, Vera Molnár, François Morellet, Horacio García Rossi, Francisco Sobrino, Joël Stein, and Yvaral (Jean-Pierre Vasarely, son of Victor Vasarely) were among the group's members.

10   Judd met the Swiss architect and artist Max Bill (1908–1994) in the 1980s through his friends and gallerists Annemarie and Gianfranco Verna.

11   See, for example, Kandinsky's *Transverse Line* (1923), Kunstsammlung Nordrhein-Westfalen, Düsseldorf.

12   "Root, hog, or die" is a nineteenth-century American expression that developed from the colonial practice of turning pigs loose to fend for themselves. It is often used as an idiomatic expression of self-reliance.

13   Stella refers here to either *Morris Louis*, French & Company, New York, April 10–May 2, 1959, or *Morris Louis*, French & Company, New York, March 26–April 16, 1960.

14   Alexander Eliot (1919–2015) was an American writer and author of *Three Hundred Years of American Painting* (New York: Time, 1957).

15   *Jackson Pollock*, Marlborough-Gerson Gallery, New York, January 14–February 15, 1964.

16   Clement Greenberg, "After Abstract Expressionism," *Art International*, October 25, 1962, 24–32.

17   Yves Klein's exhibition *The Void*, Galerie Iris Clert, Paris, April 28–May 12, 1958, consisted of an empty, white-walled gallery.

18   Max Jakob Friedländer (1867–1958) was a German curator and art historian specializing in early Netherlandish painting and the Northern Renaissance.

19   Stella's *Aluminum Paintings* (1960) consist of twelve canvases coated in an aluminum-hue metallic paint. See Lawrence Rubin, *Frank Stella: Paintings 1958 to 1965; A Catalogue Raisonné* (London: Thames & Hudson, 1986), 65.

20   "At the opposite end of the group is Frank Stella, whose paintings may be the most 'difficult' in the show.... He believes that too much nineteenth-century Romanticism still prevails and that sloppy looking around in canvases by the sentimental viewer should come to an end." Samuel Wagstaff, "Paintings to Think About," *ARTnews*, January 1964, 62.

21   Robert Rosenblum (1927–2006) was an American art historian and curator whose scholarship focused on European and American art from the eighteenth century to the twentieth.

22   Kazimir Malevich, *Suprematist Composition: White on White* (1918), The Museum of Modern Art, New York.

23   Judd studied with Meyer Schapiro (1904–1996) while a graduate student at Columbia University. Schapiro was an influential art critic, art historian, and professor. Judd included nine books by Schapiro in his library in Marfa, Texas.

24   Elaine de Kooning, "Pure Paints a Picture," *ARTnews*, Summer 1957, 57, 86–87.

"Geometry and Art"
Panel discussion with Charles Parkhurst (moderator),
Ernst Benkert, Francis Hewitt, Anthony Hill,
and Ed Mieczkowski
April 2, 1964

This panel discussion was held in conjunction with the exhibition *Paintings and Drawings and a Motorized Construction by Karen Hewitt* (April 4–18, 1964), organized by Ernst Benkert, Francis Hewitt, and Ed Mieczkowski, three artists who worked as a collective under the name of the Anonima Group. Anonima was presenting its first show in New York at a rented space at 23 West Fifty-Sixth Street, which is where this discussion occurred. Judd was acquainted with Benkert through the Allen-Stevenson School, a private all–boys school on Manhattan's Upper East Side where Benkert taught English and where Judd taught shop and world history from 1957 to 1959. The British artist Anthony Hill also participated in the panel; Charles Parkhurst, director of the Baltimore Museum of Art at the time, moderated.

From 1959 until 1965, Judd wrote monthly exhibition reviews, primarily for *Arts Magazine*. In 1964, he wrote the essay "Specific Objects"; it was published in *Arts Yearbook 8* the following year.

CP   [Charles Parkhurst] What is the intention of the use of geometry in painting?

DJ   [Donald Judd] To somewhat answer your question, I don't think geometry has any general application. And as far as my own work is concerned, which is about the only work I can talk about, it's not the basis of it and it has no particular meaning to it. Geometry and scientific information, or sensations, rather, optical sensations, are just a means — you pick up a couple you can use for other purposes. And I don't see that they are in any way a principle. I don't see that they're a basis for geometric art, which I don't think is what mine is, though it looks like that. I don't think it's any different than anyone doing quite a different kind of art now, say a John Chamberlain sculpture. I think Chamberlain — who is, in a way, doing somewhat descriptive sculpture, descriptive movement of natural appearances, in a very oblique way — is pretty much doing it the same way I want to be doing it. Despite this distinction of description, that's the main reason I'm using geometric work, probably — to get rid of any natural references or descriptive qualities in my work. But I don't see it as any more than a means to doing something I want, which is completely aside from the question of geometry.

US   [Unknown speaker] It's not a philosophy?

DJ   No, geometry isn't a philosophy at all. It's just a means.

EM   [Ed Mieczkowski] I would possibly like to amplify that a little bit. I think one of the important developments in the current century right now has been the release of what I would roughly call the elements in painting, or even sculpture, if you will — the release of things like tone, value, line, patches of color, the elements of the work, from any necessity to recur to what we usually see when we look at the world. The elements of a painting are now at the painter's disposal. And the problem then becomes, how do you distribute these elements, how do you scatter them around, how do you, shall we say, sow your field? I like that idea that it's all going back again to the fact that we've got to take the measure of a surface. If some geometric preparation engenders or brings about coincidences, things that we can't anticipate, surprises, then geometry does then become, in effect, a very friendly and warm thing, rather than looking toward any perfect figure, rather than subscribing to any kind of view of life, such as Kepler's, who I think at one time said, "All things strive to the form of the circle."[1] I can't quote him directly, but what he was implying there is that we're all really balloons if we could be, but the tragedy of life is the fact that we aren't!

Taking it back again, I think that geometry is roughly a very friendly affair for the painter, that it is not so much the imposition of principles upon the surface; it's just simply a playful application of some maintained for only a short time. You try, and, after a while, you get tired of it, dismiss it and try another.

DJ   That makes it pretty much the same as expressionism. In other words, it isn't distinctively geometric. In other words, your way of going about it is pretty much the same as, say, Jackson Pollock did it. He's intuitively measuring out the canvas as he works.

CP   Mr. Judd, a reviewer of your recent show at Green Gallery [images 2, 3] said he knew what you liked, and he mentioned your "overall rectilinearity" and your frame – unlike a balloon – and the regularity of your structural pulses, which I didn't quite understand, and your positive and negative spaces.[2] But he said what he wondered about was fundamentally why you liked these things. This was the one thing he never could understand. I don't know whether you read the review and had a chance to think about it, but would you like to comment on the review at this particular point?

DJ   I think I like it for the same reason that Chamberlain likes
        the smashed-up automobiles. He likes them because they
        have something to do with him. I can make something out
        of rectilinearity, but I don't think it has any special key to
        the universe or anything. It's my particular way of work-
        ing, but it isn't a reflection of any kind of order, which I
        think is an idea that must go back to [Victor] Vasarely, say,
        the European artists, certainly back to Mondrian.

This discussion was sourced from an audio recording. The original sound tape reel
is in the Ernst Benkert papers, 1962–1971, Archives of American Art, Smithsonian Institution, Washington, DC.

This is an excerpt of Judd's most substantive remarks during the panel. Considerable portions of the recording are inaudible, and Judd spoke infrequently.

1   Like many of his European contemporaries, the astronomer Johannes
        Kepler (1571–1630) believed the circle to be a divine shape, and so ini-
        tially assumed that planets traveled in circular orbits. His discovery that
        planets move elliptically around the sun is now known as Kepler's first
        law of planetary motion.
2   *Don Judd*, Green Gallery, New York, December 17, 1963–January 11, 1964.
        This exhibition was Judd's first solo show to include works in three di-
        mensions. "On the one hand there are several qualities it is clear enough
        Judd likes: overall rectilinearity, regularity of structural pulse, play between
        positive and negative spaces and structural mirroring of all kinds." Michael
        Fried, "New York Letter," *Art International*, February 15, 1964, 26.

Interview with Bruce Hooton
February 3, 1965

This interview is one of twelve that editor and publisher Bruce Hooton conducted for the Smithsonian Institution's Archives of American Art Oral History Program. In addition to Judd, between 1965 and 1966, Hooton also interviewed Jim Dine, Elias Goldberg, Leon Golub, Stewart Klonis, Claes Oldenburg, Hilla Rebay, and Vaclav Vytlacil.

The year preceding the interview, Judd first hired Bernstein Brothers Sheet Metal Specialties, Inc., a sheet metal shop located near his apartment and studio at 53 East Nineteenth Street, to fabricate his works. Judd's use of fabricators generated a diversity of responses from critics and artists.

With the close of Green Gallery in July 1965, Judd joined the Leo Castelli Gallery, New York, participating in his first group show with the gallery later that year (December 14, 1965–January 5, 1966).

B H   [Bruce Hooton] I don't understand the new geometric art, frankly. I mean, people are complaining. Norman Mailer complained just the other day in *The New York Times* about the square look of things, you know, everything is kind of simplified and square, and too simplified.[1] He made a model of a whole building that went off this way and that way. [*Laughs*] I mean, he's a nut, but I don't know what — things are not simple, certainly, but should they be simplified?

D J   [Donald Judd] Well, I really only know about myself, my reasons for doing it. They certainly aren't connected to the old geometric art. You know, it's [my work] not geometric in that sense. One of the reasons, I guess, that my stuff is geometric is that I want it simple, and I want it nonnaturalistic, or nonimagistic, or nonexpressionistic. The simpleness, as far as I'm concerned, goes all the way back through my other paintings, almost to when I first started working.

B H   Where did you first work? I don't know where your family is from.

D J   I was born in Missouri and lived around the Middle West, moved to Philadelphia during World War II — no, just before it, before Pearl Harbor.

B H   Before '41, maybe?

D J   Yeah, and then we moved to New Jersey, and I went to the Art Students League.

B H   So, that's where you studied, actually?

D J   Yeah, for about three years — three and a half years.

B H   With whom?

D J   With Louis Bouché for the first two years, I think; one year with Louis Bosa; about a year with Will Barnet; and summers with several people — [Reginald] Marsh, [Robert Beverly] Hale, and [Robert Ward] Johnson. I don't know if you remember him, he used to teach contour drawing.

B H   What's his first name?

DJ   I can't remember his first name. He's dead now. He died
not too long after I left. And Bernard Klonis, too. Yeah, I
went to school here – dates are hard – well, '48 or so, and
then I moved here in 1953. Before that I commuted in
from New Jersey to save money, because I was doing both
Columbia and the Art Students League.[2]

BH   Did you take a degree at Columbia?

DJ   Yeah.

BH   In what? In art? In art history?

DJ   In philosophy. [*Laughs*] I figured I had a major in effect
down at the League.

BH   You must – Reinhardt, when did you first meet Reinhardt?

DJ   A couple of years ago.

BH   Were you painting or working more or less the same way
before you met him?

DJ   I don't remember especially being influenced by him. I
admired his work, but also that of quite a few other people. One thing: I was a painter until maybe '62 – I'll have
to figure out the dates – and then I started doing three-
dimensional things. The paintings are not geometric, exactly, but it's there. Geometric art as such doesn't mean all
that much to me. A lot of the people I admire, previously
or now, aren't doing it. I don't feel the connection in that
way, with my own work.

BH   A drawing I saw of yours over there at the gallery had a
kind of inverted Stonehenge feeling [image 4]. There was
a certain monumentality, even though –

DJ   It's a blatant post-and-lintel arrangement.

BH   There's no kind of philosophical point to the whole thing?
I mean, what would one say if one decides to cut out certain things in the same way that one decides to throw paint,
or one decides to not throw paint, or to simplify things?

DJ   Well, I am not interested in the kind of expression that
you have when you paint a painting using paint and brushstrokes; I'm not especially interested in it, and people have

already done something with it and are still doing it. I think if someone younger is doing it now, he's probably using another related form, or he's getting into something which is rather played out and narrow. Of course, that doesn't mean that people like Newman who still use it are that way. But I think that's one particular kind of experience. It implies a certain immediacy between you and the canvas, or rather you and the experience of any particular moment. I think what I'm trying to deal with is something more long range than that quality, in a way, more obscure, perhaps, more involved in things that happen over a longer time. At the least it's in another area of experience and not as expressive itself.

BH   In other words, you're trying to lay the foundation for a thought. One might say that you try to kind of stop time for a minute.

Certainly abstract expressionism in its lesser form is a great teaching gimmick across the country, because anybody can do it. It's a great thought – anybody can throw paint.

DJ   Well, that can be said of drawing, or anything. It depends on – anybody can do it if it isn't too good. But I'm not especially against abstract expressionism. I think it's just as difficult and just as good as many other forms have been. And it had a superfluous number of followers.

BH   As any group does.

DJ   Yeah, and that certainly helped to run it down.

BH   It gave ammunition to people who were totally against it.

DJ   Yeah, and it was accepted too rigidly, and I think that –

BH   That's actually what killed it.

DJ   I think that there was more of a reaction against it than probably should have occurred. Then also, several of the main people failed. I think [Franz] Kline's painting went downhill, and de Kooning's. Pollock died, of course. And Pollock and de Kooning are more of the typical expressionists.

And Newman, whose work I think is even better than Rothko's, is not characteristically expressionist.

BH   They include themselves.

DJ   I don't think there's especially been any public reaction against it. And I don't think there's been any public reaction against them.

BH   Against abstract expressionism?

DJ   Well, against Newman and Rothko. They've been very influential with a lot of people my age.

BH   About the idea of simplicity?

DJ   Usually when someone says a thing is too simple, they're saying that certain familiar things aren't there, and they're seeing a couple, maybe, that are left, which they count as a couple, that's all. But actually, there may be those couple of things and several new things to which they aren't paying attention. These may be quite complex. At the moment when someone says it's too simple, they mean that it doesn't have the composition that the abstract expressionist painting, or cubist painting, or whatever – going back – had. It doesn't have a lot of parts working against one another, a lot of colors working with and against one another. If it doesn't have this, therefore it's simple to them. Now, actually, it may have other things which are really pretty complex. They may be read all at once, which I think is important to most of the best work going on now. It has to have a totality to it that previous work probably doesn't have, but still, within that, it's not all as simple as you say.

BH   If you're going to do a box, the line has to join at the right spot.

DJ   Yeah. Boxes, they're pretty simple. [*Laughter*]

BH   But, I mean, it has to join with something – there's a Chinese phrase for it that I can't remember, but the totality which the line does – it has to complete itself.

DJ   The corners all have to join. Even in a box, after all, just on the top you've got four edges there. And then all the edges, four more down the sides. It really isn't all that simple. And that's just a plain box. But one of mine has subdivisions in it — a trough cut out and a lot of subdivisions [image 5]. Those subdivisions are progressive, and the progression in there is really pretty complicated. It looks like a trough with a lot of arcs in it, and it's very simple if you don't start to think about the progression along there. If you take that into consideration, you could say it's reasonably complex.

BH   Did you see the Whitney show?[3]

DJ   Yeah.

BH   What did you think of that?

DJ   I thought it was better than usual. More current.

BH   I did too. [*Laughter*] It really looked like what the Whitney Annual ought to look like. Even though I may or may not like everything.

DJ   That's about the first time, yeah.

BH   That's true. I really felt that too. They have to be good now. But essentially, just what little I saw of that *Box Show* last night and the Whitney show — I hate to say that I was kind of impressed by both shows, and even *The Box Show*, what little I saw of it, was very impressive.[4] I mean, it's kind of overwhelming, but you know there's tremendous activity going on.

DJ   There's a lot of interesting things. It's pretty good work. I think if you say "a lot of very good work," you cut it down quite a bit, but if you say there's "a lot of fairly good work" —

BH   Fairly good work —

DJ   — there really is an enormous amount.

BH   And it's incredibly varied. I mean, the whole —

DJ   Yes.

BH   I was with [Paul] Georges for a while last night.[5] Went to a fellow by the name of Beauchamp's — Bob Beauchamp — whose paintings I don't like too much.[6]

DJ   I don't either.

BH   But his drawings I think are extraordinary, and he has a whole drawing show that is worth looking at. They really are kind of interesting. I mean, they are really good. And then Georges pipes up and says he thought they were good too, and he said, "If America had sixty more years of peace, or fifty more years of peace, we'd produce an art that is overwhelming." I think that is true.

DJ   Peace and money.

BH   Well, yes. Peace without depression. He really is kind of interested in art, he's an art lover.

DJ   Despite my defensiveness about the complexity that these things have, they probably are simpler. I very much don't think that they're simpler in quality. If anything, it's perhaps more complex in quality.

BH   But in what way?

DJ   I certainly think they're stronger in quality. The strongness is one reason why they are somewhat simpler. They have to work all at once. The older painting – well, it does have an effect all at once, I suppose, but it's of a lesser intensity than a lot of the American work in the last ten or fifteen years. You really only comprehend it after you look at it part by part. I think most of the new work is intended to have much more impact at once. You certainly see things later. I think it's meant to be understood more as a single thing – from Pollock on to the present.

BH   Well, Pollock actually worked very simply, and he worked very directly.

DJ   Yeah. Pollock is not an ordinary painter; he's not an expressionist in the usual sense.

BH   No, not at all.

DJ   He's always been pulled in with them, but I think he's a much more radical artist – more than de Kooning. As far as the second generation goes, I think they really missed the whole boat on his importance.

BH Pollock?

DJ Yeah.

BH What about [Arshile] Gorky?

DJ Oh, he's a nice painter, but – I like them. Some of the drawings are very nice, but I think he's a pretty old-fashioned
painter. I don't think he did anything as unusual as Pollock.
Pollock looks unusual and radical even now.

BH Yeah, there's no question about that. Well, a genius is a genius; there's only about five geniuses in every fifty years.

DJ Not so few as that.

BH Hopper may be one, and [Winslow] Homer one, and
Eakins.

DJ I'll take Hopper out – I'll leave the other two.

BH What?

DJ Hopper's a good painter, but take him out of that rank.

BH Well, Eakins and Homer –

DJ Eakins and Homer, I think.

BH Eakins and Homer, Hopper, and maybe Pollock – there
aren't many more.

DJ Not Hopper.

BH Not Hopper? He's out?

DJ He's too late on that, and also –

BH You think he's not good?

DJ I think he's good, but I think he was too late to do what
he was doing and to do it at a first-rate caliber, for a lot of
reasons.

BH There's a point in that.

DJ He's a good painter, and I think he's got a lot that is per-
tinent to American art generally and even to, oh, Newman, almost anybody. I think that spareness and simplicity is pervasive, also in Hopper. It goes all the way back to
Homer and beyond. There's probably more in the American tradition than people give the place credit for. I think
there are certain elements you could probably trace back,
maybe even as far back as – I've forgotten his name –

[Robert] Feke, I guess.[7] Or [John Singleton] Copley, especially something like Copley's portrait of Paul Revere, where he made a right-angle triangle.[8] The thing is relatively uncomposed compared to European work of the time. I think it would have been somewhat irritating to Europeans of that time.

BH   It didn't carry all the capitals.

DJ   Yeah, it could get a little too simple.

BH   I've always kind of defended Hopper in the sense that if one had to find a painter of, say, from 1910 to 1950 — it's one of my great arguments against the bad abstract expressionists — that if one had to find a painter that really represented America, that really described America, say, sixty thousand years from now, or two thousand, or five thousand, one would see in Hopper — or if literature survived too, someone like Hemingway, [Thomas] Wolfe, or [Theodore] Dreiser, or [John] Dos Passos — all the loneliness of America, and the sparseness and everything. I always said that if you think you're doing so well, then hey, the only painter in the last fifty years that's going to represent what literature talked about, assuming that literature speaks the truth from time to time, then Hopper's it. And I always ask, "Who are the writers who are abstract expressionists?" Kerouac?

DJ   No, but description, I don't think, is all that important as the art representing a period much later. For one thing, you really don't understand that much about any period from its art. I think you probably overestimate that.

BH   Well, they either glorify it or attack it.

DJ   Well, I think even if they like it, you're bound to miss a great deal that was in it at the time.

BH   That's true.

DJ   You see it considerably pared down. You don't know all the associations and what it can mean in all sorts of ways. But especially, you see the force of it, and I think something more complex than just description, in Hopper's case. Well, for example, Asia House has Chinese bronzes over there.

BH   I saw them.

DJ   And they are thoroughly unintelligible as far as the reasons go. They don't say anything about China at the time, but they're extremely powerful things. Somehow there is something this powerful in the culture at that time, and that's all you know. I think that's all you can deal with, and I don't think the fact that Hopper shows what the place looks like is all that important. I sort of – I like it, I have a certain nostalgia for it. I recognize this very much in Hopper. It does look like the United States; it looks like the '30s and my first impressions of everything, all of which I have to deal with and which get mixed up in my work and probably get mixed up in everybody else's work too. But I think it can come out in more complex ways. I think some of the things I deal with Hopper probably has dealt with also, since it's somewhat the same environment, and I have pretty strong reactions to what this country looks like. Mix it up with the fact that it looks pretty dull and spare, and you like this, and dislike it, and it's very complicated.

I'd like to present this more forcefully than Hopper, but not as description. But I think you have to – whatever the environment looks like does enter into people's art almost invariably in one way or another; it's very remote or it isn't. I know in my work it has to have a certain amount of ordinariness. I admire other people's work that is more exotic, such as [Lee] Bontecou's and [Lucas] Samaras's, but I suppose I work in a way within limits of ordinariness. Those limits come from what's around you, and you know what this range is. I think maybe an artist like Bob Morris may have this problem too; it may have something to do with what it looks like – simple shapes and –

BH   In the cubist period, that was really what they were interested in, not the look of Paris – that's what really killed the School of Paris, even though it looked like Paris. In Hopper, certainly a strip of road with trees couldn't be anything else than America, but he's the only one who did it.

DJ   Well, I think there are artists who are more or less contemporary with Hopper who are more relevant. I think that an artist like Stuart Davis[9] has more to do with what the United States is actually like than Hopper. But also you have the big problem here, too, that you don't represent exactly the United States or the culture. You're in it and it gets mixed up in what you're doing, but you're one out of the other two hundred million and you only know little parts of it, and I think that no one is going to represent it in a very broad, grand way. Anyway, the culture is not only American.

BH   I guess that comes from being literary in nature. Tolstoy, to my mind, represents Russia.

DJ   Tolstoy may not be showing that much of Russia at that time, even. It's hard to tell. You tend to associate the quality of the period with what's lasted – what's still good. And that quality becomes the whole period. Whatever didn't get written about or painted just goes.

But I don't much like the idea of representing the United States in my work. It's just that you live here and you are involved in your sense of what's around you – your sense of what's ordinary, for example, that I talked about.

BH   Is that true of most artists you know?

DJ   Is what true?

BH   I mean, about that feeling – do you think they would all agree with that?

DJ   Well, I don't think anyone now would say that they're painting the state of the culture of America. I think that's too grand and pompous a thing for anybody to claim. You're only dealing with whatever you know, which is a

very small part of it, and later on it'll look like it has something to do with the period. Obviously, the artists have
something to do with one another. They tend to set up
certain common qualities among themselves.

BH   Did you meet, then, after you started painting?

DJ   After I started painting?

BH   Well, I mean in this whole thing – Stella, for example, I
remember a few years back, in '60, a kind of showing –

DJ   Yeah.

BH   In '60, '61?

DJ   I met him maybe –

BH   Your first show was just last year, wasn't it?[10] Did you meet
painters working in a similar manner before your show,
like Frank Stella or Dan Flavin?[11]

DJ   I might have met Stella four years ago, but I didn't especially know him. I got to know him somewhat in the last
couple of years. I've known Flavin for about four years,
and of course he hadn't shown yet.[12] I don't know how
it may look to other people, but I think their work looks
pretty diverse. Stella is opulent, for example –

BH   Opulent? Silver paint and –

DJ   And the purple, in general, and the weight and opulence
of some of his paintings, which I like very much, but they
are very alien to me.

BH   What do you think of Louise Nevelson?

DJ   Nice, but nothing special.

BH   Quite an opposite to – do you like her son, Mike Nevelson? Have you seen his sparse pieces of wood?

DJ   Well, they're all right. I don't think they're remarkable.
There are some other people along that line. He's not
too far from Gabe Kohn, and he did those things a long
time ago.

BH   No. That's true. Raoul Hague, what do you think about
Hague?

DJ   About the same thing. I don't think they're unusual artists.

Nevelson's, they're nice – I guess that's not a good word. I think they're good secondary artists. I don't know how to evaluate them.

B H   Pastiche, in one way or another – sort of put together.

D J   No, it's on the level, but I'm not interested in all that composition within the little boxes, and then the black monochrome is a little swank and easy. I like – I guess the things by Newman are the best around.

B H   That's certainly a switch from what I heard in New York. Newman was around early, but for about eight years they really gave him the –

D J   Yeah, I know. I don't know too much about that. It's sort of interesting. Well, you see, I suppose his looked a little geometric. But again, I don't think – I don't quite understand the opposition between him and Pollock. They probably thought Pollock was acceptable because it looked like expressionism.

B H   Yeah. And came out of surrealism.

D J   Yeah, and yet to me Pollock is just as radical and unlike expressionism as Newman.

B H   I couldn't agree with you more. I never thought about that before.

D J   And I sure don't think Newman has anything to do with the old-fashioned European geometricism, which I assume they linked him with. I think his development at that time was connected with Pollock.

B H   You know, they always say about Ad Reinhardt that he is a kind of Lutheran minister. Is there something like a certain morality involved in your attitude toward art?

D J   Well, there's a morality in that you want your work to be good and serious art, I suppose. I think most of the art now is involved with a denial of any kind of absolute morality, or general morality. I think most of us in one way or another are involved in ideas of a fairly loose world, however it's expressed, whether obviously, like [John]

Chamberlain, or just accidentally, or like Newman — his paintings are so open, you know, that they can't be read in the old ordered sense that Mondrian and other European painters had. But I don't think that geometricism is any more moral or serious than loose painting, or work like Oldenburg's, or Lichtenstein's, or [H.C.] Westermann's. I don't think there's anything pure about it being geometric.

BH   You remember Plato, of course, on art, about the representation of objects as being the death of culture, or the death of civilization, so in that sense there could be, according to Plato, a morality implied. Oldenburg making hamburgers — because hamburgers we have, and tables, and they represent things, and they had them, and he wanted to do away with art.

DJ   Well, his [Plato's] ideas of form, pure form, are extremely uninteresting. I don't think geometric art — I don't like to call it that, but it's handy — I don't think it's any more pure than pop art or anything else. It doesn't have anything to do with purity. There's a certain type of quality involved that can't be gotten any other way. I have no real interest in objects or anything I can see around such as what Oldenburg does. Obviously, Oldenburg's interest in what he can see around him is more immediate than mine; he has to deal with that sort of thing. I like his work a lot, but I don't have that kind of interest in that sort of thing, and I don't want to be prescriptive or naturalistic in any way, so for the time being I'm left with fairly geometric sort of arrangements, because that doesn't have any of these things. I can't tell, it might prove too narrow, I don't know, that's up to me, or — the geometricism is there by default. I never worked that way; I never had anything to do with the usual geometric art; I didn't know that much about European developments along that line — neoplasticism, or constructivism, or any of those things.

BH   I talked to a man in a store a long time ago in New York, three or four years ago. He had a little shop in North Carolina, I think it was, and his family made furniture. He was the son of a wealthy furniture manufacturer whose name I don't remember, even his. And he was very open and straight, and he started talking, and he said, "I cracked up, and I was in Connecticut in a mental hospital, and they taught me – part of the therapy was making frames." And he said, "I knew when those two ends joined, I knew I found them." And he set up a frame shop, a little gallery in North Carolina somewhere – Greensboro or something like that. As I say, is there anything to that? When two ends join, is that – ?

DJ   Well, in any one art, there are a lot of technical things that you can get to like. Some things are a lot of dull labor, I suppose. I also don't mind other people building them, but the way things go together and are made is interesting to me; I like that a lot. I pay a lot of attention to how things are done, and the whole act of building something is interesting.

BH   When you do it actually, do you feel the edges of the wood go together?

DJ   Well, when it fits, it's very nice. It's very exasperating when you can't get it right. Building things can be really boring, too. After all, the work isn't the point; the piece is. I've had a tinsmith make a few when I've gotten hold of some money. I'm just as satisfied with their joints, maybe more so, than I am with mine. Also, I can't make as many.

BH   Do you know the work of Ernest Trova?

DJ   Yes.

BH   What do you think of it?

DJ   I think it's – I didn't see the last show. I saw the one before that.

BH   It's obviously being sold – a lot of money in bronze and aluminum.

DJ   It's expensive.

BH   It must have cost a fortune when he did that show. A thousand dollars.

DJ   My work is not that expensive. I can get a pretty large piece of galvanized iron for $150.

BH   How does his work fit in? Is that kind of surrealism – ?

DJ   Well, I didn't see this show. I saw the one last year. It was played up as pop art.

BH   I don't remember that one.

DJ   But so far it seems pretty dull to me. No particular invention.

BH   It seems too easy.

DJ   I guess so.

BH   Even though it's complex and difficult to do, it seems like anybody could come in once you had the idea and do it. That's not true of really good art, I think.

DJ   Well, it's good if it's unusual. I don't know about difficult. Maybe it's difficult to understand important things. I don't think it necessarily has to be difficult to make. Obviously, I think that's irrelevant.

This conversation was sourced from an audio recording and a transcript, which vary slightly from each other. The original sound tape reel and archival transcript are in the records of the Oral History Program, Archives of American Art, Smithsonian Institution, Washington, DC.

1   Norman Mailer, "Cities Higher Than Mountains," *The New York Times Magazine*, January 31, 1965, 16–17, 30, 32, 33, 40.

2   Judd attended the Art Students League, in New York, from 1948 to 1953, while also working toward an undergraduate degree at Columbia University. He received his BS in philosophy from Columbia, cum laude, in 1953.

3   *Annual Exhibition of Contemporary American Sculpture*, Whitney Museum of American Art, New York, December 9, 1964–January 31, 1965.

4   *The Box Show*, Byron Gallery, New York, February 3–27, 1965. Included in this show was Judd's first progression: a twenty-five-and-a-half-inch red, round-front progression in wood from 1964.

5   Paul Georges (1923–2002) was an American figurative painter.

6   "Bob Beacham" is the spelling provided in the transcript at the Archives
        of American Art. The editors have rendered the name here as "Bob Beau-
        champ"; Robert Beauchamp (1923–1995) was an American figurative
        painter. In the 1960s, Beauchamp and Judd were both represented by
        Green Gallery, New York.
7   Robert Feke (c. 1705–c. 1752) was an American portrait painter.
8   John Singleton Copley (1738–1815) was an Anglo-American painter, fa-
        mous for his portraits. His *Paul Revere* (1768) was not publicly displayed
        until 1928, at the Museum of Fine Arts, Boston, where it was subsequently
        gifted in 1930 by Revere's great-grandsons.
9   Stuart Davis (1892–1964) was an American artist known for his bold, col-
        orful paintings influenced by jazz, advertising, and urban life. Davis iden-
        tified his art as American, writing in 1921: "I too feel the thing Whitman
        felt – and I too will express it in pictures – America – the wonderful place
        we live in." In 1962, Judd reviewed Davis's solo show at Downtown Gallery,
        New York, in *Arts Magazine*. Noting Davis's "amazing continuity," Judd's
        review began, "There should be applause. Davis, at sixty-seven, is still a
        hot shot." Judd, "Stuart Davis" in *Donald Judd: Complete Writings 1959–1975*,
        55–56.
10   *Don Judd*, Green Gallery, New York, December 17, 1963–January 11,
        1964. This exhibition was Judd's first solo show to include works in three
        dimensions.
11   See "New Nihilism or New Art?" (1964) in this volume, 28–58.
12   Judd met Dan Flavin in 1962 at a gathering in a Brooklyn apartment or-
        ganized to discuss the possibility of a cooperative artist-run gallery. See
        Michael Govan and Tiffany Bell, *Dan Flavin: The Complete Lights, 1961–
        1996*, exh. cat. (New York: Dia Art Foundation, 2004), 183. Flavin's first
        exhibition of all fluorescent light works was at Green Gallery, New York,
        in November–December 1964.

Interview with Bruce Glaser and Lucy R. Lippard
December 8, 1965

This conversation was conducted as a follow-up to "New Nihilism or New Art?," a radio program hosted by art historian Bruce Glaser that featured Judd as a participant (see 28–58 in this volume). Quoting from the original broadcast, Glaser and art critic Lucy R. Lippard ask Judd for clarification concerning his statements on nonhierarchical composition and his problem with the term "reductive" as applied to his work.

In the fall of 1965, Judd presented work in the VIII Bienal de São Paulo (September 4–November 28, 1965), his first significant international exhibition. This iteration of the São Paulo biennial also included works by Billy Al Bengston, Robert Irwin, Barnett Newman, Larry Poons, and Frank Stella.

BG   [Bruce Glaser] Why do you want to avoid compositional effects? You said that most effects tend to carry with them "all the structures, values, feelings … of the whole European tradition, which suits me fine if that's all down the drain." When in fact there is only optical effects, whereas [Victor] Vasarely has to have at least three or four squares, slanted, tilted inside each other, and all arranged, et cetera. And I ask, "It's too busy?" And you say it is to someone like [Larry] Poons, and that Vasarely's "composition has the effect of … order and quality that old European painting had, which I find pretty objectionable."[1]

Now. What I want to ask you here at this point is — I was wondering if you wanted to say a little bit more about that old order and quality and this kind of busyness that you seem to be talking about. I asked if it was too busy and you said yes, it is in terms of someone like Poons.

DJ   [Donald Judd] I don't remember the Poons remark.

BG   You actually said it. It's on the transcript.

DJ   Am I criticizing Poons?

BG   No, no.

LRL   [Lucy R. Lippard] In other words, Vasarely is busy compared to Poons?

DJ   It's not that Vasarely's busy. My objection isn't that he's busy. It's that in that busyness or in that multiplicity, there's a certain structure that has qualities which I don't like.

BG   What are those qualities?

DJ   Qualities of European art so far.

BG   Well, what are those qualities?

DJ   They're numerable and complex. The main way of saying it is that they're linked up with a philosophy.

BG   Which philosophy?

DJ   Rationalism.

BG   Who do you think of specifically, a painter or philosopher – Descartes?

DJ   Descartes, yeah.

BG   Do you mean to say that your work is apart from rational-
      ism?

DJ   Yeah. It's all a rationalist's phantom land. All of those are
      systems built beforehand, a priori systems. They express
      certain types of thinking and logic, which is pretty much
      discredited now as a way of finding out about what the
      world is like.

BG   Discredited by whom?

DJ   Scientists. Both philosophy and science.

BG   What is the alternative to a rationalistic system in your
      method? It's often said that your work is preconceived
      before you do it, that you think the plan out. Somewhere
      during our discussion you talk about that. Isn't that a ra-
      tionalistic method of working?

DJ   Not necessarily. That's much smaller. Whether you think
      it out while you work on it or you think it out before-
      hand is a much smaller problem than the nature of the
      work. What you want to express is a much bigger thing
      than however you may go at it. Poons works out the dots
      somewhat as he goes along, figures out his theme before-
      hand and works them out also – makes changes as he goes
      along. Obviously, I can't make many changes, so I do what
      I can when I get stuck sometimes.

BG   In other words, you might be referring to an antirational-
      ist position somewhere way before you start actually mak-
      ing works of art.

DJ   I'm making it for quality that I think is interesting and
      more or less true. The quality involved in that kind of a
      composition isn't true to me.

BG   What about someone like Piero della Francesca? Would
      you say he was too rationalistic or what?

DJ   Not for his time. But I like him.

BG   Can you be specific, in your own words, how it consciously
      reflects an antirationalistic point of view?

DJ   The parts are relatively unrelational. The business of relat-
      ing parts is –

LRL   In other words, if there is nothing to relate, then you can't
      be rational about it, because it's just there.

BG   It's almost an abdication of a kind of thinking – a logical
      thinking, in other words. A plus B equals C, or if you have
      A and you have B, therefore you will have C.

LRL   It's a pure creation. It's making something without –

DJ   I don't have anything against using some sort of logic
      like that either. That's simple. When you start relating
      parts – well, in the first place, you're assuming the work of
      art is painting; most of the structure comes out of paint-
      ing, not sculpture, in our Western tradition. You're as-
      suming you have a vague whole that is the rectangle of
      the canvas and definite parts, which is all screwed up, be-
      cause you should have a definite whole and maybe no
      parts, or very few. The parts are always more important
      than the whole.

BG   And you want the whole more important than the parts?

DJ   Yeah, the whole is it.

BG   Now it's becoming clear. This is the first time I've heard
      you explain yourself a little bit more clearly. That's good.

DJ   The big problem is to maintain the sense of the whole
      thing.

BG   You really want to return it to a kind of mythical situation
      of, like, Athena springing full grown from the forehead of
      Zeus. Is it the same idea, that there's no gestation? There
      is a kind of gestation –

DJ   I'll think about it. I'll change it if I can.

BG   But it's always thought of as a whole thing.

DJ   I want it to exist as a whole thing. That's not especially
      unusual; painting has been going for that for a long time.
      You've got people like Oldenburg and, I don't know – a
      lot of people have a whole effect to their work.

LRL   What makes the space that you use that different from neo-
      classical sculpture? I think I know, but I want to ask. What
      are you after in the way of new space? Under, around, in-
      stead of compositional space?

DJ   In the first place, I don't know a heck of a lot about neo-classical sculpture, outside of vaguely liking it. I'm using actual space because when I was doing paintings, I couldn't see any way out of having a certain amount of volition-ism in the paintings. I thought that also was a quality of Western tradition, and I didn't want it.

LRL   But you said that at one point, when you had that horizontal with the five verticals coming down from it, that you weren't opposing them at all but using them as a whole, and that kept it away from being compositional [image 6]. Still, after all, you are opposing them, because vertical and horizontal are opposed. Perpendicular is an opposition, and if you've got space in between each one, then it makes them parts.

DJ   Yeah, it does somewhat. The big problem is that anything that starts to not be absolutely plain begins to have parts in some way. So, it's possible for the work.

[*Break in recording*]

DJ   The thing is to be able to work and do different things and yet not to break up the wholeness that a piece has. You see, the piece with the brass and the five verticals is first, to me, that shape. I don't think of the brass being opposed to the five things in the way [Naum] Gabo or [Antoine] Pevsner might have an angle like this and then another one sort of supporting it or related against it on a diagonal. Also, the verticals below the brass both support the brass and pend from it; the length is just enough from it so it seems that they can hang as well as support it. They're sort of caught there, and I didn't think they came loose into parts. If they were longer and the brass obviously sat on them, then I wouldn't like the piece.

BG   Two other questions about the relationship with the neo-classic. You obviously have an awareness of constructivist work and Gabo and Pevsner. I was just curious – what about the Bauhaus? You keep talking about standards and austerity; is that only in relationship to the idea that you want to get your work there, whole, all at once? Or are you really interested, or fascinated, or do you think that there is really anything in the idea, the Bauhaus dictum, that less is more?

DJ   Not necessarily. In the first place, I'm more interested in neoplasticism and constructivism, all of it, more than I was before, perhaps, but I was never very influenced by it. I'm certainly more influenced by what happened here in the United States rather than anything like that. So my admiration of Pevsner and Gabo is sort of in retrospect. And I considered the Bauhaus too long ago to think about it, and I never thought about it that much, and any general statement like that I'm not inclined to agree with.

BG   The one question that's always been in the back of my mind – well, before I get to that major question, I've always had the feeling, and now I have some qualms about it, asking this – if there was always some kind of negativism or nihilism in your point of view? In a sense, you kind of wanted a non-European tradition, which I get, and you explained yourself well about why you wanted to do it. But nevertheless, even this explanation – would you say that you find any sympathy or anything from an ideological standpoint that appeals to you in a nihilistic point of view?

DJ   No.

BG   Not at all?

DJ   I don't consider it nihilistic or negative or cool or anything. Also, I don't think that's a quality that's posited in my work, that I object to the Western tradition – it's just something I don't want to do. That's all. I want to do something else. That doesn't mean I'm against something and it shows in the work.

BG   Don't you see art as kind of evolutionary? You talk about what art was, and now you're saying art isn't about that – that's all old hat. You've actually written this –

DJ   It's old hat because, as I said, it involves all those beliefs, which I really can't accept in life. I don't want to work with it anymore. It's not necessarily that any of that work has suddenly become bad in itself. If I get hold of a Piero della Francesca, that's fine.

LRL   I understand the limitations that you think painting has, which you've written about a couple of times – the limitation of the rectangle and so on.[2]

DJ   In the first place, I object to the whole reduction idea, I've decided finally –

LRL   Finally! [*Laughter*]

DJ   It wasn't so bad, but it's getting to the point where it's really cockeyed.

LRL   Why?

DJ   Because it's only reduction in these things that someone doesn't want. If my work is reductionist or something, it's because it doesn't have the elements that people think should be there, and it has other elements –

LRL   But it's going off in another direction.

DJ   It has elements there that I like, which are somewhat new.

LRL   Yeah, it doesn't stress the negative, like within [Kenneth] Noland –

DJ   You think Noland has all these things that he doesn't have in his paintings, and yet there's a whole list of things that he does have that painting didn't have before. Why is it necessarily a reduction? Just because it's spare doesn't necessarily mean it's a reduction.

LRL   It's less to look at.

DJ   I don't think that.

This conversation was sourced from an audio recording, which is significantly damaged. The original sound tape reel is in the Lucy R. Lippard papers, 1930s–2010, bulk 1960s–1990, Archives of American Art, Smithsonian Institution, Washington, DC.

1   Glaser refers here to statements made in an interview conducted with Judd in 1964. See "New Nihilism or New Art?" (1964) in this volume, 28–58.
2   See Judd's "Specific Objects" (1964) in *Donald Judd Writings*, 134–45.

"The New Sculpture"
Symposium with Kynaston McShine (moderator),
Mark di Suvero, and Barbara Rose
May 2, 1966

"The New Sculpture" was held in conjunction with *Primary Structures: Younger American and British Sculptors*, at the Jewish Museum, New York (April 27–June 12, 1966). This exhibition, organized by Kynaston McShine, the museum's curator of painting and sculpture, contributed significantly to the codification of the group of artists associated with "minimalism," a term that Judd and many other artists repeatedly rejected. Forty-two emerging British and American artists, mostly in their thirties, were invited by McShine to participate, including Carl Andre, Anthony Caro, Walter De Maria, Dan Flavin, Judd, Robert Morris, and Anne Truitt.

In "Statement" (1966), his contribution to the *Primary Structures* exhibition catalogue, Judd objected to what he called "several popular ideas," namely the terms "reductive," "minimal," "ABC," "non-art," and "anti-art" to describe the new work of the time, including his own. Nevertheless, despite Judd's disavowal and that of many other artists, critics such as Hilton Kramer in *The New York Times* did not hesitate to repeat the terms "minimal" and "ABC art" as catchalls for the various kinds of works reflected in *Primary Structures* and other exhibitions during the mid- to late 1960s. Judd wrote in 1969 (in "Complaints: Part I"), only a few years after the exhibition, that he "hated the *Primary Structures* show at the Jewish Museum in 1966, both itself and its title – 'primary' sounds Platonic."

Although Robert Morris also participated in this symposium, his statements have not been included here, per his request.

BR   [Barbara Rose] I think one might begin this discussion by remarking that the sculpture in this exhibition broke down quite clearly into two groups of work: the open, linear, flat, and planar works, mainly by the English sculptors such as Anthony Caro, Phillip King, Gerald Laing, Michael Bolus, and David Annesley, and on the other hand, the volumetric sculpture, mainly by Americans, which depended on single indivisible volumes. Most of the work of the former was polychromed. Some of the American work was painted, but often only one color was used.

KM   [Kynaston McShine] I knew that color would be an important factor while selecting the show. I also realized that the intrinsic color of the material would often be significant, not in the old sense of the patina of a bronze, but in such a way that color and structure are unified.

BR   [Ellsworth] Kelly paints his pieces, but Don Judd uses color by coating aluminum with commercial metallic glazes or by using the intrinsic color of the metal. Of course, that gives quite a different effect from his earlier painted wood or painted metal pieces.

DJ   [Donald Judd] I think it would be best of all if the material had its own color which was intrinsic and not applied. But there isn't much color of this sort to work with. So far, the only thing that really had a lot of color is plastic. For example, Larry Bell's coated glass boxes are really pale. And most of the metals are gray in one way or another.

KM   In Judd's wall piece the transverse rod has been colored blue, while the galvanized aluminum boxes have been left in their original state. In the similar floor construction which faces it, there is no applied color [image 7]. Since the pieces are quite similar, I wonder how you decide about color?

DJ   I don't work from any general principle. I select what happens to be in accordance with my purpose. As I said, I'd rather they'd color the material than paint it, because by adding paint you're adding some other standard or authority, which is somehow redundant. But it gets pretty tricky as to what color to use. In fact, the bare tube is not uncolored; it's been anodized. Therefore, it has an extra layer, which has been oxidized. But all that tends to become picayune…

BR   To change the subject, I wanted to explain the appropriateness of the participation of [Robert] Morris, Judd, and di Suvero in this symposium. They were among the first to establish and make explicit new positions in sculpture which made possible some of the developments this show has focused upon.

In di Suvero's work, there is a kind of dynamic tension of structural relationships and a directness of impact that have influenced many young sculptors, particularly those in the Park Place group.[1] Morris was one of the first, if not the first, to use simple unitary volumes rather than to make sculpture that depended on a relationship of parts. Several works in the show by other artists derive directly from prototypes he executed in plywood from 1961 to 1965, which were exhibited at the Green Gallery and widely reproduced in photographs. In these works, he used the room as a general environment for works which related to the floor, wall, and ceiling in unprecedented ways. Judd was among the first to use identical or repeated elements to work with mathematical sequences, particularly those extendable to infinity. Like Morris, he too used simple volumes and nonrelational composition.

I think it is important to point out how these three artists developed precedents which prepared the way for the kind of work we're seeing now. Di Suvero's work, although more romantic than the sculpture in the show, must be counted as part of the general space —

US   [Unknown speaker] Which we perceive is untrue. We've learned it, yet you're still operating in its terms.

MDS [Mark di Suvero] When you talk about my space and say that it's suggestive, that is right. But that shows a weakness on my part, that I think that space should be *warped*. The mere idea that man could not find one side of its infinite surface until the eighteenth century is incredible. This is knowledge we must have like a part of our fingertips.[2]

DJ Those kinds of things are very tricky in application to art. Art is not science, and whether it is behind science or not is a very complicated question. If it's dealing with a specific scientific problem, certainly it's following, but on the whole it is not doing that. Usually science is just a mine for technique. Nothing much else.

MDS They used to talk about the interchange between art and science. I think that it meant something then and it still means something now. It's a special kind of approach to a problem which is explorative. I mean, in a true sense, art does not explore, as opposed to the tools which you use. You use a man as a tool. And I object to that, because I think that we should use everything we have in the communicative world.

DJ I think there's a big gap between the discussion of Euclidean and non-Euclidean geometry and art, and that the two should be left in the different areas in which they are – the sort of context in which it developed. And on that score, I want to ask Mark whether he agrees with Hilton Kramer that the new sculpture is anonymous and impersonal, and whether he finds this objectionable, since it is an aesthetic position opposed to his own.[3]

MDS I think *Primary Structures* is the key show of the '60s, and that it has introduced a new generation of artists. As for whether the work is anonymous, all work is anonymous that doesn't have any name. Some of it is beautiful. The Ron Bladen, for example, is a great piece. It expands our idea of scale and really changes our knowledge of space. Some of the work presents itself as manufactured object, and the very sense of objectness eliminates it from what I think is the most crucial part of modern sculpture. I think that my friend Don Judd can't qualify as an artist because he doesn't do the work. And there is more and more of this kind of thing, which to my mind is the negation of the object by making an object. But this is not grappling with the essential fact that a man has to make a thing in order to be an artist. As far as I'm concerned, those works which give me that sense of radiance which I find I need in a work are those that have been actually worked over by the artist. I think that all those pointed-up bronzes, the pointed-up marbles, the expanded bronzes from the casts are meaningless.

DJ   Now, wait a minute. The point is not whether one makes a work oneself or not. The point is that it's all a case of technique that makes the thing visible, so that I don't see in the long run why one technique is any more essentially art than another technique. And there are presumably an infinite number of techniques. I don't see why someone shouldn't go out and find the one that suits him, whether or not it conforms to the manipulatory technique that's been going on for some time or to a new one.

BR   Here is the crucial question – whether an abstract aesthetic conception which may be manufactured or fabricated is as much art as the personal manipulation of materials. I think the heart of most of the objections to the new work is that people feel that since they can't see the artist's fingerprints, it's not a personal statement.

MDS   In a sense, it's a question of the ability to be terrific in one procedure, or the willingness to make mistakes. You never discover broken color by just sitting there analyzing color charts, although theoretically you could. But it has to happen with actually working with paint on canvas. That doesn't mean that I don't like work that doesn't have fingerprints. For example, there is Carl Andre's line of firebricks. It is really nihilistic, but because it is beautiful, it gives you a sense of joy, as few of the works in the show do. But that is because I think that at the core of modern sculpture is space, and most of the artists in the show have avoided dealing with space, although some of the British ones have tangled with it.

BR   I couldn't disagree more. What is interesting about the good new work is that it encloses space rather than cutting into it. It works with interior volume rather than mass, changing our conventional notion about space. In fact, I began by observing that the work breaks down into two groups. Of the pieces which cut into space in the manner of Tony Caro's work, none begins to approach the level of Caro's sculpture, which stands out in a way that divorces it from work derived from it. And then, on the other hand, there is the volumetric work, of which Morris's and Judd's pieces would be examples, which deal with space in an entirely different way, by displacing it and enclosing it.

MDS   You mean the monolith, the old-fashioned monolith? The obelisk in Central Park?[4]

BR   No, I think that the volumetric works in the show operate differently from the monolith in the manner in which they displace great chunks of space, and in that one often had the real sense that they are hollow shells and not solid.

DJ   Anyway, Mark is defining space as something that is moved by the forms. If it isn't moved, if it's static, and then, according to his definition, it isn't really space. But space that is shifted around or activated in one way or another is not what interests me.

MDS   The people who change space through a new sense of scale are the ones I dig the most. Giacometti certainly does it, although he has to use the figure. But he actually changes the size of the space.

DJ   I hate that kind of space and purposely avoid it, because it's an anthropomorphic kind of space.

BR   To go on to another point, Hilton Kramer listed what he believes were the precedents for the new sculpture in the works of the constructivists, [Naum] Gabo, [Georges] Vantongerloo, Calder, David Smith, and Louise Nevelson.[5] I don't agree that their work has any kind of direct relationship to the new sculpture, except perhaps in the scale of Calder's and Smith's works or in their relative simplicity. The roots of the new work, it seems to me, lie more specifically in painting, in that it grows out of a dissatisfaction with the limitations of painting. I know, for example, that Don and Bob were both originally painters. Let me ask you then, why did you stop painting and start making sculpture?

DJ   I became very tired of several major aspects of painting and felt that I couldn't do anything I would ever like with any of them. In the first place, I was tired of the fact that it's a rectangle, and in the second, that it's so many inches from the wall, and that no matter what you do, you have to put something within the shape of the canvas. For example, if you put a series of circles within the canvas, that leaves all that border around the circles. On the other hand, if you decide you want to emphasize the rectangularity of the canvas, then you have to use elements that enforce it – that is, correspond to the edges in some way. That really leaves you no choice. Also, paintings are invariably canvas and I'm very tired of that particular surface, and of oil paint, too, so it seemed a good thing to give up. Painting seemed very restricted. No matter what you did, you couldn't make it strong enough and clear enough. So there was nothing to do but quit on it.

      Apropos of sculpture, I never took sculpture as a model, although I was impressed – not influenced, exactly, but pushed somewhat – by quite a few people, for example by [Lee] Bontecou and [John] Chamberlain, who at one time I thought did stronger work than I could possibly do. And one of the reasons I stopped painting at the same time was that Oldenburg's work was much stronger than anything I could possibly make in a painting. So the new developments in sculpture don't exactly amount to a revolution. It didn't come overnight. I think it's had a pretty normal development. And you don't want to get saddled with a lot of people who are supposed to have influenced you who didn't influence you. For example, even though I admired Smith's work, I never seriously considered it as an influence. But Kramer mentions that Smith's last show was an influence. Now, chronologically, that's impossible, because it was last year, and everybody was pretty well along in what they were doing by then, so Smith's late pieces could not have been an influence. In fact, sculpture always looked archaic to me. It always had the kind of space Mark talked about, and it always had related forms and a certain hierarchy of parts – the major part, the minor part, and so forth. These were things I wasn't interested in and which I certainly was trying to get away from in painting.

BR   But that's what I mean about painting being a primary source for a number of the ideas in the new sculpture. For example, the elimination of internal compositional relationships was accomplished in painting by Pollock and Newman. That is why I feel the antecedents for the new sculpture can be found in painting rather than in sculpture.

DJ   Yes, but I'd say, at least for myself, that those antecedents are extremely general, and that they mostly concern scale. Almost everybody assumes that broad scale is desirable now. Nearly all the best works have it.

KM   How about Russian constructivists, were you interested in their work?

DJ   I think everybody considered constructivism, neoplasticism, and cubism past history by the time Bob and I were developing our work. Mondrian was dead and gone and an Old Master when I thought about painting. Recent American painting seemed much more actual.

KM In the new work, repetition is a very strong element. Why do you think this is so?

BR Repetition is a method of structuring; rhythm is important to art. The three repeated diagonals in Ron Bladen's piece give a particular kind of emphasis and the impressive sense of monumentality, or static majesty, if you like.

KM But it's not really static, because part of the experience consists of just walking around it.

BR Let's put it this way: the viewer moves, but the forms don't leap or jump around. They remain, at least in comparison with open-welded or assembled work, relatively static. They really stand still. That's one of the big differences between Mark's position and the new aesthetic. And the content of the new work is quite different from the more emotional and romantic content of earlier work.

DJ Mark states that sculpture imitates movement in a way. You know, the gist of it is that a certain anthropomorphic attitude runs through his work. One finds it not only in his work, but in the general history of art for the last several hundred years. Although I like his work very much, I would object to this quality if I were doing it. Smith, too, I think, does a great deal of alluding to other things. The general structure even in the last pieces is rather figurative. He has a box there and a box there, which is very relational and allusive. And that particular quality I find pretty unbelievable philosophically and pretty uninteresting. I'd like work that didn't allude to other things and was a specific thing in itself which derived a specific quality from its form.

But I think that my work and Bob's work is art in the same sense that work has always been art. It intends to have a certain quality which deals with what you think about the world, and whatever art is, and I don't think it is essentially any different than art has always been in that respect. And it's certainly not impersonal, anonymous, and all that sort of stuff. I'd rather stay clear of the word "spiritual," since I don't like its old meaning. I think that a given thing creates an interesting space, but that you don't need to set up a certain amount of motion to make it interesting — that a surface in itself is interesting. You don't have to set a form at an angle and relate something else to it. If you have a rectangle of a certain size and certain surface and material and it has the quality you want, then it's sufficiently interesting, and you don't have to work it into some other context to make it interesting.

MDS You talk about your art in a pure, rational fashion, while the formation of values, as you know excellently well, is not based upon this rational cognizant sense. And when you talk about space, you're ignoring the mathematical perception of space. That connection you're making is exactly the kind of analogy making that I object to.

BR Do you feel your work has expressive quality?

DJ Yes, of course. I don't exactly like talking about "spirit," "mysticism," and that sort of thing, because those words have old meanings, and I think they may as well be dumped because their old meanings are stronger than the new meanings.

MDS It's true that what I do really like in a piece of sculpture is to feel from it that sense in which it is not an object, in which it possesses that thing which is not visible to our eyes, which you may call mystical or spiritual. For example, the rock at the Met isn't a rock; it's truly an archaic Apollo. I find that this object art, this "ABC art," is often a special kind of commercial acceptance of the technological world that disavows all of the joy and the tragedy and accepts regimentation, which is what you mean by repetition.[6]

KM Don't you think it's a criticism of the regimentation, though?

MDS   I think it's as much a criticism as anybody who wears a
      gray flannel suit.[7]
BR   Essentially, what Mark is saying is that the joy and the
      tragedy should be in art, whereas what those who accept
      the aesthetic of abstract art feel is that the joy and tragedy
      should be in life, and that the aesthetic emotion, which is
      different, should be in art. But I want to return to the ques-
      tion of scale. You are obviously creating problems for the
      collector who lives in a high-rise apartment and for the
      museums which have limited space. In one sense, the re-
      fusal to compromise on the issue of scale becomes a part of
      the quality of the new work, which is clearly monumen-
      tal sculpture and not coffee-table knickknacks or lobby art.
      But where can this oversize art be accommodated?
DJ   I don't think you worry about where it's going to go. I
      think if you worried about that you wouldn't get anything
      done.
MDS   You use the word "scale" very loosely. Size is meaningless;
      size is stupid, eventually. The biggest man in the world is
      probably the stupidest man in the world.

Questions from the audience:

LS   [Leo Steinberg] I'd like very much to know from Don
      whether the knowledge and the sensation of the hollow-
      ness of their pieces are part of their aesthetic presence.
DJ   I intend my pieces to be hollow. The sheet metal is obvi-
      ously only so thick, and everyone knows how thick it is,
      so that you are aware of this big space inside. That's also
      why the tube in the piece with the four boxes is open, in
      order to show that it is hollow [see image 7].
MDS   I find the two pieces that are clearly hollow inside the most
      interesting in the show. For example, one has a sense, as
      one looks inside the Larry Bell, of knowing that it's hol-
      low, and one experiences a visual contact which you get

neither in painting nor in ordinary sculpture. You know
that it is hollow and you see it constantly reflecting. On
the other hand, knowing that Ron Bladen's piece is hollow,
you still sense that it is not. What he has done is worked
with the center of gravity, which is a really invisible point,
and he's managed to do something that gives me a sense
of awe.

FS [Frank Stella] I would like to ask Don how he feels about
the difference between the way the volumes are experi-
enced in the wall piece and the floor piece.

DJ The volumes are the same, of course. But I think the one
on the floor looks larger because you see all the sides. And
the sense of the volume is probably changed somewhat by
the fact that you don't read the dimensions the same way
in the wall piece, since you're lacking one side to look at.
This has the effect of flattening the piece, which decidedly has a face, while the one on the floor can be looked
at from all sides, making you aware of just how large that
cube is. So there is a difference. Some will prefer one over
the other. But it seems to me that any place you put the
piece is all right, whether it is on the ceiling, wall, or floor.
And I don't think that the ones I have on the wall are reliefs, nor do they have the same kind of format that paintings have. For a while, I didn't know what to do with the
wall pieces; then I figured out that if they project a certain distance and are a certain size, then they get outside of
the whole display effect that you have in painting, which
I dislike. And while it's true that the position does change
the shape, I don't think that one is especially more sacred
than another.

This symposium discussion was sourced from an archival transcript in the Barbara Rose papers, 1962–circa 1969, Archives of American Art, Smithsonian Institution, Washington, DC.

1   The Park Place Gallery was an artists' cooperative space in the 1960s in SoHo, New York, consisting of five sculptors (Mark di Suvero, Peter Forakis, Robert Grosvenor, Anthony Magar, and Forrest "Frosty" Myers) and five painters (Dean Fleming, Tamara Melcher, David Novros, Edwin Ruda, and Leo Valledor). Paula Cooper worked at Park Place from 1964 until its closure in 1967. Cooper later opened a space on Prince Street, the first commercial gallery in SoHo. Judd's first show at Paula Cooper Gallery was the *Benefit for the Student Mobilization Committee to End the War in Vietnam*, October 22–31, 1968. For a further discussion of the history of the Park Place Gallery, see Linda D. Henderson, "Dean Fleming, Ed Ruda, and the Park Place Gallery: Spatial Complexity and the 'Fourth Dimension' in 1960s New York," in *Blanton Museum of Art: American Art Since 1900*, ed. Annette DiMeo Carlozzi and Kelly Baum (Austin: Blanton Museum of Art, 2006), 379–89.

2   The transcript attributes both this response and the preceding (assigned here to Mark di Suvero and an unknown speaker, respectively) to Barbara Rose, as part of her most recent response. The revised attributions used here attempt to account for suggestive shifts in voice and opinion, but cannot be confirmed as definitive.

3   See Hilton Kramer, "'Primary Structures' – The New Anonymity," *The New York Times*, May 1, 1966, 147. Kramer (1928–2012) was an American art critic and editor. In December 1959, Kramer hired Judd to review exhibitions for *Arts Magazine*; Judd continued to write for the magazine, with only a few interruptions, until March 1965.

4   In 1881, Egypt gifted a large obelisk, commissioned by pharaoh Thutmose III around 1450 BCE, to New York's Central Park.

5   "There are sculptural precedents for what the new sculptors are doing – precedents to be found in the work of Gabo and Vantongerloo and Max Bill, in Calder and David Smith and Louise Nevelson – but these are less immediately relevant than the inspiration that has been drawn from recent painting." Kramer, "'Primary Structures' – The New Anonymity," 147.

6   Di Suvero refers here to terminology used by Barbara Rose in her article "ABC Art," *Art in America*, October–November 1965, 57–69, which was one of the first essays devoted to defining minimalism as a style.

7   *The Man in the Gray Flannel Suit* is a 1955 best-selling novel by Sloan Wilson about a man trying to find success and purpose by climbing the ranks of the business world.

"Is Easel Painting Dead?"
Panel discussion with Barbara Rose (moderator),
Darby Bannard, Larry Poons, and Robert Rauschenberg
November 10, 1966

This panel was the first in the Critic's Colloquium, a series of conversations on art hosted by New York University. Barbara Rose, the panel's moderator, and Judd met at Columbia University, where they were both graduate students in art history and studied together under Meyer Schapiro and Renaissance scholar Charles Tornay. Rose earned a PhD and later included Judd in numerous exhibitions she curated and wrote extensively about his work.

Judd had exhibited with Larry Poons in two shows at Green Gallery, New York: *New Work: Part I* (January 8–February 2, 1963) and *Contemporary American Group Show [New Work Part III]* (May–June 15, 1963). Of Poons's work, Judd wrote in "New York Letter" (1965) for *Art International* that "Poons is one of the best of the younger artists. His work is already a substantial achievement. Its affinities, incidentally, are with the best American art and not with optical art…. It's very important that Poons, and others, have discarded the old intellectual basis of art, particularly the old compositional order, and developed ways to deal with live ideas and senses of order, relative order and chance."

Other panels in the series were "The Art Student and the Future of the Avant-Garde," moderated by Sidney Tillim; "The Meaning of the Formal Statement," moderated by Annette Michelson; and "Art and the American Place," moderated by Max Kozloff.

BR [Barbara Rose] Last night I was speaking with Barnett Newman about the topic of this symposium – is easel painting exhausted? – and he said, "Who paints on an easel?" And I guess that's the point – nobody. Artists today paint either on the wall or on the floor.

The question is a little broader than that; I suppose the real question is: "Is painting itself dead?" Or, what do we mean by an "easel painting" in this context? We mean simply an art object that hangs on the wall and that is painted on a two-dimensional cloth support with brushes. I've invited the artists you see up here with me tonight because I think that their work – the work of Darby Bannard, Robert Rauschenberg, Donald Judd, and Larry Poons – represents stands, either pro or con, in terms of this question: "Is painting dead?"

Robert Rauschenberg's last show was a show of sculpture.[1] Recently he has devoted himself increasingly to making mixed-media theater events. Don Judd, who began as a painter, rejected painting on some grounds, which he has made very clear in various theoretical articles that he's written, in order to enter the field of three-dimensional structures. Larry Poons and Darby Bannard, who both were working toward minimal, reductive solutions in their paintings in the early '60s, have recently turned away from such reductive solutions toward a denser, more complex art. Obviously, they think that there is still a large potential for easel painting, or for painting, to be clearer. On the other hand, there does seem to be – because so many artists do seem to be turning away from painting, in the direction of either three-dimensional structures or shaped canvases or various kinds of hybrids – certain dissatisfactions with the convention of easel painting. And I thought we might possibly probe some of these tonight.

To begin, I'd like to ask the artists questions about their stand on the question. I'd like to ask Bob Rauschenberg first whether he thinks that there is any potential left in painting – or, why did you stop painting yourself?

RR [Robert Rauschenberg] I didn't really stop in the sense of just stopping. I found that doing something other than painting in the studio, some experience, seemed to me to be useful just in the general category of keeping alive.

BR Insofar as I know your work, I don't remember ever seeing works of yours that were just simply paint on canvas. Did you ever just do paintings on canvas?

RR Well, I never was convinced of that divine space like a canvas. I always recognize any canvas as a piece of cloth. It is just through the economy of lumber and structure that a fabric is woven horizontally and vertically and that it stretches most expediently in those directions, and I never had a concept to change that shape.

BR Was it pictorial space that you were dissatisfied with, or was it just the sacrosanct idea of the painting as a two-dimensional object?

RR I always knew it was a three-dimensional object; I mean, there was no doubt about that. One was manipulating an object. I just couldn't see the other, so that it was very easy to move out off of that surface, out into the room. And once you're in the room, well, then your medium can take any shape.

BR I have always seen your paintings to an extent as a reaction against flatness in painting, and the reason that the contents of the work finally spilled out into the room was because the space of the painting was inadequate to hold them. I don't know whether that's right or not, but that's one of the ways that I see them.

RR I was already out in the room. By the time you stretch the canvas, you're out in the room. [*Laughter*]

BR Yes, I guess that's true. But specifically, can you see yourself painting again?

RR I can't, but you could, maybe. [*Laughter*]

BR   Well, why wouldn't you want to paint again?

RR   It's not that I wouldn't want to paint again – I will.

BR   Do you find working in theater events more exciting, or do you find that there is some kind of experience there that is more immediate to you? I just wonder, why are you concentrating your activity in that area now, as opposed to painting?

RR   The criticalness of doing something live and the difficulty that one runs into doing theater.

BR   So, you think painting is dead, then [*laughter*], if theater events are live?

RR   It doesn't have to be.

BR   Well, do you think it is?

RR   But I don't know too many ways of – with my own personal experience, I don't know too many ways of being satisfied with a fixed relationship without resorting to illusion and that kind of illusion that painting is, like, right here now. I just couldn't mix those two.

BR   So in other words, you can't really see yourself painting again?

RR   Yeah, I can. I mean, there's nothing wrong with paint, there's nothing wrong with canvas. There are other things to paint on; canvas is interesting, not *as* interesting, but it is interesting to paint on. [*Laughter*] Once you have some idea about composition and that fixedness, there ought to be something you can do about it if it bothers you. And there are things that you can do about it.

BR   What I was trying to find out was whether it did bother you enough so that you don't want to do it anymore.

RR   Right, but that doesn't eliminate painting and the possibility of painting. [*A few claps in the audience*] Painting is just one thing that you do. [*An audience member yells, "Bravo!"; laughter*]

BR   Darby Bannard has prepared some sort of statement, and although I didn't ask for statements, I expect that his attitude will be rather different. I'd like to let you read it, if you want to.

DB   [Darby Bannard] All right. It's a short statement.

The subject of the discussion tonight is a tradition or convention of art making called easel painting, which could be defined as painting done on a flat surface all of which may be seen at once. Now, if a convention or a tradition or a method of making pictures is to remain vital, then the artists contained within that convention have to paint vital paintings. And if the tradition is exhausted, that means that the artists within that tradition are painting bad paintings. And that would mean that there would be no good easel painting done within a recent period of time, which you could make, arbitrarily, the last year, or two years, or six months. Which would mean, in turn, that artists such as Kenneth Noland, Helen Frankenthaler, Frank Stella, [Jules] Olitski, Lichtenstein, Larry Poons, et cetera – you can supply your own – have not painted good paintings in the last year. [*A few claps; an audience member yells out in agreement with Bannard*]

BR   [*To the audience*] Would you reserve your remarks for the question period? I would appreciate it as a mark of courtesy. [*Laughter and applause*]

DB   If they have painted good paintings in the last year, then easel painting, as a convention of art making, is not exhausted. Now, it might be better to ask if easel painting as a convention is doomed because other conventions will supersede it. I simply think that the answer to that is no, because the combinations that can take place between paint and canvas are infinite. And consequently, there's no –

BR   But they are infinitely viable? I mean, that's the question. Of course, they're infinite in one sense, but are they infinitely viable?

DB   They are as infinitely viable as the people want to make them.

BR   If we look at it in a total historical context, though, we see
      that easel painting has not been a permanent convention;
      I mean, it's about five hundred years old. It dates from the
      time when painting came down from the walls and off
      the manuscript page and became a portable object. And I
      don't see why we can't see a point either in the immedi-
      ate, the near, or the distant future when it will be an out-
      worn, exhausted convention.

DB   It is possible that everybody will give it up tomorrow. But
      the point is that people are using it now well. So conse-
      quently, there is no reason for them to give it up, because
      you can do a great deal with it.

BR   Would you agree with that, Don? Would you agree that
      the activity is such that the convention is obviously still
      very vital?

DJ   [Donald Judd] Yeah, on the whole, I would. Unfortunately,
      I would.

BR   You would? Well, that seems to be in contradiction to a
      statement that I have here that you made two years ago,
      in which you said [*laughter*]: "Oil paint and canvas aren't
      as strong as commercial paints and as the colors and sur-
      faces of materials, especially if the materials are used in
      three dimensions. Oil and canvas are familiar and, like the
      rectangular plane, have a certain quality and have limits.
      The quality is especially identified with art.... Three di-
      mensions are real space. That gets rid of the problem of il-
      lusionism and of literal space, space in and around marks
      and colors – which is riddance of one of the salient and
      most objectionable relics of European art."[2]

DJ   That's all true enough. But let me explain, because it's a very
      complicated subject and I don't want to answer yes or no.
          In the first place, you have two cases: one, the social
      one that Darby was just talking about, in which you prove
      that it's still alive because so many people have done good
      work in the last year or ten years or whatever. Obviously,

it's true that there has been good work done in that time. So, if you just take that, it is obviously proven that it's still alive and kicking. Then, there's what I think about my own work and think about painting, which is something else. Obviously, I don't want to do it myself and have a number of objections to it.

BR   If it's good enough for the others, why isn't it good enough for you?

DJ   Because you don't establish universal criteria like that. That's all. I like painting done by a number of people. In many cases, I like that painting better than three-dimensional work that would supposedly have some affinity with my work; so, it's a complicated situation. And also whether something is a painting or is not a painting, that is, a certain kind of form, is not the only thing involved. There are other kinds of forms, other techniques involved, other qualities involved, and all of those balance against one another. Both Stella and Poons have a certain kind of order that I like, which, say, unlike painting itself, is radical and new and something developing. So I may like the order, and sort of feel, well, sorry that it's in painting. So it's ambiguous –

BR   Why are you sorry that it's in painting, then? That's what I'm trying to get at.

DJ   Well, again, this is my feeling about it. It's not a general judgment.

BR   What is wrong with painting?

DJ   I think that the most general thing that you can hold against it is that, willy-nilly, it's still somewhat pictorial, no matter how abstract. Somehow or another, you're too inclined to –

BR   By "pictorial," you mean pictorial space? What do you mean by "pictorial"?

DJ   Pictorial, in almost any way you can go at it, even if it was completely blank –

BR   I don't understand what you mean by "pictorial" in that sense.

DJ   It's somewhat contemplative, slightly passive in quality.

BR   And you see three-dimensional objects as more aggressive and active?

DJ   I guess so, yeah [*laughter*], but anyway – we need a definition of painting, because obviously it is changing and it can change.

BR   It has changed, obviously. In 1947, with his drip paintings, Jackson Pollock stopped using the technique of hand painting with brushes. Since then, Morris Louis has spilled and stained paint; Jules Olitski has done paintings with spray guns. Do you think that these technical innovations are enough to reinvigorate the tradition?

DJ   Well, I would consider all of that still painting. To define it simply in its most conventional way, I'd say that it's a rectangle on stretchers –

BR   Then shaped canvases are not paintings?

DJ   – not quite – an inch or two from the wall, using oil paint on canvas and usually something within the rectangle. The minute that you have a variation on one of those aspects, such as it being shaped, or such as the surface being, say, metal or wood or something other than canvas, then you're somewhat away from traditional painting. So, you don't have a simple case.

BR   I suppose the point is that the tradition of easel painting has been breached the moment you have a shaped canvas.

DJ   Well, easel painting was breached when Pollock and Newman and those people started.

BR   What, with the mural-scale picture?

DJ   Yeah.

BR   In other words, you feel that one can date the end of the easel convention to the late 1940s?

DJ   Yeah, they did, I guess, and I would agree with that. As long as it's not portable, it's not easel –

BR   And the painting done now, in other words, you feel is beyond that convention, is a different sort of thing, anyway?

DJ Yeah, it's a different kind of painting. I guess you can call it painting. But certainly very different.

BR But if I've understood statements you've made elsewhere, you've felt that there still was something implicitly limited about paint on a two-dimensional support. If I understand it correctly, it was the space, the illusionistic space of painting that you were objecting to.

DJ Yeah, I object to it a great deal. I think that it almost has it willy-nilly no matter what happens.

BR Darby, do you think that's sufficient grounds for rejecting painting?

DB No, because I think a canvas is sufficient grounds for paint. [*Laughter*] The point is that there is no reason, because you have an annoyance with the fact of a rectangle on a wall, that this has to be extended into making a materially different kind of art. In other words, it's mixing quality and materials, it seems to me. You're saying that because this thing has a certain factual existence and you can describe that existence, the next step is that it is irksome. And it's in between those two thoughts –

DJ Its quality comes from its shape and materials, in part.

DB Sure it does, but what of it?

DJ It's those shapes and materials which I object to. It's not an annoyance – it's a real, thorough dislike. I think it has emotional, philosophical, social implications and so forth and everything that you can name. I think it's something that shouldn't be there.

RR I don't think art could ever be defined negatively. Everything that you could want it to do that it's not doing is historic.

BR But do you feel that an art form, say painting, could simply no longer be viable? I mean, art, per se, of course obviously can be changed in any way the artist wants to change it, but –

LP [Larry Poons] But Barbara, what is this thing that you keep referring to as reviving something, like something is dead? That is what struck me about the original question that this talk is supposed to be about. I started to ask myself, "Now, how could this question be asked in a serious way?"

BR   One reason I asked the question was because I've been doing some reading and I came across some quotes like this. Thirty years ago John Graham wrote: "The problems of pictorial form have been all solved and easel painting for private patronage is dead. The generation which has seen this take place is as usual not fully conscious of it."[3] Now, that was thirty years ago. Certain things have happened in the interim – new materials –

LP   Certainly, and I think that the things that have happened in the interim, especially in the last five years, have led to the asking of this question. But it is generally an uninformed art public, who do now happen to comprise the majority of the so-called art scene, who is asking this question. Simply because these people, I feel, are very uninformed or uninspired when they see what you might call traditional two-dimensional painting, whether it be Rembrandt or Louis. They're not moved by it. But luckily for them, they were able to grab hold of something in pop art, you might say, that began to make them feel that art really isn't evading them – that if they like pop art, they are interested in art. But then they still run up against people like Louis and Noland or Newman, and they run into a blank wall with them. So, it seems to be a natural impulse for them at that point to ask the question, "Well, maybe it's dead?" Because they just don't really dig it. I agree with Darby when he made the inference that if easel painting is dead, then all the people that are making easel paintings are exhausted. Meaning if easel painting is exhausted, then it means that Darby is exhausted, it means Noland is exhausted; it means that a lot of great painters are exhausted, and that's not true! [*Applause*]

So then the whole question that comes up then is: "Why is this a question asked in a serious manner?" I can only relate it back to the large scene that art now more or less belatedly enjoys. I guess there is a lot of money floating around, but that's about it. People are asking this question because they are not really moved by traditional art. And I'm not saying just because they don't like Louis or Noland – that's one thing – but I also feel that a great majority of them, if they came face to face with a Tiepolo, would not be moved by that either. They would rather look at some extreme example of pop art and grab hold of something there.

RR   You are implying that there is some kind of standard.

LP   Yes, there is a standard of quality you can't ignore –

RR   I can.

LP   – which is still continuing in easel painting, and if it wasn't continuing I wouldn't say so, or wouldn't if I didn't believe it.

RR   If it were continuing, you wouldn't have to say so. [*Laughter*]

BR   Well, I think that there's two interesting points. At least two. [*Laughter*]

All right, why is this a question now? It occurred to me that it was a question not only because of the large uninformed public, but also because in the art schools, one sees students turning away from the convention of easel painting. One sees them making either three-dimensional objects, or various kinds of kinetic work, or any number of things other than paintings. Painting seems to be capturing the imagination of the young less.

LP   I don't believe that's true.

BR   It may or it may not be. It has just been my observation that carpentry kits and spray guns have come to take the place in art schools that –

LP   Well, you certainly don't object to Jules Olitski using a spray gun and to putting him into a different category of painting simply because he uses a spray gun. He also still uses a brush.

BR   No, I think that what's emerged so far is that perhaps the specific convention of easel painting is dead and has been dead since the late '40s, since Pollock, at any rate. But what we mean by painting at large –

LP   Well, what do you mean by "dead"?

BR   I mean that nobody important is working in it anymore. [*Commotion in the audience*]

LP   Is that what you think?

BR   No, I meant in the sense of the small-scale cabinet painting.

LP   Oh, well, easel painting in itself is – just like Barney told you, "Who paints on an easel?" – so, I mean, really your question is about two-dimensional flat painting.

BR   Okay, fine, I would revise the question. [*Laughter*]

DB   Well, I think there is another simple way of looking at it.

LP   Another one?

DB   Like the other simple ways. [*Laughter*] I mean, art has gotten to be very popular.

BR   Look at all the people here.

DB   A lot of people are interested in art.

LP   I would not say abstract art. Art in general, yes, but only a certain portion of art has become very popular. I am not talking about op art, either. I'm talking about what we would term the carrying on of the tradition of flat, two-dimensional paintings, which is not essentially any more popular than it ever was.

DB   I wasn't talking about tradition or anything else. I just mean that there are more people numerically who have a great deal more interest in art than they did before. Many, many times more people are interested in art, and this generates a certain kind of environment. It's an environment in which art gets publicity and money and lots of other attractive things. This attracts young people to go into making art. You get many more people making art than ever before, and you get many more people making more variations on art than ever before. You have many more people going into painting, for example, who might not really be interested in painting. But they are interested in the fact that this is an exciting environment. So therefore, those people do something else eventually. They do other things than painting. Some people paint, some people make, let's say, objects, some people go into the theater, and each person does the things that his talent leads him to do as soon as he finds his talent. Then the people who do the other things turn around and see where they have been before – that is, painting – and they say, "I think painting is no good because it was limiting me." But the people who are still painting look at the paintings that they're doing and say, "This is what I like because I know how to do it, and I know how to handle paint." There's plenty of paint. [*Laughter*] There's plenty of canvas. And they continue doing it. So there we are. [*Laughter*]

LP   Well, Bob, there's also plenty of people. As you know.

DB   And there is more, all the time, of everything.

BR   Well, do you think that's a bad or a good thing?

DB   I think it's great, because it means more money, more publicity. [*Laughter*]

BR   More artists. More paint.

DB   Well, I don't care about that. [*Laughter*]

RR   I've heard often that business that art has been overpublicized and so many people are interested in art. Even their credentials have been doubted, the idea of credentials and of snobbish breakdowns about who's interested in what and for what reasons and all that. I think that it's a kind of self-consciousness that makes one talk about that in art because that's really the way nearly everything is.

DB   Yeah, I wasn't saying it was bad.

RR   No, I'm not saying it's bad or good. I'm saying that I don't think that's particularly unique to art.

DB   Oh no, not at all. Absolutely not.

RR   I mean, there are automobiles and things like that that have certainly kept their relationship to art. I really don't feel smothered by too much attention and understanding and appreciation and interest in art. But that's not because I am setting up these hierarchies where you can say that this person does have an interesting attitude about art or a serious one. I don't think it was ever that simple. You read art history and you see that great patrons existed all over who had all kinds of peculiar relationships to art. A painting had two societies. I think that art is going to maintain that, and I think that it's just as useless today as it ever was.

DB   What, art?

RR   Yeah.

LP   But it is certainly not useless to somebody capable of appreciating it on a very intense personal level.

RR   I don't mean "useless" that way.

LP   Well, I mean, it's certainly not useless categorically. It is very essential to some people in regard to making it or viewing it.

DB   It is overtly useless; in other words, it has no substitute.

LP   Well, it doesn't drive a car for you, and it doesn't walk down the street for you, no.

RR   It can't even really last for you.

LP   No, it can't.

RR   One painting that may have absolutely cut your life in two might not work three years later.

LP   I once mentioned something to a painter friend of mine: "Well, it seems that I no longer get a great kick or charge out of making a painting, and it's really getting to be a lot of work and not much excitement involved in doing it anymore." His answer to it was that there are plenty of other places in life to find excitement. [*Laughter*] And I believe it. It's true. To try to justify one's whole life and existence in the studio, you know, is a kind of useless and senseless thing to do.

RR   Why would you have to justify it? All you have to do is walk out the door. [*Laughter*]

LP   Well, as you said, a painting is not even capable of making you laugh. Sometimes a painting is not capable of doing anything to you. The only relationship that you have to the painting is that you did it, and that's it.

RR   I haven't had that experience too often. [*Laughter*]

BR   I want to get back to something that was implicit in what Larry was saying, which is that there are really two publics now for art. There is the general public and they're willing to seize on things that are not painting, things like, say, kinetic art, or whatever the new gimmick of the year that The Museum of Modern Art is throwing out. [*Laughter*] But, on the other hand, there is a more limited public that is interested in traditional art. And by "traditional art," as you defined it, or "traditional painting," you said merely a two-dimensional canvas. Isn't that how you redefined it?

LP   Flat, two-dimensional.

BR   Yeah, a flat, two-dimensional canvas. I don't know, do you think that's true? Do you think that there are two publics for art, and does it make any difference to which you address yourself?

LP   I definitely think there is a public that's intimidated by paintings such as Louis's. These are the same people who are intimidated when they walk into, say, the Metropolitan and are forced to look at a Cézanne. They really feel intimidated by it, because there may or may not be, in the situation that I'm talking about, a rapport between them and the painting, as there would be no rapport between them and a Louis. And I would say that the majority of people now – because the art scene is too large, I would tend to believe – fall into that category. And the other category

of people involved in the art scene who are not painters, the public, are involved in, as you described, flat, two-
dimensional painting.

RR   How can you judge a public that way?

LP   Well, it's just instinctual.

RR   You'd have to spend your whole life studying personalities or something, and I'm sure it wouldn't come out to
"this kind" and "that kind."

LP   No, I'm sure I'm making very, very broad generalizations,
and I'm aware of it.

RR   There are lots of people that just make you sick to your
stomach when they are talking about your work or a
friend's work or any work. I would really not say that they
might not know – I mean, that what they're saying may
not be what they are going through, but those things don't
necessarily … like, you don't get articulate or something
like that.

LP   I'm not talking about social articulation, I'm talking about
the emotional response that these people deal with when
they view art. I'm not really talking about whether somebody is articulate or not. I'm talking about whether someone is genuinely moved by a painting.

RR   But what are they doing there?

LP   They're there because of what has happened in the last five
years in art – the emergence of an art form which opened
the door, so to speak, to a lot of people who had never really before been interested in art, who all of a sudden, because of this and because they could grab onto things, literal things, literary things, about the art, got in the door.
I feel that there's a great majority of them around today
who are comprising a large part of the art scene.

BR   I'd like to ask Don, who has been so quiet, whether you
feel you're working for a limited public or a larger public,
or whether you think the public you're working for now
is larger than the art public was a couple of years ago.

DJ   Well, first, I agree with what Bob said. I think that the public is a very bad thing to talk about in regard to any discussion of art. In the first place, you really don't know anything about it. It's the public, and that involves some people who know a great deal about it [art], it involves a lot of people who don't know much about it. You don't know anything about what is being thought about your work, on the whole, so I don't see that reference back to the public or politics or museums or markets or any of that really being very useful in talking about the subject. I think it's one of the big faults of a lot of criticism that it does refer back to those sorts of things a great deal.

BR   Well, it's part of the total picture. You may object to it as a discussion of art, but it is part of a larger view.

DJ   But I think it usually doesn't say much about the work involved.

BR   Well, at any rate, the kind of work that is being done now, it seems to me, does differ from conventional easel painting in its scale, at least. The kind of scale that artists are using is simply a scale which demands a public viewing.

LP   You mean there are other kinds of art making being done.

BR   Yes. In other words –

LP   Well, that's true.

BR   Well, easel painting was painting which was made for middle-class domestic patronage. It was made to be put into houses. It was made for, conceivably, a different social milieu. I mean, Larry, you know the difficulty that your large canvases have in getting into people's houses.

LP   That's not a problem.

BR   It's really not? You still feel that it's private patronage and not public art that you are interested in?

LP   Well, actually, the origins of the money for purchasing the paintings are different from the intentions of the artist and the results that he achieves.

BR   Well, I wonder if artists do intend –

L P   As a matter of fact, most of the work being done in this country today is quite evidently still twenty-four-by-thirty-inch paintings which are meant to hang in people's houses. Ninety-nine percent of the painting is, actually. It hasn't died out at all. I'm sure there are more paintings being painted now for people's living room walls and over the fireplace than were painted five hundred years ago. Many, many more.

R R   Yes, but there are lots of other things that weren't being done then, too. I think what Barbara is alluding to is that at a certain point it seemed that the painter became conscious that someone was going to see it. And he couldn't anymore rely on a kind of eternal sentimentality or familiarity or classic concepts which were more or less historical, but realized that there was some kind of lacking there, or wanted to try something else. There really is no need for paintings to get so big if you really aren't taking into consideration that someone has to remove the staircase or break out a window to get it into their house, or taking into account that in order to see the whole painting, they'll have to walk from one side of the room to the other. That's no coincidence – something happened. Those are not large easel paintings.

B R   Larry, do you think that there's a reason why the painting has to be very big now?

L P   Well, of course, it almost goes without saying that certain possibilities for painting are definitely the possibilities of scale. Instead of saying "big" paintings, I would rather say "large-scale" or "small-scale" paintings, because bigness really is not the issue.

R R   It can be. We never had so many big paintings around.

L P   Well, it can be, yeah, if the painting is just big, period. But if the painting happens to be a remarkable painting, you cannot separate that from its physical dimensions. Therefore, it is a marvelous painting or a remarkable painting despite its size, meaning the size really is of no importance in the painting.

BR   Yeah, but what I was asking is, do you think large scale is necessary now? I mean, why –

LP   Well, I just told you. It does become necessary for an artist for one reason or another. In my case, I have two reasons, but I don't care to talk about the second reason. [*Laughter*]

BR   That's very mysterious.

LP   But primarily, the first reason is the reason that I operate on in my studio. The second reason is a social reason which is of no importance to anyone except myself.

BR   Well, that's one of the things that I was asking about before, but if I can't get an answer, I can't get an answer. What do you mean by the way you operate in the studio?

LP   Well, the way I go about painting a painting, no matter what dimensions it is.

BR   Yeah, but nonetheless, you have been working on a large scale.

LP   Oh, well, I mean, Barbara, to put it in the simplest sense: twelve square inches of cobalt blue is one experience, 100 square feet of cobalt blue is an entirely different experience. Now, if I want to deal with the experience of a one-foot-square blue painting, I will paint a one-foot-square blue painting, and vice versa.

RR   But that is not a familiar academic idea in art.

LP   Well, I don't know, why are those Tiepolos at the Metropolitan so enormous?

RR   Probably because they were commissioned for a particular space or something. [*Laughter*]

LP   Were they, Barbara?

BR   Um, I don't know. Yes, I think they were, yes. Specifically. [*Laughter*]

LP   Well, you might say that in a certain sense, the artist still is working on commission nowadays, except he is commissioned to a gallery. So he paints all his work on commission to a gallery.

BR   That's not really true.

RR   That's not true.

LP   So, therefore, the artist does, in a certain sense, limit or restrict his work, if it's going to be in a gallery, to a certain size.

BR   Do you, Larry?

DB   Let me try to get you out of this. [*Laughter*]

LP   If I definitely want a painting to be shown in a gallery, I'm certainly not going to make it sixteen feet tall if the gallery is only nine feet tall. [*Laughter*]

BR   Yeah, but would you make a sixteen-foot painting, anyway?

LP   Of course.

BR   Okay.

DB   The thing is that I think what Larry was saying, actually, which nobody took him to say, was that painting, as self-conscious as it is now, any aspect of a painting that you make is an ingredient of the painting, and one of the aspects of painting nowadays is scale, shape, size, and what the outside perimeter of the painting is like. And Larry said that he had a reason for making a big painting, just as someone would have a reason for putting a stripe across it, or a blob of paint, or painting a face, or anything. But it's a reason.

LP   The question of making a large painting is not blowing up a small painting into a large painting. The painting could not exist in the same sense, being smaller than it is, or any other dimension than it is. The final aspect of the painting is that it is the painting, whether it be ten inches or nine feet tall. You know, that's the final thing about it.

BR   Okay, but what I'm asking really is, do you think there is any going back to easel-painting scale, or do you think we're now stuck for the duration of painting with a mural scale?

LP   People every day paint small paintings.

BR   Yeah, are they any good?

LP   Of course they're good. [*Audience member yells, "Mine are!";
     laughter*]

RR   One is never stuck with anything in art. I mean, there
     are people everywhere doing all kinds of things. Art isn't
     something that a few artists do and cram down the pub-
     lic's throat.

BR   No, but it does seem that there comes a point past which
     there isn't any going back to what was done previously.

RR   Nearly always.

DB   You won't do anything previously in terms of the whole
     painting. In other words, nobody is going to paint a paint-
     ing now — I mean, it's unlikely that anyone will paint a Pi-
     casso 1912 cubist painting. But somebody might paint a
     painting that had the same color brown in it, or had the
     same line in it, or was the same size, or had other ingredi-
     ents, because these ingredients are for everybody. Every-
     body can have it.

RR   Or look just like it. [*Laughter*]

DB   And if they use enough of these ingredients, it will look
     just like it; that's right. And that would be real crazy,
     wouldn't it? [*Laughter*]

BR   I meant very specifically if you thought that there was a
     possibility for going back to small scale.

DB   You can't have an irreversible material position. The only
     material changes that are made, actually, is that materials
     get better, I think, and that it's unlikely that people will
     use inferior materials anymore.

BR   How about the new materials? Do you think they make
     a difference? Do plastic-based paints make a difference?

DB   I don't know.

LP   They certainly have made a difference in that certain
     things now are possible to do which were impossible to
     do with oil paint.

BR   Like what?

LP   Let's see. [*Laughter*] Well, I think that it was pretty much impossible with oil paint to paint, say, 120 square feet of an area and have it be the same color and have it be absolutely soaked into the canvas, so that there was no surface shine or no light-reflective qualities on the surface of the painting, which is now possible to do with acrylics and water-based paints. You could, of course, paint 120 square feet with oil paint, but the result would have a sheen to the surface, you see, which would reflect light.

RR   That's just different. Why is that better?

LP   What? We're not talking about good or better –

RR   There's some implication that – no, Darby said –

LP   – we're talking about certain things that are possible now to do with new materials in painting. You might say that it is possible now to work overall on a painting in a much different and more quick or immediate fashion than was possible with oil paint.

DB   When I said that materials were better, I was going under certain assumptions, like, for instance, that you could do this when you couldn't do it before or that the paint lasted longer. Therefore, you assume that paint, when it lasts longer, is better. You don't have to make that assumption at all. It's not necessary to make these assumptions. I was just saying that from a manufacturing standpoint, these materials were better. And so these are more easily manipulatable, which is much better for painting.

BR   Well, I think that we have unanimously decided, at any rate, that painting is not dead. Perhaps we can –

RR   Easel painting.

DB   Painting houses isn't dead either.

BR   Well, that easel painting is not dead, or that painting on the two-dimensional support is not dead.

DB   I'm so glad. What if we had decided –

LP   What would have happened if we had decided the other way? We'd have to go out and hang ourselves. [*Laughter*]

BR   But what do you feel are the central problems facing

painting today, then, if it is still a very lively and viable tradition?

DB It's not the basic problem of painting, because painting doesn't have problems. Only painters have problems. [*Laughter and applause*] The basic problem with painting is that nowadays, you have to absolutely start from scratch. Everything you do has to be invented by yourself. This gives painters problems, because they don't have any tradition to work with. They can't work under a master and then paint like him, and improve a little bit on him the way they used to do. What you have to do is you have to invent — in other words, you can't even start with painting anymore. You might say you want to start with structural objects, or you might want to start with any combination of any materials or any events or any things that can make an artistic entity. You have to make decisions at such a low, basic level that it takes you about twenty years to even decide what kind of medium you want to work in. And this is a problem for painters, no doubt about it — for any artist. Once you get up to a certain level of development in the kind of art you have chosen, you have to continually refine and choose, refine and choose, refine and choose — on and on until you've got yourself a mature style. The reason it's a problem is because it is so long and so tedious and so difficult.

BR Do you think that there are more possibilities open to the artist? That there are simply more choices?

DB Well, there have always been the same number of choices.

BR Have there?

DB Yes, but the point is that there haven't been the same number of choices that people knew about. [*Laughter*] There are more things being done by more people today, so you can look and see them being done. Like, this whole business of Happenings and all the rest, this instant or self-motivated theater, theater on a scale where you didn't have to go through all the problems that theater entailed before – this is something which is fresh and new, and it is a choice that people can take, and a choice that a lot of people will take from now on. Doing this kind of thing – small-scale theater motivated on yourself, just like you'd make a painting – that's something new, which you might call upgraded, because this exists as a thing now. People can look at it and see that it's there and do it, whereas they wouldn't have done it before because they just didn't think of it, you see?

B R   Do you think there is any pressure brought to bear from this sort of proliferation of choices? Do you think that painting in any way is being pressured by, say, the kind of three-dimensional structures that Don makes?

D B   No, because people who don't want to paint don't paint anymore, that's all. In other words, if somebody isn't interested in painting in what you call the traditional way, which is painting on a flat surface, then they do something else.

B R   Well, it seems to me that what Larry was saying about wanting the kind of sensation that you get from a large area of pure color has as its goal the same kind of immediacy or directness, the same kind of sensation that, say, Don is after in his work. Does that make sense to you?

D J   Yeah – [*Laughter*]

B R   Well, do you have any of the same concerns as painters, or do you see any kind of similarities between what concerns you and painting?

D J   To some extent, the kind of order involved, and certainly the kind of immediacy in large-scale color.

B R   Would you say that's common to both painting and sculpture?

D J   Yeah, the scale and the relative simplicity and the wholeness of the things. I don't think the various things, as long as they're visual, can stand altogether independently of one another, though. So that if one seems very lively and very strong, another one can exist alongside of it if it isn't that lively or strong. So you do have a problem of value back and forth between various kinds of techniques.

BR   Do you think that painting is as lively and as strong as three-dimensional structures at this point?

DJ   Probably right now, but even that you asked the question is rather unusual, you know, because four years ago or five years ago it was obvious, apparently to everybody – though I didn't think it was that obvious – that the leading art was painting and that anything else was a much more minor activity.

DB   You can make the point or ask the question, "Is painting as lively and strong as professional football?" [*Laughter*] Now, there's an awful lot of people who would say, with some justification, that painting is not as strong and lively and vital as professional football. [*Applause*] The point is that each has its own qualities and there's different ways of dealing with watching professional football on TV and with watching a painting or building your automobile or making a milkshake or whatever. Each one of these things can have its own type of vitality. If you get involved in measuring vitality comparatively, then it's impossible. But if there are good paintings being made, as I said originally, or good structures, or whatever, then this tradition or sphere of art making is functioning and it's vital.

RR   There are a couple of things – like, I don't really know whose business it is whether good paintings are being made or not.

BR   It's the critics' business, presumably.

RR   Well, they don't have much business. [*Laughter*] The other thing is that I don't see this dramatic breakdown of painters now stopping painting and doing something else. Some of the most incredible pieces of sculpture in the world were done by painters, or were done in a time when one didn't care whether one was a painter or one was a sculptor. It seems to me that a painter just does whatever he wants to do, just like a sculptor does.

BR   I am getting the impression from what you say that you feel the arts are closer together than perhaps they once were.

RR   Well, I do think that, but I think they weren't ever as far apart as has been implied by this exaggeration about whether you are doing three-dimensional or whether you're doing a flat something. Usually what art is is that someone has an idea, or has a reaction, or a feeling, and it concerns them so much that they do something about it.

BR   There is one question which, it seems to me, concerns all of you, although in different ways, and that is the question of pictorial space, and what that means in terms of what is possible in a painting. If I understand the direction of everyone's work, it has been – for a time, at any rate – an anti-illusionistic direction. It has been in the direction of making the object more actual and more concrete. It has led Bob, for example, to allow objects to spill out into the room. It has led Don into three-dimensional work. It has led Darby and Larry into something quite different. Do you think that the question of the kind of space or the kind of illusionism that painting offers is a central one today?

DB   It may be a central question. By saying it's a central question today implies that it's on everybody's mind.

BR   Isn't it on your mind?

DB   Not particularly, no.

BR   What do you think about most in terms of making a painting if it's not a spatial consideration?

DB   You have to make a spatial division. I do for myself. I make a spatial division of a certain special sort on the canvas, and this is a consideration for me, but what it is is part of building a painting. In other words, I don't worry particularly about spatial considerations that don't have anything to do with the paintings. I don't worry, for instance, about whether I should be involved in this kind of space, because I find this kind of space comfortable. Consequently, I continue to use it. If I found it uncomfortable and limiting, well, then I'd use another kind of space.

BR   I'm very much interested in the concept which Sidney Tillim used in talking about Larry's painting, which is the concept of "bulked space."[4] In talking about the dynamics of Larry's paintings, he said that there were no longer these positive and negative values, but rather that the whole space seemed to be positive, and that it seemed to be a different kind of space. Do you think that the space in painting today is of a different sort? I guess I should direct it toward you, Larry, since it was a remark that was made about your paintings.

LP   It seems to me that the issue of positive and negative space somehow has always been resolved in paintings throughout history. The way positive and negative space, you might say, is resolved today is still resolved essentially the same way — meaning essentially, you really don't have any positive or negative space. It is all one space, so to speak.

DB   I think, in addition, the critics are very worried about space — more than anything else — because they have a history of spatial paintings.

LP   I think there are new ways —

DB   I have never seen a critic come up and say, "There is a blue-green, I have never seen a blue-green in a painting before, and that's a red-hot item, and I'm going to write it up as being blue-green." Rather, it turns out that they talk about the space and the different things that are happening in the space and use such terms as "positive" and "negative" and so forth because recent art history has been a history of what you might call a spatial revolution beginning with impressionism and the cubists and so forth, and with abstract expressionism. We have always been worried about space, so it's space, space, space all the time. And space is just one part of a painting. The size and the space that's used in the painting is just one little ingredient.

LP   Well, it's also the space created by the painting – within the painting.

DB   Right.

RR   But I think only of surface, unless there really is space. And that's what you're saying?

BR   Well, I'm asking a question about space and about the kind of space that's being used in painting today.

DB   That's good. What he said about surface, that's what I think about, too, because that's what you have: you have a surface. If you choose to have a surface.

LP   Well, I think, Barbara, maybe there has been a tendency in the last five years to treat space from the edges of the canvas toward the center, working from the edges in rather from the center out to the edges. I think there might be that tendency now, but it is all essentially to the same purpose.

RR   And one's as big a trap as the other. [*Laughter*]

LP   What kind of trap are you talking about?

RR   Well, how can painting from the center out be any better than painting from the edge in? [*Laughter and applause*]

LP   I didn't say one way or the other was any better. I just said there has been a tendency, I think starting with Pollock; you see many of his paintings in which the edges are really relatively free, very, very much less dense than what is happening on the inside of the painting. Somehow the painting seems to start at the edges and grow in.

BR   Or start at the center and grow out. [*Laughter*]

There is something I do feel is new about the way that space is being used in abstract painting today, and I see it in Darby's work, and I see it in Larry's work. I just wonder if this is conscious, whether you're trying for a different kind of space? It seems to me that there is a new kind of illusionism in painting, but it's of a different sort, and I particularly remarked on this in your recent paintings.

DB   Well, I think that one thing that we might have in com-
     mon is that we order things so consciously – make a con-
     scious order out of them. In other words, the things have
     a definite relationship which we think about beforehand,
     but that's just a different method of putting things on the
     canvas. It may create a different spatial situation, but the
     fact that it's a different spatial situation is just a fact; it's not
     an element of quality.

BR   Let me put it this way: in older art, you get space behind
     the picture plane. The feeling, the sensation, I often get
     about the new abstract work is that there is a kind of illu-
     sionism, but that forms are, because of the nature of the
     interaction of adjacent colors, being projected forward.
     In other words, it's not value contrasts that are doing this,
     but it's the power of colors to either recede or to go for-
     ward. When I first saw Larry's paintings, I had the sensa-
     tion that the dots were actually suspended between me
     and the ground. And I got that same feeling about the cen-
     ters of your new paintings – that they come forward.

DB   That's right, but that's a tool that you use.

BR   Why do you use it, though? I mean, do you think there is
     some kind of tendency now to –

DB   Because it makes another complicating factor to use. Just
     like you use a different color. You use something that
     goes in front of – one thing goes in front of another visu-
     ally. And then you've got something else in your roster of
     materials.

BR   But do you deliberately want to create this sort of space
     in which the –

DB   Well, I do. I like things shuffling behind, curling behind,
     and forward.

BR   Yeah, but do you feel that that goes on behind the frame,
     or in front of the frame? That the illusion takes place, in
     other words –

LP   Well, I think that it might be an intricate balance arrived at where it is neither in front nor behind. You know, it's behind and in front at the same time, so to speak. There is a deep space involved.

BR   How can it be both —

LP   That's a deep space. You can see it as deep space one second and as absolutely flat space the next second.

BR   So, you like that interchange? Do you also like that ambiguity?

DB   Yeah, sure. It's nice. [*Laughter*]

RR   But Barbara, that's nothing new for painting.

BR   I just want to know if that's deliberate. I mean, these are effects that I perceive, and I want to know if it's deliberate.

LP   It is new in the traditional sense, Bob, of painting where there really was a background and a sky twenty miles off in the distance, and that sky, because, say, it was blue, was always way back there in the distance no matter what you did, because you had a figure in front of it proclaiming the space there, and the sky proclaimed its space back here. There was the illusion of perspective and distance between these two points. I'm saying these points exist today in painting, except they're intermingled, meaning they're there, and there's a balance reached between going back and going forward.

BR   It sounds like Hans Hofmann, somehow.

RR   No, [Josef] Albers.

BR   No, it sounds like push-pull. I mean, do you have in mind the kind of thing that —

LP   Well, I don't know, because I never studied with Hofmann or read anything about that.

RR   I think these things are so stretched in your painting that that element is no longer just simply part of your material or a decision, but is actually your content. And I think that's the main difference.

LP   It's also what?

RR   It's part of your content. It is your content.

BR   What's that?

RR   Well, you're certainly not interested in little dots! [*Laughter*]

LP   No, certainly not. You see, the dots are simply a means to use color, and color is a means to produce what I've been talking about.

BR   I think one question that might be interesting to consider is the question of simplicity versus complexity. I got the impression from Darby's remarks that he thinks that art should become more complicated.

DB   Yeah, overtly complicated. I think my paintings should become more complicated [*laughter*], so I'm making them more complicated.

BR   Why do you feel that?

DB   Because I made lots and lots of very simple paintings about five years ago which consisted of, say, a circle on a background. And I just ran through all my colors doing this [*laughter and applause*] and I decided that I had it within my power to make more complicated paintings, so I did.

BR   I want to ask Larry: why have you been using more complex systems? I mean, the recent paintings are more complicated.

LP   Because I have become, you might say, interested in this backward and forward thing and in equivocal balance between these two things. In order to get that equivocal balance, I needed to use more color. You might say the only basic change, Barbara, from the paintings five years to now is the use of more color, meaning from basic two-color paintings to now eight or nine or ten colors in a painting.

BR   There are different shapes, though – different elements.

LP   No different shapes. The first paintings were all dots. But during the first year the ellipses came into the painting.

BR   I just wonder whether you feel that that point at which you and Darby were both using fairly simple solutions came out of that original reaction to abstract expressionism, and whether now, perhaps, we are witnessing another kind of reversal where things are going to start getting complicated again?

DB   Well, the thing is, if you want to use color, you have to think about it beforehand, because if you use color right on the canvas, it gets all muddy [*laughter*], and if it gets all muddy it doesn't show like the original color as you planned it. If you want to use twenty colors in the canvas and you want each color to be distinct so that people can recognize it as the color, then you have to make each of these little colors separate, or big colors, whatever you want to do. But if you mix it up, the color is going to get lost, and consequently, that's part of the reason that our paintings look the way they do.

AM   [Audience member] Can you repeat that, please?

DB   I couldn't possibly repeat it. [*Laughter*]

BR   How do you feel, Bob, about simplicity versus complexity as something you're interested in?

RR   Well, I know that you can put on paint without thinking about it. You can just see a can of red and, without making a sketch for it and predetermining its relationship to the entire thing, do something about that, and it isn't necessarily muddy. [*Applause*] But it's the complications thing that I don't know about.

BR   Your art strikes me as fairly complex, and I wondered whether you feel that there is a kind of superiority to the notion of complexity just as an idea.

RR   I never felt that making a painting was very simple, and that probably shows. [*Laughter*]

LP   Barbara, you mean by "complexity"– you know, just not black and white? What do you mean?

BR   I just mean more elements doing more things, as opposed to less elements doing less things.

RR   They ought to do as much as they can. [*Laughter and applause*]

BR   Well, how do you feel about that, Don? It seems to me

that in your work, you're repudiating the notion of complexity. That you're trying for relative simplicity.

DJ   Okay. I'll get to that in a second. What I wanted to say, though, when I grabbed the microphone before is the receding and coming forward of, say, Larry's spots, or any such activity, is one of the things that I hold very much against painting and one of the things that I don't think should exist, and they definitely have certain meanings.

BR   Why?

DJ   I think that it ties into the whole European tradition – the whole complex of philosophical and emotional attitudes.

BR   In what way? How does advancing and receding tie in, and which philosophical –

DJ   Because it's a projected space and illusionism, and that's a way of projecting – the whole business of anthropomorphism, really.

BR   How is illusionism anthropomorphism? I don't understand the connection.

DJ   It is in that context, because it comes right out of that painting. Now back to simplicity and complexity.

BR   No, I don't understand how illusionism and anthropomorphism are related.

DJ   Because you're making an illusionistic space. You're attributing qualities to it. You're making a fake realistic space and attributing certain qualities to it, which is what has been done all along. And I think that, as a credible position, is impossible.

LP   Well, I don't know if I get you, but what is illusionistic, say, about a white painting that's all white, half of which is painted another color white, and one quarter of the painting is painted red? Now, there is a distinct physical law that says the red is going to be more outstanding than the off-white and the pure white. So, what's illusionistic about that? It seems to be a physical fact, or part of our physical reality, that certain colors and certain relationships of colors are this way, or this is the way they do appear to us in a given situation. The painter works, I feel, in this situation.

DJ   Well, I think in that case, obviously, the red does come forward. And I think –

LP   Well, what's illusionistic about that?

DJ   Well, because it's not forward and it seems to come forward, and that's illusionistic.

LP   So then you're saying that physical reality in itself is illusionistic.

DJ   It's not altogether physical reality, because you're creating another surface on the white, one that's slightly back of the red, and this tends to read as imitation space. Possibly there's a way out of this, so that you can make these sensations so definite –

LP   You can equivocate through the act of painting – you might be able to achieve a neutral zone where all these different elements or colors actually exist on one plane and also do exist on the other plane, too. And through the act of painting you can paint and achieve that; you see, that's where the illusion comes in.

BR   Do I understand you correctly, Don, that you think that all pictorial space is illusionistic?

DJ   Well, by definition, I mean, pictorial space –

BR   There's no such thing as a flat painting?

DJ   No, there isn't, so far. I think it's probable that someone will manage to make one. You might make, as I was going to say, the sensation so definite or specific enough as to stay on the surface and not negate it, but so far, no one's made a painting [like that]. I think Frank's paintings come closest to being actually flat. I think that you can't have any illusionism in any sense of it without getting back to this old quality that painting has had all along, which I think is not especially credible.

RR   Aren't you saying, then, that the reading of a painting is where the correction should take place?

DJ   No, it's decidedly in the painting.

RR   Because, like, when I look out here, I can certainly see the red blouses and the orange dress more quickly than the bright blue and green back there. Now, are those people sitting in the wrong seats? [*Laughter*]

DJ   [*Laughter*] Those people aren't paintings out there. I mean, that's not a painting.

RR   But you're talking about a kind of morality about –

DJ   Look, if the laws of perception – if you are going to use just an optical thing like that, it has to be made so definite that you don't have an illusionistic surface, so that you don't somehow destroy the surface you are working on.

DB   But the other possibility would be that some of the things we've inherited from the European tradition are just fine and that they are very good things to use. They remain with us, and we can handle them, and we can use them in our own context.

DJ   As I said, it's a question of credibility and what you believe, and I can't believe any of it.

BR   You can't believe in illusionism?

DJ   I don't believe in any of those qualities, illusionism, among others – that kind of illusionism, anyway, because there are other kinds.

DB   You'd look at a Flemish painting, for instance, and you wouldn't believe that that person was really in front of that background, because I wouldn't believe it either. But I wouldn't make any decision about the quality of the painting related to the belief I had. In other words, I don't feel undermined or fooled by the –

DJ   No, but your credibility, your belief in the painting and its quality are, in a way, two different things. Again, it's a gradation. The only work you really believe in completely would be your own –

LP   Well, the question of belief –

DJ   Now, wait a second –

LP   That's nonsense.

DJ   Now, be quiet, Larry, will you? [*Laughter*] – and after that
        it shades off in various ways depending upon the time and
        the period and the people involved, so that you believe
        certain elements in someone else's work and you disbe-
        lieve certain elements. Like, I believe something of the
        order that Larry has in his paintings, but I disbelieve the
        kind of illusionism.

DB   Belief is a function of words, isn't it? It's a function of a
        question that's formed. I can't find myself believing in
        something until I can articulate it. I have to believe that
        something is a certain color, believe that there is a fact
        or believe that an event happened in Chicago, let's say. I
        have a certain degree of belief that this is true because the
        newspaper says or doesn't say so. But when I'm looking
        at a painting, I don't have any such thing as belief; I only
        have observation of these facts that are there.

DJ   That seems a contradiction of the whole experience to
        me, because I think it's very much a question of belief in
        it and just what's believed and what kind of enthusiasm
        you have for it.

DB   In other words, when you look at a painting, you form
        questions about it, and then decide whether you believe
        the answers that you give the questions.

DJ   It's often not that verbal. I think it's visual, pretty much.

RR   Then you'd have to be lying in order to make the surface
        true, right? Like, if red would appear to come forward,
        then one can put red on that surface, and it does stay ex-
        actly where it is. Then you would have to figure out the
        extent of the simplemindedness of people in order to pre-
        sent a nonactive, nondistorting surface.

DJ   I don't know. I gave it all up, you see. That's somebody else's
        problem. I really don't know how you make a live painting.

RR   Isn't that in those forms, too? Like the cubes that are on
        the wall, one right beside the other? You're certainly not

interested in the little mechanical or manufacturing dis-
crepancies there. You really do want that to stay just where
it is.

DJ Yeah.

RR What about the distortion when the light passes through
the glass and hits the wall, and all of a sudden you have an
illusionary thing that this one is closer to you than that
one, because of the size or density of its shadow? Because
that happens, too.

DJ Which ones are you talking about?

RR The ones you had at Leo [Castelli]'s against the wall.[5]

DJ With the amber plexiglass [image 8]?

RR The shadows were really quite extraordinary, and I tried to
ignore them, but they certainly defeated what you wanted.
[*Laughter and applause*]

DJ All I can say is that they don't seem illusionistic in that
sense to me. You are bound to have a certain amount of
reflection, and you are changing position when you look
at a three-dimensional thing. In a sense, that's an illusion
just in the technical meaning of the term. But I distinguish between that as an illusion, which I think is a perfectly matter-of-fact illusion and has no connections to
the other kind of illusion, which I think has definite philosophical meaning. You're going to have illusion forever
in art.

RR You live with illusion.

BR Even in non-artistic situations?

RR I mean, illusion, that's what it is. It's in the eyeballs.
[*Laughter*]

LP Well, he wants to keep it there, you see?

RR We've all got very different juices and they perform very
differently, and there is no way of seeing anything.

BR Well, um. [*Laughter*] There's not much you can argue with
there.

This panel discussion was sourced from an audio recording and transcript, which vary significantly from each other; deference has been given to the audio in these instances. The original sound tape reels and archival transcript are in the Barbara Rose papers, 1962–circa 1969, Archives of American Art, Smithsonian Institution, Washington, DC.

Not included here is an extensive question-and-answer session held at the end of the panel, which began with an angry audience member lambasting the panel participants for a number of minutes.

1   Rauschenberg exhibited *Oracle* (1962–65), a five-part assemblage of sheet metal with iron, rubber tires, glass fragments, batteries, wire, and electrical and electronic components, at Leo Castelli Gallery, New York, May 15–June 19, 1965.

2   See Judd's "Specific Objects" (1964) in *Donald Judd Writings*, 138, 141.

3   John D. Graham, *System and Dialectics of Art* (New York: Delphic Studios, 1937), 125.

4   "A distinguishing feature of the paintings by Noland, Louis and Poons is that traditional dark-and-light contrasts have been exchanged for the contrasts of hues which are usually of equal value and intensity. Thus the entire planimetric field becomes a chiaroscuro-less 'positive' form, 'bulked space' as it were, rather than space that has been carved into traditional, structured figure-ground relationships." See Sidney Tillim, "Optical Art: Pending or Ending?," *Arts Magazine*, January 1965, 19, 21.

5   *Don Judd*, Leo Castelli Gallery, New York, February 5–March 2, 1966.

"A Painter Interviews a Sculptor (on Painting)"
Interview with Jo Baer
1966–67

Judd and the artist Jo Baer met in the summer of 1962. Baer and the artist John Wesley were married in 1960 and were together for eleven years; Wesley and Judd remained close friends throughout Judd's life.

In the 1960s, Baer conducted a handful of dialogues with artists. She wrote in *Jo Baer: Paintings 1960–1998* that they were "a project undertaken at the moment when it became clear that some artists and myself were forging a new movement. I gave it up only because my schedule of exhibiting commitments had become very demanding." These dialogues include, in Baer's words, "a poem from Carl Andre, set questions from Robert Smithson, an exchange with Sol LeWitt, citations from Dan Graham and Mel Bochner, an interview with Don Judd."

JB   [Jo Baer] There are four aspects of "ordinary painting"
      which you listed in your article called "Specific Objects"
      in *Arts Yearbook* 8, 1965.[1] They are:

      1.   The main thing wrong with painting is that it is a rect-
           angular plane placed flat against the wall.
      2.   Everything on or slightly in the plane of the painting
           must be arranged laterally.
      3.   Almost all paintings are spatial. Two colors on the same
           surface almost always lie on different depths.
      4.   Oil and canvas are familiar and, like the rectangular
           plane, have a certain quality and have limits. The qual-
           ity is especially identified with art.

DJ   [Donald Judd] There are two ways in which something is
      alive: first, whether it is still being done well, whether first-
      rate work is still being produced, in which sense Barnett
      Newman and Rothko are still live artists. Secondly, and
      fairly narrow historically, whether it is something for artists
      whose work is developing to consider or not. In which case,
      for the most part, Newman and the others aren't, and by
      now, almost no painters are. What I want to say, what really
      seems to be dying off is conventional painting. I don't like
      conventional sculpture either. I couldn't care less about con-
      ventional sculpture. I bothered with conventional painting
      six years ago and haven't bothered with it since, except ev-
      eryone brings it up. Other people bring it up, that's all.
JB   Is this total condemnation, or do you see any chance for
      paintings at all?
DJ   I think another kind of painting, like Bob Irwin's, has not
      all the aspects of the old painting.
JB   Why do you call that painting?
DJ   Primarily, I guess, because it's parallel to the wall. I guess
      it has to be two-dimensional.
JB   But you do draw, and drawings are also two-dimensional.

DJ   I just put them down sometimes so that I won't forget an idea. They're sort of materialized ideas.

JB   I guess they could be useful in getting to what you want, which is an art object?

DJ   Yeah. But otherwise I don't think it's too interesting.

JB   So you don't think these sketches of ideas can stand as, or be, a work of art?

DJ   No, I guess not, because I want to make something that I want to look at. I don't want to make something that stands for the thing I want to look at.

JB   But aren't there levels of complication, complex ideas or qualities, in fact, that a sculpture cannot make apparent in just the act of looking?

DJ   You don't just look at the damn thing. One look at it is, by definition, complex in quality. That doesn't mean it's an idea as an idea, or that it stands for something.

JB   But ideas are real too?

DJ   Anyway, I'm interested in *visual* art.

JB   From what you're saying, one could guess that you don't much like conceptual art?

DJ   I don't give a damn for the whole thing, because you can't really see it.

JB   Couldn't the literalness and fidelity to the complication of an idea, an "idealized" work, sometimes seduce you?

DJ   I want something you can see – thoroughly visual art – not so-called idea art. Any good work has ideas, that's why it's good visually. If a thing is interesting visually, it's obviously complicated as far as ideas go, and call it feelings, whatever – I don't like the disassociation between the two. I think illustrating a point is pretty uninteresting.

JB   Personally, I find that paintings can be richer in ideas, if somewhat poorer in presence, than three-dimensional objects. The flat wall concentrates the mind of the viewer rather wonderfully. But objects standing alone enjoy the power of greater "thereness."

DJ   Objects can be mixed up with other things, which would
      certainly be an undercutting of a presence: I never meant
      mine to be inconspicuous or to get mixed up with other
      things, to be minimal or whatever, in a way which is some-
      what contemplative. That's what I object to in painting,
      because it does lie back, and ordinarily it's contemplative.
      In a way, there's no way out of it. That may be what you
      mean in not being immediate or whatever. It's a slightly
      passive aspect. I don't think on drawings, I really think in
      my head. The drawings accomplish almost nothing. Oth-
      erwise they're done because someone wants to buy one, or
      just for the hell of it. I also don't think in articles. I think
      walking around, that's all, like everybody else. Thinking
      for yourself and thinking to communicate something to
      someone else are two different things. This is writing, and
      I don't want to get that into painting: a discussion of vi-
      sual art, that's a verbal situation.

JB   To be contemplative is to think about things. Is "thought,"
      for you, something which occurs in between writing and
      the verbal?

DJ   I don't think that way. That doesn't mean anything to me as
      far as I think. Work should be made to be thought about.
      That's not what I mean by "contemplative." "Contem-
      plative" is some sort of word that stands for a quality that
      I sort of ascribe to painting in general, going on back,
      which is just sort of dying out now.

JB   But aside from their surface to-ings and fro-ings, paint-
      ings are also objects that occur.

DJ   They're rather small, flimsy objects that occur primarily
      at the sufferance of a rather big object, which is the wall.
      Your really big object is *really* that wall.

JB   Well, boxes are a sufferance of a room's space, too.

DJ   But a box or anything else three-dimensional is at least
      free on three sides or whatever. It only lies or is attached
      on one side. Ordinarily, it's freer, freer of support.

JB   Paintings are also three-dimensional, just less obtrusively so. And they may be appendages on a wall, but so are so-called three-dimensional objects either on floors or walls.

DJ   Actually, in a way, a three-dimensional work occurs in an area the way painting occurs within the wall area, so I think that reduces the power of the form.

JB   Then perhaps the major difference between paintings and sculptures lies in the greater presence that three-dimensional objects provide?

DJ   If I accept presence, then that presence has to be the all-important quality, not a word that I use. I don't like paintings lying back against the wall. It's personal with me.

JB   But since you also use the wall, are you saying that only works which obtrude from a wall in an aggressive way are valid?

DJ   If it turns out that my work isn't any good, then it's invalidated. I use the wall as I'd use a floor, but if it doesn't come out a certain distance, it's a bas-relief. And because of that quality, I thought for a while there wasn't anything I could do on a wall. Anyway, the main thing for anyone now is to invent his own means.

JB   Have you a position on what makes a work of art good?

DJ   The persistent characteristics of good art are very general and not always present, such as large scale, wholeness, unmodulated color, and an emphasis on materials.

First published: Jo Baer, "A Painter Interviews a Sculptor (on Painting): Donald Judd Interviewed by Jo Baer, 1966–1967," in Jo Baer, *Broadsides and Belles Lettres: Selected Writings and Interviews 1965–2010*, ed. Roel Arkesteijn (Amsterdam: Roma Publications, 2010), 91–92.

1   See Judd's "Specific Objects" (1964) in *Donald Judd Writings*, 134–45. The list given by Baer is composed of direct (but not adjacent) quotes from "Specific Objects," 136–38.

Interview with Barbara Rose and Frank Stella
1966–67

Like Judd, art historian Barbara Rose was a student of Meyer Schapiro's – the influential art critic, historian, and professor – while at Columbia University and became an art critic for hire. Her 1965 essay "ABC Art" offered a definition of the characteristics of "a new sensibility," which Rose traced back to two origins: the innovations of Marcel Duchamp and Kazimir Malevich. Intertwined with the essay were statements by artists whom Rose identified as being part of this "new art," including Carl Andre, Richard Artschwager, Ronald Bladen, Dan Flavin, Judd, Robert Morris, Richard Smith, Frank Stella, Richard Tuttle, Andy Warhol, and Larry Zox. In both interviews and writings, Judd addressed his problems with the term "ABC art" and other similar descriptions.

Between 1965 and 1969, Rose also interviewed gallerists Richard Bellamy, Leo Castelli, Ivan Karp, John Lefebre, and John Bernard Myers; curator Henry Geldzahler; and artists James E. Davis, Lee Krasner, and Tom Wesselmann.

Rose and Stella were married from 1961 to 1969.

BR   [Barbara Rose] We are going to resume our interview with Mickey the Dummy.[1] [*Laughter*] Would you tell us what your opinion of the Oblomov theory of your painting is?[2] That is, that it's the product of intense feelings of ennui and anomie?

FS   [Frank Stella] I just try to do the best job that I can to make Leo [Castelli] and you and all the people out there happy. [*Laughter*] And Ed Sullivan, too.

BR   Well, since you reneged on your promise to quit painting at the age of twenty-five, do you feel that many people were disappointed by the fact that you didn't quit?

FS   Yes, I think my failure to not continue painting has disappointed a lot of people.

BR   On what did you base your original decision to quit painting?

FS   I had done enough painting.

[*Break in recording*]

BR   You said that your work is not sculpture. If it isn't sculpture, what is it?

DJ   [Donald Judd] I don't know what it is, and I don't feel that I have to give it a title. So I don't feel required to say what it is.

BR   Well, why don't you feel it's sculpture? What is it that differentiates it from sculpture?

DJ   Because of the generally figurative organization of sculpture, sort of the core structure and the chronically composed nature of sculpture.

BR   In other words, the main difference between your work and sculpture is that you feel that your work is not composed?

DJ   Yeah, not composed and not arranged on a central core.

BR   Well, you said "figurative"; do you mean that you feel that sculpture in the past has always been figurative?

DJ   Yeah.

BR   All of it?

DJ   Yeah.

BR   How about constructivist sculpture? Do you feel that con-
     structivist sculpture is essentially figurative, too?

DJ   Yeah.

FS   What's the core in a plexiglass [Antoine] Pevsner, or some-
     thing like that?

DJ   Usually it's composed in some way. One of them, for exam-
     ple, crosses on an X shape, so that's still like a piece of sculp-
     ture on a pedestal, with sort of a central axis or whatever.

FS   What about something like David Smith's "gate" pieces?[3]

DJ   Well, those are pretty recent. I haven't seen them, and I
     haven't thought about them that much. That might not
     be, but most of Smith's work is decidedly figurative.

FS   Right. But these are based on something like a portal.

DJ   Yeah. Well, they might be something else.

BR   You feel that your work is not axial, in other words? It's
     not oriented on an axis? Well, obviously, it's not.

DJ   I guess not on that kind of axis, anyway.

BR   If your work isn't composed, how do you arrive at it?

DJ   Full blown in the middle of the night. [Laughter]

BR   How do you arrive at the conception if it's not composed?

DJ   It's not composed in the sense that you try to arrange the
     parts a great deal in relation to one another or play with
     the parts in the process of making the thing. What Frank
     said the other day on the television – the correctional idea
     phrase was nice.[4]

BR   What do you mean?

DJ   Frank said he didn't want to do correctional painting,
     which was nice. That is, you're always involved in getting
     the rest of the painting up to something you like and mak-
     ing changes and adjusting everything, and finally you get
     everything adjusted. Which is a real pain in the neck.

BR   In other words, you don't want to make any adjustments?

DJ   No, I don't see why you should make any adjustments.

FS   What I mean is that the adjustments are totally in terms of the final results. In other words, the adjustments you make are when you begin with the piece: the four boxes are adjusted, but after that, there's just one adjustment.

DJ   You figure it all out ahead.

FS   You don't correct it, at least, in working. Well, you might correct it with the next piece. In other words, if you felt that the intervals were too wide, then you would – would that be a correction, or a different piece? I mean, you could correct it by doing another piece.

DJ   I suppose it would be a correction. That stack that Henry [Geldzahler][5] bought is an inch further out from the wall – it sticks out an inch further than the first set that I made.[6] So I thought it didn't stick out just quite enough.

BR   Do you think of each piece as a correction, for example, of the piece that's gone before, or an improvement in some way?

DJ   No, because I can't afford to do a number of pieces that are like one another.

BR   But I mean, do you analyze, for example, the last pieces you've done and try to make modifications in the next series?

DJ   Not so much. They tend to be kind of separate things.

BR   Then, in other words, you don't look at your work critically?

DJ   Well, no – [*Laughter*]

BR   Well, why would you change a mode of working? I mean, why would you make a new set of decisions?

DJ   The pieces are rather different from one another, so that you can't just build another piece that's a correction of a previous piece.

BR   No, I don't mean a specific correction. But, for example, are you never dissatisfied with what you've done? And if you are dissatisfied, then do you try to make something that will be more satisfactory?

DJ   I suppose so, but I'm not so dissatisfied lately. [*Laughter*]
     The change sort of takes care of itself. The change from
     the wooden pieces, which now look kind of foreign to
     me, to the present pieces took place without any partic-
     ular anxiety over the first case.

BR   You're making it sound very mystical. I mean, you never
     crystallize your thoughts about these matters?

DJ   Yeah, but it's not a case of enormous worry or anything. I
     decided that the paint on the wood had a certain kind of
     generality which still had something to do with the qual-
     ity of painting, say Newman's big surfaces or something,
     and that again was something I didn't want, and I saw a
     way how I could get rid of it by using actual materials.

BR   And you don't feel that applied color, for example, gives
     that same effect that the painted wood gave?

DJ   No, because it's such a peculiar kind of color, and there's
     not that much of it, either.

BR   In other words, you feel your color now is no longer at all
     related to painting color?

DJ   Well, I wouldn't want to say that absolutely, but there's a
     certain austerity that a big surface painted one color and a
     particular texture of cotton canvas and oil paint on it and
     so forth has. A particular kind of quality which I can't re-
     ally pin down.

BR   Yeah, which wood would have more than metal?

DJ   Yeah, and when you paint over the wood, it's still some-
     what that same quality, because it sinks in a bit. It comes
     out matte. And as nice as that is, that's I think too easy a
     kind of generality to get hold of now.

FS   To get back to the noncomposing idea: if you take, say, the
     piece with the four boxes and the blue channel running
     across in front of it [image 9], how do you manage to deal
     with that in noncompositional terms? For example, from
     the head-on view particularly, when you have the bar go-
     ing across the four boxes, you have the proportion of the

channel to the surface of the box, for one thing, which is a relationship that has to be worked out in some kind of way, plus you have the thing of the contrasting surfaces; you have a color problem. You have essentially a kind of blue and silver, or blue and galvanized metal. I mean, in spite of the fact that the organization may be simpler than most kinds of common thinking about composition, or organization, or whatever you want to call it, as far as making sculpture and painting goes, you're still dealing with that same basic problem, and you have to make it convince you it will work out in some kind of way. You're dealing with that kind of problem. So how is that noncomposing?

DJ   Well, to some extent, it still is.

BR   Yeah, but essentially what you're getting at is that the composition is nonrelational.

DJ   The thing is that it's primarily a whole, and it's not so easily broken down into parts. Now, that is the main thing all along.

FS   Well, all right. Are you saying that because you give yourself pretty much a given unit — in other words, the very fact that you're working from standard units, because the channel comes in certain sizes, right?

DJ   Yeah.

FS   So you have a lot of decisions made for you. If you have such and such a size channel, or choices of channel, then you're going to use them, and then, roughly, the choice of the boxes that you're going to build for it are really well decided, in a way. In other words, it'll be relatively easy to find a size that'll go for each width channel.

DJ   Actually, I had the channel, having gotten a piece on Canal Street some time ago. I cut out the face of the boxes in paper, and for a long time I juggled the face of the size of the boxes. [*Laughter*] They were hanging down.

BR   But you begin usually with a sketch, right?

DJ   No, usually sketches are sort of after the fact.

BR   You mean you just carry these ideas in your head?

DJ   Sketches aren't necessary. They don't tell me much about it.

BR   Yeah, but how do you decide to produce a piece?

DJ   The ones that feel right. Same old story.

BR   Yeah, I know, but I mean, you just carry these around in your head, until one day, you call up and you have it done?

DJ   One day I get the money to have it done.

BR   Oh, but you don't put down your ideas in any notational form?

DJ   Yeah, sometimes I put them down just to record the idea.

FS   Do any pieces or ideas seem really necessary or have priority? Do you ever get involved in a piece you feel you have to get through?

DJ   Well, I obviously tend to do the pieces I like best and am surest of.

BR   In other words, you get a certain number of ideas and then some develop priority, because you don't build them all, obviously.

DJ   Well, some seem like a sure thing, better ideas. Often, it's ones I'm sure of against ones that seem to be a considerable gamble. Because obviously you can't afford to lose $500 to $700 on a stupid idea.

BR   Why? What would be a gamble as opposed to a sure thing? I mean, what would be the difference?

DJ   Well, some particular form that didn't feel quite right but might be – I might think interesting, you know.

FS   Say if I were a wealthy patron and you have a series of ideas for, say, your next group of work that you're going to do, and in the normal course of events you're going to be able to build – you're going to get the money in a fairly normal way as a result of working and whatnot, and you're going to build those pieces. And I come along as Patron X and say I'll match that amount of money and whatever money you need to build only the bad ideas, only the gambles, only the things you're unsure of. Would it be interesting to you to see the body of work of the ideas with less risk against the ideas that have the maximum risk? I mean, do you think anything like that can change your thinking?

BR   Why are you thinking of these half-assed questions?

FS   You don't think that's a good question? No? All right. Go ahead.

BR   No, answer it if you've got an answer to that.

DJ   No, it divides it up into two categories which I'm not especially interested in putting one against the other. The pieces I'm pretty sure of always seem pretty risky, anyway. So it's not exactly such a safe bet. I thought for sure that show[7] didn't mean anything to anybody, and me included, when I put it up [image 10].

BR   So, there's a certain degree of surprise until you actually see the things manufactured.

DJ   Two of those pieces I hadn't seen on the wall before.

BR   When you actually see them installed, then, there's a certain degree of surprise? I mean, you really only know if they're successful once you've seen them installed?

DJ   Right. Yeah. And sometimes I'm not sure for a while either.

BR   So, in other words, your ability to visualize is very important – how accurately you can visualize, let me put it that way.

DJ   Yeah.

BR   Okay. You've so far differentiated your work from conventional sculpture by saying it's not involved in composition, or not involved in conventional composition, at any rate.

DJ   It's involved in proportion. That's what Frank's talking about, certainly.

BR   What, then, are the main considerations in your sculpture?

DJ   Getting the size right is obviously very important. And I suppose you could call it composition in the sense that you juggle an area in a painting. The only thing I'm juggling – well, you can call it one proportion, or you can call it –

BR   Do you think proportion is the primary element involved?
      Relationships?

DJ   Yeah. Just what size it is is highly important to me.

BR   How about materials? Do you think much about mate-
      rials and color?

DJ   Yeah, materials and color, what size it is.

FS   So, it's sort of like architectural composition rather than,
      say, painting or sculptural composition. Somehow it in-
      volves more generalities and is less kind of concerned with
      specific details, in the sense that architectural composi-
      tion has to deal with texture, with materials, but only in
      a way that it fits into the whole and how it relates to the
      space – whereas textural concerns in, say, sculpture, and
      particularly bad sculpture, get to be overly artistic, overly
      involved with details like expression and their own tac-
      tile values and their own aesthetic values. In other words,
      the aesthetics of a kind of bronze patina is a little different
      from the idea of, say, the way Mies [van der Rohe] wants
      bronze to be used, bronze plaques and bronze siding or a
      kind of bronze decoration to be used in something like
      the Seagram Building.

BR   Do you agree with that?

DJ   It's a long question. [*Laughter*]

BR   Well, I mean, essentially, do you think that your consider-
      ations or method is closer to architecture than sculpture?

DJ   Yeah, obviously, it's something like architecture. More like
      architecture than like previous sculpture. But I also think
      the decisions are specific. It's specific, which material you
      choose.

BR   But you definitely feel different materials give different
      qualities? You don't feel neutrally toward your material?

DJ   No. Choosing to do the stainless steel took some think-
      ing, because I'm sort of wary of stainless being a pretty el-
      egant material, you know.

BR   Well, I think that's a fairly elegant piece.

FS   Maybe it's not fair to characterize a more traditional sculp-
        ture in this way, but, say, if a traditional sculptor wants to
        get some kind of expressive quality out of the materials –
        in other words, if stainless steel is used by, say, Brancusi,
        or maybe Rivera, or somebody like that, they want the
        beauty of the stainless steel. But if you are presented with
        the problem of stainless steel, you are worrying about how
        it can use its own properties to work in with your organi-
        zational ideas in this sort of overall point of the piece, the
        overall way of the piece. In other words, you don't take
        your cue from the materials, but you want the materials
        to do more of what you want it to do.

DJ   Yeah, but would that be any different from Brancusi? Or
        anyone else? You're choosing materials because they pro-
        duce a certain quality.

FS   Well, of course, but they basically molded it; they always
        molded the material, and David Smith scars it. And actu-
        ally, in a way, you really let it alone more.

DJ   But it's still serving my purpose, though, all the same.

FS   Yeah. Right.

DJ   And, you know, you're using a quality that it has. I like its
        qualities better than anything I could do to it, anyway.

BR   Okay. Can I ask a few questions? Thank you.

DJ   He's not so dumb. Mickey isn't dumb. [*Laughter*]

BR   Anyway, do you feel your work is related to painting in
        any way?

FS   Oh, what a boring question. [*Laughter*]

DJ   Yeah, to some extent. I mean, obviously, it's related to
        painting and to so-called sculpture and so forth. I'm not
        saying it's brand-new and divorced – it's connected to
        paintings –

BR   Well, my feeling as I've watched its evolution is that it
        evolved out of a criticism of painting.

DJ   I guess so, but it's better than painting.

BR   On what grounds?

DJ   Well, in the first place, I couldn't think of anything I could
       do with it that I wanted to do with it. So primarily on per-
       sonal grounds. But after that, that it was a rectangle, that
       it was parallel to the wall, and that it was almost unavoid-
       ably illusionistic, and that none of the color or materials
       could be specific enough. There wasn't much you could
       do inside of the rectangle because everything had to re-
       late to it; otherwise you'd break it up too much. So you
       didn't have many choices to work with. It seemed kind
       of contemplative, splayed out against the wall like that. I
       didn't like that.

BR   You don't like the idea of your work being interpreted as
       objects for contemplation?

DJ   No, I guess not. Painting seemed kind of passive –

BR   Uh-huh.

FS   It's the easiest thing.

BR   Do you see any problems in – well, using this work? I
       mean, it's too large, really, for most people's apartments. Is
       it intended for private collections? Or what is it intended
       for? How is it intended to be seen?

DJ   It's just intended to get done, that's all.

BR   You never think, in other words, about the context in
       which it might be shown? Inside? Outside? Museums?
       Apartments?

DJ   Not too much, because I don't think I have much control
       over it. Therefore, it's not a very interesting problem. I'd
       think about it a lot if I could control where it was going to
       be and could do something about where it was going to be.

BR   But you must be aware that it doesn't fit into any of the
       contexts that are provided for collecting works of art at
       this point. Doesn't that ever occur to you?

DJ   No, what can you do about it?

FS   Write letters?

DJ   [*Laughter*] You know, if that's what I want to do, that's all
       you can do. It doesn't happen to be especially saleable or –

BR   Well, ideally, where do you think it should go? I mean, where do you think it should be placed, suppose you did have some control?

DJ   Ideally, I'd like to build the architecture for it as well as —

BR   Ah! [*Hums a tune*] In other words, you visualize it in an architectural context?

DJ   Well, everything is in an architectural context. It's inside or outside, other than the high plains.

BR   All right. [*Laughter*]

FS   I want to ask one small last question. You use a negative sort of inflection in speaking about illusionistic space in painting. Why is it a negative proposition? For example, let's say I allow a negative thing toward traditional naturalistic illusionism. But what would be the matter with, say, a good workable, abstract, illusionistic space, say [Jules] Olitski, or Bauhaus, Kandinsky?

DJ   Because I think it's still illusionistic in the same sense that the old naturalistic illusionism is illusionistic. I think it's just one thing. There's just less of it now than there was before. Essentially, it's the same sort of phenomenon.

BR   As long as it suggests any kind of depth, Frank, it's illusionistic.

DJ   Which has objectionable qualities.

FS   Abstract illusionistic space, even though it's the same kind of depth, it's really not the same kind. For one thing, it's shallower; and for two, when you don't have the implication of a horizon line, you have a different kind of illusionistic space. The classic illusionism in the West is like looking out the window, right? When you look out the window you see the ground line, you have the trees, you have the light and dark, you have the top and bottom and all that —

DJ   You have things one in front of the other.

FS   Right. But you look up, say, and you don't look out the window. Say you're standing in the middle of a meadow, and again you have the same kind of illusionism, but if you look straight up – and the problem of the horizon is not there on the picture plane if you're looking straight up – then you have the infinite, but it's still naturalistic illusionistic space, or the way we see.

DJ   Mm–hmm.

FS   So it's still a different kind of space. It's a new abstract illusionistic space in, say, Olitski and in some of the things suggested in Kandinsky, which was obviously oriented toward a kind of stargazing –

DJ   You really talk fast.

FS   – and that's different. You have to say that's different from the classical illusionistic space in the West, which has to do with the horizon.

DJ   It's somewhat different, but I don't think it's essentially different. It's another emphasis. It's a decreased amount of illusionism on one end of the scale where it's dying out or something, but I don't think it's essentially different if there's any at all. That was very important to me, because it –

FS   Take Pollock. Pollock would be another example. In a sense, Pollock is that, too.

DJ   Yeah. I think the illusionism in there is a real illusionism. The same as ever, even though it's shallow and even though it's in a very peculiar context.

FS   I would say that it works in real painterly, successful terms. It does the job that it has to do, and it doesn't bring back open space or get in the way. You don't feel like it's landscape or something like that. It's its own space, which is suitable for its own ends.

DJ   No, I don't think it feels that much like landscape, but it still feels like –

BR   Depth?

DJ   Like depth. The way you experience things as you see them, I guess. So it's part of a description of seeing things.

BR   Well, it's not actual; I mean, painting space is not actual.

FS   Yeah, but wait a second. In Pollock, and even in some
       works of Olitski's, there's a little bit of illusion, right? But
       in the best examples, where it works best, what you get is
       a physical illusionistic space created by the actual mate-
       rial itself – the paint. That's the way the paint works, and
       you bring some illusion to it, but it develops the surface
       softness, the kind of give and the interlace of the web of
       Pollock. It develops a kind of optical give or shallow illu-
       sionism that works. So why –

DJ   I think it works great, you know. But I don't want the
       quality. I'm not criticizing whether it works or not. Ob-
       viously, it works for their purposes. You know, [Larry]
       Poons's things work for Poons's purposes. But that both-
       ered me a lot in painting, that there was just nothing you
       could put on that surface that really would stay put. And I
       couldn't think of any way to solve it. To me, that meant it
       had all the implications of naturalistic illusionism, which
       got mixed up in rationalistic philosophy and all those ab-
       struse things.

FS   Yeah, but what are the implications? Meaning that com-
       position is limited?

DJ   I mean generally, in a way, reading a sort of anthropo-
       morphic view, which is a big objection to the whole of
       traditional painting. That quality, again, is – it's sort of a
       description.

FS   In other words, you're saying that there's no abstract paint-
       ing? Right? It doesn't make abstract painting possible?

DJ   Yeah. I guess – I suppose – maybe so. Maybe so. It still has
       a certain amount of ordinary naturalism to it. Certainly,
       Mondrian has, because of the double space that the white
       has. So obviously the blue dots [in Poons] stand out in
       front of the yellow ocher.

BR   In other words, there isn't any absolutely flat painting?

DJ   No. I sort of tried to think of doing that, but I didn't think that seriously about it. That's why I like those [John] Chamberlains, because the surface is –

FS   Yes, but what they create is a mirror depth, actually. It does the trick, except that you read the reflections, so you get that manifest illusion. But theoretically, the hard lacquers or the hard surfaces should do it. But they don't. Why isn't it the same problem? If you're saying you have to have anthropomorphic and therefore nonabstract connotations to something like Poons – that there is no abstract painting because of the problems of the way the paint works – well, it seems to me you can make that same argument for any colored surface, and why can't you get the same feeling out of the sheets of galvanized and stuff like that? You see the reflections, you feel the space, or even if you feel the actuality, isn't that an anthropomorphic feeling, a reaction, so it doesn't get to be totally abstract?

BR   You're trying to say that human beings can't have abstract sensations?

FS   All I'm trying to say is that – yeah, right, I'm trying to say that that's what it finally comes down to. His assertion about the nonabstract quality or inability to read Poons abstractly is essentially saying the same thing.

DJ   It doesn't matter to me that surfaces reflect, or shine, or whatever, because that doesn't come under this kind of space, and it's especially that kind of space which is sort of the center of the old naturalism.

BR   Which kind of space?

DJ   Well, that something has space behind it, or around it, or the colors move in and out on a flat surface. Now, you know, there's all sorts of illusionism. But another illusion can mean something that doesn't have anything to do with this problem. So, I'm not against any other illusions, just this particular one at the moment.

FS   Well, how do you feel about, say, mechanical illusionism? Say –

BR   Trompe l'oeil.

FS   Well, not so much trompe l'oeil. I mean, like, orthographic drawing or whatever –

DJ   No, I don't mean that kind of illusionism. I mean the fact that things are always appearing different from what they are, or a surface is shiny, like [Larry] Bell's boxes. Or, say, that purple paint looks different depending on where you stand because it reflects in a different way.

BR   You're saying that that isn't involved with the problem of illusionism?

DJ   No, that's another illusionism, but one that's chronic to art.

BR   Do you think there's a current revival of monumental art, and do you think that there are a number of people involved? I mean, obviously, there are people now working in a related direction which is unlike the sculpture that was produced during abstract expressionism, and it's much more monumental. But do you think in general there's a revival of monumental sculpture?

DJ   When was the first monumental sculpture that you're reviving?

BR   In the twentieth century, there hasn't been much of it. There's been very little monumental sculpture in the twentieth century.

DJ   "Monumental" is what – is big? And public?

BR   Yes, I guess so. Big and public.

DJ   Well, I don't care whether mine is big and public, or big and private, or small and public, or in what regard. So in that sense, it's not monumental. I wouldn't want it to have a quality in front of some big building that it might not, that it wouldn't have on a smaller scale inside of somebody's house. I wouldn't want to make awesome or imposing sculpture in a conventional sense.

BR   Do you think that the younger sculptors are reacting to, say, for example, David Smith? I mean, do you think that they're reacting to the idea that the whole cubist open-welded tradition is exhausted? Or do you feel that the cubist open-welded tradition is exhausted?

DJ   Yeah, but I always thought so, and I took it quite naturally, so there's no real problem. I can't really have reacted against it. I always liked Smith, but I always knew I'd never on earth do anything like that. So it wasn't such a live problem. And I never had any idea of doing sculpture, anyway.

BR   So, in other words, really the work or the sculpture arose out of you thinking about painting problems and your feeling about the exhaustion of painting, rather than the exhaustion of sculpture?

DJ   Yeah, because I always considered it another kind of form which I wouldn't have done under any circumstances, anyway. Because even more than painting, well, it [sculpture] was cubist when painting certainly wasn't. So that indicates its state.

BR   Well, do you think that the new sculpture is postcubist? Or do you think of your work as postcubist?

DJ   Well, I don't think it's cubist. So I suppose it's post. [*Laughter*]

BR   Do you think that the shaped canvas is any kind of solution to the problems of painting as you outline them?

DJ   I think any difference from the several standard qualities of painting taken away from usual painting thereby is an improvement.

BR   And those standard qualities are rectangularity, illusionism?

DJ   Parallel with only an inch or two behind them.

BR   So you think that the shaped canvas is at least a partial solution? But obviously you must think it's only partial, because you're not doing it.

DJ   Well, it was occupied at an early date by an obscure painter named Frank Stella. [*Laughter*]

BR   Do you think that there's any relationship between constructivism or de Stijl sculpture and your own work?

DJ   No, I have never paid much attention to it, and I'm sort
     of sympathetic now, because in retrospect –

BR   Well, I think it was really very little studied or known in
     this country among artists.

FS   Was it ever very well known?

DJ   I haven't seen much.

FS   Mostly what we know are photographs.

DJ   Yeah. I've seen very few pieces. I've seen a couple of Pevs-
     ners that I liked a lot. But it certainly wasn't an influence,
     because all that stuff looked very small scale, very com-
     posed, ideal, and historical.

FS   I think a lot about the scale; for example, I often felt that
     everything before I started to paint or before, say, abstract
     expressionism was small scale and dainty. But on the other
     hand, if you take, say, [Naum] Gabo or Pevsner or a lot of
     that constructivist stuff, that was really done because of
     limits and stuff, and a lot of that was confused, because –

BR   Well, they were products like [Vladimir] Tatlin's Monu-
     ment to the Third International.[8] It was never built. So it
     was obviously supposed to be enormous. But your notion
     of scale, in other words, comes out of painting, or comes
     out of American painting?

DJ   Yeah.

FS   Also, you know what, there's an interesting point here.
     You say that most of it [constructivist art] seems small to
     us, and it was small, and most of it was models, but they
     had an idea of big pieces and monumental pieces – but
     the fact still remains that they never found the real kind of
     scale. In other words, there's the mock-up and then there's
     the giant piece. But a whole lot of my efforts, and I think
     Don's a little bit, are directed toward a real kind of, you
     know, scale, a real kind of size. It's not either a model size
     or a huge blowup, it's a kind of real, actual size that's sup-
     posed to do the job. That's it. It's not supposed to be made
     smaller or bigger than is really convincing. It's supposed

to do what a monumental piece can do if the scale and the thing is right, if you find a kind of viable size, a viable scale and structure.

DJ   Well, I think if they had built those big pieces, it would probably still have a smaller internal structure than, say, someone making a big piece now.

BR   Yes, they would have modules and things of a different sort.

DJ   Because you've got all those parts in a Pevsner.

BR   And all those relationships.

DJ   Which bring it down to a smaller scale, and that's again a carryover from the old tradition, the kind of painting that was involved – and they paint all those little figures and landscapes.

BR   Do you think that your work can be subjected to conventional formal analysis? Do you think it's meaningful to subject it to formal analysis?

DJ   Yeah, I guess so. If a piece doesn't work, there's probably some reason – I mean, if it's not so dumb that there's no reason at all. If it gets beyond a certain point, there's nothing much you can say about it – you know, a certain point toward badness – you can't really criticize it. But if it's just a little bit bad, then there's usually reason for it.

FS   Like making the tubing thicker, change the color?

DJ   Yeah. Like, how far down the top should go on that one in the middle of the room was a delicate calculation [image 11]. I called Bernstein up at the last minute and told him to put it up a quarter of an inch.[9] He thought I was crazy.

BR   Do you think that the question of the artist's intentions is important at this point? I mean, do you think it's important for one to know?

DJ   I think that's always useful and interesting information.

BR   Well, how would you describe your intentions?

DJ   I think that's a long story which –

BR   Tell it.

DJ   That takes a while because – well, like the business with space. That goes back five or six years or something, you know, so those are sort of problems I've forgotten about.

BR   Think about them.

DJ   Yeah, but then you have to collect all those and get them together.

BR   Well, think.

DJ   It's a big undertaking, and —

BR   Think. Go on. Give it a whirl.

DJ   Well, we talked about painting. So, I had all those objections to that. I did quite a few paintings that I thought were pretty good paintings, but which I was never satisfied with, about three years before I did three-dimensional work. Then overlapping the last couple of paintings, I did a couple of things which were — one was a relief that came out quite a ways [image 12]. Well, the first one was a very shallow relief, then there was another one that was even more of a relief [image 13]. Both on the wall. And almost at the same time a freestanding piece [image 14]. And they surprised me quite a bit.

BR   They seemed much more satisfactory?

DJ   Well, for one thing, I found them a lot harder to understand, and I didn't quite know what to make of them. And in a way, they looked a hell of a lot stronger and better.

BR   Do you remember why you did a relief in the first place?

DJ   I couldn't do anything with that damn painting. I curved — you know, the first one, the first idea was the relief with the curved top and bottom [see image 12]. That was the very first thing to do with painting. And actually, I did that with a piece of canvas first. I just built a little wooden structure at each end and curved the whole piece of canvas because I'd painted out everything on the surface and I didn't know what to do with that blank surface.

BR   Oh, was there a painting under that?

DJ   No, this one doesn't. I threw it out. I mean, this got to be such a mess that —

BR   But originally it was a painting? You mean it originally
      had some kind of shaped front?
FS   Yeah, it was a [Enrico] Castellani or a [Lucio] Fontana or
      something?
DJ   This isn't anything you've seen.
BR   No, the first relief you did, you painted over a painting?
DJ   It was a piece of canvas. It was a painting, about thirty-six
      by forty-five, or something or other.
BR   And then you made it a monochrome, and then you built
      the box.
DJ   I got it down to texture and monochrome, and I still didn't
      like it. And then I curved both ends outward, top and bot-
      tom. But it was pretty messy by then. So after a while, I
      threw it out and then did it over with the top and bottom
      galvanized.
BR   Do you think painting has anywhere to go? Or do you
      think it's in a corner?
DJ   I think it is kind of in a corner, but I don't think you can
      really say what's going to happen.
BR   How about sculpture?
DJ   What sculpture? All the sculpture?
BR   Conventional sculpture. Welded sculpture. Open-assembled
      sculpture.
DJ   I think it will probably just peter out. And the people who
      are doing it and doing it well, like di Suvero, will go on
      doing it. But the others, I think, will do something else.
      Like, [David] Weinrib and Frosty Myers and people like
      that seem to be moving into something that isn't quite like
      the old composed sculpture.
BR   Yeah, how would you characterize it? I mean, it's differ-
      ent, there's no question.
DJ   I don't know how to characterize it, but the parts aren't
      composed in the way di Suvero or earlier people would
      compose it.
BR   Well, it's more environmental.

DJ   There are many more parts, so that you can't read the re-
      lations in the same way.

BR   It also comes out of painting.

FS   It's additive and anecdotal.

BR   Yeah, it's additive, anecdotal, environmental, and basically
      pictorial.

DJ   It's so additive, though, that you sort of lose control of the
      sum of the whole thing. See, with di Suvero or Smith or
      somebody like that, you can say, "Well, it's a major part,
      it's a minor part, and this goes to that."

FS   Yeah, Mark's things are totally composed. You've got to re-
      alize they're very composed. They're composed all the way
      down to the detail and the opposition materials, and down
      to the bends of the metal and contrast with the texture of
      the board and the bolts, and all of the bolts are placed.

BR   What would you say is the most interesting development?
      Would you rather call your work something other than
      sculpture, like "three-dimensional work" or something?

DJ   Yeah. I don't like "sculpture." I never wanted to get mixed
      up in it. Anyway, just to be literal, the word means sculpting.

BR   Well, yeah, but there's no other word in the language for
      three-dimensional art. I mean, we have three visual arts
      and —

FS   There's music. [*Laughter*]

BR   Music, dancing, and Rauschenberg. Did you ever want to
      fill the gap between art and life?

DJ   No, I don't know anything about that gap.

BR   Do you feel there is a gap between art and life?

DJ   No, I can't even think of that.

FS   How about art? Is making objects that you want to make,
      is that — do you consider that an art practice? What are the
      final criteria for success? Whether or not you like it? Or
      do you feel it has to appeal to some kind of general artis-
      tic problem?

DJ   I think the only criteria is whether you like it or not. What else is there to go on? You assume that if you like it, then hopefully somebody else will like it, so that makes it public art, because that's the only way you can get at the rest of the people.

FS   You don't think the question of art is a problem of defining it or having a useful word like "art" around? I mean, what you're doing comes under the category of art. Do you think art is just a total convention that's not really meaningful or useful in any way?

DJ   I don't think it's very useful. I'm willing to let anybody call anything art.

FS   You don't think it's meaningful, either? In other words, are you an artist?

DJ   Yeah. No, I think I'm making art, but I'm saying that anybody else can call whatever they choose art.

FS   Yeah, but is it important to you? I mean, you say you think you're making art. Now, that's a lot different from what you said before.

DJ   Which was what?

FS   That the word "art" doesn't have any meaning, and the final criteria is just whether or not you like it. You say you're making art and all that counts is whether or not it's just something you like – does art consist in being just what you like?

DJ   Yeah, maybe so.

BR   Yeah, but I like all that chocolate, but it's not art.

DJ   I'm not sure that all that stuff is essentially that different from art, anyway.

BR   Chocolate?

DJ   Yeah.

BR   Can you eat art? And if not, why not? [*Laughter*]

DJ   Really, it seems a little continuous with your reasons for liking art, and all the other things you might like.

BR   Then, in other words, you don't think there is such a thing as the aesthetic emotion?

FS   Okay. How about –

BR   Wait a minute. Wait a minute. Wait a minute. We're really on Don's home territory now. [*Laughter*]

DJ   I can have aesthetic emotions about most anything. I think art is very variable.

BR   You don't think there is a specialized aesthetic emotion which has to do only with art?

DJ   But look how much is art, anyway, just by an ordinary –

FS   The aesthetic emotion is actually probably strongest when it's not dealing with art. The art emotion is actually the least common denominator. Most people get stronger aesthetic emotion out of things relating to sex or money or, say, a beautiful table, or a beautiful girl, or –

BR   Stop giving yourself away, Mickey. [*Laughter*]

DJ   But I don't think it's that distinct from all those things.

BR   Do you think it's distinct at all?

DJ   Yeah, I think so. Yes. But maybe not so much; the difference in nature is perhaps more defined.

BR   Do you think it's possible to communicate anything in art?

DJ   Yeah, I guess so.

BR   What?

DJ   A general attitude toward things at large, I guess.

BR   What things at large?

DJ   Everything. That's a big question. I think it communicates. I think I have some sense of the quality in other people's work, or what they mean.

BR   In other words, what is possible to communicate is only quality? I mean, you can't communicate anything more specific than quality?

DJ   The quality that is there implies certain other things; it wouldn't be as it is if they didn't think certain things.

BR   Who?

DJ   Well, for example, Frank and Poons said something – I've forgotten what it was – it was very much alike, which I

never heard either one of them say and which was completely expected, some attitude that is pretty chronic, about
the nature of their work.[10]

BR   Well, they both said that they try for a certain kind of quality.

DJ   Yeah, it had something to do with scale or something like that. It implied more than that. It implied an attitude that there's also un-art. Could art occur outside of an artistic context? Which would be a case where you'd have a painting implying something that someone who is not an artist also might feel, or think, or act upon.

BR   Can you think of anything else?

FS   Well, just, do you think in terms of good and bad art? How do you think we should deal with bad art?

DJ   I think good and bad art's more interesting than art – I mean, than the idea of art and non-art and all that. There's more distinction there than there is between what is art and what isn't art and all the rest of that.

BR   Yeah. Yeah. That's a very good point.

FS   I can say just for myself, I learn a lot – I've learned almost more from bad art, and I think a lot of people do. I learn more from bad art than I do from good art, because it really helps you. It's easier for you to see what you think by looking at bad art than it is, at least for me, to see what I think from looking at my own art, or even the art that I like. In fact, I have the least reaction to art that I like. I don't think why or anything. I just like it. But on the other hand, if I see bad art, I can give you reasons why I think it's bad. The only way I get the positive values is by describing what I don't like, and then I take that to mean that I like the opposite.

DJ   It's not very laudable that it serves just a teaching purpose. That's not saying much for it.

BR   Do you think there's such a thing as avant-garde art anymore? Or do you think that that's a kind of outworn concept?

D J   Well, it sounds kind of outworn. But on the other hand, you have just a few people doing the best work and the most radical work and so forth. It doesn't seem as separate, perhaps, from the general body of what's going on as maybe it used to be, or as isolated in some group as it used to be. I'm not sure it's outworn, I guess, because you have a few people who are doing the best work and in a way inventing something, sort of leading. I suppose that's what an "avant-garde" meant.

       Actually, there's no avant-garde because there's no rear guard that amounts to anything. So there's just the people that are good, and then there's —

B R   And then there's the Art Students League.

F S   Where's pop art?

B R   Yeah, what's pop art?

D J   I don't know. I mean, you've got to define the question.

B R   Yeah. Did you go to Claes [Oldenburg]'s show?[11] I didn't see it, but I heard it was great.

D J   I just went to the opening and couldn't see it very well. I didn't go back.

B R   I didn't see it.

D J   He had a lot of things painted. A lot of ghost models which he brushed over.

B R   With paint?

D J   Yeah. Which was a dumb idea. Very sensitive and aesthetic and stupid.

B R   What would you do if there were no demand for your work?

D J   Well, very little of it would get made.

B R   But you'd still continue to do it, I mean?

D J   Sure. It's too late to change. You either quit at twenty-five or that's it. [*Laughter*]

B R   What do you think of Tony Smith's work?

D J   I've only seen one piece. I saw that one piece at the Wadsworth.[12]

B R   It looked very advanced.

DJ   It was black, though. [*Laughter*]

BR   Well, do you think your concept of an avant-garde now is involved with feeling impelled to push on? I mean, once a position has been established, to find an antithetical position?

DJ   I think that sounds too historical.

BR   Do you subscribe to the notion of a dialectic?

DJ   Between who and who?

BR   Well, in the sense that Michael Fried talks about.[13]

DJ   No, I don't think things are all that historical.

BR   Well, but, the whole description of how you evolved your work…

DJ   It is very important when you're developing it [your art], because you're learning from what's going on around you, and you're staying away from certain things maybe just because they're well done. But on the other hand, it's mostly getting you out of what is current at the moment. You're not going to some fixed future position; you're just going off and doing something that you think is interesting and presumably new.

FS   Yeah, but dialectic is not going to a fixed position. It's just going on to a position which –

BR   Which hasn't been occupied.

DJ   But it sounds as if that position is there to be occupied. That position wasn't there. You invented it.

FS   Yeah, there is a necessity to dialectic. Not to say where or what that position is, but there's going to be a position there. In other words, there's always going to be that position. It doesn't care how long it takes us to get there, but it's going to move toward a position, which is going to be a renewed position. It's not going to stop. I mean, all I'm saying, I suppose, is that in the long run, history is not going to stop. There's got to be a future.

DJ   Obviously, you're not going to want to do what's been done.

BR   Why obviously?

DJ   Because somebody else invented it.

BR   Well, so what?

DJ   You're never going to understand it, that's why. I mean, I admire Newman's paintings, or Pollock's, or Matisse's, or Frank's, or whoever, but you're never on earth going to understand those paintings sufficiently to copy them well, even if you wanted to do that, because actually, it's not a language. They invented the forms, and they're the only people who are really going to know what it's all about.

FS   Yeah, and also, one of the things I thought about or said once is that you can learn and you can guess and you can research it enough to get some idea of the forms and why they did them and what they did. But you're always guessing, or you're on very shaky ground, if you kind of have to re-create the emotional atmosphere or whatever it was that made them do what they did. And if you can do that, I mean, it gets to be like – you're not schizo or whatever it is, but you're destroying yourself as a personality. So if you were able to do it, you would make it not as yourself, anyway, which would be pretty hard to do, but it would also be ultimately about as destructive a thing as you could do.

DJ   Yeah. You know, I like Matisse, I've always liked Matisse, but at one time, the funny shapes he puts in the paintings, especially the sculpture, they're really alien. You can't imagine just what they come out of, what kind of an emotional –

BR   Do you think your work is involved with – I've already asked about the aesthetic emotions – but an emotion or a feeling of sorts?

DJ   Sure. What else?

BR   Is it characterizable?

DJ   No, I think it should be too complex for that. But it certainly, I think, it has –

BR   A personal necessity?

DJ Yeah, I guess so.

BR I've heard it described as puritanical masculinity, but —

DJ I don't think it's puritanical.

BR You don't think of your work as puritanical?

DJ No.

BR Do you think of it as deeply sensuous and ingratiating?

DJ Yeah. [*Laughter*]

FS Do you think it can ever get to be more than an assertion? In other words, you can describe what you like and describe it as quality, but do you think there's any way of a —

BR That's verifiable.

FS Yeah, that's verifiable. Or at least desirable?

BR Verifiable through consensus only.

DJ Do you mean verify the quality that's there?

FS Yeah — do you think you have the ability to convince at least someone or somebody? Or if you could convince somebody, does that only mean that they happen to think like you do? Or do you think that you can have some kind of mildly objective situation? In other words, do you think that you have any confidence in your ability to convince someone about the things that you feel strongly about in terms of quality?

DJ I don't see how you can convince anybody to understand and like the stuff without their really doing so, you know. I mean, you can always help by explaining things. You can at least make them willing to look at it, which is sort of a step.

BR Well, what would be some of the information you would give to help someone understand this work?

DJ Oh, boy. Why don't we just run along with little questions, so that this sort of thing comes out, instead of attacking it in such —

BR One criticism of the new abstract art is that it's not humanistic. Do you feel your work is in the tradition of humanism?

DJ No. I hate humanism.

BR   Well, why do you feel negatively about humanism?

DJ   It's a particular philosophy which is now in its old age and no longer very interesting.

BR   Well, what's replaced it?

DJ   I don't know. You don't have to name what's replaced it. Humanism is sort of resurrected Renaissance literature and whatnot run by Mark Van Doren and other dumb people who — Joseph Wood Krutch, especially, I think is my favorite humanist.[14]

BR   Oh, that's *Saturday Review* stuff.

DJ   But that's also what humanism is in art, insofar as it still exists. It's [Leonard] Baskin and so forth. And it's the same sort of simpleminded, stupid level with the same lack of —

BR   Well, no, take Meyer Schapiro.[15] Now, obviously, he's in favor of the humanist tradition in art. But you can't put him on the same level with these people.

FS   I don't think he'd be in favor of it now. I mean, in favor of applying it to contemporary work.

BR   Oh, I think so. I think that's the kind of humanism that more sophisticated people —

FS   I mean, I don't think he would criticize, say, Don's work or my work. He wouldn't criticize it as being antihumanistic in the way [Hilton] Kramer might object to it.[16] I mean, I think Schapiro would take some other kind of tack.

BR   Well, no, I think essentially the objection is that it doesn't have any emotional content, and it doesn't relate.

FS   I don't think he'd say that. I think he'd imply some qualitative formal argument, saying in some way it's not a good painting, or something like that, not saying it's less human as art.

BR   Yeah, I think you're probably right. But essentially — I mean, people are still looking in art for some quality which is related to —

DJ   That art is a very particular kind of art, based upon human bodies and landscape and so forth. And that's had its day,

and I have another kind. It's no less humanistic to make
something than it is to paint people and landscapes. So, it
seems very obvious.

B R   Well, how about the criticism that there is a lack of feeling among the educated classes?

D J   You mean the really educated classes?

B R   Well, that was, you know, Kramer's review of Frank's show.[17]
That was the point of it.

D J   Oh yeah. I think that's silly and foolish.

B R   Why?

D J   Because he has a very infantile idea of feeling. He doesn't
like Baskin, I can say that for him. He once said that Saul
Baizerman was one of the great undiscovered, less discovered artists of the twentieth century. For example, he compared Baizerman to, I think, Michelangelo and such lumi-
naries. Which means that his idea of the quality in both
Michelangelo and Baizerman is pretty warped. So he's seen
rather superficial things in the old artists and likes those
and expects them in present art. I don't think anyone now
likes older art any the less for what they may be doing.

B R   Well, what kind of Old Master art?

D J   I much prefer my idea of Michelangelo than I do Hilton
Kramer's idea of Michelangelo.

B R   What older art do you like particularly?

D J   Oh, most of it.

B R   No, I mean, you must have certain preferences. Everybody does, things that have to do with taste and sensibility. Who are your favorite artists?

D J   I really do like a lot of them.

B R   Rubens?

D J   Rubens is a great painter.

B R   Rubens is a great painter, but –

D J   Did you see the one in Washington? Were you there?
You weren't there; who was with us? Oh, Glo [Bell] and
[Larry] Bell. After the opening. They've got one there of

Daniel in the lions' den, and the painting is solid lions except for Daniel.[18] It's a really nutty painting.

BR   Yeah, but who – [Frans] Snyders did the animals, didn't he?[19]

DJ   Yes, probably. The animals aren't by Rubens.

BR   I think that Snyders did the animals in Rubens's paintings.

DJ   But again, that's Rubens's idea. That's inhumanistic art in humanistic times, or –

BR   Oh, because they're animals?

DJ   No, because somebody else painted them.

BR   Aha! A small concept of executive art from –

DJ   Rubens was a real manager. My ideal. I'll have my own palazzo and I'll run diplomatic errands for Johnson.

BR   That's very interesting. [*Inaudible*] Listen, I'd rather have Barney [Newman] for president than Johnson. I'm not sure. Barney for secretary of state. He ran for mayor of New York; did you know that?[20]

DJ   Yeah, he told me.

BR   But I mean, so much has been eliminated from contemporary art or contemporary avant-garde art; do you think it's impoverished? Do you think in comparison with Donatello, do you feel your work is impoverished? Or in comparison with Rubens?

DJ   Decidedly not. What's been eliminated is the aspects in the old art. That's been eliminated. But you've also invented all sorts of new things. So there are aspects there that didn't exist before, which you assume are just as plentiful and full and luscious and ripe as the old art was. So why is there necessarily less in it? I object to your "minimal" phrase and "reductive" and all the rest of it.[21] Going back to [Kenneth] Noland's work, I don't think "reductive" is a very good –

BR   Well, I wasn't using it in terms of content, but in means.

DJ   If you just consider technical things, I don't think their work was reductive, or that that's a very apt description of it.

BR   Why not?

DJ   I don't think my work, say, is minimal and –

BR   Why not? I mean –

DJ   Because there's not essentially any less.

BR   Well, there are fewer elements, for one thing.

DJ   But you have other things. You have a much greater scale, you have more color. You have more emphasis on material.

BR   You don't have more colors.

DJ   So what? A lot of red is better maybe than three colors, who knows?

FS   It may be more complicated.

DJ   My first piece was just a box, pretty much, and I thought it would be too simple. But boxes are fairly complicated things.

BR   How – "fairly"?

DJ   Well, you've got eight edges.

BR   Yeah, but they're all the same.

DJ   What, in one piece?

BR   Yeah. The edges are all – I mean, they're straight edges.

DJ   Sure, but there are eight of them. And you can't see all of them, of course, but you see four. Well, you see seven. You see seven at once.

FS   The whole idea of what you see and don't see, and you know the edges are there – that's a complicated idea to begin with.

DJ   Yeah. You see seven of them at once, all from a different angle. A simple box is really a pretty complicated thing.

BR   But we have a knowledge, we have a foreknowledge of it, so it's not as complicated as a created form which we don't have a foreknowledge of.

FS   I think it's complicated every time you stop, and no matter how long you stop, but if you really stop to consider it, or even look at one – any kind of box, any kind of thing – it's complicated.

DJ   You don't necessarily have to have thought about it before, you know. Like, I don't look too closely at the lampshade; I don't think about it too much, the lampshade. Somebody makes a big form like that and really does something with it, then you give it a lot more thought.

FS   Well, you usually end up in most of those situations with the lampshade. [*Laughter*]

DJ   I decidedly don't think that Noland or Frank or anybody is reductive.

FS   Isn't there a lack of invention if you stay with a reductive format, in the sense that you deal mostly with cubes or rectangles?

BR   Don doesn't like reduction.

FS   Or, say, you deal with geometric elements; you're going to have a certain lack of invention there.

DJ   No. I don't see why it's any less inventive than, say, di Suvero's juggling with shapes. Do you think it's less inventive when you do, say, a triangle than a pentagon?

FS   Yeah, in a sense.

[*Break in recording*]

BR   You thought what? Go ahead.

DJ   They [my early works] occurred in a context that had all sorts of possibilities, and I still think that the work I'm doing can go in all sorts of directions; all sorts of things can be done with it to develop pretty naturally. And I don't have to get into my weekly crisis over the whole thing, which I used to do, and it definitely isn't some sort of closed or given situation.

BR   What were you going to say?

FS   I think that if you do anything or you follow it through, you're a victim of your own basic premises somehow. It amounts to a preference for one thing over another. [*Inaudible*]

DJ   Obviously, artists are going to make their own conventions.

When they become boring to you, it's time to do something about it and change it. I think it's fine if it's a radical change, like Chamberlain's change from what he did to what he's doing now.

FS Okay. But what happens if the change is from good to bad? Take, for example, my own work. [*Laughter*]

DJ I doubt that you think that.

FS Well, in a way, I do. I think in terms of convention. The set of conventions that I was working with before were more necessary and more consistent and had more reason to be, had greater necessity, and they were also harder to do. What I'm doing now – its greatest virtue seems to be that it has a promise for the future. In other words, it promises to keep me working, and I flatter myself; I can say I've already made something good and I know where I am.

DJ The big question is whether you're tired of the earlier ones or not.

FS I'm tired enough to stop doing them. I mean, I wasn't forced to stop doing them. I could have kept doing them.

DJ Things keep developing from the pieces. I've got far more ideas than I'll ever be able to build. I'm not worried that I'm running out of possibilities.

This discussion was sourced from an audio recording and a transcript, which vary slightly from each other; deference has been given to the audio in these instances. The original sound tape reel and archival transcript are in the Barbara Rose papers, 1962–circa 1969, Archives of American Art, Smithsonian Institution, Washington, DC.

The transcript gives two conflicting dates for the interview: a typed date reads "December 18, 1967," which has been crossed out by Rose in pen and replaced with "Fall 1965." Due to references within the interview to events occurring in 1966, the editors have dated the interview to 1966–67.

1 A note on the transcript reads: "The 'Mickey' referred to in the course of the discussion is a reference to 'Mickey the Dummy,' a fictional persona invented by Frank Stella for the purpose of interviews."

2 *Oblomov* (1859) is a Russian novel by Ivan Goncharov. The main character, Oblomov, is a young, incurious, inattentive, procrastinating aristocrat who never leaves his bed. Rose refers here to Brian O'Doherty's description of Stella as "the Oblomov of art": "These paintings are semi-icons for a spiritual blank. They make Mr. Stella the Oblomov of art, the Cézanne of nihilism, the master of *ennui*." O'Doherty, "Frank Stella and a Crisis of Nothingness," *The New York Times*, January 19, 1964, 21.

3 Smith's "gate" pieces are some of the final works in his *Cubi* series (1961–65).

4 "I wanted to solve, particularly, the spatial problem of depth and the problem of what happened to the painting as it faded out around the edges. A lot of abstract expressionist painters seemed to me to have found one part of the painting that they really liked, one part where it came off, where it worked. And then they spent the whole rest of that time working on that painting trying to nurse the painting into a situation that would show off the one good part.... I didn't want to be involved in the kind of painting that was mostly – mostly correctional, mostly kind of nursemaid kind of painting, trying to nurse something up that was supposed to be fresh and direct to begin with." Frank Stella in USA: *Artists*, episode 2, "The New Abstraction: Frank Stella and Larry Poons," directed by Lane Slate, aired March 29, 1966, on WNDT, New York, 28 min.

5 Henry Geldzahler (1935–1994) was a Belgian-born American curator, art historian, and critic.

6 The first stack Judd made, in spring 1965, contained seven galvanized units with each unit measuring nine by forty by thirty inches. The next stack, also in galvanized iron, was fabricated from the end of 1965 into early 1966, with eight units each measuring nine by forty by thirty-one inches.

7 Judd's first solo show at Leo Castelli Gallery, New York, ran from February 5 to March 2, 1966.

8 Vladimir Tatlin's Monument to the Third International (1919–20) was a design for the Communist International headquarters. It was realized as a model, but never built.

9 Judd worked with Bernstein Brothers Sheet Metal Specialties, Inc. from late 1963 until the end of his life. Although they moved to Long Island City by the end of 1964, their shop was originally located in Manhattan, at 191 Third Avenue.

10 Judd refers here to an attitude expressed by both Stella and Poons in "The New Abstraction: Frank Stella and Larry Poons." During the course of the episode, the two artists communicate a number of shared stances; it is unclear to the editors which is under discussion.

11   Rose likely refers here to either *Recent Work by Claes Oldenburg*, Sidney Janis Gallery, New York, March 9–April 2, 1966, or *An Exhibition of New Work by Claes Oldenburg*, Sidney Janis Gallery, New York, April 26–May 27, 1967.

12   Judd refers here to Tony Smith's *The Elevens Are Up* (1963) when it was exhibited in *Black, White and Grey*, Wadsworth Atheneum, Hartford, Connecticut, January 9–February 9, 1964. Discussing Smith's "four-by-four-by-eight black boxes" in his review of the exhibition, Judd notes: "The boxes are plywood, mock-ups for welded metal ones. This is the first I've seen of Smith's work. The boxes can be arranged in any way. Two are stacked parallel to the other two, separated by a narrow aisle." Judd, "Black, White and Gray" in *Donald Judd: Complete Writings 1959–1975*, 117–18.

13   See Michael Fried, introduction to *Three American Painters: Kenneth Noland, Jules Olitski, Frank Stella*, exh. cat. (Cambridge: Fogg Art Museum/Harvard University, 1965), 3–53.

14   Mark Van Doren (1894–1972) was an American poet, writer, and teacher. Joseph Wood Krutch (1893–1970) was an American naturalist, conservationist, writer, and critic.

15   Judd studied with Meyer Schapiro (1904–1996) while a graduate student at Columbia University. Schapiro was an influential art critic, art historian, and professor. Judd included nine books by Schapiro in his library in Marfa, Texas.

16   Hilton Kramer (1928–2012) was an American art critic and editor. In December 1959, Kramer hired Judd to review exhibitions for *Arts Magazine*, and Judd continued to write for the magazine, with only a few interruptions, until March 1965.

17   "[Stella's work] is part of the revolution in sensibility we are witnessing at the present moment – a revolution characterized by its happy preference for blunt and impersonal physical sensation and its indifference, if not its outright hostility, to interior experience.... It ... says something authentic – unhappily authentic – about the life of feeling among the cultivated classes in our society." Hilton Kramer, "Representative of the 1960's," *The New York Times*, March 20, 1966, 135.

18   Peter Paul Rubens, *Daniel in the Lions' Den* (c. 1614/16), National Gallery of Art, Washington, DC.

19   Frans Snyders (1579–1657) was the first specialist of the animal still life. He was a close friend of Peter Paul Rubens and was often employed by him on the still life and animal sections of Rubens's paintings.

20   In 1933, Barnett Newman and his friend Alexander Borodulin ran for New York City mayor and comptroller, respectively. Fiorello Henry La Guardia was elected in November 1933, the first of his three terms as mayor. See Ann Temkin, ed., *Barnett Newman*, exh. cat. (Philadelphia: Philadelphia Museum of Art, 2002), 22–24.

21   Judd refers here to terminology used by Rose in her article "ABC Art," *Art in America*, October–November 1965, 57–69.

"The Antihierarchical American"
Article by Amy Goldin for *ARTnews*
September 1967

In March 1965, Judd stopped writing for *Arts Magazine* as a critic for hire; he had
been reviewing exhibitions for the magazine since December 1959. Two months
later, Amy Goldin began writing reviews for *Arts's* "In the Galleries" section.

Throughout this article for *ARTnews*, Goldin and Judd contrast American and
European art sensibilities. As Judd states, "Primary and secondary forms, some
things being *naturally* subordinate to others. The great Chain of Being and all
that. A very played-out, European idea. I think Americans have always tended to
escape from it." Judd reiterated this idea a year later in his June 1968 "Statement,"
writing, "The United States is still a hierarchical country, sort of a large oligarchy,
though apparently not as hierarchical as Europe, which may be the difference between European and American art; my work and that of most artists is opposed
to that hierarchy."

"They have some very nice chimneys over in Paterson," Don Judd said calmly. "They taper, and they're rectangular."

Dutifully, the remark was entered in my notes. I have never been in Paterson. Next, I thought sourly to myself, you ask who's his favorite movie star.

I was chatting with Judd, but it was not the minutiae of his taste that I was after. It might be possible to deduce an artist's aesthetic criteria from his eating habits and his ideas about the solar system, but such Talmudic procedures are a severe strain on my ingenuity. The trouble was that asking Judd for a direct explanation of terms like "antistructural" and "anticompositional" never seemed to lead to anything useful. I had heard him explain what he meant by "hierarchic form" in symposiums and had read interviews with him in magazines, but I still remained baffled and intrigued.

When primary structures first appeared they were generally explained as a dialectical response to the dazzle of op and pop, or even abstract expressionism. An equal and opposite reaction in the direction of quiet matter-of-factness. But a genetic account of a style, no matter how accurate, does not give us the answers we need. The revision of sensibility that primary structures demanded of us has been, to a great extent, accomplished. Accustomed to judge inexpressiveness as artistic failure, we learned that it was possible to admire the work of artists who found emotion crass and aesthetically irrelevant. We learned to distinguish the individual qualities of Smithson, [Ronald] Bladen, [Robert] Morris, [Tony] Smith, LeWitt, all working more or less within the same style. But the process softened the original hard outlines of primary structure as a visual idea. We are left uncertain about where its unity lies, about the formal core of the style.

My conversations with Judd were undertaken in the hope of locating criteria – which never materialized. Judd does not have a legislative temperament. He is always careful to present his ideas as personal observations and private preferences. Yet everything he said was remarkably serious and unwhimsical – intellectually he is not at all playful or self-indulgent. His reluctance to interpret his artistic judgments as binding anyone else to his conclusions, I finally decided, is a matter of principle. It is not simply a fastidious dislike of overstatement, but a belief in the contingency of artistic statements. It is not the flabby contingency of taste: a work of art is good if you like it and can get something from it. Judd's caution is grounded in a recognition of historical contingency. He feels that artistic ideas are not good and usable for all time, but that their value depends on historical ideas of reality. Somehow art should be true to the fundamental assumptions of the society in which it is produced.

What follows is a reconstruction of a conversation with Judd. In the course of a discussion of American art, terms and phrases of his that had been hopelessly opaque to me before took on meaning. Readers less dense than I may find these explanations unnecessary. For them there may be a compensatory interest in seeing those terms at work in an unfamiliar context.

I suggested above that Judd's artistic truthfulness is not a matter of flavor (art vaguely reflecting the Spirit of Our Time) or of images (Modern Mechanical Man). It is rather a question of using contemporary principles, modern forms of organization. I had often heard him say that the hierarchic principle, for example, was outmoded, false, and basically irrelevant to American art.

But what on earth does a hierarchic principle look like?

Oliver Larkin's *Art and Life in America* lay on the table between us. Judd opened it to Benjamin West's *Penn's Treaty with the Indians*.

"See how the groups are balanced off against each other," he said. One group, dominated by the figure of Penn, holds the center of interest, while subsidiary groups of declining importance fill the picture. "That's European composition, the hierarchic arrangement of parts."

I decided to risk an intuitive leap. "But it's not completely European," I said. "Look how isolated from each other the groups are. It's only the horizon and the little bit of landscape that ties them together. And there's all that sky off by itself."

Judd nodded. "Poussin would have balanced the foreground groups with architecture in the background," he agreed.

His vocabulary was beginning to get through to me. "So that's what you mean by composition!"

He seemed mildly surprised. "It's the usual idea of picture making, isn't it? To get the parts working together to fill out a major form?"

"So you think of 'composition' as being intrinsically a hierarchic idea." I had to think that one over. "Hierarchy" is usually a neutral descriptive term, but clearly it had other meanings for Judd. A unit in a hierarchy is defined by assigning it a role in a total process. That role is its "meaning." I remembered that Judd dislikes having his work interpreted, that he refuses to have a meaning assigned to it. I remembered being rebuked as a child and having my duty explained to me as the inevitable consequence of my role in the scheme of things. "The notion of hierarchy has social and political implications for you?"

"Yes, certainly," he replied. "Primary and secondary forms, some things being *naturally* subordinate to others. The great Chain of Being and all that. A very played-out, European idea. I think Americans have always tended to escape from it."

"What I've never understood is how you *can* get away from composition. You always have wholes and parts in art, no matter how far you reduce the number of parts. And the whole is always *some* sort of structure composed of parts."

Judd frowned. "What about nonstructural painting, like Newman's and Stella's?"

"I could never see why they were called nonstructural," I admitted.

"It's because the rectangle of the canvas itself is the dominant form. The parts of the picture don't combine to make a portrayed form in illusionistic space. The canvas's rectangle was never so important before."

"Matisse? Mondrian?" I protested. "You can't say the shape of the canvas was trivial to them."

"It's still a container, something taken for granted, something the picture fits *into*. In nonstructural painting the canvas shape itself is the result of the working together of the parts." Reaching for the Larkin he added, "The emptier you let the canvas be, the more the rectangle of canvas dominates. The whole idea of letting the canvas be empty – not trying to fill it – is pretty much an American idea." He turned to [George Caleb] Bingham's *Fur Traders Descending the Missouri*, with its expanses of sky and water, the image suspended between them. "You wouldn't find big flat areas like that in any European painting of the period," he said. "Americans generally have been bolder about using unmodulated surfaces."

"Shaker architecture," I suggested.

"And lots of plain ordinary brick buildings or the New England salt boxes. There are plenty of unremarkable buildings that are unstressed and unauthoritative in form."

"What about American sculpture? Do you think it shows the same qualities?"

Judd began leafing through the book.

"It seems as if sculpture never really got off the ground in this country, until David Smith." He kept looking through Larkin's illustrations. "Sculpture's difficult. Mostly there's not much of a market. And it's expensive to do."

"That's a nice girl, though," he remarked in a more cheerful tone. He was pointing at Erastus Palmer's *The White Captive*. "As a *girl*, I mean." Then, turning more pages, "I like [Jean-Antoine] Houdon, too, although he's not American.[1] He has that unstressed quality, that absence of any dominant emotional tone. He measured everything. You know that for his portrait of Washington he made a life-mask to work from?" He was clearly impressed with such regard for accuracy. "Like Eakins, Houdon was very factually inclined."

"Do you like Eakins?"

"Yes." Judd flipped through an Eakins catalogue I had brought and smiled at the *Nymph*. "You know that painting of Wyeth's?" he asked.

"*Christina's World*." Christina is obviously an offspring of the nymph, but Judd does not hold the nymph's errors against her. The painting is a good example of what Judd thinks of as the peculiarly American sense of composition – the willingness to leave a lot of space empty, the willingness to put down a strong diagonal and let it stand without a counterbalancing thrust. He also admires [John Singleton] Copley; he returned several times to the early portrait of Paul Revere.[2] He was especially struck by the awkwardness and energy of the right arm, with its blocky triangle of white sleeve. He showed me that there is only one other line in the picture that even begins to parallel its thrust. Both the shape and its isolation from the general form of the body delighted him and seemed peculiarly American.

In the context of the discussion about hierarchic form, Judd's idea of "American" began to make sense. I realized that harmonized, aligned relationships and amalgamated motifs were anathema to him. For Judd, the forms in the work must be isolated in order to feel free and "normal." Their subordination to a pattern of predetermined rhythm strikes him as false and coercive, a travesty of the independence and individual character of objects in real life. This hypothesis was strengthened when he began to talk about Winslow Homer, another favorite.

"What gets me is the funny way he cuts his figures off and sticks them in unexpected places," Judd remarked. "You know *The Turtle Pond*?" He looked for it in a book from his bookcase. "I guess it's not in here." Taking a used envelope from the table he began to sketch its composition.

"Homer's cutting makes his figures blockier – they become more of an area and less of a figure. That's directly against the whole anthropomorphic way of European thinking. Figures in European painting always have a stressed quality."

"A self-consciousness about being human? Maybe, but do you think that's a compositional thing?" I asked dubiously.

"Maybe not. But in Homer you get a funny, spotty sort of composition. The forms land in odd, surprising places." He poked at the scattered apexes of *Kissing the Moon*.

"Of course, partly what makes that possible is that they're marine paintings," I observed. "That way he doesn't need to worry so much about gravity. You *know* that water supports weight. Homer is visually rather thin, anyway. Even in the oils he's often perfunctory about any consistent treatment of massiveness. Do you think of that lightness as something characteristically American?"

"Well, a lot of the painters of the '20s and '30s — O'Keeffe, [Charles] Demuth, [John] Marin — they didn't take volume seriously. I like linearity, but of course I like things broad and large scale, too. The problem is how to reconcile them."

Judd looked appropriately worried as he said this. It seemed to me that he didn't need to brood about it. His statement was a very apt description of his own work, particularly the wall pieces. There the linearity is not simply a function of the clarity of contour of his boxes but, explicitly or implicitly, characterizes the total form.

"And 'nonrelational'?" I asked. I had figured that one out. It seemed to me to describe a state of affairs in which the parts seemed neither to disperse nor to cohere, a state in which the totality of the structure was neither threatened with dissolution nor overemphasized. Now it made sense, like Judd's answer to his concept of hierarchy. He confirmed my general idea without appearing to be very satisfied with it.

It seems to me that in our conversation I failed to consider an element that is very strong in Judd's work — the peculiar sort of stasis he achieves by equalizing directional thrusts. One of his pieces, for example, is fundamentally a long, open-ended box, but made by a series of cross-sections at right angles to the main axis. It has to be read in both directions at once. This not only slows down the perception of the piece, but gives it a built-in ambiguity that actually reinforces the singleness of the total form. The stillness of Judd's recent work is independent of the inertia of mass; it results from the interpenetration of forces at right angles to each other. But "forces" is too strenuous a word, its connotations are all wrong. Physically it suggests a commotion, but to emphasize the regularity of Judd's "forces" might bring out the military associations of the word. And, as his pejorative use of "hierarchy" indicates, the idea of natural forces under formal control is deeply repugnant to him. He aims at an air of unconstrained resolution and unargued clarity. To me his stillness often looks fresher and much less clumsy than the equally static organization of Homer.

Judd might agree, but he would probably credit the superior reality of his medium. He is disturbed by the ambiguity of pictorial space. (How hard it is to make a picture stay exactly on the surface, where he believes it should be.) It thwarts what seems to me to be his overriding aim — the precise statement that emphasizes coherence while avoiding any suggestion of physical or emotional pressure.

As an artist Judd wants his "statements" to be without the reverberations implicit in exclamations, questions, and arguments. He aims at the steady, even inflection that people use for obvious matters of fact. Yet the absence of emphasis does not mean that he wants either a cerebral or a neutral look. There is no attempt to tease the spectator into pure thought or to seduce him into making his own feelings a part of the aesthetic experience. Judd's color alone would contradict such an assumption. He often chooses unmysterious, high-keyed reds and blues, unrestrained colors with pronounced emotional intensity. He uses Harley-Davidson's Hi-Fi color bombs sprayed over metallic primer or automobile paint.

Judd's chief worry about color is to avoid having it act like a second surface, a skin lying on top of the form. "Of course it is a skin, physically," he admits, "but it shouldn't look like one." He says he has found it oddly impossible to use a dark red on curved surfaces. Nor would he use a dark color on interior surfaces where it would go black in the shadow, for Judd is generally concerned with evening out and minimizing the effects of light.

Judd's work carries a sense of easy, absentminded orderliness that has nothing to do with grace. Nor do his regular structures carry implications of law, of disorder overcome. When he writes or talks, Judd sounds as if he were looking for words for a new sense of order, one that cannot be assimilated to the principles of organism or of balanced weight. His intuitive feeling that such a new order will be specifically American seems fanciful, but a corroborative voice appears in the following quotation from Patrick Heron, a British critic who is here reproaching American artists for their chauvinism (Judd showed it to me as a perfect statement of what he does *not* believe):

> The British 'middle generation' *never* fell for this: we never abandoned the belief that painting should *resolve* asymmetric, unequal, disparate formal ingredients into a state of architectonic harmony.... That obvious 'unity,' of image or format, which the American cultivation of the symmetrical canvas (or 'composition' – a nice, old-fashioned word which still nevertheless serves) produces so easily – this is a unity not worth having. Indeed, it has short-circuited the whole process of pictorial statement, which should involve an elaborate, intuitive adjustment and readjustment of initially warring and disparate elements, until they finally click into the condition of *balance*.[3]

The qualities that Judd identifies in American art need not be peculiar to it in order to become the foci of a peculiarly American style. It is undeniable that the disjunctive angular openness that intrigues Judd in American painting appears more significant in the light of recent stylistic developments. It is the sort of discovery that is a part of the artistic imagination. Traits previously uncherished and undiscerned lay the groundwork for a new style.

First published: Amy Goldin, "The Antihierarchical American," *ARTnews*, September 1967, 48–50, 64–65.

1   Jean-Antoine Houdon (1741–1828) was a French sculptor known for his portrait busts.

2   Copley's portrait of Paul Revere is also discussed in "Interview with Bruce Hooton" (1965) in this volume, 72, 80n8.

3   Patrick Heron, "The Ascendancy of London in the Sixties," *Studio International*, December 1966, 280–81.

Artists' symposium for *7 for 67*
With Emily Rauh (moderator), Mark di Suvero,
and Ernest Trova
October 1, 1967

Held at the City Art Museum of St. Louis, this symposium was moderated by Emily Rauh, curator of the museum's exhibition *7 for 67: Works by Contemporary American Sculptors* (October 1–November 12, 1967). The show, which included work by Christo, Mark di Suvero, Judd, Claes Oldenburg, Lucas Samaras, George Segal, and Ernest Trova, marked Judd's first exhibition in Saint Louis.

Today, the museum is known as the Saint Louis Art Museum; Emily Rauh, later Emily Rauh Pulitzer, went on to found the Pulitzer Arts Foundation, Saint Louis.

ER   [Emily Rauh] As I'm sure you all know, this afternoon – or
today – we are opening, officially, the exhibition of works
of seven sculptors. We're very pleased to have with us this
weekend three of the artists whose works are in the show,
Mark di Suvero, Donald Judd, and Ernest Trova.

We thought this afternoon we would talk in an infor-
mal fashion about sculpture, the show, their work, what's
going on in general. I don't really know. And we'll see
what develops. We've been talking all weekend and I hope
that this afternoon is as enjoyable as the rest of the weekend has been.

We might start with sculpture in general. Why are
these men making sculpture? I have a feeling that today
sculpture is one of the areas of the arts that is most vital,
the most interesting, where the most searching questions
and solutions are being sought after. I think all art is always solving problems, is always searching for new solutions, and in sculpture, it seems to me, there is more exciting work going on than ever, at least in recent history.
I think, in a way, it's a little like science, that the interest
in certain areas shifts from time to time. At certain moments in history, something like pathology or genetics is
where the really exciting work seems to go on, and then
it shifts to something else. I have a feeling that in recent
years this is true in sculpture. One of the reasons, I think,
is the whole new vast area of materials that are available
for sculptors to work with. I think all of the men on the
panel today started off as painters, so it might be interesting to know why you switched from painting to sculpture, or if you have switched completely, which I think,
for instance, in the case of Ernie Trova, is not so. But what
do you find is the relationship between your painting
and sculpture?

ET   [Ernest Trova] Well, in my case, I think it would be that the
opportunity to make sculpture was the essential reason that

made me continue. The opportunity alone was the deciding factor.

ER	And if given complete freedom of choice in activities, ma-
terials, et cetera, you would rather make sculpture?

ET	No, I'd rather do both simultaneously, actually. The week
is seven days, I guess – do certain things on Mondays, certain things on Tuesdays – no reason why we can't do it all.

ER	What about you? Why did you find you turned from paint-
ing to sculpture?

DJ	[Donald Judd] Finally, I couldn't do anything with paint-
ing and decided I thoroughly hated the whole thing. I
painted for a long time, and finally a number of the aspects of it seemed to be completely restrictive, and I was
painting paintings one by one rather than ones that had
anything to do with one another. It was a pretty difficult
and boring activity, so I wanted to find something that I
could work more loosely in – where the whole thing had
more natural development.

ER	And the development is between one series of pieces, and
the next in sculpture, or is it a more conceptual thing?

DJ	Well, obviously, one piece produces further ideas about
other pieces, and so forth. With only the first couple of
things I did in three dimensions, there seemed to be a
great number of possibilities and something really to think
about. With the paintings, I would get one painting I
would rather like but which wasn't altogether satisfactory,
and it didn't seem anything that had any openings or any
possibilities – not connected paintings of any kind.

ER	Your work, from what I've seen, has gotten bigger and big-
ger in scale. Is this a part of the fascination with working
in sculpture, and where is this leading?

DJ	The bigger scale is, in part, money.

ER	And if money were no problem at all, what?

DJ	They might be very enormous, I think. [*Laughter*] The
first three-dimensional ones I did were plywood. Plywood

comes in a four-by-eight sheet, and other than joining it ad infinitum, there's not much you can do to make it any larger. I didn't want too many joints. Also, I wasn't working in a very big loft. So a large piece at that time would be maybe one. I remember one that was four by four by seven feet long or something, or eight feet. So it was within range of plywood, pretty much.

ER   And now in metal, it's a question of production – I mean, it's a question of money. But if that were aside, it's a matter of whatever industry could produce.

DJ   Yes, that's right. Obviously, metal's by the pound, and it goes up immensely. I think, though, outside of that, perhaps you get into it, and your thinking – thinking or feeling or whatever – gets a little clearer on it. The scale does increase somewhat. But the last paintings I did were already large-scale painting, so the scale was pretty much already there [image 15].

ER   What about the color that is applied to the sculpture, the paint skin on your work?

DJ   Well, I don't want to do only more or less gray-colored things. And other than anodizing, which has a lot of restrictions as to the size of the tank and everything, there aren't any natural colors in the materials. So that in order to have, say, the brown, whatever it is upstairs, or the green, it has to be painted, and I prefer it was in the material, but I don't know how you can do that other than plastic and such things as anodizing.

ER   How crucial is color in your work, Mark?

MDS   [Mark di Suvero] Immaterial. I can't be grilled, come on. I think as far as painting and sculpture go, they're two totally different things, and what we've all ended up doing, we're going to do best.

ER   When do you come to a conclusion about the color for your piece? Such as *Blue Arch for Matisse*, where color is obviously a fairly crucial part of it, or you wouldn't have called it that?

MDS   Well, I think that sculptors learn a lot from painters, and when sculptors try to put color on top of the sculpture, it generally ends up being bad. I really had a long series of failures because of it. But there's some people who seem very natural with color. It's always been a hassle for me. It's never finalized. The color always changes. People rub it; it goes — rust comes through.

ER   In your work, you incorporate metal and wood that you find in the area around where you work. Do you conceptualize the form of your sculpture before you look for the materials? Does it develop as you find the materials? As you work along, you pick up more and more. What is the progression of the material and the idea that go together to make up the piece?

MDS   Emily, I think that we work with what we have, huh? And I think in abstract art it really doesn't matter what the materials are. You end up only seeing the skin of the thing. If I use wood, I know that on the inside of the wood, it can be as polished as this table or whatever, the floor, but if a work is at all structural, it doesn't matter what the external material is. It's only a concept.

ER   Do you find this to be so with your work, Ernie? What about the external, the surface — how does it relate to the image?

ET   Well, I have preferences that I would like to deal with. Certain materials I find interesting to experiment with. But like Mark said, if I wasn't using bronze, I'd be using something else. So it really depends on what you have available, and if you have nothing available, then you paint. [*Laughter*]

ER   So that theoretically, if everything was available, sculpture would become larger and more important and richer.

ET   We'd build cities and things of that nature.

DJ   Uh-huh.

ER   Exactly.

ET   Very much like what Disney is doing in Florida. There again it's a financial problem.

ER   But the direction is not to make the small object that is within the room, but to organize the work around the object.

ET   In between, outside the room, everything, all sizes, all dimensions fit in spaces. Make things for rooms, for outside of rooms, for cities – I don't think we should be limited by size, that's usually a hang-up. So working with certain materials, we're often limited by material itself.

ER   If the work can be mass produced, if the direction is toward casting, where you can make any number of castings, then can't it be done in a much larger edition, much less expensively, where many more people could have it – which would be the same thing I would think true in your work, Don, where it's not casting, but fabricated? If you're making eight boxes, you can make twenty-eight boxes, or fifty-eight boxes?

DJ   It gets somewhat cheaper. They don't seem to give me much discount on that sort of thing.

ER   But the cost involved is not just the fabricating, it's the idea, so that if they were more and more –

DJ   No, see, if you make a great many, say, of one given piece – if you made a dozen and the whole dozen could be sold, obviously they could be sold, because you wouldn't have to get that much out of each one.

ER   Would this be a goal, to work toward getting the cost down so they could be mass produced and exist everywhere?

DJ   It's not too live a goal. I want to make one piece at a time. If there are ten copies of it or one, it doesn't matter too much. I want to get sufficient money out of it to live and make the next piece or the next several pieces. So however the market's arranged, it's somebody's – the dealer's problem, or whatever.

ER   But with yours, it has to be in a specific kind of space. They're so big that with smaller houses – there aren't very many houses or apartments that can hold the kind of –

DJ   People should live in larger houses. [*Laughter*]

ER   So what you're doing is not necessarily for a specific audience, but specifically for you.

DJ   No – yeah – the pieces are made for me. I have no idea what the audience is like – any idea, some generalized idea of the public. I don't see how you could work from that premise, anyway. It's just something very vague that you don't know anything about. Obviously, you're making pieces for yourself.

ER   Right, but aren't you also making pieces for a kind of space?

DJ   Yes, to some extent, varying from piece to piece. They need a good deal of space around them. Sometimes they have to do with a particular dimension of a room, sometimes they don't. And they could have even more to do with a particular dimension of a room. But again, that gets into something more ambitious, making your own room and so forth.

ER   Is the complete simplicity and unclutteredness of your work in any way a reaction to the complexity and clutter of our visual environment?

DJ   Not really; the reaction might be that something like 99 percent of the usual environment's a total failure. So it might be a reaction to that, but not to complexity or clutter or anything like that. It's just that most of what you see doesn't amount to much. Architecture or anything else – I don't know. I'm not too keen on the word "reaction," actually. It implies what it says and means it's not quite accurate.

ER   Are images in your work, Ernie, the starting point, the kick-off point, or is it the formal aspects?

ET   Well, I believe the image is a nucleus on which I base new work. New work comes out of old work. I would say yes.

ER   Mark, do you think of – do you have in mind things like bridges, architectures, structures?

MDS   When Don was talking about the space within a room

and the way he makes it so austere, I sort of think about Lucas's room, the Lucas Samaras room, which to me is the most beautiful experience here in the museum.[1] A moment of spatiality in it which really gives you a sense of liberation without – without any fear. There's a tremendous amount of beauty just using commercial materials, and this is the kind of possibility that I think artists like Don and Samaras are beginning to explore, and that possibility seems much more open and wild in sculpture than anything that has preceded it since – you know – in the past here in America. Do you like it?

ER   Yes.

MDS   Why?

ER   Because of the unending possibilities in, I think, both of these pieces you're talking about. The infinity of directions, in dimensions of the Samaras room; the transformation of the environment as the amount of light changes is an extraordinary thing. The mood involved. Agree?

MDS   Yeah … I don't know. Everything that's said about art, especially off of these kinds of platforms, becomes like a lie no matter what happens. These filters – it's a nonsense, artificial, non-one-to-one relationship, and it's a real denial of the art process. It becomes one of the horrors that artists end up being subjected to. [*Applause*]

ER   On that note, maybe we should let the audience subject us. Are there questions that people in the audience would like to ask? Yes?

AM   [Audience member][2] Could the men each talk about one work that's on exhibit?

ER   Mark, would you like to talk about *Elohim Adonai*?

MDS   No. Ask Ernie.

ET   Well, I have one piece that's three tons and I've never touched it.

ER   But other people have?

ET   Yes, yes.

ER   And therefore it continually needs to be repolished.

ET   I think you're aware of this.

ER   Would you like to talk about, say, the brown boxes [image 16]?

DJ   No.

MDS   I would.

ER   All right.

MDS   I think that's probably the most radical piece in the show. The last time I was on a panel with Don, we ended up fighting pretty roughly.[3] The piece itself, I think, is a really – it's a totally negative piece in the sense that it throws off all your judgments about what sculpture should be. Everything you've learned sculpture should be, it isn't.

DJ   It's not sculpture.

MDS   Cause it's nothing – you think it's not a sculpture? Do you think it's not sculpture?

DJ   Yeah, I don't think of them as being sculpture.

MDS   Yeah, what do you think they are?

DJ   I don't know. That's somebody else's problem.

MDS   Why do you take the name away?

DJ   Sculpture?

MDS   Yeah.

DJ   I do when I can. I don't use the term.

MDS   Yeah, right. You call them "objects."

DJ   I don't call them anything. I don't need to call them anything.

MDS   No, I like to think of them as sculpture, and I know why. It's the same kind of negativity that Mondrian gave to all those people who originally looked at – you know, they came out of painting looking for brushstrokes and so on. Does it have to be that? I think those brown boxes are a very fine piece, and what happens is they deal with space – that kind of a blank refusal in a very, very powerful way.

      I know the first time that I saw Don's work, it left me nonplussed [see images 2, 3]. That was in the Green Gallery years ago.[4] But since then I've seen the tremendous influence that this kind of an expression to the world around us has had as a moving force amongst the young sculptors all over the US and Canada – in the cities, the same kind of draw that de Kooning had in painting. There were many young de Koonings painting like de Kooning in the late '50s. But what's happened is now there are a lot of –

DJ   They're no longer painting.

MDS   Yes, they are. Some of them are, but there are a lot of people who have taken Judd's idea and really repeated it, essentially, and there's that funny thing that that repetition does where it gives you that sense of blankness – it's as if the saccharine has been taken out of the – that horribly sweet, you know, that Greek sculpture, that classic period, not the good archaic things. I think it's a radical piece. Don, you want to say something about it or defend yourself?

DJ   No. What you want is a simple explanation. Obviously, nobody can give that or paraphrase. So that's why I don't want to answer. If you can ask something, a given question about it that I can deal with, I can give you some sort of answer. If you ask enough of them, maybe you'll learn something about it. But if you just ask some general question, I can't get at anything, because it involves too many things.

AM   I'd like to ask Mr. Judd: aside from people living in larger houses, where do you think that your work could be placed? In museums, outside? In a home? Exactly where?

DJ   No, I don't really think of it at all. Since I can't control the kind of space they go into, I don't think about it. It's a pointless thing to worry about. I sort of invent places I'd like to live in – if I could build one – but otherwise I don't think about spaces they can go into, and I don't see why they can't go into all three of those places. I think people are great suckers to live in such small spaces. I think it's a very bad development. And it's very expensive, too, and it's still small.

AM   [*Inaudible*]

DJ   Little bit. I don't have too many there now. It's a very crowded loft.[5] I have some big things by other people, which sort of pushes mine out. They're right in there where we're living. I don't know.

AM   [*Question relating to use of boxes*]

DJ   I do, but I'm very much against the practice. They used to use one of them at the Green Gallery to sit on, and I was always quarrelling with [Richard] Bellamy about it.[6] They're not made to put glass on or sit on or anything else.

AM   I'd like to ask Mr. di Suvero what *Elohim Adonai* means and what he meant to represent by that sculpture.

MDS Well, it's easier to reply to the first part of the question than the second part. The word "God" in Hebrew is unutterable, and so it has many different covers, and I had originally meant that all titles on any sculpture are meaningless and at best they can reflect a different preoccupation than the truly sculptural. I think that all sculpture that makes it acts in a way of praise to the world. What it represents is nothing, because I think that any art that ends up being representational is less than what it hopes to represent. It should be itself.

AM   Mr. Trova, how did the figure of the falling man begin?

ET   Began as a drawing and used it later in paintings and then three–dimensionalized it.

AM   What does it represent?

ET   It represents a man falling.

AM   Mr. di Suvero, why do you use sculptural media instead of other types of material?

DJ   The big question again.

MDS Yeah, I think that the only way I can answer is that I used to – I found the cheapest way to work was working with discarded timbers, and I found that they did a certain line drawing in space which seemed to satisfy, I don't know, a structural need in me. That's why I continue to do that. I like to put things together.

RW   [Rodney Winfield][7] I would like to ask the gentlemen at the table if they could be objective about something which interests them. What would you people like to really talk about?

DJ   Nothing. The work's upstairs.

ET   In Rodney's case, I'd say come over some afternoon and we'll have lunch.

AM   It's interesting you don't feel like talking about anything. All of these people are here this afternoon on the assumption you were going to talk about something, and I think it's reasonable to assume that you would be interested in what you're talking about.

DJ   The chronic fallacy.

ER   Is this perhaps more a sociological problem?

MDS   Mm-hmm – listen, that's what we dread, you know.

AM   I'd like to ask Mr. Trova if you feel there is any loss in having someone else create your work for you, or do you feel the sculptor should be directly involved in his material?

MDS   Ernie, listen, I don't think anybody creates things; we just re-form them.

AM   It's to Mr. Trova. I'd like to know if Mr. Trova feels something is lost by having someone else create the work for him.

ET   Well, number one, Mark can answer for me, I mean, adequately, and I concur with what he said, but no, I don't feel any loss at all, absolutely none. I wish that I would have more people helping me produce my things. If you can come around Saturday afternoons I think I can put you to work, I always need some help.

AM   I'd be interested to hear what your opinions of form are. Painters are usually turned on, so to speak, by color. Sculptors are usually turned on by form. What about form? How do you feel about form?

ET   I feel fine.

DJ   In the first place, I wouldn't want to split it up the way you've split it up so. Painting isn't primarily color, and sculpture – whatever – isn't primarily form. The term "form" is pretty hard to handle.

MDS   Don, don't you think that there's a difference before there was – I mean before, historically – there was a kind of very rigid idea about form? Recently, I think that with the new geometries, with the new concepts, what becomes much more important is the destruction of form, the deformations, the warpages, the use of light, whether off a reflected surface, or as a source of illumination, projection, and so on. I think it's just part of a continuing revolution against that, you know, hysterical, reactionary society which we're all bound up in. We're living right now in a murder society. We're all criminals here. We're all participating in a war which is obvious murder of innocent people, and I think that when you get to that point, you can't make forms which really praise society.

ER   And yet this is what you're trying to do with something like *Elohim Adonai*, which is a praise.

MDS   Well, it sure ain't for the society, then. It's for – I think, then, it's for the flower children, for the people who have a little bit of peace and love, and not, you know – it isn't for those people who are accomplices to the acts of destruction that we do so frequently to each other. That limits the audience.

AM   Mr. Judd, I'd like to know why the *Store Fronts* are considered to be art.[8]

DJ   Those aren't mine. It's really Christo's problem, who made them. But my answer on all that is that if somebody wants to call something art, he's perfectly right to call it so. You can call it bad, or be bored with it, or whatever, but if he says it's art, it's art. I think that sort of takes care of all possible situations on that subject. [*Laughter*]

MDS   Bravo.

AM   I'd like to ask if there are any contemporary artists who influenced your work, and if so, who, to Mr. – I'm sorry, I can't pronounce your last name.

MDS   You know, every artist only continues from where other artists began, and I … no, I wouldn't like to answer your question, like influences and so on. That's for art historians, and supposedly you're supposed to – you know, if we do anything here, you're supposed to look at the work a little clearer. I think art history blinds one. Okay?

AM   Can you name some of the sculpture which you personally like and collect? Give an example of your taste.

DJ   Yeah, I can. I don't have my hands on all that I want to get them on yet. I have a painting by Frank Stella, a piece by Dan Flavin, a piece by Bob Morris, a painter named Yayoi Kusama, a piece by Craig Kauffman, a piece by Samaras, and a number of other people owe me pieces. Larry Bell and Bob Irwin and Carl Andre. And if I had some money to work with, I could get one of Newman's paintings, perhaps one of Mark's pieces, or whatever. You get quite a list after a while. Conceivably, there's two or three dozen people whose work I would like to have, either alive or recently dead, which is pretty good. Quite a bit of good work.

AM   [*Inaudible*]

DJ   The space between the boxes is very important, so that's my doing. As I told somebody the other day, it wouldn't do even an inch or so one way or another. They should have a fair amount of space around them and they should have reasonably even light, and my control in the matter depends on whether I'm there or not when they're set up, and lot of circumstances.

AM   [*Inaudible*]

DJ   Yes, of course, again, that's a very general question. You're asking me what the work's all about, and I can't answer just like that.

A M   [*Inaudible*]

E T   Well, we all have a personal stake in these things. I can't
say which one would work for you, but I work partially
with some rationale and partially with my instinct. I can't
pinpoint it. I think we use all these elements somewhere
along the line.

E R   Isn't it really very hard to separate out the material from
the form? From the sculpture, I mean; it all goes together
part and parcel.

E T   It all ends up one thing.

A M   Have any of you really started to alter [your work] in a
large way?

M D S   I'm still stuck in the same place. I think that – I've found
that my progress is very, very slow, if there is any. It seems
a lot of time I just repeat. What about you, Don?

D J   It's the same thing. It changes slowly, and perhaps it's
doubtful if you can call it progress, as Mark implied. But
there is a change, so the pieces a couple of years old start
to look rather peculiar after a while.

E R   So it's a problem of being too intimate with the work in
the very moment that it's being done to be able to abstract yourself enough for, say, progress, difference, change,
something – a variation – but it's not necessarily progress
until you get a little bit of perspective.

D J   I don't know, maybe the person gets organized somehow,
maybe it's not progress – like, [David] Smith does good
sculpture for twenty, twenty-five years. I like ones in the
late '40s, early '50s as much as I like ones a couple years
ago, from just before he died. So they changed a great deal,
but I don't know that *Hudson River Landscape* is somehow
an earlier stage before the late pieces. It's an earlier stage
if you start putting it into a big schema, maybe, and calling it art history and so forth. But as far as Smith's work
goes, that's one thing, later work is a different thing, and
it's pretty even up.

ER   Yes. I think "progress" has a qualitative connotation that really doesn't belong in terms of the development and change in the work. I mean, once an artist becomes mature, it would be a question of different approaches, not necessarily a better solution.

DJ   Yeah, you'd want to do something new because you don't want to keep – you get bored with doing the same thing over and over again. But the new thing is not necessarily superior, perhaps.

ER   Right.

Well, I think since these men have done, essentially, their work long before they came here and that it's on view in the galleries, and this is, after all, the medium in which they have chosen to speak, that it would be good now to go to the galleries and to look at the actual works themselves. Thank you.

This symposium discussion was sourced from an archival transcript in the archives of the Saint Louis Art Museum.

1   Thirteen works by Lucas Samaras were included in *7 for 67*.

2   The transcript of this symposium does not distinguish between different audience members, with the exception of one named speaker (Rodney Winfield, also named here). Correspondingly, all audience responses have been rendered here as from "AM," though there are clearly different speakers participating.

3   Di Suvero refers here to a symposium in which he and Judd participated for the exhibition *Primary Structures*. See "The New Sculpture" (1966) in this volume, 90–102.

4   Judd participated in six shows at Green Gallery, New York, between 1963 and 1965.

5   Judd refers here to 53 East Nineteenth Street.

6   Richard Bellamy (1927–1998) was the founder and director of Green Gallery, New York.

7   Rodney Winfield (1925–2017) was an American artist, designer, and professor who lived in Saint Louis at the time of the symposium.

8   In 1963, Christo began making works titled *Show Cases* – small display cases and cabinets that he would alter by lining them with fabric and paper. In 1964, he expanded the practice to include *Store Fronts*, which were similar to the *Show Cases* and *Show Windows*, but larger.

"Art Notes: A Box Is a Box Is a Box"
Article by Grace Glueck for *The New York Times*
March 10, 1968

Only five years after his first solo exhibition of work in three dimensions at Green Gallery, New York (*Don Judd*, December 17, 1963–January 11, 1964), Judd presented his first large-scale museum exhibition, *Don Judd*, at the Whitney Museum of American Art, New York (February 27–March 24, 1968, extended through April 14). Conducted at the time of Judd's Whitney exhibition, the interview presented in this article by art journalist Grace Glueck took place at 53 East Nineteenth Street, where Judd had both a loft and a studio.

Judd's Whitney show was also reviewed in *Arts Magazine*, *Artforum*, *The Village Voice*, and *The Christian Science Monitor*, among other publications. Critic Elizabeth C. Baker wrote in *ARTnews* in April 1968 that the exhibition showed "a remarkably cohesive development and, within boundaries chosen for their deliberate restraint, a rapid expansion of confidence and invention."

What's Donald Judd doing?

"Making mischief," suggests one Establishment artist, deadpan.

Understandable. So simple they seem to have generated themselves, Judd's stripped-down structures (now on view at the Whitney Museum) don't exactly tie in with the traditional concepts of art [images 17, 18]. A row of eight stainless-steel cubes, four by four by four feet. Eight ten-by-ten-foot aluminum rectangles, lined up in the middle of the floor. A wall piece — five iron verticals, topped by a brass bar. No "composition," or inter-related parts — the work is a whole, perceivable all at once. No "allusions" — the pieces are actual, specific facts of themselves. No "message" — except that a box is a box is a box.

"One of the most original and stunning accomplishments of the 1960s," writes the Whitney's associate curator, William C. Agee, in the catalogue for the show. "A pivotal figure in the creation of a fundamentally new attitude toward the art process."[1]

In his loft off Gramercy Park the other day, the pivotal figure, somewhat on the burly side, shrugged mildly over the acclaim. No, he was not the center of a movement — he couldn't stand the idea of that. What's more, he didn't like the term "minimal" applied to his and other new work — not only because it made it seem less than what went before, but because it suggested a "movement."

"My stuff is just a little progression, like adding up the grocery bill," Judd said. "There's no mathematical mystique to it. If it seems a reaction to European art, it's because it doesn't involve incredible assumptions about everything. It's not a general statement. I can't even begin to think about reflecting on 'universal order,' as the Europeans did. The work is — well, just like lining up eight boxes."

He didn't intend any statement at all? Judd, a type who pauses thoughtfully in conversation, paused thoughtfully. "I suppose inevitably it does say you can't make such statements about the world as have been made by old painters and sculptors." He smiled. "Don't get me wrong. I like European art — I just don't want to do it."

Judd is by no means an evangelist, or even a plumper for, the kind of work he does. "I don't know any artist who wants a closed situation where one kind of work prevails – though I think some critics do. Let everyone do what he wants. If someone says his work is art, it's art. I like having new things happen."

Judd, forty, lives two floors above his studio in an art-crammed loft that also houses his wife, Julie, and Flavin Starbuck Judd, his month-old son.[2] ("Flavin" for his friend Dan Flavin, the fluorescent bulbist, and "Starbuck" after a relative of his wife's.) "We didn't want an ordinary name – we'll call the cats and dogs John and Mary." His ambition is as single-minded as his art: "All I want is more money – to make more pieces."

First published: Grace Glueck, "Art Notes: A Box Is a Box Is a Box," *The New York Times*, March 10, 1968, 23.

1   William C. Agee, *Don Judd*, exh. cat. (New York: Whitney Museum of American Art, 1968), 9. With notes by Dan Flavin and selected writings by Judd.

2   Julie Margaret Hughan Finch (1941–) is a dancer and social activist. She and Judd married on March 14, 1964; they divorced in 1978.

Interview with Lucy R. Lippard and William C. Agee
April–June 1968

For this interview, Judd and art critic Lucy R. Lippard met on three separate occasions, each time in a different location: Judd's studio, on the second floor of 53 East Nineteenth Street; the Whitney Museum of American Art, New York; and Judd's loft, on the top floor of 53 East Nineteenth Street. The portion of the interview conducted at the Whitney took place partially within the exhibition *Don Judd* (February 27–March 24, 1968, extended through April 14) and includes contributions from William C. Agee, the show's curator.

In his opening remarks for the *Don Judd* exhibition catalogue, Agee contended that "this exhibition … brings together for the first time the full range of one of the most original and stunning accomplishments of the 1960s." Judd's first major solo show at a museum, *Don Judd* contained over thirty works made between 1963 and 1968. As Elizabeth C. Baker noted in her April 1968 review of the exhibition for *ARTnews*, "The fact that he [Judd] previously had had only two one-man shows in New York galleries does not indicate how influential he has been for the past five years."

L R L   [Lucy R. Lippard] Then, what – biographical stuff? It seems as good a way as any to warm up. Like, you know, the first paintings you ever saw, and your finger paintings. Go right back.

D J   [Donald Judd] I didn't do any finger paintings.

L R L   You were brought up where, in Kansas City? Or just outside Kansas City?

D J   No, several places. We lived in Omaha and moved to Des Moines, moved back to Omaha – wait a minute, Kansas City wasn't the next –

L R L   You were born there, weren't you?

D J   No, near there, but we didn't actually live there at the time.

L R L   Excelsior, isn't it?

D J   Yeah, Excelsior Springs. The Whitney catalogue is wrong; it's Excelsior Springs, not Excelsior. Boy, I've forgotten that sequence.

L R L   You're not that old. Some of these little old men being interviewed on these things, they can remember every single thing, prenatal on.

D J   Omaha. Maybe it was Omaha, Kansas City, Des Moines, and then back to Omaha. Then to Dallas, then to Philadelphia, then to North Jersey.

L R L   What are the ages involved? When you were in Kansas City, were you old enough to go to the Nelson-Atkins?

D J   Yeah, but I don't think I got to the Nelson-Atkins until – well, maybe I did, yes. I believe I did get to it once, I think, pretty early on, and then once just after I was out of the army, in the summer of 1948, I guess [image 19].[1] But I was up there once before that. One summer I was staying with my grandparents – I usually stayed with them when I was a teenager.

L R L   Was that your only exposure to seeing any art? Because there isn't much out there.

D J   Well, almost. When we were in Omaha – I was maybe ten or eleven or something, which would be the second

time we were in Omaha – they had just opened the Joslyn Memorial.

LRL   Yes, I saw it this fall.

DJ   Did you? I thought it was awful even then.

LRL   It's pretty bad now.

DJ   Yeah, it was brand-new, and they didn't even have the
plants in, and the whole thing was classical all the way. And
at the time, there were hardly any paintings, even. They
built a stupid, classical building.

LRL   Now they have sculpture all hidden in the bushes. It was
the damnedest thing. They have lots of leaves and things
and the sculpture kind of coyly peeking out from under.

DJ   It really seemed stupid. And I don't know whether this impression is from having seen the Nelson-Atkins the first
time when I was a teenager or seeing it that summer just
after I got out of the army, but the irrelevance of the whole
thing, you know, and the lack of contemporary things and
also that extremely stupid building – they were all irritating somehow. The building has no architecture at all and
cost a fortune in the 1930s or something. And they could
have gotten an awful lot of art for all that useless architecture when nobody was paying anything for it.[2]

LRL   Well, the Oriental collection is good, though.

DJ   Yeah, the Oriental collection is very good, and they have
a few nice old paintings. They have a nice, very funny
Rembrandt – peculiar Rembrandt – a very sort of mis-
shapen man's head. And a nice Poussin – it looks like
Poussin. Anthony Blunt says it's not a Poussin, but anyway,
whatever it is, it's a good copy or something.[3] There are
a couple of little Seurats. There were a lot of nice single
things, but they had really at that time nothing contemporary short of – I don't know, maybe they had a [Thomas
Hart] Benton or a [John Steuart] Curry or something.

LRL   Well, it's still a very weak contemporary collection, because there was a clause in the – they were telling me –

DJ   Yeah, they can't buy anything unless he's been dead for twenty years.

For about a year in Omaha, the second time, when I was ten or eleven, I studied art with a woman who had a little, very minute school downtown in Omaha. I copied things out of books and did a few watercolors out the window and things like that [image 20].

LRL   Was it your idea or your parents' idea?

DJ   My idea. It was nice. She was very amiable and didn't try to make me do anything, so I liked it.

LRL   Did you go in the army right after high school?

DJ   Yeah.

LRL   And you were in high school where?

DJ   North Jersey – Westwood.

LRL   I see. So all that western business was early?

DJ   Yeah.

LRL   And did you come to New York and see art and stuff here?

DJ   A little bit. I remember we went to the Metropolitan a couple of times, but I didn't really know much about it. All I knew about, really, were various Old Masters or something, from reading *The Book of Knowledge*[4] or looking through portfolios that the *Omaha World-Herald* put out; it had mostly Old Masters, and Curry and Benton and Jon Corbino. They had a few Americans. It was that sort. I think maybe they had a Matisse and a Picasso.

LRL   Did that stuff turn you on at some point?

DJ   Yeah, I was very interested in it, except my idea of art was a very archaic one, because all the things reproduced were old European paintings.

LRL   Where did you go in the army?

DJ   I went to Korea. There was no war on. This was 1947.

LRL   What were you doing in Korea at the time?

DJ   Occupying the place. Keeping the Japanese out. The United States went in as if the Koreans were the enemy.

LRL   That's funny.

DJ   Well, it's Japanese owned, and then it was partitioned in the treaty between Russia and the United States.

LRL   Were you over there about the same time Sol [LeWitt] was?

DJ   When was Sol there?

LRL   No, I guess he was – it must have been later. After he went to college.

DJ   I don't quite know how old – oh, people my age went in after college, so they were in the war.

LRL   Yeah, pretty smart idea to manage that.

DJ   I wanted to get it over with. I thought they'd get me anyway. And also because the GI Bill was still in effect and it was due to run out that October, and I went in June. It was fairly good then; I really got a lot of education out of it.

LRL   What did you do when you got out of the army?

DJ   I got out the end of November 1947. I didn't want to start college in the middle of the year, so I went to the [Art Students] League and then –

LRL   With who?

DJ   Let's see. [Louis] Bouché in the morning for painting, and maybe a fellow named [Robert Ward] Johnson in the afternoon for drawing, I believe. It's quite a while ago. Johnson is dead. He was very obscure and deservedly so.

LRL   Isn't that funny? The history of the league is funny, because when you think of Don studying with Bouché –

DJ   Yeah, isn't that strange? I really didn't know anything.

LRL   But you did know by that time – you were very clear when you went straight into the league; you knew it was art.

DJ   Yeah, I intended to study art. But at that time, I wanted to go to college first and get it over with – I seemed to think it was necessary – and then study art. But in that time at the league, I got into a little too much. That year, when I went down to William & Mary, in the fall of 1948, there really wasn't much art there that I could study, and it became obvious that I wanted to get on with it. So I gave up that idea and went back to the league full time.

LRL When?

DJ So, it was only one year there at William & Mary.

LRL William & Mary – coming from the New York art scene to William & Mary; you couldn't have picked a worse place. I didn't realize you went back that far.

DJ Well, you know, it was the stereotyped idea of going to college and all that. Also, I figured out that if I went to the league full time, I could go to Columbia nights and summers, and it really wouldn't amount to all that much longer. Which it didn't, really.

LRL Were you a graduate student at Columbia?

DJ Yeah, later on. There was a gap of two or three years. Then I went up there to see if I could get an art history degree.

LRL Did you?

DJ No, I gave it up after a while. I took all the courses, but I never did the essay [thesis]. The main reason, really, for taking the master's was practical.

LRL I got mine – purely practical.

DJ I was desperate to somehow make a living, and it became obvious that a master's degree wasn't sufficient to stay in New York. I just couldn't use it, anyway.

LRL I don't know. I got my master's degree while I was doing research, and that master's really did a lot of good.

DJ Did it?

LRL I had The Museum of Modern Art background and a tremendous amount of experience; I didn't need anything. But I got the master's – I never took anything modern – and the minute I got the master's from the Institute [of Fine Arts at New York University], then I got paid much better for the research – like, a dollar an hour more, which made it two fifty an hour instead of one fifty.

DJ I didn't know that. I was thinking of teaching.

LRL I just kind of fell into research.

DJ   Yeah, I would have liked the research better than teaching.

LRL   Oh, it was tremendous. You were very much on your own. You didn't have to be at any place at any time. It's like writing.

DJ   But the art history — a fair amount of it was pretty interesting. I had one course at Columbia while I was an undergraduate, and it was all chronology; really horrible. So, I hated art history. That's why I didn't major in it. It was Northern Renaissance painting, and it was just one date after another.

LRL   Then you went back to the league after William & Mary — who were you working with then?

DJ   Well, Bouché for two years in the morning, painting. Various people for drawing in the afternoon, Bernard Klonis … I think [Robert Beverly] Hale for his anatomy thing, either in a summer or some such session.

LRL   There really wasn't anybody at the league who was, like, avant-garde, was there?

DJ   Not really. [Vaclav] Vytlacil would have been the most so, and [Morris] Kantor, I guess. The league has been pretty dead for a long time.

LRL   Well, I know Larry Poons is teaching there.

DJ   Yeah, that's a rare thing. And there's a story on that which is incredible. Some girl — a girl who's on the Board of Control, which is made up partly of students; she's a student — said she suggested him at one of the meetings, and no one knew who he was. It was only last year or something. They took her word for it that he should be hired, without anyone else, presumably also Stewart Klonis, even knowing who he was. Which indicated the caliber of the people that — it's really a big waste, though, to have facilities and all that, and then run a school in such an incompetent way.

LRL   It is a big waste. Well, the School of Visual Arts is going to take it away from them, to some extent.

DJ   Yeah, I mean, they're much, much better.

LRL   But still the league is where poor innocents go when they come in from out of town. It remains that kind of thing.

DJ   Well, at the time, it was about the only thing that existed. Bouché wasn't so bad for the two years, probably, or at least the first year – for one year, anyway. It was probably no loss to study with him. But the second year, I was pretty dissatisfied with him.

LRL   What kind of work were you doing?

DJ   Just realistic painting from the model. But he had kind of an ordinary approach to it; he was very against any sort of schmaltzy things. That was sort of nice. After you got a little interested in composition and color or something, which I did in the second year, he was useless.

LRL   It's sad. Who were you seeing outside and stuff? Were you aware of the things that were going on in the late 1940s? Let's see; by this time, by the time you came back, it was – well, the end of 1948?

DJ   Yeah, the end of 1948. No, not much. I'd say in the third year – there was two years with Bouché, and then a third year – I know I did know of Pollock. I knew of de Kooning and those people.

LRL   Did you go to art exhibits? I guess [Charles] Egan [Gallery] was the only thing around.

DJ   I didn't know much of – I saw [Franz] Kline's second show, which may have been in 1952 or something; I remember that because I was impressed by it.[5] But I really didn't know much about them. Also, I didn't understand what I did see. So it was sort of –

LRL   Who were your friends? Just people you knew at the league?

DJ   Yeah, most of them.

LRL   You didn't have any connection with the kind of –

DJ   No, I didn't know anybody. All the people who I thought were kind of good at the league have gone some place away. They're not painters. A lot of them I don't think are even doing art at all.

LRL   Then there wasn't any Tenth Street yet. Did you see the Ninth Street show?[6] I guess that one you'd have to know about to be involved.

DJ   No. It's too bad. I really didn't know anything about all that. I remember the third year, I had Louis Bosa, who is pretty much a jerk. *Time* magazine had something on Pollock, and Bosa was making fun of it. And I really didn't especially like the paintings, but I remember I resented Bosa's ridicule of them. I took the realistic work seriously, so that it was a real barrier. And also, the people around the league doing abstract work were really such dolts that it made me unduly –

LRL   What kind of work was it? Neoplasticism, or –

DJ   All sorts of schmaltzy, semiabstract stuff. A guy named [Richard] Bove or something – he went into a teaching career; he's at Pratt and all that. He was sort of the big abstract successful man around the league. Another one named Vincent Malta has never been heard of since. And they were sort of Picasso-y – Malta's were sort of Picasso-y, semiabstract shapes. It seemed dead already. So that sort of kept me from becoming interested in it.

LRL   So then you got out of the league; what did you do?

DJ   I got pretty dissatisfied with the league and, actually, with realistic work in general, because I couldn't ever do anything with it. It seemed such a hopeless thing. I left the league in 1953, I think. The last year was only mornings, anyway.

   Several years after that were miserable. But that first year was really miserable, because I was pretty timid and all that. As I said, I took this realistic work seriously, and giving it up and doing something more or less, even semiabstract, which they were for quite a while, was pretty traumatic.

LRL   That's funny. You just didn't lead into it.

D J   No, it was pretty horrible. I was really green.

L R L   And how were you making a living?

D J   Well, just after I moved in, which would be the late fall of 1953, I guess — no, I moved in in the summer; I sublet Bosa's studio in the summer of 1953 — they tore down the skylight over me, and it was really miserable, too. Then I worked at Grand Central Art Supplies that fall and through Christmas.[7] Oh, and I guess then at Columbia library, in the spring for a few weeks, part of the summer — or, I don't know, maybe it was six months; I don't know how long it was. Maybe the spring and summer at Columbia library. Then I got a job at a settlement house on Avenue D — Christodora House.[8] That was every afternoon — I don't know, 2:30 to 6 or something. I think it was $100 a month. Living on $100 a month was out of this world. That's why I began to think about making a living, because I really —

L R L   I did that when I first started here in research. But I had an eighteen-dollars-a-month apartment. I didn't have to have a studio space.

D J   Well, this one was just twenty-seven dollars; what they call a railroad flat, I guess, in a little building on Twenty-Seventh Street.[9] I had two places in that building. The first on the first floor, and then on the second floor in the adjacent building, which was just like it. The first floor had mice and even rats, and it was really formidable.

L R L   Let's see — oh yes, I forgot to ask: what did your parents do? What did your father do?

D J   My father worked for Western Union Telegraph Company. He started out as an operator. Later, he was manager of one of those little offices they have. And then various supervisory jobs.

L R L   Was there any problem about the art thing? Were they horrified when you —

D J   They didn't put up any active objections, except they were pretty sullen and uninterested in it all. They were very quiet and very uninterested, and now and then, you know, they'd say something derogatory, just as they were derogatory about most things you can think of that one should be. The whole impression, too, that I had from them and the Middle West and everybody was that art wasn't something that anybody did. So, it was very much –

LRL   It just happened on the periphery of society.

DJ   Yeah, well, out there, people just didn't do such a thing, so that it was a very outlandish thing to do. It's sort of outside the whole realm of possibilities.

LRL   That's funny; that's exactly Bob [Ryman]'s story from Nashville, and it struck me as peculiar. I've never had to live in those places.

DJ   I mean, it's as if they were so implicitly against it, they just didn't bother. I don't think they took it seriously. I think my mother kept thinking – well, around twenty-five or twenty-six, I'd go off and get serious and do something, the one thing I never did.

LRL   Are they surprised about the success now?

DJ   Yeah.

LRL   Do you have more than one brother and sister?

DJ   Just one sister.

LRL   And she ended up in art, too?

DJ   No, she's married to a man who teaches physical anthropology out in Portland, Oregon.

LRL   How did she happen to get on *Arts*?[10]

DJ   Oh, let me see, what did she want to do? She had a little training after college as a secretary. She wanted a job that was somewhat interesting. That seemed like it might be interesting to her, so she went and applied, and they happened to need somebody.

LRL   What galleries were there at the time?

DJ   You can't overstate the whole negativism of the middle class, Middle West, whatever it is. It's not the Middle West, really. I think it's more a middle-class thing, say, the nouveau middle class. It's not some old middle class that's been around a while.

LRL   It's middle-middle class? Upper, lower, middle.

DJ   It's not upper-middle class at all, and it's not exactly lower, but it's a very – it has to do with it all being new. It's first-generation middle class, in a way. Just as my parents are pretty much off the farm.

LRL   So, they are still concerned with other things, I guess is what it is.

DJ   Well, their idea of middle class–ness and properness and all that I think was very narrow and conformist. Also, a lot of these people, as my father did, worked for big companies, and, I don't know, it seems like it must have been highly conformist. My grandparents – at least my grandmother, whom I knew best, is certainly freer as a person than either one of my parents.

[New tape]

LRL   Well, we'll begin with this business about sculpture again. Do you still consider that it's not sculpture?

DJ   It's not sculpture.

LRL   Why not?

DJ   In the first place, "sculpture" seems like a more archaic term than "painting," so it doesn't apply too well to anyone anymore. And then on top of that, its format and composition seem – very much sculpture is not identified with the term.

LRL   But couldn't there be nonrelational sculpture, just like painting is still painting even if it's nonrelational, even if it's not compositional?

DJ   There could be, except for the fact that it means "sculpting." Seems very awkward.

LRL   What in God's name would you call it, then? You just call it "three-dimensional art"? I've got to call it something.

DJ   I'd probably not call it anything.

LRL   But isn't "sculpture," kind of by definition, mass? If there is a definition of "sculpture," it is three-dimensional art, isn't it?

DJ   Well, it's three-dimensional all right —

LRL   But not necessarily art. [*Laughter*]

DJ   Not necessarily art. Usually, it is massive. For the most part, it has been fairly compact, and it's located in the center.

LRL   Yes. Something like Bob Morris's new things — is that sculpture? I mean, that's not sculpture, because it's three-dimensional in a sense?

DJ   He calls them "sculpture." Let him define his. He doesn't mind the word. But I mind the word.

LRL   You really do mind the word?

DJ   Yeah. Also because I never thought about sculpture — almost never. The work didn't have anything to do with current sculpture.

LRL   It seems like too much sculpture now is nonsculpture, if you want to think of it that way. Just generically, it seems simpler to call it sculpture, and you're usually so direct and simple.

DJ   It's simple for me not to call it sculpture, because I never dealt with it. I never dealt with anybody's [sculptural] work beyond a few things of David Smith's, when I was a painter. Otherwise, I never thought about sculpture.

LRL   Everybody's always very defensively saying, "New materials have nothing to do with my work, I'm not dependent on new materials." Which is just obvious in some cases; in some cases, it isn't. But you seem like the only person who has actually called materials an integral part of the work, just in the sense that it's a new material and a new surface, and a new way, you know, a new thing.

DJ   Obviously, it's pretty important to me. There aren't very many things there ever, and the material you've brought in is part of it.

LRL   [*Laughter*] Would this have been the, what I called – I won't
       call it that again – the jungle gym [image 21]? I called it that
       in the first show.[11]

DJ   I call it the bleachers.

LRL   The bleachers, yeah. Well, anyway, that stepped piece
       with the dark blue that's in the middle.

DJ   It's purple.

LRL   It is purple? That's funny, because I'd always thought it
       was dark blue. When I looked at it in the show, I said,
       "My god, it's purple." Would that have been an entirely
       different piece, then, if you had it fabricated in steel or
       something?

DJ   Little bit neater in steel. I don't think it would have
       changed too much.

LRL   It wouldn't change it? No. I love that piece. Has anybody
       bought it?

DJ   I gave it to Julie [Finch].[12]

LRL   Good, because that takes care of that.

DJ   That ties it up.
           You think about materials that you can afford to buy
       and deal with. So at the time, it was a problem, and I wasn't
       thinking –

LRL   Because you'd have to be a millionaire to really deal with
       the material you'd like to deal with.

DJ   You'd have to work up to it; I don't think about that.

LRL   Flavin says he doesn't want any development; he's damned
       if he's going to develop. Do you feel the same way about
       stylistic development? It seems like there's been some kind
       of move into more open things recently. Do you think of
       that as being something you're moving into, not neces-
       sarily an advance, but just something else you're involved
       with now? Or does it coincide with the boxes?

DJ   It changes slowly. I don't think much about that sort of
       thing – about how it's going to develop, or how it's going
       to change, or what the next work might be like. It doesn't

have much sense of futurity. It's always a case of the next few pieces I'm making.

LRL   You pretty much exhaust a series when you do it?

DJ   No, because they cost too much, so that the whole collection of ideas – well, it will eventually be built.

LRL   Like when you die and somebody finally realizes what it is you've been doing. [*Laughter*]

DJ   The idea dates back to the time of the galvanized stuff, the idea of the stainless steel and plexiglass. The galvanized was cheap, and this is pretty expensive, so it got done now; it didn't get done in '65. So there's more and more of a chance.

LRL   I'll just describe it for the tape. It's the piece with the yellow plexi [image 22] – you call them stacks?

DJ   Yeah.

LRL   It seemed at the beginning, when you started working with clear things, that it was sort of a contradiction to a lot of mass and stuff that you'd been involved in. Is it a completely different intention – the plexi thing, with the light going all the way through it, and the galvanized stack [image 23]?

DJ   No, I think they're connected. In the first place, I never wanted them to seem all that heavy. I'm against heaviness –

LRL   That was probably just the plywood thing?

DJ   Yeah. This piece actually is pretty heavy, but of course it's –

LRL   The orange one – it should have a catalogue number someplace – the orange one with the pipe [see image 5].

DJ   No. No pipe.

LRL   But with a pipe shape – aluminum. It's on page 21.[13]

DJ   It's heavy in weight, and it's pretty closed. Yet you can see into it enough so that the whole interior gets opened up.

LRL   Yeah. And the color is luminous – luminescent.

DJ   Cadmium red light. That's true of all this cadmium red light.

LRL   I had never thought of cadmium from a light point of view.
          What about the hollowness, then? I remember when it was brought up at the Jewish Museum thing,[14] and I al-

ways thought that was a spurious issue – like, who gives a damn, unless you're working in something where you can actually see in, and then it's a point you're making? But do you think of them as closed boxes, whether they're hollow or not?

DJ   Well, they shouldn't seem heavy.

[*William C. Agee joins conversation*]

LRL   Well, seriously, Mr. Judd [*laughter*], what about the monumentality thing? If it's going to stay light, what makes a monument? Obviously not just weight, but it's one of the clichés about –

DJ   I hate that whole idea.

LRL   Barbara [Rose] said in the "A New Aesthetic" thing that the most reassuring thing about your work was that it was heading toward a new monumentality.[15]

DJ   The words "monumentality" and "monument," Morris's "public" and "private," are thoroughly anathema to me.

LRL   How big would you get if you could get –

DJ   Oh, I'd get very big, but I don't think there's any distinction between public and private or monumental or whatever, and a public work, big or small, is the same as one that simply is not big or small.

LRL   Yeah. "Public art" does sound as though it's going to be bad enough for the masses to appreciate.

DJ   Yes, it sounds like nineteenth-century decoration. I was surprised at Bob's distinction. Maybe there's more to it.

LRL   I think what he means is that there's no private and intimate associations, don't you?

DJ   It's a dichotomy of some kind, and I can't connect either end of it. It's, again, something that I didn't think about.

[*Interruption*]

LRL   A lot of people were very surprised that this was so col-
      orful and sensuous.

DJ   It's the lighting. The lighting is sensuous.

LRL   It is the lighting that does it? [*Laughter*]

DJ   I'm against the lighting. It's too dark. In the first place,
      the whole idea of spotlights is bad, which really just came
      home to me here [the Whitney]. It's obviously set up
      to show paintings a little and a little sculpture, and the
      light should be bright, flat, even, and simulate outdoor
      lighting.

LRL   When you conceive of a piece, do you conceive of it pretty
      much with the color and surface? Or do you wait for the
      color to come along?

DJ   No, pretty much altogether.

LRL   That's what I was trying to get at. Doesn't color make it
      less neutral if you want a neutral quality?

DJ   I'm not interested in neutral qualities.

LRL   Didn't you used to be? I mean, the word comes up all the
      time; I was just reading through some of your writings,
      and the word "neutral" does come up a lot.

DJ   No, I don't know – I don't remember anything from you,
      but that's Barbara Rose and all those –

LRL   I use the term all the time. No, you've got it, though. You've
      got it in your – well, "neutral context" is what you talk
      about. Does that make sense or not?

DJ   Well, I don't know how I used the word. I certainly don't
      mean neutral art.

WCA   [William C. Agee] I think, Don, where you've used the
      term "neutral" before is in describing other peoples' forms.

LRL   But you use it as a complimentary term, usually. You do
      use it often.

WCA   Usually, yes. You have used it in the context of, I think, the
      disposition or the formation of certain forms – that is, a
      form that does not emulate something else.

DJ   Well, yes, I guess maybe in the arrangement of it.

W C A   But that certainly is something much different from the work of art which turns out to be neutral.

L R L   Oh, yes. I didn't mean that you would walk right by without seeing it, because it was so neutral. But it is a matter of neutralizing – if you can call it "neutralizing" – or canceling out the other factors of the environment. Your work kind of does that. It exists in its own space, and it's very directly there.

D J   It might be the business of perspective about order or something.

L R L   You wrote something about [John] Chamberlain that sounds like some of these. You said about his reliefs: "They are extreme, elegant in the wrong way, immoderate."[16] Do you think of your things that way at all? They are pretty snazzy and elegant in the wrong way, no?

D J   No, that's John Chamberlain.

L R L   If it weren't John Chamberlain, would it be you?

D J   "Elegance" is a very bad term.

L R L   Yes, it's one those European terms that you want to get away from.

D J   Yeah. It's a bad quality in art, incidentally.

L R L   What constitutes elegance?

D J   A work that's pat and too easily understood.

L R L   But it's used in a lot of different ways.

D J   "Elegance," by now, I think, could be a favorable term, but it's a derogatory term.

L R L   You meant it favorably there, didn't you? "Elegant in the wrong way."

D J   Oh, yeah. It's qualified. It's favorable there.

L R L   I've never used the word favorably in my life. I practically always use it derogatorily. But most of the time, people don't realize that I'm using it derogatorily.

D J   Yeah. [Robert] Indiana's paintings are elegant, I'd say. I shouldn't have said that.

L R L   Why did you pick cadmium red light? I remember saying it was like Yves Klein because of his blue.[17] But it doesn't have anything to do with your choice of one color?

DJ   Not so much that it was one color. First, in a general way, I like the quality of the color.

LRL   The lightness that –

DJ   Yeah, its particular brightness, a particular value, and so forth, which makes the three-dimensionality of the pieces most clear. If you go to cadmium red deep, it's too dark.

LRL   It goes into the shadows.

DJ   Cadmium red medium is sort of too sweet, or too blue, or something. I really disliked both cadmium red medium and cadmium red deep.

LRL   What about the aggressive quality, did that come up at all? Or that's an accident?

DJ   My answer depends on what you mean by "aggressive." I'm a little wary of that.

LRL   Well, it's probably the associational things that I'm thinking of. Just fire-engine red, which isn't really cadmium red light; it's kind of cadmium red medium, I guess. But red is thought of in that whole psychological color scale – even though most people don't think of that anymore; I don't even think of it, really – but that color red still holds these connotations. I guess it's just something that's been wiped out.

DJ   No, I don't think about that – but it's important that it was highly visible. It's very important that it wasn't a quiet color of some kind.

LRL   And that the edges really showed.

DJ   Yes.

WCA   Modulations of hue and value almost always give some illusion of depth, as shown –

DJ   It's not that it's a rule and regulation or something like that. It's a quality to it that makes up a whole complex of ideas and whatnot that, you know, I don't believe in, or object to, or so forth.

LRL   But you don't think of the idea as particularly important, do you, as an idea?

DJ   Which idea?

LRL   Any idea, such as the thing somebody would think about first in the work; the idea of this painting is that it be flat, or that it be mathematically involved, or anything else.

DJ   I don't quite know. I mean, it's not a case of idea, pure and simple, I don't think. Hardly ever.

LRL   Well, it's this whole conceptual art business, which Sol says and doesn't entirely believe. He's still very visually oriented and wants to be, but his thing about the idea that it's the machine that makes the work – would you agree with that? Or would you just prefer not to think about the idea at all, and just art as art, like Reinhardt?

DJ   I don't like the separation of idea and emotion or whatever. I don't think things occur like that. I don't know what a visible idea would be – or a nonvisible idea – that has to do with visual art.

LRL   Well, I think a nonvisible idea is clear enough.

DJ   Well, I mean, yeah, but by an artist. It's interesting if you can see it; the main thing is if it can be seen. Otherwise, it becomes another kind of art – it becomes philosophy, or something else.

LRL   Yes, and literature.

DJ   It's the visible kind that I really want.

LRL   What's the four-by-six-foot "space-lattice" that Smithson mentioned in that Philadelphia catalogue a couple of years ago?[18] He said you'd made an X-shaped "space-lattice" [image 24].

DJ   Oh, it's not an X – it's rectangular. It's this drawing – no, there's no drawing downstairs. It's a piece with the pipes which you didn't see. It's made up of iron pipe. It was made by a plumber friend of Lee Lozano's.

WCA   That was the first freestanding construction that you did, wasn't it?

DJ   No, it's after the bleachers. It's maybe '65 or something.

LRL   What is it, a rectangle and a pipe?

DJ   Yes, well, say you had a freestanding thing, and you come around here, and another set of pipe comes across here. There's one that comes across here too; they cross in the center. Then three rectangles of pipe, pipe here – four corners raise them up, pipe in three tiers, say one, two, three, and then in the center one, there's –

LRL   It kind of relates to the plexi box, too.

DJ   It's a perfectly nice piece. But it was never put back together again after it was shown at Welfare Island in a show that di Suvero organized.[19] One of the few pieces that wasn't destroyed by the people coming through.

LRL   Wasn't it a show for four delinquents or junkies or something?

DJ   Something – I don't know.

LRL   And they all dashed into the sculpture – so much for that. "Don't do nuthin' for me."

DJ   I guess it was pretty hard to disturb.

Smithson was just trying to upstage Sol or something. That's what that was all about.

LRL   Well, there was all that crystallography thing.[20] How much did the crystallography business have to do with it? I didn't know anything about crystallography when all that was going on. Now I know more. Tony Smith was involved in it. So I read a few books, and now I have some foggier idea. But what was it?

DJ   Nothing.

LRL   I never got a very clear way it could apply to your work. Just a conception of the order and disorder, the plane of disorder that interested you?

DJ   No.

LRL   Nothing?

DJ   Smithson loves to confuse art and science, and I'm opposed to such things.

LRL   I don't know why everybody is so pristine about that, because I certainly think that, you know, science and art
aren't the same thing, and that should be so blatantly clear
by now that I don't know why everybody is worried about
mentioning that they've been interested in anything any
more than they're interested in anything else. It's all outside art, so I don't know why it should be a taboo subject
the way it is.

DJ   I don't know. It's not taboo to me. I'm interested in geology, but it doesn't mean much in relation to what I do.
I'm interested in a lot of things. I'm interested in my Land
Rover, which – they can all mean a little bit, maybe, but
it gets pretty vague. [*Laughter*]

LRL   Now, there's still something else about this – do you call
this thing a "space-lattice," or was that just Smithson?

DJ   No, that's Smithson's.

LRL   Oh, good. I'm glad to get that clear in my mind. The other
idea of Smithson's that I kind of liked was about the plexiglass box again [image 25] – I keep going back on this – his
idea of antimatter sort of seemed like a nice way of thinking that the space was inside and outside.[21] That's why I
liked it so much in that plastic show,[22] because everybody else was, like, overcome by plastics, and this is one
of the few pieces that was both plastic but mainly something else, because it was so clearly defined as to what it
was. The plastic was just an integral part of it and nothing else.

DJ   I don't know what antimatter has to do with it.

LRL   Remember a couple of years ago when they discovered
that antimatter wasn't going to exactly mirror matter? I
don't know enough about it, but there was a sort of mirror set up, and it turned out that antimatter had an identity all its own.

DJ   I don't know.

LRL   I don't know – it was just a conceit about the work, really.

Now, so much for that. Why were the ends on that [piece] steel? Mainly to keep it tighter?

DJ   No, because I wanted steel ends, solid ends. I could very well make a plain plastic box; then it could be all glued together and so forth. This can't be, because the ends are too heavy.

LRL   And then the ends were the reason for the axis things, rather than you having planned on the wires inside?

DJ   No, I planned on the wires. It was thought of like it is. A plain plastic box seemed too simpleminded.

LRL   You've never done one, have you?

WCA   It might be too pretty, almost, somehow.

LRL   Well, it would begin to look like a display item, too. This made it *sculpture*. [*Laughter*]

WCA   The steel ends, too, seem to give it an anchor, give it more of a definition than an all-plastic box.

LRL   Also, it makes it harder to define, and it does make it more complex, the whole thing.

DJ   It would be too light, too.

WCA   All plastic would just seem to levitate.

LRL   The floor is so important for that.

      I seem to be out of questions as such. Got any for me, Bill?

WCA   You raised the question of art and science. I think one thing that might be interesting to talk about is there's still a general misconception about Don's work that mass somehow plays an ultimate role, that he's interested in it for its own sake, and therefore, it is correlated with science.

LRL   I don't think anybody really thinks that about it. I think his work is freer from that than almost anybody else's. It's become clearer and clearer –

WCA   Well, I'm thinking only about the progressions – the wall pieces. I think somehow that should be aired in the interview.

DJ   Well, I think I aired that somewhere.

WCA   But this is something else.

LRL   This is hot air. [*Laughter*]

DJ   It falls in with what I said before. The mathematics or the
      arrangement of the parts is part of the work, just the way
      the material, or color, or whatever is, and it is not some
      sort of underlying order or great organizing thing.

LRL   Since most people don't realize what the progression is, or
      don't even realize it's a progression, it looks like it might
      have been an arbitrary grouping of different sizes and forms
      against each other; doesn't that become very relational?
      Or do you just – "To hell with how people look at it"?

DJ   No, I don't think so. I mean, it would seem very different
      to me if I had set out to work out by eye the one set that
      belongs to the Whitney, on the wall [image 26]. By then it
      was too boring to work on. It was a terrible idea.

LRL   You actually just did the thing? What would be the differ-
      ence to working it out by eye and –

DJ   The progression served the purpose.

LRL   How would it have been different then?

DJ   I think it would look it. In which case, I wouldn't like the
      quality of it.

LRL   It would look what?

DJ   It would look as if it had been worked out. You don't have
      to understand just what progression it is, or how it's ar-
      ranged, to know that there's some sort of scheme.

LRL   Well, as long as you know there's a scheme. I started think-
      ing about everything like this in the last five years or so,
      but I think most people don't think much about schemes
      in art. Which is one reason I think it's just as well to let
      people realize that some of this goes on, that it is a vehicle
      for, you know, a part of the work, like everything else is a
      part of it. I'm speaking as a critic and a kind of educator.

DJ   Yeah. When you look at one of Poons's paintings, you
      don't know what that very complicated scheme is that he's
      dealing with. Or if you realized it, you'd have to sit there

a few days to figure it out. Which isn't a very entertaining business.

L R L John, a friend of mine, did it. It was fascinating, though, once it had turned out. Poons, I don't think, was very happy about having it exposed as such. But I like the feeling that there is a type of thing under there, and if I hadn't read about Poons and known about Poons's work and so on – if I had just come in as somebody from, oh, Oshkosh or Europe or someplace, and was interested in art, but just hadn't been exposed to this sort of thing – I wouldn't know that that structure existed under there. And I find that it does add to my aesthetic pleasure, even though I don't know what it is. I can't ever track down those Poons things any more than I can immediately see anything in your thing.

W C A It is based on some kind of progression or grid or something?

L R L Yes, almost all of them. I don't know what about the one at the Whitney, but it works out absolutely beautifully. John's got a little diagram.

D J Where they hit on a grid or something.

L R L It's like, one dot is here, then the next one is here, and the next one is here, and so on. It's all worked out on a grid. They get very complicated. And sometimes he turns the whole thing upside down and the rotations get very involved.

W C A My reaction is the same. I know there's a grid under there, but I mean, my question is: how is it worked out?

L R L I think the important thing is feeling that there's a grid under there and the hell with how it's worked out.

W C A Does he use three grids? Or more?

D J It varies a lot from painting to painting. I know in some of the earlier ones, or that drawing that I have, anyway – [*begins sketching*] say, take one corner of the painting somewhere. The first dot might be here. Then you go over there, and it might be here –

LRL   Clockwise and counterclockwise part of the ways.

DJ   – it might be here. It might be there and on that one, and
      so forth. Or there might be two of them. Or one might
      be an ellipse over here.

LRL   Then it would follow through that this one in this row
      would be here, or here, or here, depending on the scheme.
      Maybe not that pattern is retained, but the reason be-
      hind these being there is retained throughout the whole
      thing.

DJ   But you see, at the time when Poons first showed these
      paintings, and when I was sort of getting interested in
      some way of organizing things – well, with that box that
      has the sections in it [see image 5] which you saw at Green
      [see images 2, 3] – [23]

LRL   The cadmium?

DJ   Yeah. I was thinking about some kind of order that didn't
      involve this compositional order that everything had,
      which seemed to have such a general character and to, you
      know, imply an underlying order of some kind of things –

LRL   A general underlying order?

DJ   Yeah. So the progression seemed like a very brand-new
      thing to me.

LRL   I think it was for most artists. We were all very naive – I
      mean, even paying attention to progression, because –

DJ   I don't mean progression as a thing; I mean being able
      to use some other kind of order, an alternative to all that
      composition, because at the time, there was almost no
      other thing that I was aware of. When I did the progres-
      sion, it seemed like an absolute alternative to all other
      kinds of form.

LRL   Did you know Max Bill's things?[24] Because his work looks
      like, I think, what you think of as European in general. It
      is based on the same kind of order.

DJ   Those orders – he ends up with an organic sculpture,
      though.

L R L   No, no, not those. Well, Lohse – I guess it's Richard [Paul] Lohse I'm talking about, the guy who does the squares. It's Bill's paintings that are done on – not organically, but they look like variations on early [Josef] Alberses.

D J   Yeah. Those paintings of [Victor] Vasarely and all that are, you know – there may be some of that in it, but they wind up looking compositional.

L R L   Well, that's what I mean; they look compositional. I don't know how systematic Vasarely is; I don't know enough about his work. But Bill, I know, does stick to a definite thing, which is as definite as Poons's –

D J   Poons's looks compositional. I wanted mine just a plain other kind of order. Poons's paintings, which sort of interested me, had some of what I was interested in. Also, they had a loose element in there, an accidental element. And then also – which I always objected to whenever I got too much of it – the compositional part. Sometimes he'd do paintings which are too compositional. Another sort of form of buildup that really got like that silk screen that the Wadsworth put out,[25] you know, just a group –

L R L   Which I have, yes.

D J   I have it too. A group on either side. I really decided that I hated that thing.

L R L   Was that the time you were doing the sectional thing?

D J   The single, big, lumpy pieces seemed to have a certain – some connection; I wasn't going to pay much attention to it. It's just sculpture, in that, after all, Brancusi –

L R L   Your single lumpy pieces?

D J   Yeah, single pieces. The singleness had a precedent. It was a certain kind of form that you could take further, in a way, and make it more conspicuous, but –

L R L   The precedent being Brancusi or whatever?

D J   – but using some kind of series or progression seemed more unusual.

L R L   It still seems unusual.

DJ   The progression?

LRL   Yeah, but I mean, it does seem a kind of different order.

DJ   I don't think you read it as compositional order, though.

LRL   Well, again, you can be perverse and read anything as compositional order, because you can read this as just a rationalization of … you know, you compose something nice, but you've got a reason for not thinking you've composed something nice, because you have a system that dictated it to you – but then, you chose the system, which is the same thing as composing. So in a way, it's not all that different.

DJ   Choosing isn't the same as fiddling with all those parts. You choose the overall result just as you choose the color, as you choose the material, or whatever.

LRL   Yeah. I'm just thinking, though, logically, that it can all be read as the same thing. It's a much finer point than that other –

DJ   That composition has definite meaning to me in all respects.

LRL   Yeah, but it means balancing things against each other.

DJ   Adjusting them to one another, and making a whole out of a great number of parts – which to me, I think, makes a weak whole and weak parts.

WCA   I don't know whether you talked about it before, but for the purposes of the interview, I think it's very much worthwhile exploring the way Don works, the element of chance, risk involved –

DJ   The financial risk.

LRL   And then there's his image, which is not one of a sensuous sculptor. [*Laughter*]

WCA   – the fact that it may simply just not work, although I don't think that has ever happened. I think the common idea of his way of working is the Tony Smith idea that came from that one piece: that you call up a fabricator and order a six-foot –

DJ   Tony has never worked like that before.

WCA   No, I think that was that one piece. But *Time* and *Life* picked up on it,[26] and that's the image, with the result being the misconception, the idea that working this way is somehow an abrogation of the artist's responsibility – di Suvero's comment.[27]

DJ   Mark di Suvero is more agreeable now. He takes the Jewish Museum episode back. He apologized, actually, when he ran into me on Max's street. I felt awkward that he was bothered to apologize.

LRL   Well, it was an awfully stupid thing for him to say. He probably realized that it was – I don't think he probably worried about hurting your feelings so much as having everybody know what a stupid thing it was to say.

WCA   But from that, though – I do think that seems very simple and obvious, and it is to us – from that, then we get into the way that Don works and the way a piece is developed, which I think is worth exploring. It doesn't just happen. After Don gets down on paper a drawing of what he wants, there's the question of working with the fabricator on what kind of joint, what kind of structure, what kind of support you can use. If something cannot be worked out, Don presumably has to modify what he's doing. The point is that Don just doesn't get the drawing down and it's just made. And again, I think that's worth getting down on tape.

DJ   They always make the second version better.

LRL   Yeah, Bob Morris said an interesting thing when he gave his talk at E.A.T.; he said something about how working with the fabricator had literally been changing the way he thought of his work.[28] Do you think it's made that much difference?

DJ   No, maybe not that much.

LRL   It's like working in public instead of private, too, isn't it? I mean, isn't it different, being in a studio, than being in a factory full of people?

DJ   Oh, I don't know. It doesn't bother me.

LRL   It doesn't make any difference?

DJ   Most of it is talking. There are all sorts of limitations that come up which constantly change something. I don't see that it enormously changes my work. Somehow, the whole process affects it or something, but I don't know – the metal only goes together in a certain way, or certain kinds of metal do so-and-so. It's full of details.

LRL   Have there been any accidents that you have been able to use? Have there been things that have come out of the fabrication process, or materials that were forced upon you, that you used again for other reasons?

DJ   Pretty much no.

LRL   Pretty much no? I should think that would be one of the vaguely experimental qualities of working with industry. Not experimental in the sense of dabbling, mixing things, and so on, but –

DJ   Usually I know what's going to happen, though. My interest in stainless steel comes out of what it can do and so forth. It's not exactly the result of making a piece –

LRL   What happens if the plexi gets scratched up badly if somebody owns it?

DJ   Throw it away and get a new set.

LRL   Get a new set? Not just the plexiglass?

DJ   No, replace the plexiglass.

LRL   Have you got any stipulations when you sell something as to what the collector's responsibility is, as far as that goes?

DJ   Total. They never bother me again.

LRL   They can scrape the paint off it if they want?

DJ   Oh, no, they can't do that.

LRL   Was that really Leo Castelli who did that? Remember that famous David Smith story? I just discovered that that was true. There was an *ARTnews* editorial several years ago – oh, six, eight, ten, or more.[29] It said someone had bought a David Smith – it was about the collector's responsibility.

DJ   David Smith wrote a letter.[30]

LRL Yes, that's right, and then there was an editorial letter. Somebody had bought a red piece of Smith's, and the buyer had shaved off the red because he wanted it in stainless — liked it better in another color. And, needless to say, Smith — of all people to do that to —

DJ   I'd object to that.

LRL Obviously.

WCA Well, what happened?

LRL It turned out to be Leo, apparently. He's the one who did it for the collector. I can't imagine why that didn't come out in Tom Hess's editorial; it seems like the kind of thing Hess would do. Now we're getting this rumor down for posterity. Someday I'll have to put a footnote if I find out it's wrong.[31]

DJ   Well, I don't want to have to restore everything forever and ever. We can't do that. That would be a lifetime job.

LRL Obviously Reinhardt was still repainting things. He only had about twenty-five pictures left, because he had to have them repainted. Two of them were covered with white when he died. But the life expectancy for these things is forever, isn't it?

DJ   It depends on how somebody takes care of them. They're made as art just as anything has ever been made as art.

LRL But would it bother you if you go to somebody's house and somebody had kicked in the sides and made dents — if somebody's child had been consistently running a bicycle into something?

DJ   I wouldn't fix it for nothing.

LRL No, no. Hell no, nobody does. I don't think that's the problem.

DJ   Well, yeah, I'd have to see the piece damaged; I don't like that.

LRL I think that more of this ought to be done. I think the artist's responsibility does keep going.

D J   Well, I don't want to see the pieces destroyed. They're too much money and trouble to make.

L R L   Once you've made the piece and sent it out, it is still your piece, to some extent.

D J   But it really becomes impossible to keep track of them or save them, because so much happens.

L R L   But all the early things of Frank Stella's — the *Black Paintings* — I saw another one in Ottawa, a great, bagging, bulging, warped thing with the canvas just hanging off. Those lines are pretty soft anyway, and when you take away the top surface —

W C A   Well, that sounds like a restretching.

L R L   If I were Frank, if I knew that this went on at all, I think I would specify when it was sold or something that you'd have to restretch it once every five years.

D J   In the first place, they ought to quit moving all the art around. It's not up to that. People who own it should keep it. Don't lend museums anything. [*Laughter*]

L R L   Your things get treated worse, too, because they look so tough, and guards are leaning on them.

D J   Yeah, the guards don't do anything.

L R L   In the Philadelphia show — I was just going through the LA sculpture show in Philadelphia — [32]

W C A   Oh, a travesty!

L R L   I dragged, personally, three people off things. One guy was kicking a plastic [Peter] Agostini thing.

W C A   I dragged five kids off. I counted something like one guard on the second floor, where the major part of the show, or a large part of the show was — and this was at a peak hour on a Sunday afternoon. While I was dragging a kid off a David Gray, another kid, I believe of the same family, was pulling and succeeded in dislodging one of the butts from the Oldenburg pieces. He was a very small but very strong child.

L R L   They all are.

WCA   That was a disgrace.

DJ   You're going to have to divide up the museums in due time, I think, into public, educational museums and –

LRL   Specialize. But that would be terribly sad, because when you think about how many artists come from, like – well, I think of Bob [Ryman] in Nashville; he had never seen any art, and when he got here and was just seeing something, bang! That really turned him on.

DJ   Well, I don't know. Perhaps it wouldn't have to be very strict, but just to cut it somewhat.

LRL   The other thing would be the pieces like yours – everybody could have double copies of them, one to keep away and one to have out.

DJ   Yeah, if you keep the bloody kids away. But also, you should be able to see the pieces. Some shows are so crowded that it's heartless. And what's the point of that? I mean, you couldn't look at that [Alexander] Calder show at the Guggenheim a couple of years ago.[33] I tried, but gee whiz.

WCA   That art of Calder's – even Calder's things were so beat by the end of that show.

LRL   Especially Calder's. But they had made this big point of letting people play with them. They were fools. Anybody with museum expertise knows that even if you don't let them play with them, they get busted.

WCA   Well, the very fragile mobiles, of course, but even some of the bigger ones.

LRL   Some of those mobiles are pretty tough. They're so beautifully balanced.

DJ   I think with Reinhardt's paintings, or Newman's, where there are not so many of them and they get worn pretty quickly – the museum should build a special room or museum. Walter Hopps had the idea of little separate museums where people – did he tell you about it?[34]

WCA   No, where? You mean just a –

DJ   Wherever. Maybe a Reinhardt museum, or a Newman museum, because those things aren't going to last. And you let the people in on a quota, like the Barnes or some such thing.

LRL   And you take all the sharp instruments away from them – their shoes, their hatpins.

DJ   Or in a special section.

LRL   Dress them in padded pajamas and gloves and things.

DJ   In the special section, you charge them five dollars a head and provide more guards or something. If they pay five dollars, they get a little bit serious.

LRL   Yeah, but what about the poor guy who is serious as hell, but can't pay five dollars?

WCA   Can't pay!

DJ   Everybody can afford five dollars.

LRL   Have artist's passes or something?

DJ   Or then go talk to somebody.

LRL   Can you remember the time when you couldn't possibly pay five dollars if you wanted to go to three museum shows in a week? It was over half your income.

WCA   I still can't.

LRL   You must have been in that state like everybody else. Then you have to start pulling strings.

DJ   Well, they could have credentials or something.

LRL   Oh, what time is it? Shall we – ?

WCA   12:35.

LRL   I'm famished. Do you want to keep going?

DJ   Not especially.

LRL   Are you still getting warmed up?

DJ   I'm always ready to quit. [*Laughter*]

[*New tape*]

LRL   [James] Fitzsimmons wants to use this.[35] Do you object to having another interview? It seems silly. I ought to write an article on you; I've been meaning to for years. The only other thing I've ever done with you is interview you.

DJ   I'd rather have an article because, for one thing, I'm gloomy about a lot of things lately. Also, apropos of interviews, I do all the talking, and nobody else sits down and thinks about the work, and I'm sort of beginning to resent explaining it myself.

LRL   Yes. I don't blame you. There hasn't been a real article on you yet, a really exhaustive thing.

DJ   I'm beginning to think about it a little bit – you know, why should I pass out all these explanations? I don't really want to.

LRL   Yes, that makes sense.

        When did the breakthrough come, as far as seeing things? Or was it very gradual? Did you suddenly become aware of the kind of abstract art that was being done?

DJ   It was kind of gradual. I'm just trying to think; probably – well, I was aware of de Kooning and liked him pretty early. So that, let's say, in '54, maybe '55, there were some semiabstract paintings, there were some landscapes, a little bit of de Kooning, but they're not really that loose or anything, not all that expressionistic, a little de Kooning influenced. I liked those very flat paintings [by de Kooning] – *Excavation* and *Attic* and *Asheville* and such things. Except that I was taking it backward. I mean, it wasn't a very beneficial influence. I was making – I was conservatizing or something. I kind of liked Pollock, but I didn't understand it then. In general, Pollock is the one I liked most. But it never seemed possible for me to actually use the technique or anything like that. I assumed that dripping was all Pollock's and best left alone. So I never did anything like that. I did do, maybe in '56 or '57 or something, some relatively loose painting, just expressionist in general [image 27]. Loose painting really didn't do what I wanted, because it always seems a little unnatural, even though I got so I could sort of do it pretty well.

LRL Who were your heroes? You couldn't have been painting away in this total void for all that time.

DJ Not by then. I admired – it was more general than any one artist. By maybe, say, '57, I was sort of influenced by the whole thing, not so much by one man as the scale that all the work had, and the singleness it had, and the comparative uniqueness that each one of those people had. It was Pollock or Newman or Rothko or some of Guston's paintings.

LRL You couldn't have been much aware of Newman, because he didn't show at all. The *New American Painting* show[36] at the museum –

DJ No, I didn't know too much about Newman. I had seen reproductions.

LRL Because until the French & Company show – [37]

DJ Yes. I saw a horizontal Newman at Betty Parsons pretty early. It has a horizontal band, one end of which sort of goes dark.[38]

LRL Yes, that's right – Betty Parsons. Did you start going to her – she was around in '46.

DJ Yes, I saw some things there. I saw the show of [Bradley Walker] Tomlin's – a couple of those I liked. And I think I did see a couple of Pollocks there. I saw Pollock's show[39] at Janis – what – just after he died, I think? *The Deep*?

LRL Yes. He went with Janis in '52.

DJ *The Deep* was in the show. And I didn't like *The Deep*, I remember. I liked most of the paintings, but I thought *The Deep* was sort of schmaltzy. I remember that. But I was very impressed by the show generally.

LRL That wouldn't have been '52. It wasn't after he died.

DJ I think maybe it was just after.

LRL He went with Janis in '52, and the first show, I think, was '53.

DJ   I think in a group show I saw some of those later paint-
      ings. Let's see, and I saw *Gray Ocean* or something or other
      in, of all places, the National Arts Club.[40]
LRL   That's the one that the Guggenheim has.
DJ   Yes.
LRL   But the National Arts Club!
DJ   It was a good show. I don't know what it was doing down
      here. Along with a nice Stuart Davis, I remember.
LRL   What about Ad [Reinhardt]?
DJ   I didn't know much about him really until later.
LRL   Because he was at Betty's all along, in a show almost ev-
      ery year from '46 on –
DJ   I must not have paid any attention, if I saw them at all. The
      earliest I remember are the black paintings, which I saw –
LRL   They were first shown about '56, '55.
DJ   Yeah, and I probably didn't see them until '58 or something.
      It wasn't too early.
            I saw Newman's show at French & Company.
LRL   Yeah. Did it bowl you over?
DJ   I liked them. I wasn't exactly bowled over. By then I took
      what I wanted out of the things for granted, you see; the
      scale, the importance of color, and all those things. So I
      had already accepted that. It depends on which painting,
      in a way. I really like *Vir Heroicus Sublimis*. The one that's
      blue with the stripe down the middle, *Cathedra* or some-
      thing, I thought was too hazy, the blue was too hazy.[41]
LRL   Is that the big blue one, the one that was in the Guggen-
      heim?
DJ   Yes, the one with the big stripe down the middle.
LRL   White stripe?
DJ   Well, it's really a little bluish, maybe. It looks blue, anyway.
LRL   But it's a big painting?
DJ   Yeah.
LRL   That's the Newman that I think probably did me in most.
      I really liked that one, if it's the same one.

DJ   There were a few vertical black and whites, and I didn't like them so well; and some I've seen since I've liked a lot. I don't know if they're the same paintings or not. They seemed a little like stripped-down Mondrians with the stripe moved to one side or the other. And I sort of objected to that composition – what I took to be composition. Sort of like a single panel out of a Mondrian, so the stripes flipped this way or flipped that way. But when I saw a vertical one at the Whitney a few years ago, I didn't really like that at all. So it's hard to know.

      I saw a show of Rothko's pretty early at Janis, in '55, '56, something like that.[42]

LRL   Then the same thing goes for that? Or –

DJ   Yeah, except probably in a way it was a little more influential because it was earlier. I didn't quite understand it. I didn't try to do anything like it, but I knew that it was much stronger than anything I could do or think of – I mean, unique and all those things. So the possibilities, or the – well, the general implication of the thing impressed me. But I wasn't going to go off and do Rothkos or anything. Pollock is really the primary artist, I guess.

LRL   Did you go to Tenth Street much when that started, from '57 on?[43]

DJ   No. I had just one connection with it, in maybe '55 or something.

LRL   It was maybe later, Tenth Street wasn't really going – Tanager I think was '57.[44]

DJ   It was the Camino Gallery. It was '55 or '56. Somehow or other, I met somebody there; I can't remember. And three or four people came up to look at my paintings with the possibility of inviting me into the gallery, which they did. One of them was Leon Smith, and the other – Ruth Abrams I guess was one of them. And I was in a group show there.[45] Then this stupid little gallery uptown offered me a one-man show.[46]

LRL   Panoras?

DJ   Yes.

LRL   I read a review of that.

DJ   Yeah. So I had a one-man show there instead of at Camino, and I don't even remember if Camino wanted to give me a one-man show. At any rate, they did offer membership. And I was in a big, an enormous group show there.

LRL   How did they hear of you?

DJ   I don't know how. I met one single person somehow.

LRL   Were communications in the art world just a lot slower then? I always suppose people now don't know anybody, but it seems almost every studio I go to now – going from, you know, the weirdest kind of connections through which I might hear of somebody – always, eventually, the person turns up to know somebody I know, and the network seems much tighter than maybe it was before.

DJ   I really didn't know anybody.

LRL   I wonder if that was something generic in the early '50s.

DJ   I probably could have been someplace else because I worked by myself there for a long time without much knowledge, except of some of these things by accident – for some reason, seeing Kline's show. Nobody was in the gallery at all, including Egan. An absolutely empty gallery. A pile of drawings, oh, about a foot high was on telephone [book] paper.

LRL   You should have got hold of one of those. You should have sold – probably could have gotten about twenty-five bucks apiece.

DJ   Yes, I should have stolen – no, I think they were about a hundred. I think there was a little sign on them or something. I should have just slipped through and stolen a couple.

LRL   Yeah, it wouldn't have been a bad idea.

DJ   Too honest. I made a big mistake.

LRL   David Diao had some [Hans] Hofmanns that he got – he didn't steal them, but when the whole Hofmann estate was finished at Kootz [Gallery], everything had been listed and taken away and divided up and everything, and then suddenly they came across these four or five drawings that somebody had forgotten.[47] So [Samuel] Kootz just handed them around the gallery. Two or three painters lived on it for a year. [*Laughs*]

What about the magazines? Did you read any magazines?

DJ   Well, *Arts*, yes. I read *Arts* and *ARTnews*, pretty much. I used to buy it in the art store when I worked there, which was late '53. And *Arts* wasn't bad when Belle Krasne had it, and they commissioned Kline and all sorts of people to do covers.[48] It actually had a little life there for a while — two years, that's about the life span of a magazine.

LRL   I guess so. At least in spurts; it can be reincarnated now and then. *Art International* had slightly longer than that, I think. Four years.

DJ   Yes, two or maybe three. [*Laughter*]

LRL   Pre-me. I was the kiss of death on that magazine. [*Laughter*] The minute I got there, the whole thing blew up.

DJ   Yeah, he's [James Fitzsimmons] not — you know, he doesn't —

LRL   He couldn't care less, and he just isn't interested in any of these things.

DJ   He doesn't have any articles, really. It all seems to be money business.

LRL   No, it really isn't; that's the amazing thing. He's much more honest than it sounds. I've had a number of people send him things, and he says, "Oh, don't have any more of your friends send me things, I'm so full of stuff." So then you peer into the magazine to see what's been so marvelous that he wouldn't read other peoples' manuscripts, and it's always the same old show.

DJ   Well, I'd heard that a lot of the articles on European artists were bought articles.

LRL   Really? Because he claims they aren't, and I tend to believe him, just because I don't think he's a liar, whatever else he may be. [*Laughs*] Also, he claims he doesn't have any collection at all, but somebody told me he had a tremendous houseful of paintings that he took in return for favors or something. So that's a lot of baloney.

What about the writing business? When did that start?

DJ In '59.

LRL How in the world did you – you went back to graduate school starting when?

DJ In '58, maybe.[49] I was in a seminar of [Meyer] Schapiro's.[50] It was the American Painting 1940–1950 seminar that everybody else was in.

LRL Barbara was there too?

DJ No, she wasn't in that seminar. She was in other classes, but not in that one. Schapiro said that Tom Hess wanted some reviewers, if anybody would be interested.[51] A couple of us raised our hands; I thought I might need a part-time job, so I raised mine. I was teaching mornings at a school, but it was beginning to look –

LRL What school?

DJ Allen-Stevenson School, a private school. I taught shop and, at one point, world history. One course of world history in the middle of a whole morning of woodshop.

LRL That's great! [*Laughs*] Had you gotten a degree by this time? Did you go through Columbia?

DJ Yeah, I had a bachelor's, but I didn't get the master's. But anyway, the school was getting rid of part-time people, so I thought maybe I had better take what I could just in case.

LRL How long did you write for Hess?

DJ I wrote for three months, I believe, beginning in the fall of '59. It would have been September, October, November. And he seemed to raise so many restrictions and objections that I went to *Arts* to see if they wanted anybody, and when they did, I just sent him a short note saying that I was leaving.

LRL   I can't imagine – was your style the same then? I can't
      imagine *ARTnews* putting up with it at all.

DJ   He didn't really. It wasn't the same, no; it was a little more
      complex.

LRL   And a little more ordinary?

DJ   Ordinary, yeah. It wasn't so highly developed. But he didn't
      like it. He wanted it to be more poetic, and he said I wasn't
      saying anything.

LRL   Yes, the same *Art International* syndrome.

DJ   Yeah, he had all sorts of things. There was one point – I
      had used "focus" or "locus" or some such word in a re-
      view, and he said he didn't want any Latin-derived words.
      So that got so dense I couldn't see how I could manage.

LRL   Jesus, that's quite a prescription. That's everything.

DJ   Yes. I couldn't see how I could get around all those things.
      So that sort of finished it off. Oh, and also because they
      would cut reviews.

LRL   That's why I've never gotten near *ARTnews* – although
      I'm doing something for them for the summer issue, but
      I'm putting a stipulation on it. Fitzsimmons has almost
      never cut anything of mine. Now and then – once, or
      about three times a year, he'll change one word and just
      completely screw up a sentence and completely change
      my meaning. Jo Baer did that thing on [Edward] Kien-
      holz.[52] Did she tell you about all this?

DJ   I saw it. I haven't read it.

LRL   He cut it. He wouldn't send her proofs. He promised to
      send her proofs, and he didn't. She had footnotes twice
      and he cut out one set. And she wrote him mad as hell.
      I don't blame her, because he just didn't warn her. Or,
      he wrote her and said, "The article has been printed and
      I left out one single footnote," something like that. And
      I was mad as hell because I had vouched for him, sort of. I
      said, "If he said he'll send you proofs, he'll send you proofs."
      And he didn't – the bastard. Anyway, he wrote Jo this long,

involved letter about how terrible women writers were, and he said that in all the time he –

DJ Just what Jo wants to hear.

LRL Yes. Exactly. [*Laughter*] And then he sent me a carbon. He said that in all the time he'd been editing, he had never had a complaint about editorial practices from a man, but the three times he'd had it, it was always from a woman, and so on. And that amused me, because I think women are touchier about having things messed with in general.

DJ I was always highly touchy.

LRL Then you were. [*Laughs*] Like Bob Morris was saying the other day – that "Anti Form" article in *Artforum*, he didn't choose the title.[53] I said I didn't know what the title was about, and he said that he didn't choose it, he had left it up to them, and that he wouldn't do that again. And I thought, "Wow! Imagine doing that!" That is something that I would never think of. Of course, *New York* magazine did that to me. They made up a title, but it was that kind of cliché you expect.

DJ You can't allow them to title it. *Arts*, when Francis Kloeppel was the editor dealing with cuts and things – [54]

LRL He's a pretty straight guy.

DJ Yeah. They were always very careful about it. And I would always put up a last-ditch defense; I didn't want Francis to do anything.

LRL It doesn't occur to me that anybody has any right to do anything unless they tell me about it.

DJ Now and then, he was right. But ordinarily he was wrong, by my thinking, in one of various ways. So I'd always fight for what little he did against the things. But they were on the whole pretty good.

  But Hess – one of the first reviews I did[55] was a group show at Tanager Gallery, and there were seven people in it.[56] Sally Hazelet, now Drummond, came down in August to open up the gallery so I could see the group show, which was to be opened in a couple of weeks. And I thought her paintings were among the nicest ones there. So I described them and so forth, the various artists – all of it was just a few lines – and I put her few lines at the end of the review, because I wanted to say just a little more. Well, apparently, they needed space or something. They just clipped her off the whole thing completely. So she wasn't even in the show. And she apparently had come from the country or some damn thing to open the gallery.

LRL   Did you explain it to her?

DJ   No, I never saw her. I don't know her. And I did like them best and so forth, but they just didn't come into the magazine. So I was mad about that right from the beginning.

LRL   That's what I've always heard about *ARTnews*. I don't understand how people can write for them when that's what they do. I mean, Scott Burton said – and Gene Swenson; of course you don't mess with Gene Swenson, but in those days you could mess with him a little more – they say that Hess would completely change the meaning of the thing.[57] Like, you know, he reviewed the [James] Rosenquist show, and he gave it a good review, and Hess would flip things around so that it became a bad review. I don't know how anybody in the world would put up with this. People go right on writing for Hess. It's strange. I don't think it's just the women. I can't believe that it's just the women. [*Laughter*]

DJ   Oh, no.

I didn't want Francis to do anything. He was against all colloquial use and any sort of slightly loose use of language.

LRL   Yeah. Well, Fitzsimmons changed – Nam June Paik had that robot thing that was shitting the stones. So I had said it "shat shiny, white stones," or something like that. Fitzsimmons changed it to "passed."[58]

DJ   That's really awful. [*Laughter*]

LRL   "Passed little white stones." It didn't mean anything anymore.

DJ   That's what Francis Kloeppel would do, you know. Also would want to make it proper. A couple of times he tried to put "Miss" in front of some woman artist's name, and we would have a fight about that. You don't put anything in front of men's names or married women's names, but for some reason you put "Miss" down –

LRL   With married women you're supposed to put "Mrs." I always call women by their last names, but people really think it sounds funny.

DJ   Not anymore.

       I can still go through the reviews and recognize Francis's words, though, because they're so outlandish.

LRL   [*Laughs*] That's funny.

       Well, in '59, you went to graduate school. Why did you suddenly go to graduate school? Were you getting more interested in a kind of intellectual approach to art? Or was it strictly for practical reasons?

DJ   Yeah. After the work for the settlement house, I worked for the PAL [Police Athletic League] for a couple of years, and the whole thing was so miserable.[59] There was so little money in it. It was all so grim. I didn't see any other way out of the thing. Any little job would have been fine, but there weren't any little jobs.

LRL   How come you were never a guard in the museums?

DJ   Oh, I was a guard in the army now and then, and I hated it. [*Laughter*]

LRL   That's right. Weren't you an MP [military police] or something?

DJ   No, I was an engineer. I wouldn't have been an MP. But we didn't have too much – we had some guard duty. And it's torture.

LRL   It's a good way to get an art education.

DJ   I suppose so. Flavin seems to have met everybody he knows at The Museum of Modern Art.

LRL   Yeah, to say nothing of the social contacts. Well, Flavin
       was a monster. I overlapped a couple of months with Fla-
       vin when he was a guard. I remember from the first day
       when I went down there, he clamped on to me and took
       me off and told me which paintings were bad and which
       were good and the whole business. I think it was before
       he met Sonja [Flavin]. I think he did that to all the girls
       who were working there, sort of impressing people. But
       God knows I never would have forgotten his name. I re-
       member he left the room he was supposed to be guard-
       ing, and we walked around and looked at the pictures and
       stuff. I thought it was funny.
           Let's see then; what about sculpture? All this talk is
       about painting and sculpture –
DJ   Sculpture had next to no effect on me. The only time that
       it could be called an influence was in some of the first sort
       of abstract things, maybe '55 or something like that. I liked
       the lateral arrangement in some of David Smith's things.
LRL   The kind of drawing in space things?
DJ   Yeah. And the lateralness of the whole thing – single-plane
       business. It was sort of a little bit of an influence for some
       of the paintings. But it was, you know, fairly brief and
       minor. And I always liked David Smith, but it seemed
       comparatively old-fashioned compared to the paintings.
       It didn't seem like a real – well, like Stuart Davis. I always
       liked Stuart Davis. But at that point, you're not going to
       learn anything from him. Which is what I thought of
       Smith, too. Otherwise, there really wasn't anybody else.
LRL   What about Ad? When did you become aware of the black
       ones – you said '56 or something? Were you ever particu-
       larly aware of him as being a kind of influence?
DJ   No, he's no influence, because I don't remember. But I
       might have learned of him maybe in '58. I don't know.
LRL   I've been going through his papers and things, and it's
       fascinating how he really had been around for so long. It

is interesting how he wasn't included in anything, which was [*inaudible*]; he was in thousands and millions of little group shows and everything.

DJ   He certainly had a raw deal. I like the black paintings. And I admired the whole body of work and the effort, and at the time was really envious of somebody who really had something of his own he could deal with and work with and all that, since I didn't. It really seemed great to have your own problems. But by then the singleness, which is one of the really contemporary things the paintings have, was evident to me. So it was too late to be influenced by that. And I was against the degree of tonality that the paintings have, which I thought was somewhat old – the blackness makes tonality, as well as what's new about it.

LRL   As well as what?

DJ   New factors in it. But also it's a certain tonal quality there, dark tonal characteristics. By the time I really looked at them, I already disliked that sort of thing and had had a lot of trouble getting rid of it. So for that reason, I considered them less new than, oh, say, Newman or Pollock or something. And also, you see, he's a somewhat otherworldly artist in some sense, which I always find strange, and I admire quite a few people who are somewhat like that.

LRL   Like who?

DJ   Well, [Robert] Irwin, I would think. And [Larry] Bell to some extent. Even Flavin to some extent, because it is light and all that. To me, it's not a criticism of them; it has to do with what I can't – what I don't want to do. For me to do it seems excessively mysterious somehow.

LRL   That is a quality that is very much through all of the figures.

DJ   I think it's very interesting, you know. It has a lot of possibilities. By the time you get those three or four people together, it's a fair chunk of things. And I think they're all very good.

LRL   You know, right after we had lunch with Bell after his last business, I went out to Vancouver and saw his new pieces. Have you seen them?

DJ   I saw the big glass mock-ups in his studio, but they weren't coated or anything yet, or colored.

LRL   I like them better than anything I've seen of his before. I've never really been a wholehearted fan of Bell's, but I've been waiting for him to get to something that is just a little more – I don't know – and he's really seemed to do it.

DJ   Especially after this last trip, I think he really has possibilities there. Just generally my whole impression of him is good. He really sounds serious. He really seems to be thinking it out. So I think he's really going to be very good. And I've thought Flavin was first-rate for a long time.

LRL   I've always thought Flavin was first-rate. There's always been something that bothers me, and there's still something that nags me about Flavin. I don't know how much of it I'm mixing up with the constant personal angles I seem to have with Flavin. [*Laughs*] The minute we start speaking, some other things come up, and that's the end of it again. It's ridiculous.

DJ   I remember some objections he had to something.

LRL   To practically everything. But I've committed myself completely as far as Flavin is concerned, and I do think it's one of the best things – there's no question.

DJ   I can't quite give a reason why I wouldn't want to do it or why somehow it's against me – an objective reason. I mean, I can't see any reason why they shouldn't do something like that.

LRL   Well, in some ways, some of your plexiglass things get a slight quality of that, but I know it's not what you're after.

DJ   A little bit, maybe. But at a point, it gets too dematerialized or something for what I would want to do.

LRL   But it also does have something to do with, I don't know, attitude, sensibility, or whatever the word is, but it comes through the work. It isn't just that light is slightly diffused. It's the reasons for choosing a slightly different light.

DJ   Right. It's very much the reasons in back of the whole thing.

LRL   It's fascinating to hear people say that Flavin is a cold, hard, classical artist, because it just seems so appallingly obvious that he isn't. I don't know how much he aims at that at times.

Now, Reinhardt I'm doing a book on – I'm involved in that thing now –[60]

DJ   So that's some of the reason, too, why Reinhardt would not be a direct influence. It's also like that, somewhat.

LRL   Was it at Columbia that you started kind of meeting people?

DJ   To some extent. Actually, I met a lot of people reviewing, of course. Once you start doing that in a regular way – first, you meet people in galleries, and then you meet artists. I did meet some people at Columbia.

LRL   When did you meet Flavin?

DJ   '63, maybe? No, it has to be earlier than that – '62?

LRL   We were seeing a lot of Flavin around '61, right before they were married. We were married around the same time, and we were kind of racing to see who was going to last longer.[61]

DJ   It must have been '62, because I had a show at Green late in '63. I knew Ivan [Karp], of course, from reviewing shows at Castelli.[62] Ivan thought he had the makings of some new small gallery, or he had some people on his hands. Though I wasn't really that eager to show, and I never asked him to do anything; some of the other people had I guess, and some hadn't. So he had a bunch of us get together to make this new gallery. Of course, none of it ever came to anything.

LRL   Who were they?

DJ   There was me, and Flavin, John Anderson, Idelle Weber,

Sheldon Machlin, and Ralph Ortiz. I think that's the whole list.[63]

L R L   Dear God, that really is a motley – it could have been another Green Gallery if the quality had been a little higher. [*Laughter*] You and Flavin were the only ones that had anything in common of that group.

D J   Yes. And then Dan's work seemed interesting when he told me about it. I think he had some photographs and drawings with him or something. So it seemed interesting.

L R L   And he was doing light things by then too – the *icons*.[64]

D J   Boxes, right. And also since I was interested in boxes and three-dimensional things –

L R L   Yeah. And you were doing – I may have gone through this before, but it still isn't clear in my mind – the Panoras show was what, '57?

D J   '56, maybe? It's pretty far back. So those are just semi-abstract cubist paintings of a vague kind.

L R L   And then you didn't show at all in group shows or anything?

D J   No.[65] The Panoras show was sort of because I felt I should do something. You know, it was a long time to – well, it all seemed very hopeless; I mean, no way of making money, and you weren't doing anything that had anything to do with anything but yourself. So it was sort of just a formality to have a show. I didn't think the paintings were all that developed; I didn't expect to stay there or stop there with them. They were all fairly well resolved, though, for what they were.

L R L   Was there any like – there was a review of it, because I saw it.

D J   Yes, the reviews really weren't bad, but it didn't mean anything.[66] I wasn't disappointed or anything, it just didn't mean anything to me. But I became more and more dissatisfied with the paintings; I was really unsatisfied for a long time with all the paintings and didn't really want to show

them. Just about when I began to get things I liked, Dick
[Bellamy] came along, so that worked out very smoothly.[67]
And then when I first started doing three-dimensional
things, it was a lot clearer and better.

LRL   What is this painting over here on the floor?

DJ   It's a failed painting. I never managed to solve it.

LRL   What years was it from about?

DJ   '60, maybe, I don't know — '59, '60, probably. I couldn't make
anything out of it. I kept painting things in and out.

LRL   The stripes were supposed to be all one color?

DJ   Yeah, I tried it all sorts of ways. So I'm going to throw it
out. That painting, the red one back there with the gray
stripes, I like pretty much [see image 15]. It's in the rear. Have
you seen it?

[*Break in recording*]

DJ   I'm very much in favor of being honest about the matter of influence and all that. I don't see any reason why it
should be obscured or falsified or anything.

LRL   It's ridiculous to make one be ashamed of having been
influenced. I mean, you'd just stay in a void forever if you
weren't.

DJ   That's what I was in before. So —

LRL   What, a void? [*Laughs*]

DJ   All that time on Twenty-Seventh Street.

LRL   An uninfluenced void?

DJ   Yeah. I don't like to be given influences that didn't exist, though, like [Anthony] Caro or Smith — I mean Tony
Smith —

LRL   Oh, Tony Smith couldn't possibly be an influence on
anybody.

DJ   It's incredible. It's impossible. Or Anne Truitt, as [Clem-
ent] Greenberg — did you read that thing in *Vogue*?[68]

LRL   No, no. Do you have that? I'd love to borrow it; I should

get hold of that. I had a big fight with him right after
that –

DJ   Buy it, because I want to write an answer in *Artforum*, because it's really impossible. It's a falsification.

LRL   Yeah, well, the Anne Truitt thing, the whole business – in
the LA catalogue, it was dated wrong, her show.[69] Was it a
year? He pre-dated it a year.

DJ   Yeah. I think it's corrected; it's right in this issue [of *Vogue*].

LRL   And I picked it up – I told him that, and he was furious
that anybody had noticed it, apparently. I don't know –
you couldn't make out whether he had done it on purpose
or not.

DJ   I was strongly suspicious of that. I noticed that it was
wrong because I reviewed the show which he mentions
in the *Vogue* article.

LRL   I remember seeing it because I was interested in Ad by
then. Rita Reinhardt was telling me that Anne Truitt came
to Ad like a student, like an admirer, to talk to him and to
ask him how he mixed his colors and everything long before that show, and she was perfectly honest about it, that
that was a tremendous influence. But of course Greenberg won't mention Ad. He has awful things to say about
him now.

DJ   Yeah, it came out very funny. He said in the article they
were influenced by Newman. Well, I thought they were
wrapped-around Reinhardts, which I said in my review.[70]
So it was so funny when it came out as influenced by
Newman!

LRL   It's that whole Newman-Reinhardt business going again.
Greenberg says Ad was a vicious schmuck and – you know,
incredibly bad words to say for a man who was so totally
unmalicious and such a nice guy.

DJ   That whole – Barney's bite there is pretty bad. It's all sad.
And also Reinhardt apparently cordially hated Pollock.
The whole thing is very sad.

LRL Reinhardt hated Pollock?

DJ Yeah, he said something to me one time really bitter against Pollock. So it's grim all around.

LRL That's funny, because I never got that. We talked a lot about Pollock; he always seemed pretty – you know, like, "Well, I wasn't his type, but he was okay."

    Did the reviewing help the writing? Did it help you crystallize your own ideas at all? Or was it just separate from it?

DJ I think it was primarily separate. I did see a lot of work, which helps.

LRL I should think having it put down why such and such isn't good would, in a way, sharpen your idea of where you were headed.

DJ No, not really. I don't tend to learn that way.

LRL Just by seeing?

DJ No, I mean I don't learn any more by writing it than I do by thinking of it without writing it. It's just harder work.

LRL You're never going to write again?

DJ I'm pretty fed up with *Artforum* and Greenberg and [Michael] Fried and all that, so I may write –

LRL You notice my absence from *Artforum* in the last year. I'm staying out of it.

DJ I think it's really gone over the hill. So I may write a denunciatory letter to the editor.

LRL Oh, don't start writing letters to the editor. [*Laughs*]

DJ No, just one. It sort of piled up all around too much – really since Greenberg put that review in there[71] and mentioned me in the *Vogue* thing. It's so bad you can't really let it go.

LRL I have to read the *Vogue* thing, but it was pretty much the same thing as he did in the other –

DJ He said, "One of the leading minimal sculptors Donald Judd didn't even recognize the value of Truitt's work," or some such thing – "he wrote an uncomprehending review."[72] It's not uncomprehending. I said it's junk. I said it looks like serious art, and it isn't. It's just wrap-around Reinhardts.

LRL It's funny to see him – like, that's such a misstep, such a stupidity for him to bank on Anne Truitt. I mean, of *all* things…

DJ It says directly that that show preceded any three-dimensional thing that I was doing, or anybody else.[73] Which is not true. I mean, you've got shows at the Green Gallery that year, one of which did precede that show.[74] Obviously the work was being done before that. It had to be.

LRL When I write my article on you, I'll have a good chance to get my two cents' worth in about that part.

DJ I'm very sour about the whole thing.

LRL It's amusing to me. I told him when I had this argument with him that he hadn't written anything since 1962 that showed that he even had any idea or understood what was happening. I said, "You're just too far out of it to tell." And he said, "Well, Anne Truitt," mumble mumble. And I said, "Well, that's the greatest indication, there it is."

What's this thing? Is that one of the [Fred] Sandbacks?

DJ Yes.

LRL Or is it just some wire?

DJ No, it's a Sandback.

LRL That's my first Sandback. I've been hearing about it.

DJ That's one in the flesh.

LRL Gee, that's pretty dematerialized.

DJ Yeah, that would be a case too. I really couldn't do anything that – also [James] Turrell probably, if I could ever get hold of one and just look at it –

LRL I have a feeling just from looking at that article that I've seen one. I mean, I can picture very carefully – imagine a projected thing, you know, with one side cut off or whatever it is.

Let me see, one of these notes says "Run through anthropomorphic bit again." [*Laughter*]

D J   Oh, that's a long time ago, and I'm weary of it. It goes as far back as when I quit painting and drawing figures and landscapes, you know, when I first became what I thought was abstract, which wasn't really very abstract — in that you can't sit and draw something out there as if some-how you're putting it down on paper. Which was a very live, hard problem at the time. I used to go down and try to draw things off the dock at Twenty-Seventh Street — drawing, say, the limb of a tree on a piece of paper as if there's something in the tree that you're putting down on the piece of paper. And it became pretty obvious after a while that the thing was only a tree and that the gap be-tween the tree and what I had on the paper just was a lot of baloney.

L R L   That's the old Greek thing. This is not a pipe.

D J   It was really pretty horrible. I mean, I was very bothered by it. But, see, once you quit believing that you can see something in a tree and get it down, that it's really in the tree, then that's it. It took a long time to get rid of all the qualities that you think you've got to get rid of. I evidently didn't recognize a lot of it at first. At least I saw that I re-ally couldn't go ahead and just plain draw trees and things.

L R L   I have the same feeling about writing today and theater and everything — the whole part of writing fiction, what have you, that I'm not really involved with. It's like that ba-sic thing is wrong with it, and it's just hopeless. That whole business can't be done anymore, character, plot, and ev-erything. There's nothing left but words — but then, what do you have? Because words are so damn loaded. There seems to be no way out of it.

D J   Well, I didn't know what else I could do, really. I couldn't believe that, and I didn't know what else you could do.

L R L   It must have been a big decision to go off the wall when you started the three-dimensional things. Or did that just seem natural?

DJ   It seemed very dangerous and unlike me. It sort of scared me.

LRL But you didn't feel you were making sculpture even then? I mean, it didn't occur to you that that would be –

DJ   No, I knew it wasn't sculpture. I just knew it really didn't make sense to call it sculpture then.

LRL Let's see – had you seen Stella's notched things and so on? Was Stella a kind of an influence? Certainly, people like Sol – Sol admits –

DJ   A little bit, except it was really – the *Black Paintings* were sort of a confirmation of an idea I already had. One thing I was always against was geometric art; I didn't want to really get into that, because I tied it up with Mondrian and a general purist quality, which I didn't want. So you had the problem of geometric art that had other qualities, not necessarily pure. So I had some of that idea. When I saw Frank's, they certainly were not purist. You see, it sort of confirmed that line of thinking. And by the *Aluminum Paintings*, I was already doing three-dimensional paintings or something, I think, by the time that show occurred; I'll have to check the date.[75]

[*Break in recording*]

DJ   When were the *Black Paintings* shown?

LRL The *Black Paintings* were shown in November '59, I think.[76]

DJ   Well, I think by the *Aluminum Paintings*, I already had some reliefs and some of the first three-dimensional things.

LRL Yes, the *Aluminum Paintings* must have been shown in '60, '61 – '61, I guess.

DJ   Anyway, I was so fed up with it that intermediate stuff like that didn't seem logical.

LRL You were radically fed up. [*Laughs*]

DJ   Yeah, I didn't want to fool around with sort of an alteration of a shape or something. And also, one main thing I disliked was the thing being parallel and back against the wall. Frank's still are, of course – his paintings. So it just sort of carried through a couple of those reliefs and beyond rather quickly. Or actually, the ones right on the floor [image 28] are almost simultaneous with the reliefs [see images 12, 13].

LRL   How about Bob Morris? Was he around then? Did you know Frank? You knew Barbara at Columbia, sort of.

DJ   Yes, a little bit. I didn't know Frank for a while.

LRL   Was Frank really all that – I don't really know him. I've always been kind of curious as to how much – I remember about '63, '64 people constantly quoting him and talking about things he'd said and everything, and it seemed like his ideas were very powerful, or ideas were being attributed to him that were powerful at the time. Did he do a lot of talking that would have been influential? It must have been earlier than that; it must have been '62 or something. I don't know who I'm thinking of that told me this, but I had the impression at the time that Frank was kind of an intellectual genius hiding out up there and talking to his friends and sending his ideas out through people.

DJ   He probably was, but I didn't really, somehow, get any of those ideas. I don't remember receiving any.

LRL   There was a very special kind of atmosphere going on, and he seemed very influential. I remember taking Maurice Tuchman around the studios and telling him that I thought Frank was probably the influence, as much as anything, on these people, because that was whose name I was hearing mentioned.[77]

DJ   Well, I knew his work was influential. I only knew the work, and that's what I thought about. I don't remember any ideas all that clear of Frank's.

LRL   I wonder if that was just some myth that I thought up. I bet I know one person I got it from: it was Flavin, because I was seeing –

DJ   His work was very influential, certainly.

LRL   Yeah, the work certainly was, if not the influence on, at least the precedent for a lot of things that went on afterward. But I think it was Flavin that I got that impression from.

DJ   I don't think Dan liked him as much as I did for a while.

LRL   I don't think he liked the work so much as that was where I got the impression of you talking to Frank.

DJ   I don't know how much – I didn't talk all that seriously to Frank.

LRL   So it really was more the work. Probably it was more the work, and the ideas that it brought up, as you say, confirmed or – I guess I was thinking partly of Sol. Sol and Flavin were the two people I knew before they started doing this kind of work, so I talked to them a lot during the sort of transition. It must have been the two of them somehow that I got that impression from. What about Morris? From '59 to '61 is the period when all this was germinating and before anybody really had shown.

DJ   I didn't know him. I think the first piece I ever saw was *Slab*, in some group show at Green, about the same time I was – maybe it was the same show I was in or something, I don't know. The one show in early '63, I know he had the piece he calls *Column* in it.[78]

LRL   A gray column, yeah. The dark gray stone?

DJ   The same gray. *Slab* I was sort of curious about. I wasn't crazy about it; I was a little interested in it. *Column* I disliked. I remember Lucas [Samaras] and I kept shoving it around the room so as to get it out of the way of everything else. [*Laughter*]

LRL   That's right; Lucas was at Columbia then too.

       Did you go to Hansa around that time?[79]

DJ   No, I never did. I remember I was assigned once to it by *Arts* or *ARTnews* but never found it, and that was my last chance to ever see it, I guess. I never did see it.

LRL   I only went once or twice, and I don't remember having
      gone — I remember shows that were there, but I don't re-
      member anything particularly about the gallery or any-
      thing. Now it's become this myth, and I can't remember
      the great experience of walking in and walking around.
          What about Rauschenberg? And what about [Jasper]
      Johns, especially, who seems to be —
DJ   Rauschenberg, of course, was never an influence.
LRL   No, I don't mean influence so much as what —
DJ   When I was at Columbia, Jasper was just showing a paint-
      ing or something at the Jewish Museum. Schapiro had got
      it in. I guess that was sort of a break for him or something.
      Some group show.
LRL   *The New Abstraction* — was it that late?[80]
DJ   Maybe. I don't know. No, no, it was before that. It would
      be in '59, I guess.
LRL   I don't think I'd ever been to the Jewish Museum that early.
DJ   I sort of like the quality of Jasper's paintings. There's a cer-
      tain ironic quality or something.
LRL   Actually, the quality of his flags is slightly like the striped
      thing that you have back there [see image 15]. The surface —
DJ   There's a certain form I like — the one upstairs with the
      copper is a circle [image 29], which … but then [Kenneth]
      Noland was doing circles, too.
LRL   I don't think you can really track a circle down. [*Laughs*]
DJ   It's a little hard. And those paintings are rough because I
      wanted to make this surface simply a surface.
LRL   What do you mean? You mean it's a way of getting away
      from the illusionism of —
DJ   Yeah; if you painted flat and smooth, then it certainly really
      looks spatial. So I made it rough so that you could make
      a more definite surface. And the roughness, especially in
      that painting back there, is somewhat like Jasper's. But I
      don't know if it comes from Jasper or not. I can't remem-
      ber. I'm not inclined to think it does.

I also liked Yves Klein's paintings, which were shown at Castelli pretty early.[81] And they also have a rough surface. There's more of a connection with Yves Klein. Also, I consider all that brushwork in Jasper very old-fashioned. So, you know, that was one of these things, like the tonality in Reinhardt. I liked the work, but that was a factor that negated an influence.

LRL   What do you think about – well, I can imagine what you think about it, so I'll just ask it as a lead-in question: Fried's theater business?[82] I remember the first review I wrote on you – do you remember, I said they looked like Greek podiums?[83] Something for Greek –

DJ   Fortunately, I don't remember that.

LRL   [*Laughs*] I shouldn't bring it up. It's the first review I'd ever written.

DJ   Let it die. I think Fried's article is stupid. When it first came out in the fall, I glanced through it and saw that it was comparing me and Morris and Tony Smith back and forth and that there was something about theater, and I didn't read it. And after about five or six months, people kept asking me what I thought of it. So I read it. It's just as stupid as I thought it was when I didn't read it.

LRL   It's pretty incredible.

DJ   The theater – that's just baloney. And the literal –

LRL   And there again, it's this whole thing where they just can't see, where there's something completely blocked –

DJ   You know, that's ridiculous, as to why it's any more theater than anything is.

LRL   Than any other kind of sculpture. Like, Tony Smith, when he dims the lights, is, granted, getting into some kind of thing –

DJ   That's just junk to me. I'm not sympathetic.

LRL   – but then so is Irwin. And everybody lights their own shows, so in that sense, everybody's lighting is theatrical.

DJ   Unfortunately, I didn't light mine at the Whitney.[84]

LRL   Yeah. [*Laughs*] That's the second plug we've gotten in against that lighting on this tape.

DJ   And "literal" – it just comes out of a definition he's got for painting and sculpture, that there are two polarities. So you can't take that seriously; if you take it seriously, you have to accept his definition, which seems to me conservative and stupid. But I was really appalled that he would quote Tony Smith and then use it against me or Morris. I mean, what Smith says is – and I think Morris is pretty alien too, so I don't really want to be compared with those people –

LRL   Comparing you and Morris has become something that – at the beginning, everybody, including me, including Barbara, everyone just lumped it all together, you know, especially you and Morris, because you were shown together, you were at the same gallery and at the same time, and all this business. And then it became important to me, anyway, to start splitting you up, so I did a lot of – I kept saying, "Judd is this and Morris is this." I remember doing it, I think, two or three times, trying to pin down the differences. Now I guess it's obvious enough, especially after the felt show.[85]

DJ   Well, the whole Dada business which he does have – did have, when I first saw work of his, a fair amount of work, which was at the Gordon on Fifth Avenue.[86]

LRL   That's right. That was – what was that show? I didn't see it.

DJ   Oh, it was the worst, most crowded show with four Japanese [artists] and Morris.

LRL   Four Japanese and Morris. [*Laughs*] I remember getting the notice for it. I have a clear memory of the whole Gordon thing. And I never made it.

DJ   He had the box with the sound of its own making and a couple of other sort of Dada things in there, homespun Dada. As well as the big, simple shapes. The cloud in it, I think, and the column, and a couple more, one or two more.

LRL   You never did a round piece? That was Morris, *Wheels*?[87]

DJ   Yeah.

LRL   I had a big argument with somebody who should have known better, who said to me the other night – and I can't think who it was; it was a couple of months ago, and I can't think who – but he said that was yours. And I said no, it couldn't have been yours. I mean, even if I had never seen the piece, it couldn't be yours.

DJ   No. I dislike that piece a lot.

LRL   How has the teaching been working out?

DJ   I'm not doing any teaching.

LRL   Weren't you at Yale this year?[88]

DJ   Well, yes, that seminar one day a week for six weeks.

LRL   Oh, just for six weeks.

DJ   Yeah. I only teach in case of future poverty.

LRL   It's creeping up on me.

      Let's see… I can't make head or tail out of these notes of mine, I don't know where my head was. [*Reads from notes*] "Even reliefs not frontal entirely," "What about clear plastics?," "Look up at an angle business."

DJ   Well, you knew from the side of the reliefs their shape.

LRL   I guess it was something about the difference in the aesthetic between the relief and the sculpture. The relief is a half-baked sculpture, because it is only half a shape instead of a whole shape –

DJ   Yeah, I thought it was rather half-baked. The reliefs – you know, there are two ways out of painting: one is just directly putting things on the floor in three dimensions, and then there's the reliefs. And after maybe a year or so, the reliefs seemed insufficiently different from the paintings, so I thought at one point there really wasn't going to be anything I could do on the wall – about the time of the Green Gallery show, one-man show, late '63. By then I was already tired of the reliefs and didn't intend to do anymore. But there's a little piece there I had made which belongs

to Hanford Yang and was in the Whitney show, and I sort
of thought about that, and it seemed that if it were narrow like that and long, and at least projected as much as
it is wide, you'd get around the effect of something being
splayed out against the wall [image 30] —

LRL   That's what my next question was.

DJ   — which I didn't want. Then also, maybe a little bit later,
not long — it was a little while after the show, I guess,
maybe that winter — it occurred to me that it projected
more than it was wide, or deep, or however you want to
consider it, up and down. It at least projected enough
past a certain point that it wouldn't seem spread out like
that, and it wouldn't have the quality of a relief. So there
really seemed to be none of that flattened quality left to
these things.

LRL   Yeah. Of course, I guess the fact that one side is up against
the wall — I mean, one side of everything is up against the
floor, or up against something, unless there was a hidden
side, or you were to hang the painting in the air…

DJ   Well, it's the difference between when you put the book
against the wall [*gestures with book*] and half of it is against
the wall, but if you put it this way, the thing is coming up. It
seems much stronger. You have more possibilities. But the
degree of projection is very important. So when that occurred to me and I started thinking about it, then it seemed
to have a lot of possibilities. But really, at one point there,
it looked like that was it as far as walls were concerned.

    I can't wait until we leave.

LRL   I'm never going to get out of here [New York] because
I had taken on all this stuff before I knew I had the Guggenheim; I had taken on jobs enough so that I could get
through the summer, and now I have to do them all.[89] And
I want to get them over with before the summer, so I'm
just rushing furiously.

    Let's see; I've never been altogether clear on the way

you use "specific" and "general," which is – have a drink.
[*Laughs*]

DJ   That's a little hard. Incidentally, and to get it down, that
      "Specific Objects" article, despite what people think, was
      not meant to be a doctrinaire, dogmatic, or definitive, or
      anything article.[90]

LRL   It wasn't? The tone of it wasn't doctrinaire and definitive.

DJ   I didn't think so, but people keep using it that way. The
      magazine wanted something on what they call a big bunch
      of three-dimensional art that's being done, and so they
      asked me to do it, since they knew I was doing some-
      thing like that. And it was just really meant to report all of
      that stuff, and all of it was very diverse and not capable of
      coming under any heading but an extremely general one.
      And "Specific Objects," which is my title, and I liked, isn't
      meant to be about my work; it's just meant to be about
      any of that kind of thing that isn't painting or sculpture. I
      liked the article a lot.

LRL   Yes, it's a good article. A lot of people have heard you say
      things that you've never written, that you've said after you
      stopped writing, pretty much, which are kind of doc-
      trinaire, so that they think they're pinning – since they
      haven't got it down in print to quote you – they're pin-
      ning down all those assumptions, or just even the way you
      sound when you say things. They're pinning it all back
      into that article or something.

DJ   I don't like doctrinaire.

LRL   Yes, that's because it's kind of an unpleasant word. [*Laughs*]

DJ   I'm in favor of being certain, or definite, or whatever, but
      I think it's important as to whether it's about your own
      work or someone else's. And I think I have a right to be
      as definite about my own as I want to be.

LRL   Yeah, well, it's always interpreted as being about every-
      body else's.

DJ   But I don't like things to be carried over without qualification to other people's work, which people love to do all the time. Or to be used without any distinction as to whether you were saying it about your own work or somebody else's.

LRL   You have more trouble with that because of the critic thing. I mean, you've obviously had more to say about other artists than any other artist has because nobody else has had to review, so it's —

DJ   It's getting to be a long time ago now, though.

LRL   Yeah, but people remember. [*Laughs*]

DJ   I don't mind saying that I think somebody's work is lousy or mediocre or something if I think so.

LRL   Yeah, exactly. But that article made it so clear — like, you talked about Oldenburg, that you couldn't possibly —

DJ   Yeah, that's not talking about my work.

LRL   [Lee] Bontecou and the people you had in that article couldn't possibly be demanding that they do what you do, because it's —

DJ   I don't want that, anyway.

LRL   Oh, they did that with me. I wrote a bunch of reviews — it was just a "New York Letter." I called it "New York Letter: Rejective Art."[91] [*Laughs*] That's when I started using that word.

DJ   I'm not in favor of that word, either.

LRL   I'm in favor of it more than any other, but I'm not in favor of any words anymore. But anyway, Fitzsimmons left off the "New York Letter," and it was picked up as an article and made into my major thing I'd ever written about the whole business. So when people want to read what I said about that, the whole business, they go to that article, and it's just a bunch of reviews. It was the Finch [College Museum of Art] show, and Sol's show, and it was never intended to be any kind of ultimatum, or even any completed thoughts on anything. It's the old image business.

DJ   I didn't like Morris's article in *Artforum*[92] because I don't know who he's talking about, whether it's himself, or whether it's my work, which I think sometimes –

LRL   [*Inaudible*]

DJ   Well, his earlier articles say that too. At one point he goes on about reliefs, and I don't know what he's talking about.

LRL   That kind of has to be you. I don't know what else it could be.

DJ   Whether he's cutting his throat about all those old lead reliefs he did, or whether it's me, or the business about being on the wall…But if he's going to talk about me on the wall, I wish he'd mention me and make it clear who he's talking about.

LRL   Yeah. Well, this last article, I thought, was very different from the others, because this last one was the first one that I thought could have been written by – I could have written it, or it could have been written by a critic; it sounded like a critic's writing somehow, which his other things haven't. Only some of them might sound like a historian's writing. The "Notes on Sculpture" sounded much more clean and hard and very much his identity.[93] They are maybe making the same mistake people do about you, but I read them as being about his sculpture, period – you know, to hell with what he thinks sculpture should be. I'd read them –

DJ   I think it should be written about what he thinks his work should be.

LRL   Yes, but this antiform thing –

DJ   I don't say people shouldn't paint gray sculpture [*laughter*]; after all, I can have colored sculpture if I want. To hell with Bob Morris. Well, this one seemed muddy, certainly.

LRL   But I remember when we were – I should have brought that article, the interview thing that Bruce Glaser did, and then we did the section up here, getting into something about generalizing that I'm too foggy to pin down now.[94] I wanted you to say more. That's where this note came from.

D J   It's a long story. I know I read it. That's important, because one of my problems for a long time was that I didn't seem to know enough about anything or believe enough to make such art as people made.

L R L   Yeah. That's amazing. [*Laughs*] I like that statement.

D J   You know, they're making all this grand art, and I really couldn't make such grand stuff as that. So it was really very much a problem of belief in what you knew or something. So after a while, it occurred to me that maybe they believed too much. They really didn't know any more about what they were talking about – except they thought they did – than I did.

L R L   Mmm. Did you read Ad's writings around that time? Because I think Ad's writings really do get a lot of that down.

D J   Yeah, maybe – I don't know if I read them that early.

L R L   They're worded so differently from anything you could put down.

D J   One thing about Reinhardt's things is that right away you realize that it is dogma all right, but it's obviously his dogma, which is a little more palatable than Morris's crisscrossing.

L R L   Yes. Well, Morris's pseudo-scholarly thing – Ad was lucky that he had a style that –

D J   By the time you got through twelve rules for the new academy or whatever it is, it's a one-man academy, you know very well. So that's okay.

L R L   Yeah. It's the "not with them guys" joke.[95]

D J   It made Ad a little hard on a couple of panels; one panel, I was on with him. In conversations, public conversations – he was okay in private – he was not at all –

L R L   I never really heard him in public except for a couple of lectures that he gave at the Jewish Museum, which I must say he handled very well. But in a symposium, he'd be bound to be up against it – I've heard transcripts and so on.

DJ   I was on a symposium with him up at Yale. Oldenburg
     was on it. Fairfield Porter was the moderator.[96]

LRL Well, at least they realized there should be a moderator.
     [*Laughter*] The most moderate moderator probably that
     ever existed.

DJ   But Ad only went through his lists, and I really wanted to
     talk to him. I don't know really how to handle panels or
     what to do anyway, so I didn't do very well at all. But I re-
     ally wanted him to try to talk to me.

LRL It was very difficult to ever get him to, even in private I
     think. Did you know him privately?

DJ   Oldenburg did well, but he did it by himself. He talked
     about his work and was very nice. We weren't talking
     to one another, certainly. And I wish that would have
     happened.
         I didn't especially know him [Reinhardt], but actually,
     we met several times on street corners around here [53
     East Nineteenth Street], because he lived somewhere in
     the neighborhood. He'd be nice to talk to on a street cor-
     ner or at a party; he was quite responsive then.

LRL Oh, he was a hell of a lot of fun to talk to, but it was very,
     very difficult to pin him down on any kind of ideas. He
     was very bright, but everything was tremendously indi-
     rect. You'd ask a question, and he'd come back to it three
     hours later in some funny little glancing way, and if you
     didn't catch it – I always wondered how much I missed.

DJ   Schapiro, in this seminar, invited Reinhardt up one time
     and Newman up one time. I was sick at the time New-
     man was there.

LRL Not together?

DJ   No, no, not together.

LRL That's something I would like to have seen.

DJ   So I missed Barney's, which was just too bad. I was there
     when Reinhardt was there. In the first place, everybody
     was assigned an artist's work, and I don't think anybody

was assigned Reinhardt's work, which was funny. But they started asking about Kline and all these people, and I think he really got sore about it. He said almost nothing during the whole two hours. It was very awkward. Schapiro was trying to fill in while Ad was just sulking.

LRL Well, Ad probably knew that there was the Newman thing, too — that they'd had Newman.

DJ Well, the students didn't care about him or his work. They wanted to know about the New York School.

LRL Ad was very, very sensitive about not being included in the New York School. All his friends were in it. And even though he didn't want "to go with them guys," he wanted very, very badly to be in the *New American Painting* show.[97] And I think that was one of the great blows.

DJ I thought he was right, but he sure didn't say anything. So I thought thereafter, until I really met him and talked to him, that he never talked. [*Laughter*]

LRL Oh, no; far from it.

Well, what went on at the symposium?

DJ It was pretty inconclusive.

LRL What was the subject supposed to be?

DJ God knows. If there was one, I don't know.

LRL The millions of fascinating panels that have gone on, fascinating only in terms of juxtaposition of personalities — that's my picture of panels. It's a performance thing completely. I don't think anything ever gets said on panels.

DJ Maybe art, or non-art, or some such thing.

LRL Fairfield Porter was there for art. [*Laughs*]

DJ I had nothing to say about non-art much.

LRL I've finally gotten out of that business too. It's maddening, when you write, to find all your sins popping up at you all the time. I change my mind constantly about how to say things, and yet there's always that backlog and never any way of getting rid of your mistakes.

Back to the "specific and general" thing. What makes

any kind of object – an Oldenburg, or yours, or anything –
any more specific than any other? Is it the wholeness?

DJ   It's not a case of being objects or not. It's a case of the
meaning of the work, or the credibility of the work. And I
think it's probably always going to be true that work prior
to someone's is perhaps going to seem to be too general,
or too incredible, or something. There's a quality in Barney's work – he's still doing it and it's not long gone, even
at the earliest, but it's obviously of another generation and
so forth. There's a quality in there that you can't quite believe. He talks about such things as sublime and awesome
and so forth.

LRL   But he's the only one that really does do that. Nobody else
ever did.

DJ   Well, I don't know; doesn't Rothko?

LRL   Rothko never has. Rothko is very down-to-earth. Rothko
is very close to Ad in the things he's written and said, oddly
enough, now and then. In 1943, he did a statement with
[Adolph] Gottlieb that was all about myth and so on,[98] but
since then his statements have been very clear and good,
and he says he mistrusts people who talk about their art
in terms of things like sublime.

DJ   That's hard for me to take, too. Except I think Barney is
a more down-to-earth painter than Rothko. But you see,
that's a kind of generalizing that I can't accept. What the
hell's sublime? Where is it?

LRL   That's what I'm trying to pin Greenberg down on in these
arguments. Like, what do you mean by "quality"?

DJ   The only sublime thing I know of is me. [*Laughter*] Sort of
like Cassius Clay. That's it. It's sure not out there anywhere.

LRL   But that's one way something can be general – just like being before you and being incredible. But what about things
that are like yours? What makes Anne Truitt bad? No, not
Anne Truitt; take somebody whose work you kind of respect, but you think is general as opposed to specific.

DJ   I think there's less of it now among people more or less
      my age. Flavin is a very different case. But in a way, it's not
      general in the way that prior art seems.

LRL   Do you mean by "general" or "generalized" that it can be
      read in a lot of different ways?

DJ   Yeah. Claiming too much about things in general.

LRL   Whether it claims or not, though, isn't it partly a matter
      of how much evocation is there for the viewer to hang
      on to?

DJ   Partly, yeah. It suggests too much or seems to be saying
      too much about everything. Which you can't believe. If
      somebody is saying the world is sublime, I can't really be-
      lieve that he knows any more about it than I do. It's okay
      for Barney; he's a great painter, and he's older. But some-
      body tries it now it —

LRL   But then you get somebody like Oldenburg; Oldenburg
      evokes all kinds of things.

DJ   I don't think Oldenburg is what I would call anthropo-
      morphic, in the usual sense.[99]

LRL   Really? Why? Because I think Oldenburg is one of the
      most anthropomorphic artists, and I don't think that's a
      bad thing, particularly. I know what you mean by "anthro-
      pomorphic," in that the David Smith things look like —

DJ   Yes, but that kind of anthropomorphism is within a cer-
      tain range where you believe the anthropomorphism.

LRL   You believe it as an image —

DJ   David Smith is seeing it out there, and it's in the work.
      He's feeling it out there, and it's in the work, and it's be-
      yond him. Oldenburg's is so far over the hill that it's only
      Oldenburg, you see, in which case it's sort of turned full
      circle and isn't really anthropomorphic in the old sense.

LRL   Well, I think what the Oldenburgs produce are abstract
      suggestions, which is the curious thing about it. A New-
      man produces figurative suggestions – not figurative,
      representational suggestions; what he evokes is, like, you

know, the sky: the great big thing. And yet Oldenburg, who is making real-life, ordinary objects – complete figuration or whatever – all the evocation from those things is abstract. They're things that you can't pin down quite – sensuous reactions, I think, kind of visceral and all that business. It's not like being in love to look at an Oldenburg or anything. I mean, you can't find –

DJ   They're not really about the objects.

LRL   They are about the way they're made, aren't they?

DJ   You take an older painting of an object – I'm trying to think of an example – well, I don't know, [Chaim] Soutine and *The Chicken*: it seems to have something to do with the chicken. But it's obviously what Oldenburg feels *about* the chicken. There's no question about that.

LRL   You mean what Soutine feels – ?

DJ   No. With Soutine, it might possibly have something to do with the chicken. [*Laughs*]

LRL   Oh, yes, I see what you mean.

DJ   He's reading into the chicken. With Oldenburg, it's Oldenburg's interest in these things. So there's really nothing about the ice-cream cone as an ice-cream cone.

LRL   I don't know how you really split that. I can vaguely sense what you're talking about, but I don't think that it makes any sense as far as –

DJ   But look, you feel something about a certain object. It's obvious.

LRL   Oldenburg obviously feels good about the fact that an ice-cream cone can melt and is a fluid that's solid and things like that.

DJ   Look, yeah, you know you feel all these things about what you see and deal with –

LRL   But it wouldn't make any difference to him if it tasted sweet, I suppose?

DJ   No, I don't quite mean that.

LRL   In other words, it isn't that you buy your kid an ice-cream cone that Oldenburg is dealing with? Like, Soutine might be saying, "Bring in the chicken, Sandra."

DJ   No, more than that with Soutine, especially earlier work. It's even more intrinsic to the object with the earlier work.

LRL   You mean the burlap and the newspaper – *papier-mâché* –

DJ   What they feel about things when they're looking at them.

LRL   Oh, earlier Soutine works?

DJ   Yeah, well, earlier art in general. You look at all the things you look at or deal with, and you know you have feelings about them; it's pretty obvious. But the fact is that they have no feeling or meaning or anything in themselves.

LRL   They're absorbent, in other words, instead of reflective?

DJ   Well, after all, there's just nothing there, really, but whatever they are. So ordinarily, you go around, and it feels like so-and-so, or this room feels like something to me. But I know that somebody can walk in here and the room could feel like nothing, or as it is, it's factual, it's just what it is, and that's all. So now Oldenburg, instead of walking into the room, say, and putting down his feelings about it as if those feelings were in the room, deals with his feelings as his feelings, which become with him a much more extravagant, gross, bigger thing than ordinary description. If he did that as traditional descriptive art, it wouldn't be convincing, because nobody would believe that objects are that wild. So it's gone so far that it really isn't anthropomorphic in the old sense. Which I think is very nice. It's an interesting thing.

LRL   But when you use the word "anthropomorphic," you have to be dealing with man.

DJ   But anthropomorphic to me is sort of the whole philosophical credible context of traditional art.

LRL   Well, see, that's never been really clear to me. I always thought you were using it in a narrower sense. Does the word really mean all of that?

DJ   I think so. I mean, the whole European tradition is involved in an anthropomorphic kind of art, because always it's —

LRL Well, is Mondrian?

DJ A little bit. I mean —

LRL His writings are. His writings on plasticism and neoplasticism and whatever the —

DJ Yes, but a lot less so. I mean, this changes a lot according to the period. It's obviously in the writings where he's talking about the sky and all that.

LRL No, but when I was thinking about anthropomorphism — an-thro-po-*morph*-ism — I don't say the word as often as you do —

DJ I never say it. I haven't thought about it in years.

LRL Almost a year ago, you were in a symposium, having to stand up against it again.

DJ That's because people bring it up. I haven't thought about it since I quit making curved lines in those paintings. I guess that was sort of the last gasp.

LRL I think it's partly because it's just such a funny word to come up that people hitch on to it. The thing about words is that it's greatly underestimated how words are thrown around. I mean, that's why I'm coming to you with this "specific and general" thing. There are maybe fifty words a year, or twenty — ten words a year that anybody really thinks about.

DJ Yeah, it's really a joke.

LRL You can make a little list of the ten words a year. And you get really preoccupied with things like titles. I swear to God, I'll never title anything again. Like *Eccentric Abstraction* — I'll never![100] I was so very naive about that. I thought I was titling a show; I had no idea I was naming a fucking movement or something. Now I would like to call everything just "Things I like now" or "Something I think I like now."

DJ It's really because you have mixed — you have a small public and, especially, a small, ignorant public.

LRL   But it's not the small, ignorant public that's picked it up.
       It's people who want to blame something on any kind
       of thing.

DJ   Sure. But you don't have people who are very knowledge-
       able in the museums, or anywhere, really. So they latch on
       to a thing like that because it's handy.

LRL   But it's putting me off words, which are the only thing I
       have. I don't want to be completely put off words. [*Laughs*]

DJ   But anyway, all of European art is really involved in read-
       ing things into things. You look out there and somehow
       what you feel is supposed to be out there.

LRL   But you use "anthropomorphism" as a kind of synonym
       for "humanism." It's a word I used to use, but –

DJ   Yeah, that whole kind of philosophy and so forth. The
       whole rationalistic philosophy is involved in it. In other
       words, you can look out there and feel something about
       it and then deduct something from that. I'm pretty sure
       I can look out there and not learn a damn thing just by
       looking or feeling.

LRL   Well, where is it coming from, then?

DJ   What you actually know is just plain knowledge, that's all.
       Otherwise, you don't know anything.

LRL   But what is just plain knowledge? I mean, knowledge has
       to come from someplace.

DJ   It has to be more or less scientific. In other words, you don't
       know anything about the world except what's scientific.

LRL   That's what I'm told. And I believe it or I don't believe it,
       I suppose. So that's belief. I mean, fact is more belief than
       anything else.

DJ   Yeah. It's belief that it's round and all those things.

LRL   Or just that glass is really silicone, and so on. I mean, just
       anything has to be believed. You can't go around testing –
       it would be great to have somebody take five minutes of
       their life and spend the next sixty-five years of their life
       testing everything in that five minutes to be sure that they

had nothing put over on them. [*Laughs*] You could spend the rest of your life doing it.

DJ   Right, and obviously you don't want to do that. I'm willing to accept all that as fact.

LRL   Where do you stop accepting something as fact? If Barney Newman says that painting is sublime – but you don't want to accept that as a fact. You can't.

DJ   No, I just accept Barney as a fact.

LRL   Ad says he's painting colorless paintings; is that a fact? But it wasn't colorless, and so on. I mean, the facts start backing up and that's where there's something in there between the specific and general.

DJ   The facts about art are very shady business, I guess.

LRL   And what are the facts about your things?

DJ   Well, the facts about science are somewhat clear-cut.

LRL   The facts would be about three-dimensional, weight, color.

DJ   Yeah, but that's not what I'm talking about, because those facts are only part of the whole thing. I mean, art isn't a factual matter really, anyway. I'm not saying that art is. We're talking about what you believe about the world, which is pretty much a factual situation.

LRL   Which is in your art, though?

DJ   Yeah. So if that attitude toward the whole thing does turn up in the nature of the work, it doesn't mean that the work is factual, in the sense that science would be.

LRL   But in a specific sense, any work is factual, obviously, because any work is the fact of being there. You can do the most godawful purply sunset, with ladies dancing, and crosses in the sky, and it's a fact.

DJ   Yes, that's not what I mean. It's important to me that people don't say things about what exists or happens or occurs generally that don't happen or occur. It's important that the extent of knowledge is made clear so that it doesn't get muddled. They know so much about geology; they know so much about physics; and at any one time, it's a certain point. They don't know more than that. And since that constitutes knowledge and is reasonably factual, although always somewhat uncertain, that's what should be taken seriously or believed, if you want, and not some great general statement about it. You don't know much about astronomy, say, or something like that. So people shouldn't really believe in astrology. [*Laughter*]

LRL What sign are you, Don?

DJ I'm down on astrology. It seems to have cropped up lately as a —

LRL It sure has. But what sign are you?

DJ Gemini. But I think it's a lot of baloney.

LRL But to get back to the work itself —

DJ What you want to believe in — you're dealing with one person who has to deal with a number of necessary things and so forth, feel certain things, and it's all a very local situation. Which I think should be paid more attention to, in a sense, instead of worrying about the justification or belief in much larger things you can't know about.

LRL In other words, it really comes down to perception and things like that?

DJ Yeah, perception, but also belief, and what you consider important, and so forth.

LRL But I still don't see how you can use "more" or "less specific" as a kind of criteria. Aside from all its evocative business — that's finally clear to me, I can see that. But —

DJ It seems to me that if it's specific, it doesn't deal with general beliefs in that way.

LRL Do you care about what people think when they see it?

DJ I may care, but I never think about it.

LRL I mean, you have to care, if you care whether it is non-evocative or evocative, because if you didn't give a damn whether people saw your things as jewel boxes, or sunsets, or God knows what, then you wouldn't think about this at all.

DJ   I get reasonably irritated when it's misinterpreted.

LRL   But it's always misinterpreted, isn't it? Has it ever been interpreted right, as far as you're concerned?

DJ   No. No.

LRL   I don't think it will be, either, will it?

DJ   I don't know. Not exactly. But they could do a little better, I guess. You're not making things regardless of other people, I suppose, in the ultimate sense. But primarily, I make them to suit myself.

LRL   I think any good artist does.

DJ   And I really don't speculate about the audience, because what can you speculate about? There are all sorts of people, and they're very different. Some are nincompoops, and some aren't. And what is there to think about in the whole matter? I want to believe the damn thing. I mean, you're making it so that it will be credible for yourself. It has to suit me. I assume that if I like it and it means something to me, it will mean something to somebody else. That seems to me the only assumption you can go on. Because you certainly can't deal in some hypothetical public and —

LRL   No. If people are worrying about what people are thinking all the time, you'd never get anything done.

DJ   Who are you going to think about, I mean?

LRL   Those are the people who have something for everything, and you can tell the art at a glance if it has something for everybody.
      Well, I finally got that pinned down, that general and specific —

DJ   It's really very much a matter of making believable art, though. Sort of hitting it right for all these things that you may have wanted, which certainly for a long time didn't seem to go together as possibilities, as things that could be somehow together.

LRL   Like what?

DJ   Well, one thing, about the time that I was doing those paintings back there and then going on into the reliefs and three-dimensional things, was to keep up sufficient scale and still have the work kind of thin, or sharp, or something. I don't know how to describe it. Or broad without having mass, or scale without having mass. That seemed kind of incompatible at one point, and then it turned out it can be perfectly compatible.

LRL   That you could believe any of it?

DJ   They were two ideas that didn't seem to go together.

LRL   I suppose that's really what any kind of advance in art is about. It has nothing to do with beauty or ugliness; it certainly has nothing to do with this formal advance thing anymore. That really has been discredited in a way that — two years ago, I never would have believed it could have been discredited that much. It was slow. I mean, the artist probably realized it, but advance has to be, if anything, something that wasn't expected in any direction rather than a straight line.

DJ   Form was certainly important, but that's after the fact.

LRL   What is? Form?

DJ   It's always there, always important, but it's kind of after the fact, and if it's considered only by itself, you have rather meaningless discussion. When I did those reliefs — back to the scale and thinness and so on — the whole curve was very broad; then the top and bottom ends were very thin, and they seemed to follow from the curve, because they were in at the ends of the curve. I liked that a good deal — that you had a very thin element and yet it was just sort of a logical end of the whole big curve, whatever you call it. Then in the boxes, you've got all those sharp corners and angles and lines, and yet it's part of very broad sides and top. So that was very nice.

LRL   I never thought of that, particularly.

DJ   How else can you get — what is it? — one, two, three, four,

five, six – six infinitely thin lines out of the same number
of broad areas, four around and two on the top – no, you
only have five broad areas and six lines.

At least the bourbon is good for my throat.

LRL   Yeah, I think maybe we should have started on it a little
      earlier. [*Laughs*]

DJ   We'd have really been looped by now.

LRL   The best interview I ever had – actually, I have never
      done any interviewing; I think the time I was here with
      you and Bruce[101] was about the only … I went down and
      talked to Poons before [*inaudible*]; it was Rosenquist, be-
      cause I knew him, and it was easier. We ran all over town.
      I didn't know him very well, and it was the first article I
      had ever written, and I gritted my teeth and started writ-
      ing an article. We went to, I don't know, museums and bars,
      and we went to the Battery and ended up back down. We
      spent the whole day just racing around town furiously,
      drinking like mad, and I wrote all these notes. It was really
      magnificent – I kept having the feeling, "Oh, yes, mmm,
      that's really being said now." And I came home with just
      this hot little wad of notes, and I couldn't read anything
      out of it. I've got to get a pocket tape recorder.

DJ   Was it Rosenquist or Poons?

LRL   Rosenquist, not Poons. But the self-conscious part of the
      tape recorder –

DJ   Well, we're so used to it. I should have had one. I used to
      take down notes very carefully. I reviewed a show of Jas-
      per's and went down there and all that; it would have been
      funny if I had the tape.[102]

LRL   It would have been great. In fact, whenever I go to a lec-
      ture or symposium or something, if it isn't taped, I wonder
      why the hell it isn't taped. It's a mass of information that
      obviously computers are going to have to be around to do
      something with, because there's just too damn much of it.
      But every little word is valuable. The times I've sat around

trying to think of who said what at a certain symposium, and people have been talking about it since but nobody can remember exactly how it was said, and it's misquoted and becomes mythology…and ten years later, you read it, and you don't know about all that, so you quote it again. It's too bad. You've got to get a little tape recorder that hangs in the pocket somehow, so that you can walk all over town and get a recording. Then everybody would lose all self-consciousness about it. You'd start having really wild things and revelations. [*Laughs*]

DJ   That's pretty funny with Jasper, though. Me as a young reviewer, though I was older than Jasper.

LRL   Are you really?

DJ   Yeah. Jasper was a young artist. He had all the paintings around the studio, and I was looking at them all. Jasper wouldn't any more let anybody review his paintings in a studio than he would –

LRL   And that whole slightly patronizing thing that when you go to a studio for the first time as a reviewer, for some reason, no matter how much you like the person and you can talk, there's always this slight thing: "I did come all the way down, I took a bus, and I came down to see your bloody things, and I won't be able to say something about them."

DJ   The seniority business is a little aggravating sometimes.

LRL   It's very strange, too, because it's true that not only do people who invented something early and didn't show it get completely forgotten, but it's the age at which you have your first one-man show that makes a difference to people, that classifies where you are. I find myself saying "my generation" to people. And they say, "Well, what's your generation?" I mean, people who came into the art world about when I did. So I start listing people, and their ages range from twenty-five to forty, and then I begin to wonder why the hell I'm talking about "my generation," because I think of my generation as being people who may be older than I am, because I started seeing things as soon as I got to New York. They're always older than I am, as most people I knew were. I think of being exactly your age and Sol's age and so on, even though you were around before that time.

DJ   It's relevant to when your work got organized and all that. On the other hand, you may think, as I think, that my work is as good as anyone's. And yet, you know, the whole thing grinds on for years as to when it sells and all these things.

LRL   And, of course, time can be just missed, too.

DJ   It doesn't have anything to do with the caliber of the work. Look at all those paintings that Frank did and didn't sell. Now people sort of sneak them out for $20,000 from somewhere.

LRL   Frank is an odd case, because his first show was at the museum and everything.[103] It's very peculiar — it's the first of something that's going to happen more and more often. It's a phenomenon.

DJ   With a smart public, you would have gotten sales then. Should have.

LRL   I had no idea, frankly, that you were in New York that early, that you have had that long —

DJ   I was here [New York] since '53. And in school before that.

LRL   You were here since early '49.

DJ   '48.

LRL   For some reason, that seems like a long time. The '50s I can conceive of, because I came in a '50s year. [Laughs] But anything in the '40s begins to sound like forever.

DJ   I could have been a second-generation abstract expressionist if I had tried.

LRL   You could have been almost a first-generation abstract expressionist. [Laughs] Except nobody was.

DJ   I think Helen Frankenthaler is the same age as I am.

LRL   Is she really? Isn't that funny.

DJ   It's strange.

LRL   There it is. That's exactly what I mean.

DJ   Sol had dinner at David Lee's, and Bill Bollinger was there.[104] I think that David is exactly my age, because we went to school together in Virginia years and years ago. Bollinger must be, like, twenty-one – no, not twenty-one, but twenty-five. And Sol is forty. But we had all come in at approximately the same time, and there was no age gap at all. Whereas Frankenthaler and some of the twenty-one-year-olds who are on another kick completely would be – I shouldn't be talking. It's pretty funny.

LRL   You mean the who-got-there-first business?

DJ   No, just the whole seniority and the time it takes to get some money out of it, and proper attention, and so forth.

LRL   Do you think that it really is a very different situation now than it was ten years ago? People are always saying there are so many galleries now, and everybody has instant success, and so on. And yet I still know people that I knew – Ryman is obviously the best example, for me, anyway; I think that's damn good work and always has been as good as most things going on. And I don't think it'll – you know, "It's never going to get recognized"; "Eventually it will."

DJ   Who?

LRL   Bob. This is the stuff I grew up with, and I'm convinced by it, anyway. But everybody says it's so easy to get a gallery now. He's got a tremendous underground reputation with a lot of kids now, but that doesn't mean anything overground any more than it did ten years ago, or fifteen years ago.

DJ   In that sense, I don't think it's that much different. In the first place, there aren't many galleries that are real galleries.

LRL   When you start weeding, you really – I don't go to but about seven galleries anymore.

DJ   Sure. It doesn't take long to get it down to that, and they're the only functioning ones, really. And the whole business of getting some attention and getting some money and all that is really extremely slow – which is something else Greenberg says in his articles. He says, "Well, in only two years, all these people have gotten something or other" – whatever it is, I've forgotten. And Hilton Kramer in the *Times* talks about the fast turnover in fads and all this.[105] But, boy, it looks slow to me.

LRL Yeah, and even to me. This is my tenth year in New York, and I'm constantly aware of it. It's like there are anniversary flags out all over the place, because ten years does make a difference, I guess. When I think of where things were then and where things are now, it's all been creeping – this has all been happening all that time. I mean, since I came to New York, I've been involved with the kind of things I like now, but it's just been crawling along.

DJ Sure it has. The red box there [see image 5] – I couldn't sell that out of the Green Gallery show in '63. And the one that's wrapped is from the show, the one I made. This is the third copy, which is all I make.

LRL Were you doing it in an edition?

DJ We made an edition of three because I wanted to keep the first one. That's the third one. It goes to Dallas. I just made it – someone just made it. I couldn't have sold it then; didn't sell it then, rather, or only one piece out of the whole show, and that for nearly nothing.

LRL What sold?

DJ Philip Johnson – the one like that with the pipe [image 31], but he didn't pay very much.

LRL How much did he pay?

DJ Three hundred dollars. [*Laughter*]

LRL God, who was involved that he had the sense to buy that? Whose advice was he taking? Dick's?

DJ Dick's, I think.

LRL I suppose it also makes sense that an architect would dig this stuff earlier than most –

DJ   According to the story, Dick pretty much just told him to take it.

LRL   That he wouldn't be sorry.

DJ   And that's why I was so low, because I realized he was just taking it to make Dick happy.

    Well, anyway, you know, now I could make a dozen of them. Don't intend to. But that's pretty slow interest in the piece.

LRL   Of course, one thing people don't take into consideration is just this whole time it takes for an artist to develop, too. You've been – well, God, it's about twenty years, isn't it?

DJ   For me, it's very slow, because I was very slow getting organized. For some reason, I'm very slow thinking things out. I don't really know why. Perhaps accidents of who I knew and had gotten information from. Perhaps if somehow or other I had met the New York School people or something, it would have been different.

LRL   It's funny how much the social thing finally does come into it. I guess my sophistication as far as abstract art – I was involved in abstract art, I thought, when I came to New York. I had lived in Paris, but I didn't know anybody in Paris; I just went around and looked at the [Pierre] Soulages. But when I came to New York, I didn't know anybody. I knew a few abstract painters, and they were doing good things, but it really was Bob [Ryman] who was the breakthrough as far as I was concerned, to find out what it was really about, finally, without any of the romantic shit that I had all along with the Parisians and poor people – I mean, not artists, but other people. And I suppose I could have gone another five years without ever meeting anybody who made – and I never would have done anything about art criticism. It might have been a damn good idea.

    It certainly goes for artists, too. It's been fascinating to hear how little, how few connections you've had, because you're not a very social kind of person, so you weren't going to go immediately meet everybody at the Cedar [Street Tavern].

DJ   I knew about the Cedar. In the first place, I thought it was a very bleak place. I didn't really like bars, because I knew a few people in the league who pretty much drank themselves out of the world. Especially one good painter I knew who drank so much that –

LRL   Who?

DJ   Oh, you don't know him. He was the best student that I knew of at the time, but he got drunk mostly every night.

LRL   That almost happened to Pollock. I was reading his biography at the museum, a kind of diary set up in the museum catalogue; he was very close to that all the time at the early stage there.[106] But the amazing thing with Pollock was that he had lots of people who really – I don't know how they saw it in the stuff he was doing, but they really did see it. Benton was absolutely convinced he was a great artist. So there was something there. Who knows what reason; maybe it was because he was a romantic guy or something. Maybe it was just completely extraneous. But somehow, there were enough people right from the beginning who were convinced that he could do something. His own letters read just like everybody's, like yours would read, like anybody's would read, about working and getting depressed about what you're doing and not getting anyplace. But there was this odd reception. Robert Coates at *The New Yorker* was the very first person to really dig Pollock and immediately said, just like Greenberg said, "This is it; this is going to be something." It wasn't that fantastic painting at that point; at least it doesn't look like it now. But anyway, still, he didn't believe in himself as much as the other people did. He was constantly at the edge of dropping the whole business and drinking himself to –

DJ   This fellow was trained as an asbestos steam-pipe fitter. He belonged to the union. So I assume that's what he went back to do. It was really, really bad. The last time I ever saw him, we had a very bad time. He was kind of looped, as usual, and I was doing the realistic paintings, but they were rather flattened, a little Matisse-like or something. And he was really sore. They were a little abstract or something, and he really raked me over for it. So I figured I'd had enough of that, and I never did see him again.

LRL   Do you know what happened to him at all? You just know he never showed up on the surface? Maybe he met a nice girl, kicked the drink, and is painting beautiful paintings someplace else in Arizona or some place.

DJ   I bet he's not painting paintings. Obviously, I guess, he'll never do anything now. But he was very serious about it. And just getting mad like that over what, after all, is an aesthetic difference to the rest of the world is something. Except I didn't appreciate it then, because I was —

LRL   Is it harder to work once you're successful, sort of? Does it get in the way a little?

DJ   Well, I think it's easy —

LRL   Phone calls and stuff like this?

DJ   Well, that's a pain in the neck, but there's a lot more money, which makes it easier. And I can do a lot more. I can do pieces that I couldn't have done before. Though you can still go broke at sort of a higher level.

LRL   Yeah, yeah, I guess it's easier. It's hard to go back down. Have you had any bites to do anything big? I won't say "monumental" — just big?

DJ   I don't like "monumental."

LRL   I know you don't. We went through that the last time. [*Laughs*]

DJ   Well, okay. No, not really, except that a couple of years ago or so, or a year ago, Henry called about something for the World Trade Center.[107] I assume it's by recommendation; I guess he made up a list. I guess if it came across – to have a lot of money available – I mean, you could build something big. And then there's Lippincott to be fairly big, probably more than I could build on my own.[108] Bob built a piece there.

LRL   Morris?

DJ   Yeah.

LRL   They did the new one for the –

DJ   Right. So they want to do something, I guess, and will probably do it eventually.

LRL   Do they [Lippincott] pay for it? I mean, is that a kind of commission?

DJ   They pay for the construction and labor. And then if they ever sell it, you split it or something.

LRL   Really? I didn't realize that. What did Morris do?

DJ   The one at Albright-Knox [Art Gallery],[109] a channel; it goes up and down.[110] It's made of channel beam, U-shaped beams – U or H, I don't know.

LRL   Where does it go?

DJ   It goes in sort of a shamrock shape on the ground. It's pretty big. Anyway, it's a lot more aluminum than I could afford, even if I were extravagant – the amount of money that I put into the Whitney show.

LRL   Do you think there is such a thing as "monumental"? Or the word is just –

DJ   No, I don't see why there's any difference. That's another thing I disagree with Morris about. In one of the articles, he had "public" and "private." And I don't see why on earth there's any difference between the two. Why is it monumental? It's just bigger than what you might do in here. I don't think it should differ in quality; it's just bigger, that's all.

LRL   Well, it's a nineteenth-century connotation, the word "monument"; sculpture went all the way from figurines to things you had in the house and things you had in

the garden, and things you had outdoors and in public
were monuments, because they were commissioned *as*
monuments.

DJ I think very much that it should be substantially the same
thing, whether it's big or little.

[*New tape*]

LRL What are you in the mood for, Don? Do you want a question on David Smith, or do you want a question –

DJ Nothing. But any questions are better than ad-libbing.

LRL Right. By the way, Eugene Goossen showed in that lecture he had at the museum last time a David Smith which
I'm sure nobody ever saw, because he said it was in a private collection or something.[111] It was a stack. Did you
ever see that thing? Obviously, it didn't have any effect
on you, because it doesn't look like your work. But it
was an amazing piece. You could see all the art historians gasp and wishing that somebody could have seen it. I
don't think it was shown. It was in 1956 or something. It
was just a straight rod with rectangular boxes on it. A very
good-looking piece.

DJ There was something called *Totem* in the French & Company show.[112] But I didn't see the show; I hated the word
"totem" so much that I didn't want to see it.

LRL This I suppose could have been called *Totem*, but I don't
think it was – I mean, it wasn't. It's the only one like it, and
somebody has it in a private collection.[113] I just wondered
if, by any possibility, you had ever seen the thing.

DJ No. Anyway, if the stacks were freestanding, I'd hate them.

LRL [*Laughter*] If they were freestanding – or on a pole, even
better.

DJ Yeah.

LRL Let's get some more on that biographical stuff, because
that gets us going. What did you do in Korea?

DJ   I don't know – I was put in the engineers. I was trained
      for the infantry, but by some piece of –
LRL   Trained to walk.
DJ   I was trained to fight. By some fluke, I was put in the en-
      gineers when I got to Korea. Which was real luck.
LRL   What did the engineers do?
DJ   We were attached to Kimpo Air Base, the main air base
      near Seoul. It involved building a number of useful things,
      and it was interesting and pleasant. The Koreans did most
      of the work, either managerial or labor.
LRL   Were you building and things like that?
DJ   Yeah. Ditches to building – well, I was in charge of finish-
      ing a boiler plant at one point. Really, I didn't have much
      to do with it. The Koreans were contracted for the job, so
      they were really the ones who were building it. A bunch
      of officers would come around. I would just report on it. I
      learned enough about it to make a very impressive report.
LRL   Everybody had such funny Korean – Sol was with the
      PX [post exchange] and would have such things as free
      liquor –
DJ   Well, it wasn't fun, but it wasn't bad either, because there
      was no war. And you were pretty autonomous. Like, it re-
      ally was my boiler plant, and other than the final deadline
      or a couple of things, nobody really cared. The same with
      the other jobs.
LRL   How long were you over there?
DJ   Eleven months – almost a year. I quarried rocks for a wall
      in Kimpo for a while. It just meant blasting out the side
      of a cliff down along by the river.
LRL   Did you dig the whole Oriental thing? Or were you not
      the least bit interested in it?
DJ   What's the Oriental thing?
LRL   Did you look around for art and dig things up and so on,
      as some people seem to have done?
DJ   I wasn't too interested in art. A little bit. But for one thing,

we had no leave, which meant that legally we couldn't go into Seoul. I did go in a few times, but between sort of moderate interest in it and restrictions on really looking around, I didn't see much. I bought a few things, but I really didn't see much. I saw a few buildings.

LRL   What are your objections to the art technology boom? Have you any idea of technology having something explicit to do with art, aside from the building?

DJ   I don't know that I have any objections to it. The first thing, though, is that it has to be art, which isn't so easy to do.

LRL   Do you think there's a kind of wide open field where technology is going to help artists get into things that haven't been done before? Or is it all just going to limp along?

DJ   I think primarily it's wide open, but as I said, it has to be art. You have to have uses for it. It doesn't do any good just to apply a little technology from somewhere to either good or bad art as it stands.

LRL   I couldn't agree more. I haven't seen anything so far, but it does seem like there's just so much that could be done.

DJ   There's a great deal that could be done, but –

LRL   It doesn't interest you as such? The performance thing obviously doesn't.

DJ   Well, no, I'm not at all against other people doing it and so forth. But it's very far from my way of thinking of things.

LRL   Why? Where does the gap come from?

DJ   Well, it's partly not visual. It's time, for one thing. The time is not visual. And then – or maybe just to break it down more simply, it is time, and I'm not interested in something that occurs in time.

LRL   But it doesn't necessarily have to mean kinetic things – something to do with light, for instance, doesn't have to be time; it could be a static light thing, like Turrell.

DJ   I suppose so. But the quality of light is –

LRL   Well, it's too ephemeral for the kind of thing you do. But

I'm just curious whether anything like this could ever particularly turn you on.

DJ   I don't know that it's ephemeral or anything. I like other
people who have used it. Turrell seems interesting; I haven't
seen any actual pieces. And certainly, I like Flavin's work. It
has a quality which is very alien to me and that I couldn't
think about.

LRL   Do you like Len Lye's things?

DJ   Oh, not really. A couple sort of have possibilities, or are
sort of close, but he turns it into an awful lot of symbolism and baloney.

LRL   It depends on what way you look at it, I suppose.

DJ   The thing – the one down from the ceiling, the flip-flop
that made a noise, then the big belt was electric – [114]

LRL   The belt put a thing on the top that made it ring a bell,
sort of every time it came around.

DJ   I didn't see it then, but it was controlled by a current;
where it's primarily movement, then it begins to get interesting. Where it's just symbolism or something, it's a
real bore.

LRL   I don't know what I was trying to get into with this technology thing.

DJ   Well, if you use some sort of technique, or use anything,
material or whatever, that has to be highly important in
the work, which is pretty obvious. And ordinarily, such
as occurred in *9 Evenings*, it's something just tacked on to
work that has nothing to do with technology, or even particularly advanced work of any kind.[115] If somebody just
does sort of ordinary Rauschenberg mishmash and then
uses a little electronics in it – I mean, it's just Schwitters's
collages with a little electronics, that's all there is to it. So
whatever technique, technology, or device, whatever you
use, it has to be the main thing in the work.

LRL   Why does it have to be? If the art is going to be the main
thing, does technology have to be involved?

DJ   The art is involved; it's both things together that are the
        main —

LRL   But if technique is just a medium?

DJ   Nothing is just the medium, though. We don't care about
        it for its own sake. I mean, materials I'm interested in are
        materials that I like ordinarily other than art. They're no
        more important than quite a few other materials that I can
        think of.

This conversation was sourced from a damaged audio recording and multiple transcripts. The original sound tape reels and archival transcripts are in the Lucy R. Lippard papers, 1930s–2010, bulk 1960s–1990, Archives of American Art, Smithsonian Institution, Washington, DC.

The editors have chosen to arrange this conversation in respect to both likely chronology and readability.

1   Judd enlisted in the United States Army on June 28, 1946, and was assigned
        to the Corps of Engineers in Korea. He was honorably discharged on November 20, 1947.

2   See Judd's "Kansas City Report" (1963) in *Donald Judd Writings*, 104–12.

3   Anthony Blunt (1907–1983) was a British art historian and an expert on
        Nicholas Poussin. Judd included eight books by Blunt in his library in
        Marfa, Texas.

4   *The Book of Knowledge*, published in 1910 by Grolier, is a multivolume encyclopedia for children.

5   *Franz Kline*, Charles Egan Gallery, New York, November–December 8, 1951.

6   *9th Street*, 60 East Ninth Street, New York, May 21–June 10, 1951. This seminal exhibition of the New York School was organized by artists and hung
        by Leo Castelli in a condemned building in New York's Greenwich Village.

7   Judd likely refers here to either Grand Central Artists' Materials or New
        York Central Art Supply (both former art supply stores in Manhattan),
        but confirmation could not be obtained.

8   Christodora House, which operates today under the name Christodora, was founded in 1897 as a settlement house for immigrants to New York. In 1928, a new home was built for the organization at Avenue B and East Ninth Street. It occupied this building – which still bears the name Christodora House and is now luxury condominiums – until the late 1940s, when the City of New York condemned the building, forcing Christodora House to relocate its activities. When Judd worked at the organization beginning in fall 1954, it operated out of the Jacob Riis Houses, on Avenue D between East Sixth and East Thirteenth Streets.

9   Judd refers here to 302 and 304 East Twenty-Seventh Street.

10   Marcia Judd Lamb (1932–1992) worked as a secretary at *Art Digest/Arts Magazine* in the 1950s. (The magazine's name changed to *Arts Magazine* in 1955.)

11   *Don Judd*, Green Gallery, New York, December 17, 1963–January 11, 1964. This exhibition was Judd's first solo show to include works in three dimensions. Lippard wrote in her review of it, "The most successful piece, and the one least derived from the mainstream of geometrical abstraction, is a stepped jungle-jim object, which retains the rather menacing anonymity of the room as a whole." Lippard, "New York," *Artforum*, March 1964, 19.

12   Julie Margaret Hughan Finch (1941–) is a dancer and social activist. She and Judd married on March 14, 1964; they divorced in 1978.

13   Lippard refers here to William C. Agee, *Don Judd*, exh. cat. (New York: Whitney Museum of American Art, 1968). With notes by Dan Flavin and selected writings by Judd.

14   Lippard refers here to a symposium that Judd participated in for the Jewish Museum exhibition *Primary Structures*. See "The New Sculpture" (1966) in this volume, 90–102.

15   "A New Aesthetic," symposium with Ronald Davis, Dan Flavin, Robert Kauffman, and John Harvey McCracken, moderated by Barbara Rose, May 6, 1967, Washington Gallery of Modern Art, Washington, DC.

16   Judd's original text reads, "They are extreme, snazzy, elegant in the wrong way, immoderate." See Judd's catalogue essay "John Chamberlain" (1965) in *Donald Judd Writings*, 173.

17   "Like the late Yves 'le monochrome' Klein, Judd has appropriated a single color for his own." Lippard, "New York," 19.

18   In an essay on Judd, Smithson referred to Judd's 1964 work *To Dave Shackman* [see image 24] as a "space-lattice." Smithson, "Donald Judd," in *7 Sculptors*, exh. cat. (Philadelphia: Institute of Contemporary Art, University of Pennsylvania, 1965), 14.

19   *Welfare Island Art Festival*, Welfare (now Roosevelt) Island, New York, summer 1964. For more information on this festival and its organization by di Suvero, see Linda Dalrymple Henderson, "Park Place: Its Art and History," in *Reimagining Space: The Park Place Gallery Group in 1960s New York*, exh. cat. (Austin: Blanton Museum of Art, 2008), 8.

20   "The formal logic of crystallography, apart from any preconceived scientific content, relates to Judd's art in an abstract way." Smithson, "Donald Judd," 16.

21   "What is outside vanishes to meet the inside, while what is inside vanishes to meet the outside. The concept of 'anti-matter' overruns, and fills everything, making these very definite works verge on the notion of disappearance." Smithson, "Donald Judd," 16.

22   *Plastics*, John Daniels Gallery, New York, March 16–April 3, 1965.

23   Judd refers here to *Don Judd*, Green Gallery, New York, December 17, 1963–January 11, 1964, in which the work under discussion was included. This exhibition was Judd's first solo show to include works in three dimensions.

24   Judd met the Swiss architect and artist Max Bill (1908–1994) in the 1980s through his friends and gallerists Annemarie and Gianfranco Verna.

25   Larry Poons, *Untitled* (1964), one in a portfolio of ten screenprints titled *X + X (Ten Works by Ten Painters)* published by the Wadsworth Atheneum, edition of 500.

26   In 1967, an article in *Life* magazine referred to Judd as "chief box-man" and quoted him repeatedly: "'Whether one makes it oneself or doesn't,' says Judd, 'it's all a case of technique that makes the thing visible, so that I don't see in the long run why one technique is any more essentially art than another technique.'… 'Soul is at the bottom of the barrel,' says Judd." "Shape of Art for Some Time to Come," *Life*, July 28, 1967, 38–43, 44A. The next year, a reviewer in *Time* magazine wrote that the works in Judd's Whitney exhibition were "chilling," "commercially fabricated," and "have all the cosy warmth and intimacy of an assembly line or a bank vault," further describing one of the stacks as "a machine-produced, 20th century revision of a medieval illuminator's stairway to paradise." "Art," *Time*, March 22, 1968, 54.

27   See "The New Sculpture" (1966) in this volume, 90–102.

28   E.A.T. (Experiments in Art and Technology) was a New York–based nonprofit that promoted knowledge sharing and collaboration between industry, science, and the arts. It was founded in 1966 by Billy Klüver, Fred Waldhauer, Robert Rauschenberg, and Robert Whitman and was active through the 1980s.

29   Thomas B. Hess, "Editorial: Notes from Utopia," *ARTnews*, May 1960, 23.

30   Smith wrote three letters to the editor about this incident: two announcing the situation and his displeasure with it, "A Protest Against Vandalism," *Arts Magazine*, June 1960, 5, and "Letters," *ARTnews*, Summer 1960, 6, and one announcing its resolution, "Rescue Operation," *Arts Magazine*, November 1960, 7. The work in question, *17 h's* (1950), was repurchased by Smith, repainted, and given to his daughters.

31   Lippard's account is accurate; *17 h's* was sold by Leo Castelli to collector Edward J. Gallagher in 1959 and stripped of its cadmium aluminum red paint at Gallagher's request. See Susan J. Cooke, ed., *David Smith: Collected Writings, Lectures, and Interviews* (Berkeley: University of California Press, 2018), 338.

32   *American Sculpture of the Sixties*, Los Angeles County Museum of Art, April 28–June 25, 1967; Philadelphia Museum of Art, September 15–October 29, 1967.

33   *Alexander Calder: A Retrospective Exhibition*, Solomon R. Guggenheim Museum, New York, November 6, 1964–January 31, 1965.

34   Walter Hopps (1932–2005) was a curator, museum director, and a cofounder of Los Angeles's Ferus Gallery. As the curator of the VIII Bienal de São Paulo, September 4–November 28, 1965, Hopps included Judd's work.

35   James A. Fitzsimmons (1919–1985) was the chief editor, publisher, and owner of *Art International*.

36   *The New American Painting*, The Museum of Modern Art, New York, May 28–September 8, 1959. This seminal exhibition organized by curator Dorothy C. Miller presented the work of seventeen painters: William Baziotes, James Brooks, Willem de Kooning, Sam Francis, Arshile Gorky, Adolph Gottlieb, Philip Guston, Grace Hartigan, Franz Kline, Robert Motherwell, Barnett Newman, Jackson Pollock, Mark Rothko, Theodoros Stamos, Clyfford Still, Bradley Walker Tomlin, and Jack Tworkov. It toured eight European countries in 1958 and 1959 before appearing in New York.

37   *Barnett Newman: A Selection 1946–1952*, French & Company, New York, March 11–April 5, 1959. This exhibition was organized by Clement Greenberg.

38   Newman's *Horizon Light* (1949) was exhibited in *Ten Years*, Betty Parsons Gallery, New York, December 19, 1955–January 14, 1956.

39   Judd likely refers here to *Jackson Pollock*, Sidney Janis Gallery, New York, November 3–29, 1958.

40   Jackson Pollock, *Ocean Greyness* (1953), Solomon R. Guggenheim Museum, New York.

41   See Judd's "Barnett Newman" (1964) in *Donald Judd Writings*, 152–59.

42   *New Paintings by Mark Rothko*, Sidney Janis Gallery, New York, April 11–May 14, 1955.

43   In the 1950s and 1960s, many cooperative and artist-run galleries opened and operated in New York's East Village. The majority of these galleries were located on Tenth Street, whose name became shorthand for the larger scene.

44   Tanager Gallery, founded in 1952, was one of the first and most influential of the Tenth Street galleries. It operated until 1962.

45   *Mid-Season Salon*, Camino Gallery, New York, December 14, 1956–January 3, 1957.

46   *Don Judd*, Panoras Gallery, New York, June 24–July 6, 1957.

47   Artist David Diao (1943–) worked at the Kootz Gallery during 1966, the year the gallery closed.

48   Belle Krasne Ribicoff (1924–) is an American editor, critic, and university administrator. She was an editor at *Art Digest* (later *Arts Magazine*) from 1949 to 1954, the last few years of which she was the magazine's editor in chief.

49   Judd began graduate work in art history at Columbia University in fall 1957 and completed his coursework in fall 1961. No degree was conferred because he did not complete the requirements.

50   Judd studied with Meyer Schapiro (1904–1996) while a graduate student at Columbia University. Schapiro was an influential art critic, art historian, and professor. Judd included nine books by Schapiro in his library in Marfa, Texas.

51   Thomas B. Hess (1920–1978) was an American editor, art critic, and curator. He was on the editorial staff of *ARTnews* from 1945 to 1972 and the magazine's editor from 1965 to 1972.

52   Jo Baer, "Edward Kienholz: A Sentimental Journeyman," *Art International*, April 1968, 45–49.

53   Robert Morris, "Anti Form," *Artforum*, April 1968, 33–35.

54   Francis Kloeppel was an associate editor at *Arts Magazine* at the time.

55   See Judd's review of *Members* (1959) in *Donald Judd: Complete Writings 1959–1975*, 1.

56   *Members*, Tanager Gallery, New York, October 15–30, 1959.

57   Scott Burton (1939–1989) was a sculptor and performance artist who both wrote and edited for *ARTnews* in the 1960s. Gene Swenson (1934–1969) was a critic at *ARTnews*.

58   The work in question is Nam June Paik's *Robot K-456* (1964), built in collaboration with Shuya Abe; it "shat" white beans. Lippard's published text reads, "The element of chance, of outrageous humor and a Dada disregard for finesse and propriety are conspicuous in a hilariously dilapidated armature of a robot that bows, nods, raises its arms, twirls a pinwheel nose, gut and penis, wiggles silly soft breasts, lurches forward in a parody of walking, makes gruesome sounds, and passes a shower of tiny pale pebbles." Lippard, "New York Letter," *Art International*, January 1966, 93.

59   In 1958, Judd taught art to underprivileged children at the Police Athletic League, New York.

60   Lucy R. Lippard, *Ad Reinhardt* (New York: Abrams, 1981). Judd included this book in his library in Marfa, Texas.

61   Lippard married Robert Ryman in 1961. Lippard and Ryman divorced in 1968; Flavin and Sonja remained married until 1979.

62   Ivan Karp (1926–2012) was an art dealer, author, and gallerist. He was the associate director of Leo Castelli Gallery, New York, from 1959 to 1969.

63   "In 1962, a group of young artists gathered to discuss the formation of a
       new cooperative gallery in Brooklyn. Both Karp and Richard Bellamy,
       the best eyes in New York at the time, were also involved in the negoti-
       ations. The diverse members included Weber … Dan Flavin and Donald
       Judd … Cora Ward … Sheldon Macklin [*sic*], Tom Wesselmann and Rafael
       [*sic*] Ortiz. Weber explains 'we'd go around once a week, once a month,
       to various galleries, and [looked at] other artists to see if we wanted other
       people in our group. By the time we were ready to get together, every-
       one had gotten a gallery.' Although this co-op never developed beyond the
       planning stage, through the process Judd and Flavin became close friends
       and soon were represented by the Green Gallery." Sid Sachs, "Idelle We-
       ber: New Realist," in *Idelle Weber: The Pop Years* (New York: Hollis Taggart
       Galleries, 2013), 8.

64   Flavin completed a series of eight works known as *icons* between 1961 and
       1964. Judd permanently installed two of the eight, *icon III (blood) (the blood
       of a martyr)* (1962) and *icon VI (Ireland dying) (to Louis Sullivan)* (1962–63),
       at 101 Spring Street.

65   Judd participated in two group shows at Panoras Gallery before his 1957
       solo exhibition there: *Four Americans*, October 10–22, 1955, and *Don Judd
       and Nathan Raisen*, September 4–15, 1956.

66   Reviews of Judd's 1957 solo exhibition at Panoras Gallery include Barbara
       Gilbert, *East*, June 20, 1957; C.B., *New York Herald Tribune*, June 30, 1957;
       "Don Judd chez Panoras," *France-Amérique*, June 30, 1957; Vernon Young,
       "In the Galleries," *Arts Magazine*, June 1957, 58; and Edith Burkhardt, "Re-
       views and Previews," *ARTnews*, Summer 1957, 77.

67   Richard Bellamy (1927–1998) was the founder and director of Green Gal-
       lery, New York.

68   Clement Greenberg, "Changer: Anne Truitt," *Vogue*, May 1968, 212–13,
       284. One year after this article's publication, Judd argued that Greenberg
       had become "ignorant and hysterical," citing "Changer: Anne Truitt" as
       an example. See Judd's "Complaints: Part I" (1969) in *Donald Judd Writ-
       ings*, 200–209.

69   Greenberg in fact dates Truitt's exhibition accurately. *Truitt: First New York
       Exhibition* showed at the André Emmerich Gallery, New York, from Feb-
       ruary 12 to March 2, 1963; in his essay for the exhibition catalogue *Ameri-
       can Sculpture of the Sixties*, Greenberg cites *Truitt* as having appeared "early
       in 1963." Greenberg, "Recentness of Sculpture," in *American Sculpture of the
       Sixties*, ed. Maurice Tuchman, exh. cat. (Los Angeles: Los Angeles County
       Museum of Art, 1967), 25. *Truitt* is also dated to the correct year in the vol-
       ume's bibliography.

70   See Judd's review of *Truitt* (1963) in *Donald Judd: Complete Writings 1959–
       1975*, 85.

71   Judd may refer here to Greenberg's contribution to the *American Sculpture
      of the Sixties* exhibition catalogue, in which Greenberg compares Judd and
      other so-called minimalists unfavorably to Anne Truitt: "Truitt's art did flirt
      with the look of non-art, and her 1963 show was the first in which I no-
      ticed how this look could confer an effect of *presence*.... Truitt's sculpture
      had this kind of presence but did not *hide* behind it. That sculpture could
      hide behind it – just as painting did – I found out only after repeated ac-
      quaintance with Minimal works of art: Judd's, Morris's, Andre's, Steiner's,
      some but not all of Smithson's, some but not all of LeWitt's." Greenberg,
      "Recentness of Sculpture," 25.

72   Greenberg's original text reads, "Truitt's first New York show, at the An-
      dré Emmerich Gallery, in February 1963, met incomprehension (from,
      among others, Donald Judd, today a Minimalist leader, who reviewed the
      show for *Arts*)." Greenberg, "Changer: Anne Truitt," 284.

73   "If any one artist started or anticipated Minimal Art, it was she, in the fence-
      like and then box-like objects of wood or aluminum she began making,
      the former in 1961 and the latter in 1962." Greenberg, "Changer: Anne
      Truitt," 284.

74   Judd's work was shown at two exhibitions at Green Gallery, New York,
      in 1963: a group show, *New Work: Part 1*, January 8–February 2, 1963, and a
      solo show, *Don Judd*, December 17, 1963–January 11, 1964. The latter ex-
      hibition was Judd's first solo show to include works in three dimensions.
      The Truitt show under discussion is *Truitt: First New York Exhibition*, An-
      dré Emmerich Gallery, New York, February 12–March 2, 1963.

75   Judd's first three-dimensional paintings date to 1961; the first three of
      Stella's *Aluminum Paintings – Kingsbury Run, Luis Miguel Dominguin*, and
      Marquis de Portago – were completed in 1960 and exhibited that same year
      in *Frank Stella*, Leo Castelli Gallery, New York, September 27–October 15,
      1960. See Lawrence Rubin, *Frank Stella: Paintings 1958 to 1965; A Catalogue
      Raisonné* (London: Thames & Hudson, 1986), 95.

76   The inclusion of *Club Onyx* (1959) in *Selections*, Tibor de Nagy, New York,
      April 7–25, 1959, marked both Stella's first professional exhibition and the
      first showing of his *Black Paintings* (1958–60). Lippard likely refers here to
      Sixteen Americans, The Museum of Modern Art, New York, December 16,
      1959–February 14, 1960, in which four *Black Paintings* were included. See
      Lawrence Rubin, *Frank Stella*, 57–86, and William S. Rubin, *Frank Stella*,
      exh. cat. (New York: The Museum of Modern Art, 1970), 155–56.

77   Maurice Tuchman (1936–) is a curator of American art. He studied un-
      der Meyer Schapiro with Judd and Barbara Rose at Columbia University.

78   Two group exhibitions at Green Gallery, New York, in 1963 included
      works by both Judd and Morris: *New Work: Part I*, January 8–February 2,
      1963, and *Contemporary American Group Show [New Work Part III]*, May–
      June 15, 1963. *Slab* (1962) appeared in *Group Show*, June 12–July 21, 1962,
      and *Column* (1961) in *New Work: Part I*. See Judith E. Stein, *Eye of the Six-
      ties: Richard Bellamy and the Transformation of Modern Art* (New York: Far-
      rar, Straus & Giroux, 2016), 276–77.

79   Hansa Gallery was one of the first Tenth Street galleries. Initially on East
      Twelfth Street and then on Central Park South, it operated from 1952 to 1959.

80   *Toward a New Abstraction*, Jewish Museum, New York, May 19–September 15,
      1963.

81   *Yves Klein: Le monochrome*, Leo Castelli Gallery, New York, April 11–29,
      1961. This was Klein's first solo exhibition in the United States.

82   See Michael Fried, "Art and Objecthood," *Artforum*, Summer 1967, 12–23.

83   "Some of the pieces resemble the kind of podium upon which Greek
      drama is often enacted in the modern theatre. Deadpan, even mute, these
      box-like forms in a white room are an odd combination of the clinical
      and the dramatic." Lippard, "New York," 19.

84   *Don Judd*, Whitney Museum of American Art, New York, February 27–
      March 24, 1968, extended through April 14.

85   *Fiberglass, Felt*, Leo Castelli Gallery, New York, April 20–26, 1968.

86   *Boxing Match*, Gordon Gallery, New York, February 27–March 24, 1963.
      The exhibition included works by Shusaku Arakawa, Ay-O, Morris, and
      Masunobu Yoshimura. See Judd's review of *Boxing Match* (1963) in *Don-
      ald Judd: Complete Writings 1959–1975*, 90.

87   Lippard refers here to Morris's *Wheels* (1963), which was exhibited in *Box-
      ing Match* (see note 86). Judd wrote of this work, "The proportions of the
      wheels are dumb." See Judd's review of *Boxing Match* (1963) in *Donald
      Judd: Complete Writings 1959–1975*, 90.

88   Judd taught a seminar on sculpture at Yale School of Art and Architecture
      from October to December 1967.

89   Lippard was awarded a Guggenheim Fellowship in Fine Arts Research in
      1968.

90   See Judd's "Specific Objects" (1964) in *Donald Judd Writings*, 134–45.

91   Lucy R. Lippard, "Rejective Art," *Art International*, October 1966, 33–36.

92   Morris, "Anti Form," 33–35.

93   Robert Morris, "Notes on Sculpture, Part 1," *Artforum*, February 1966, 42–
      44; "Notes on Sculpture, Part 2," *Artforum*, October 1966, 20–23; "Notes
      on Sculpture, Part 3: Notes and Non Sequiturs," *Artforum*, June 1967, 24–
      29. See also Morris, "Notes on Sculpture, Part 4: Beyond Objects," *Art-
      forum*, April 1969, 50–54.

94   See "New Nihilism or New Art?" (1964) and "Interview with Bruce
      Glaser and Lucy R. Lippard" (1965) in this volume, 28–58 and 82–89,
      respectively.

95   "Ad liked to retell one of President Franklin Delano Roosevelt's jokes. A Sunday school teacher asked her class, 'Who would like to go [to] heaven?' All hands were raised but Johnny's. 'Don't you want to go to heaven, Johnny?' 'Yes, teacher, but not with them guys.'" Irving Sandler, "Ad Reinhardt: My Gadfly and My Friend," *The Brooklyn Rail*, January 16, 2014.

96   Panel discussion with Donald Judd, Claes Oldenburg, and Ad Reinhardt, moderated by Fairfield Porter, May 1966, Yale School of Art and Architecture, New Haven, Connecticut. Yale was unable to locate a recording or transcript in the university's archives.

97   *The New American Painting*, The Museum of Modern Art, New York, May 28–September 8, 1959 (see note 36).

98   This statement by Rothko and Gottlieb was sent to Edward Alden Jewell, a critic at *The New York Times*, in response to remarks he had made on an exhibition they both appeared in; Alden published the statement in his column. See Edward Alden Jewell, "'Globalism' Pops into View," *The New York Times*, June 13, 1943, X9.

99   For further commentary on Oldenburg and anthropomorphism, see Judd's "Specific Objects" (1964) and "Claes Oldenburg" (1966) in *Donald Judd Writings*, 143–45 and 180–84, respectively.

100   *Eccentric Abstraction*, Fischbach Gallery, New York, September 20–October 8, 1966. This exhibition was organized by Lippard.

101   See "Interview with Bruce Glaser and Lucy R. Lippard" (1965) in this volume, 82–89.

102   See Judd's review of *Jasper Johns* (1960) in *Donald Judd: Complete Writings 1959–1975*, 14.

103   Lippard refers here to Stella's inclusion in *Sixteen Americans*, The Museum of Modern Art, New York, December 16, 1959–February 14, 1960. However, Stella had shown work in five previous exhibitions: a solo show in Malden, Massachusetts; a group show in Oberlin, Ohio; and three group shows in New York (at Tibor de Nagy, Leo Castelli Gallery, and the National Arts Club), all in 1959. See William S. Rubin, *Frank Stella*, 155–56.

104   Bill Bollinger (1939–1988) and David Lee were American artists.

105   Hilton Kramer (1928–2012) was an American art critic and editor. In December 1959, Kramer hired Judd to review exhibitions for *Arts Magazine*; Judd continued to write for the magazine, with only a few interruptions, until March 1965.

106   Lippard refers here to a chronology of Pollock's life published in a Museum of Modern Art exhibition catalogue; it includes excerpts from diaristic letters written by Pollock. See "Chronology by Francis V. O'Connor," in Francis V. O'Connor, *Jackson Pollock*, exh. cat. (New York: The Museum of Modern Art, 1967), 11–78.

107   "Henry" may refer to Henry Geldzahler, but the editors have not been able to confirm this reference.

108   Judd worked frequently with Lippincott, Inc. of North Haven, Connecticut, between 1978 and 1986.

109   *Plus by Minus: Today's Half-Century*, Albright-Knox Art Gallery, Buffalo, New York, March 3–April 14, 1968.

110   Morris's contribution to *Plus by Minus*, an untitled, temporary structure, was later remade by the artist for the Solomon R. Guggenheim Museum, New York, as *Untitled* (1971).

111   Lippard likely refers here to Smith's *Five Units Equal* (1956), though it is also possible that the work in question is *Four Units Equal* (1956), which Smith altered later the same year and retitled to 5½. See Rosalind E. Krauss, *The Sculpture of David Smith: A Catalogue Raisonné* (New York: Garland Publishing, 1977), 70–71.

112   Smith made ten numbered assemblages under the name *Tanktotem* between 1952 and 1960.

113   For a nuancing of this claim, see Krauss, *The Sculpture of David Smith*, 70–71.

114   Len Lye, *Loop* (1963), Art Institute of Chicago. This work was first shown in New York in *On the Move*, Howard Wise Gallery, January 9–February 1, 1964.

115   *9 Evenings: Theatre and Engineering*, 69th Regiment Armory, New York, October 13–23, 1966. This project, initiated by Billy Klüver and Robert Rauschenberg, paired engineers from New Jersey's Bell Laboratories with artists to produce nine original performances utilizing new technologies.

Interview with Margot Willett
May 1968

In his 1964 review of the exhibition *Twentieth Century Engineering* (The Museum of Modern Art, New York, June 30–September 13, 1964) for *Arts Magazine*, Judd wrote disapprovingly of architects who were "prone to elegance and not especially imaginative," arguing that "much of the engineering is better architecture than most architecture." The sharpness of his criticism of contemporary architecture would permeate his public statements and his writings on the relationship between art and architecture for the rest of his life. In this conversation with Margot Willett, for example, Judd decries the "compositional fiddling around" found in much new architecture.

At the end of 1968, Judd purchased 101 Spring Street, a five-story cast-iron building in the SoHo neighborhood of New York; he and his family moved in the following year. Judd restored the building, which had been used for manufacturing, and began to install his work and the work of other artists. As he wrote in 1977, in the essay "Judd Foundation," 101 Spring Street marked the beginning of his architectural work and the further development of work related to architecture: "The interrelation of the architecture of 101 Spring Street, its own and what I've invented with the pieces installed there, has led to many of my newer, larger pieces, ones involving whole spaces."

M W   [Margot Willett] What I wanted to start out by asking you is, how much influence did growing up in the Midwest, in Missouri, have on your awareness of art and your contact with it?

D J   [Donald Judd] I don't know how much influence growing up out there had in general.

M W   Well, did it affect you in any particular way?

D J   There's next to no art whatsoever.

M W   In other words, you weren't exposed.

D J   Not much.

[*Break in recording*]

D J   Well, it has to do with several events, which I'm just going to go through. This sort of covers my whole knowledge of it. I did go to a small – it wasn't a school, I guess it was just an art teacher, in downtown Omaha, when I was about ten or eleven. And she was very ordinary as an artist, but I liked that.

M W   What kind of work were you doing?

D J   Little watercolors out the window or whatnot, you know [see image 20]; even things copied from books. But I liked it, and she was nice about it all.

M W   What got you to start going to art school in the first place?

D J   I guess I must have liked to draw, I suppose, and all that.

M W   Starting from when you were very little?

D J   Yeah. I remember doing things in school, on the blackboard, like kids do.

M W   Finger painting and all.

D J   No, I think at least it was before finger painting in the Midwest. I never did that till I taught students.[1]

M W   You've worked with finger painting with students here?

D J   A little bit. I taught a couple of semesters.

M W   After this first exposure, when you were in Omaha and taking art lessons –

DJ   Yeah, it was very short, maybe about a year. Then we moved.

MW   To Missouri?

DJ   No, let's see; I think we moved to Dallas.

MW   Did you do anything in art then?

DJ   No, not in Dallas. I don't quite know why.

MW   So did you sort of hold off on art until you came to the east?

DJ   Yeah, except that I was always interested in it.

MW   You weren't one of these industrious little prodigies who drew on the sidelines when you were supposed to be doing your schoolwork?

DJ   Yeah, pretty much. Also, I often didn't get along with art teachers … or sometimes I did. It was a matter of chance, whether the school was useful or not.

MW   Was that because you didn't like them telling you what to do and the way to do it?

DJ   Yeah. It could work out two ways. One I had in Philadelphia would give us projects.

MW   When was this?

DJ   We went from Omaha to Dallas and from Dallas to Philadelphia – Philadelphia about '41 or something. I remember she wanted us to do a poster on the war, and I didn't want to do posters; I didn't want to deal with the lettering. I didn't want the lettering on top of the picture, or something like that. So it was a semester-long fight – [2]

MW   Great battles between you and –

DJ   – in which I got a D. It probably wasn't a great battle, but it was, you know – it's life, I guess.

MW   Did you come to New York after that?

DJ   We moved to northern Jersey. But one sort of useful thing in Omaha was that the *Omaha World-Herald* put out a portfolio of reproductions.

MW   Whose reproductions?

DJ   From Old Masters to what they considered contemporary

art, which was [Thomas Hart] Benton and [John Steuart] Curry and Jon Corbino and such people. But it had, I remember, Rubens and Corot and Velázquez – I guess the whole range of Old Masters. That's about all I'd seen. That was very interesting to me.

M W   You never took an art history course or anything like that?

D J   Not at that time. I was only ten or eleven or so. Also, I read the sections in *The Book of Knowledge* and such things on art, so I had some idea of the history and what things looked like.[3]

M W   Do you think these early Old Masters, whom you first saw at this age, had much to do with your feeling?

D J   They gave me the initial idea that that was art, which was a big mistake.

M W   You don't feel that way at all?

D J   Yes, it's art, but I mean, it's not the only kind. See, they had nothing else, they had almost nothing – maybe they had a Matisse.

M W   But nothing very contemporary. What Old Masters do you really like?

D J   Quite a few of them. You know, what everybody else likes.

M W   You mean da Vinci and Michelangelo and people like that?

D J   Yeah. Especially Piero della Francesca.

M W   What do you feel about the European tradition? Did you object greatly to that?

D J   No – you see, at the time, I assumed that that was art, from what I got out of the portfolio, and the books, and, say, the Joslyn Memorial in Omaha, which was brand-new at the time. There wasn't anything else.

M W   How about now?

D J   Well, I think it's the European tradition and history.

M W   It's to be looked at as history.

D J   Yeah.

M W   Do you think this is because of the compositional effects of the European styles?

DJ   Well, yeah. It's the quality and meaning of the thing, which comes out of a completely different society. I can't imagine what art that comes out of, say, a small town like Venice in the sixteenth century would have to do with a contemporary situation. There's an enormous gap there. You can't use any of those things.

MW   What about the general principles behind, say, landscape painting, or just figure painting? I mean, are they obsolete?

DJ   I can't imagine why anybody would want to paint figures or landscapes now.

MW   When you started out, didn't you start out in painting?

DJ   Yeah.

MW   You did a bit of abstract expressionistic type of work?

DJ   Some. I started out painting realistic things. I was taught them in the Art Students League. Also because of what I knew, which wasn't, as I said, very much.

MW   When was the Art Students League – when did you attend?

DJ   A little bit in '48, and then there was a gap, and then '49 and on, for two or three years.

MW   What about this painting? Is this just because you felt that one starts out in painting and branches from painting, or because you hadn't really tried other media at that point?

DJ   I didn't know what I wanted to do or what could be done with it. I was interested in it, and I liked things that had been done, so it seemed like something I wanted to do, but I didn't know what I could do with it or anything. You really don't know anything about it when you start. You don't know the possibilities.

MW   What made you give up painting?

DJ   Well, that's a lot later, after an awful lot of paintings.

MW   How long did you paint, until about the early '60s?

DJ   Yeah, the last painting I think is about '61. I left the league in '53, I think, so it's from '53 to '61.

MW   What kind of paintings were these?

DJ   Well, they varied a great deal. The earlier ones after I left the league were sort of cubist in a way, based on landscape, pretty much, with areas more flattened and more parallel to the picture plane than occurs in a regular cubist work. Maybe the closest person would be Léger or something. Again, that was without – I knew of Léger and those people, but without too much study or attention to them. See, once you start to pay attention to somebody you're sort of like and trying to be like, then the possibility of the whole thing really comes home, and you leave.

MW   Did you lapse into a more abstract expressionist type of painting later?

DJ   Yeah. The thing got too cubistic and too small-scaled, or began to seem so to me after a while, and too spatial. So, I wanted to bring the picture plane – what else to call it – make it more a matter of surface, more a matter of a single plane, and increase the scale and increase the color, which wasn't always allowed. So, for a while, since most of the painting was of that nature – was loose – I did some fairly loose paintings. But that whole kind of looseness is very much against my way of working.

MW   Then somebody like Pollock would be completely against your way of working?

DJ   Yeah, it is, finally, except that I thought Pollock was the best painter.

MW   Because of his style?

DJ   I admired Pollock more than any other of the contemporary painters, but it's not something I can use myself, except in a very general way as to scale, or the importance of the surface, or something like that. The looseness and the drip thing and all that was impossible.

MW   Was impossible?

DJ   Yeah; I didn't even really try, actually, to do any such thing. I knew that it was too particular to Pollock to be of any use.

MW   How big were you working – how big were the canvases you were working on?

DJ   They got pretty big the last couple years I was painting, '59, '60, '61. At first, they were sort of curved lines on a single-colored ground. Then I got tired of the organic quality of all the curved lines and also the space they made because they curved away. I made them straight [image 32].

MW   Did you know Stella at this point?

DJ   Well, I'd seen the paintings at the Modern museum in that show he was first in.[4]

MW   How did you react to his shaped canvases?

DJ   Well, the black ones weren't shaped, and I thought they were very good; I was very impressed by the black ones.

MW   You did like them?

DJ   Yeah. I forget when that show was, though – '60?

MW   I don't know.

DJ   And then by the aluminum show, I think I was doing three-dimensional things.[5]

MW   You started doing this in about '61, '62?

DJ   Yeah, the three-dimensional ones, sort of. I can't quite remember all of the dates, but somewhere around there.

MW   That doesn't matter. Did you find the edge of the canvas, the rectangular edge of the canvas, confining to you?

DJ   Yeah, it was a real pain in the neck.

MW   [*Laughs*] And this is what really started you on three dimensions?

DJ   Well, I've said that in print, gone through that whole list of things.[6] The rectangle seemed to be hopeless. The fact that it was ordinarily about an inch and a half from the wall, a conventionally structured distance; that it was a particular relationship; and then the lines always made space on the ground or a general color, no matter what you did, and they were always within the general … at least in my opinion. Frank's overall system was very alien to me. He seemed to have a logical way out of some of those things.

MW   Because of the shape?

D J   Yeah, because of the shape; they're further out from the wall; and because the configuration was overall.

M W   How are you differentiating between the confines of a rectangular surface in a painting and the confines of, say, a box? I mean, they both are a format.

D J   Sure. Anything is a format, if you get interested in it. One's a format that a million people have used and which seems dead as hell, and the other's one I thought I'd found for myself.

M W   So, the aliveness was in your personal discovery of it?

D J   Yeah. The boxes are going to – perhaps by now, boxes of that shape could be very tiresome for somebody.

M W   Do you have intentions of expanding beyond – well, you aren't doing just boxes at all.

D J   No, but I'm not doctrinaire about boxes or anything. They give me something within which to work; they seem to have a lot of possibilities.

M W   Do you attach any suggestive elements of internal feeling or inner life in these boxes? It seems that there's a great emphasis on shape in much of your work, and in this emphasis on shape, there's almost a hollowness. And I personally get an exciting, internal sort of vibrating feeling inside, and yet at the same time it's very mysterious, because you can't get in it.

D J   I don't quite know what you're asking.

M W   What I'm saying is, was it intentional for you to remain strictly with the external appearance of the box, or –

D J   No, no, the hollowness is important. It is important that the thing is, say, made of sheet metal, and obviously, as everybody knows, sheet metal is very thin, and the interior is empty. Also, a lot of pieces work with the internal space. This is one of the first pieces on the floor, and you can see down into and all that. Some of them, the whole interior is opened up. So it very much is a case of what's inside of it or what's outside of it.

M W   Or at least suggesting.

D J   Well, I hope it doesn't suggest. I'd rather it was just plain there.

M W   This is very important to you, the assertion of the concreteness and the "thereness" of the object as sort of existing in its own reality without any interpretive connotations.

D J   Yeah, without interpretive – but that doesn't mean you're just making something that is there and doesn't have qualities or ideas or something. Say one of those concrete blocks is just over there, which is sort of interesting if you're speculating on things, but ultimately, it doesn't say very much.

M W   How do you differentiate between something – aside from the fact that you've constructed your forms and your shapes – between, say, something like that, or like that?[7]

D J   One has a quality or number of qualities and ideas that I like, and those don't; those are – those just exist the way everything else does. They're not necessarily of any particular interest.

M W   Because they're not art?

D J   No, they're not art now.

M W   But they could be made into art?

D J   Yeah, I'm willing to let anybody make them art by calling them art.

M W   You are?

D J   Yeah.

M W   You think anything can be called art?

D J   Yeah. It depends on your interest in the thing. I don't pay much attention to them, I work on them –

M W   They're part of the environment.

D J   Yeah. Nobody else has paid much attention to them. They serve Con Edison's purpose of connecting things. So I'd say, in that sense, they're not art. I'd say if anybody becomes interested in them, in a serious sense of interest in something, it could be called art.

MW   How are you differentiating between a functional inter-
     est and –

DJ   The complexity of one's interest in it, and the range of
     meaning it might have for someone, and so forth. The
     man who made the radiator is more interested in those
     than the man who made the blocks, for example, but it's
     all very situational.

MW   This whole situation is something I wanted to ask you
     about. Do you ally yourself with the term of "literalist
     art"?

DJ   No. I think it's stupid.

MW   You do think it's stupid? Why?

DJ   It's somebody else's term, and it doesn't mean anything to
     me. From what I can get out of it, it's meant to be derog-
     atory somehow. I don't know what it is that's being literal.

MW   Well, there's the aspect of literalist art that they claim to
     have the art object as a part of the whole entire art sit-
     uation, which the artist, I mean the viewer, is also a part
     of. The viewer is looking at the art object, and he sort
     of controls the light and space and everything, and yet
     the art object itself is supposed to be confronting the
     viewer. As you were speaking before in regard to the cin-
     der blocks, or the cement blocks, or the radiator, or your
     work – your work confronts the viewer as something dif-
     ferent from the environment that the radiator may be in.
     Do you include the viewer as part of the whole, say, per-
     ceiving situation?

DJ   You don't have any art without a viewer, but I don't really
     think of other people and their reactions or their view-
     ing it. I'm the viewer, in that case. So I'm making for my-
     self and for me to look at. Now, it can exist otherwise.

MW   Otherwise from what?

DJ   From myself, or from a viewer. If you put anything, any
     collection of things, out somewhere where nobody can
     see them, then they're just a bunch of objects.

MW But that isn't in accordance with what you just said; you said you were making them for you, in essence, and yet they are on display for other people too.

DJ Yeah.

MW And had they not been on display for other people, I'm interpreting what you said as they would just be objects.

DJ No, you'd still have one viewer, and that's me.

MW Which is the most important.

DJ Yeah. In a general way, you want people to see them, but there's nothing in all that that I take into consideration, as far as other people go.

MW How they will react to it?

DJ Yeah. There's nothing to think about; it's all too general a situation to think about, and they're too various, as far as kinds of people go.

MW What do you feel about the public now?

DJ I think it's reasonably awful.

MW Are they ignorant?

DJ Yeah.

MW How about as compared to something like the '50s?

DJ I don't know, there are probably six more knowledgeable people now than there were in the '50s.

MW Six?

DJ Yeah, which makes twelve altogether or something. I think most of the people involved in art are very ignorant of the whole thing, which includes everybody but the art-ists. That's sort of come along to me more in the last year or so. It's not an assumption I started with; I assumed that the whole thing is more professional than it really is, or more serious, and there really is not very –

MW You assumed?

DJ Yeah, a few years ago. And as I found out more about the museums – and I knew about criticism, of course, from writing criticism – museums, and buyers, and so forth … it seems pretty hopeless sometimes.

MW   You think the museums and the dealers are also sort of
      ignorant about the whole scene?

DJ   Yeah. Museums are really bad in a lot of respects.

MW   Are they out for themselves and not for what they're ex-
      hibiting? Or are they exhibiting only because –

DJ   Yeah, in a general way. A lot of it seems routine. They have
      to fill the space, and it gets kind of predictable. You run
      into an awful lot of people who don't know what it's all
      about, or aren't willing to deal with it seriously, or even
      install it seriously, and it gets pretty depressing. Some guy
      wants a big show costing a lot of trouble and a lot of
      money and the gallery a lot of growth, and he just wants
      the show. He may not be willing to work on the installa-
      tion. They usually won't handle things directly because –

MW   He just wants a final product?

DJ   Yeah. They're not professional in the way they handle the art.
      You go out and talk to them or something, it turns out they
      don't know anything about it, really. You're just somebody
      who has a certain reputation, and they all want to throw a
      few pieces in. It's very glib, really, and depressing, generally.

MW   Do you find a difference in your relationship with artists
      now, as [compared to] before? With the exception of your
      being more established in what you're doing now. Is it a
      more affable, less competitive, less heroic situation now
      than it was in the '50s?

DJ   I don't know much about the '50s directly, because I was
      here in New York, but I worked by myself, and I really
      didn't know anyone. I didn't know any New York paint-
      ers till the second or third generation.

MW   Okay, well, never mind the '50s. What about now?

DJ   I don't think it's especially different.

MW   It's not a competitive situation?

DJ   No. I only feel competitive when people whose work I
      don't like very much receive undue attention. That makes
      me – I don't know if it's competition or not; either way

it's irritating. But I'm very much in favor of people whose work I like.

M W   Going back specifically now to your boxes, or your forms: how do you feel about the unity that you display in five or six different boxes on your wall? Is it the one theme that is carried through which brings a wholeness to it? I know that you're fairly interested in creating or maintaining the importance of the whole situation, as opposed to all the separate parts that go into an object.

D J   Yeah, primarily, they should be single things, because, as I've said, I don't want them to seem to be made of parts.

M W   But you have intersecting – or not intersecting, but you have spaces cut out in such a way that it may disrupt that unity or that wholeness.

D J   It depends on which piece you're talking about. I don't think it disrupts the wholeness; they're obviously parts of some kind that you can count. Take six boxes on the wall horizontally [image 33]. You know right away that it's six things, but it's primarily a row, so the row is a single thing. You can just look at something – you look at the blocks; you can see right away that they're four, but the grouping of four is so random or so lower level that it has very little coherence. It's just sort of a neutral numeric coherence: one is up, and two are paired, the other one's by itself, down, and so forth, which would be very much what I would be against. So if you line them up, they're in a row, and the fact is that it's a row first, so that the parts are then pretty neutral. They're parts only if somebody really wants to define them as something or give them a name. They don't become parts in the way something like this does. I want a pretty flexible situation; I don't want to get into the position of doing single unbroken lumps of some kind. That was never my idea.

M W   If there's such an importance in maintaining this wholeness, this unity, I would think that varying the textures –

say, galvanized steel and plexiglass, or something like that –
would be a disturbing element and would cause the viewer
or cause the sensation to focus more on the respective tex-
tured parts, the parts being in this sense a textural thing,
than on the whole surface itself.

DJ   Well, I don't think that happens. It depends on my sense
of it and what would do it, what would break it up or not.
Usually there are no more than two different surfaces, and
they occur in the same place throughout the piece. I don't
think it breaks up the unity of the piece. If you use more
divergent textures, maybe it would.

MW   What were some things that made you start working
in steel and aluminum and plexiglass, as opposed to the
boxes – the wooden ones you started out with?

DJ   Primarily, I wanted a harder surface, and one that was
more conspicuously hollow.

MW   Even the plexiglass ends of some of the boxes emphasize
the hollowness of it too [see image 8].

DJ   But the wood tended to – you paint the wood, and the
paint soaks into the wood. It looks sort of like oil paint
or Liquitex or something applied very flatly on a canvas.
There's a certain quality there that I'd like to get away from.

MW   What about something like plaster? That would be the
same sort of thing, I imagine.

DJ   Yeah, if you painted plaster, you would end up like a fresco.

MW   Yes, but you never worked in any sort of plasticized or
comparable media, either in sculpture or –

DJ   No, I never did ordinary sculpture.

MW   You never did any sculpture?

DJ   No. I went from painting to those things, so I don't have
much connection to sculpture. I thought most of it was
pretty bad.

MW   What's the difference between a box, or the three-dimensional elements of the box, and the three-dimensional
elements of sculpture?

D J   Sculpture is, so far – obviously they're both three-dimensional, but sculpture is a very traditional thing, and primarily it's based on this part-by-part composition we're talking about, which I find very –

M W   Dissatisfying?

D J   Yeah. It goes back to being based upon gesture, figures, or landscape, or whatever. Given that so many things in it are traditional, I'd just as soon the word was left where it is.

M W   What about somebody like Tony Smith – how do you feel about his type of work?

D J   I think it's sort of half-baked.

M W   Why?

D J   I think it's the old gestural sculpture in a somewhat simplified form, that's all. By the time he did it, there were already plenty of people doing it. A lot of Park Place people were sort of like that.[8] It was a not very amazing thing to do.

M W   But he is visually – has the same sort of reaction as some of your work.

D J   Most of his pieces are very composed. There are only the box and those two piles he calls *The Elevens* that I first saw in the Wadsworth, which was the first time I ever saw the piece, that are fairly simple and really composed.[9]

M W   But something like *Die* and *Black Box* –

D J   I reviewed this show at the Wadsworth Atheneum, and I couldn't see anything to *The Elevens*, or *Eleven*, or whatever it's called.[10] Maybe it's just *Eleven*, because there are four boxes, two of them right on top of one another, side by side, two pair. I hated them being black, because it seemed such a weak color, visually. Black sort of destroys edges and turns a square thing into an amorphous thing.

M W   Just because it sort of negates an edge?

D J   Yeah, you can't – none of those things shows up clearly.

M W   You can't differentiate, yeah. Well, he's beginning to work – he's done a couple of things in color now, some models.

D J   Anyway, I think he's just sort of an ordinarily competent
       sculptor, not of great importance.

M W   What about [Robert] Morris?

D J   Anyway, back to Smith for a minute. I still don't see any-
       thing to *The Elevens*. I was a little interested, but I couldn't
       make sense out of it.

M W   You can really see, I think, his architectural influences in
       a lot of his work. Much more than, say, in yours and in
       Robert Morris's.

D J   Yeah. I suppose so. Architecture's a fairly backward pro-
       fession.

M W   What's going to happen now, though? Architecture's go-
       ing to have to be brought up to date, or people are going
       to be in trouble.

D J   I hope so. They're full of that sort of compositional fid-
       dling around.

M W   But that's a necessity; you have to have a compositional
       setup.

D J   Not like that –

M W   But you're dealing with a mass then; you're not dealing
       with an art object, you're dealing with people.

D J   Sure, but you can build – you don't have to build with a
       lot of intersecting verticals and horizontals, which they
       love to do.

M W   How do you build?

D J   When they put up, say, a plain, ordinary steel frame build-
       ing before it's covered by whatever junk they cover it with,
       that building isn't composed; it's a big cage, and it's not
       bad before they cover it all up. When [Paul] Rudolph or
       somebody, like – [11]

M W   Yale Art and Architecture.

D J   – yeah, Yale Art and Architecture school builds, they'll
       come up with a vertical and then cross it with a horizon-
       tal. You end up with something that looks like it should
       have been made in the '20s. With crisscrossing verticals

and horizontals and all sorts of interplay, you sort of have a big quandary –

MW   How do you escape it?

DJ   Well, the cage, for example, would escape it, because they're joining for the structure, and the things don't criss-cross and become composed in all sorts of ways.

MW   Then you have to put a series of cage-like structures –

DJ   Well, I don't know; I haven't thought about how I would build such a big building, but there are certainly alternatives. There's one, right away: leave it as a cage somehow. Some of the glass-fronted buildings, you don't get that much composition.

MW   Going back to your use of materials and the almost industrial quality of a lot of this work: do you think this could be mass-produced?

DJ   It could be, yeah.

MW   Wouldn't that distort it?

DJ   No.

MW   If you mass-produce an object, you're losing, it would seem, a lot of the artisan's sensibility about the object itself.

DJ   Why? It'd be the same object. In fact, if they had to build, say, thirty of them, they'd get a lot better at it than they are now. The work would get better, for one thing.

MW   But that's extending and expanding beyond the limit of an artistic creation.

DJ   Why is it? It would be just what I had them make, so why would it be any different?

MW   But it's not what you're doing.

DJ   Which is not what I am doing?

MW   I mean, the fifth thing that's being made is not – doesn't still hold, or doesn't seem to still hold.

DJ   But it would be identical.

MW   But why is it art, then?

DJ   Because I liked the first one, and it's identical to the first one. Except that, as I said, it would probably be made a little better, because if they have to make a thing again and again, then they'd get better at it, learning how to make it well. It doesn't matter in what numbers it occurs. Why should it? You couldn't tell the difference between the first one and the thirtieth one.

M W No, this is the whole point. I mean, this is what I'm saying: that it would seem to disrupt – I suppose that's a traditional point of view, by saying that it would disrupt the connotation you want to attach to an art object, if it's being mass-produced. It's turning into any object that could ever be made, then. You're differentiating very little between –

D J Sure, but that kind of uniqueness is fairly superficial. I don't think it means much that there's only one.

M W Well, for centuries, there hasn't been just only one of a certain kind of thing, but it's always had the artist's own feeling, and its own approach, and its own sensibility to it.

D J But all of those things I can make in something that could theoretically be duplicated. My work, I think, has all that too. But it occurred – it might not have occurred, it just happens to occur – that all of that can be duplicated by somebody else, if you can trust them to do it.

M W Where do you think you're going to go from here with this kind of work? Do you have any ideas of expanding beyond, say, the color and the materials that you're using now, and the shapes?

D J Oh, I just have ideas for pieces a few months ahead of time. I'm not given to speculation for numbers of years. I have some idea of the pieces I want to do next and various possibilities.

M W Do you think you'll ever work in another medium, as you see it now? You're really happy with what you've got now?

D J Yeah, it lets me do what I want to do. I would build buildings if I ever got a chance.

M W But you could have that chance.

DJ   Oh, I don't know; I don't know where you would begin.

MW   You could make cages.

DJ   Well, that isn't quite the building I would build. That was just an instance of something that isn't composed and so forth.

MW   Well, okay – thank you, very much.

This conversation was sourced from an audio recording. The original sound tape reel is in the Archives of American Art, Smithsonian Institution, Washington, DC.

1   Judd taught art at the Brooklyn Institute of Arts and Sciences from 1962 to spring 1964 and shop and history at the Allen-Stevenson School, a private all-boys school on the Upper East Side of Manhattan, from 1957 to 1959.

2   According to Roberta Smith, "Once, when he was in eighth grade, he designed a war bonds poster for his art class assignment, but he refused to put any slogan on it because he felt the sentiment would ruin the poster. He and the teacher had a serious disagreement about it; after that 'she didn't say anything but she gave me a "D".'" Smith, "Donald Judd," in *Donald Judd: Catalogue Raisonné of Paintings, Objects, and Wood-Blocks 1960–1974*, ed. Brydon Smith, exh. cat. (Ottawa: National Gallery of Canada, 1975), 4.

3   *The Book of Knowledge*, published in 1910 by Grolier, is a multivolume encyclopedia for children.

4   Judd refers here to Stella's inclusion in *Sixteen Americans*, The Museum of Modern Art, New York, December 16, 1959–February 14, 1960. However, Stella had shown work in five previous exhibitions: a solo show in Malden, Massachusetts; a group show in Oberlin, Ohio; and three group shows in New York (at Tibor de Nagy, Leo Castelli Gallery, and the National Arts Club), all in 1959. See William S. Rubin, *Frank Stella*, exh. cat. (New York: The Museum of Modern Art, 1970), 155–56.

5   Judd's first three-dimensional paintings date to 1961; the first three of Stella's *Aluminum Paintings – Kingsbury Run*, *Luis Miguel Dominguin*, and *Marquis de Portago* – were completed in 1960 and exhibited that same year in *Frank Stella*, Leo Castelli Gallery, New York, September 27–October 15, 1960. See Lawrence Rubin, *Frank Stella: Paintings 1958 to 1965; A Catalogue Raisonné* (London: Thames & Hudson, 1986), 95.

6   See Judd's "Specific Objects" (1964) in *Donald Judd Writings*, 134–45.

7   Willett refers here to objects in the room in which the interview is occurring; these objects are not identified in the audio recording.

8   The Park Place Gallery was an artists' cooperative space in the 1960s in SoHo, New York, consisting of five sculptors (Mark di Suvero, Peter Forakis, Robert Grosvenor, Anthony Magar, and Forrest "Frosty" Myers) and five painters (Dean Fleming, Tamara Melcher, David Novros, Edwin Ruda, and Leo Valledor). Paula Cooper worked at Park Place from 1964 until its closure in 1967. Cooper later opened a space on Prince Street, the first commercial gallery in SoHo. Judd's first show at Paula Cooper Gallery was the *Benefit for the Student Mobilization Committee to End the War in Vietnam*, October 22–31, 1968. For a further discussion of the history of the Park Place Gallery, see Linda D. Henderson, "Dean Fleming, Ed Ruda, and the Park Place Gallery: Spatial Complexity and the 'Fourth Dimension' in 1960s New York," in *Blanton Museum of Art: American Art Since 1900*, ed. Annette DiMeo Carlozzi and Kelly Baum (Austin: Blanton Museum of Art, 2006), 379–89.

9   Tony Smith, *The Elevens Are Up* (1963), edition of three.

10   *Black, White and Grey*, Wadsworth Atheneum, Hartford, Connecticut, January 9–February 9, 1964. See Judd's review of *Black, White and Grey* (1964) in *Donald Judd: Complete Writings 1959–1975*, 117–19.

11   Paul Rudolph (1918–1997) was an American architect and the chair of Yale's Department of Architecture from 1958 to 1965. He designed the Yale Art and Architecture Building (completed in 1963), now known as Rudolph Hall.

"Don Judd: An Interview with John Coplans"
From the exhibition catalogue *Don Judd*
1971

Published in the catalogue for the exhibition *Don Judd* (Pasadena Art Museum, California, May 11–July 4, 1971), this interview – conducted by John Coplans, the museum's senior curator from 1967 to 1970 – was then reprinted in the summer 1971 issue of *Artforum*. In "Complaints: Part II" (1973), Judd wrote, "Obviously Coplans didn't worry too much about the catalogue. He was supposed to write an essay but wrote six columns instead since he had an interview with me to fill up the space. That had been made to provide an accurate chronology for his essay. At the last minute he asked permission to print the interview in the catalogue, which I gave out of weariness. I was never asked if that interview could be printed in *Artforum*. Coplans probably got paid for it."

Following the exhibition, Judd installed three of the works from the Pasadena show at his home and studio spaces – one at 101 Spring Street and two at La Mansana de Chinati/The Block. One of the pieces, a large site-specific work from 1969, hastened Judd's rental and eventual purchase of the two large hangars at the Block. As Judd recounted in his 1985 essay "Marfa, Texas," "In addition to my developing idea of installations and my need for a place in the Southwest, both due in part to the harsh and glib situation within art in New York and to the unpleasantness of the city, I had set a deadline for finding a place. Bill Agee, then director of the Pasadena Art Museum, where I had an exhibition in 1971, had agreed to ship a large piece the museum had borrowed anywhere in the Southwest within a year."

JC   [John Coplans] On what basis did you formulate your early work?

DJ   [Donald Judd] Two things: the public situation and my own situation. Through most of the '50s, the dominant style was very loose painting – it was all abstract expressionist painting, so there was almost no idea for art that wasn't very sloshy and organic. The idea of geometric paintings was a very rare thing, so the few people who worked that way weren't the ones who were most regarded, like Barnett Newman or Ad Reinhardt. On my side, the person who impressed me most was Jackson Pollock, and though I never really got close to working like Pollock, I was very far from being interested in the geometric artists and very suspicious, very uninterested, and very wary of the style. I always liked Mondrian, and I liked Frank Stella's *Black Paintings* when I saw them. But, on the whole, I disliked the quality of geometric art. I guess I didn't understand Newman's work until later. Ken Noland's circles were geometric, in a way, even though some of them were sloshy. But with geometry, one important idea was available: it could be used in a nonneoplastic way, an impure way, without the purity that geometric art seemed to have. Mondrian, though really great, is too ideal and clean. In another way, Reinhardt is too. That was not a believable quality for me. Stella's painting had a possibility that became evident of an impure geometric art. And that's the only connection I had to Stella's work: his *Black Paintings* were a suggestion of new possibilities with geometry.

JC   It seems that in your early paintings, you were quite free from any rigid ideas about the use of materials, especially in the thickness of the skin of paint you used.

DJ   Yes, I was trying to make the surface nonspatial and flat. It has to do with trying to make it just surface, without any idea of purity of materials, color, or any restrictive notion, such as using three colors.

JC   What about your adoption of symmetry in the early '60s?

DJ   I know it was a move lots of people made to get away from
      the relational aspects of European painting – especially
      the idea of balancing forms – but at the time, it was pretty
      scarce, really. There was very little plain symmetry; there
      was Noland's painting, or [Jasper] Johns's targets, but Johns
      usually had something at the top anyway.

JC   Were you at all interested in the assemblage aspects of
      materials?

DJ   No, just the idea that there was complete freedom in the
      use of materials, but not in a rational, technological, or
      scientific way. That you could use anything you wanted
      to. I didn't see any reason for not using a particular mate-
      rial, but I was pretty uninterested in anything that actu-
      ally existed.

      I think Johns is a good artist, but I am not as crazy about
      him as a lot of people were. I was interested in some of
      his flatter surfaces – the texture might have a little bit to
      do with that – but from the beginning, I was very critical
      of all that brushwork. I got to like it better, but for quite
      a while, I thought it was pretty backward stuff compared
      to Pollock. I still do, some.

JC   There is a progressive development from a flat, painterly
      surface to relief.

DJ   Two things were going on in the painting: some of the
      earlier ones were organic and had curved lines; secondly,
      they were illusionistic to some extent, and I very steadily
      got tired of both things and tried to get rid of spatial il-
      lusionism, but I couldn't get rid of it. So even in a paint-
      ing like the red one with the gray stripes, painted in 1962,
      which is just all surface, there is still a spatial play around
      the lines [see image 15].

JC   By "spatial play" I suppose you mean figure/ground in-
      terrelationships, et cetera.

DJ   Yes. And one also had the problem that there were at least two things in the painting: the rectangle itself and the thing (image) in the rectangle, which is true even in Newman's. You couldn't get around that. The only paintings that didn't have that kind of problem were Yves Klein's – the blue paintings. But for some reason I just didn't want to do monochrome paintings.

JC   So you moved progressively from painterly low reliefs into more dimensional work?

DJ   Yes; one of the first three-dimensional ones started off as a piece of canvas from a failed painting that I tried to turn up, but I couldn't make the canvas turn up evenly. So after a while, it occurred to me to change the material and use something that would curve naturally. I threw out the piece of canvas and replaced it with galvanized iron. The relief is galvanized iron and painted plywood [see image 12]. It's the first really three-dimensional relief. The one with the pipe is 1962 [see image 13]. I went from low to high relief and then to freestanding works.

JC   What was the impulse to move from the wall to fully three-dimensional floor pieces?

DJ   First, I did the pipe relief and kept it on the floor [see image 14]. It was a big thing when sitting on the floor. I left it on the floor, and that didn't seem to bother it much. It was meant to go on the wall, but it looked all right on the floor. And then the whole situation of the wall was tiresome, but I was also tired of low relief. It seemed a method that would solve a lot of problems, and it did, to some extent, but it still shared the nature of painting in that low relief is rectangular and goes back against the wall. And I didn't want it to sit back against the wall. A piece that was completely three-dimensional was a big event for me.

JC   All your materials of this kind were just what you could find lying around?

DJ   Yes. A lot of it was primarily because it was cheap, and also I didn't care about it being precise. The piece with the

horizontal pipe is made out of printing material skids, sal-
vaged wood. It was pretty roughly made because I didn't
care about it.

JC   Does it have a bottom?

DJ   No, it's open at top and bottom.

JC   You seem to have broken the frontality in the next piece.

DJ   Yes, the pipe piece has two sides instead of four sides. The
      back is nice, too. The next three-dimensional piece is a
      right-angled floor piece with a bent pipe [see image 28]. The
      wood was purchased for this. The bent and welded pipe
      was found.

JC   It's very frontal.

DJ   No, it's a regular three-dimensional piece. The earlier
      pipe piece is decidedly more front and back. The sides
      don't amount to too much. This one really works; it's very
      definitely four-sided and opened up. It's a normal three-
      dimensional piece. The space is uncontained, and the con-
      struction and dimension are a function of the pipe. The
      arms of the pipe are of a different size; that's why it's not
      symmetrical.

JC   It's a big shift from symmetry to asymmetry, which you
      didn't maintain very much, did you?

DJ   Basically, I don't have anything against asymmetry – it's
      composition that I don't want. Neutral, plain asymmetry is
      all right. The bent-pipe piece is asymmetrical. The asym-
      metrical disposition is determined by the pipe, which I
      found that way, so that the pipe is a given thing. This gets
      around why one arm should be different from the other.
      Otherwise, it would get into composing, and it doesn't
      really look that way. I think you realize that the pipe has
      determined the shape of the piece. In the red box, I did a
      great deal of juggling to make it uncomposed [see image 5].
      I spent a lot of time determining where the trough should
      be on top of the box, having to do with it not being in any
      particular or obvious spot. It couldn't occur across one of

the quarters; it couldn't appear to occur at some definite, measured spot.

The wall reliefs and the freestanding pieces occurred right together. I didn't really get fed up with reliefs until the time of the Green Gallery show, or just before it [see images 2, 3].[1]

JC   Your material and techniques began to improve.

DJ   Yes, I got better and more interested in making the pieces. In the early ones, I didn't really care if the wood was sloppy or bad. And I still don't care the way some people care.

JC   Is there a reason for that?

DJ   Because precision doesn't have that much to do with it. I want my work well made, but I don't necessarily want it made with a great deal of precision.

JC   You mean industrial precision?

DJ   Yes; a certain amount of variation doesn't detract from them.

JC   Is the large relief pegboard [image 34]?

DJ   No, I hand-drilled nine hundred–odd holes.

JC   What was the idea of piercing the surface like that with small holes?

DJ   To make it more definite.

JC   In what way?

DJ   Just the surface. Without the holes, the metallic finish would be too illusionistic, too soft. It's to make a firmer surface. The edges are metal painted black.

JC   What about this long rectilinear one with holes at either end [see image 30]?

DJ   It's dated 1963, which is a big shift, and though very small, it's important. It's five by thirty-two by five inches, painted wood and an aluminum tube. At the time of the Green Gallery show in 1963, or just before, I finished the big relief of one-half-by-three-inch strips with the metal top and bottom. After that, I was tired of the whole relief idea against the wall and the rectilinear format, a painterly format. That situation really seemed to be dead. At first, it was just a casual thing. I had gotten the tube to figure out what I could do with it, but when I made the pipe and thought about it for a couple of months, it seemed to avoid all those things I didn't like. It wasn't rectangular, it wasn't back against the wall – which was the main point – because it was long and because of its projection. It doesn't look like the extension of a canvas anymore. And it comes out as far as the height of the front. The narrowness and horizontality keep it away from the whole idea of paint-ing. It is a box with an articulated interior, more than any-thing else. The horizontality and the projection are im-portant. Afterward, it occurred to me that the idea would work if the pieces were projected, and that the painting situation would be completely avoided if they projected more than they were wide, top to bottom.

JC   The progressions, stacks, and wall boxes develop from it?

DJ   Right, because of the projection. Also the idea of cantile-vering: it is like a form cantilevered off the wall, as against a painting that clings to the wall. One is aware of the weight of the pieces thrust forward and the fact they're being can-tilevered off the wall.

JC   The ladder piece seems to be a very important piece [see image 21].

DJ   Yes, it's the first big piece. It's also the first free, open, dimensional sculpture. It has the right angle and all those things too, but you can see through it. It's painted red and purple.

JC   Your predisposition toward red arises from what reason?

DJ   I like the color and I like the quality of cadmium red light. And then, also, I thought for a color, it had the right value for a three-dimensional object. If you paint something black or any dark color, you can't tell what its edges are like. If you paint it white, it seems small and purist. And the red, other than a gray of that value, seems to be the only color that really makes an object sharp and defines its contours and angles.

JC Red also has a saturated quality that seems very strong in all your work.

DJ I didn't want any bland colors. I would be more interested in them now, but at the time, I really hated them. At the same time as I was interested in developing plain surfaces, I was also interested in developing colors in a strong way.

JC Rather than being ambiguous, they were as clear as they could be.

DJ Yes, there is certain range. A dark chartreuse in which I did one piece has about the same value. I never used it, but I thought cerulean blue would do too. From the point of view of light, these colors define the angles very well. If you went down to cadmium red medium or deep, the form would be fuzzy, so the only point about the color was its capacity to define the form with clarity.

JC The Green Gallery show was in 1963. By this time, the question of sculpture without a base was central to your work. Did you now consider yourself a sculptor?

DJ I had always considered my work another activity of some kind. I was surprised when I made those first two free-standing pieces, to have something set out into the middle of the room. It puzzled me. On the one hand, I didn't quite know what to make of it, and on the other, they suddenly seemed to have an enormous number of possibilities. It looked at that point and from then on that I could do anything. Anyway, I certainly didn't think I was making sculpture. I liked Mark di Suvero and David Smith, but I didn't think what they did had much to do with me.

JC What about Anthony Caro's work?

DJ He didn't show in New York until 1964, and his work looked as if he were one of di Suvero's followers.

JC About this time, you wrote the "Specific Objects" article?[2]

DJ   Yes, but it was published much later than it was written –
     about a year later.
JC   Wasn't that a declaration of your situation?
DJ   I don't know. They just gave me a job of reporting. People
     talk about it being about my work, a manifesto and things
     like that, but really, I was earning a living as a writer, and
     it's a report on three-dimensional art.
JC   Who else, apart from Dan Flavin, was around? What was
     Robert Morris doing at this time?
DJ   It was a little while before I saw anything of Morris's, but
     Flavin was the only artist I knew who I thought was trying
     to do something out of the way. It's surprising, but there
     wasn't much around. There were Flavin's boxes and noth-
     ing else for a couple of years.[3]
JC   There's a surprising connection between some of Flavin's
     early work (the colored boxes) and yours.
DJ   I knew him before he did the green box.[4] I considered
     him the only interesting new artist.
JC   Did Stella know you and your work at the time?
DJ   Yes, he was interested.
JC   Did you discuss your sculpture with him?
DJ   Not too much.[5]
JC   The shapes in the Green Gallery show were more or less
     simple, geometric ones, often with diagonals?
DJ   I didn't want to make just lumps. I didn't want to make
     just a red box. That seemed too easy and pointless. I just
     didn't want to follow Yves Klein and make monochrome
     paintings.
JC   Also, I assume in not wanting to make boxes, you steered
     clear of anything mysterious, that all your sculpture was
     open to the eye and plain. I mean in the same way you
     were trying to get rid of illusionism, you were also trying
     to get rid of any anthropomorphism or surrealism.
DJ   Yes, I hate all that stuff.
     Back to the beginning: there was hardly anyone around

at the time I did my first work, but not much later, in the *Primary Structures* show, there were dozens of people.[6]

JC   Do we need to go into this whole question of *Primary Structures*?

DJ   I think it's a stupid name and was a stupid show. When I did my pieces, I finally felt I was doing something on my own, and suddenly, a few years later, similar things were occurring here and there. On the other hand, I figured it would all pass, which it did.

JC   I think it was surprising, however, to see so much sculpture without a base suddenly appearing on the scene.

DJ   That was almost completely my idea.[7] There are two things, both a little remote, that have anything to do with it: di Suvero's pieces tended – because of his studio, probably – to be rather low, six or seven feet high, with posts standing on the floor. They didn't stand on a base. John Chamberlain, I suppose, was the other. Also, Chamberlain's use of volume was important to me.

JC   But as far as I remember, he never made a specific point of having sculpture directly on the floor.

DJ   True; the ones that really sat on the floor were later on. So it's kind of remote, but there is that idea in di Suvero. And then the other thing was that Lucas Samaras did a four-by-four-foot piece in Sculp-Metal, I think, and it was right down on the floor.[8] It was more like a painting when it was put on the floor, because it was very flat. A little like Carl Andre's pieces, but it had a mound in the middle. I don't remember it too well. Andre was doing carved vertical pieces. I like Andre's work, but I don't like being put in the same time as him.[9] The absence of a base, as far as I knew, was completely my idea. It wasn't like Flavin, who was a contemporary, and it's not as if Andre took place in the development of the idea.

JC   There seems to be definite drive in your work to purge it of all iconic qualities, especially in the color.

DJ   I wanted to get rid of all those extraneous meanings – connections to things that didn't mean anything to the art.

JC   What do you consider art is about, then?

DJ   About what I know. The iconic quality, by definition, refers to other things.

JC   What about the question of scale and size?

DJ   That was very important to me in all the earlier and later paintings which had to do with that. In the paintings, I learned to use scale, size, direct color, and those things. As far as scale and size go, I don't think there's anything in my work that doesn't occur in common with or that isn't like most good New York art. I think my use of scale and size isn't that much different from Stella's, or Newman's, and so forth. I think it's a general broad scale that I thought was very good, and in which I worked, that I adopted from the situation.

JC   What determined your pieces?

DJ   It had to be a broad, single thing. I have a real hatred of small scale and small units. Not size, but small scale. As Newman remarked: a small work needn't necessarily be small in scale. I don't think I've contributed anything new in the way of scale. Broad scale is a pretty common thing in New York; I don't think there is a substantial difference between Ellsworth Kelly, Stella, Newman, di Suvero, Chamberlain, and whoever. The thing that is very different is Larry Bell's work, which is completely outside of broad scale.

JC   What about the use of polychrome?

DJ   Well, that was one of those big fake challenges. Every few years, somebody would come along and talk about when is somebody going to do polychrome sculpture. So in a way, it's a bit of a cliché. It was new in actuality, but I didn't make so much of it – I sort of took it for granted.

JC   In the Green Gallery show, you used color to neutralize the origins of the material.

DJ   You knew it was wood. The early ones were rough be-
      cause I just didn't care. In the later works, the color is dif-
      ferent. I'm not saying the color isn't very important. Some
      things seemed new to me. I took the color for granted
      because, for one thing, my paintings were colored; so
      obviously, I wasn't going to go and do uncolored three-
      dimensional things.

JC   Then after the Green Gallery show, you began to get the
      idea of working in metal?

DJ   Yes, but not right after. The Green Gallery show was from
      December 1963 to January 1964 or so. The first metal
      piece, I guess, was done in something like April 1964.
      I went to Bernstein's for the relief with one thousand
      holes in it.[10] That's the first time I went there, but Bern-
      stein said it would cost too much to do. There was no
      way to do it other than for me to drill it by hand, because
      it was cheaper. That was before the Green Gallery show,
      and that's a metal piece. Then, I think, in the spring of
      1964, I took the wooden box with the trough in it – the
      one that projected from the wall – to Bernstein to have
      it covered in galvanized iron. Anyway, that piece – even
      though it has wood underneath, which I had made – was
      ostensibly made of metal. Bernstein, at the time, was a lit-
      tle crude and not used to my ideas, and the wood con-
      struction made it difficult to do too carefully. They had
      to work against the wood. In a few months, I had it made
      over again in metal [see image 1]. The first big piece Bern-
      stein made must have been sometime before the Tibor de
      Nagy show in 1964.[11] They made the oval piece [image 35].
      It's not too well made, because they didn't realize how
      I wanted it. Bernstein made it as he would have made a
      ventilating duct. The pieces for the São Paulo biennial
      are the next lot.[12]

JC   Why the switch into metal?

DJ   I learned to do a better job at carpentry, but the main thing was that the wood was a little bit absorbent, the way canvas is. It wasn't hard enough of a surface. It also had to be a thick surface, and I wanted a thinner, more shell-like surface, so that the volume inside would be clear. Half-inch plywood is a pretty indefinite material; it could be any thickness once the piece is built. Also, I wanted to get out of painting pieces.

JC   You wanted to use materials that had self-colored surfaces?

DJ   Yes, but the painting was a problem. The reason for using galvanized iron was that it didn't have to be painted. The first oval piece was painted red. I'm still painting pieces because I can't find enough of a range of color in the materials. I consider everything to be color, including gray, so that business of gray not being a color that Morris talks about is nonsense.[13] But I don't want to use gray all the time, which is the color of most metals. The anodizing is an improvement because it colors the metal, so that's some possibility. The use of metal is just to reduce the number of ambiguous elements in the pieces, to define them more rigorously. The first floor pieces to follow the Green Gallery show are the plexiglass boxes with metal ends [see image 25]. They begin in 1964.

JC   So you added plexiglass to metal?

DJ   Yes, though I first used plexiglass in the wooden piece with a diagonal step in the Green Gallery exhibition [see image 3].

JC   Why the use of the plexiglass?

DJ   It has a hard, single surface, and the color is embedded in the material. In some cases, it also gives access to the interior – to a varying degree, however.

JC   With the wall pieces, I imagine the use of the plexiglass is important because the observer can see through the piece.

DJ   The use of plexiglass exposes the interior, so the volume is opened up. In the large piece owned by Pasadena [see image 9], the viewer has a clear idea of the volume because he knows how thick the walls are, even though it can't be seen into. It's fairly logical to open it up so the interior can be viewed. It makes it less mysterious, less ambiguous. I'm also interested in what might be called blank areas, or just plain areas, and what is seen obliquely, like the stack with the plexiglass top and bottom [see image 22]. When viewed frontally, the sides are seen obliquely, so the color and the plane and the face are somewhat obscure compared to the front. It's the other way around when seeing the side. In most of my pieces, there are no front or sides — it depends on the viewing position of the observer. It's obvious that the floor pieces have no front.

JC   The horizontal wall boxes don't seem to be explored in their variations as much as the stacks.

DJ   It has a lot to do with money. There has been quite a demand for the stacks and next to none for the four or six boxes in a row [see image 8]. Along with that, the six boxes in a row are bigger and consequently cost more than the stacks to make.

JC   The big and small stacks spread from floor to ceiling; the large, nine inches from the floor and the ceiling, and the small, six inches.[14]

DJ   Yes, there is the premise that the piece fits into the space.

JC   Was it at all important to you the way the stacks visually bite into the wall surface?

DJ   No, the wall goes through the piece, and that's all.

JC   But it opens the sculpture.

DJ   Yes, but that has to do with verticality. It's like one of the things I said before: I like David Smith's work, mostly, but I dislike all vertical, gestural sculpture. One reason I like di Suvero's sculpture is that it isn't so gestural. Somehow the stack going from floor to ceiling and the fact that it's not a column and not resting on its base saves it from that figurative business.

JC   All your pieces are pretty light in weight.

DJ   Yes, they're light pieces. For the most part, I've always been interested in making light pieces. I dislike sculptural bulk, weight, and massiveness. The big box shown at the Metropolitan Museum weighs four thousand pounds, but it doesn't look heavy, even though it's a great big tube covering an incredible volume of space [image 36].[15]

JC   I understand the stacks exist in the following variations: galvanized iron, copper, and stainless steel, and there soon will be one of brass. Then there are the various stacks of different-colored plexiglass with each type of metal.

DJ   Yes, first you have the solids, then plexiglass top and bottom, and finally the wraparound plexiglass sides.

JC   Do you work in editions in the stacks? Are there more than one of some combination of material?

DJ   No, they are all unique. Again, it's a question of money. If I had had more money, a lot of possibilities would have gotten done at one shot. That's somewhat true of the stacks. The ones of galvanized iron were made first because they were the cheapest to make. On the other hand, it's five years or more since I made the first stacks, and in that time, many more ideas have occurred, so I probably couldn't have made them all at once. So there is the development in the materials to allow for a wider range of plastic in different colors – some transparent, translucent, or opaque. I didn't think at first of opening them from top to bottom. That only came later. And I didn't think of the wraparound until after that.

JC   You never painted any of the stacks?

DJ   I painted one, which is the beginning of the wraparound idea; Leo Castelli had it in his tenth anniversary show.[16] It's galvanized iron with painted green sides. It's painted in the same way as the wraparound, but the plexiglass seemed to be an improvement on painting.

JC   What about the question of editions, as far as your work is concerned?

DJ   Not much is in editions. The small painted and unpainted galvanized round-fronted and square-fronted progressions are in editions of three.[17] I'm interested in ideas I can work with, and the stack proved to have a lot of possibilities. In a way, when one gets one part set, it gives more leeway on the other things, because it is very hard to deal with all things at once. So once I thought of the idea of the stack, or a certain scheme, and once I see a couple and spend time with them, further ideas occur.

JC   Why do you make the small progressions in editions of three?

DJ   It's just a question of money. People seem to pay just as much money for small things made in editions as for unique ones. And without money, I can't make more sculpture – that's all. The stacks could have been done the same way, but as things developed, the stacks turned out to be unique. Also, I don't sell as many stacks as progressions.

JC   Important to your work after the Green Gallery show in 1963 is the idea of having your sculpture fabricated, of not having to make them by hand yourself.

DJ   The paintings were handmade, but none of the three-dimensional work is meant to look handmade, including the wooden ones, which I made in as matter-of-fact a way as I could. Wood, being what it is, tends to look more manipulated than metal. I kept down the handcraft aspect. Other artists play it up.

JC   You did gain a great freedom, though, from being able to send your work out to be made.

DJ   I guess so, but I don't make a great thing of technology and all that. In the first place, I use an old-fashioned technique – basically a late nineteenth-century metal-working technique. I don't romanticize technology like Robert Smithson and others. I think generally you are forced into more modern technologies, but the technology is merely to suit one's purpose. It's not something myste-rious or something that sanctions the work.

JC   Do the progressions come after the stacks?

DJ   No, the progressions sort of come all together. They and the stacks originate from that one wood piece with the two holes in either end [see image 30]. In fact, because of the wooden piece, the progressions slightly precede the stacks. True, with the wood piece, I started to think about equal-izing the projection and the height, but the idea of the progression occurs in the red wooden box with the semi-circles cut out of the divisions.

JC   Were the interior divisions based upon the idea of a math-ematical progression?

DJ   Yes, the first real wooden progression was done from the cut semicircles left over from that box. It's decidedly a pro-gression, with half an inch being added each time.

JC   Then you seem to have done some plain, roundnosed nonprogressions?

DJ   Yes, but you're going too fast. The small one with the alu-minum tube was in the Green Gallery show. It had an alu-minum tube and a wooden structure. That was 1963. Then in the spring of 1964, I did the one with the trough that Stella owns [see image 1]. That box really projects and is the beginning of the idea for the stacks.

JC   It's cantilevered out from the wall?

DJ   Right. The first one done prior to Pasadena's boxes is a com-bination of two things: it's got the horizontal element – the bar – and it has boxes that project as much as they are high – thirty inches. After that, I did the one Stella owns and another one or two; then I ordered the plain, round-sided, and round-fronted single boxes all at once. I don't know whether I ordered the metal stack or not; I think the metal stack was a little bit later. I think the single small box preceded the big stacks. So at São Paulo in 1965, there was the long progression and the smaller Pasadena-type boxes.

The stack had just been finished and wasn't in the show. It must have been made in the first half of 1965.

JC   What about the cantilevering of the stacks?

DJ   I think it's pretty much just a practical matter.

JC   Then why didn't you project them more? What determined the amount of projection?

DJ   I didn't want to make too much of the cantilevering – it's a way of getting them in a row up the wall. They couldn't come out too far in relationship to the width, and I didn't want any kind of engineering problem. The projection was a very precise relationship to the width of the piece. The first stack was a thirty-inch projection as against forty inches wide. I changed the next one to thirty-one inches by forty inches. I don't like any dramatic quality or incident or anything archaic. The boxes just hang on the wall in a practical manner.

JC   And the progressions?

DJ   There are two kinds of progressions. In the first, the spaces or intervals are equal to the solids. I'm not doctrinaire about symmetry, so when the whole idea of the progressions developed, I saw a way of having asymmetrical pieces that didn't involve composition.

JC   Would you define "composition"?

DJ   Typical part-by-part play, as in David Smith, or in all earlier painting and art, or European art.

JC   You mean to take variously weighted parts to make them visually balance?

DJ   Yes – Mondrian is typical. The idea of taking some little part down here to adjust it to balance some big part up there.

JC   Okay, but you also compose.

DJ   Yes, but I wouldn't want to call it that. I mean I'm working with the form. I know I'm doing something with the form, but I wouldn't call it "composition" because I hate the term.

J C   You mean that all your ordering of form is arrived at or
        deduced as a whole in advance?

D J   Yes, that's what I was going to tell you. You see, the thing
        about my work is that it is given. Just as you take a stack or
        row of boxes, it's a row. Everybody knows about rows, so
        it's given in advance. Now, it's also given if it's a fairly simple
        progression, because everybody knows right off the spaces
        are given by the mathematics. In one of the progressions, I
        used the Fibonacci series. In another, I used the kind of in-
        verse natural number series: one, minus a half, plus a third,
        a fourth, a fifth, et cetera. No one other than a mathemati-
        cian is going to know what that series really is – you don't
        walk up to it and understand how it is working – but I think
        you do understand that there is a scheme there, and that it
        doesn't look as if it is just done part by part visually. So it's
        not conceived part by part; it's done in one shot. The pro-
        gressions made it possible to use an asymmetrical arrange-
        ment, yet to have some sort of order not involved in com-
        position. The point is that the series doesn't mean anything
        to me as mathematics, nor does it have anything to do with
        the nature of the world. The progressions consist of several
        variations – round nosed, square nosed, and those with a
        tube and boxes underneath. There are also the progressions
        that have no tube and the big progressions that have a tube.

J C   Why were the boxes at the bottom and not the top?

D J   It would have turned the top into teeth and made the bar
        look like a base. In the piece in Robert Rowan's collec-
        tion and in Pasadena's, there is a certain equivalence be-
        tween what is supported and what is hanging [see image 6].
        I fiddled with Rowan's for a long time so that the verti-
        cals wouldn't appear to be hanging. They are attached to
        it and support it, but I didn't want them to look as if they
        were hanging.

J C   You seem to have some difficulty in the stacks and the pro-
        gressions with the amount of shadows cast.

DJ   It has to do with the fact that museum lighting is pretty
      bad. The Whitney show was especially bad because of the
      spotlights.[18] All my pieces are meant to be seen in even or
      natural light. The shadows are unimportant; they are just
      a by-product.

JC   What about the horizontal wall pieces?

DJ   Some of them go to the side walls, and the intervals be-
      tween the walls and the boxes are identical. So they are
      related to the architecture like the stacks, but horizon-
      tally instead of vertically. The height of the boxes from the
      ground is also critical. The viewer is meant to see a little of
      the tops of the boxes, but the ceiling height doesn't mat-
      ter. They should be hung at either sixty-two or sixty-three
      inches. The choice of that height is meant to avoid flat-
      tening the boxes when they are on the wall. If the viewer
      can see a little of the top plane, it's going to keep them
      three-dimensional.

JC   And the floor boxes?

DJ   The floor boxes obviously come from the Green Gallery
      show. They are even the same size. If they were any larger,
      they would have been too gross or monumental. They
      have to look static, without movement. I am interested in
      static visual art and hate imitation of movement.

      The floor boxes with plastic sides and top started out
      in a practical way: I wanted them to be portable and
      shippable – a knockdown piece. Thus they are designed to
      be taken apart. The stacks didn't start out that way. The first
      boxes incorporating plexiglass are a little fancy technically
      and required four tension wires to hold them together.
      The pebbled finish in the plexiglass is because I didn't
      want the interior to be seen into at that time [image 37].
      I wanted the finish translucent; however, you can see the
      struts inside a little bit.

      Sometime later I had the idea of the clear boxes [see
      image 25]. None of the plexiglass boxes has a bottom; thus

in the clear ones, the floor can be seen through the box. This opens the box up. The whole scheme has to do with defined ends and open body; this has been a sort of steady idea. Once I got the design of the wires, better I was able to make the boxes of transparent plexiglass.

JC   What about the boxes with a recessed top?

DJ   I made a chartreuse wooden box with a trough that was a little larger than the red box. I got tired of the trough, or something that just cut across the top like a trough or a cut, and I wanted to do something more with the top, but with a single box. I thought it was too much like putting an element in it to keep cutting it, so I made a hot-rolled steel box and painted it [image 38].

JC   What do you think the effect of lipping or recessing the box is?

DJ   The surface is pushed back. It occurred to me if you took one of the sides and pushed it in, it would open the top surface up. I was always interested in edges and flanges. I was also interested in a certain quality of thinness and edgeness in the paintings. It defines what the boxes are made of by showing the thickness of the sheet metal, and thus becomes less arbitrary, more rigorous, with a more precise knowledge of the thickness of the material. So it shows, or makes, or emphasizes the edge more clearly. One thing I liked about the red box when I originally made it was that now I had a broad shape with several edges, which I couldn't get in a painting.

There are also plexiglass boxes with stainless-steel tubes through the center. They are without frontality and have an axis running in two directions. Another kind of tube is the double-walled box [image 39]. You get two different types of space – the compressed space formed by the two walls and the open tubular space.

JC   Some of the boxes have the insides lined with color [image 40].

DJ   The box with the plexiglass inside is an attempt to make a definite second surface. The inside is radically different from the outside; while the outside is definite and rigorous, the inside is indefinite. The interior appears to be larger than the exterior. The plastic is very slippery in look.

There is one thing I know how to do very well, and that is to produce a plain, austere piece. It's a quality that I like, and I get very skeptical about it. But I like to try other things to see what happens to the shape and surface. Also, I like to try different colors on the same form by using different materials. Brass, for example, is very yellow. I have very ambivalent feelings about plexiglass and don't like it too much as a material. In part, it's a sort of slippery and slightly disagreeable material.

JC   Don't you think that your color on the recent progressions is pretty opulent?

DJ   Yes, it's a pretty strange thing. I never use more than two colors on the progressions, and they are very often just plain aluminum and one color. One thing I have never liked is dividing a single surface with a color; color is always identical with a single surface. The reason I have two colors in the progressions is obviously that the tubes and the boxes are two different things.

JC   What about the environmental quality of the honeycomb and the galvanized sheet piece [images 41, 42]?

DJ   I still intend to do discrete pieces, but I get a little tired of them. My work goes back and forth. I got a little tired of big pieces that just sit there in an indefinite space, so I wanted to do something that deals more with the space of the room. I don't know about it being environmental — it is just a piece that does something with the space of the room.

JC   The 1966 piece that seems like a wedge on the floor is very anomalous [image 43].

DJ   The pierced metal has to do with opening up the surface like the plexiglass. Obviously, by piercing it, one can see into it. The wedge relates to a parallelogram, but it's made to be a very low piece.

JC   It's the lowest piece you have ever made?

DJ   Yes. It's only eight inches high, and that height is very important. I thought if it was too flat, it would just lie down on the floor, which is the same objection I have to painting.

JC   Sculpture seems to have less attention than painting.

DJ   Obviously, paintings are easier to handle, to buy, and put in people's houses, et cetera. Also, since painting has been the medium in which most of the best work and innovation has been done, it has more prestige. I think a lot of people still believe that painting is the main thing, so it's easier to sell.

JC   In your more recent pieces, you have enhanced the scale. Is this a result of better access to technology and money?

DJ   Yes. I think about what I can actually do, which has been true all along, ever since money and labor got into it. The plywood pieces took so long to make. I don't have too great a sense of progress – of change, either. I like to work back and forth. There seems to be a lot more variety in my work than is casually apparent.

This conversation was sourced from an archival transcript in the Judd Foundation Archives, Marfa, Texas, as well as from its first two published versions.

First published: "Don Judd: An Interview with John Coplans," in John Coplans, *Don Judd*, exh. cat. (Pasadena, CA: Pasadena Art Museum, 1971), 18–44; reprinted: John Coplans, "An Interview with Don Judd," *Artforum*, Summer 1971, 40–50.

1   *Don Judd*, Green Gallery, New York, December 17, 1963–January 11, 1964. This exhibition was Judd's first solo show to include works in three dimensions.

2   See Judd's "Specific Objects" (1964) in *Donald Judd Writings*, 134–45.

3   Flavin completed a series of eight works known as *icons* between 1961 and 1964. Judd permanently installed two of the eight, *icon III (blood) (the blood of a martyr)* (1962) and *icon VI (Ireland dying) (to Louis Sullivan)* (1962–63), at 101 Spring Street.

4   Flavin's *icon VI (Ireland dying) (to Louis Sullivan)* is painted cadmium green
     light. Judd met Flavin in 1962 at a gathering in a Brooklyn apartment or-
     ganized to discuss the possibility of a cooperative artist-run gallery. See
     Michael Govan and Tiffany Bell, *Dan Flavin: The Complete Lights, 1961–
     1996*, exh. cat. (New York: Dia Art Foundation, 2004), 183.

5   See "New Nihilism or New Art?" (1964) and "Interview with Barbara Rose
     and Frank Stella" (1966–67) in this volume, 28–58 and 148–84, respectively.

6   *Primary Structures: Younger American and British Sculptors*, Jewish Museum,
     New York, April 27–June 12, 1966. See "The New Sculpture" (1966) in
     this volume, 90–102.

7   Judd's first work in three dimensions on the floor dates to 1962. The only
     baseless work to appear in *Primary Structures* that dates this early is Tony
     Smith's *Free Ride* (1962); Smith made at least two other baseless works the
     same year, *Die* and *Black Box*. See *Primary Structures: Younger American and
     British Sculptors*, exh. cat. (New York: Jewish Museum, 1966), n.p.

8   Lucas Samaras, *Untitled (Floorpiece)* (1961), The Metropolitan Museum of
     Art, New York.

9   Carl Andre was making baseless sculptures that sat on the floor as early as
     1958; see, for example, *First Ladder* (1958), Tate, London.

10   Judd worked with Bernstein Brothers Sheet Metal Specialties, Inc. from
     late 1963 until the end of his life. Although they moved to Long Island
     City by the end of 1964, their shop was originally located in Manhattan,
     at 191 Third Avenue.

11   The exhibition was in fact in 1965: *Shape and Structure*, Tibor de Nagy,
     New York, January 5–13, 1965. Judd refers here to an untitled 1964 piece
     in galvanized iron that is similar to but has different dimensions than the
     work referenced in image 35.

12   VIII Bienal de São Paulo, Ibirapuera Park, São Paulo, September 4–
     November 28, 1965; National Collection of Fine Arts, Smithsonian Insti-
     tution, Washington, DC, January 27–March 6, 1966. This iteration of the
     Bienal de São Paulo also included works by Billy Al Bengston, Robert Ir-
     win, Barnett Newman, Larry Poons, and Frank Stella. Judd attended the
     opening of the biennial in Washington, DC, with Larry Bell, Dan Flavin,
     Barnett Newman, and Larry Poons.

13   See Robert Morris, "Notes on Sculpture, Part 2," *Artforum*, October 1966,
     20–23.

14   Each stack unit is installed six or nine inches from the floor, with six- or
     nine-inch intervals between each unit, generally up to ten units.

15   *New York Painting and Sculpture: 1940–1970*, The Metropolitan Museum of
     Art, New York, October 18, 1969–February 1, 1970.

16   *Ten Years*, Leo Castelli Gallery, New York, February 4–26, 1967.

17   Judd's roundfront progressions were made in multiple examples as
     unique works.

18   *Don Judd*, Whitney Museum of American Art, New York, February 27–
     March 24, 1968, extended through April 14.

"Around Barnett Newman"
Article by Jeanne Siegel for *ARTnews*
October 1971

This interview was organized as part of an oral history of the influence of Barnett Newman and conducted in conjunction with the first large-scale retrospective of his work (*Barnett Newman*, The Museum of Modern Art, New York, October 21, 1971–January 10, 1972). In addition to this interview with Judd, the article also included contributions from eleven other artists.

Judd saw Newman's 1959 exhibition *Barnett Newman: A Selection 1946–1952*, at French & Company, New York (March 11–April 5, 1959), which included twenty-nine paintings and was the largest show of Newman's work up to that point; it was organized by critic Clement Greenberg. Meyer Schapiro, the influential art critic, historian, and professor, had asked all of his students at Columbia University – including Judd – to attend the exhibition. In "Barnett Newman" (1964), his first article on Newman's work, Judd wrote that it was "a large and magnificent show of paintings."

Judd and Newman met for the first time when Newman fact-checked the article, and the two became friends. (The article, which had been written for the German journal *Das Kunstwerk*, was not published as planned, but was later run by *Studio International* in February 1970.) After Newman's death in the summer of 1970, Annalee Newman, Newman's wife, gifted a number of items to Judd, including two of Newman's painting scaffolds and one of his painting palettes. Judd installed these items in his Art Studio and also installed two of Newman's prints (one from the *18 Cantos* series, the other from the *Notes* series) in his Architecture Studio.

JS   [Jeanne Siegel] You stated, in 1964, that you thought Bar-
      nett Newman's paintings were some of the best done in
      the United States in the last fifteen years and that New-
      man was the best painter in this country.[1] Do you feel the
      same way today?

DJ   [Donald Judd] I don't know if he is the greatest, but he's
      one of very few. I'm in favor of comparing artists, but it's
      a very difficult thing to do. Anyway, he's one of the best.

JS   At that time, you saw his work as a very definite statement
      about the rectangle.

DJ   I think certainly that he and other people developed the
      rectangle as a thing itself.

JS   Do you believe that he was directly responsible for any-
      thing that you were doing in the early 1960s?

DJ   No, I don't think so. The timing was sort of wrong,
      somehow – my timing. The moments when I came to
      figure certain things out didn't quite coincide with the
      ones when I could have used knowledge about his paint-
      ings, so that I really came to like them after the point
      where I could learn anything from them, beyond a couple
      of general things, such as scale, primacy of wholeness, and
      color, and so forth. It's a very big point, but I didn't learn
      it only from him, but from all of the New York painters.
      It's nothing that Rothko didn't do too, or Pollock. Also,
      Pollock was the first artist that I was really impressed by
      of that group. I'm still impressed by Pollock.

      When I saw Newman's show at French & Company
      in 1959, I thought the paintings were good, but I was kind
      of critical of him because of the geometry, which I think
      was probably the problem Barney got into with every-
      body in the 1950s. I think people misread that geometry;
      I misread it too. I attributed all that geometry to Mon-
      drian and the Europeans. Though I like Mondrian, I felt
      it could only be used one way and that was the end of it,
      so I had a lot of trouble getting into it myself.

JS   Wasn't the main objection to Mondrian's paintings that they were built up of relational elements?

DJ   The relational elements and just the quality of it, the pure and ideal. I was never interested in a pure kind of art. That was the main thing I held against geometry and primary colors and such things. Now, though, I wouldn't distinguish between pure and impure. It's a writer's cliché. But I guess, too, at French & Company, I took Barney's paintings – I remember some of them, particularly black-and-white paintings, which I think now aren't at all like that – as sort of blown-up sections of some of Mondrian's paintings, where the stripe would be over on one edge, which Mondrian does all the time. Except Barney would have nothing but white canvas with a stripe at one edge, and it looked like a section. So I kept thinking of the stripe, as in Mondrian, moving to one side rather than simply being there as it really is in his paintings.

JS   When did you change your mind?

DJ   About '64, that was all finished.

JS   Do you think there are young artists today upon whom Newman had a direct influence?

DJ   I'm not really interested. I've seen a fair number of paintings around. They don't look very interesting to me. As you can probably figure out, I'm pretty skeptical about painting. But that sort of thing isn't retroactive; it doesn't apply to Barney or Stella. I don't think anyone has come along doing interesting painting in quite a while.

JS   What about an influence on Dan Flavin? By the way, Flavin told me that you introduced him to Newman.

DJ   We were all on a panel together,[2] Barney, Dan, and myself, at the Richmond [Professional] Institute in Richmond, Virginia,[3] and somehow we got to talking about Charlottesville, and Barney wanted to go there. So the next day a guy named Livingston at the institute took us up there, and we saw Monticello and the buildings on the campus.[4]

They were pretty interesting. Barney liked the pillars on the main building. The pillars as line and the space behind them. I don't know. I first saw Dan's work before he used the fluorescent tubes. In his first show he had one, two, three, four tubes, and that reminded me of Barney. I see things that I'm interested in that he was interested in, too, maybe, that are closer connections than those general things. But it's in retrospect. That is, for example, pieces with narrow shapes – evenly spaced; or some of the pieces that have narrow spaces of one kind or another. They're usually part of a very broad area. That's certainly true of the stripes.

An incredible quantity of thinking went into the lines in Barney's paintings. I'm not talking so much about placing as the possibilities of the line. You know – broad, narrow, and so forth. That's really amazing. I think about things like that in my own work, but I'm mildly surprised that he can think so much about a relatively unmomentous matter. It's funny. It's a very philosophical matter, I guess. Presumably there are an awful lot of things to think about – it's strange to think about a single form over and over again.

JS   Do you have a preference for any particular painting of Newman's?

DJ   I tried to buy *Shining Forth (To George)*. It's one of his best paintings, but it's a personal painting, too, because of George.[5] I saw it when it was just finished, in a show at the Jewish Museum. Then, not too long afterward, it was in the Janis Gallery.[6] I didn't see very many Newmans after the French & Company show, so I think maybe it was one of the first big ones I'd seen since I'd changed my mind on the whole subject. And it's also a spectacular painting.

JS   What about *Who's Afraid of Red, Yellow and Blue II*?

DJ   That's nice. It's a very nice painting. Barney and Dan Flavin and I went down to see the big one after he'd finished it. I was very surprised by [the] bright color and I guess, actually, the red, yellow, and blue.

Vir Heroicus Sublimis is a red painting – it has plenty of red, white, and off-red, a red-brown stripe – but anyway, decidedly not primary color. I guess I was surprised by the use of primaries because of my own bias against primaries and the fact that it didn't have any of that quality. I disliked primaries in Mondrian's paintings, at least as something for me to use. But this painting doesn't have anything to do with that sort of use of primaries. Also, an interesting thing about the red–yellow–blue paintings, too, is that they're very flat and comparatively nonspatial, compared to his earlier paintings. They have a very mechanical surface. He was using a roller.

One thing I objected to in the French & Company show in several of the paintings, for example, *Cathedra*, a big blue painting, was the brushwork and the airiness.

JS   There is brushiness in *Shining Forth*.

DJ   Yes, but it's not used to make air or illusionistic space. It's used as the nature of the edge, the process of making the edge. That has to do with brushwork as contrasted with making space. *Cathedra* seems to go way back, while the late ones are very, very flat. In *Red, Yellow and Blue III*, it's only one stripe that's a little spatial – the blue is glazed or something, so it's a little indeterminate, but the red is just red paint.

JS   Certainly Newman was the most successful in eliminating illusionism. For instance, compare him to Rothko.

DJ   That is pretty recent in Newman's painting. However, Rothko's whole way of working depended on a good deal of illusionism. I think it's very aerial. The whole thing is about areas floating in space. Compared to Newman, there is distinctly a certain depth. But I finally thought that all painting was spatially illusionistic, even when it was flattened as much as Barney had flattened it, or as I tried to in my paintings. Barney's quite a bit less illusionistic than others, but they're still involved in a certain amount of space. *Shining Forth* is all about where the space occurs, even though it's only canvas.

I went to Annalee [Newman] to see the paintings Barney had been working on when he died, and he had a great big one finished and some unfinished. They're like the *Red, Yellow and Blue* ones. He was using a roller on these. The big finished one had a very wide central band and two big areas on either side, and all the areas were flat – rolled on.[7] It was exceedingly flat. It's really just a layer of paint. Also, he had some triangles stretched that he was going to work on. So far I haven't been too interested in them; I need to think about them more. I wasn't so keen on them in the Knoedler show (in 1969), but then they were on velvet walls.[8] Maybe in another context and more time to think about them I'd like them better.

JS   The idea for the triangular paintings grew out of his sculpture *Broken Obelisk*.

DJ   I don't like the obelisk. I don't know what it's all about. I can't make any sense of it. I have no interest at all in obelisks. I didn't understand why he was interested in the obelisk as a form. And it didn't seem interesting to break it. Why not just do a big line or band or whatever? And the precarious perch seems tricky, or cute, or something. I like the first sculpture he did, in 1950.

First published: Jeanne Siegel, "Around Barnett Newman," *ARTnews*, October 1971, 42–47, 59–62, 65–66; reprinted: Jeanne Siegel, *Artwords: Discourse on the 60s and 70s* (Ann Arbor, MI: UMI Research Press, 1985), 42–62.

1   See Judd's "Barnett Newman" (1964) in *Donald Judd Writings*, 152–59.

2   "Art, Non-Art, Anti-Art," panel discussion with Dan Flavin, Donald Judd, Allan Kaprow, Barnett Newman, and Ernest Trova, March 25, 1966, Richmond Professional Institute Spring Arts Festival, Richmond, Virginia. The editors were unable to locate a recording or transcript of this discussion.

3   The Richmond Professional Institute was particularly known for its School of Art. In 1968, it merged with the Medical College of Virginia to form Virginia Commonwealth University, whose art department is today known as VCUarts.

4   Judd refers here to the campus of the University of Virginia, in Charlottesville; the school's campus and the neighboring plantation of Monticello were both designed by Thomas Jefferson and together constitute a World Heritage site.

5   George Newman, Barnett's brother, died in 1961; *Shining Forth (To George)* was made later that same year.

6   The Janis exhibition in fact preceded that at the Jewish Museum: *Eleven Abstract Expressionist Painters*, Sidney Janis Gallery, New York, October 7–November 2, 1963; *Black and White*, Jewish Museum, New York, December 12, 1963–February 5, 1964.

7   Original note from *ARTnews*: "In point of fact, Newman painted with a brush all the final coats of his pictures. He sometimes used rollers to lay on the undercoats. (Ed.)"

8   *Barnett Newman*, Knoedler & Company, New York, March 25–April 19, 1969. Newman's first solo exhibition in ten years, it was also his last solo exhibition before his death, on July 4, 1970.

"Excerpts from a Conversation between Elizabeth C. Baker,
John Chamberlain, Don Judd, and Diane Waldman"
For the exhibition catalogue *John Chamberlain*
October 26, 1971

This conversation between art critic and editor Elizabeth C. Baker, John Chamberlain, Judd, and curator Diane Waldman took place in conjunction with Chamberlain's first major museum retrospective, *John Chamberlain: A Retrospective Exhibition*, curated by Waldman at the Solomon R. Guggenheim Museum, New York (December 22, 1971–February 27, 1972).

In his first review of Chamberlain's work, published in *Arts Magazine* in March 1962, Judd opened by stating, "The only reason Chamberlain is not the best American sculptor under forty is the incommensurability of 'the best' which makes it arbitrary to say so." He continued to write frequently and favorably of Chamberlain's work for the rest of his life.

In his essay "Chamberlain: Another View" (1963), Judd described Chamberlain's 1961 sculpture *Mr. Press* in detail, noting, for example, that "the color, as is apparent, is structural. The combination of pastel colors and dark and intense ones is characteristic, novel, and excellent." By 1970, Judd had installed *Mr. Press* on the fifth floor of 101 Spring Street.

DW   [Diane Waldman] Did you start out as a painter?

JC   [John Chamberlain] Oh, momentarily.

DW   Well, how long – about a year?

JC   I was still in art school.[1] I walked past the sculpture studio one time, and I saw all these little people standing on stands.

DW   Little sculptures or little people?

JC   Little sculptures, and I did about three takes. It was just fantastic to see about thirty little people standing around, and I thought it was marvelous. It enlarged the whole space of the room, and I was convinced that was the room to be in.

DJ   [Donald Judd] That would probably be a real solution to the population problem. Just reduce the size of the people.

JC   I think they're probably doing a good job on themselves. Then I got in there, and I found Joe Goto working.[2] He had left school, but he came back to use the studio, and it was fantastic the way he was welding things. I didn't particularly see his sculpture in some kind of context, because he was sort of making large horses – you know, that style that he developed in the beginning of the '50s. I don't know if you know him at all. But it wasn't the welding that was the thing, but that he made connection by welding. I mean, his connections, they were well welded as they say – the welding was good and all that, but it wasn't good welding that was appealing: it was that he made great connections. He connected, and that was an interesting point.

Then a David Smith sculpture showed up – one of the early *Agricolas* – and it was sitting up in the museum, so I would go look at it, and it was the first piece of sculpture that I saw that was just itself. I mean, it wasn't representing something, and it wasn't telling me that I should do this or that. It was just there by itself, and that fascinated me. And I think there was a Giacometti that they put up at the head of the stairs. They have a great open space there.

DW   Where was this?

JC   In the Chicago Art Institute.

It was one of the four figures crossing the square, but it took up the whole space that Giacometti was able to maneuver. The sculpture intrigued me in terms of presence and volume – but the volume that delineates, like, say, the negative areas. Well, the negative area around the Giacometti was tremendous. That was about the same time that de Kooning won a prize there for a painting that they own called *Excavation*, which was very large to me; then I saw it subsequently three other times, and it got smaller and smaller – it was very funny. In other words, the presence of it is only allowable in terms of your experience, somehow. But with those sculptures, the presence was sustained. In other words, there's a larger presence available in sculpture than there would be in painting, so I made a choice there in terms of the physicality of it. But David's piece intrigued me because it was like meeting another person, you see. And they were bare, so to speak, like all their parts were available for inspection.

DW   Did you like his [welded] connections?

JC   His connections didn't intrigue me in the same way I was affected by Goto's number.

DW   No, because recent criticism has emphasized his importance as a welder.

JC   I still think he's a painter, although I think that there's something about the weight that he liked. I mean, he knew that a lot of things could be done to steel, but I don't know that he really did all those things to it. I don't really know how to say it, because possibly I don't want to say it, but I just think he painted.

ECB   [Elizabeth C. Baker] Because you read them two-dimensionally?

DW   Many people do.

JC   Yeah, I don't think that their presence is as big as they want to get. Anyway, I feel that is part of why I disagree with

David, but I have to say that for me there was a turn-on in 1952.

DW There really isn't any good sculpture that avoids the pictorial.

JC No, I think that we're all 2-D. The majority of people are 2-D; there's very few people who are 3-D. And they're all so used to getting the information from painting. I mean, what is it about sculpture that is different from painting? You know, I go back to the presence of it, and I find that when I take even small sculptures to people's apartments, it wipes the place out. And a lot of people don't like to be wiped out that way, see?

DW But isn't it also, then, a problem between the sculptor and his work? Maybe that relationship doesn't work well either.

JC You have a lot of people trying to make sculpture, and they're more interested in making sculpture, let's say, than they are in paying attention to what the information of the material tells them, which I always thought was one of the first places to go. You find the material, and it excites you. What does it do that's really indigenous to your soul? And you play with it.

DW Was it that way for you with the automobile?

JC Well, I was looking around for another kind of material, because I ran out of material. Then I had a studio, and nothing happened there. I made some drawings and things like that and couldn't figure out anything. Then I went to Larry Rivers's place, and he had some old car parts out there – a '29 Ford – and it was a different proposition. All of a sudden, I liked them, for some reason. Then a couple of months later, it occurred to me that there were all of these junkyards around, and it was fantastic – just free material. Free material at that time was essential. And here it was, free steel that was already painted. You couldn't beat it with a sledgehammer; that was all right. Along with anybody else who happened to be around, I kept pointing at it, and, in the case of Larry's place, I kept tripping over it, and finally it got through.

DW   But to him they were just cars?

JC   Yeah, he was going to put it back together or something. I don't know. Beat him to it.

But I feel that there's a certain honesty about how you come about your material, whether it is at the movies – it just happens – like how I found out about foam rubber. Like it's always around, but it has to be indicated by some means other than the "Well, I think I'll give it a chance" number. Rather than that, you really discover it. It's a common material; you finally discover it.

DW   You like the fact that it's common?

JC   Oh, yeah, all the material I work with – I mean, all that material is common, but what you do with it is what's uncommon. What you do with materials is going to alter it for anybody doing it later. If you don't find your materials by some means indigenous to your trip, if you just take it because it looks like an "in" material, that's sort of a shitty way of doing it. But really to "fall in love" and then deal with it like you would something in that way – well, you come to another side of it, and you come to another side of yourself, I think. I mean, art has to be something besides the line, color, texture, and the three dimensions.

DW   When did you find these pieces at Rivers's?

JC   About '57, I guess.

DW   When did you leave Chicago?

JC   I left in '54 and then went to Black Mountain.[3]

DW   And you were at Black Mountain for a year?

JC   Yeah, and then I came to New York.

DW   Who was at Black Mountain then?

JC   Charles Olson, Bob Creeley, Robert Duncan. When I was there it was just poets. Stefan Wolpe was there and Joe Fiore was there and Dan Rice was there; a few other people. Fielding Dawson was there.

D W   What was it like?

J C   Well, it was very interesting, because I felt that the object has its own life and its own qualities; I couldn't ever get any conversation in Chicago about it, but I went to Black Mountain and I found out about it immediately. They were all thinking the same thing. So it was one of those moves – something moved me, so to speak, and it was the right move. I mean, it's like how Pound talks, and how Williams talked, and how Olson talked. They all had different estimates about how form was built. So it was all very interesting, and it fit in with an attitude I had. I wanted the sculpture to exist on its own terms, coming through the process of myself. You know, do you like the material, or the material is what you liked and what's available? And a few other things like that. I suspect that if everything were reduced to glass, you'd do something with glass, because that's what you'd have. I found that the particular principle of compression and wadding up or manipulating with the fingers, so to speak, whether you use the machine or not, has a lot of application to a lot of different materials, and I only use materials that deal with that. Even the paintings, by using the veil method, are a compression of some kind. So it all has to do with if it's sexual, it's squeezing and hugging. And if it's instinctive, it has to do with fit and balance; if it's emotional, it's presence; and I don't know how it gets to be intellectual.

D W   How much manipulation did you do in the early pieces?

J C   A lot. There were times – like, I remember Creeley and I got drunk one night, and we just threw a lot of shit in the pile and kicked it around a few times, and then we looked down and gee, it looked beautiful. That happened a couple of times. On a couple of other occasions, I would get a thing built up and get a fantastic view from one side, but the rest of it was off, like, way over. You could never do anything more to it because the one side was so beautiful, so I had to destroy it. I mean, beauty was in the fit and, say, the color combination, or something like that. In other words, it would have two or more components going for it with one view only, and there was nothing I could do around it. It was impossible. But on some occasions, it just depends on where the vibes are and how the energy bursts out.

DW Don, what did you mean when you used the term "redundant" in referring to John's sculptures?[4]

DJ I was trying to use it in a particular way; I was saying something about the volume exceeding the structure. That and the fact that the appearance was concealing. The incredible volume – the volume exceeds the structure – it doesn't fit so nicely as structure usually does. The structure sort of rattles around in this big space.

JC I think he means that the volume has a lot to do with the fit. The fit of a lot of pieces has a great deal to do with the volume in this particular case, because there's air between it. But I think that because of the kind of material it is, and it was worked at different ways at different stages, that in the buildup and assembly of such things, a presence occurs. It's a presence which is met also by the balance and the rhythm of the balances and the fit. I think this gives it what Don says is volume, which I say is a presence.

ECB Both of you have used the wall, and I'm interested in how you feel about using the wall.

JC Well, I don't care too much for the wall. It allowed me to use that material in a bigger aspect. It's like this piece Don has, *Mr. Press* [image 44], that he doesn't want to take off the wall because there's too much to move, see. But if it were that big out in the area off the wall, it would even be worse.

DW What is the biggest piece you've done?

JC The piece I did for the World's Fair. It's fifteen by eight by four feet.[5]

D W   Did you think in terms of working that big before?

J C   No, I didn't care. I think even this paper bag, about six inches high, is pretty big.[6] I like that size better. It becomes terribly immediate, and if the scale is dealt with, then the size has nothing to do with it.

D J   Do you get the same immediacy if you have to enlarge it?

J C   No, I don't think you have to at all.

D J   Between it, would there be an equivalent immediacy?

J C   It would be a whole different number. I'm just talking about the size. It would probably be impossible to make that paper bag at that large a size. The delicacy wouldn't be there, because of the weight.

D W   How did you arrive at the paper pieces?

J C   I had some idea that if you blew up a bag and then you popped it, that maybe you could catch the energy of the pop, somehow, and then it turned out that when they got wadded up, whatever happened at the end of the fingers seemed to be more urgent and viable. So after a few of them, I felt that by looking at the outside, I would feel the inside. That interchange – between the energy of the pop and what it might amount to, or wherever the hell that thought came from – that changeover was fine. And then, all right, so paper is very delicate, and it can burn, and somebody will pick it up and throw it away very easily, so I sort of put color on it. I painted it little bits at a time with resin and let the resin run down in the crevices and things like that, and it gave it the support it needed without being completely coated and destroying the delicacy of the paper. Then whatever paint – or, in this case, watercolor – that was thrown picked up the color through some of the resin and didn't make it just all dreary brown. Some of them were pretty fantastic.

D W   Why did you decide to use foam?

J C   Well, the foam is very interesting to me. I thought it was very funny. And you can see the humor. I mean, it's really instinctive and sexual. I tried working it several different ways, and I returned to the first way, which was tying it and squeezing it. I'm not too happy about it all, but, you know, there are a couple of good pieces somewhere.

DW Did you like the idea of the cord?

JC No, that doesn't matter.

DW Donald talked before about "composition" as a term that had a lot of meaning.

DJ Well, I was talking about whatever you want to call it – I mean structure, composition, form, or anything in the pieces, in contrast to their appearance of not having any at first. But they really look like folded metal.

DW They look like what they are.

DJ Yeah, at first. It's hard to see the structure, or fit, or whatever.

JC Yeah, all right, there's another thing going down with me right now: I wanted to do some stainless-steel sculpture, and this was on the tail of doing the transparent sculptures that I did at Larry Bell's last year. I wanted to do the stainless steel and coat them. It all sounded pretty good until I thought about it for a while, and I found out that the material of the steel and the size would prohibit any color on it, because it was just added. The sculptures looked like they didn't need the color, which would only be like putting on a coat. But that kind of color is necessary to plastic. It really works in defining the form of the clear plastic.

DW I think that's why your color has always been good, even in the early crushed pieces. It was never additive color – it was always an integral part of the form. I remember that in the late '50s and early '60s, most polychrome sculpture was bad. It was simply painted on the form, which yours never was.

JC Well, at first, because it's inherent in the whole project, rather than something added.

DJ I was pretty interested in the two movies that you showed at Hunter.[7] The very Chamberlain color.

ECB   What's the connection between the two of you?

JC   We both have a certain sympathy toward each other's work. In this case, Don's probably the only person who has that much sympathy toward my work. And I think that's because he liked my paintings.

DJ   Yeah, I did, but I liked the sculptures, of course.

JC   There's been nothing said about the paintings that I know of. Since I haven't gotten much feedback, I don't know if the process, or if the finished product, whatever it is, says what I feel. Which is several things.

ECB   Such as?

JC   Well, one is about arriving at a color through veils. There's a lot of coats of paint with very little color in a lot of clear. You just keep putting it on like that; finally, after a while, it builds up to a color, but it isn't a color that's mixed and then put on. And then in that superstructure of a set of squares, there is an idea about them being deep at some level with the color buildup. There was the idea that they would change color as the light changed, as most of them do; some of them change color as you walk past them. But I was particularly interested in how to arrive at color.

      There was a thing that occurred during the process of the big ones; in painting them, I had to mask everything off to paint one section. I found that when I painted it, I could paint as long as I wanted. Listen, in one of them – I don't remember which one – I put down silver, and I was going to put on candy yellow. I put on three coats of candy yellow, and it turned pea green; it was fantastic. I took the masking off, and, you know, I just liked the color. It fits. So any color that you arrive at seemed to fit in any conjunction with the other colors. In other words, there was no finding the color in relationship to what was already there, but you arrived at the color by another means – by the process. I mean, you just looked at the color – the paint made the color, and you looked at it, and you could see there was nothing more to do to it. Any color went with any other color as long as the color was arrived at by some other means that was just as viable as one's *choosing* a selection of colors. Rather than selecting color, you have to make sure that in the manner of painting, whatever you do feels good to you, or something like that.

ECB   How technically is it put on?

JC   Spray gun to mist method. You put on a color and you can change it.

DJ   One thing I liked about the paintings which interested me, because I've gotten into that with my paintings, is they're just plain surface; they don't have any spatial business. It's just a matter of surface. When you laid a color on, it didn't produce a spatial situation. It was just as you said, a veil over a coat over another color, which meant, just like putting a little liquid on the table, you don't change the surface; it's just a case of one thing over another, and it's the same surface.[8]

JC   An absorption, perhaps.

DW   I think a lot of people were negative – extremely negative about them. I got that reaction. They looked like geometric paintings, and I remember that people were offended by the color.

DJ   The thing is they aren't geometric paintings, really. They're not involved in geometry, but in their surfaces – the arbitrariness of them gets them out of all that composition. They looked like latter-day [Charles] Biedermans, or something like that. Initially, I think maybe that's how people thought of them. Some big revolutionary change of mind on John's part.

JC   I liked the material of the paint; really, that was where it went. But I had other concerns. All of those, I think, are important, so that you keep the development up without losing the balance. I think you just keep working; sometimes you can't work. You know, any of us could sit down and figure out a million-dollar project, but if I were to stick you in three acres in Maui and tell you that you got to come out of there with something tangible that hasn't been there, that becomes another form of limitation. The limitation is all around. If you had a whole plant as a resource, you could be just as befuddled as if you had to deal only with this table. So whatever comes along is fine with me — all I have to do is like it.

DW   But don't you think the form was uncharacteristic?

JC   No, because I liked it. I like [Josef] Albers's work a lot, and I felt that this came closest to it without any of his problems.

DJ   Mostly, I'm sorry people have the presupposition of geometry versus anything else.

DW   You mean that it has to be one or the other — a fixed order, or that it represents two different kinds of mentalities?

DJ   Yeah.

JC   That's what artists are. The artist is coming out of some kind of dissatisfaction into some kind of company where you can deal with all that, and everyone feels that.

DW   Another thing that was upsetting was the type of color that was accepted at that time — 1965.

DJ   Maybe they would have accepted it on his regular pieces. It was exceedingly out of context in terms of most geometric work, but that depends on what was meant by "geometric."

JC   Well, lacquer's a very old medium. That's the oldest paint. And because it has a transparent quality and so on, I was interested. In California, they call it candy apple, which is a certain kind of base that reflects through the clear with just a few drops of color in it. I was interested in that luminescent sort of thing and the fact of its thinness and how to control it by multiplying. I found out a lot about color myself.

ECB   That gives a certain depth to the surface, though, doesn't it? I mean, it's not space in the sense that you were speaking of, but it's not an opaque surface either. It has a kind of optical depth.

DJ   It's part of the surface; you take it as a variation in the surface.

ECB   But you feel like you could see into it a bit, don't you?

DJ   Well, I don't think so in these paintings. If you add a slight layer here, you've got something to see into. But that's a physical thing; it's not that you're creating two or three inches of illusionary space alongside. What you're looking into is really just the paint – the two or three layers of lacquer, that's all.

JC   I like the idea about the color. There is no bad color; there's no color decision to reject, because everything is colored.

DW   But isn't that essentially a part of your thinking, even in the early sculptures? In other words, that there was no color relationship that was inherently bad.

JC   Well, perhaps, but I didn't know it as well as I did after I did these paintings. These forced the point somewhat.

DJ   I think the earlier pieces are more relational in color.

JC   I don't remember ever tearing a sculpture apart because the color was disagreeable, but I tore them apart because the form didn't fit.

ECB   But when you started making the colored pieces in the beginning, weren't those found colors? And then at a certain point, didn't you change parts of the color?

JC   Yeah, about '62, I started painting them. I felt that the material needed a little help.

DW   So in this sense, you were really creating – you had the material, but it wasn't a form, and you were creating it all, weren't you?

JC   The material and the use of it. The process of the material makes the use.

DW   But it's not preexistent.

JC Yeah, well, there were some attributes, though, that were perfectly normal in this case. I always liked the color change because of the way the color's put on. I think if it was just one flat color, one color, one coat and that's the color, these would change color as the light changes.

DW Why didn't you paint the galvanized pieces?

JC I thought the earlier pieces didn't go as far as they should, and I imagine that I painted them to get another element, whereas the galvanized pieces don't need to be painted.

DW Why?

JC Well, they extend pretty much – they have their own color.

DW Where were the early galvanized pieces from?

JC I had boxes made and went to a place on White Street and crushed them.[9]

DW Did you have particular shapes made, or just boxes?

JC There was something like thirty boxes, and some boxes had liners in them. The liners gave it body and added dimension – a certain weight that I had in mind.

DW What about process?

JC Well, as I think back on it, it's only recently that I can say anything about it, really, and as I remember even as – ever since I got impressed with the sculpture, it's always been that I really don't remember if I have ever done anything where process wasn't the point of view. In other words, I went through the number, but whatever came out was what came out. Nothing has ever been premeditated. It's only recently that the process has been a big enough number to talk about.

DW Well, it was to a certain extent in the '50s, though. What about Pollock?

JC Well, that's how I look at it. I think that's true; I believe it was. He wanted to get away from easel painting and had some ideas about mural painting. But that was only the size and the scale. In other words, his breeding had something to do with the scale he wanted to choose. He was wrapped up in this fine-art number, like easel painting and mural painting, and he wanted to be free, later on, to walk around the painting.

DJ Those paintings, too, have a sort of concealment of something like your sculpture, which is curious. You know, everybody's work is sort of unintelligible; they really do tend to look like junk or car parts or something. They don't make sense initially — you don't know what they are, or it doesn't look aesthetic, or it's beyond what other people's work would look like. In a way, that geometric scheme is sort of a concealment too, like a randomness of car parts, or junk, or something. The plastic pieces I know very well; sometimes the composition or the form doesn't show, and it just turns into junk or something. It's peculiar — all that structure isn't evident at first.

JC I find that rather than dealing with composition, to me composition has some sort of pre-idea of the order of a certain given space of a given area that's been composed. And in this case, it has to do with fit — how the parts fit, and where they stand, and in what kind of balance and rhythms they give off as vibration, in terms of my choice, which would be close to a kind of partnership in terms of the balances and rhythms that have to do with me, plus the material as it's fitted. Now all those pieces are very well fitted, and I think that's a more interesting attitude toward looking at it than just composition. Composition could be like taking something out here or there that could be the composition, and it wouldn't matter whether I touched it or not. But the sculptures have to do with contact — either when you can touch yourself or when you shake hands with somebody. Shaking hands has a lot to do with fit; it also has to do with the vibration of the person you shake hands with — whether you prefer it or not, whether you feel cold hands or sweaty hands — it's all these points about shaking hands, but it's fit, and you can tell a lot that way.

First published: "Excerpts from a Conversation between Elizabeth C. Baker, John Chamberlain, Don Judd, and Diane Waldman," in Diane Waldman, *John Chamberlain: A Retrospective Exhibition*, exh. cat. (New York: Solomon R. Guggenheim Museum, 1971), 15–21.

1   Chamberlain attended the School of the Art Institute of Chicago on the GI Bill from 1951 to 1952.

2   Joseph Goto (1916–1994) was an American sculptor known for his abstract expressionist welded steel works. Goto studied at the School of the Art Institute of Chicago in the late 1940s.

3   Black Mountain College, founded in 1933 by John Andrew Rice near Asheville, North Carolina, was an experimental college with many influential teachers and students in the arts and letters, including Josef and Anni Albers, Ruth Asawa, John Cage, Robert Creeley, Merce Cunningham, Willem and Elaine de Kooning, Francine du Plessix Gray, Buckminster Fuller, Franz Kline, Jacob Lawrence, Kenneth Noland, Charles Olson, Arthur Penn, Robert Rauschenberg, M. C. Richards, Dorothea Rockburne, Ben Shahn, Cy Twombly, Susan Weil, and Vera B. Williams. Black Mountain College closed in 1957.

4   "The work is in turn neutral, redundant, and expressively structured." See Judd's "Chamberlain: Another View" (1963) in *Donald Judd Writings*, 115.

5   Chamberlain refers here to *Untitled* (1963–64). According to Julie Sylvester, "The sculpture was rented through the Leo Castelli Gallery to the New York State Pavilion at the World's Fair in Flushing, New York, in 1964. It was lost and never returned to the gallery." Sylvester, *John Chamberlain: A Catalogue Raisonné of the Sculpture, 1954–1985*, exh. cat. (Los Angeles: The Museum of Contemporary Art, Los Angeles; New York: Hudson Hills Press, 1986), 80. Judd made the following note in his copy of this book: "This work was on the ground at P.J.'s [Philip Johnson] place. I offered to store it at 101 Spring Street. The next I knew P.J. and D.W. [David Whitney] had thrown it away 'as junk.'"

6   Chamberlain's paper-bag sculptures, described in full a few responses later, date to 1969; these works were at first untitled, but later named the *Penthouse* series by the artist. See Sylvester, *John Chamberlain*, 112–13.

7   Chamberlain premiered *The Secret Life of Hernando Cortez* (1968) and *Wide Point* (1968) at Hunter College in February 1969. Judd wrote of the films: "As I said, Chamberlain's color is great and this is conspicuous in the three movies that he made, two of which were shown at Hunter College, one whose name I don't remember [*Wide Point*], and *The Secret Life of Hernando Cortez* (Fernando Cortés is the correct spelling). The unnamed movie had no plot and was primarily the color of interiors. The plot of *Cortez* was pretty casual: what to do next, having arrived in Veracruz. Like the reliefs the movies suggest ways out of old ideas or simply enforcement of the medium." See Judd's note from November 1988 in *Donald Judd Writings*, 507.

The Chamberlain Building, part of the Chinati Foundation, was conceived of and installed with works by John Chamberlain. In addition to twenty-two sculptures by Chamberlain, the installation includes a large foam coach made by Chamberlain, *Barge Marfa*, in 1983. Flanking the north and south sides of *Barge Marfa* are two televisions, which screen *The Secret Life of Hernando Cortez* on loop.

8   Judd owned six paintings made by Chamberlain in 1964, during which time Chamberlain was working with auto lacquer resins and spray applications. The paintings owned by Judd have both metal flake and metal relief elements.

9   White Street runs through the New York City neighborhoods of TriBeCa and Chinatown in Lower Manhattan.

Interview with John Fekner
October 1971

In 1971, Judd installed a large work in hot-rolled steel at the Solomon R. Guggenheim Museum, New York, for that year's iteration of the Guggenheim International Exhibition (February 12–April 11, 1971). The show focused on the emergence of so-called minimal and postminimal work by twenty-one artists, including pieces by Carl Andre, Dan Flavin, Judd, Richard Long, Robert Morris, Richard Serra, and Lawrence Weiner. In this early site-specific work, Judd designed the inner circle to follow the slope of the Guggenheim Museum ramp, while the outer circle remained level across the top of the piece.

This interview, undertaken later the same year, when Judd's work at the Guggenheim was still resonant, was conducted by John Fekner for his painting thesis course at the New York Institute of Technology.

JF   [John Fekner] Is your format for working something that
      will continue in the future in the same vein as your pre-
      vious work?

DJ   [Donald Judd] I don't think very much about what will
      happen. I really don't worry about the future, because
      people worry too much, and it's really a sort of useless ac-
      tivity. So I just go along doing what I have to do at any
      given time. Since it's my work and what I want to do, it
      has a certain continuity, and I wouldn't expect it to make
      a drastic change. But obviously, it just changes of its own
      … I get bored with a certain thing, quit doing it, and do
      something else – but I wouldn't go out and get involved
      in any organic pieces or something like that.

JF   Do you feel that viewers of your work see it in the way
      you want them to see it?

DJ   I really don't know; I make it to suit myself. I don't think
      about what they're thinking about it. I don't know what
      they think about it. All you know is what is current,
      comes up in the magazines, and that usually is not too
      knowledgeable.

JF   Are you satisfied by what they see?

DJ   No, I think that art criticism is pretty low level – it's all
      the same.

JF   I can see people saying you're still dealing with elements
      and composition, even though you're trying to get away
      from that. Is that correct?

DJ   Yeah, I'm not really interested in that. Presumably, every-
      body has the freedom to think about it the way they like,
      so I guess they can talk about it the way they want, but
      if there were to be anything fairly intelligent about it, I'd
      assume I'll do just what I want to do, which is certainly
      not composition.

JF   Would you pursue your own direction in art even though
      you were not getting the response from the critics or
      viewers?

DJ   Yeah, I think so. At one time, there wasn't such a thing. One time, there was a little bit; then there was a fair amount, and so forth. It's sort of a by-product; if it brings in money, there's a lot to make. If I didn't make money, I might have to use other materials, I suppose. Metal costs a lot, so if you were forced not to do the metal, then there are other mediums to use.

JF   So the transition from cheaper materials to metal was due to an increase in your funds?

DJ   Yes, I've always thought about just what I'm able to do. I really don't want to sit around thinking of a $50,000 piece, because the matter is I'm not going to get $50,000 to make it, so it doesn't get serious. If you get a $50,000 grant to make a piece, then I'll think about it and take it seriously. I really want to think about just the pieces I want and can do.

JF   Was the circular piece in the Guggenheim show [image 45] made before the show or for it?

DJ   Yes, it was made for the show, paid for by me and not the Guggenheim, which was important for me. It has to do with a number of pieces, some of which I have done right outdoors on slopes. So I was sort of anxious with the Guggenheim slope to use the ramp; I wanted to use that. The idea started off with a square rectangle piece, and then obviously it occurred to make it circular to fit with the building.

JF   What is the relation between you and who picks you for the show?

DJ   Well, they picked the artists. It was Diane Waldman's show. She picked all the artists – no, Ed Fry, not Waldman.[1] They picked all the artists they wanted in the show, but then after that, the artists were allowed to do what they wanted for the show. It was a very open show; they didn't go around picking pieces that were already made.

JF   So you felt that you used the structure of your piece in the form of the museum?

D J   Yes, I wanted to try doing that, because I had never done anything like that before.

J F   How do you feel about using metal instead of plexiglass, in which case the pieces have a cooler, finished look?

D J   Well, it has to do with the quality of what I want to make, of course, the nature of the piece: what the materials are, whether it should be something very well made or just something made. Some of them, usually the ones with stained glass or plexiglass, have to be made with just an industrial sense, but it's a little more than that.

J F   Where your piece was in the museum – did you intentionally present your work as an obstacle, giving off the feeling of stagnation to those who came across it?

D J   The ramp's pretty narrow, and there wasn't much room. If the ramp was bigger, it probably would have been bigger, but I really wasn't trying to block off traffic.

J F   While reviewing art shows, critics always seem to ramble on, using their own flamboyant writing techniques to express their own creativity, before getting to the main brunt of the essay. How do you feel about this?

D J   Well, I generally don't like it. It's sort of a standard thing, to put it in the beginning of something before telling you what they want to say. Sometimes they spend a lot of time saying what they want, whether it has to do with the show or not. It's okay, but it's something they should put someplace else. It's partly because they aren't allowed to say too much anymore.

J F   To some people, a critic will function as a judge, either swaying them to a show or away from a show. Do you feel this is a negative point or a good point for a critic?

D J   Well, I think that's okay, but it depends on how it's taken. I think that everybody makes a judgment whether they think something is good or bad or whatever, so I don't mind anybody saying that or writing that in public. The effect it may have has to do with the people who are being

affected. What they ought to realize is that it's just someone else's judgment, which has a great deal to do with his
history, so you have to have some idea of him. If you just
take some critic's word for it, and you don't know much
about him and his thinking, it's sort of silly; you don't
know what he's worth. The public is a little gullible if it
behaves like that. If the critic tries to act like a judge, I
think he's being rather pretentious; but if he says, "That's
a lousy piece of art," and you take it as just his opinion,
then that's all right.

JF   Shouldn't people seek out their own preferences by themselves?

DJ   Basically, that's what it's all about: they can do their own
thinking. It's not a public situation.

JF   Shouldn't art criticism be extraneous to the art field and
not so much a part of it?

DJ   In the first place, it's on another sort of level; it's not sufficiently independent. Well, maybe one thing – it doesn't
get paid much, which causes trouble in any activity. You
can't make a living out of it, so you get a lot of people on
a part-time thing. Maybe if it paid well enough to write
at a reasonable rate, instead of an article and a review every month, a person could live on doing four periodicals a
year; then that would improve. It's sort of a cross between
publicity and reporting, or just as a newspaper reports; it's
sort of serious art history – it's a real mishmash.

JF   Do you feel you are in a position to disregard the critic
altogether?

DJ   Well, I was in that position, but they haven't been all that
favorable, so somehow or other I have managed along
without any great praise from critics.

JF   So now you're in the position where you're not going to be
troubled by the critic and just concerned with your work?

DJ   I'll continue to do what I want to do. You don't always
want to be criticized; it's nice to be praised and all that, but

it has everything to do with where it comes from, and, as it usually is, it's just publicity. "Well, it's great, it sells, you can do things" – mostly what it is is publicity. A big article in most art magazines is just selling art; that's what it really does.

This conversation was sourced from an archival transcript in the Judd Foundation Archives, Marfa, Texas.

1   The exhibition was cocurated by Diane Waldman and Edward J. Fry.

Interview with Barbara Rose
For the film *American Art in the 1960s*
Summer 1972

Produced and directed by filmmaker Michael Blackwood and written and narrated by art historian Barbara Rose, the 1972 documentary *American Art in the
1960s* includes interviews with artists Carl Andre, John Cage, Ronald Davis, Dan
Flavin, Sam Francis, Helen Frankenthaler, Robert Irwin, Jasper Johns, Judd, Ellsworth Kelly, Edward Kienholz, Roy Lichtenstein, Morris Louis, Kenneth Noland,
Claes Oldenburg, Jules Olitski, Robert Rauschenberg, Larry Rivers, Ed Ruscha,
George Segal, Frank Stella, Andy Warhol, and Jack Youngerman; master printer
Ken Tyler; gallerist Leo Castelli; and critic Clement Greenberg.

This interview was filmed at 101 Spring Street, in the second-floor living space
and on the third floor, which Judd used as his studio.

BR   [Barbara Rose] How did you feel about abstract expressionism?

DJ   [Donald Judd] That's sort of a general question. I like Jackson Pollock's paintings a great deal.

BR   Did you feel they were different from action painting? What was it about Pollock's work?

DJ   Well, action painting is just [Harold] Rosenberg's label.[1] I think Pollock is a more unusual painter than the rest of them. Also, I think, on the whole, that he invented the large scale and the overall image. I like de Kooning's paintings along about the late '40s – paintings like *Excavation*, I think, is one of them – very linear paintings.

BR   What was your attitude toward Tenth Street[2] and the second generation?[3]

DJ   It looked kind of sleazy [*laughs*] – looked very derivative.

BR   Did you formulate ideas that were antagonistic to the de Kooning style? Your early thinking – did it come from thinking about Pollock?

DJ   Well, to some extent. I made several general assumptions, after a while, based upon some common things in Pollock's painting, Newman's, Rothko, [Kenneth] Noland maybe – though that was later.

BR   What were those assumptions?

DJ   Well, obvious things like the scale, the importance of color, generally overall or unitary sort of arrangement – the importance of the primary state of the things you're really interested in. If you're interested in a color, make the color important. You don't have to make it fit into something else.

BR   You began as a painter; why did you stop painting?

DJ   In the first place, I painted for a long time – about ten years. I couldn't get what I wanted. That was the most general statement. There were several problems that I finally couldn't resolve in painting, and I would get something in one painting that I would like and other things I didn't like so much, and the next painting would have something else that I would like and other things I didn't like. Nothing ever worked together. So, the paintings occurred one by one. There was something always unresolved. With the first three-dimensional things, several of the things I was interested in occurred all at once, as a normal, logical thing, and that seemed impossible in the paintings.

As a sort of specific thing about painting, I didn't like the flatness. I didn't like them being against the wall. I couldn't get around the problem of there always being something within the rectangle, so that then you had the rectangle as a major thing and the thing within it as a major thing, which gave you two things – and that division seemed impossible.

BR   When did you make your first object, and what was it?

DJ   I think the end of '61, beginning of '62. They overlapped a couple of the paintings.

BR   Was there any specific source for your beginning to make objects?

DJ   No, I just sort of – it came out of the paintings very much. There is one early relief that's earlier than that [image 46]. It's actually four small brown paintings joined with a red cross in between them; it's recessed. So it was actually a relief. Then another one – I couldn't get the ends to curve properly. I got a painting down to where it was nothing but a surface, kept painting it and applying paint and fooling around with it and still didn't like it, and then finally I bent up the ends. I couldn't get the ends to curve properly, so I sliced –

BR   Did you think of these early reliefs as three-dimensional paintings?

DJ   Yeah – well, I thought of them as reliefs, which is low by definition: a low flat thing against a wall. The one I was describing, I chopped off the ends, then, and put galvanized on – curved the top and bottom with sheets of galvanized iron. Then I didn't like the whole surface I'd originally been using, so I threw that away and used plywood in the center, and that's the piece that Lewis Winter bought a long time ago [see image 34].

BR   What artists influenced your development? What artists were you thinking about?

DJ   Well, it all has to do with what I said before about the abstract expressionists. Some general assumptions come out of their work. I was on the whole not influenced by any sculpture, because I didn't think I was doing sculpture and still don't, contrary to Richard [Serra]. I liked di Suvero's work, but then, it was very far from anything I wanted to do, so it was not really an influence – but it was there as something pretty powerful and interesting. And [John] Chamberlain's, but again, it was too far away from anything I was interested in. But the real influence, something that is in the work, is the three or four general assumptions that come from Pollock, Newman, Rothko, and so forth.

BR   What were these assumptions?

DJ   That you have a single unit, but that the painting, in their case, is more or less one thing. That any color is a primary consideration. That whatever form there is – configuration, whatever it is – is a primary thing. And none of these things is subordinate to anything you can think of, like other images, or the depiction of realistic things, or things like that, and scale.

BR   Were you involved with eliminating depiction and illusionism? What were your attitudes toward –

DJ   It's not a case of elimination. It's what I wanted. I was totally uninterested in those things and couldn't work with them; I didn't want to work with them. I wanted to work with what I was really interested in. In the first place, I didn't know that originally and as I found it out, that's what I wanted to do. The main thing is what the person is actually interested in. It's not a case of getting rid of things he has no interest in dealing with.

BR   So you had no interest in dealing with illusionism or depiction?

DJ   No.

BR   Was [Jasper] Johns's work important in your thinking?

DJ   Yeah, somewhat. It came a little late. I first started seeing a lot of John [Chamberlain]'s work almost at the time I was doing my own first three-dimensional work; I hadn't seen much prior to that. And I considered it sculpture, and I thought sculpture was very foreign to what I was doing, so I kind of disconnected it. The volume of John's work and that idea of volume was important to me. So that was an influence, and I learned something from that. That was the main thing, I think – the volume was really the essential thing.

BR   You mean in Johns's sculpture?

DJ   Are you talking about Jasper or Chamberlain?

BR   I'm sorry. I was talking about Jasper Johns.

DJ   No, I was not very interested in Jasper; I was talking about Chamberlain. I'm not as overcome by Jasper as a lot of people. I'm a little bit interested in Jasper's paintings because of the surface, but it was still an illusionistic surface. In the paintings, I was very much trying to make an ordinary flat surface, and to some extent, the roughness in his paintings suggested that. But still, he was making a great deal of space. His brushwork was all about depiction, so I wasn't interested in that.

BR   What was radical about Stella's work?

DJ   Well, I was especially interested because, as I think I wrote someplace,[4] it was geometric work, and I was certainly interested in geometric work that didn't have a sort of clean quality that all previous geometric work had had – the certain quality of Mondrian and all that, which seems too clean and ideal for me. While I like Mondrian a great deal, I hadn't wanted any quality like that in my work. I tended to consider all geometric work to be like that. So it was interesting when I saw Frank's *Black Paintings* at the Modern that they were geometric but did not have any quality at all like that in the previous geometric work.[5]

BR   What was different about them?

DJ   Well, they are exceedingly unideal, for one thing. I can't say what quality they had, because that's too complicated to say.

BR   Do you think there's an American attitude toward geometry that's different from Bauhaus attitudes?

DJ   Oh, yeah, very much.

BR   How would you characterize it?

DJ   It's a little hard. On the whole, I'd say that Mondrian is very much a European artist and comes out of general European thinking, which has a lot to do with idealism and deductive systems and whatnot. This is all getting a little simple, but the American geometry is more pragmatic or something – that's a dangerous word, but – it's certainly not about ideal forms or systems. When Frank makes a certain configuration, or [Ellsworth] Kelly makes – and Kelly has some of that European idealism – but when Kelly puts a square into another square, he's more interested in a specific situation: the square and the square that it's within and all that. With Mondrian, you're always referring to some other ideal scheme sort of beyond the particular painting. It's also a case of generations.

BR   Do you feel the generation of the '60s was very different from abstract expressionists in terms of their aesthetic?

DJ   I don't think so. [*Laughs*] You're getting rid of that? You want a big issue out of that? You had more things introduced – like, the abstract expressionist situation got pretty monolithic there with all the second-generation people in the galleries. And so at the end of the '50s, I thought it was pretty impressive; I was very happy to see Chamberlain come along, and [Lee] Bontecou and Jasper and Rauschenberg and all that, to break up that single aesthetic, which it certainly seemed to be going to. But I think if you sort of forget the second-generation abstract expressionists and just consider the people who were good, and then a lot of people in the '60s, I don't think there's such a great break between them. Like, a lot of Frank's assumptions come out of abstract expressionism. Obviously, somebody doing somewhat descriptive work like Jasper or Rauschenberg are antithetical to somewhat abstract art. I don't see it as any great break between the two.

BR Did Newman's 1960 French & Company show have an effect on your thinking?[6]

DJ Somewhat, but I was also skeptical. I like *Vir Heroicus* [*Sublimis*] a great deal, and that comes under the heading of the general assumptions I was talking about. Some of the paintings, I thought, looked like they came from Mondrian's, which I think was a big mistake – some of the black-and-white paintings where the black line is all the way over to one side, it looked just like a quadrant out of a Mondrian. I don't think so now, but that's what I thought then. I was a little skeptical of them. The *Vir Heroicus* I liked a lot.

BR There is the whole issue of relationships and the fact that Newman was not involved in internal relationships within the work. Wasn't that very important in the development in the art of the '60s? That elimination of relationships within the work?

DJ Well, there are relationships within the work, but they're not compositional in the ordinary sense.

BR Well, is there a different attitude toward composition in '60s art generally?

DJ Oh, yeah. Oh, you mean [different] from the abstract expressionists? No, I don't think so.

BR Well, from European art?

DJ Very much from European art.

BR What is the difference, say, in the American attitude toward composition from the European?

DJ   All the European art was very compositional and, I thought, not very good, either, in the '50s. The only painter that I liked a lot was Yves Klein.

BR   Because it didn't have composition?

DJ   It didn't have any composition, but it also has a quality that I don't think is especially American. But I felt the whole juxtaposition of little things against one another was incredibly unbelievable and tiresome in European work.

BR   Do you think your background in pragmatist philosophy influenced your thinking about art?

DJ   Yeah, I think so.

BR   How?

DJ   I studied all that at Columbia, but I was already inclined to think that way when I got into their department; actually, it was just a case of recognizing something and liking it.[7]

BR   Specifically what?

DJ   Well, for one thing, being very skeptical of general statements and large schemes and all things that pretend to say more about the world than the information they actually have, and certainly empiricist philosophy is all about that sort of thing. I like very much people like – not people like, but David Hume.

BR   Do you think of your work as a philosophical statement?

DJ   Yeah, sure. All art has to do with philosophy, among other things, but the general point is that you deal with what you know and what you can do in a particular situation, instead of trying to ascribe a great deal of things to the rest of the world or saying things in very general ways.

BR   How do you feel about the term "minimal art"?

DJ   Well, I don't like it. What's minimal about it?

BR   Do you think there is a group of artists, whose work in some way is related, who could be called minimal artists?

DJ   No. No, I never did. I think that people who would be called minimal artists weren't all doing work at the same time. I think Carl [Andre]'s work was a little later in development than mine and [Robert] Morris's.[8] And in the beginning, I didn't know Morris, and Morris and I didn't know each other's work. Also, I don't think there's much connection between me and Morris, whom I consider sort of variously a plain Dada artist and an unplain one, or something.

BR   Do you feel close to other artists who have been called minimal artists, such as Andre and Flavin?

DJ   Well, I've known Flavin for a long time, and yeah, I do feel close to Flavin, but I think there's not much similarity in my work and his. There's a couple of common aspects of it, maybe, use of things in sequence and whatnot, but his interest in light and all that is very alien to any way I could think. So, that's very different.

BR   How about the group of California artists who use literal and specific properties of materials, like [Craig] Kauffman and [Larry] Bell and [Robert] Irwin?

DJ   I like Larry Bell's work a great deal, but I also feel, as with Flavin, it's very different stuff; I would never have thought of it. His interest in surface phenomena and light and all that is very foreign to my thinking.

BR   Do you think that there are common denominators that relate all of American art of the '60s?

DJ   A few, but you get very general if you talk about them. I think in twenty years, it all will look a little more similar than it might have looked at the moment. Someone like Claes [Oldenburg] is using single, more or less unitary objects too, even when he's involved in an object that looks like a real object. But still, the color is very important. The object is more or less unitary. The scale is large. Two common things, but they're very general.

BR   So in other words, the categories "pop" and "minimal" are really very arbitrary?

DJ   Yeah. I don't like them at all.

BR   Do you think that sculpture is exhausted?

DJ   In the first place, I never thought of my work as sculpture to begin with. Serra considers his work sculpture, and I think he's perfectly allowed. I'm not sure just what Carl thinks, but I think he considers it sculpture too, and I think his is certainly going. Flavin doesn't consider his sculpture.

BR   If your work isn't painting, and isn't sculpture, what is it?

DJ   I think it's just something else. I don't really have to –

BR   It's not another category.

DJ   As I've said, I'm doing more or less discrete objects, and some pieces are involved with the land, if they're outside; some are involved with the room. It's quite possible that someone new coming along wouldn't be able to do anything with discrete objects, in which case it might be finished, which is okay. It all changes.

BR   How do you feel about David Smith?

DJ   I think he's a pretty good artist, but I don't think he's a great artist, in the sense that Pollock was.

BR   Why not?

DJ   I don't think the invention is that great – the quality of it. I think what Pollock invented is an incredible invention in all respects, and I don't think David Smith invented that much.

BR   Could you talk more about Pollock's inventions?

DJ   It sounds banal, but just the idea of using drip paint, I think, is an unbelievable invention, and the results of that: the immediacy of the material, the emphasis on the material, and the form that he could actually make with it. Also, I think that on the whole, he invented the scale, and the overall single unit, and many of the things which have been pretty standard by now.

BR   Do you think that the emphasis on the specific qualities of materials relates to Brancusi's doctrine of truth to materials?

DJ   Maybe a little bit, but I have never really thought of Brancusi very much. My connection with that would be out of Pollock's use of paint and not out of Brancusi. If the thinking involved in the work is empirical, you're going to make something with empirical situations, like the use of a given material. You don't want, as in all earlier painting and sculpture, to obscure the material or deny it, to some extent.

BR Do you feel that your work is related to older art, or that it's a radical break?

DJ As I said, I think it's related to the abstract expressionists. I think the abstract expressionists and at least certain subsequent American art is a fairly radical break from earlier art, but still, there are connections to Matisse, and Picasso, and all that.

BR Do you think that there's such a thing as a mainstream tradition to which one has to relate oneself?

DJ No, I don't think so. Since I think that, say, Oldenburg is as good as Stella, as good as Flavin, as good as Bell, and so forth, there's not one single kind.

BR Do you think that growing up in the Midwest affected your thinking and the kind of art you produced?

DJ Maybe; I've thought about it. I think that probably I got very used to being out there – to ordinary situations – so that it makes me a little incapable or disinterested in sort of exotic kinds of art, at least if I make them. I like other people's exotic art, like Lucas Samaras's. I don't think it would be possible for me to make an art that was really too strange or exotic or anything like that. I think it has to have a certain ordinariness – it perhaps comes out of what you get used to visually.

BR Did that museum in Kansas City affect your thinking?[9]

DJ Well, I sort of hated that museum. The museum is a major collection of Chinese art and the normal number of Old Masters, and I took it as history and resented the fact – and I saw it a long time ago, maybe when I was twelve or thirteen years old – resented the fact that there was nothing there that had been made within thousands of miles of it. No sign of any – there wasn't even any Indian art. I mean, at least they could go out and talk to the Omaha Indians and get something. But there was no sign of anything that had been made in the whole Middle West.

BR   Do you think the new interest in American Indian art is significant in any way?

DJ   It's not so new, because there have always been people interested in it. Yeah, I think so. I think the Indians produced a great deal of art, and they're still producing art. They're also the people who are right here, so they're the ones you know about and deal with. And more than you would think, the colonists, so to speak, are still living among them, and that's bound to have a considerable effect. It's entirely a different culture. It isn't a European culture like all the people who came here, almost. Just being curious about it and the nature of it and some of the possibilities it has, I think, is pretty important.

BR   Do you think the situation in 1972 is very different from the situation in 1962, when you first began making your three-dimensional pieces and the Green Gallery was opened?

DJ   I think what will happen and what's possible are very different. It may be just me and my knowing less about what's going on, but it seems less lively now than it did then. Because suddenly, in '62, you had Oldenburg and Chamberlain and di Suvero and Stella and Jasper and Rauschenberg and Bontecou, and you had a whole bundle of artists who suddenly were being shown. So, it seemed pretty lively to me. It doesn't seem that way now.

BR   Has the direction of your work changed?

DJ   Well, somewhat, but it doesn't change very fast, and I don't try to make it change. It just goes along from one piece to the next and changes at its own accord. The larger pieces are mostly recent. The pieces outdoors are in the last two or three years.

B R   What is it that switched your focus to environments and sites, as opposed to isolated museum objects?

D J   Well, just about that: I got a little tired of them being single objects. If you take an object, even though you like it a great deal, or a single thing, and you put it in a space like this, it's very much by implication – spatially, it trails off into all directions, into indefinite space. So to some extent, like the wall that went around Leo [Castelli]'s front room [see image 42], it was an attempt to deal with the whole space and make it clear, rather than let the space generated by the object just sort of trail off in four directions.

B R   Do you think that there is a dialogue among artists?

D J   No. [*Laughs*]

B R   Do you think that there was?

D J   I guess there was in the '50s, but I don't see other artists very often. And they certainly don't talk about art, so there's not much. I think they pay attention to each other's work, to some extent. They're not nearly as sociable as they were in the early '60s, or even before.

B R   Why do you think that's the case?

D J   I don't really quite know. I think it's mysterious. Do you have any idea why? All busy making money or something?

B R   Do you think that the American artist works in greater isolation than the European artist?

D J   I don't know. I don't know that many European artists.

B R   You're living now in this new loft building in SoHo.[10] Do you think that SoHo in general is another Tenth Street?

D J   Yeah, I'd say it's another Tenth Street, also in the fact that Tenth Street after de Kooning didn't produce anything but mediocre art. In the first place, I don't like the name SoHo, which sounds like London, and I don't like the development that's occurred here in the last three years. I'm sorry the galleries came down. There's not that much sign of the work being done being all that good. And there's a great deal of real estate development going on, and everything's getting so expensive that there won't be any artists here pretty soon.

BR   Do you think that criticism is important?

DJ   I think theoretically it's important, in that it's discussion and should occur. It would be very nice to have discussion about the work and all that, but I think that its level is so low that it's insignificant. At a high level, I think that it would be very nice to have it.

BR   Do you think it ever had a significant importance?

DJ   Well, it's a comparatively new activity, for one thing.

BR   How would you describe the Rosenberg versus [Clement] Greenberg debate?

DJ   In the first place, I really don't know much about Rosenberg. I haven't read most of his stuff, and I haven't thought about it. I was never overcome by the idea of "action painting," or the label. And of course Greenberg I dislike by now.

BR   How would you describe Greenberg's influence?

DJ   A few years ago, I thought it was very bad, in the sense that he was trying to set up a monolithic situation, and I think that's against the whole idea of contemporary art here and in Europe. Going on the general idea that art is produced by individual people, anything that sets up an overall scheme is bound to be false. He's not setting up some ideal state, but he's setting up an ideal historical scheme, and that's bound to be false too. The history's using the people, not vice versa.[11]

BR   Why are you opposed to idealism?

DJ   Because it's based on general ignorance.

BR   Do you think critics have the power to establish taste?

DJ   I don't know. I think probably Greenberg's the only instance. In taste, you're talking about the general public, and publicity cuts a lot of ice with the public, but I don't think there's really been any big sales job, except maybe Greenberg's.

BR   What do you think is the most pressing problem facing artists in New York today?

DJ   Well, two or three things. The obvious one to me is money to make pieces with, to work with, which is getting scarcer and scarcer. And secondly, general mistreatment of their work – and them, too – by museums and other institutions that are supposed to be supporting them.[12]

BR   What kind of patronage do you think is needed?

DJ   My general idea on that is that you have to have three or four schemes, on the grounds that probably one of them alone is going to fail, and what you have right now is one alone, which is the galleries and their business. The museums aren't independent, so they follow the galleries. I suggest maybe a loose government grant to almost anybody saying that he's an artist – not much money, but maybe enough to live a year on, or to do a couple of pieces with – without any distinction in the caliber of their work. Then the galleries as they're run, as businesses, letting things fall as they may as business, and then the museums, as very independent from the galleries, supporting the work by purchases, and perhaps grants, and showing it in a good way, which they don't now – a responsible way. And probably an artist organization, which could somehow get money and give money itself to people who need money to work, and also defend themselves against the general debasement which the museums cause.

BR   Do you think that artists are rebelling against the market-gallery-museum situation?

DJ   Yeah, I think so.

BR   In what ways?

DJ   You're asking what they don't like, or what they're going to do about it?

BR   What do you think is happening in terms of the revolt of the artist?

DJ   As I said, we formed an organization to try to defend ourselves somehow.[13] So far, that's about all it amounts to. The major thing we're going to do is, in the fall, put on – in a space that we'll rent – Hans Haacke's show that was refused by the Guggenheim Museum.[14] We figured that was a clear, self-interested thing to do. It was a clear-cut case of censorship or something, and the obvious way to correct that is simply to give the show. So we're going to do that. Also, we sent a long letter last week to Documenta, complaining about the general abuses there. We're going to run an ad in the Kassel newspaper.

The shows in the museums debase the work by putting it in categories and in group shows that are meaningless, and by handling the work badly and destroying it, and by bad installation, and just by general mistreatment of the artists. Like the letters from Documenta telling people what they're going to put in the show that say, "Well, we want something else." The artist wants one thing, and Documenta says, "We don't want to have anything to do with it." They didn't even ask me; they just told me, "There's a piece in the show, and would you please correct this enormous pile of information and send it back."[15]

BR   What do you think is the motivation behind conceptual art?

DJ   I don't know enough to want to talk about it. I kind of like Joseph Kosuth and Bernar Venet as people, and unfortunately I don't know enough about their work to say anything. I'm very much, of course, for my own interests, for actual visual art.

BR   Do you think it's a rejection of the market, a rejection of the gallery situation, refusing to produce commodities?

DJ   Not really. I understand Kosuth has a carpenter over there working away – just as I have a carpenter working away – improving his living conditions. So I don't think so.

BR   How is your work made?

DJ   It's made in a sheet metal factory over in Long Island

City.[16] It's mostly plain sheet metal work, or it's made of large plates.

BR   You don't miss the fact that you have no physical contact with the work?

DJ   No, it's just work to me, which I'm happy to get out of.

BR   Can you describe your procedure from the beginning to end of a piece?

DJ   The thing that really interests me most is just sitting around thinking about the pieces and figuring out what I want to do. When I get that figured out in a loose way, I go and talk to Ed Bernstein, and he usually tells me that the material doesn't come that size, or it can't be cut that way, or that the alloy is wrong, or there's some big hitch, and so I have to think about it some more. And then when it becomes sort of possible, we talk about how it can be assembled and how it can be put together. That sometimes affects its appearance, and it's a great deal of talking at that point, but once he's got it straight and he can make a working drawing, that's the end of it, and it's made there in the factory. Usually it comes out all right, and now and then it doesn't.

BR   Do you think your working with a factory has anything to do with Warhol setting up his studio as a factory?

DJ   Did Andy do it because I did it, or what?

BR   No, do you think there's any connection?

DJ   I don't think so. Not that I know of.

BR   Well, it's a divorce of the artist from the work.

DJ   You see, I'm not much interested in technique, or technology, or any of that. The factory does that work because I can't do it myself. It takes machines, and it takes a labor force, and I don't want all those machines, and I certainly wouldn't want several workers that I'd have to deal with all the time and pay every week. To me, it gets what I want. So it's just a technique. I don't see any reason why anybody else should want that technique, especially.

BR   Is New York the center of an avant-garde today?

DJ   I thought we'd sort of demoted the idea of an avant-garde; if you put down the avant-garde, then it can't be the center. Obviously there seem to be more artists here than anywhere else, but I've always considered Los Angeles a pretty serious place. So I think a lot of the people out there – several people, I think – are as good as a lot of people here. I don't think it should occur all in one city, anyway. There's no reason for it to be centered here.

BR   What is your objection to the term "avant-garde"?

DJ   Well, I think maybe you can quote Flavin on that.[17] It sounds like Greenberg's historical main line; it requires a point of some kind that's the leading point. Maybe it's just too simple. I think that art sort of moves on. I don't know about progress, but at least it changes. And some things at times seem too old-fashioned to deal with, perhaps. There's some kind of movement there. But if you're talking about an avant-garde, it seems too directed to a single line.

BR   Do you think that the fact that there's an economic crisis and a political crisis is affecting American art now?

DJ   Yeah, it's certainly reducing the money, which means a lot less gets done.

BR   How about the morale of the artist, given the political crisis?

DJ   Well, I think the whole thing is very depressing. I've been very depressed about dealing with the situation – politics here in New York City, which I've found out more and more about, and certainly the war in Vietnam and the whole social situation. But then, it hasn't been any good ever since I remember; I went to high school through World War II, and somebody's been fighting ever since. It's not new that it's miserable.

BR   Do you think that artists are fighting the feeling of frustration? Do you think that people feel frustrated now or that they are fighting back?

DJ   Well, I hope the organization will fight back; I think people have felt frustrated about it. And I think it's very interesting, as I told you, in that organization, that all those
diverse people –

BR   The organization of sculptors.

DJ   Well, isn't supposed to be sculptors; that's sort of a background. It just happens to be only sculptors, which is sort
of too bad, but it really wasn't meant to be sculptors. But
it's interesting that they're all keen on it remaining an organization and that it hasn't split up after six, eight meetings or something.

BR   Can you tell me about the new work that you're installing at Castelli's?[18]

DJ   It's all happened very recently, and it's kind of a complicated situation. I was going to do a large piece for the
ground floor of the building here which involved seven
boxes open front and back. It's a little bit like a small piece
that I had in Sonnabend a couple of years ago in Paris.[19]
It's a comparatively old idea, but none of the pieces has
ever been made except that one small one. It started out
with that idea. And all of these were squares.

     Showing the piece at Castelli's came up because Rich-
ard Serra asked me if I wanted to show a piece in a show
that's basically his. He has a large, open, low piece that
takes up most of the room, and to one side, behind some
pillars, there's about twelve feet by fifty or sixty. I've never
really looked at Leo's space all that carefully; when I went
over there, I was hoping to use the piece I was going to
make downstairs over there, so as to double up on the
money and save it and get some of it pawned off on Leo.
But the squares came out too much into the space, and
the columns were in the way of the piece, so I was thinking about all that, and also, I thought you'd have to get way
back into Richard's piece in order to look at mine. Something about that arrangement bothered me. So I thought

about that awhile and thought that if the squares were turned into parallelograms, they'd still come out just as far as the squares would have, but the fact that the main axis is directed sideways or at an angle to the pillars seemed to avoid the pillars somehow and also turned the main axis away from Richard's piece [image 47]. And I hadn't used parallelograms for quite a while.

BR   Why do think that more and more artists are interested in doing a piece for a specific environment or a specific site?

DJ   That's very general. I think it's true enough … I was just trying to think why it's true in a general way. In a way, it seems a continuation of a general empiricism that most people have, maybe. It is another thing you can deal with in a particular fashion, and certainly Larry Bell, Flavin, that group have done it for quite a while.

BR   Why are artists turning toward environments and works that are made for a specific show or a specific site? For example, you and Richard Serra both have done works commissioned for specific architectural sites.

DJ   Hmm. That takes a really general answer. I don't know.

BR   Well, what led to your making this piece that you're going to show at Castelli's?

DJ   It's hard for me if I'm speaking for everybody; that makes it a little hard to deal with. Like, Flavin's been using rooms for quite a while; in the Kornblee show three or four years ago — [20]

BR   Isn't it that the object can't be perceived apart from its environment?

DJ   People make single pieces, and I intend to keep on making single pieces that can go anywhere.

BR   What is it you want to communicate in this piece that's new, that's different from the single objects?

DJ   I felt the piece I was going to put downstairs — that was made particularly for that spot; it was made for downstairs [image 48].

BR   In this building.

DJ   Yeah. Now, that piece wouldn't have worked at Leo's be-
       cause of the axis — the general axis — and because there's
       not enough room between it and the pillars. Then also
       there's a problem because that wall is free on both ends at
       Leo's. So the piece had to make sense in relation to a wall
       that had no corners. Also, I wasn't too keen on something
       centered on that wall. This piece — because they're all par-
       allelograms — will be somewhat off-center, because you
       have an angle left over at one end.

BR   Are you involved in the way in which the work is
       perceived?

DJ   On the whole, I don't think about that. In the first place,
       I don't think about any viewers, I just think about what
       I'm interested in. So I never think about viewers. But
       certainly it's about the way I'm perceiving it. Like this
       piece: because they're all turned at an angle — all the boxes
       are turned at an angle, and they're all parallelograms — I
       think that forces me or a person to look at it from an an-
       gle. When you look at it from straight out, all the spaces,
       or some of the spaces, anyway, will be closed by an angle.
       So it has a good deal of variation within what happens as
       you move around.

BR   People have said that your work has a degree of illusion-
       ism, that the fact that you have to perceive a series of
       forms from a certain angle makes them diminish in size
       and space because of the angle of vision. Do you take that
       into consideration? Is that a problem?

DJ   I generally don't think about it. Perspective and light and
       all that, I take as things that exist in the world. I don't re-
       ally consider them. As I said a long time ago, the one il-
       lusion that I really didn't like was the one that occurred
       in painting — the spatial illusion. I don't use the word, but
       all art has illusion of one kind or another, and obviously
       the pieces are going to occur in perspective and occur in

some kind of light and cause shadows and all that, which
I don't care about.

BR How do you feel about the fact that this piece has to be
made in plywood because there isn't the money to fabricate it?

DJ Well, I'm interested in what it looks like in plywood. I'm
used to metal and would rather have made it in metal, but
it would have cost a great deal, and I've been sort of waiting around hoping to get money to make large pieces in
metal, so I haven't done any large pieces for a while. It
seemed better to go ahead and work in what's possible, as
I've certainly done before, than to stew around. The plywood won't be painted or anything, it will be plywood,
and I hope it carries as a material. It might be all right.

BR What is it that you want the viewer to get out of your
work? What is it you're trying to convey, principally?

DJ I can't state that. That's too complicated – too complex.

BR Are you involved in impact?

DJ I don't consider the viewer. I don't know about all that.
I'm interested in what I want to think about – what I want
to do. And if I like it, that's all I want. I don't think about
what anybody else is going to think about it.

BR Well, what is it that you get out of it?

DJ It's too complicated. You're talking about a general quality that is very complex, and it has a lot to do with what
you've thought for a long time, and I don't see how I can
state it. When, finally, you come down to what anybody's
work is about, you can't really state it just like that. To even
make an attempt at it takes a sort of construction of terms
and ideas, and it takes a lot of space.

BR Do you feel there are any shared premises among artists
working today, or is everybody off in their own individual ivory tower?

DJ I think there's certainly a great deal of individuality, and
I think that's one of the definitions of present art. I think

there are certain common things. What you were just talking about, being interested in particular spaces and particular spaces outdoors, is certainly common to a few people.

BR   You've no idea why that is such an important development?

DJ   It interests me. I can't find a general statement about it. I got involved in it – somewhere about the time of the Whitney show, early in '68 or before then.[21] I tried to figure out a piece for outdoors, and I never got it to work. It was sort of a series of tubes going down a slope, and it always was a contradiction to the slope. Having spent a lot of time trying to figure it out and figure out how the tubes wouldn't turn into steps and could rest on the slope without bearing part of each tube, I gave it up. After that, I took the whole problem very seriously and tried to figure out something I could do.

BR   Why does your work keep getting larger and larger?

DJ   Money, for one thing – mostly it's the possibilities in money. I only think about pieces that I really make; I don't make drawings or models or theoretical pieces. So if it seems possible to make a piece like the one that was in the Metropolitan show [see image 36][22] – like, if there is seven dollars or $8,000 possible to spend, then you think about a piece that can be made. I don't think about pieces that cost $20,000 to make.

BR   But what is the point of making them so large? What is it that the large scale does for the work?

DJ   Love of the large scale. I like the large scale a great deal. There's a big difference between, say, that tubular piece upstairs and a smaller one in the same scheme that's only three by six feet, and it seemed to me it's space and scale.

BR   Which, what – gives it greater impact, or is it more impressive, or what is it?

DJ   Space and scale – they're very likeable things. The bigger –

BR   The better?

DJ   The better… I don't know about that. I'm not keen on gi-
      ganticism. I don't like monuments either, come to think
      of it. I think I would have made large pieces a long time
      ago if there were any possibility of a large piece, but it was
      just impossible. Plus, I think you get more used to yourself
      all the time, so you're able to handle a large piece – deal
      with the scale in a more familiar way.

BR   Do you think that there's a problem about the relation-
      ship of painting, sculpture, objects to architecture?

DJ   There seems to be in the minds of architects, since they
      don't really use them. I think on the whole, the artists are
      better than the architects, which is a problem.

BR   Do you think it's significant that Castelli has opened up
      this new large space downtown?[23]

DJ   Yeah, he certainly opened it up because he thought a num-
      ber of his artists wanted a larger space to show in. The only
      thing is that it's behind a small elevator, so it really doesn't
      do you much good. I haven't shown anything there yet.

BR   What will happen to this piece that you're constructing?

DJ   Each parallelogram comes in four sheets, so it unscrews
      and comes apart. The piece is to go after that. It's to be
      shipped to [Rolf] Ricke in Cologne and to be shown
      around November, I guess.[24]

BR   It's not just a potlach situation, where these things are cre-
      ated for an event, and then they're discarded?

DJ   No, I'm against that. I want them to last a while; I don't
      like to see them destroyed or worn out or ruined. And
      even plywood in that quantity is too expensive to be casual
      with. We're still talking about a couple thousand dollars.

BR   How do you feel about earthworks, land art? Man shap-
      ing nature?

DJ   There's several of the artists whose work I don't like so
      much involved in it, so that sort of cuts my interest. Basi-
      cally, I'm not against it. [Michael] Heizer's work I haven't
      seen, so it's hard to say, and he seems the most interesting.

But I haven't seen any, except photographs. So, I don't know what I'm talking about; it's hard to say anything about it. I'm not particularly interested in Smithson's work, or Morris's. But there's no reason why it shouldn't be perfectly interesting and viable.

This conversation was sourced from an audio recording and a transcript. Sections of the recording are not included in the transcript and vice versa. The audio recording is in the Michael Blackwood Collection, Harvard Film Archive, Cambridge, Massachusetts. A copy of the transcript is in the Judd Foundation Archives, Marfa, Texas.

First published (excerpt): *American Art in the 1960s*, directed by Michael Blackwood (New York: Michael Blackwood Productions Inc., 1972), 16 mm, 57 min.; reprinted (excerpt): *The Artist's Studio: Donald Judd*, directed by Michael Blackwood (New York: Michael Blackwood Productions Inc., 2010), DVD, 29 min.

1   Harold Rosenberg (1906–1978) was an American writer, philosopher, and art critic. He coined the term "action painting."

2   In the 1950s and 1960s, many cooperative and artist-run galleries opened and operated in New York's East Village. The majority of these galleries were located on Tenth Street, whose name became shorthand for the larger scene.

3   Rose refers here to the second generation of abstract expressionist painters.

4   "Several of the artists have invented elements which might be considered an advance beyond the earlier abstraction; Frank Stella, for example, has made something new of geometric painting, made it more concrete and increased its scale." See Judd's "New York City – A World Art Center" (1962) in *Donald Judd Writings*, 81.

5   Judd refers here to *Sixteen Americans*, The Museum of Modern Art, New York, December 16, 1959–February 14, 1960, in which four of Stella's *Black Paintings* (1958–60) were included.

6   The exhibition was in fact in 1959: *Barnett Newman: A Selection 1946–1952*, French & Company, New York, March 11–April 5, 1959. This exhibition was organized by Clement Greenberg.

7   Judd received his BS in philosophy from Columbia University, cum laude, in 1953. He began graduate work in art history at Columbia in fall 1957 and completed his coursework in fall 1961; no degree was conferred because he did not complete the requirements.

8   See "Don Judd: An Interview with John Coplans" (1971) in this volume, 347, 361n9, for more on the timing of Andre's development in relation to Judd's.

9   Rose refers here to the Nelson Gallery and Atkins Museum, now known as The Nelson-Atkins Museum of Art. See Judd's "Kansas City Report" (1963) in *Donald Judd Writings*, 104–12.

10   Rose refers here to 101 Spring Street.

11   Judd would go on to criticize Greenberg's theory of art-historical development – most famously laid out in Greenberg's 1960 radio broadcast and essay "Modernist Painting" – in his writings, as well. See, for example, Judd's "Complaints: Part 1" (1969) and "A Long Discussion Not About Master-Pieces But Why There Are So Few of Them: Part 11" (1984) in *Donald Judd Writings*, 206 and 383–84, respectively.

12   See Judd's "Complaints: Part 1" (1969) in *Donald Judd Writings*, 200–209.

13   Judd was a member of Artists Rights Today, an association formed to further legislation affecting the arts. Other members included Lynda Benglis, John Chamberlain, Roy Lichtenstein, Marisol, Robert Morris, Robert Motherwell, Claes Oldenburg, Robert Rauschenberg, James Rosenquist, George Segal, Richard Serra, Andy Warhol, and Tom Wesselmann.

14   Hans Haacke's work *Shapolsky et al. Manhattan Real Estate Holdings, a Real-Time Social System, as of May 1, 1971* (1971), which documented the fraudulent activities of one of New York City's biggest slum landlords, was to be included in the artist's 1971 solo exhibition at the Solomon R. Guggenheim Museum, New York. When the artist refused to pull or alter the work, the Guggenheim canceled the exhibition weeks before the scheduled opening. See Judd's "Complaints: Part 11" (1973) in *Donald Judd Writings*, 240–41.

       The discussed 1972 staging of Haacke's canceled exhibition did not come to pass. *Shapolsky et al.*, however, was shown in the United States that year, in the group exhibition *Art Without Limit*, Memorial Art Gallery, University of Rochester, New York, April 7–May 7, 1972.

15   Judd refers here to Documenta 5, Kassel, Germany, June 30–October 8, 1972. He wrote of the exhibition, "It was awful this time too. They sent a letter that seemed to be missing its first half informing me that some small unspecified piece would be in the show and ordering me to check a bundle of papers they had sent. I told them I didn't want to be in their show.... It seemed to be that my piece was to be token history in some category for large pieces by younger artists." See Judd's "Complaints: Part 11" (1973) in *Donald Judd Writings*, 246.

16   Judd worked with Bernstein Brothers Sheet Metal Specialties, Inc. from late 1963 until the end of his life. Although they moved to Long Island City by the end of 1964, their shop was originally located in Manhattan, at 191 Third Avenue.

17   "The term 'avant-garde' ought to be restored to the French Army where its manic sense of futility propitiously belongs. It does not apply to any American art that I know about." Dan Flavin, "Some Remarks...Excerpts from a Spleenish Journal," *Artforum*, December 1966, 27.

18   *Richard Serra – Don Judd*, Leo Castelli Gallery (downtown), New York, May 20–June 10, 1972.

19   *Don Judd: Structures*, Galerie Ileana Sonnabend, Paris, May 6–29, 1969.

20   Flavin's work appeared at Kornblee Gallery, New York, four times during the late 1960s: in two solo exhibitions, both in 1966, and two group exhibitions, both in 1967.

21   *Don Judd*, Whitney Museum of American Art, New York, February 27–March 24, 1968, extended through April 14.

22   *New York Painting and Sculpture: 1940–1970*, The Metropolitan Museum of Art, New York, October 18, 1969–February 1, 1970.

23   In 1971, Leo Castelli opened a downtown location of his gallery at 420 West Broadway, in SoHo.

24   *Donald Judd*, Galerie Ricke, Cologne, November 4–December 1, 1972.

Interview with Richard Stankiewicz
For the film *Four Sculptors*
1973

Filmed on 16 mm, *Four Sculptors*, directed by Carl Howard, includes interviews with artists Louise Nevelson, George Rickey, and George Segal, in addition to Judd. This interview was conducted at 101 Spring Street by the sculptor Richard Stankiewicz, who is known for his work in metal assemblage.

RS   [Richard Stankiewicz] Before we get on to you and your
     particular work, I would like to open with the most gen-
     eral thing of all, which is why anybody bothers to make
     sculpture in the first place.

DJ   [Donald Judd] That's a question. [*Laughter*] Basically, I
     guess, I'm making it for myself. Newman has a sort of fa-
     mous statement where he said he made paintings because
     he wanted something to see, so that's the main thing, that
     I want those things to exist and I want to be able to see
     them.[1] And despite all of the complications of money and
     showings and all that, the fact that they go somewhere else
     and become public is sort of a by-product. One of my big
     problems – which is one of the points of this building[2] –
     is to have space to see things. I just had one loft for a long
     time, and there wasn't room to have very much there.[3] So
     I hope to have a lot of things around to be able to look at.

RS   What do you have, four floors?

DJ   There are five and two basements.

RS   So making sculptures is a self-serving activity for you.
     [*Laughs*]

DJ   I would say it is highly self-serving. It is hopefully non-
     serving as far as everybody else goes.

RS   Yeah, well, as far as anybody else goes, could it be the op-
     posite? I don't want to use an antagonistic and hostile –
     it's a little too warlike, but is there some kind of aggres-
     sive element in relation to everybody else?

DJ   Even if it is, just the way I do it – and to hell with tradi-
     tion and everything else – the main thing is that I don't
     think you can think about what other people think, since
     you don't know that much about what they think. You
     don't know who's involved, and just as a practical matter,
     it isn't possible to consider what they think, anyway. I only
     know what three or four other artists think, and I'm not
     too sure about that even, so –

RS   I know, so really it isn't –

DJ   Yeah, you know, it's somehow, as with anybody's art – all art – it turns out to be somehow partially intelligible to other people. Which is based on the premise that if it's intelligible to me, then it will be. You don't really know why it works that way.

RS   Would you agree that, as a communication, the thing works in proportion – that your responses are like other people's, rather than different?

DJ   Probably. One thing is that people aren't that different from one another. So that, despite considerable peculiarities, there's still a lot of things in common. That works for very old art, new art, and so forth. It's mysterious that you can get anything at all out of it – ancient Chinese art, or something. I assume that people are pretty much alike.

RS   I think that it is the thing, though, that lots of people forget or don't think about, and also this most recent romantic tradition that the artist is a very different person. I wanted to see if you agreed that an artist succeeds in getting through to other people only because he's like them and not because he is different from them.

DJ   Well, the fact that he gets through to them is because he is like them, but the capacity to do that, maybe, is being different. Probably the difference between people who are artists and people who are not artists is just a measured percentage or something, a very small percent. But that small percent seems to be pretty crucial.

RS   Yeah, I think it is. But we all belong to the same race. What generally is the reason?

DJ   Generally, some necessity for having, again, something to look at. You see what I mean? It's very important when something happens visually to me.

RS   Well, I know a lot of people who have seen your work, and not everybody I know likes it.

DJ   [*Laughs*]

RS And a lot of people say, "Well, I don't see anything, nothing is happening." What's happening?

DJ It means they think that nothing is happening. I mean, there's nothing you can say to that; that's their judgment about it, which is perfectly reasonable, and there's no answer to that, I guess.

RS What's your feeling about the kind of sculpture that involves all kinds of dynamic movements and asymmetry and a shooting up into different directions?

DJ I don't want to do that kind of sculpture. You probably know that I did paintings for a long time and went right from the paintings to three-dimensional work, and it had very little to do with any of the sculpture that was going on. I never thought of myself as being a sculptor. I still like David Smith's work and di Suvero's and so forth – I like di Suvero's a great deal – but that was sort of a definition of what I didn't want to do, insofar as three-dimensional work goes. It has to do with imitation of movement and the number of parts and all that sort of thing.

RS You don't really get involved with it.
    It would appear that your work is conceived entirely before its fabrication.

DJ Pretty much so. But we do a lot of talking before it actually gets made, because we usually have a lot of problems.

RS "We"?

DJ The guy at the factory, Ed Bernstein,[4] and myself. I think about how it is supposed to look, and then we have the problem of how do you put it together. Is the material available, how long it is, how wide it is, how clean it is, and how much does it cost, all that stuff. But since there really isn't any room to work on it – change it while it's being made – you have to get it all figured out ahead of time.

RS Do you think that you miss some things?

DJ Yes, sometimes they're wrong. But you make a guess at it. You know the proportions, the measurements, how thick the material should be, and so forth. Now and then it's all wrong.

RS   In what way?

DJ   The sizes can be wrong. It's not in proportion. And sometimes it's just a dumb idea and you didn't realize for some time.

RS   Well, with this fabricating system that you have, it's pretty much go for broke every time. You present your design, and the guy makes it, and you don't have the adventure, the accident in the process, or changing your course in midstream, so to speak.

DJ   Yeah, it can't be changed while they're working on it. But see, I'm not interested in changing it, either. If I were to change it, it would be a correction, just a correction of a mistake. It is certainly not a way of working on it. The way you work, or di Suvero works, or Smith – the process of actually working on it is crucial to the thing, because something is happening at every point, you're thinking about it. But I want to think it out ahead of time.

RS   The advantages in my own work – my process – is what I describe as a series of embarrassments, because I don't know what is going to happen next, and when I do, it only presents a problem. I stumble from one emergency to the next until it is finished. Your process is radically different: by the time you're done thinking about your thing, presumably, it's predetermined, and the making is out of your hands.

DJ   See, there's some of that in thinking about it. When I first think of the piece, a lot of things I don't know about it; there's sort of a general idea that finally comes together. You may not know the size, the material; a lot of things have to be figured out, especially how to make it. So some of that thinking is like the process of actually working on a piece and changing it, except you don't have anything there to see yet; you may be very wrong. It may turn out to be very wrong when it's finished.

R S   Well, it would seem to me that since you do plan every-
      thing in advance of the making, and you know there must
      not be any mistakes – ideally, it would seem to me, this
      kind of predetermination would limit the amount of
      complication in the work. I should think that it's a very
      restricted amount of complication and interrelationships
      of parts that you can predict.

D J   Yes, well, see, I'm not interested in them [complication
      and interrelationships] anyway, so it's no loss; I mean –

R S   You mean this in regards to very simple forms, and very
      few of them are intentional, regardless of the process?

D J   Yeah.
          There's a piece downstairs that is set up now that I
      first did three or four years ago – sort of a big aluminum
      box with a second top on it [image 49]. I first made it and
      I thought the top was to be a one-and-a-quarter-inch
      sheet of aluminum, three or four inches above the box.
      Well, when we set it up, it was terrible.

R S   Why?

D J   It was the space; it just didn't work. It was an enormous
      space. The second top looked too thin and sort of shrank
      back from the edge of the tubes – from the edge of the
      box – so that instead of it coming out as a box, it sort of
      came out as a box with an inward slope at the very top.
      So it was in storage for a long time, and then we set it up
      a few months ago. I started to move the top up and down,
      and then a couple of inches, then one inch, then three-
      quarters, then a quarter inch, then I finally decided it had
      to be a half-inch sheet of aluminum. All that monkeying
      with it in a way is similar to the way you would work, or
      di Suvero.

R S   I was just thinking that this is a very close and sensitive
      concern for relationships.

D J   Yes, but that doesn't show, finally. Nobody will know,
      when the piece is finished, that I monkeyed around with

it. The process of working on it and the way of thinking doesn't show, which is what I want. Anyway, I'm not interested in complicated art. I can see that someone could make a very complicated kind of art that didn't involve composition or part-by-part working or the process of working – probably somebody will, but it isn't within what I can think about.

RS   Did you write a piece once about relational and non-relational art?

DJ   It's in the yearbook of *Arts Magazine*, I think.[5]

RS   Yeah, I read it, but I can't quite place it.

DJ   It was pretty general, because they wanted me to sort of talk about what was going on at the moment, which covered an awful lot of ground.

RS   Do you care to sort of characterize the idea of relational –

DJ   I consider almost all sculpture and painting up to Pollock to be relational, in that one part is just opposed to another part, or parallel to it, or in some connection to one another. I haven't really been thinking about what I didn't like for a long time. I guess one thing – basic thing, too – is that the parts dominate the whole of the thing, so that you have a somewhat indefinite whole and very strong related parts, and that is one thing that I object to, too. I thought, "Well, if these relations were that interesting and sort of the core of the piece, why not make them the whole piece?" You find them in a big, fairly complex piece of di Suvero's, all these things going on in a very tight, intelligible structure. But this is my sort of thinking about them – I saw that this was so important – why not clear up the lesser parts and make it the whole thing?

RS   Well, you couldn't, for instance, define a man without his context in his environment and in nature and in the world – in the universe. Any definition of an isolated person is a fiction. What would you say to the proposition that an individual element in the sculpture really has its interest and its meaning in relation to other parts, and by itself, it's —

DJ   Well, I understand it, you know, and you can't take this as criticism of sculpture and expect to have a change. You don't want to come along and say that the thing that it is, that is basic to it, is wrong and somehow should change, because the whole thing is a stand-up. I mean, it's an impossibility — which is one reason why I don't go off and do something by myself. I know that the kind of form or structure in the thing can't be taken out of the context; it's the way of working and so forth. But it drives me nuts when I was trying to — I didn't get into this in sculpture, but when I first started painting, it was sort of vaguely ignorant or cubist or something, and there was a lot of juggling and placing of areas in relation to one another and all that. Eventually I developed a dislike for all that fiddling around in the way of working.

RS   Yeah, I can see that it can get sort of messy.

There are other kinds of relationships besides the relationships of sizes and directions of parts in sculpture and so-called visual dynamics; people are introducing things like movement, sound, proximities, sensing, reaction, and so on. Do you have any notions about that?

DJ   That's fine. It depends on how you use the words "relation" and "composition" and so forth. I just always used them in connection to the previous work, so that I didn't use them for my own work — which in some light or sense had relations too, I guess. I know the proportions and sizes are very important.

RS   I just wondered what your thinking was about the introductions of other elements, like sight, light, and movement. Can you imagine yourself ever working with movement?

DJ   No, but it's fine for other people to do it. I don't know quite why, but I wanted it to be static, apparently.

RS   [*Laughs*] Your antimovement is antirelational.

D J   Well, the original antimovement was the imitation of
       movement – again, in the previous painting and sculp-
       ture. I'm certainly not against people making sculpture
       that moves, which I think is a great idea and probably will
       sometime develop far beyond what it is now. And as far as
       light goes, I think that Flavin is the best artist around. It's
       just a case of my not understanding it, not being able to
       use it. That has no principles or anything involved: that's
       just a matter of what I can do.

R S   It appears that the use of elements like light, sound, move-
       ment, and so on are not your thing to do, as you feel it, and
       yet presumably you won't always be working exactly as
       you do now. Do you have any ambition for future work?
       Or, what direction do you think it will take, or would you
       like it to take?

D J   I'm pretty much inclined to work in the present, so that
       I usually don't have predictions. My work has slowly
       changed, and it's a very sort of uneventful thing. I never
       feel that I have to change. It seems to be, I don't know, some
       sort of point you're working toward, or which you have
       passed, or something like that. So it just sort of goes along.

R S   You feel you can plan your individual works, but you
       don't try to determine the evolution of your thinking?

D J   I think it takes care of itself.

R S   All right.
           What role has boredom got in your scheme of –

D J   Well, obviously, you get bored with a certain type of work,
       so you don't want to do it anymore. And, if so, you can't
       even think about it anymore, so it doesn't get done, any-
       way. Instead, it moves you along a little. But that happens
       pretty naturally. If the pieces don't get made, which often
       happens because of the money involved, then they begin
       to seem too alien to think about.

R S   I just wondered about that.

D J   When it's finished, that's it. In the '60s – I don't know, '64 or

'65 – I did a couple of what we call progressions and long horizontal pieces on the wall. At the time, there wasn't much money, so one small one and one large one got made, and one out of wood, I think, and metal. There's a great many possibilities both in cutting the material and the kind of progressions, the numbers involved. Only one got done in '66 [see image 26]. And since then, I've done more, but with the same progression, which only amounts to three or four, the same sort of numerical scheme and dimensions, because the time passed when I could think of how the thing worked, as far as numbers go. I made a couple of new ones that have different colors, different materials, because it's a more general thing, and you can substitute and play around with them, but the scheme itself and ideas just went past its time, and it wasn't possible to work with it in the way that it should have been worked with. After a while, you don't quite understand it, either, just as you don't understand other peoples' work or earlier work, or enough to imitate it or develop from it. You don't quite understand that you're the owner of the work.

RS   What you are saying reminds me of what Hans Hofmann once said, which was, "I love to not know what I'm doing."[6] It sounds a little bit funny in relation to your work, maybe, but I would like to ask you what you think the role of the unconscious is in the making of your works – the conceiving of your works?

DJ   Well, I don't really know what the unconscious is, but it [the work] can't be too cut-and-dry or it isn't interesting; it's just an optical thing. If the pieces are too evident or you're too sure of it, then you're not going to be interested in it, because it's really the thinking about it that's interesting. After a while, a lot of things that all seemed to be separate, which didn't work together, finally sort of coalesce; it begins to make sense, and certainly many things you don't know about, which I guess is the unconscious part. But a lot of it is conscious, and it's just history: you settled it, it's disappeared, and it becomes your ordinary way of working.

Perhaps the whole point for your way of working is to get to the point where it is natural, so that it's not a case of extreme problems from point to point – which when I was doing paintings was always the case. Each one was sort of a separate thing and wouldn't lead to similar ones, or there wasn't any context that developed. Each painting would have things that I liked a great deal and things that I thought were necessary, and the next painting would be the same thing, but they weren't the same things I liked, and you could never put the two sets of things you liked together – so that it was sort of a square wheel going on, you know? It was very difficult and highly unnatural. When I started to do three-dimensional work, it came together, and there seemed to be a lot of possibilities and a lot of room to think.

RS   I'm interested in the idea of trepidation in painting and sculpture – the idea of terrible fears, and courage, and so on. Having the courage to work as you work regardless. One kind of internal courage is indicated by Picasso, who said when he was in a jam about a painting, he would decide what it was he liked about it and what he didn't like in the painting; then it was a simple matter to erase the part that night. His working process might be individual to him, but a thing like that takes a lot of courage, because you're really hanging on the cliff when you do that. I wonder if you had these crises? Surely you must have, but what are they like?

DJ   Well, I never think it's too great of a crisis, but you do get to know what you like, and you can be wary of that. Also, I think as far as Picasso goes, you have to be wary in both directions. You can't destroy what you like to just get something newer, or –

RS You can reduce it to a kind of logical puzzle or game of
some sort, where you can say that he likes what he doesn't
like and he doesn't really like what he likes, so he's choosing what he likes – [*Laughs*]

DJ The main point is, I think, that you don't really want to
play it safe all the time. I think probably most people didn't
develop by playing safe, and if it's related to boredom, too,
you just don't want a sure thing. So you like the chance of
making a piece and seeing how it will turn out.

RS Yeah, I can see it can be a sure thing or a sure death. But I
don't know your early work or anything like it; was it simpler, if it's possible, or more complicated than it is now?

DJ Well, the paintings before the end of the painting were
pretty simple. The real early work was, as I said before, sort
of half-baked cubism, sort of naturalistic, half-baked cubism. But the paintings, for the last couple of years before
I quit doing them, which was '61 or so, were pretty simple, and certainly were connected to the painting that was
going on. But I guess that was also simplicity – that sort
of simplicity that I'm especially interested in.

RS Do you think for most people that the natural tendency is
to work from complication down to more and more simplicity? Reduction?

DJ Not really. One's early work is unclear and therefore often created with complexity. Then it becomes clear that
almost everybody's work seems to be simple. Early Cézanne is muddled and the middle one is clearly the right
one; what looks like complexity is simplicity. The attitudes
and the conscious, unconscious, or whatever you're talking about is highly complex, much more than in his earlier
work. Also, I think that all good art is about the same as far
as complexity, or the same degree, regardless of whether
it is visually complex or visually simple. Which means
that if someone came along and did exceedingly complex
work visually, that finally it would have the same degree of

simplicity or complexity that most work has. There seems to be some point at which it is intelligible or makes sense to you, a certain quality that you see in the work which is intelligible to you, regardless of whether it's complex work or simple work.

RS   Along with the idea of reduction and simplicity are certain other things that are happening where the so-called art is taken out of the gallery and out of the environment of art altogether. People might take a bulldozer and dig a hole in the ground in the middle of the desert – create a theatrical event and call it a Happening. All these are on the fringes of the traditional painting and sculpture idea. Do you think that valid? Would you call that art, or would you call it amusement, or –

DJ   No.

RS   Is it necessary to call it anything? What is the value of it?

DJ   I'm willing to call art whatever anybody says is art. I'm not going to object to that. I don't see any point in saying that something is not art if somebody says it is. Something that I said before – I'm really interested in things that you can see. To correct it a little bit: see more or less at once. As far as working with the land goes, that's a perfectly reasonable thing to do, I think; that's another possibility, along with a great many possibilities. As far as Happenings go, you know, I liked Oldenburg's. Some I don't like, but that's a different case to me; it's a performance of some kind. It takes place in time and it isn't what I want the most. It's certainly something that's nice if somebody is interested in it, but it's like all the other things that could possibly happen. What I especially want to occur are visible, reasonably static things.

RS   I can't get it. You want things to last a bit in time, anyway?

DJ   Yeah.

RS   I take it you don't believe in the gesture, the affirmable doing of something? You like to think.

DJ   I like to think a lot about doing it before doing it. Yeah, I guess so.

RS   But your notion about the process of making your sculpture – as long as you get what you imagine in the end, it doesn't matter whether you make it or the factory makes it, or anything of the sort. A lot more is involved in the process. What I was starting to get at, though, was you seem not to be concerned with the process of the actual making of the sculpture.

DJ   You know, I guess not.

RS   Are you involved in the material, and the modeling of the material, and the ideas they get from the material as they work with it? This is not your method. You imagine the thing, and then you get it executed. Therefore, I think, you're more interested in the object than in any performance.

DJ   Yeah.

RS   And therefore, in connection with these earthworks and Happenings and so on, I gather you're not really interested in them as performances. Because as a gesture, as an act, they're ephemeral, and after they're done, it's vanished away forever, like a theatrical performance. And you like to have a concrete object.

DJ   It's a case of priorities, and the thing I really want to see are the things that are visible that aren't performances. Obviously, other kinds of activities exist all over and they are perfectly legitimate, but I'm not necessarily so very interested in them. Things are what I'm most interested in. When art starts to drift off into other kinds of activities, then I'm less interested. That doesn't mean those activities aren't very interesting to the people doing them, aren't perfectly legitimate. And as far as working with the land or earth or anything, that lasts longer – it's not about weighing a single performance. As far as materials go, I think about the material a lot. You look around the factory and at certain ways of working, and certain materials suggest things – but then again, that's all before the piece. Once the piece is started, it goes through just as it was planned.

RS   It's just maybe a kind of expanded-time existence that happens to a person like myself. I would pick up ideas in the process of making a sculpture, and I might change my course and revise the image as I go along. And if it's true, as you say, that you get ideas from the materials and processes that you see in the factory, you get your intentions modified, but not within the time span of one piece – from one piece to the next.

DJ   Yeah, that's right.

RS   So it's a different kind of time operation, but the same process happens.

DJ   Yeah; as I said earlier, it's not that different a way of working, but the result, finally, is very different – the terms of the process, or terms of aesthetics, or something. It makes a big difference to me that nothing in the process shows in the work.

This conversation was sourced from a transcript and from the film *Four Sculptors*; the transcript includes material from outtakes. The 16 mm footage of *Four Sculptors* is in the M. E. Grenander Department of Special Collections & Archives, University at Albany, State University of New York. A copy of the transcript is in the Judd Foundation Archives, Marfa, Texas.

First published (excerpt): *Four Sculptors*, directed by Carl Howard, hosted by Richard Stankiewicz (Albany: Educational Community Center, University at Albany, State University of New York, 1973), 16 mm, 56 min.

1   In a 1947 statement for *The Tiger's Eye*, an art and literary magazine, Newman wrote, "An artist paints so that he will have something to look at; at times he must write so that he will also have something to read." Newman, "From 'The Ides of Art: The Attitudes of Ten Artists on Their Art and Contemporaneousness,'" in *Barnett Newman: Selected Writings and Interviews*, ed. John P. O'Neill (New York: Knopf, 1990), 160.

2   Judd refers here to 101 Spring Street.

3   Judd refers here to 53 East Nineteenth Street.

4   Judd worked with Bernstein Brothers Sheet Metal Specialties, Inc. from late 1963 until the end of his life. Although they moved to Long Island City by the end of 1964, their shop was originally located in Manhattan, at 191 Third Avenue.

5   See Judd's "Specific Objects" (1964) in *Donald Judd Writings*, 134–45.

6   "At the time of making a picture, I want *not* to know what I'm doing; a picture should be made with *feeling*, not knowing." Elaine de Kooning, "Hans Hofmann Paints a Picture," *ARTnews*, February 1950, 40.

Interview with Ian North
May 30, 1974

In the spring of 1974, Judd traveled to Adelaide, Australia, to execute a commission from the Art Gallery of South Australia for a large triangular work in concrete, sited outdoors at the rear of the museum. This commission was organized in conjunction with the exhibition *Some Recent American Art*, organized by The Museum of Modern Art, New York, which traveled to a number of venues throughout Australia in 1974, including the Art Gallery of South Australia (May 31–June 30, 1974).

Ian North, curator of paintings, conducted this tape-recorded interview with Judd in his office at the Art Gallery of South Australia. A note on the transcript in the museum's archives reads, "The interview was recorded for the gallery's archives. It was a relaxed occasion, Judd lounging in a visitor's chair, wearing embroidered cowboy boots, and speaking his mind freely."

This is the first interview in this volume in which Judd mentions Marfa, the small town in West Texas where he began to live and work in the early 1970s.

IN   [Ian North] Don, can I first ask you what prompted you
      to come here?
DJ   [Donald Judd] Well, let's see — obviously a chance to make
      a piece [image 50], which was a lot of my reason.
IN   Who organized it, who put pressure on you to come here?
DJ   Jenny Licht wanted me to, and she brought John Baily
      down, and John Stringer, and the other guy from the
      Modern — [1]
IN   Waldo?
DJ   Yeah, Waldo Rasmussen, and Leo [Castelli] came to the
      dinner [in New York] too. Jenny had been talking about
      my coming over and my making a piece.
IN   You said you'd like to spend longer in Australia, mainly to
      look at the countryside.
DJ   Yeah. I was a little reluctant to come for such a short time.
      I would rather have brought my children and all that and
      spent two months or something wandering around.
IN   How does the work that you're producing for us relate to
      work which you have been doing in the immediate past?
DJ   Well, as I told you, there is one other concrete piece that
      belongs to Philip Johnson [image 51], which was a circle,
      and I can't quite remember when it was made; it was
      made two or three years ago. And the chances for a con-
      crete piece — actually, the chances for any large permanent
      piece — are rather scarce.
IN   Yes, that surprised me a bit.
DJ   We sell a lot of pieces, but they're all sort of moderate,
      household-size pieces. In order to make me happy, or
      sort of minimally happy, because it isn't all that fast, we try
      to make two or three large pieces each year. The smaller
      pieces support the bigger pieces.
IN   I'm surprised that you haven't made more pieces in con-
      crete, in that it's a fairly cheap medium.
DJ   It wasn't cheap in Connecticut. I expected it to be cheap,
      too. The circle cost $8,000 to make.

IN   That astonishes me.

DJ   Of course, I didn't pay for it; Johnson paid for it. This
      shouldn't cost that much – the circle involves all that
      formwork.

IN   How preconceived was the triangular piece which you
      are doing for us?

DJ   It's not very preconceived.

IN   How much of its form did you have in your mind before
      you saw the site, before you actually came here?

DJ   Well, I thought I was going to have to deal with a flat site,
      because John Baily said it was flat. The concrete pieces
      were sort of developed in terms of a slope, so I really didn't
      have a piece for a flat site. So I've been thinking rather
      steadily for however long this came up – three weeks ago,
      or more than that, maybe – about what I could make in
      concrete that would be suitable for a level spot. Some-
      where in the back of my mind was an idea to make it tri-
      angular. Actually, the idea was to make triangular steel
      pieces, as well as concrete pieces.

IN   This is the first triangular piece?

DJ   This is the first triangular piece of any kind, little or big.
      Everything got abruptly reversed when John met me at
      the airport and realized after he got home that it [the
      site] was sloped. So then I could have gone back to the –
      usually an idea has a number of possibilities. Johnson's
      piece, where the slope, the bevel, was on the outside – the
      bevel could be on the inside, so in a way you have two
      pieces there; the other circle could have been used here.
      But again, that's pretty predictable. I know it would have
      been a nice piece. But also now that I've seen the first
      thing, it's a sure thing, and I'm inclined to – it's more fun
      to take a chance on it.

IN   I'm glad you did.

DJ   Wait until you see it first before you say that. [*Laughter*]

IN   Did you envisage that the triangular piece and perhaps

your sculpture in general would relate to the physical environment, as with the beveled edge? Had you conceived
that to apply generally to your sculpture?

DJ   The siting?

IN   The siting, but also the beveled edge following the contour of the land; was that conceived to be a regular feature, as it were, of your work?

DJ   Yeah, I've been trying to figure out something with some
way to use the slope of the land for a long time. I think it
actually started with Johnson. A long time ago, he bought
eight big boxes that go in a row [see image 16]. They are in
a slightly sloping field, and he never quite leveled it off.
They were supposed to be level. We sort of argued about
it. It isn't too tilted. Anyway, around about '68 or so, '67, I
think I was trying to figure out something that would go
on a slope, and nothing came of that for a long time.

IN   Did you conceive of works which on a flat surface relate
more specifically to the environment than might have
been the case in your past work?

DJ   Well, I used indoor pieces, which relate to the space they
are in. The first one, I think, was a row of six or eight
boxes – it can vary – between two sidewalls, on the wall
[image 52]. It was in a show in Dartmouth somewhere round
in '66, I guess.²

IN   It seems to be generally true of minimal art that it does
relate very much to the space it's in.

DJ   Some does and some doesn't. There's a range, of mine and
other's. Some of mine is freestanding in the normal sense
and some of it isn't. Some of it has a vague relationship to
space and some of it is quite particular; it couldn't even
be moved, like the concrete pieces.

IN   I'm sure a lot of people imagine the triangular form of the
piece sprang directly from its site, but it's by coincidence
that it just happens to be placed on a triangular corner
of land.

DJ   Yeah – it is becoming trapezoidal now that they took the
      wall out down there. It got clear more or less as I arrived
      here; I don't know how much the land suggested it or not.
      I had it in mind before, but its position in the land is pretty
      particular. I fooled around with it quite a bit.

IN   So you see the development of your work more toward
      larger outdoor pieces which relate to the environment; is
      that a fair statement to make?

DJ   Well, either large indoor or large outdoor pieces, either
      one. I'm interested in larger pieces.

IN   May I quote you from the MOMA catalogue?[3]

DJ   It depends on what they've said.

IN   It's a little piece published in 1968: "I wanted work that
      didn't involve incredible assumptions about everything. I
      couldn't begin to think about the order of the universe or
      the nature of American society. I didn't want work that
      was general or universal in the usual sense. I didn't want
      it to claim too much."[4] That's perhaps indicative of your
      present attitude, too, is it? What sort of thing are you aim-
      ing to achieve in work like you are doing for us?

DJ   I think it's too complicated – and then again, it's too
      general – to get into saying why. You like to figure out
      work that you want to do because it corresponds or suits
      a lot of your thinking, attitudes, and all that. It's very com-
      plicated, because it stands on a ten- or twenty-year history,
      depending on where you cut it off, so I'm not keen on
      making any general statements about why I do it.

IN   I thought that would be your reaction, and I'm sure that
      if I was in your position, that would be my reaction too,
      if I may say so. I just thought I would try daring the ques-
      tion anyway.
          What sort of influences have affected your sculpture?

DJ   Well, almost nothing has affected it. I don't think of it as
      sculpture. I was influenced, or whatever word you use, a
      lot over the years by painting done in New York.

IN   Hard-edge?

DJ   No, not really; Pollock and those people. Hard-edge in a way didn't exist then. Anyway, it's another concoction. I think it came later.

IN   So you don't think of it as sculpture, but just as things you make.

DJ   Yeah, well, it's sculpture in a way. "Sculpture" is not a very useful word. And then there's sculpture by David Smith or somebody – I liked it, but I don't know if I got anything out of it for myself.

IN   I've got the feeling that you are working rather away from what might be generally conceived to be influential traditions. You mentioned that you went to Paris and didn't go to an art gallery, and so on. How do you see your work in relation to the so-called post-object movement, if it's not too general a question?

DJ   Oh, not at all, I suppose. I don't know. Obviously, I'm interested in being able to see something, so I'm not very interested in literary art. Art's always declining into literature or realism or something. It's just a chronic state of things.

IN   In many ways, you are trying to strip a lot of formal aspects from your work?

DJ   Well, no, I have my own formal aspects. As I've written it out someplace, I don't consider it a reduction or anything like that.[5] There are certain things you don't understand or you don't like, and you get rid of them, and you invent other things which suit you. So you haven't lost anything in terms of quantity of things that are involved.

[*Break in recording*]

IN   Don, you seem to be orientating yourself more toward living in Texas than in New York. I gather you want to begin making works in Texas?

DJ   Well, it's a very little town; there are a couple of hardware stores with shops attached to fix windmills, tanks, and things like that, so they might be able to weld rough pieces, but they couldn't do anything like the chartreuse piece upstairs.

IN   What's the name of the town, by the way?

DJ   Marfa.

IN   So the New York environment is –

DJ   They have a good factory there. Most of this stuff is made in New York. The smaller stuff – well, they've done some big metal pieces, too.[6] The main thing is, I've kept a lot of my own big pieces. One reason for the two aircraft hangars is to have the space to set those pieces up.[7]

IN   Are the airplane hangars in the same little town?

DJ   Yeah. I bought a block with hangars like this and this [*gestures*] and some space in between them. I'm mainly there because I wanted to get land outside of town.[8] It's very empty; it's near Mexico. We've been going to the Southwest for a long time.

IN   What's your attitude toward the New York art scene, if it makes sense to use such a term?

DJ   Well, I don't have all that much to do with it. My idea of things is probably what they'd call elitist a couple of years back: I don't think there are all that many good artists. My friends would certainly miss not seeing me. But I'm not fond of all those other mediocre people, who get to be a pain in the neck. Unfortunately, the neighborhood where we lived has turned into some sort of artistic neighborhood.

IN   South Houston?

DJ   Yeah. It has become a real sore subject.

IN   Who are your friends or the people you admire?

DJ   Well, I'm going to miss somebody – Flavin is an old friend, John Chamberlain, Larry Bell. Some people I admire I don't know so well: Claes Oldenburg, Richard Serra. Carl Andre is a middling friend – I don't know him really well.

IN   Any painters?

DJ   Frank Stella. I liked his painting, but I don't – we are both
       unsociable, so I seldom – we were on good terms, but we
       just never see anything of each other.

IN   Agnes Martin?

DJ   I've met her. I like her painting, but I've only met her once
       or twice, and I haven't seen her for years. I'd like to. She
       has been down in New Mexico for some time.

IN   It seems obvious that you don't consider that the
       galleries – in particular, perhaps, the so-called public gal-
       leries, like The Museum of Modern Art – are all that cru-
       cial to the development of your art, anyway?

DJ   The Modern museum is useless. Almost useless, anyway.

IN   Too much behind the times?

DJ   Yes – Jenny Licht is an exception – too much behind the
       times. They have very little to do with what is happening
       in the last twenty years; in fact, I don't know if they have
       had anything to do with what's happened since the '30s,
       if then. Their claim to fame is that they showed Picasso
       in the '30s, and he certainly didn't need it all that much.
       [*Laughs*] I'm not sure that they have ever done too much.

IN   What about the Met?

DJ   Well, the Met's just a historical museum. That big show
       they had was a sort of fluke.[9]

IN   The Guggenheim and the Whitney?

DJ   The Guggenheim and the Whitney are more sort of
       down-to-earth institutions. They are both a little indis-
       criminate. I get a bit aggravated when they show every-
       body, and the Whitney has those big annual things.

IN   I saw one of those. Gosh, there was a lot of rubbish there.

DJ   Yes, they're usually pretty trashy, not very interesting. But
       then, they buy things in a fairly early stage, and they gave
       me a big show, and I guess everyone else would have
       thought it was such an early stage.[10] That was '68, but I
       suppose it helps – but that's as far as these things help.

IN No plans for exhibitions of work in Australia?

DJ No – me, no. Somebody wants to buy a stack; they called Leo about it.

IN From Sydney, probably.

Don, you were just saying that The Museum of Modern Art justifies showing works of younger artists by placing labels on them to tone down their individual importance. I think this is probably a fairly common institutional attitude. I guess it's a bit disappointing.

DJ Well, as I said, they think so much of themselves they can't give anyone the honor. They did show Frank Stella, a big show, and Claes, a big show.[11] That's good, but in a way, it's pretty late; both could have been shown five or seven years ago.

IN Do you think it's really important that a gallery does show artists' work early? Are artists really that dependent on a museum?

DJ No; in terms of selling, or their reputation, and all that, it doesn't seem to matter much. Claes and Frank did perfectly well without the Modern.

IN Well, how do you feel about this show?[12]

DJ Well, as I was saying, it's a lot of people, and each one has three or four things, and it's strange to see it all together, because you never do see it all together; you usually see one person's show. And it's strange to see so few things [by each person]. It's better than nothing, but it would be very hard for somebody to judge what the different people are like.

IN How do you feel about seeing the artist's work not only out of the context that you are used to, but also in another country? How does that seem?

DJ Well, I think I would feel the same if I saw the show in Cleveland or some other American city that doesn't have all the art. New York has the galleries; it doesn't have that many museums. They don't show that much publicly.

IN   Have you seen your own work on display in this gallery?
      How does it look?

DJ   Yes, I was upstairs just now. It seems to be going all right.
      They don't have the stack up; the floor drops, so it might
      be difficult.

IN   It's going to be very hard for a lot of the public to come
      in cold from the suburbs.

DJ   Also – it's a little bit by chance – it's going to be a really
      quiet show. There is a sort of common factor, by Jenny's
      selection. There are a great many relatively quiet works
      there. Which wouldn't happen if there was a big Serra or
      a big di Suvero, Chamberlain, or a big piece of Flavin's; it
      would change things.

IN   It's a pity, really; we are getting a bit of a distorted picture,
      in a way. She's only called it *Some Recent American Art*, of
      course, which is logical. You don't want too great a diver-
      sity in one show. I think it's confusing. There's no lyrical
      abstraction, no new realism.

DJ   All to the good, as far as I am concerned.

IN   Yes – irrelevancies?

DJ   A lot of people, at least for a show like this, are a high pro-
      portion of people whom I like.

IN   What do you think about lyrical abstraction, new re-
      alism? Well, I put the word in your mouth, perhaps:
      "irrelevancies"?

DJ   They are not very interesting. On a personal level, lyri-
      cal abstraction is a very watered-down painting that has
      been going on for a long time. The other one's a revival
      of something that's been dead from time to time. It has
      nothing interesting.

IN   I just wondered if there was an indication in what you
      said of some sort of developing mainstream or whatever
      of American art around at the moment, which these other
      movements – lyrical abstraction, anyway – are a part of.

DJ   I'm wary of mainstream theories because I think art should be diverse, but I think after a certain kind of work doesn't produce anything first-class for a certain length of time, I think you call it quits; if everything you see confirms this, it must be. There hasn't been good realistic work for decades. Hopper is a pretty nice painter; he's not a first-class painter, but he was an old man.

IN   I must say how surprised, how unimpressed I was by people like [Philip] Pearlstein, [Chuck] Close, and so on when I saw them at the Whitney.

DJ   Yes, I think they are a real bore.

IN   I'm surprised at the promotion they've got; I don't understand it.

DJ   Yes, there are obviously a lot of people who like them – *The New York Times* and people like that.

IN   What do you feel about the critical scene in New York?

DJ   That's a sore subject. I don't think there are any critics of very good competence there.

IN   Do you feel that, on the one hand, some are too conservative, and perhaps on the other, others are too willing to embrace everything that comes along?

DJ   Yes, a great deal of them are conservative, and they are not even … I don't know. It seems there should be, both in politics [and art], there should be intelligent conservatives, but it never seems to happen. They are very strange. In *The New York Times*, [Hilton] Kramer and so on, they are actually dumb in terms of what they like.[13] I remember seeing something written about [Pierre] Bonnard, which was just stupid: he didn't have anything to say about something he actually liked.

IN   I see. A lack of a sense of real perspective.

DJ   The rest of it is a combination of publicity and reporting. Not much thought and not much accuracy. Anybody who reads the stuff in ten years must be very wary of the facts.

IN   What do you think of Lucy Lippard, more specifically?

DJ   Well, she's not too bad, but, you know, she's not very clear on what she likes, and she's sort of sloppy and fast about writing anything.

IN   Ursula Meyer?[14]

DJ   I don't have much of an impression of her. Lucy's a little fashionable, too. In order to write about something, it takes a lot of thought, a lot of development. They just don't put that into it, and because they are used to writing for publications, they don't have the time or get paid enough for that to be done.

IN   No. It's a bit of a farce, having weekly columns and so on, really.

      You wrote reviews at one time.

DJ   Yes, you can write reviews, maybe, but they aren't long enough to think anything out. But some of the people are writing both reviews and articles; you can't write an article like that, it's impossible.

      I just wrote an article on Malevich in January.[15]

IN   What for?

DJ   *Art in America.* I didn't know all that much about the history. It's not a great article; I mean, I hope it is fairly accurate or reasonable, but it was just the sort of beginning. It's too big a thing to write with all that frequency.

IN   Yes. I've written newspaper criticism at times; I became increasingly upset by the implication of what one was doing, sort of hipshot judgments and so on. I suppose you can justify it to yourself in that it does at least give some publicity to the whole thing. That's about all. Sort of a notification process.

DJ   It's easier to justify it, in a way, in the newspapers than in the art magazines. You get these long articles that are pretty pretentious and serious in the art magazines at the rate of once a month. They are done by standard hacks, and I don't think they can think in any way; I know they can't think at that rate. Most of that fills the art magazines. They at least should be more serious.

IN   The whole situation seems to suffer a bit from overkill. There's just too much stuff, too much bunk; you know, this tray is full of stuff most of which you can't read. There's no time to read it. It's like that every day.

DJ   I don't read all that stuff. You get used to it. I'm interested in doing my own work, I'm interested in a few other people's; in one way, the whole thing gets narrower. I'm more intolerant of other people than I used to be. I don't know. I just don't have much regard for the big mediocre base, which is supposed to be the base for the better work and all that stuff. I think it is done by a few people.

IN   What about the art schools in New York?

DJ   They are pretty bad. This all gets pretty negative. The School of Visual Arts in New York is probably the best of them; at least they have some actual artists teaching for them. The Art Students League has gone down.

IN   It used to be important, didn't it?

DJ   Yeah. It has the students of the students of the first generation in the 1920s.[16] Just incredible.

IN   That happens here at this art school [the South Australian School of Art], actually.

DJ   The art school is almost full of instructors that you have never heard of. They are the best pupils of the guy who died, who was in most cases the pupil of the previous guy who died. It is really a strange place.

IN   A side note, not really relevant to this talk: I remember studying from a book called *The Natural Way to Draw* by Kimon Nicolaïdes.[17]

DJ   Yeah, I've used that book. I still have it. I don't know what they can do about schools. I don't think there is anything to teach except what the person is interested in.

IN   I gather that you have been living off your sculpture for quite some time?

DJ   Yes. Might help my intolerance a little, because it means that I have to deal with other people. Makes you less patient, I suppose. There are more people involved. You expect more to happen, too; you find out I wrote about people's work, "Yes, it might have possibilities," and almost invariably, how it was then – it doesn't change. You expect almost all the time that they won't ever develop.

IN That's right; promising young artists hardly ever fulfill their promise.

DJ The ratio is tremendous; it is a real reality that 98 to 99 percent of the young artists you run into, the younger ones, are never doing anything lasting. While you want this to happen, this makes you very skeptical, too.

IN Perhaps this is a definition of the fact that good work can only be produced by very few people; you judge good work by everybody else's. You seem to be suggesting that it is most futile to overpromote the scene, the whole deal, because few good people are going to rise up, anyway; the rest aren't going to be anything.

DJ As long as there's some interest in it, actually, everyone is eager for somebody good. Contrary to the rubbish you get in those magazines, the whole thing is so damn slow.

IN The development of things?

DJ New people don't come along at any great rate. So you get eager for something to happen.

IN You sound slightly – I got this impression right along – you are a little bit detached from the whole thing in America, and perhaps a little weary of it.

DJ I'm tired of the art business.

IN Has this been a long-standing attitude, or one which has developed through specific experiences?

DJ It develops. It turns into – it all gets serious. At first, it's nice –

IN People interview you in their offices.

DJ The money thing is a strange thing. At first, it's really nice to have some money coming in. You don't have to work at some job for it. For a while, it all seems pretty pleasant, but that all slowly gets serious, a lot of people get interested in it, it turns into a real business; it is a real business now. It's kind of depressing.

IN   You mean generally, or with respect to your own work?

DJ   With respect to me, and I see other people in the same boat.

IN   And it confuses the real issues that you are interested in?

DJ   I'm not really confused about it – I make a big distinction between money and art – but it means that you are back in the society and subject to some of the ordinary things that go on in the society. Some of the dealers – Castelli, fortunately, is fine, so in a way I consider him a buffer against all this. Some of the dealers are just real ordinary, you know, businessmen.

IN   Most in Australia are; there's hardly any really dedicated dealers in Australia. Might be dedicated dealers, but not dedicated to art, that's for sure.

DJ   These people are pretty depressing.

IN   What do you think of the post-object thing of trying to buck the dealer system?

DJ   I don't believe those guys. [Joseph] Kosuth is a first-class operator. He's okay, but then, he's making money.

IN   Most of them put out their hands in Australia for not money for artworks, but money for them to live well while they are doing things, to get big fees and so on, so it's the same thing.

DJ   I'm skeptical. Those claims tend to disappear after a couple of years. You get all this hullabaloo at the beginning, but it all seems to disappear in two or three years when somebody gives them a check.

IN   The artwork might be devalued, but the artist certainly isn't by all this. On the contrary.

    Getting back to the work at the gallery – a twenty-five-foot-sided triangle: is it very large for your work?

DJ   Yep. Some of them are longer, maybe; Johnson's is pretty

big for [a work of] mine. I did a twenty-five-foot square
in Holland in metal [image 53], which was later destroyed,
because it was just a temporary exhibition; that's one of
the largest ones. Some are longer. I have one in a building
in New York maybe sixty feet long [see image 48].

IN   Was the one in New York an outdoor piece?

DJ   No, it was plywood boxes; they could not last outdoors.

IN   You wouldn't mind if they were made out of something
else?

DJ   Yes, they could be made out of concrete.

IN   Don, have you got anything in the Tate Gallery?

DJ   Yeah, they have one piece, but that goes on the wall.
Medium size.[18]

IN   I thought you did. I remember seeing it there when I was
there.

DJ   The Tate's very peculiar. Now and then they send a letter
to Leo or [Nicholas] Logsdail about buying a big piece,
but they never do it.[19]

IN   What do you think of the London art scene?

DJ   Well, it is pretty dim.

IN   Seems to be very much taken over by dealers selling conservative work to the rich.

DJ   Yeah, there is not too much going on. This gallery that
I showed in, Lisson, is very small, and he sells next to
nothing.[20]

IN   Oh well.

      Let's hope you can show some work in Australia again. I
think there is a considerable reception for American work
in Australia, really.

DJ   You see, I don't have any sense of it.

IN   I think this is so. I think Australian art has been looking
to America for quite a while now, particularly since the
early '60s, and accelerating really up to the end of the '60s.
The postpainterly abstraction thing to, more recently, the
post-object thing. A great deal of interest.

D J   The main thing is that they should be regarded as an international art, not American art. You can't give the United States any credit for it. No one likes the United States government, no one who makes art. It should disperse.

      Europe is picking up, you know. It seems to be spreading.

I N   Somehow I find it hard to see your work developing in Europe, though.

D J   They buy a lot of stuff. I don't know. The Europeans are very strange; they make very strange art to me, which I don't find interesting.

I N   Introspective and expressionistic and –

D J   Symbolistic, which I find a terrific bore.

I N   It seems so pretentious, once you become a bit of a disbeliever in that kind of thing – that those sorts of values can be effectively conveyed in art.

D J   There's been a criticism of American art correlating with the United States itself and all that stuff. It's pretty basic to everyone's attitude that everybody [in art] worked against that society, the general nature of the United States. That's what I meant about the money. I wanted to get clear of the whole damn thing, and selling your work and, of course, getting the money to make bigger things and all that, which involves selling, sort of pulls you back into it, even if it's in somewhat of a buffered way.

I N   That's right; capitalism has a way of taking things over.

D J   Yes. Kind of depressing. My kids go to school and see all these attitudes; all these things you forgot about thirty years ago turn up again. I would like to be able to ignore it.

This conversation was sourced from an audio recording in the Research Library of the Art Gallery of South Australia, Adelaide.

1   At the time of the interview, Jennifer Licht, John Stringer, and Waldo Rasmussen held curatorial positions at The Museum of Modern Art, New York; John Baily was the director of the Art Gallery of South Australia, Adelaide.

2   *Donald Judd Visiting Artist*, Hopkins Center for the Arts, Dartmouth College, Hanover, New Hampshire, July 16–August 9, 1966.

3   Jennifer Licht, *Some Recent American Art*, exh. cat. (Melbourne: National Gallery of Victoria; New York: The Museum of Modern Art, 1973).

4   See Judd's "Statement" (1968) in *Donald Judd Writings*, 196.

5   "I don't think anyone's work is 'reductive.' The most the term can mean is that new work doesn't have what the old work had. It's not so definitive that a certain kind of form is missing; a description and discussion of the kind present is pretty definitive. New work is just as complex and developed as old work." See Judd's "Statement" (1966) in *Donald Judd Writings*, 179.

6   Judd worked with Bernstein Brothers Sheet Metal Specialties, Inc. from late 1963 until the end of his life. Although they moved to Long Island City by the end of 1964, their shop was originally located in Manhattan, at 191 Third Avenue.

7   In 1973, Judd purchased La Mansana de Chinati, a complex of buildings located in Marfa, Texas. Referred to casually as "the Block," it encompasses a full city block, and includes two large airplane hangars where Judd installed his art, built his library of more than thirteen thousand books, and lived. See Judd's "La Mansana de Chinati" (1989) in *Donald Judd Writings*, 588–91.

8   Judd purchased his first ranch, Casa Morales (formerly the Morales Ranch), in 1976. See Judd's "Ayala de Chinati" (1989) in *Donald Judd Writings*, 592–94.

9   Judd exhibited four works in *New York Painting and Sculpture: 1940–1970*, The Metropolitan Museum of Art, New York, October 18, 1969–February 1, 1970.

10 *Don Judd*, Whitney Museum of American Art, New York, February 27–March 24, 1968, extended through April 14.

11 *Frank Stella*, The Museum of Modern Art, New York, March 24–June 2, 1970; *Claes Oldenburg*, The Museum of Modern Art, September 23–November 23, 1969.

12 North refers here to the exhibition *Some Recent American Art*.

13 Hilton Kramer (1928–2012) was an American art critic and editor. In December 1959, Kramer hired Judd to review exhibitions for *Arts Magazine*; Judd continued to write for the magazine, with only a few interruptions, until March 1965.

14 Ursula Meyer (1915–2003) was a German-born American artist, professor of sculpture, and the author of *Conceptual Art* (New York: E. P. Dutton, 1972).

15 See Judd's review of *Kazimir Malevich* (1973–74) in *Donald Judd Writings*, 254–66.

16   Judd refers here to the first generation of abstract expressionist painters.
17   Kimon Nicolaïdes, *The Natural Way to Draw: A Working Plan for Art Study* (Boston: Houghton Mifflin, 1941). Nicolaïdes was an instructor at the Art Students League. Judd included this book in his library in Marfa, Texas.
18   In 1973, the Tate purchased a round-front progression in copper.
19   Nicholas Logsdail (1945–) is a British art dealer and the owner of Lisson Gallery.
20   *Don Judd*, Lisson Gallery, London, January 22–February 9, 1974.

"'Plain Old Art' Creates New Space in Environment of PCVA"
Article by Beth Fagan for *The Oregonian*
November 10, 1974

This article was written on the occasion of *Judd*, an exhibition at Portland Center for the Visual Arts, Oregon (November 2–December 1, 1974). For this show, Judd created a large site-specific work in plywood that was fabricated by students and dismantled shortly after the exhibition closed.

Donald Judd conceded in an interview while he was completing work in Portland Center for the Visual Arts that some of his work could be called architectural. Not in the sense of constructing a piece, but in the sense of a piece creating its own space.

"It's really plain old art," not architecture, Judd said, "because it's absolutely useless. Architects always have to consider function, which is a perfectly serious matter."

"Here (the PCVA work), I don't have to worry about function."

The only change he has made in PCVA is a linear wall piece of plywood sheets on three of the room's sides [image 54].[1]

It is rare, in either sculpture or architecture, to be alerted to the sense of space, but this appears to be at least one aspect of response to Judd's work.

Encompassing the total space it occupies, and creating a new space, it is impossible, at least for us, to pry it loose from that space for consideration only as an object.

A possible reason is that the piece has the same natural, unpretentious quality, unrelated to iconography, of space itself.

It seems to exist with space comfortably, and in different ways, depending on where one is in relation to it. It has the feeling of always having been there.

There are, of course, many other aspects of Judd's work, exhaustively explored in the many articles on his work.

Judd confirmed that Giuseppe Panza is interested in the PCVA work,[2] possibly for the new Long Beach art museum, designed by I. M. Pei, and scheduled to open in two years.[3]

"He would buy it on paper, so to speak, and remake it later," Judd said, adding that the work "could go anywhere."

He said Panza is acquiring a lot of work for the Long Beach museum, as he has for the Mönchengladbach museum [Museum Abteiberg] in Germany; that he is setting up his own museum in connection with some Swiss banking institution, and also is thinking about buying ten sections or a ten-square-mile area in the desert, where Judd and possibly other artists would do outdoor works.

Judd said Panza also has his own collection with rooms for individual artists in Varese, near Milan.

He said it's an old palace, that the old stables also have large rooms, and that work includes his, Dan Flavin's, Carl Andre's, Bruce Nauman's, and Robert Morris.

"He also has about one-third of the pieces in Oldenburg's *Store*, about a dozen Rothkos, and several pieces by Bob Irwin. A lot of pieces take up whole rooms."

Judd says he disagrees with Panza opening a stable door and showing each room. "It's a one-shot view. If I were doing it, I'd want to have some reason to be there. I want to live with a space. If I had this room (PCVA), I'd want to put in a table or bed and live with it. I like doing permanent installations."

Judd said he still is doing freestanding pieces that deal with immediate space around them, "shading off into general space," but that he's now trying to deal with space in a more complete way.

He said there is a handful of artists who are, and that they all have separatist ideas about each other.

Mentioning specific incidents, he said artists are providing a lot of the steam to architecture, but that the architects get paid and tend to ruin the ideas. "I think visual art is much livelier. All the thinking is going there, not in architecture."

"I'm interested in real architecture too, art and function, and I try to do it for myself. But it's hard to get the two together."

"I have a couple of plans for entire buildings, and a very good plan for one I want to build in the desert for myself."

Judd lives both in New York and the Big Bend area of West Texas, and said the proportion of time he's in each place is slowly changing in favor of Texas.

"I have a building in New York (in the Cast Iron District) and two airplane hangars in Texas – mostly because I can have a lot of pieces of my own."

He said each floor of the New York building has one function, and so do the two parts of one hangar and three of another in Texas.

"Each space has one function, even though it has a lot of different pieces. In some cases works have been done for particular spaces, and some are just freestanding."

Judd said that instead of working with predetermined spaces, he'd like to try, at least once, an entire building. "But I'm very aware of differences between architecture as both art and function and plain art."

Mel Katz, Portland artist and board chairman of the PCVA, says Judd "has created his own aesthetic."

In one of the many articles on the artist, he is described as a "100 percent American artist who did not go to Europe before reaching his artistic maturing," and "a man deeply committed to the understanding of his culture."

First published: Beth Fagan, "'Plain Old Art' Creates New Space in Environment of PCVA," *The Oregonian*, November 10, 1974, B15.

1	A short, unsigned text on the same page that described Judd's work at Portland Center for the Visual Arts in greater physical detail accompanied this article: "Wall Work New," *The Oregonian*, November 10, 1974, B14.
2	Giuseppe Panza di Biumo (1923–2010) was a prominent Italian collector of modern art. See Judd's "Una stanza per Panza" (1990) in *Donald Judd Writings*, 630–99.
3	In the 1970s, I.M. Pei designed a new building for the Long Beach Museum of Art. It was never built.

Interview with Friedrich Teja Bach
May 5, 1975

Donald Judd, Judd's first retrospective exhibition, at the National Gallery of Canada, Ottawa (May 24–July 6, 1975), opened a few weeks after this interview with art historian Friedrich Teja Bach was conducted. In conjunction with the exhibition, the National Gallery of Canada published *Donald Judd: Catalogue Raisonné of Paintings, Objects, and Wood-Blocks 1960–1974.*

Also published at this time was Judd's *Donald Judd: Complete Writings 1959–1975,* which gathered his to-date exhibition and book reviews, articles, and letters to the editor. Found in these collected writings and echoed in this interview is Judd's commitment to empirical epistemology. In his reviews, Judd praised Lee Bontecou's "pragmatic" and "immediate" scale and the "empirical" quality of Claes Oldenburg's man-made, anthropomorphized objects. "I am, if you want to put a label on it," Judd affirms to Bach, "a thorough empiricist."

FTB   [Friedrich Teja Bach] In the last years, a large body of your work has been designed for particular exterior and interior places. What do you think caused you to stress this quality in your work, as opposed to your earlier work?

DJ   [Donald Judd] Well, it is not that recent. The first piece like that, which went from wall to wall, I made in the summer of 1966 at Dartmouth [see image 52].[1] There was another one a couple of years later at the Sonnabend gallery.[2]

FTB   But still, it is a different quality compared with the more self-contained "specific objects" you did earlier.

DJ   Yes; if you take a freestanding piece, it controls a certain amount of space, but that space, at a certain distance from the piece, goes off into whatever the rest of the room is. So if you make a piece for the room, you are defining the whole room, or at least a good portion of it. Those are two different things, and I am actually interested in both of them; I don't think it's a case of better or worse, it's just logical that if you once get interested in doing so much with the space, you try to do something with the whole space that is available.

FTB   Your interest in outdoor works is a more recent phenomenon.

DJ   It's hard to make big pieces, because it costs so much. I have been interested in outdoor pieces since the beginning of 1968, but there wasn't any chance to make one.

FTB   Already some of your earlier work revealed a tension, a play between the inside and outside of the object. This feature of interplay of inside and outside now seems to be developed even further in your outdoor work, in a way creating a reconciliation between object and nature. What would you say is the nature relation of those pieces you did for outdoors?

DJ   The relation to nature? Well, first, it very definitely is just a relation to a certain piece of land.

FTB   Yes, the way I phrased it is too abstract.

DJ   It has to do with a particular piece of land, just as you deal with a particular room. Beyond that, more generally, I am interested in leaving the land, or nature, if you want to use the word, alone. I rather would like to deal with land that hasn't been moved around a great deal. I am generally opposed to all the leveling, asphalting, and redoing of land.[3]

FTB   Your earlier work sometimes has what one might call an alien presence, whereas your outdoor works seem to have a more friendly relation to nature.

DJ   I don't know; I don't think it should necessarily get along with the land that well. It deals with the slope, what's there, just as the Guggenheim piece deals with the Guggenheim [see image 45], but I think it should be a very distinct thing from the circumstances.[4] The concrete pieces look pretty in photographs, but they don't look so in actuality when you see them.

FTB   Most, maybe all, of your work is untitled, and one has to refer to it either by the names of people who commissioned it or by the forms it suggests, like "ladder piece" or "honeycombs." Do you think that specific titles would be inadequate for your work?

DJ   Yes, I think they would be misleading. They don't have anything to do with any things, so they shouldn't be titled. I mean, there is no title that could be given.

FTB   Like some of your concrete outdoor works, your recent plywood pieces break with your previous dealing with color or with richness of the material. Do you remember any of the motivations to make that shift in material?

DJ   I think that plywood is like galvanized iron, which I have always used; it's a plain material, it's an ordinary commercial material. I link it to the galvanized iron, and also, I don't especially distinguish between the pieces that have lots of color and those that don't have very much color. To me, the galvanized iron is colored, the plywood is colored.

FTB   Richard Serra suggested that the feature of going from floor to ceiling in Brancusi's wooden *Endless Columns* for the Brummer Gallery might have had something to do with your "stacks." [*Shows Judd image of* Endless Columns *from* Brancusi, *by Sidney Geist*][5]

DJ   I never knew they went from floor to ceiling. I never looked at [Sidney] Geist's book, it's the first time I saw it; Brancusi did this?[6]

FTB   Yes; he had to cut them in order to get them into this room.

Your work, as a whole, is a kind of definite departure from anthropomorphic forms, but nevertheless it maintains a sense of human scale.

DJ   The scale is not "human scale," it's my scale. I make them. I am interested in big pieces, but I am not interested in pieces so enormous that you cannot see the whole thing. I am against a monumental quality, which I consider old-fashioned. I think if you made a big outdoor piece that went beyond the range you could see, I wouldn't like it.

FTB   How would you describe the beholder-sculpture relationship in the case of the Guggenheim installation, or your galvanized sheet piece, or the honeycombs, or the more recent Portland piece [see images 42, 41, 54]?[7]

DJ   Again, I never think about the viewer; it's all my work and defined in my terms, and the rest of it I don't know anything about. All those distances and possibilities that evolve from it are what I am interested in.

In the Portland piece, you can see across the top; it would be a very different piece if it were two feet higher — it wouldn't even make sense if it were above your eye level.

FTB   Your work is not environmental.

DJ   No, I don't really think of it as environmental.

FTB   Do you feel that the feature of rearrangement or permutation, when your pieces are arranged differently according to a particular place, is more a by-product of what happens, or do you think it's an important aspect of your work?

DJ   It is a little bit of a by-product. I mean, I would prefer to make the pieces and leave them alone; I don't like to have them torn down. That's a waste. Ideally, if I had the space, I would just make them for myself, for a certain room, and leave them alone. Also, you know, the pieces are not so determined.

FTB   You once talked about the problem of order and systems in relation to basically rationalistic philosophy as the basis for European art, in the sense that it is based on preexisting, a priori systems. Now, in a way, the horizontal progressions you did in the '60s reveal a similar kind of a priori system as a quality. Would you agree?

DJ   No, they are just local; they are like finding a material. They are just a local sort of order.

FTB   What do you mean by "local"?

DJ   It is like one, two, three, four. It's one thing when you write about the philosophy of mathematics, but in a daily way, we just count things. That doesn't mean anything in particular.

FTB   What I meant are the specific changes of distances.

DJ   Those things in the progressions were just fancier than this, that's all. I mean, a doubling progression is pretty obvious, and I think the point was that anybody could see that there was a scheme there. I'm not interested in juggling it; I want it to be apparent that there is a scheme, and it's given, just the way the rows of boxes are, one, two, three, four. So those things are not in any way mathematical – or mysterious, either. I wouldn't include mathematics in "a priori"; mathematics is a pretty practical, obvious thing.

FTB   When you started out with your work, people referred to it in what I think was a basic misunderstanding as rigid, depressing, nihilistic. Particularly after living here in New York City for a while, I have the feeling that your work has – I can't find a better word – an optimistic quality, rather than a negative connotation.

DJ   Yes, I don't think it's nihilistic or any of those. I would rather have it called optimistic.

FTB   You made some strong statements against the European tradition of art. Now, I always had the feeling that by "European tradition" you meant post-Renaissance art. In other words, I feel from your work that you might be interested in trecento art, or, let's say, Piero della Francesca, that in your work, particularly when you used colored plexiglass and metal, there is a reconciliation of spirituality and material – that there is almost, in a sense, a remembrance of a sacred quality there.

DJ   To be very general, art is supposed to be about such things as living and dying and time and such long-distance problems. Also, I like Piero a great deal. And I like some European painters after that; I like Poussin and Ingres a great deal. You know, it's just that things come from another time and you don't understand them, you never understand them, and thinking, you realize, to some extent, what the thinking of the society was, and you disagree with them. I like, say, Spinoza a great deal, but I'm not going to believe in all of that.

FTB   Again, there would be the question what "system" means in Spinoza's case and what in your case –

DJ   I am, if you want to put a label on it, a thorough empiricist.

This conversation was sourced from an archival transcript with handwritten corrections by Judd in the Judd Foundation Archives, Marfa, Texas.

1   *Donald Judd Visiting Artist*, Hopkins Center for the Arts, Dartmouth College, Hanover, New Hampshire, July 16–August 9, 1966.

2   *Don Judd: Structures*, Galerie Ileana Sonnabend, Paris, May 6–29, 1969.

3   "Here, everywhere, the destruction of new land is a brutality…. I've never built anything on new land." See Judd's "Ayala de Chinati" (1989) in *Donald Judd Writings*, 593.

4   *Guggenheim International Exhibition 1971*, Solomon R. Guggenheim Museum, New York, February 12–April 11, 1971. The outer circle of the referenced work is level, whereas the inner circle follows the incline of the ramp in the Guggenheim.

5   Sidney Geist, *Brancusi: A Study of the Sculpture* (New York: Grossman, 1968), 72.

6   Although Judd had not encountered Geist's *Brancusi* at the time of this interview, he later included a 1983 edition of this book in his library in Marfa, Texas.

7   For more on what Bach calls "the Portland piece," see "'Plain Old Art' Creates New Space in Environment of PCVA" (1974) in this volume, 458–61.

"Eight Statements"
Article by Jean-Claude Lebensztejn for *Art in America*
July–August 1975

Art historian and critic Jean-Claude Lebensztejn solicited thoughts on Matisse from eight contemporary artists on the occasion of *Henri Matisse: Dessins et sculpture*, at the Musée national d'art moderne, Centre Georges Pompidou, Paris (May 29– September 7, 1975). Though commentary from Carl Andre, Roy Lichtenstein, Brice Marden, Paul Sharits, Frank Stella, Andy Warhol, and Tom Wesselmann was included in the *Art in America* article, only Judd's contribution is reproduced here.

Judd installed two prints by Matisse – an etching, *Reclining Nude, with Crossed Legs* (*Nu allongé, jambes repliées*), and a drypoint, *Seated Nude, Torso Leaning on Knees* (*Nu assis, le torse appuyé sur les genoux*), both from 1929 – on the second floor of his Architecture Studio in Marfa, Texas, where they remain today.

DJ   [Donald Judd] Though it's not that far back, I don't tend
to think of Matisse in terms of what I might think about
my own work. It never occurred to me to use something
out of his thinking or work. On the other hand, as with
all first-rate work, it shows you what can be done. And
I've thought for a long time that Matisse was probably, before Pollock anyway, the best artist in the twentieth century. I'm much more interested in Matisse than in Picasso;
I've never been very interested in him. And the only thing
that worries me about a statement like that is Mondrian.
I'd hate to get into the business of comparing Mondrian
and Matisse. That's a little painful.

They're very different in terms of scale. That's what
bothers me. Naturally my general bias is toward completely
unrepresentational work, so that makes me want to prefer Mondrian. The only thing is that Matisse has the scale,
and I think he has greater variety in what he's doing – in
all ways he just has the edge as an artist.

JCL   [Jean-Claude Lebensztejn] You said that the difference
between Matisse and Mondrian was a difference in scale.

DJ   It's obvious that in Matisse it's greater scale and they're
bigger. Greater internal scale. But size is something
too – perhaps if Mondrian had had more money and
lived a while longer, maybe he might have made larger
paintings. It sounds a little silly for that to matter so much,
but it does matter. And it makes Mondrian seem like a
generation earlier than Matisse. It seems like Mondrian
belongs to Malevich's generation, while Matisse would
be almost a generation after that, though actually, I suppose, Mondrian and Matisse must have been about the
same age.

When you get to the cutouts and some of those big
late Matisses, they have a larger internal scale that's more
like the work that was done here after World War II. I
don't think Picasso ever did it with that kind of internal

scale. He did *Guernica*, and *Guernica*'s a big painting, but it doesn't have the scale of those cutouts of Matisse's.

JCL   What do you think makes Matisse's scale impressive?

DJ   Well, it's not only Matisse – scale is important to almost all the art made since the '40s. As a general statement, I think it has to do with making the main aspects of art more important: color becomes more important, shapes become more important, space becomes more important – everything about it is developed beyond what had been possible before. In an old painting of Matisse's, say in the '20s or something – and they're nice paintings, too – what was buried in all the figurative elements becomes in the cut-outs very separate and large and important.

JCL   What about the relationship between color, surface, and scale?

DJ   I guess you could say that you can't have one without the others. Shape and color, and obviously surface, can't be developed without scale. It's a desire to have all these things strong that produces a larger scale.

Matisse took shapes he'd been using all his life and cut them loose, made them independent things, which makes a lot of sense. Those are shapes that he'd been using since 1910 or something. You can trace the shapes back – he certainly modified them – they become simplified, but they're the same kind of shapes. He really likes a certain kind of shape and he's stressed it until it's become almost the only thing, which makes perfect sense to me. While Picasso stayed with a sort of modification of shapes and colors and all that stuff which has to do with representation.

JCL   You think Matisse was more interested in the abstract use of the shapes than in representation?

DJ   Oh sure.

JCL   Why do you think, then, he retained representation?

DJ   For one thing, in order not to be representational, it's almost unavoidable that you use a geometric scheme; the only way to be so-called abstract so far as I know is to use completely geometric means. I can see, given the kind of shapes Matisse was interested in, that abstraction wasn't really very possible for him. In order to continue to be interested in the kind of shapes he was interested in, they still had to have some kind of representational appearance, because they're strange, irregular shapes.

JCL   What about in early Kandinsky?

DJ   I don't think they're very abstract. Usually they're painted in a kind of descriptive way, and there are a lot of things that appear that are a little bit descriptive.[1] Pollock's abstract, though, he's an exception. He's an abstract painter who isn't geometric.

JCL   Is he the only exception?

DJ   I wouldn't say so. I was very reluctant to get into completely geometric work. I felt it was pretty strange. I came by it in a very difficult way, so it's always been an important thing to me. To me it's very important not to be in any way representational. I have no use for it.

JCL   But at the same time you had some kind of reluctance about geometry?

DJ   I was reluctant to get myself completely into only using straight lines. And rectangular surfaces. There were other shapes I was interested in, I guess. Maybe it was the same problem with Matisse except he didn't give up those shapes. But you know, I felt eventually that I wasn't interested in shapes. I think there's an important philosophical difference. I'm in no way interested in any kind of representation. I think I would share that with Mondrian. I couldn't see any reason to suggest a piece of a leg or anything like that. But the way those late collages of Matisse's work, in terms of color – the importance of color and surface and scale and all that – they're abstract paintings. Loose use – "abstract" is a sloppy word; but compared to everybody else, they're abstract paintings. All the descriptive parts are not immediately descriptive the way most representational art is, but they're just sort of residual description. It's as if he'd done this knee fifty times until it's just Chinese writing, just the image.

JCL Matisse's impact in this country seems to be fairly recent. Stella seems to have started thinking about him only in the late '60s. His earlier concern seems to have been with abstract expressionism.

DJ You'd probably find it true of almost all the people you talk to here. Though I was interested in Matisse before I was ever interested in any American. Still, the real force and kick and example is Pollock and Newman and Rothko and so forth. It's the immediate situation that provides the force, but then of course you go back – after a while, again – you go outside of your own circumstances and start looking at earlier work or work from other kinds of societies.

JCL Rothko once said that he had learned the most about structure from Matisse, because Matisse was the first painter who produced surface paintings.

DJ I didn't know that. That sounds very accurate and interesting. Surface is very important, obviously, and it's all pretty much on the surface, it's in a very shallow space.

JCL On the other hand, Carl Andre the other day wrote in his interview that what he found interesting in Matisse was an interlocking of spaces on the surface, which he called impressionism of space.

DJ I remember sending him a Matisse cutout, one with a garden or something, with columns – I can't quite remember. It's very big.

JCL Oh, very big – *Decoration with Masks*?

DJ It has a generally flat surface, but then certain things – the head or the mask, whatever, occur, and there's a sudden recession. The perspective which is not normally used at all is suddenly used, and you get a hole dropping back there,

for a few feet or something, so you get this strange contradiction on a flat surface. Shapes are side by side, then you
have that sudden hole. It's pretty distant from the changes
that occur in easel painting.

First published: Jean-Claude Lebensztejn, "Eight Statements," *Art in America*, July–
August 1975, 71–72.

1   See Judd's review of *Vasily Kandinsky, 1866–1944: A Retrospective Exhibition*
        (1963) in *Donald Judd Writings*, 92–97.

Interview with Michael Blackwood
For the film *Masters of Modern Sculpture Part III*
September 1975

Produced and directed by filmmaker Michael Blackwood and narrated by artist Mary Miss, the 1978 documentary *Masters of Modern Sculpture Part III: The New
World* includes interviews with Carl Andre, Louise Bourgeois, John Chamberlain,
Christo, Mark di Suvero, Herbert Ferber, David Hare, Michael Heizer, Judd, Edward Kienholz, Ibram Lassaw, Robert Morris, Louise Nevelson, Barnett Newman,
Isamu Noguchi, Claes Oldenburg, George Rickey, Theodore Roszak, George Segal, Richard Serra, David Smith, Tony Smith, and Robert Smithson.

While just a short excerpt of this interview appears in *Masters of Modern Sculpture Part III*, a longer portion of it is included in Blackwood's 2010 film *The Artist's Studio: Donald Judd*, which opens in the summer of 1972, with an interview of
Judd by the art historian Barbara Rose at 101 Spring Street (see "Interview with
Barbara Rose" [1972] in this volume, 394–420). The film then turns to footage
shot in September 1975 of Judd and his family in Marfa, Texas, and on the second
floor of 101 Spring Street, of which this interview is comprised.

MB   [Michael Blackwood] Why did you come to Marfa?

DJ   [Donald Judd] It's empty, and the desert's nearby, and it's
      near Mexico. Arizona is very crowded, and Nevada, Utah
      are too far north, really. I like less people and more space,
      I guess. I don't like dense country. It's easier to think out
      here because it's not so busy. It's too busy in New York,
      and a number of things that are kind of disagreeable. So
      really there's more time to think. Nothing gets made out
      here, but maybe it will when we get organized. I like the
      Southwest a great deal, and most of the Southwest is rather
      crowded, and this isn't; and I wanted to be near Mexico,
      since I like Mexico. I don't want to actually be in Mexico,
      because they don't want longhaired folks in sometimes.[1]
      So it makes me a little leery of putting a lot of pieces
      down there, plus the fact that I can barely deal with this
      government – not with two of them.

MB   It will be a permanent place?

DJ   Yeah, it's permanent. And I need a lot of pieces for myself
      to look at in order to be able to think and feel that there
      is something relatively permanent versus all these tempo-
      rary exhibitions.

MB   As an observer and critic of art in New York in the early
      '60s, what did you admire and respect at the time?[2]

DJ   The work that was actually going on – I'm bound to
      make a list, and I'm going to forget somebody. But I was
      impressed with Oldenburg's *Store*, which was what – '59,
      maybe?[3] Frank Stella's paintings, and [John] Chamber-
      lain's work; go a little further back, [Kenneth] Noland's
      paintings – they're a little bit prior to this, not much. And
      I've been impressed for years with Jackson Pollock's work.
      Newman's work I got to know a little later. I first saw a lot
      of his paintings at a show at French & Company maybe
      in '60, '61; I'm not sure.[4] I liked them; again, I was still kind
      of wary about the geometry. I met him in '64. I liked him
      a great deal; he was a good friend. He was a great painter

and a smart man. I was very upset by his dying. He was the only one I knew of all those artists, the older artists. Pollock, of course, was dead, and he was really the only – I guess I met de Kooning – he was the only one sort of around New York, too.

MB   What art could you say that preceded you was really meaningful in your development? I mean, since you say some of it was too long ago – did you like anyone? What do you think was influential in your thinking?

DJ   Pollock's the most important case. I was impressed with Pollock's work really early on for me, because I was pretty slow in all this, and it took me a long time to get myself organized. But I knew it was very good. It's hard to just take anything out of Pollock's work, which is one good thing about it, I guess. I mean, what can you do with a drip scheme that looks like Pollock's? But there are general things, like the scale, and the frontality, and all that, which you can get out of it – which everybody did get out of it – and it has remained one of the main factors. It's the level of development, and what can be done, and all that, which is a big example; not so much what it's like or anything, but simply what can be done as a painting or work of art. So I was pretty seriously kicked along by Pollock's example.

MB   What about sculpture at the time?

DJ   Well, there wasn't any sculpture at the time but David Smith. I mean, di Suvero is not a bad artist, but he's not a great artist. The first group of things looked pretty good, but still, it seemed rather too late to make something like that. He's probably the best younger artist who's really doing sculpture – though I guess you can call Chamberlain's work, maybe, really sculpture.

      As I said, I was very wary of geometric schemes, so it wasn't easy to come to using all that.

MB   Why?

D J   I liked organic shapes, I guess; I don't know. [*Laughs*] It's the same old objections most people have – it's too schematic, or too rigid. But, again, I got to dislike the organic sort of line or shape, because it always referred to something else. The geometric shapes don't refer to anything else.

At that time, any geometric art, certainly three-dimensional art, was nonexistent. There was very little geometric art, and there was a terrific bias against it, so that both Reinhardt and Newman, who were the only two – well, there was [Ellsworth] Kelly, too, but he wasn't so well known, and there was Leon Smith – but there was a tremendous bias against it, and it was considered rigid or something, and it was also considered old-fashioned. It was certainly considered nonexpressionistic, which everything was. When I began doing three-dimensional pieces, and until I met Flavin, there was nothing in New York that was geometric. Then his early boxes with lights on the wall were more or less geometric, and then there really wasn't anything for a long time.[5]

I always liked Mondrian's paintings a great deal, and I associated geometry with the quality of those paintings, which is quite idealistic, and purist, I guess, and all that. It didn't occur to me for years that geometry could occur with other qualities, in another way and out of that context, so I had it pretty seriously tied up with Mondrian. But once you use colors that are not primary colors like that, and once you get out of the compositional grid scheme and so forth – once it's frontal, once it has a bigger scale, you know, a lot of things, it becomes a very different thing. I like color, and the materials tend to be gray, which is fine, but it's only gray, so that you have to anodize them, which is the most natural thing to do, in a way, because it does look like material, or paint them, which looks pretty artificial. And copper and brass and some of those have quite a bit of color, but if you want red, what can you do? Anodize it or paint it. I don't plan on being stuck with tan and gray. [*Laughs*]

MB   Is the intent to give the things a sort of weightlessness also?

DJ   No. I've always been wary of them being – seeming heavy, so that's another general idea. Painting them or anodizing them doesn't really have anything to do with that, though, I don't think. Obviously, when they're parts, it separates parts to do that, but that doesn't – that's really only important, maybe, in the progressions or the stacks, and for somewhat older pieces.

MB   The next question is, to what extent are you involved in the process of making your own works?

DJ   Not really. They're all made by the factory,[6] or Peter Ballantine, who's a carpenter.[7] I don't learn anything in the making of them, so there's no point in it, and they do a much better job than I can do. I'm interested in thinking them out, and after you've sort of thought them all out and so forth, the next big step is to talk them over with Ed Bernstein at the factory or with Peter and find out if they can actually be made or not. If that's part of the making, I'm certainly involved in that, because they often tell you it doesn't come in that size, or it costs too much, or the material will bend, or whatever. But once it's possible to do it, it's just straightforward construction.

This conversation was sourced from an audio recording and a transcript. The original recording is in the Michael Blackwood Collection, Harvard Film Archive, Cambridge, Massachusetts. A copy of the recording and the transcript are in the Judd Foundation Archives, Marfa, Texas.

First published (excerpt): *Masters of Modern Sculpture Part III: The New World*, directed by Michael Blackwood (New York: Michael Blackwood Productions Inc., 1978), 16 mm, 58 min.; reprinted (excerpt): *What Is Minimalism? The American Perspective 1958–1968*, directed by Michael Blackwood (New York: Michael Blackwood Productions Inc., 2004), DVD, 58 min.; reprinted (in full): *The Artist's Studio: Donald Judd*, directed by Michael Blackwood (New York: Michael Blackwood Productions Inc., 2010), DVD, 29 min.

1   In a letter dated June 13, 1971, sent to then President of Mexico Luis Echeverría, Judd expressed his opposition to border policies that prevented him from traveling to Tijuana, Mexico, writing, "I, my wife, my children, and another couple were not allowed through the border at Tijuana because I and the other man have long hair…. The right to travel internationally is very important."

2   Judd worked as a for-hire art critic, often reviewing over fifteen shows a month, from 1959 to 1965.

3   Oldenburg first presented his *Store* in 1961.

4   *Barnett Newman: A Selection 1946–1952*, French & Company, New York, March 11–April 5, 1959.

5   Flavin completed a series of eight works known as *icons* between 1961 and 1964. Judd eventually permanently installed two of the eight, *icon III (blood) (the blood of a martyr)* (1962) and *icon VI (Ireland dying) (to Louis Sullivan)* (1962–63), at 101 Spring Street.

6   Judd refers here to Bernstein Brothers Sheet Metal Specialties, Inc., whom he worked with from late 1963 until the end of his life. Although they moved to Long Island City by the end of 1964, their shop was originally located in Manhattan, at 191 Third Avenue.

7   From 1971 to the end of Judd's life, Peter Ballantine was the primary fabricator of Judd's works in plywood.

"Artists at Home: Donald Judd"
Article by J. Nebraska Gifford and M. B. Shestack for *Cue*
April 10, 1976

Cue: The Weekly Magazine of New York Night Life was a theater and arts magazine
that ran from 1932 to 1980. This article for the periodical – published on the closing day of *Donald Judd*, Leo Castelli Gallery, New York (March 20–April 10, 1976) –
was conducted at 101 Spring Street. By this time, Judd was living in both New
York and Texas.

Donald Judd, whose show of sculpture is currently at the Castelli Gallery (420 West Broadway), greeted us at the door of his five-storied, cast-iron building in SoHo where he works and lives.

A tall, bearded man in his late forties, and tending toward the chunky side, he wears his long hair wrapped in a small bun at the nape of his neck, Navajo style. Judd is considered one of the half dozen most influential sculptors of the past decade. There's hardly a major collection of contemporary art in the Western world that doesn't boast a Judd piece. Judd's works, sometimes difficult to comprehend because of their deceptive simplicity, are often visualizations of philosophical thought, and are fabricated from industrial materials. They have been described by critics as looking like standing boxes or sections of walls.

"I bought this building in November 1968, when SoHo was just an industrial neighborhood," he said. "I knew it was the wrong building when I bought it. Too many windows, not enough wall space, and crooked floors." Judd smiled wistfully. "SoHo wasn't a tourist trap then. Now it's a horror, especially on weekends." His geniality faltered for a split second. "And the fights I've had with the city about this building! It's made me about half through with New York City." He smiled again. "I don't even live here full time now. In fact, I'm a legal resident of Texas."

Judd has always liked the Southwest and the desert, in particular. Originally he bought some land in Baja California.[1] "But I had a fight in Tijuana about my long hair, and I figured I couldn't deal with two governments. It's difficult enough to deal with the one I have."

It isn't too surprising that Judd divides his time between New York and Middle America. He was born in his grandparents' farmhouse in Excelsior Springs, Missouri. His father worked for Western Union, and promotions within the company generally meant transfers. By the time he graduated from high school in Westwood, New Jersey, Donald Judd had moved more than six times, growing up in Omaha, Kansas City, Des Moines, Dallas, and Philadelphia.

"I do know that as we moved east," he said, "the landscape became too organized and suburbia too continuous." It was "too much moving," and Judd says he made too few friends. As a result, the moving increased his "natural shyness." He received a BS in philosophy at Columbia University (taking art courses at the Art Students League at the same time, and eventually earning an MA in art history from Columbia).[2] He lived in a cold-water flat on East Twenty-Seventh Street,[3] paying bills and rent from meager earnings as a worker in a settlement house.[4] Although the New York art scene was flourishing at the time – with Jackson Pollock, Franz Kline, and Willem de Kooning holding court at the Cedar Street Tavern – Judd kept to himself, painting flat abstractions.

"Actually, I tend to be rather down on painting now," Judd said. "I thought some years ago that painting was going to play itself out, and I've been proved right." Judd, who claims little interest in "the other arts," says that the visual arts are farther ahead in thinking than, say, literature and drama. His wife, Julie Finch, is a dancer who recently performed at Trisha Brown's studio.[5] Nonetheless, Judd believes that "ballet is like going to the Metropolitan Museum; ballet was past its time in the nineteenth century."

The sculptor admires the work of Dan Flavin (his son is named Flavin Starbuck), Larry Bell, John Chamberlain, Claes Oldenburg, and Frank Stella – "and others." Among the younger artists he mentions Fred Sandback, David Rabinowitch, and Richard Serra, "though Serra can't be considered a kid anymore, I guess." However, 90 percent of the art he sees is "junk," according to Judd.

"I'm a Guggenheim judge, and we looked through five hundred sets of slides trying to pick eighteen recipients, and it was damn hard to find anything of quality," he complained. "There are not enough good galleries. Young artists don't have a choice. The art galleries aren't serious. They're following Ivan Karp down the drain.[6] There are plenty of ways to make money by not selling art." He laments the fact that only a tiny fraction of the American population is interested in art – or has even a rudimentary knowledge of the contemporary art world. "I had dinner at the White House not long ago," Judd recalls. "It was in honor of Harold Wilson and there were all kinds of famous guests, like Cary Grant. I sat next to the wife of the president of an oil company – and she was a very nice woman – but all she wanted to know when she heard I was a sculptor was the names of the famous people I'd made busts of."

Like many artists, Judd collects the work of people he admires. He took us on a tour of his building on his way to the upper floors to see the "collection." We passed an empty floor, going up on the open-air elevator. "That's where the kitchen's going to be. We've planned for it for years, but haven't gotten around to finishing it yet." We stopped on the floor which now serves as a kitchen. It certainly didn't look like a "Donald Judd"– happily messy, with a handsome blonde woman (Mrs. Judd) looking through the refrigerator, nodding a welcome and saying, "Now I know why the refrigerator is crowded. It's full of spoiled food." The two Judd (blonde) children sat at the end of a wooden table, drawing. We stared at a bleached steer's skull on the wall. "A reminder of Texas," Judd said, taking us upstairs to a room with books, piles of clothing. From a bookcase he took a small picture – it was a small Dürer print he owns. We admired the two spectacular Barnett Newman prints.

An Oldenburg papier-mâché hot-dog piece was sprawled on the floor, throw-rug style, under a huge John Chamberlain on the wall. The bedroom (a short-rise bed in the middle of the empty floor) is lighted by a room-length Dan Flavin fluorescent sculpture. Two pairs of well-worn cowboy boots lay in the near corner. "They're Stewarts, made in Tucson," Judd said, showing us work by Ad Reinhardt (chipping) and John Wesley. The table in the bedroom – gold and black – is an original by artist Roy Lichtenstein.

"We're in New York," Judd said, picking up the thread of an earlier conversation, "because Julie wants to stay here. You know. Her work and interest in the building. I sometimes think I'd like to give up all the commercial end and just make pieces for myself in Texas. I can work there as well as here. New York is no longer the art capital. It's dispersed. Europe is more important than ten years ago. It's more hostile in SoHo than where we live in Texas."

Judd amplified on his comment. "The people in the Southwest," he explained, "are indifferent, but not hostile. There's a certain amount of antagonism toward you in New York if you have a reputation."

Judd says his life in Texas complements his life in New York. "We know lots of people, but we don't have the flow of people that we have in New York. And, in Texas, we gear our conversations away from serious subjects. The town has a terrific Anglo/Mexican split. Being strangers, we can breach that split. In a way, we're valuable. We're 'Anglos' but not part of the social system." Judd owns a block in the town – the name of which he is loath to reveal.[7] "I don't want people to know where it is. I don't want to live in a tourist attraction." He has two studios and is negotiating to buy a section of land – 640 acres – almost a fly speck in the area. "Nobody there wants to sell such a tiny piece of acreage, but I am trying to convince somebody."

Despite his panegyric for the Southwest, Judd admits that "you get used to being in a big world and knowing the range of people that you know in New York. I know everybody from some very ordinary and nice people, to very rich people, to fellow artists."

One of the very "New York things" the Judd family is involved in concerns bagpipes. He belongs to the Pibroch Society.[8] For the uninitiated, the pibroch is a classical variation of the highland bagpipe. "I'm into bagpipes," he says. "I'm beginning to learn the bagpipes." We learned that pibroch piping has nothing to do with the marches usually attributed to bagpipes. "We play classical music. There are over two hundred pieces of classical music for the bagpipe. I heard it ten years ago. It's formal, repetitious music. Not like European music at all."

For entertainment, the Judds visit with friends. "I'm fed up with movies," he comments, flatly. "But we go out to eat a lot, mostly at the same restaurants – the Nippon and the Villa Pensa.[9] And I read quite a bit." He scratched his head as we stepped on the elevator, looking up through the top grate at the view of the shaft. "I hate New York City," he said again. "It's lousy with people who give you citations for building violations." He relaxed. "The building was designed in 1870 by some architect named [Nicholas] Whyte. It's in the book on cast-iron buildings. I'm leaving next week."

"For Texas?"

"No, I have to go to Switzerland first. I'm having three shows. One at the Kunstmuseum in Basel, and the Kunsthalle in Berne, and at a gallery in Zürich."[10] Donald Judd rubbed his hands against his very un-Texas maroon velour pants. "It's the wrong building," he repeated. "No wall space."

First published: J. Nebraska Gifford and M. B. Shestack, "Artists at Home: Donald Judd," *Cue*, April 10, 1976, 16–17.

1   The authors refer here to Rancho El Porvenir, a valley near El Rosario in Baja California, on which nothing was ever built. See Judd's "Arroyo Grande" (1989) in *Donald Judd: Architektur*, 22–25.

2   Judd attended the Art Students League, in New York, during the day from 1948 to 1953, while also working toward an undergraduate degree at night at Columbia University. He received his BS in philosophy from Columbia, cum laude, in 1953. He began graduate work in art history at Columbia in fall 1957 and completed his coursework in fall 1961; no degree was conferred because he did not complete the requirements.

3   Judd refers here to 302 and 304 East Twenty-Seventh Street.

4   In the fall of 1954, Judd began working at Christodora House, a settlement house in New York's East Village that provided schooling and recreational opportunities to immigrant children.

5   Julie Margaret Hughan Finch (1941–) is a dancer and social activist. She and Judd married on March 14, 1964; they divorced in 1978.

6   Ivan Karp (1926–2012) was an art dealer, author, and gallerist. He was the associate director at Leo Castelli Gallery, New York, from 1959 to 1969.

7   In 1973, Judd purchased La Mansana de Chinati, a complex of buildings located in Marfa, Texas. Referred to casually as "the Block," it encompasses a full city block, and includes two large airplane hangars where Judd installed his art, built his library of more than thirteen thousand books, and lived. See Judd's "La Mansana de Chinati" (1989) in *Donald Judd Writings*, 588–91.

8   The organization is in fact named the Piobaireachd Society.

9   Restaurant Nippon, which still operates today, was the first Japanese restaurant in New York to serve raw sushi (in 1963). Villa Pensa, which closed around 2000, was one of the oldest restaurants in Little Italy, having opened in 1898.

10   *Donald Judd: Zeichnungen / Drawings 1956–1976*, Kunstmuseum Basel, April 14–June 23, 1976; *Donald Judd: Skulpturen*, Kunsthalle Bern, April 14–May 30, 1976; *Donald Judd*, Annemarie Verna Galerie, Zürich, April 8–May 13, 1976.

Interview with Phyllis Tuchman
June 4, 1976

At the time of this interview with art critic Phyllis Tuchman, which was conducted at 101 Spring Street, the Kunstmuseum Basel was hosting Judd's first retrospective of drawings, *Donald Judd: Zeichnungen/Drawings 1956–1976* (April 14–June 23, 1976). In an addendum to curator Dieter Koepplin's introductory essay for the accompanying catalogue, Judd wrote: "The popular dichotomy of thought and feeling provides no information and causes a lot of trouble. There isn't such a division. Feelings are intelligent because they have developed through thought and thought is felt because it has been simplified and remembered and believed through feeling."

Tuchman, then a doctoral candidate at the Institute of Fine Arts, New York University, conducted this interview as part of her dissertation research.

PT   [Phyllis Tuchman] As a child growing up in the heartland,
      were you familiar with paintings by [John Steuart] Curry
      and [Thomas Hart] Benton?

DJ   [Donald Judd] Sure. The first thing I ever saw was a port-
      folio of reproductions, probably put out by the *Omaha
      World-Herald*. It had classic European things as well as re-
      productions of Curry, Benton, and [Grant] Wood. I don't
      know if I saw actual paintings or not; there wasn't much
      art in Omaha or Kansas City. I didn't go to the museum
      until I was a teenager. I remember some Rembrandts and
      some old stuff.

PT   Did you learn anything from regional art?

DJ   Curry, Benton, and Wood were pretty bad artists. Even
      the reproductions did not hold up. I remember distinctly
      not liking the distortions in Benton. I saw Curry in the
      Capitol in Wichita, Kansas,[1] when I got out of the army
      [see image 19].[2] I was still pretty young, nineteen or so.

PT   In the army, how did you get assigned to an engineer's
      unit?

DJ   It was pure luck. I was in the infantry and was shipped to
      Korea – this was before the [Korean] War; it was a year or
      so after World War II. We occupied Korea after we seized
      it from the Japanese. At what's called a replacement de-
      pot, they called out six names, put us in a truck, and took
      us away.

      This engineering company was almost independent of
      anything. I was very lucky; I had been badly mistreated
      by the army for six months, so I was surprised by all this.
      They asked me what I wanted to do. Of course, drafting
      seemed the most interesting. But after a couple of weeks,
      it turned out that they didn't need another person. Sur-
      veying seemed the second most interesting, so I was a sur-
      veyor for a while. Then, that changed. But it was nice for
      a few months. After that, it wasn't bad either. We worked
      with Korean construction companies who did most of

the building. I learned what I could so that I could act smart when the officers turned up; they knew even less than I did about it all. I'd try to explain what was getting done. For a long time, I was in charge of installing all of the pipes and boilers and everything else in a big boiler plant. I inherited the job from someone else. It was already well underway; the Koreans were really doing it, and I was supposed to be in charge. I could talk to the officers as if I really knew what all the pipes did.

It wasn't bad. I was very lucky they put me into that unit: it was all very casual, there were no definite hours, you never really saw the officers. It was better than being left in the infantry – they just had those guys marching all the time. That's all they did, around and around.

PT   Did you ever talk to Bob Morris about his experiences in an engineering unit in Korea?

DJ   I don't know Morris very well. I don't like him, and I don't like his work. I've only talked to him a little bit – and that was years ago.

PT   Did you draw? You mentioned drafting.

DJ   A little. I would have had to have learned it the same way I had to learn how to survey. I was just doing what I was told to do.

PT   How did your sister get a job working at *Arts*?[3] Was your family interested in contemporary art?

DJ   No, not at all. She wanted to do something that had to do with art – she was interested in architecture – and went on her own looking for a job. I didn't know anyone there. She didn't want some idiot secretarial job; certainly, it was a secretarial job, but at least one in a more interesting context.

PT   You mentioned remembering a cover by Franz Kline;[4] by working there, did she make you more familiar with the avant-garde?

DJ   No; at that time, I already knew all I was going to know. I don't think she worked there when that cover and those other covers were made – that's when Belle Krasne was editor.[5] My sister worked there part time when Hilton Kramer was editor[6] and with the woman who was there between Belle Krasne and Hilton Kramer.[7]

PT   How did you chose the artists with whom you studied at the Art Students League?

DJ   There was no choice. I was very ignorant about the whole thing. I was serious about realistic art … You forget those little things. So I didn't go to [Vaclav] Vytlacil or any other guy. It might have done me a lot of good – but I got dissatisfied with it all on my own. Maybe it sticks better. Anyway, I was very slow.

PT   During the 1950s, who did you know, with whom did you discuss art?

DJ   Not many people. I was really by myself. I didn't make any effort to go down to the Cedar bar or any of those places. Once in a while, someone would haul me along. Once, I was in a group show at the Camino Gallery, and Leon Smith and somebody else came to look at my work to approve one little painting.[8]

PT   But you had two solo painting shows at the Panoras Gallery.[9]

DJ   That was a junky gallery. This guy had nothing in mind; he sold paint and rented this space – it was on Fifty-Sixth Street. It was a dumb situation. Mainly I bought supplies there.

PT   Your shows at the Panoras Gallery were reviewed, and it seemed to me that they were very positive.[10]

DJ   Yes, but it didn't mean too much to me. I wasn't satisfied with the paintings, and I felt I had too far to go. It's nice to read good reviews, but it sort of didn't register. I'm skeptical of reviewers, anyway. It often doesn't come home too much.

PT   Did you enjoy painting?

DJ   I liked it; I did it for a long time. I couldn't get it all to come together.

PT   Did you know what it was that you weren't getting together?

DJ   They were old-fashioned. They're derived from cubism, but not in a very aware sort of fashion; some of them are rather ignorant. But you just can't make a big jump. I always liked Pollock's work; I realized when I saw it that it was something important and unusual. But I couldn't make the jump from the paintings I was doing to the scale, and the frontality, and the importance of the material, and the color, and all those things. You worry about losing the little you have, which is very shaky at that point. I was very backward about it all. It took me a long time to figure it all out.

PT   What were you trying to accomplish during the mid-'50s with a limited and gray palette?

DJ   There are certain qualities in those paintings which are things I still have and am interested in. It's not easy to make those qualities stronger. There are certain colors in those paintings that I still like and use; other qualities are not so great. If you fool around with a landscape scheme that's old-fashioned, gray is the color. You can't make very bright colors if there is any kind of realism in it, and they were kind of half abstract. Also, I was making rather large, empty areas against smaller, brighter ones. They're reproduced in the Ottawa catalogue.[11] After a certain point, I was certainly interested in abstraction, but it was still based on landscape. I was very slow in taking it further.

PT   Did you find Frank Stella's stripe paintings liberating?

DJ   I was well underway at that point. They were interesting. I was wary of geometry because mostly I associated it with Mondrian. Frank's paintings have no purist — if you want to use that word — quality whatsoever in their symmetry. That was pretty interesting. When were they shown?

PT   December 1959 at The Museum of Modern Art.[12]

DJ   Maybe I wasn't so far along. I was wary about geometry; Frank's paintings were certainly well ahead of anything I could do.

PT   Do you think that their being monochromatic made it easier for you to make objects that were just one color?

DJ   That's an idea. But it's not only Frank: there was Yves Klein – it's a strong characteristic of several people, Newman, Rothko, even [Kenneth] Noland, to some extent, the limitation of color. So it's not really Frank. I'd seen and liked paintings by Klein early on. And the reduction of the number of colors – it's not a reduction of color – the reduction of the number is something that happened slowly with me, without much regard for anything else. It was an effort to get brighter and stronger color, to make more of the color. If you like cadmium red light, you make more of it. Cadmium red light is a color I always liked, but there are a lot of those colors I developed. When the color becomes very important, you have to have less colors that are shades and grays.

PT   Do you feel there's one quality that asserts your work more as objects and less as sculpture?

DJ   Yeah – color.

PT   They're objects, not sculpture?

DJ   I never thought of them as sculpture. And, as I keep saying, it did not come out of sculpture.

PT   Do you still feel this way?

DJ   Yeah. You know, I had almost nothing to do with David Smith; I always liked his work, but it just had nothing to do with me. He's not Jackson Pollock by a long shot, which I guess is one reason I wasn't influenced by him. A long time ago, I learned something from his work, or took a little bit: the lateral, sideways movement in things like *Hudson River Landscape*. I tried to use it in some of the paintings. It's very flattening, much more in the edges.

PT   Do you remember how you decided to mix wood and metal and wood and plastic?

DJ   The pieces were obviously primarily wood. It's just a case of two different surfaces, two different colors. They were wood because I never thought otherwise, I suppose, considering the money available. The plastic and the metal were much more expensive, so it wasn't very likely that it would mostly be plastic and the smaller area wood; it was the other way around. I spent a lot of time looking around. I'd see a nice piece of aluminum tubing or a strip of plastic on Canal Street and I'd buy it.

PT   Did you trim them?

DJ   No, plastic was impossible to cut – but that purple stripe on the diagonal one I had cut to order. The aluminum tubes I generally left alone and made the piece fit the tubes.

PT   Were you doing something similar to what Frank Stella and Carl Andre were doing at the time?

DJ   That's very different from me. I wasn't repeating. The very early progressions, like the one owned by Jenny Licht [see image 30],[13] that tube was a given; I bought it on Canal Street at a certain length. The piece developed from that. It's not about repeating – it actually started with seeing three of my wood plaques on the wall at the Green Gallery [image 55].[14] The repeated shapes were nice. They were shapes I'd already made. The rows of boxes and all that really come out of units I made myself to suit my own purposes.

PT   Do you feel they're boxes?

DJ   That's slang.

PT   How did you get to show at the Green Gallery [see images 2, 3]?

DJ   I lived in a loft on Nineteenth Street and Fourth Avenue; [Yayoi] Kusama, who lived below me there, helped me find the place.[15] [Richard] Bellamy came to see her work, and she brought him upstairs.[16] Not that he did anything about it right away. I never went to any galleries to try to have a show. By the time my work got to where I liked it, the show came along naturally. I didn't take the gallery business very seriously; the idea of making money from art was so remote.

I liked Kusama's paintings a great deal. She was a much better artist than I was at that time – I was impressed by all that. I have a big white painting by her downstairs.[17] Her objects went downhill. The first ones aren't bad. I bought the white painting out of the show she had at the Brata Gallery;[18] about a year ago, I found out that Frank Stella bought one out of the same show. I didn't know Frank then.

PT What was the Green Gallery like?

DJ The Green was not cohesive. Flavin, [Robert] Morris, some others, and I were certainly juniors to the pop artists – that was a pain in the neck. That was always the case. Every show, Bellamy would have a big [George] Segal in the corner which took up a quarter of the gallery. Not every show, but quite a few of the group shows. Contrary to what everybody seems to think, I don't think Bellamy really knew what it was all about. I'm mad at him for other reasons now: he kept the red box with the divisions cut into it in his backroom office [see image 5], and people sat on it all the time.

PT How important is it for an artist to invent something?

DJ It's very important, but it isn't so much to be first. It's that you've found something that does what you want. In order to do something clearly and strongly, you pretty much have to invent it. Otherwise, you're not going to know what it means. I'm the only person who knows what all those things I'm interested in really mean. Nobody else is going to do anything but ruin it.

PT What do you think is the most perceptive thing that's been written about your art?

DJ Not much, really. There's very little. I need to go back and read [William C.] Agee's piece.[19] There was a piece — it's not exactly about my work — it's about fending off some of the clichés and all that by a guy in Canada in regard to the Ottawa show.[20] It's a fairly good piece, but it's more about getting rid of some of the stupid ideas. It was in *Arts Canada* last winter. Most of the writing is very standard.

PT Do you have problems with the criticism of minimalism?

DJ Well, I hate the term "minimalism." There was in no way a group at all. It's a real concoction; it's a publicity thing, and it wasn't very good to do to pop art, either. It's just some sort of publicity thing which comes from art history, where they think everything comes from styles and groups and so forth, which is kind of doubtful anyway, if you go back and look at it. As I told you before, I didn't know all these people, and all these people developed at different times. Flavin is the only one I had anything to do with, and it's not as though we influenced each other. We were friends; we respected each other's work. And we were both doing what we were doing when we met each other.

PT Do you have any feelings about being seen as an archetype as well as a fall guy?

DJ What do you mean by "fall guy"?

PT Well, that if somebody wants to praise minimal art, they use your art as an example, and if they want to damn it, they use you as an example.

DJ They can damn it if they like. Actually, I prefer if they damn my work rather than use the word "minimal." I hate it when — and this is one of my original grievances against Morris, and also everyone else who does it — they keep talking about "minimal" art. It's just this big, vague thing. At least they can identify the people and deal with what's actually been done. But I do not think there is a group. It would be much better to clear it away and talk about the particular people and particular pieces.

I get tired of all the articles; nobody writes an article unless they love the artist, and that gets to be a bore. Somebody ought to write an article when they think the artist sucks, is not so bad, not so good, in between, when they hate him.

PT   When your wall pieces are installed, should they be a certain height?

DJ   There really is a standard height, but people don't seem to know this. I would think it would be common knowledge; somehow, they don't pay attention. There is a little bit of leeway, but it's only sixty-one inches to sixty-three inches.

PT   And is that because of your height?

DJ   Yes. But I think it could be a little bit lower for somebody else – maybe. The idea is to see a little bit of the top, because if it is dead-on, you can't see either the top or the bottom, and it flattens out. You've got to see something. I have it a little bit below my eye level.

PT   It's always so magical when you discover the sides.

DJ   You can't see the whole thing at once. That's one of the factors of three-dimensional things.

PT   Do you ever consider some of the wall environments, such as the one that is galvanized which you showed at [Leo] Castelli [Gallery] in '71 [see image 42], as murals?[21]

DJ   No, I don't think they are like murals. It's occurred to me that the galvanized wall piece which goes around is sort of like a dado, or something in architecture – perhaps a room.[22] The similarity just occurred to me; it didn't come from the idea of murals.

PT   Is it important to know about art of the past?

DJ   Anybody who knows about art knows something about the past. I spent a lot of time thinking about people like Matisse, Léger, and so forth. And I spent even more time thinking about Piero della Francesca and Poussin and all of them. I was perfectly knowledgeable about all of that stuff, as well as old architecture. I studied with [Rudolf]

Wittkower at Columbia;[23] for my master's paper, I considered writing about Puget or Ingres.[24]

PT Would you have liked to have made outdoor works early on?

DJ No, I really got interested in that in '67. I figured that was always one of the implications. A lot of the freestanding pieces weren't meant to be inside or outside; they were just freestanding pieces going either way. I like having pieces outdoors.

PT Do you think you're doing today what you would have liked to have done twenty years ago, if you knew what you know now?

DJ I think it's all pretty coherent, and it all goes along without any particular surprises. I don't think there's any big sense of progress or change; it just goes along. I like it. These things would not have occurred to me twenty years ago. The three-dimensional thing occurred to me when it occurred to me; I didn't do it before that. There is a real sequence, all the same. The big boxes downstairs [see image 48] would not have occurred six years previous to their making; though the ideas are there – the size, the scale – the whole thing wouldn't have took.

Then there's also the money question. I would have done different things in '64 if I had had the money, but they would have been along the line of what I was doing then. It would not have been drastically different.

This conversation was primarily sourced from a transcript that was heavily edited by Tuchman; an audio recording was referenced when necessary. The archival transcript is in the Judd Foundation Archives, Marfa, Texas. The audio cassette is in the Oral Histories Collection, The Getty Research Institute, Los Angeles.

First published: Phyllis Tuchman, "An Interview with Donald Judd," Chinati Foundation newsletter 12, October 2007, 52–57 (in English and Spanish).

1   Judd refers here to the Kansas State Capitol, which is not in Wichita but Topeka; its second floor features large murals by Curry.

2   Judd enlisted in the United States Army on June 28, 1946, and was assigned to the Corps of Engineers in Korea. He was honorably discharged on November 20, 1947.

3   Marcia Judd Lamb (1932–1992) worked as a secretary at *Art Digest/Arts Magazine* in the 1950s. (The magazine's name changed to *Arts Magazine* in 1955.)

4   A drawing by Franz Kline appeared on the cover of the September 15, 1953, edition of *Art Digest*.

5   Belle Krasne Ribicoff (1924–) is an American editor, critic, and university administrator. She was an editor at *Art Digest* from 1949 to 1954, the last few years of which she was the magazine's editor in chief.

6   Hilton Kramer (1928–2012) was an American art critic and editor. In December 1959, Kramer hired Judd to review exhibitions for *Arts Magazine*; Judd continued to write for the magazine, with only a few interruptions, until March 1965.

7   Judd likely refers here to Dore Ashton (1928–2017), an American art critic and editor, who, though never the magazine's editor in chief, held prominent editorial roles at *Art Digest* until Kramer's arrival at the magazine in fall 1954.

8   *Mid-Season Salon*, Camino Gallery, New York, December 14, 1956–January 3, 1957.

9   Judd participated in three shows at New York's Panoras Gallery, two group shows and one solo show: *Four Americans*, October 10–22, 1955; *Don Judd and Nathan Raisen*, September 4–15, 1956; and *Don Judd*, June 24–July 6, 1957.

10   Reviews of Judd's work in *Four Americans* at Panoras Gallery include C.B., "Art Exhibition Notes," *New York Herald Tribune*, October 22, 1955, and F.L., "Reviews and Previews," *ARTnews*, October 1955, 52. Reviews of *Don Judd and Nathan Raisen* at Panoras Gallery include *The Sunday News*, September 2, 1956; D.A., "About Art and Artists," *The New York Times*, September 18, 1956; James R. Mellow, "In the Galleries," *Arts Magazine*, September 1956, 58; and Lawrence Campbell, "Reviews and Previews," *ARTnews*, September 1956, 17. Reviews of Judd's 1957 solo exhibition at Panoras Gallery include Barbara Gilbert, *East*, June 20, 1957; C.B., *New York Herald Tribune*, June 30, 1957; "Don Judd chez Panoras," *France-Amérique*, June 30, 1957; Vernon Young, "In the Galleries," *Arts Magazine*, June 1957, 58; and Edith Burkhardt, "Reviews and Previews," *ARTnews*, Summer 1957, 77.

11   Brydon Smith, ed., *Donald Judd: Catalogue Raisonné of Paintings, Objects, and Wood-Blocks 1960–1974*, exh. cat. (Ottawa: National Gallery of Canada, 1975), 7–9.

12   Though certain of Stella's *Black Paintings* were shown elsewhere earlier in 1959, four of them were included in *Sixteen Americans*, The Museum of Modern Art, New York, December 16, 1959–February 14, 1960. See William S. Rubin, *Frank Stella*, exh. cat. (New York: The Museum of Modern Art, 1970), 155–56.

13   Jennifer Licht was a curator at The Museum of Modern Art, New York.

14   *Don Judd*, Green Gallery, New York, December 17, 1963–January 11, 1964. This exhibition was Judd's first solo show to include works in three dimensions.

15   Judd refers here to 53 East Nineteenth Street.

16   Richard Bellamy (1927–1998) was the founder and director of Green Gallery, New York.

17   Judd refers here to 101 Spring Street.

18   *Yayoi Kusama*, Brata Gallery, New York, October 9–29, 1959. Judd reviewed this exhibition and purchased one of the paintings shown in it, a work from Kusama's *Infinity Net* series. See Judd's review of *Yayoi Kusama* (1959) in *Donald Judd: Complete Writings 1959–1975*, 2.

19   William C. Agee, "Unit, Series, Site: A Judd Lexicon," *Art in America*, May–June 1975, 40–49.

20   David Burnett, "Donald Judd: The National Gallery of Canada," *Arts Canada*, Winter 1975–1976, 28–32. This was a review of Judd's first retrospective: *Donald Judd*, National Gallery of Canada, Ottawa, May 24–July 6, 1975.

21   The exhibition and the galvanized wall piece in fact both date to 1970, not 1971. *Don Judd*, Leo Castelli Gallery and warehouse, New York, April 11–May 9, 1970.

22   A dado is a painted, paneled, or decorated lower part of a wall. It can also be left plain and defined by a railing.

23   Rudolf Wittkower (1901–1971) was a German American art historian who specialized in Italian Renaissance and baroque art.

24   Judd began graduate work in art history at Columbia University in fall 1957 and completed his coursework in fall 1961. No degree was conferred because he did not complete the requirements.

"Interview: Kasper König and Donald Judd"
For the exhibition catalogue *Donald Judd*
1977

Judd dedicated his 1977 exhibition *Donald Judd: Für Josef Albers*, at the Moderne
Galerie Bottrop, Germany (May 8–June 12, 1977), to Josef Albers, who had passed
away on March 25 of the previous year. (Albers was born in Bottrop in 1888.) Also
in 1977, Judd made a site-specific work in Cor-ten steel for what became the Josef Albers Museum in Bottrop in 1983.

As an art critic, Judd wrote numerous reviews of Albers's work. Later, on the
occasion of an exhibition of Albers's art at the Chinati Foundation in 1991, Judd
wrote the essay "Josef Albers," in which he stated, "Among those supposedly interested in art, Albers's work is underrated.... I've seen a lot of paintings by Albers,
often singly, over half the world. They are always amazingly beautiful." The two
briefly corresponded, but never met.

Judd collected a number of works by Albers, installing three paintings and
two prints from the *Homage to the Square* series and one painting from the *Variant /
Adobe* series at his Architecture Studio.

KK   [Kasper König] Don, you have dedicated your exhibition at the Moderne Galerie Bottrop to Josef Albers; please tell me why.

DJ   [Donald Judd] First, because he comes from Bottrop. Second, because he recently died. Third, and what is most important, because he was a very good painter.

KK   In your review of his *Interaction of Color*,[1] you also wrote something about Albers as a teacher.[2] Have you ever taught?

DJ   I taught a little bit. I taught at a settlement house and the [Police] Athletic League in New York City – art in almost all of these cases.[3]

KK   Did you follow pedagogical principles in your teaching?

DJ   I actually came to the conclusion that it was pointless to teach anything in a systematic way, because you don't know what the student doesn't know. He doesn't need information before the fact. What I tried to do was to find out what the student was interested in and then supply him with whatever information I had. Otherwise, you are getting involved in teaching a style. Who cares about *Interaction of Color* unless you are seriously involved with that concern? Otherwise, it is of no interest.

KK   Albers is regarded as a great teacher in America. Both Albers and Hans Hofmann came from Germany, Albers because of the political situation, Hofmann from a totally different position. I think it would be interesting if we would talk about this.

DJ   I don't know. It seems to me that the description "a great teacher" is a bit questionable; I really don't know what that means.

KK   Independently of that, there are many artists who openly say they are disciples of Albers – for example, Rauschenberg.

DJ   Well, yes, but it didn't have much to do with either Albers or Rauschenberg.

KK   What, for example, is the situation of Kenneth Noland?

After all, it is clear that he only found his own way through Albers. Albers's works became an important contribution through the encounter with and through the breakup of a new artist generation in the '50s.

DJ   Yes, I mentioned that once before.

KK   Was Hans Hofmann in a similar situation?

DJ   Possibly, but I'm not interested in Hofmann; let's return to Albers. Primarily, we know that he was a good artist, and on account of that, one can explain his reputation as a teacher. Thus it became interesting that one or the other artist studied with him, as it is also interesting to know that someone is influenced by this and that, as we know it from art history. If, however, Albers was not a good artist, such an observation would be uninteresting. Thousands of people have taken lessons from him.

KK   You have expressed general objections with regard to geometric art as a possibility for your own work. That means you turned against the puristic quality which was brought in connection with this style.

DJ   Yes. Originally, I was very interested in Mondrian's work and that which was similar to him, but I also felt that the choice of color as a pure quality was strange to me. This, however, does not apply to Albers. His work is geometric and that's all, and the color is certainly not felt with the purist's nature, as Mondrian's is.

KK   Your principles in the so-called progressions, for example, do not have the characteristics of mathematics – that of structure and limitation as they are found in the works of contemporaries like Sol LeWitt, or as Albers had had them before.

DJ   One field in my work has a lot to do with Albers. I always admired his paintings. I tended to relate to him in ideas, but not so thoroughly as he and Reinhardt.

KK   You have said that to some extent, the geometry that exists in your work was taken up against your will.

DJ Well, I came to it the hard way. I was really against it for a long time; I was pretty reluctant to slowly straighten all the angles out and make straight lines. I know a lot of people who picked it up easily. I was very slow to go along with it.

KK At the end of abstract expressionism, you were a painter. Again and again, it shows in your writings that the key figures were Pollock and Barnett Newman. You could, so to speak, belong to the second generation of this abstract expressionist, gesture-like, painterly movement.

DJ You see, the whole gestural situation is very alien to me. I have some paintings that are perhaps influenced by Pollock; there are very few of them, and even now I don't like them as well as the earlier paintings, which are more parochial and of which I felt I was getting more of what I wanted out of them, even though they look more old-fashioned than these Pollock-influenced paintings. I was just sorting them out in Texas. The whole gestural thing doesn't sit well with me, either.

KK Have your works of the last fifteen years developed from your painting? Also, do you consider these works to be sculptures?

DJ Well, I just think the word "sculpture" is pretty archaic. It means to carve, and that is kind of ridiculous. I'd rather like another category altogether. Also, I associate it with composition, like David Smith. My thinking comes out of painting – but certainly I am not doing paintings.

KK Yes, that is indeed the most important part. You have eliminated the old intellectual basis of art, especially the old norm of composition in favor of a total noncomposition. It is easy to say what your work is not: it is not anthropomorphic, not landscape, not like or influenced by action, not reductive. And it is difficult to say what it is.

DJ That is always the problem. What the new work has in relation to the old work is somewhat of the same qualities in a lot of the rather large, flat planes, which were in the

paintings always set back in space, because they are somewhat based on landscape. When I tried to get more color
and make larger shapes and all that, I brought up the picture surface and tied the surface of the plane more together, but then I tended to lose some of the qualities that I
liked. This has been thoroughly documented in the transition from painting to three-dimensional objects. Another
funny thing was I was slowly appreciating Newman because of his geometry. I always liked Pollock, even when I
was in art school doing models on a stand. I realized there
was something in Pollock's work, but I didn't know what
to do about that.

KK   I do not see a clear connection between you and Newman. Is there one?

DJ   I didn't really like his work until too late for it to have any
influence on mine, which is too bad in a way, because I
saw some paintings very early and I was curious about
them. One of them had a little influence on me because
there are a couple of paintings of mine like it — a horizontal one at Betty Parsons.[4]

KK   I have never seen that picture, but I am sure it is a landscape.

DJ   No, it is only a stripe which goes into shadow. It is complex
and abstract. I was influenced by the large scale, the directness of color that goes through the work. I have never
painted fringed forms like Rothko, or stripes, or drippings.
The dripping is characteristic of Pollock; one cannot use
it. My pictures that are influenced by Pollock are similar
to his later work, where the brushstroke reemerges.

KK   To me, your work has to do with what everything looks
like, especially in the United States. Even though it's obviously not derived from the look of things, it has a resemblance to it. I would attribute the term "heavy duty"
to it; I would not even know how to translate it into
German.

DJ   I don't know this. I don't have this experience, so I am —

K K　　But you confront it a little bit when you have pieces manufactured in Europe. It's really difficult for you –

D J　　Yes, but it was difficult here, too – I just stuck with one
factory.[5] I think it might even work better in Europe, but
I have to stay put and get the factory to understand what I
want to do. Bernstein was very slow; it took two or three
years for them to realize that they were not making venti-
lation ducts, they were making art, and what they are ordinarily making they do in a rather sloppy way, like a Pitts-
burg seam,[6] where my work has to be done very carefully.
These things are invented to be done carefully; it's a new
idea that they are being done carefully.

K K　　How do they feel about it now?

D J　　They feel it's a little special.

K K　　Do you ever get any ideas at the factory?

D J　　Yeah, there are maybe one or two little things that I
thought up over there. The technology is very rudimentary.

K K　　One characteristic of your work to me reflects decision
making, and I think that is very new in art – decision making which involves, let's say, color, material, and everything
else. Intrinsically, it is an overall decision, and a lot of the
decisions you make, even if you think them out beforehand, have to be made at the factory.

D J　　Usually, the material comes first in the wrong size, or you
waste too much time and therefore it costs too much, or
the surface isn't what you thought it was the year earlier,
or you have used the same material and it changed, and
you have to start it all over.

K K　　To what extent do the economics become part of the
aesthetics – become part of your decision making?

D J　　You can't spend more than you've got. It's always very basic.

K K　　In Bottrop, since the possibility came about that you can do
a piece which will stay in Bottrop for at least five years, does
it become more substantial for you to do the show here?

D J　　Yeah, it's very nice.

K K   What is your opinion on having had large works made for an exhibition and then taken down?

D J   Naturally, I don't like such occurrences. But there are certain traditional aspects in my work – that it is art, remains art, and continues to exist as art. These "exhibitions," which disappear, appear to be performances, and that's strange to me. I'm always sorry when I see how they are taken down. To me, the exhibition in Bern should exist somewhere.[7]

K K   But this raises the question of how collections are made in public museums. I have seen pieces of yours in Washington, at the Hirshhorn Museum; in Buffalo; and other places which were so insensitively installed that I assume if you would have seen it, you would tell them to take it down.

D J   Well, I would try to get them to install them better. I know when we were doing the Ottawa catalogue,[8] photos came back of pieces installed in incredible places – one in Fort Worth is in a stairwell. Unbelievable. But there is a limit to how much fighting you can do; the work goes out to the rest of the world, and you can't check it all. I check it all before the shows, but you can't check all of the installations. There are a lot of pieces.

K K   What responsibility has the person who buys a piece, be it a collector or a museum?

D J   One of the responsibilities is to install it well, but they might have different ideas about it. A collector has a so-called progression, and after a little talk about it, I gathered that they bought it to put it over the fireplace; it would be seriously damaged by smoke. What do you do? It's horrible. You just walk out – try to forget it.

K K   The idea of conceptual art – is it completely foreign to you?

D J   Yes, these are meaningless, unless – you can't sit around and think of pieces without doing the pieces, so I tend to think in relation to what I can actually do. See, if you never see any of their results, then there is no way to think of further ones.

K K   In the last two or three years, you have done only large pieces in plywood. It probably was an economic reason behind it – to do large pieces.

D J   Yeah, but I like the plywood a lot. You simply can't do steel pieces that large.

K K   But now, for the first time, you are dealing with a very typical building material. You are going to make a large piece out of concrete in California [image 56].

D J   There were two previous pieces out of concrete [see images 50, 51].

K K   Yes, but they are sitting on the ground, like the one that you are going to do in Münster [image 57]. Is the one for California an open structure?

D J   Like the boxes downstairs [see image 48], somewhat bigger and five inches thicker.

K K   How do you view the structure under which artists can do their work? I mean, there was a lot of hype a couple of years ago – many, many people were interested in art, and what it comes down to is that there are very few who are serious about it.

D J   Yeah, there is not much of an audience. There is not that much support.

K K   You said that there should be support. What is the criteria?

D J   Well, I am here, alive, available, and all that. I have the capability to think of a certain number of pieces a year, and in the best years, there has been one large piece, and in some years, there hasn't been any large piece. At the moment things are very good, but I feel that somehow this public, which builds expensive museums and turns up crowds and all that, is not seriously supporting me, or various other people, or almost all other people doing three-dimensional work in the same situation.

K K   Okay, let's say the criteria is the quality. But who determines public money going toward art? This is a question I am confronted with all the time. What is the criteria?

People, especially in Germany, are very concerned with the word "elite."

DJ   But you have to distinguish between art and politics. Art is not politics. You have a certain number of people spending their lives [making art], and they are artists, and I think it takes that to produce good art. It's not that everybody else is able to do that or wants to do that; very few people, for one reason or another, have that capacity, and those people should be supported.

KK   In science, it works itself out.

DJ   To me, it seems rather similar. Few people can do good work, and the other ones have to support the ones who can figure it out. I don't think that this has anything to do with politics. I think that it is sort of a big confusion.

KK   Who is to determine who the legitimate artists are? That is basically what it comes down to.

DJ   That should be the artists and, when it works out, the knowledgeable people.

KK   But art has traditionally been used to perpetuate the status of those who supported it.

DJ   It has been used for a lot of things, for sure. But it is obviously not one of the things that's on the inside of the ruling situation in almost any country. The United States has not done much for the visual arts.

KK   Except when it represents itself outside of the country.

DJ   Yeah, but very little, really.

KK   But it's one of the major assets the United States has.

DJ   Yes, but the US government doesn't know that. Their present support is small, and that level started in 1966, '67 – and they just give a certain small amount of money to an awful lot of people.

KK   Have you ever been confronted by some kind of antagonism by artists outside of America – or, let's say, in Europe – where they were not willing to discuss your contributions?

D J   Yeah, I got some of that in Australia – not so much personally, but by hearsay. I remember a demonstration with a show of Oldenburg's in Amsterdam, evidently by artists. It is hard to accuse Oldenburg as being an agent of the United States. I heard a great deal about it – antagonism from the British guys.

K K   You said earlier that you feel that art could be made in any place in the world.

D J   Yes, I think so. To me, it's pretty much not a national thing.

K K   You have lived in New York for a long time; you came here in the early 1950s.

D J   1953. And I went to school before that. But I am not a New Yorker.

K K   It was possible for you to see the best art which was produced at that time.

D J   A lot of those guys were not from New York.

K K   I understand they were not from New York, but their work was accessible in New York.

D J   Yeah, but you cannot give New York any credit for that. There is nothing indigenous in New York about the art; it's just done here. It's like the scientists working down in West Texas at the McDonald Observatory – these astronomers come from everywhere; they work and they go home. It's not really much different. The business is here, and that's more important than knowledge. The market is primarily in New York. The artist is really not so visible. You see probably as much on any given day in Amsterdam about American art as you see here.

K K   You might be right.

D J   You see three or four Newman paintings [in Amsterdam]; I don't think you can see them here. There is nothing at all indigenous about the situation here.

K K   Is it attractive to you to do a show in Bottrop, because very little has happened there before?

DJ   I don't know anything about Bottrop; I went there last year. I can't give any good reason for having the show but having the show. I will have a show anywhere.

KK   Do you find in your work a development, or only a change? Is it a very definite development? Is it a development in a sense that gives direction?

DJ   I'm not breaking my head about the idea of progression or development. Work changes. I'm interested in changes, but I do not try to hurry it. It comes by itself – it does not need pressure. Surely there are certain advantages in old works; that does not mean, however, that they would be interesting to look at today. But I'm inclined to forget all of that. It is better. One grows older, and a few unpleasant things creep into the work – characteristics that one could describe as wisdom.

KK   It seems as if a clear change has taken place and that the more recent works are all very visibly joined; usually, they are open. It seems to be the intention that more and more is made visible and more transparent. Will that lead you to architecture?

DJ   Yes, I'm interested in architecture; I always have been. Often I have thought of becoming an architect, but I shy away from being a public figure. The fact that the new works appear more open does not, however, lead to architecture. I can form it always more closely and densely and therefore work back and forth with respect to time. More important is the difference between art and architecture. One cannot simply transpose forms and accompanying circumstances within art or three-dimensional objects into buildings. The function is important, even if it doesn't mean everything; it is my idea that one cannot arbitrarily ignore the function of architecture. With that I do not mean that form should follow function, but that one surely should not forget function.

KK   Today, architecture blindly follows the demands of those who pay money, or it exists in avant-gardistic hopes. Do you see light at the end of the tunnel? From where would it come?

DJ The outlook is not rosy.

KK You have said quite often that you are really interested in visual art – that in visual art, there is no separation of ideas and emotions.

DJ That's relatively traditional, too. I am interested in space and what can be seen.

KK What can be seen – but with every three-dimensional object, there is obviously something that you don't see.

DJ Yeah, that is another problem. But primarily, you see the whole, as with painting you see the whole. So I consider videotapes and performances and all that some other activity. It's not what I want for myself, either to make for myself or to see in other people's work.

KK But when you say that with a three-dimensional object there is something that you cannot see –

DJ Yeah, okay. On the one hand, you are talking about the category of art, and on the other hand, you are talking about the characteristics of mine or of somebody's work within that category. Or at the most, you are talking about the characteristics of a three-dimensional piece of art. Naturally, I am interested in the fact that you cannot see the whole piece at the same time; I have always thought about it a lot. I am reluctant to make high pieces, because you wouldn't be able to see the top.

KK I have always felt that you avoided very clearly any identification of the viewer with the work.

DJ I don't think about the viewers. I think about myself.

KK I have often found that you have consciously undermined any identification of the observer with your work.

DJ Yes, I do not think of the observer, but rather of myself. You can look over the works. That is naturally determined by the size of the body and the view of the eye.

KK   But the large-formed works of the last years are somewhat
      higher than you.

DJ   Well, large pieces are higher, six and a half feet. The one
      in Ottawa is eight feet high. I thought if you could see
      across the whole piece, you could see it – not the other
      side or the other end – you could see it as a whole thing.
      To me, it's pretty different when you look at a box seven
      feet high or eight feet high, as the one in Bottrop will be;
      you are not seeing it like a whole object placed on the
      floor, but you are seeing the underside, which in some
      obscure way is important to me. It's a big change, which
      is not brand-new this year: I slowly put them that high,
      and I slowly used the inner side as a total dimension of
      the thing.

KK   Can you tell us something about your wood works from the
      Bottrop exhibition that are 90 by 150 by 150 centimeters?

DJ   The works, which have been produced before and in the
      same size, are usually open at the top. The works in Bot-
      trop are open at the sides and represent the first of a num-
      ber of other possibilities. They have developed from the
      tube-formed works, but the idea has entered the square
      form; they are not so much horizontal, but rather static.
      Likewise are the diagonals, as well as the open diagonal,
      entirely new.

KK   For Bottrop, you produced two large new works, one of
      wood for inside and one of steel or aluminum for outside
      [images 58, 59], which will remain on loan. What differences
      exist between the two?

DJ   In this case, they are not principally different from one an-
      other. Both will be freestanding and stand on equal levels,
      because the land in Bottrop is very level. The plywood
      can't be outside; it would not hold up in the rain. They
      will be rather similar pieces – they were thought of at the
      same time, and the one that is to be outside is a product
      of the thinking of the one inside.

KK   By that, do you refer to the architecture of the pavilion at
      the Moderne Galerie Bottrop?

DJ   Certainly; I like this architecture. The glass serves as a thin
      wall of separation, and, peculiarly, one work will stand in-
      side and one will stand outside.

KK   In Bottrop, they exhibited a retrospective of your drawings
      of the last twenty years parallel to your three-dimensional
      works made for the Moderne Galerie. Tell me something
      about the dependency that exists between the drawings
      and the finished work.

DJ   The function of drawing has changed during the last
      twenty years. In the '60s, the drawing was rather inter-
      twined with the thought. What kind of possibilities are of-
      fered by the actual pieces? They are equally an inventory
      of ideas. Now, the sketches are exclusively an inventory of
      ideas and transmit no idea of the actual pieces.

KK   How much does your economic situation influence
      your art, and how much does it influence your aesthetic
      decisions?

DJ   One cannot spend more than one has. The economic sit-
      uation is always decisive: the money one has at one's dis-
      posal determines one's material and the size and character
      of the piece. In order to save money, and to prevent wast-
      ing money, we adjust the size of the piece to the existing
      material as much as possible. I hate waste. If one throws
      something away, one throws away the work of another,
      and also the basic material.

KK   We are constantly surrounded by things which are pro-
      duced to be thrown away and which are necessary in or-
      der to create or to preserve jobs.

DJ   Again, that is pure waste. Generally, one should not arti-
      ficially create jobs, because there is always enough work
      to be done. The most horrible thing is to create work
      through the sale of arms.

KK   One last question. You have studied philosophy and have written about art, but you have seldom spoken of your philosophic convictions.[9]

DJ   The matter is as follows: philosophy is my private doing. I think art is public and is a sufficient contribution for the general well-being. I am inclined not to speak about philosophical aspects. But I still think I have put things on a sound functional basis, without, however, having ideas and basic attitudes spontaneously ready.

This conversation was sourced from an archival English translation of the published interview and an undated transcript in the Zentralarchiv für deutsche und internationale Kunstmarktforschung, Cologne.

First published: "Interview: Kasper König und Donald Judd," in *Donald Judd: Für Josef Albers*, exh. cat. (Bottrop, Germany: Moderne Galerie Bottrop, 1977), 3–7.

1   Josef Albers, *Interaction of Color* (New Haven, CT: Yale University Press, 1963). Judd included this book in his library in Marfa, Texas.

2   See Judd's "*Interaction of Color* by Josef Albers" (1963) in *Donald Judd Writings*, 98–102.

3   In the fall of 1954, Judd began working at Christodora House, a settlement house in New York's East Village that provided schooling and recreational opportunities to immigrant children. In 1958, he taught art to underprivileged children at the Police Athletic League.

4   Newman's *Horizon Light* (1949) was exhibited in *Ten Years*, Betty Parsons Gallery, New York, December 19, 1955–January 14, 1956.

5   Judd worked with Bernstein Brothers Sheet Metal Specialties, Inc. from late 1963 until the end of his life. Although they moved to Long Island City by the end of 1964, their shop was originally located in Manhattan, at 191 Third Avenue.

6   A Pittsburgh seam is a type of longitudinal seam used to join pieces of sheet metal.

7   *Donald Judd: Skulpturen*, Kunsthalle Bern, April 14–May 30, 1976.

8   Brydon Smith, ed., *Donald Judd: Catalogue Raisonné of Paintings, Objects, and Wood-Blocks 1960–1974*, exh. cat. (Ottawa: National Gallery of Canada, 1975).

9   Judd received his BS in philosophy from Columbia University, cum laude, in 1953.

Interview with eighth-grade students from
Marfa Junior High School
November 1978

This interview was conducted at La Mansana de Chinati/The Block, Judd's home
and studio in Marfa, Texas, as part of a documentary film project by May Quick's
eighth-grade history students from Marfa Junior High School. In addition to the
feature on Judd, the students also made a film about Fred Shely and his Pinto Canyon ranch jun Presidio County, Texas. After researching, filming, and editing the
documentaries, they presented their films to the Century Culture Club at the
Thunderbird restaurant in Marfa on March 14, 1979. The project was sponsored by
the National Endowment for the Arts and the US Office of Education.

Quick moved to Marfa in 1958 and met Judd when he came to Marfa in the
early 1970s. She taught both Judd's son and daughter.

S1   [Student 1] Are you the one who speaks during the exhibitions? And how long do they last?

DJ   [Donald Judd] An exhibition is just the pieces, installed; they usually last a month or six weeks. And I don't speak – I avoid talking if possible.

MQ   [May Quick] Can you tell us where your first recognition was, or how it came about?

DJ   The first serious exhibition I had was at a gallery in New York called the Green Gallery in late '63 [see images 2, 3], and a small number of people thought it was interesting.[1] There are not a great many people interested in contemporary art; it's not as if there's a big wave of publicity. Slowly, over the years, your reputation builds up. It's a little mysterious to me. But I didn't make any effort to show them, and I'm not very career-minded, so I've not made much effort to promote that sort of thing.

S2   [Student 2] Do these sculptures have any special meanings to you?

DJ   Yeah, they have a lot of meaning, but they're visual, so it's not easily translated into words. It would take me a great deal of work to make any sort of philosophical statement about them, and I would have to spend a couple of months writing it all down. Obviously, they have a good deal of meaning to me.

S3   [Student 3] Have you reached your main goal in life, or are you still pursuing it?

DJ   That goal keeps changing for everybody. I've certainly done what I wanted to do in the very beginning, but then you think of more things to do, so you don't catch up. But I think I've gotten a lot more work done than I ever expected to do.

S4   [Student 4] When you first started out in your work, was it difficult? Did you have much trouble?

DJ   Yeah, it was very difficult. For a long time, all the time that I did paintings, it was to me a very difficult effort. The interesting thing that happened was when I started doing the three-dimensional work, it all became easier and happened more naturally and was generally more fun, rather than a great deal of struggle. And nowadays it's just pleasure, and I enjoy it a great deal.

S3   All these things that we see here and the designs that we see here – does that somehow lead us to know that you like making three-dimensional things?

DJ   Yes, I'm not very interested in flat things. The etchings are the only thing I do – prints – still. I haven't done any paintings since '61 or '62. I just have no ideas for them, and I'm not interested. So everything is three-dimensional.

S3   That sculpture right there, can't you put it into a picture?

DJ   Why?

S3   A painting?

DJ   No. Why? It's all about three dimensions and the space inside the boxes, around the boxes, between the boxes. It's all about space, and you can't paint the space or anything; you can only make it exist. It's about seeing and about the actuality of space.

S4   Do you actually mind if people come and talk to you and interview you?

DJ   I've been interviewed an awful lot, and I'm really worn down on it. Generally I refuse. The questions tend to be the same questions all the time, so I get tired of listening to myself.

S3   Why don't you like publicity?

DJ   Oh, I don't quite know what you mean.

S3   Why don't you like people interviewing you – I mean, I know it's because of the questions, but do you have any other reasons why you don't like it?

DJ   I'm not so interested in talking about it [the work]. I know what I'm doing, and the work itself is public; you get to see the work. I don't think it's necessary for me to come along and explain it. Anyway, there's a whole bunch of people –

museum people and art critics and all that – who can do what they can to explain it. But basically, I think that the person looking at the work should think about it and figure it out for themselves and not ask me, "Why?" Because I'm doing it, and that's enough, I think.

This discussion was sourced from a digital copy of the original Super 8 film in the Judd Foundation Archives, Marfa, Texas.

1   *Don Judd*, Green Gallery, New York, December 17, 1963–January 11, 1964. This exhibition was Judd's first solo show to include works in three dimensions.

Interview for the filmstrip *Contemporary Artists at Work*
1979

Produced by Daniel De Wilde for the publisher Harcourt Brace Jovanovich, this conversation was created for inclusion in an educational filmstrip – a form of still-image multimedia accompanied by a synchronized soundtrack – on contemporary American sculptors for high school and junior college students. Other artists featured in *Contemporary Artists at Work: Sculptors, Volume II* were Larry Bell, Jackie Ferrara, Charles Ginnever, and Beverly Pepper.

N   [Narrator] Donald Judd wants his pieces to speak for themselves. To be no more than what they are: a shape, a volume,
a color. He uses strong, clear, and often repetitive forms,
working primarily with metals, wood, and plastic. He usually leaves the surfaces of the materials untreated and un-
changed, incorporating their natural colors and textures
as part of the work.

DJ   [Donald Judd] The general historical process seems to
be for the art to have greater and greater emphasis on its
own means and its own appearance, with as few references as possible to exterior things. I don't like the piece
to show the process of its making. Often in composition,
or, you know, painting or sculpture, which I consider of an
older style, decisions are made from time to time, point to
point, as the thing is being made. Basically, I want the decisions all made beforehand, and thought out beforehand.
I tend to think of the whole piece at once – materials, and
color, and scale, and the whole thing. I'm not interested
in having a piece halfway finished and then making a big
change.

N   Once the idea for a piece is worked out, he has it constructed
at a workshop or factory according to his specifications.

DJ   There's a big gap between thinking about it and figuring
it all out and finally seeing it. And usually, I'm surprised.

[*Music*]

DJ   When I was doing paintings, I couldn't get the broad areas
and the lines to go together in any way that I liked. They
tended to turn into some sort of illusionism. And when
I made the first three-dimensional piece, it had very big,
broad areas, and the edges of the piece were the lines.

N   To produce a nonsymmetrical effect in some pieces, the composition was based on certain mathematical progressions.

DJ   I wanted it to be evident that the scheme was given, not composed – that I didn't adjust all these little parts. I think it came at a point where I didn't want to be pinned down into symmetrical schemes.

N   Judd often works in a series, such as these plywood boxes [see image 48].

DJ   Mainly, that group is open from the front. You could start off with a whole other group where it's open from the sides, but it's not a tight system or anything. If a certain piece fits the logic, but isn't good, I don't do it – that's all. I'm not interested in logic. I'm interested in the pieces.

This conversation was sourced from an audio recording and a transcript in the Judd Foundation Archives, Marfa, Texas.

First published: *Contemporary Artists at Work: Sculptors, Volume II*, produced and directed by Daniel De Wilde (New York: Harcourt Brace Jovanovich Films, 1979), filmstrip, 19 min.

"Reclusive Artist Hopes Colonists Stay Away"
Article by Shelley Gilbert-Allison for the
San Angelo Standard-Times
March 2, 1981

In 1978, Judd partnered with Dia Art Foundation, who purchased the buildings and land of Fort D. A. Russell, a decommissioned military base in Marfa, Texas. Through what was known at the time as the "Marfa project," Judd established the permanent installation of large-scale works by himself and his contemporaries. In 1986, following an ownership dispute and ensuing settlement, Dia transferred the artwork, buildings, and land to a new independent, nonprofit institution founded by Judd, which opened to the public as the Chinati Foundation that same year.

A slightly different version of this article, "Judd Chooses Marfa over World's Art Capitals," also by Gilbert-Allison, was published a few days prior in *The Big Bend Sentinel*, a weekly newspaper based in Marfa, as the third installment in a multi-author series on Judd and the "Marfa project."

MARFA — Artist colonies and large tourist crowds are two things Donald Judd does not want to see in this small West Texas town.

"I'm afraid of that idea, afraid of an art colony — just that bohemian state of things," the Dia Art Foundation resident artist said in a recent — and rare — interview.

Recognized internationally in contemporary art circles, Judd is still a relative stranger in his adopted town and he doesn't seem to mind. He moved here about six years ago from New York City's crowded SoHo district — he prefers its architectural name, the Cast Iron District — where he owns a building housing some of his work.

He has spent summers in Marfa since 1972.[1]

"Since my place in New York was overrun by people, I'm kind of touchy about privacy," the bearded, fifty-two-year-old sculptor admitted.

Yet his large modern sculptures and prints have been shown worldwide, including Europe, Japan, Canada, and the United States. He has written scholarly articles for translation and been the subject of the same.

Judd has conducted art seminars in some of the country's more prestigious schools, including Yale, Dartmouth, Columbia (his alma mater), and New York City's Hunter College.

More recently, he said, he has been asked to speak in Lubbock and Austin, but he turned down those offers, as well as others to teach full time.

"I don't like to (lecture publicly) because I'm not so public … I was a teacher once, and I've used all that up, I think."

In the past, he has taught "kids on the streets in New York" for the Police Athletic League.[2]

Today, he makes his home inside high adobe walls in the old Fort D. A. Russell quartermaster's depot in Marfa.

In 1979, he signed on as a resident artist funded by the Dia Art Foundation and is in charge of the foundation's "Marfa project."[3] Dia is a nonprofit charitable organization whose directors have been quoted in the *Standard-Times* as saying they hope the project will bring the fine arts to the widest audience possible, and "to establish Marfa as a place of culture in a quiet and peaceful environment."

They found the area, in the words of board member Heiner Friedrich of New York, "most suited for Don Judd's work."[4]

"I'm a little touchy about that," Judd commented quietly. "They (Dia) came here because I was here, not the other way around."

"The (contractual) arrangement is that they can't do anything in Marfa unless I let them, to put it bluntly – on design or anything," Judd said.

Whatever Dia's ultimate intentions, which mystify many local residents despite recent news reports, Judd's priorities do not include extensive public display of his work in Marfa. His primary concern is not to exhibit his art but "to make it and to have it stay in place forever" – a luxury not afforded by temporary museum and gallery showrooms.

To ensure that dream, Judd has "paperwork in the works" for the establishment of his own foundation in addition to one already set up to take effect upon his death.[5]

He said he doesn't expect the populace to appreciate his works, which some have likened to "giant concrete boxes," "meaningless abstracts," and "eyesores."

"I run across that in every city in Europe and the United States," he chuckled. "In the first place, art is very much a personal matter. And we're also living in a society that is, unfortunately, severely cut into pieces, where everyone doesn't know about others' activities. There's no reason for everyone to understand or like the stuff … It's nice when they do."

"I assume if it suits me and is intelligible to me, it must be intelligible, in part, to somebody else."

"I certainly do not think of the general public, because I don't know of any general public. It boils down to certain artists and museum curators – all of which amount to about twenty-four people. And with every new generation, there's twenty-four more people, and twenty-four, and twenty-four – after a while, you've got two to three hundred people."

Dia's funding does not give anyone "the right to see my work. They (the public) have no claim on it," he said.

With that philosophy in mind, Judd has designed a living-working environment with privacy built in and distractions shut out by high adobe walls. His spacious quarters, in which living, display, and studio space abut and sometimes overlap, house many of his works as well as some by his contemporaries.

The adobe walls are "primarily a work of art" and "define the space" architecturally, Judd explained. They are also for privacy. "It's where I live. If I live here, I really don't want a bunch of people wandering around," he added.

Sculptures are shipped in pieces from Connecticut, where they are manufactured in metals, wood, or concrete according to Judd's specifications.[6] They are assembled for permanent display in Marfa, often into works too large to fit through the door.

Once completed, Judd said, the Marfa project will include about half his work – including a small museum for his prints – and of the works of contemporaries Dan Flavin, John Chamberlain, and the late Barnett Newman.

Flavin and Chamberlain, both of Judd's choosing, will practice their art in Marfa periodically under Dia's sponsorship, but they will continue to live near the East Coast, Judd said. Flavin is expected to visit here in one to two months, he said.

"If this does get done, in spite of all the problems, it will probably be the greatest visible concentration of contemporary art in the world," Judd said.

The artist's interest also extends to the older architectural forms of Marfa's past. He lamented the demolition of the old Ashton house and owns doors and windows from the old Virginia Hotel.[7] He owns the old Settles house and plans to preserve it as a guest house.[8]

Plans for the many Marfa buildings purchased by Dia include renovating much of the fort into showrooms, smaller museums, and visitors' housing.

Meanwhile, the interested and curious may obtain a glimpse of Judd's world in the pasture near town. Two geometric concrete sculptures are "unofficially" on display there and by mid-April will be unveiled to the public at a reception at the site, the artist said.

Eventually, there will be fifteen such concrete pieces in a row in the pasture, placed at certain angles in relation to each other [image 60].[9]

What does Donald Judd art mean? The message is "too complicated," is his response.

"You have to look and do your best. But being art, it has to do with everything."

First published: Shelley Gilbert-Allison, "Judd Chooses Marfa over World's Art Capitals," *The Big Bend Sentinel*, February 26, 1981, 1; reprinted (revision): Shelley Gilbert-Allison, "Reclusive Artist Hopes Colonists Stay Away," *San Angelo Standard-Times*, March 2, 1981, 3B.

1   In the fall and winter of 1971, Judd rented a small house in Marfa, Texas, spending his first summer there in 1972. See Judd's "Casa Lujan and La Catorcena" (1989) in *Donald Judd: Architektur*, 26–30.

2   In 1958, Judd taught art to underprivileged children at the Police Athletic League, New York.

3   See Judd's "Statement for the Chinati Foundation/La Fundación Chinati" (1987) in *Donald Judd Writings*, 484–89.

4   Heiner Friedrich (1938–) is a German art dealer. Along with Philippa de Menil and Helen Winkler, he cofounded Dia Art Foundation in 1974.

5   Judd Foundation was conceived by Judd in 1977 to maintain and preserve his permanently installed living and working spaces, archives, and libraries in New York and Marfa, Texas. See Judd's "Judd Foundation" (1977) in *Donald Judd Writings*, 284–86.

6   Judd worked frequently with Lippincott, Inc. of North Haven, Connecticut, between 1978 and 1986. Lippincott fabricated the 100 untitled works in mill aluminum made between 1982 and 1986 at the Chinati Foundation [image 61].

7   Judd also acquired adobe bricks from Marfa's historic Virginia Hotel when it was torn down by its owners, which he used (along with bricks of other provenances) to build a wall around the perimeter of the Block. See Judd's "Marfa, Texas" (1985) in *Donald Judd Writings*, 428–29.

8   Judd purchased the Walker house (previously known as the Settles house, for another former owner) in May 1976. He used this property as a guest house and as a space for the installation of paintings by John Wesley. The Walker house was sold not long after Judd's death in 1994 and is now a private residence.

9   Judd's fifteen untitled works in concrete at the Chinati Foundation were cast and assembled on site over a four-year period, from 1980 to 1984.

"Plain Speaking from Donald Judd"
Article by Suzanne Muchnic for the *Los Angeles Times*
October 28, 1984

This article was published on the occasion of Judd's exhibition *Donald Judd: Painted Wall Sculptures*, at the Margo Leavin Gallery, Los Angeles (October 20–November 24, 1984). The show included over half a dozen multicolored pieces, a new body of work that Judd developed in Switzerland in 1984.

Until this time, Judd's works contained no more than two colors. As he wrote in his essay "Some Aspects of Color in General and Red and Black in Particular" (1993), "In the sheet aluminum works I wanted to use more and diverse bright colors than before.... I wanted all of the colors to be present at once. I didn't want them to combine. I wanted a multiplicity all at once that I had not known before." In each work, he notes, "Color and space occur together."

Donald Judd is a soft-spoken artist who has never been known for reticence. His public statements – both printed and verbal – are as uncompromising as the stark structures that have permanently etched his name in art history books.

In the early '60s, his opinionated art criticism guided the intellectual basis of the reductive abstraction that became known as minimalism. He advocated – and produced – unequivocal three-dimensional objects that occupied real space and got rid of illusionism.

This fall, in *Art in America* magazine (an influential New York journal), Judd resurfaced as a writer. "The quality of new art has been declining for fifteen years" is his opening charge in two lengthy articles that take on offending members of the entire art world – artists, educators, curators, critics, dealers, and patrons, as well as museums and publications.[1] Judd contends that, through various combinations of ineptitude, ignorance, and venality, the forces of commerce and dilution are threatening the life of art by abusing "the activity."

Judd's readers who expect him to look and act the part of a raging critic or a self-serving dogmatist may be disappointed. In Los Angeles for the recent opening of his exhibition at the Margo Leavin Gallery, he held his strongly worded position with a reserved demeanor that would win the Teddy Roosevelt seal of approval. During an interview in his Santa Monica hotel, he talked quietly about his convictions.

"I think there's an obligation to defend the activity you're involved in," he said. "The United States lacks discussion in art and all things. Artists need to talk more to everyone.

"Did I take a risk in speaking out? I took a risk to be an artist, but I didn't think it was. I just set out to do it. For me and for most artists – my age [fifty-six], anyway – there was no prospect of making a living at it. You just did it, no matter what. John Marin was considered really well off because somebody had willed him a house. Ad Reinhardt was in good shape because he had a part-time job at a college.

"That has changed enormously, so that now you have just middling artists making a living, sometimes a very good one. The finances have changed. The public is much more involved now, but it's involved in such a superficial way. It sounds sanctimonious, but I didn't go through all this – being poor for all those years and putting up with baloney from everyone – just to sell out. I don't want my art to be assimilated into junk. I don't want it to be just another product. If that involves objecting and a risk, I'll have to take it."

Charging that their fashionable art is "derivative and sloppy," Judd discounts the new breed of expressionists who have been vaunted in the press and whose works have been promoted and sold for enormous sums by shrewd dealers. And he flatly rejects the pendulum theory of art, which holds that current expressionism is a natural reaction to the perceived rigor and sterility of abstraction such as his.

"There's no real reaction because the work is not good, and that invalidates any theorizing about it. I object strongly to the division of form and content, but if art is not good, it has no human content. De Kooning was the last expressionist.

"The other implication is that my work – and lots of other people's – has no content. I very much believe that it does. My political opinions are fairly developed and they are in there. But it's better to write down political statements than to make art with slogans."

Taking the pendulum theory of art back to the era of his emergence, Judd denied the oft-stated notion that his relatively ascetic art was a reaction to the romantic excesses of abstract expressionism: "That's wrong. The Tate just wrote this down, the Whitney wrote it down, and it's just exactly false. The people I learned from were Jackson Pollock, Barnett Newman, and Mark Rothko. I learned in a very remote way. My work doesn't really resemble theirs, but I learned from them and there's no excess there. That's certainly clear. It's kind of sad and ironic, but in many ways they're still the avant-garde.

"People think that art is a freight train going by and you can only see one car at a time, but if you look around you see [Jean] Arps (and the work of other modernists) that are very fresh and alive – and tired old [Julian] Schnabel, [Georg] Baselitz, and [Sandro] Chia," Judd continued. "Baselitz is an incredibly unconvincing and trashy painter. There's always been somebody like Chia in New York painting stupid, heavy, dull, old classicism. I don't believe these people. It's insulting.

"I don't understand why the situation has become so backward. A few years ago, the dealers would have had some secretary get this art out the door; now they want to show it."

Judd says his own aesthetic concerns and "main attitudes" have changed little since his work gained attention in the '60s, but he has developed "a range" that allows greater flexibility – and a move into furniture and architecture. At the Margo Leavin Gallery (through November 24), he shows new wall reliefs made of painted metal or aluminum and colored plexiglass, as well as a 1974 floor piece of galvanized iron. His first exhibitions of wooden furniture will open at the Leo Castelli Gallery and Judd's own space in New York on November 11.[2] The Max Protetch gallery, also in New York, will unveil an exhibition of his metal furniture and architectural drawings December 6.[3]

Judd, who grew up in the Midwest, has lived in Texas since 1977.[4] He began making furniture for his children many years ago but gave it up because "it got too tangled up in art." When he came back to it, he discovered that "the secret is to take a chair as a chair. By taking it easy, the furniture came out to be relatively original. Now it has developed on its own and, in a way, it turns out to be art after all."

He maintains a heavy work and exhibition schedule, but not without obstacles. "Everybody who defends their work is going to get in trouble," he said. "I'm difficult because my pieces cost a lot to make, they are large, I insist they be installed well and that they be handled well. I've had my troubles, but I don't think I'm the most crucial case. Barnett Newman took one hell of a beating because he wanted to know where his paintings went and how they were cared for. I think that Dan Flavin, Larry Bell, and Bob Irwin are also difficult because they are very particular. You can't just make things. You have to defend their integrity."

As for expected response to his recently published criticism, Judd isn't worried. "I only got hit once so far – by Rauschenberg, because I said he did his best work in 1958."

First published: Suzanne Muchnic, "Plain Speaking from Donald Judd," *Los Angeles Times*, October 28, 1984, 89–90.

1   See Judd's "A Long Discussion Not About Master-Pieces But Why There Are So Few of Them: Part I" (1983) and "A Long Discussion Not About Master-Pieces But Why There Are So Few of Them: Part II" (1984) in *Donald Judd Writings*, 352–76 and 378–97, respectively. "Part I" was first published in *Art in America*, September 1984, 9–19; "Part II" was first published in *Art in America*, October 1984, 9–15.

2   These were in fact two separate, concurrent exhibitions, both of which opened on November 17, not November 11; art was shown at Leo Castelli Gallery, furniture at 101 Spring Street. *Donald Judd*, Leo Castelli Gallery, New York, November 17–December 15, 1984; *Furniture by Donald Judd*, 101 Spring Street, New York, November 17–December 15, 1984.

3   *Donald Judd: Architectural Drawings and Furniture*, Max Protetch, New York, December 7, 1984–January 5, 1985.

4   In the fall and winter of 1971, Judd rented a small house in Marfa, Texas, spending his first summer there in 1972. See Judd's "Casa Lujan and La Catorcena" (1989) in *Donald Judd: Architektur*, 26–30.

Interview with Pilar Viladas
1985

This conversation between journalist Pilar Viladas and Judd provides an in-depth look at the progression of Judd's property ownership and architectural work in Marfa, Texas. As it is highly referential, readers may wish to reference image 62, which offers an annotated plan of La Mansana de Chinati/The Block.

A portion of this interview was included in the article "A Sense of Proportion," published in *Progressive Architecture* in April 1985. Judd's essay "Marfa, Texas" (1985), which described the development of his activities related to art and architecture in Marfa, was published in *House & Garden* that same month. There Judd explained: "This place [La Mansana de Chinati/The Block] is primarily for the installation of art, necessarily for whatever architecture of my own that can be included in an existing situation, for work, and altogether for my idea of living. As I said, the main purpose of the place in Marfa is the serious and permanent installation of art.... Due to the prior existence of the buildings my interest here in architecture is secondary. If I could start over the two interests would be congruent. But I've carefully tried to incorporate the existing buildings into a complete complex. They are not changed, only cleaned up."

DJ [Donald Judd] I bought the first buildings in 1973, and
then the remaining fourth with the two-story building in
1974. I needed a place in 1972 to store the large piece from
Pasadena [see image 41], and so I rented the east building of
the two buildings.[1] Of course, once the piece is simply
sitting there, you wonder where it might go – I mean, it
just becomes speculation. In fact, I think I just rented the
north room of that.

The next summer, Bascomb and Harold Webb, the
father and son who owned it, said they would like to sell
it. I thought I bought the whole block for $40,000, and
then Bascomb called up the next day and said that he
thought he had said – which I'm sure that he made up
overnight – that it was only three-fourths of the block, and
the remaining fourth with the two-story building was not
included. So it was $40,000 for three-fourths, and since
it was a fairly decent price, I let it go. I think Bascomb
went home and thought he'd charged too little and went
and got out of it the next morning. Probably I could have
bluffed him out of it all. But the next summer, I bought
the remaining fourth for $8,000. It still wasn't so bad. It
had a mortgage; the mortgage is long gone.

There was no wall, of course, around the place – a city
block, wide open to the highway on one side. In fact, people used to cut straight through it on the diagonal from
the highway to the Godbold feed mill.[2] It was wide open
to Godbold and the [train] tracks on the other side. The
Webbs had torn out a lot of the walls to make doors to
drive the cars through; they had a body shop there for a
while, then they just had storage. The state police and city
police had storage for cars they'd picked up.

The buildings were a real wreck. A good portion of
the back on the north side of the Block was full of old
cars and car parts – it was just a standard urban mess. It had
originally been covered with asphalt; there were patches

of that everywhere. There was a concrete platform on the highway end, which we later tore out. And whatever graces the buildings had were pretty much destroyed by these enormous holes they'd knocked into it. All the windows were broken; the roof leaked – still leaks – and the two-story building was a wreck. So it was just like this place:[3] just to clear it up was a major undertaking.

So after I bought the buildings in 1973, I started to clean up the east building. The other [west] building I didn't work on for a long time. It was storage, and I just parked the cars in there. We just worked on the south large room [of the east building] and had the bedroom plastered – had the wall outside of there plastered, and then the bedroom plastered, which had been all divided up; it was in three parts. We tore that out and made it one room, and we turned the other end of it into the kitchen.

You know, these were World War I airplane hangars that were out at the golf course and were moved into Marfa in the 1930s by the army, and this was the quartermaster corps there. I think the army still retains, as the government always does, the uranium rights, in case I ever discover uranium. Unfortunately, the telephone poles go straight through it; there is a possibility someday of putting them underground.

So, these buildings were obviously a given – there they were – and there was nothing you could do about it. At any rate, they're not disagreeable. They're not great buildings, either, or even half great. The metal roof with the big trusses is nice, and the clerestories are nice; it was discontinuous, but I am slowly making it continuous down both sides of both buildings. And the wall is, I think, a pretty obvious thing. It had to have something around it, because it was too public, and to me, if it's that public – of course, it's more public than it would have been if it had been a residential area – the land is wasted. By putting a wall around it, you reclaim – since the buildings are not on a property line – you reclaim an awful lot of space that's nice to walk around in and use for various reasons. Without the wall, we couldn't have the swimming pool and the trees right underneath Godbold, and you wouldn't have the whole alley where Rainer's trees are, and grass, because it'd be too public.[4] Also, I like all those alleys a great deal.

The original idea for something like this [the walls] was because of a ranch which has no buildings; it's called El Porvenir, in Baja.[5] Porvenir had a very narrow valley, and I wanted to make a triangular complex, small – not big like this, but small, of adobe. But it would've been concentric walls, not as high as that, because you wouldn't have to have them that high, but you have to have them big enough so that the animals can't get in too easily. In open land, you have to have some enclosure; even in open land like a town, you still have to have enclosure. And right away it was all the same idea – that I have the wall all the way around.

At first, I didn't know where the gate would be. I was going to have it by the two-story building; it was later moved to where it is. The external wall that's level was always to have the inside wall that tilts [image 63], which is similar to the piece I made for the Pulitzers [image 64]; the piece that I made for Münster, Germany [see image 57]; and the piece that was made for Park Sonsbeek, in Holland [see image 53], which was just temporary. But this land was basically flat, and there was a slight tilt between the two big buildings, and we bulldozed that tilt – what little there was – until it became . . . I think it's something like one, two, three feet. Anyway, it drops at an angle, catty-corner. So it's not a big drop, but it's still a conspicuous drop, and it is somewhat artificial; it had to be increased. It was there, somewhat. It sure helps the drainage, and it gives you all those corridors inside – and it helps to break the force of the wind against the buildings and doors, too. In fact, the whole wall does a great deal to lower the dust and lower the force of the wind. So it's very practical that way. The dust used to be horrifying; now, between the walls and the gravel, it's really minor.

The outside wall is just determined by the property line. There's nothing you can do with the interval between the side of the building and the outside wall. The inside wall and some of the spaces toward the north of the Block are on a twelve-foot module, so you have straight alleys big enough for a car, and also in proportion to – the gate is twelve feet, the whole alley straight ahead is twelve feet, and so forth. The one straight ahead is the *decumanus maximus*, and the one crosswise is the *cardo*.[6] Except the *cardo* is supposed to be north and south, so actually, it's wrong.

The big idea about it all is to have the two walls, one level and one sloping, and then the land tilted – part of it, what I call a compound slope – and the other part level. So the whole north end is level and the south end is tilted, and then some small buildings at the north end will have roofs that are tilted. There are four buildings, but they'll just keep the same slope, across the roofs, and they'll tilt to one corner also. So the land will tilt like this [*gestures*]. That idea was pretty much there at the beginning – to do the interior wall and the interior slope.

When the kids and I actually needed to live there – [we had been living] in a little house on the edge of town[7] – I had to make something domestic out of the two-story building. All the normal domestic functions had to go into the ground floor of that building, and it became hard to get the bathroom in there. Also, at the house on the edge of town, the bathroom had been sixty feet from the house, so I was perfectly used to having the bathroom somewhere else. So in that small space between the two buildings, I put the adobe building. Then the other spaces on the other side are corresponding; the office matches the bathroom building. They're the same height as the wall, and the wall is behind them in both cases, but they project forward and fill the space as a solid, which I like a lot – the wall that comes forward is part of a volume, rather; "volume" is better than "solid" – and the one passing behind of course is a plane. Those things I like. As I said, I like the walls up against the windows. Rainer's room, for example – at the back, it has a wall less than four feet [away], because that's given by the property line. So out two windows, the wall's right there. Out the other two windows, she has a view of 130 feet or so, so it's a big extreme. One's pure mud, and the other one's grass and plum trees. I like those things.

The black building that isn't built well was not there; I put that up. Chango [Celedonio Mediano] was learning on the job, and I didn't know much about building it either.[8] But I wasn't involved, and it happened one summer. I've changed my mind about its size, and about how it should be made, and everything, so it's to come down, and two better buildings, which will be really nice, will be real architecture – one there and one in front of the two-story building.[9]

PV   [Pilar Viladas] And those will be for what?

DJ   Paintings. They're to be fireproof. They'll have either no electricity or very little – easy to switch off – and they'll be steel beams and prefab concrete slabs and a curved Quonset hut–type roof, and the axes will be crossed. The two floors and then the roof [will divide the buildings] all in thirds, going up. I can show you sketches. I really like them, and I would not be fixing up somebody else's old buildings, for a change. The plan isn't here; somebody's got it and is working on it, I'd show it to you otherwise.

Let's see – I'm working my way from the south to the north. After I fixed up the first floor of the two-story building, which is after I did the east building, I started working on the west building. The studio was first, I guess, and then the north room, and then the library. And in the middle of all that, because of being down there during the winters, I started to use that little offset on the arroyo and make it a so-called winter garden, which was meant to be green all winter, because it's very bleak. It's not finished either. So then we made the tank, made the pergola, made the garden – made a big garden; there's always been a garden, but made a real garden – and made the dog house and chicken house, the Miesian chicken coop. It's even more Miesian now, and it's pretty nice.

So the two [new] buildings of steel and concrete, which will be horizontal slabs, have to be made, and then the complex with the sloping roof at the rear, to the north, has to be made; that's four buildings. They're all adobe, and they're all, so far in my mind, the same height as the wall. The one toward the west will be a really big kitchen, because I don't think the two-story building is sufficient. There'll be a room for prints and drawings, because the light's so strong; you need someplace dark to put them. It'll only have a door and artificial light. Another one will have a piece of mine that goes around the wall and will be open to the outside, and an apartment, maybe, for somebody to stay there. It'll all be around a small pond, which will have catfish, frogs, and edible things – three ducks.

So what was there was very important, and what the place had to do was very important. Mostly it has to accommodate art, one way or another. But it also has to be liveable, pleasant. The spaces will be, when I'm finished, rather different from one another, which will be nice: very big rooms, really small rooms, spaces half outdoors, spaces really outdoors, spaces underneath something, like a pergola – open, like the winter garden is enclosed, but it's open to the sky and like a room.

P V   What are the things that for you constitute liveability?

D J   I think spaces should be pretty large, and for me, they certainly should have art. I recommend it to the rest of the world as well. You have to have different enclosed spaces – you have to have smaller spaces in order to heat them; there's no way to heat big buildings. I think you need smaller ones to do various things. But I don't think you have to get into the domestic arrangement of an ordinary house or apartment, which I guess I would think is too moderate in terms of what happens from room to room. If I were doing apartments, I guess I'd have one really big room that does almost everything, and then the smaller rooms off of that. I remember some friends who rented a place that was the private gymnasium of a big estate and looked out onto a polo field. It was really nice, and was two stories, and had a balcony above it, around the gym floor. So the kitchen and bedroom and bath downstairs and things upstairs all opened off the really big two-story space. It was terrific. And the big space did everything: you ate there, you sat around – it had a fireplace – kids roared around on tricycles. It gives you – if you can't make a lot of big spaces – it gives you one big space you can really enjoy. Because they were Italian, it was very sparsely furnished, European style, with just a few pieces of furniture, and that was it – something I like a lot. You just have a few chairs sitting around in a big space; it was all you need. I think kitchens are important, I think bedrooms are important, and should all be nice, ample. So I think the one big space is the primary thing; if you can make another big space for a bedroom, fine. If you can make another big space for a kitchen, it gets better and better.

P V   But in the Block, you have beds all over the place.

D J   Yes, because in order to live with the art, you have to be relatively comfortable. Also, I like for the rooms that have art to have some sort of function. It doesn't have to be so great, but if you can sit there and have a drink, or eat, or lie down, or read, then you look at the work. Because you can't look at the art, I think, as we're supposed to in museums and galleries, really. You walk in, you look at it, you walk out, and that's it. I can't see anything that way. I think you look at it, think about it, do something else, then look at it again, or you talk and look at it. It becomes a normal thing. You don't want to have to stand up all the time – it's ridiculous. Obviously, it can all develop into a situation where there's an awful lot of space and beyond most people's interests or finances, so if it became a popular thing it could become quite a consumption matter, but it doesn't look like it's really going to catch on. I think it's really horrifying to put the ceiling right down on top of people – a nine-foot, eight-foot ceiling is impossible.

PV   I know you said you were going to use artificial light in the room where you'll have the prints, but in the rest of the buildings, will there just be natural light?

DJ   Yes.

PV   The wall between the east and west buildings: how tall is that?

DJ   The outer wall is about nine feet, and it's as tall as at its southeast corner – which is its highest corner – as the outer wall is at its southwest corner, which is about eight feet, because the ground is tilted; the lower, inner [wall's] corner is probably about four feet lower.

    Celedonio has either supervised or built everything. Alfredo [Mediano] takes care of the art and the rooms, studio.

PV   Did you decide to make the [new] buildings you're going to put the paintings in out of concrete and steel primarily for reasons of fireproofing, or for other reasons, too?

DJ   Aesthetics is a big reason. I want to make a really nice building. They could've been adobe; the hangars, actually – and because they were moved – are steel beams and adobe walls. I'm very interested in prefab architecture, and cheaper architecture, naturally, and it's also something they can do in Marfa – something that Celedonio can do; he can put the H-beams or whatever together. At this point, I think, he's worked on the concrete pieces also. I think he knows enough about it all to make the slabs. The slabs will stack, and I think they'd be made in Marfa; if not, they can be made in El Paso. So the structure's put up, and as you put it up, you slip the slabs down the H-beam. What we can actually do there [in Marfa] is a very important principle: there's no use designing something that nobody on earth knows how to make. Obviously, the structure shows completely, inside and out, and I hope it doesn't cost a fortune. I think they should be very strong and pretty. But if I can do them, they're my first real buildings.

We're putting roofs on the two big buildings at the Fort;[10] they're big, deeply curved, Quonset-type roofs. For the moment, because of the difficulties there, the ends are corrugated iron. But I had them put in the structure in thirds and sixths, so the ends can be glass, because it's an enormous space on top of the building – the same height as the building. So those two buildings are derived from these buildings [at the Block], even though they're going to exist first. It makes an axis, too, because you see through it from side to side because of the windows, but on the top, you'll see through it end to end, in a spectacular fashion – if it's glass – running that way. So even though they're re-hashed buildings, they'll still look pretty nice.

To me, everything has a lot of ramifications. I can't rattle them off right away. Doing good architecture for less money I think is the main idea. I think it's possible; I think it should happen. I have nothing against an industrial situation – I'm all for it. I think the nature of it has to be faced: you can misuse it, just as you can misuse or schmaltzify industrial materials; you can have good plastic and bad plastic, good corrugated iron and bad corrugated iron. You could take cities like Midland and Odessa and with the same amount of money, and almost the same construction, make something really nice out of them, which they aren't now.

A good portion of Marfa was originally made of adobes. In lots of cases, the windowpanes and the doorframes came from the east. What was possible to use there, because people knew how to make it, was adobe. So all the buildings, Latino and Anglo alike, are adobes. But by the time I came along, nobody made adobes there at all. It just seemed to be a logical material. At first, I bought some from people – Toltec Motel and the Virginia Hotel, when they were torn down.[11] Old adobes are not so great; they don't like to be moved too much. But there were only so many. I suppose Chango organized it. He spoke to some people in Mexico and started to have them come up to make the adobes and lay them. Usually there are two guys working.

PV   Can you talk at all about this square that you use for the windows in the Artillery Sheds and the doors and windows in the Block [image 65]? A lot of architects are very fond of this particular form, but they use it only for windows. I found it fascinating that you use that form as a pivoting gate that is either transparent, as in the Arena gate, or solid.

DJ   The first thing about that is that long ago, there was a relief with the cross incised and divided into four parts [see image 46]. So as a form, it goes way back. It basically has to do with grids. I did the windows over at the Marfa Wool and Mohair Building – which is now the Chamberlain Building – first, and they were just very broken-down sliding doors, which were no use at all. So I threw those out, and it became a question of how to make windows out of the openings; they are divided in quarters the same way, but one panel swivels. It wasn't necessary to open them up

so drastically. I guess that quartering is the simplest form
of a grid, or it relates to the relief, and to the little house
we lived in – there were just four rooms, that's all, right
together.[12] I was a little leery of it at first, because of its
religious side. But you just have to forget those things –
anyway, the Catholic cross has a longer stem.

On the Artillery Sheds, I started off with a window –
there were several possibilities. We actually did a couple of
wooden ones – nine parts, tic-tac-toe grid; maybe even a
twelve-part one … Anyway, I started with a more complicated grid, and they were nice. They seemed too complicated. We built two or three wooden ones – Chango did –
and it was kind of a case of simplifying them, and what
would stand up in the wind. Then the possibility came
up of using the aluminum, and of course then you could
really make it stronger. But the smaller grid seemed fussy,
and I kept working at it until I got down to the four-part
one. The outside, too, is important: there's the rectangle,
and then that's divided.

The one-quarter swiveled at the Chamberlain Building, then one-half of a door swiveled, so that led to the
idea of a whole swiveling gate. That gives you a really open
space, if you want one. Frank Lloyd Wright says that half a
window is stupid – if you make an opening and then you
always have half of it closed – and I think he's right. So
when you open the thing, it's wide open, and, of course,
you can have any other degree you want. They're a little
bit hazardous if they're wide open and it's really windy;
you need a pin that'll go down. And then they provide
something that's variable, that changes and moves around
all the time. They look good closed, half open, wide open.
They also provide, when they're wide open, something
that stands out and provides a little force or a little display –
like, say, [Ludwig] Mies [van der Rohe] when he takes the
beams on the outside that stick up as a flange. They do that

in a lesser way. It's a little display of bravura, without being anything nasty. And you can get rid of it, too: just close it. I think they're fairly practical; it's a simple connection. I want to do them for the ranch houses, where it swivels, but you need three things – you need a screen, glass, and a shutter. But I think you can put them all on one pivot.

The Arena was the gymnasium at the Fort. Someone tore out the wooden floor; the floor was then covered with sand so it could be used as a horse arena. When we took the sand and dirt out, we found the big concrete strips that had supported the gymnasium floor, and they were pretty nice, with the remaining gravel between them. The Arena is supposed to have a piece of art against the walls, so the floor is clear, and I didn't see any reason to lay the whole floor in concrete, since the art is against the walls. So the floor functions as a place to be. The end toward the kitchen had to be concrete so you could have a table and chairs; you can't really deal with the gravel when you're sitting around. And the other end, which has a strip of concrete, was to be a working area, so you need a smooth floor, too. So those two areas were given, one at either end, and in figuring it out, it occurred to me that with the change of another bay – and also, I think Lauretta [Vinciarelli] volunteered a suggestion or two there, adding another bay or taking one away – that the area of gravel and the area of concrete would be the same.[13] So it's really half and half, even though the concrete's in two parts.

I put the doors and windows on an axis and cleaned up the inside; it's mainly the concrete strips and the division that make it nice, and the door-windows. So I think it made something very good out of a rather simple situation. Some of these things were given – a clerestory's always nice. It's just inevitable.

PV   Maybe it would be easy to say that it's sort of a natural progression: because your work is so rigorously ordered, it's not surprising that the buildings are so rigorously ordered.

DJ	Sure; I mean, I don't understand why things shouldn't be ordered. If people can do it, why put the windows every which way? If you don't maintain the long view, or the view across the width, you're denying the space inside. You're just losing one of the dimensions of space. I understand them [buildings] if they're strong, or somewhat assertive, if it doesn't get into the whole side of power. But I don't understand them when they're very quaint, when they're complicated, or produce a lot of commotion, which most of the buildings do now. Everything is every which way, and I don't really see the point of that. Everything is every which way anyway; why not have something that's easier to deal with?

In general, I think people should think more about an industrial architecture. It's trite, but it's a completely new situation, and it's going to be new for a long time to come. This business of acting as if everything is dead and finished – cities are going to be around for a long time.

For a long time, I didn't know what to do with that space. The two adobe walls that make it up existed, and I used to park trucks in it when it still had the big doors. I thought of putting the Northwest Coast art in it, but it's too narrow; it's hard to figure out a use for it, because it's only twenty feet across. When I settled down to live there, it finally occurred to me that that was the place to put the library. The shelves developed from two problems; they're not just straight-across shelves – I did want them to be nice-looking, but they also had to be rather deep, because the roof leaks a little bit, and at that point the dust was still a problem, and light's a problem. So the overhang is a protection for the books. It makes a module – the little shape of the shelves within the great big shape of the rectangle.

PV   What about the piece at the bottom – the sort of step?

DJ   It's to make the whole rectangle. The top comes out two boards, and the verticals come out two boards to support it; this makes the two boards at the bottom. It's not a step. I didn't want to get too close to the floor, for all the same reasons – the drips bounce up. The main idea, too, is whenever you have a long rectangle, almost the only organization possible is in regard to the length of the rectangle, and everything has to go one way or the other: halves, thirds, whatever. If you try to deny it or ignore it, you never get anywhere. Any effort at making things crosswise is a mistake.

This conversation was sourced from a transcript that includes handwritten corrections by Viladas, as well as from the published article; the transcript includes material that was not used in the article. The archival transcript is in the Judd Foundation Archives, Marfa, Texas.

First published (excerpt): Pilar Viladas, "A Sense of Proportion," *Progressive Architecture*, April 1985, 102–9.

1   See Judd's "Marfa, Texas" (1985) in *Donald Judd Writings*, 424–32.

2   The Godbold feed mill, located across the street from La Mansana de Chinati/The Block, was constructed around 1963 and operated as a commercial livestock feed manufacturing facility until fall 2018.

3   Judd refers here to 101 Spring Street.

4   Judd planted seven plum trees in line with his daughter's bedroom on the east side of the Block.

5   For Judd's original plans for Rancho El Porvenir, see Judd's "Arroyo Grande" (1989) in *Donald Judd: Architektur*, 22–25.

6   In Roman city planning, the *decumanus maximus* was the central east-west street, while the *cardo maximus* was the main north-south street.

7   Judd lived with his family in Casa Lujan, a four-room house in the Sal Si Puedes neighborhood east of Marfa, before and during the move into the Block. See Judd's "Casa Lujan and La Catorcena" (1989) in *Donald Judd: Architektur*, 26–30.

8   Celedonio "Chango" Mediano, Jr. (1951–2002), was a carpenter in Marfa, Texas, who worked on many of Judd's architectural projects and built furniture for Judd's spaces in Texas. He worked with his brother Alfredo Mediano, who also oversaw the care of Judd's art. See Judd's "Marfa, Texas" (1985) in *Donald Judd Writings*, 430.

9   These buildings for La Mansana de Chinati/The Block were never realized.

10   Judd refers here to the Artillery Sheds.

11   In 1973, Judd began using adobe bricks from Marfa's postwar Toltec Motel and historic Virginia Hotel – both torn down by their owners – to build a nine-foot-high wall on the south side of the Block. This project continued until 1979, by which time the wall enclosed the Block on all sides. See Judd's "Marfa, Texas" (1985) in *Donald Judd Writings*, 428–29.

12   See note 7.

13   Lauretta Vinciarelli (1943–2011) was an artist, architect, and professor of architecture. Judd and Vinciarelli were partners for ten years. In 1974, Vinciarelli became the first woman to have drawings acquired by the Department of Architecture and Design at The Museum of Modern Art, New York.

Interview with Russell Connor
For the television documentary *American Art '85*
1985

Judd frequently criticized large museum exhibitions in his writing and interviews. In his 1989 essay "Ausstellungsleitungsstreit," for example, he wrote that very large exhibitions "never provide a true sense of what is being done in contemporary art. Most large collections of contemporary art are also not relevant.... The best work of the time is never seen together. The organizers promote work they favor; they regard art as a 'scene,' anything that occurs. In New York City examples of this are the annuals of the Whitney Museum of forty years ago, as well as now."

Judd had two works included in the *1985 Biennial Exhibition* at the Whitney Museum of American Art, New York (March 13–June 9, 1985). To promote the biennial, the Whitney created a half-hour-long television documentary, *American Art '85: A View from the Whitney*, which aired as part of a weekly series through July and August 1985 titled *You Gotta Have Art* on Channel 13 (now WNET), a public television station that serves the New York metropolitan area. *American Art '85* was written, produced, and narrated by Russell Connor, painter and former head of public education at the Whitney. Only a brief statement by Judd was included in the documentary.

R C   [Russell Connor] You started off part one of your article by saying, "The quality of new art has been declining for fifteen years.... There have been almost no first-rate artists in this time."[1]

D J   [Donald Judd] To start from another angle on that: I think that you have a bad situation now because – this is a little more, perhaps, fundamental than that as an idea – the art in the United States originally was made in a very private way, and not necessarily to sell. And it was not very large, or, if large, it was paintings. At the present time, the art has gotten beyond the making of portable paintings or objects and beyond the cash-and-carry situation, which seems to be the only one that will work. It's necessary now to do art – or artists want to do art – that is more involved with architecture, is larger, and, in my case, with three-dimensional work, is expensive to make. And to try to do any of this is next to impossible to do, because there's no institution that will cooperate, and there's virtually no interest in having it done. So primarily what you have is a simple cash-and-carry situation, and it hasn't gotten beyond that. It's kind of like the first folks in the Amazon or something; it's a rather rudimentary civilization. It's completely going to pot, because there's no allowance for the ambition of the artist to do something beyond these small saleable things. Now you have an even worse situation, where the art is even – with all the trouble that it takes even to get it made, it now is threatened with destruction, as in Richard Serra's case.[2]

R C   What relation does this have to the problems of business as a sponsor and art being reduced to a commodity?

D J   Art's not a commodity, and everybody should fight that idea. Business as a sponsor could be all right, but they don't really know very much about art, and they don't want anything beyond these portable objects and paintings, because it's too hard for them to deal with, and too complex.

Every time you get beyond this point, there's a great deal of red tape and interference by people who don't know anything about it, until finally nothing happens.

RC   But as lamentable as business might be – as patronly and preferable to government bureaucrats or the nouveau riche –

DJ   Well, the nouveau riche are also the business people; they go hand in hand. I don't think the government should have anything to do with art, as I said in the article. I think it's an exceedingly dangerous institution. I was always against the idea of the National Endowment grants and so forth. Now they're proving themselves, as again – with the case of Richard Serra and, I think, Bob Murray and other people – to be a total pain in the neck. What little was achieved is going to be destroyed. As I said in the article, the government can buy something if they want it, just like anyone else – buy what they like. If they want statues of somebody, they can buy statues of somebody. It's harmless and you can't do anything about it, so –

RC   How does that situation as you describe it explain what we see on the walls of the biennial?

DJ   As I said in the beginning of the article, ultimately, it's the responsibility of the artists to make good art, and there's no other way around that – that's the fundamental situation. I think the government involvement in the past fifteen years, and more and more in museums, makes a greater institutional situation, and I think that institutional situation is destructive, and I think for the younger people they're probably more vulnerable to that. Everybody gets in the habit of filling out the forms for grants and competing. I was objecting the other day about competing for commissions; I don't think artists are supposed to have to compete against one another, it's not that kind of activity. So you're sucked in – in order to work, you're sucked into this bureaucratic situation. I think that kind of spreads out throughout the whole situation, and, as I said, especially with younger people. When I began, there was hardly any art situation at all, so it's hard to be corrupted by something that doesn't exist.

RC   Could you touch on that?

DJ   The commerce gets more tied into that; I think the commercial dealers and the institutions sort of come together much more than they used to. But these social reasons don't explain all these things – never. They're a factor, but they're not the ultimate explanation. You also have to have people – and this goes on to the whole article, I mean – you have to have people who will say that things are good or bad. You don't have decent criticism, you don't have support for the art that's better, and it becomes a very lax situation.

RC   I want to get into that criticism: "For a century there have usually been two versions of each art, one real, but poor and underground, and one fake, although rich and conspicuous. The latter ingests the former as needed."[3] Can you expand on that in relation to today's situation?

DJ   The art that's in the history books is ordinarily the art that has been done pretty much by the artists on their own without any great financial support – and if you go around the cities and look at what actually got done, it's art or architecture that isn't very good that received the bulk of the money and is still there. This is happening now, too, as it's always happened. You see big expensive statues – I saw some elaborate thing in Bordeaux by someone I had never heard of, done around 1850 or 1860. It probably cost half the taxes of Bordeaux for a year to put the thing together. It's not by Rodin – who was later – or anybody who, you know, you would think is important now. All the architecture that so much money is going into now is not serious architecture.

RC   A hot topic going around the Whitney these days.

DJ   It's going to be a bad building.[4] I'll say that in public.

RC   [*Laughs*]

DJ   I jumped on Michael Graves in the article.

RC   Yes, I noticed. Art and democracy – the idea that art should
be democratic – you say, "Politics alone should be democratic. Art is intrinsically a matter of quality."[5]

DJ   Yeah.

RC   What about quality?

DJ   Quality is not undemocratic. Quality is simply quality. It's
not a form of elitism or anything; it's something well done.
You don't say that a good astronomer – since I was just at
an observatory[6] – is undemocratic; he's doing a good job.
Art is a cheap target for the government because it doesn't
cost much; it's really cheap as a way to wave democracy,
and if they were really serious about it, they would be
democratic in areas where it really counts. But they can
claim, as they do, to distribute the awards to artists all the
way across the United States, no matter what the quality
is, just so someplace will get one. These things are against
the integrity of art, and any kind of fooling around with
the politics of art and the politics in art is very bad for it.
Quality in art has nothing to do with democracy. I think
it's just a cheap shot at art, and ultimately, it's a cover-up for
real politics by citizens, which the United States government does not really want to happen. The issue of democracy and art is sort of a smoke screen to keep the folks from
really being serious about the government intervening.

RC   In the biennial – as around in the galleries – there's a lot
of work which borrows conspicuously from the art of
the past, as is going on in architecture too. You say, "In art
and architecture it's impossible to use forms from the past.
They become symbols, and not profound ones either"[7] –

DJ   There's no way that you can really understand the art that
was done in the past. It's too different. You can't even understand another person's work in a way whereby you
could do it and add to it – living at the present. It's a total

illusion that you could understand anything about the art of the past and make something that looks like it in the present and have it be good art, because the gap in information and way of living and everything is too great. I think this gap is so profound; evidently, other people don't think so, but –

RC   What about in quotations, where bits and pieces are used, where they're obviously not trying to re-create –

DJ   It's ridiculous. It's a total failure of invention in the present and them doing something new. The quotations are also so incredibly trite most of the time; it's kid's stuff.

[*Interruption*]

DJ   So anyway, the Whitney should not build a building by Michael Graves. [*Laughs*]

RC   We could make a special tape with you – I'd like to hear you at great length on that.

"There's been a new fashion biannually for fifteen years. The present characteristics in common are the constant derivation, usually blown-up, and the crassness of the execution."[8] Could you talk about that? It relates also to your comment about some present artists thinking of art as a career.

DJ   I think partly the fashion comes from the fact that a great deal happened very rapidly at the end of the '50s and beginning of the '60s. For a few years, there was a constant change, and the artists, I think, in this case, were generally good. But it became the habit of the museums to think that there was going to be something new every year, and it was handy for their educational purposes to have shows of new work, which they should do, but I think it's at a pattern that they've followed since then, and they expected the subsequent twenty years to be just like those five or six years – and they weren't. You just didn't have the series of artists one after the other, two or three a year, for five years, as you had then. So they started searching for whoever was new, the two or three artists that you needed for big shows that year. If you require this newness all the time, you're scraping the barrel pretty soon. I think, as I said, that became a habit. When there aren't any new artists that are very good, there aren't any, that's all.

RC   What about the principle of the biennial just as itself, trying to embrace what they think is the most vital work that's going on? "Vital" is a word that keeps coming up.

DJ   Obviously, that's a good idea. If the Whitney is trying to show the most vital work that is going on every two years, that's a fine idea, and they should do that. The big problem is, what's vital? There's a big difference in opinion on that matter. To preface this – the criticism – the Whitney is almost the only museum that I have any kind of relationship with, so I'm not that against them. I've had nothing whatsoever to do with the Modern or the Guggenheim, for example. The only other museums that I've been involved with are the National Gallery of Canada and the Van Abbemuseum in Eindhoven; otherwise, the world is just unknown to me. My original and still remaining criticism of the Whitney Biennials is that they were always very wrong about what was vital. It wasn't that they excluded the most vital work, but they thought quite an array was vital, which made very mediocre shows all the time. And almost always, the shows have been mediocre. [*Laughs*] [Thomas] Armstrong will kill me.[9]

RC   You're giving me good stuff.

DJ   I'm not sure that I saw a biennial on Eighth Street in the early '50s, but I remember seeing the ones when they moved next to The Museum of Modern Art.[10] Except I still think that the show that I saw the Pollock in was a biennial or an annual.[11] But they had those paintings – I first saw de Kooning's *Attic* in one of the shows, and so forth,[12] so you would have those paintings, and therefore the exhibition did show what was happening at the time which was the most vital, but you also, as you had for decades, had Paul Cadmus,[13] for example, and, you know —

RC   — trying to be encyclopedic.

DJ   Yes, but Paul Cadmus was not the most vital thing happening by a long shot. And many other people who were very academic and I think very ordinary artists. So it wasn't that they excluded anybody, but they included too much junk, and that's really depressing — for every ten paintings to see one that's good. It doesn't make a good exhibition.

RC   Well, there has been a recent shift, at least in the mind of Tom Armstrong, that instead of trying to be as universal — that in the last ten years particularly, they've tried to take a stand. You applaud that?

DJ   Yes, they should take a stand. The artist has to make a judgment that's serious in order to make their paintings or whatever, and the viewer has to make a comparable judgment. You can't just play it across the board on the theory that later on you're going to sound okay because you showed Pollock very early, or Rothko, or whoever. Leo Castelli does that all the time with his shows; it looks great in the history books, but at the time, there's one mediocre show after another. If you look at the list of the names of any of those early Whitney shows, nobody now knows who they are. I've noticed that Paul Cadmus is still around, however.

RC   He is, actually.

DJ   [*Laughs*]

RC   He's a tough one for you, because I think of you, from my perspective, as a young artist, but you were a senior citizen in this group at the Whitney — you and [Jasper] Johns and [Robert] Mangold. Someone has talked about the youth cult represented in that show; do you have any comment on that, the emphasis on young career-minded artists?

DJ   Well, it's fine to be young; I'm against the career-minded-
      ness. I don't think there should be a seniority system
      whereby good artists wait for years before they get some
      sort of recognition. Lots of artists have been very good,
      very young. I think there's a certain tendency — which
      isn't very unusual now or in history — for some older art-
      ists to get neglected or taken for granted. Naturally, their
      work has a certain continuity and it's not new or fashion-
      able every year, because it's made to suit yourself and you
      don't change that much. People should have a little bit of
      tolerance for this. It's not fun for a lot of artists to be — I
      don't think this is my case particularly — it's pretty bad to
      be neglected at the end of what they may consider a pretty
      busy life. I can think of Al Jensen, for example, who died a
      few years ago; Jensen should have received more attention.[14]
      He's a better artist than his general standing in the situ-
      ation reflected. James Brooks is one of my classic exam-
      ples of a really pretty good artist; he's not Jackson Pollock,
      but still he's a pretty good artist.[15] And Milton Resnick.[16]
      I mean, these people are kind of neglected. That's not so
      sweet if you're in their position. Then when you think
      of some idiot around here getting a lot of money while
      Milton Resnick pokes along, that's not so great at all. I'm
      not sure he pokes along, but anyway, I'm making a guess.

RC   Okay, we've got a lot of great stuff, and I won't keep you
      much longer. Getting back to something you said earlier
      about the failure of criticism, in part two you start off say-
      ing, "None of the groups that can be expected to defend
      serious art do so, neither the critics, the museums, the gal-
      leries, the educators, nor even the artists."[17] Will you talk
      about that?

DJ   I think that the gap between the artists and the critics is
      enormous. Basically, the so-called critics, which I'd hardly
      be willing to call them, don't know what the art's all about,
      don't know what's going on, don't talk to the artists. There

is really no community of opinion on the matter. They're very different people, and, as I said, the gap is enormous. The artists really are – among themselves, they're artists, but somehow the minute you talk to somebody else, you are into a very alien world. I think somebody should think about that gap. I think the gap between the artists and the public is tremendous. It's one of the reasons why you can't do anything beyond this cash-and-carry system. The minute you try to talk about a large work or you deal with an institution, the incomprehension of the people at the institution is incredible. I think there's considerable hostility even to the art. I think they're kind of offended at having to deal with it.

R C   Which brings me right up to my last question. A visitor to the biennial comes up to your two works who is not very educated in an art background; would you suggest any tip as to how they might approach your work?

D J   I don't know anything about average visitors.

R C   Don't you have any in your family? I have a lot of average visitors in my family.

D J   [*Laughs*] Basically, the public is unknown to me.

R C   How would you like your work to be approached?

D J   I think people should try to look and think, and I don't think they really do that. That's the most elementary thing you can say. They don't really look at what's there and think about why it's there, what it means to be there, and that somebody, after all, is attempting to make a meaningful object, as in this case. The premise has to be that it means something. If they think about it and then figure out from their point of view that it doesn't mean anything, then it's their opinion, and at least they've made an effort. I think seldom is there any effort made.

R C   Have you seen people, like docents in a museum, try to explain work?

D J   Mostly they're not explaining anything – they're just repeating what's in the survey books, which are ordinarily clichés that are wrong. [*Laughs*] It's mostly misinformation.

RC   Anything before we close that you want to say? Any parting last words? Don't say again that Michael Graves shouldn't build a new building.

DJ   [*Laughs*] I think that I should build it.

RC   Huh?

DJ   You should tell Tom Armstrong that I'll build it. [*Laughter*]

This conversation was sourced from a video recording. The original video recording is in the Frances Mulhall Achilles Library and Archives, Whitney Museum of American Art, New York.

First published (excerpt): *American Art '85: A View from the Whitney*, directed and narrated by Russell Connor (New York: Whitney Museum of American Art, 1985), video, 28 min.

1   See Judd's "A Long Discussion Not About Master-Pieces But Why There Are So Few of Them: Part I" (1983) in *Donald Judd Writings*, 353. As suggested by Connor, this article has more than one part: see also Judd's "A Long Discussion Not About Master-Pieces But Why There Are So Few of Them: Part II" (1984) in *Donald Judd Writings*, 378–97. "Part I" was first published in *Art in America*, September 1984, 9–19; "Part II" was first published in *Art in America*, October 1984, 9–15.

2   Richard Serra's *Tilted Arc* (1981) was installed at Manhattan's Foley Federal Plaza in 1981. After acrimonious public debate and a drawn-out federal lawsuit, the sculpture was removed in 1989.

3   Judd, "A Long Discussion Not About Master-Pieces But Why There Are So Few of Them: Part I," 356.

4   In 1985, Thomas N. Armstrong III, then the director of the Whitney, developed plans for a ten-story addition to the museum's main 1966 Marcel Breuer building to be designed by Michael Graves. After significant opposition, the plan was dropped in 1989.

5   Judd, "A Long Discussion Not About Master-Pieces But Why There Are So Few of Them: Part I," 357.

6   Judd refers here to the McDonald Observatory, part of The University of Texas at Austin, located in the Davis Mountains of West Texas. He became a member of the observatory's Board of Visitors in 1989.

7   Judd, "A Long Discussion Not About Master-Pieces But Why There Are So Few of Them: Part I," 361.

8   Ibid., 365.

9   Thomas N. Armstrong III (1932–2011) was an American museum curator and the director of the Whitney Museum of American Art, New York,
from 1974 to 1990.

10   The Whitney was originally located at 8–12 West Eighth Street; in 1954,
it moved to 22 West Fifty-Fourth Street, next to The Museum of Modern Art.

11   Pollock showed work in four Whitney Annuals between the time Judd
moved to the New York metropolitan area in 1948 and Pollock's death in
1956.

12   De Kooning's *Attic* (1949) appeared in *Annual Exhibition of Contemporary
American Painting*, Whitney Museum of American Art, New York, December 16, 1949–February 5, 1950.

13   Paul Cadmus (1904–1999) was an American artist known for his satirical
figurative paintings.

14   In 1963, Judd wrote, "Now and then a chance occurs for a narrow, subjective, categorical statement: Jensen is great." See Judd's review of Jensen's exhibition *Duality Triumphant* (1963) in *Donald Judd: Complete Writings 1959–1975*, 85–86.

15   See Judd's "James Brooks: *Ainlee*" (1959) in *Donald Judd Writings*, 40–52.

16   See Judd's review of *Milton Resnick: Paintings* (1960) in *Donald Judd: Complete Writings 1959–1975*, 13.

17   Judd, "A Long Discussion Not About Master-Pieces But Why There Are
So Few of Them: Part II," 379.

"Donald Judd"
Interview with Michael Archer for *Audio Arts*
March 1986

Audio Arts was a cassette-based audio magazine founded by William Furlong and Barry Barker in 1972. Its ambition was to document the activity of contemporary artists by recording conversations held in proximity to their work. In addition to this interview, volume 8 of *Audio Arts* included contributions from Rasheed Araeen, Mona Hatoum, John Latham, Julian Schnabel, Nancy Spero, and Andy Warhol. In 2004, the Tate acquired the *Audio Arts* archive.

This interview was conducted at the Waddington Galleries, London, on the occasion of *Donald Judd*, Judd's first solo exhibition at the venue (March 5–27, 1986).

MA   [Michael Archer] We're in the Waddington Galleries, where you've just installed your latest show. Do the works, which range from colored aluminum panels to ply constructions and zinc pieces, represent investigations into concerns like those you've previously explored, or is there any departure from them – in the painted aluminum panels, for instance?

DJ   [Donald Judd] Well, always there are new things and some old things. The vertical piece of galvanized iron, or zinc, as you say, is an old idea. The piece is newly made with clear plexiglass in a combination I have never used before, but as an idea it goes back to 1964, '65. The colored pieces have only been made in the last couple of years – they're made in Dübendorf, near Zürich – and are a new idea [image 66].[1]

MA   You say they're made in Zürich. Is that simply a pragmatic decision, in that the constructors are there?

DJ   The main thing is that the color is not possible in the United States, because almost all commercial colors there have a bit of white in them, and it's impossible to get clear colors that are commercially made. In Switzerland, these colors are used for traffic signs and buses and airplanes, and all sorts of things; they don't put white in, so the color's very clear and very durable. And it's not paint – it's powder baked on. I'm not too clear about the process.

MA   Could you say something about the use of color in these works, and why you've introduced it?

DJ   I'm very interested in the material that my work is made of, and showing that material, but because any kind of material is mostly gray, that eliminates color. So there's always been this problem of how to make color and how to deal with it as a thing in itself, just as the material is. A lot of times I've used plexiglass, which, clearly, it's plexiglass and it's colored. I used to use paint, but it tended to be another surface that you put on metal, which to some extent falsifies the metal. This is still that way a little bit, but I think because of the thinness of the aluminum, it makes the coating in the color very conspicuous as that sort of thing – or at least the technique is more definite than just covering up a surface. I wanted to use color; it's something I've always liked and haven't been able to use for a long time, and this makes it possible to use a really wide range of different colors, different combinations. It's all loosely based upon a very elaborate scheme of color [image 67].

MA   Could you say something about that scheme?

DJ   The scheme's meant to be worked from – it's not meant to make rules. One of the problems at first was that I tended to go by my old rules, which all turned out to be obsolete, or react to things that I disliked in other people's work in terms of color, and that turned out to be obsolete, too. So the best rule is not to react for or against previous ideas.

MA   Nevertheless, there must be a procedure that you adopt in deciding which colors you're going to actually use on the various modules of the pieces, and also how the color interacts and relates to the color on the next module. Is there a conscious process by which you make those decisions?

DJ   Yeah, it's perfectly conscious, but it also allows for a certain amount of chance, and I don't want to pin it down too much. The scheme is based upon – it's not a tight scheme at all – it's just possibilities all pinned up on a bulletin board in a factory in Dübendorf. It's based upon not only one color in relation to another color and what they do to each other – as, for example, in Josef Albers's thinking – but also as pairs of color, triads of color. Certain pairs we take as almost a single color, like black and white. I mean, black and white is so much a pair that you just take it. So you can take black and white and juxtapose it to another pair that's very much a matched pair, that you don't think of in this very ordinary way that's more self-conscious. Red and black – together they are a very definite pair.[2]

They almost make another color. Those can be joined to more complex combinations, or they can be joined to a very close combination, like two reds together, where, obviously, you are putting two reds together. So in a way, you have a pair that's one thing that can be juxtaposed to a pair that's definitely a pair, and on and on.

MA   You mention Albers, and you also say that you're interested in looking at color in a way that perhaps avoids some of the things we associate with it. In the way that you are treating it with this loose scheme, is there any reference in your work to how color has been used by other painters or other sculptors – perhaps neoplasticists or constructivists?

DJ   Well, those are among all the prior ideas that I try to forget, and they're a little hard to forget. It's not necessarily that I dislike them. Other people put things into a different context, and you don't want the context, and as I said earlier, I try not to be for or against any of those. It's a mistake. As to the two reds, for example – there was an artist in New York named Ludwig Sander who used green and blue, slightly off from each other, in lots of paintings.[3] Well, I hated blue and green, which are close together, and especially when the value is rather close. So that's a dislike that I avoided. So I thought, "Just forget Ludwig Sander, and go ahead and do it if you want to do it." That's one way to do it. Red and black was used very much by the Russians. It's terrific. It's used by lots of people all over the world, all through history, so why not use it? That's something I liked that I used; the other is something I disliked that I used. Just try to forget all those, so you can make a new context and make a new situation, and then the colors are different.

MA   Could you say something, then, about the context that you are working in and creating, and also something about the role that you see chance playing in your work?

DJ   Chance – I suppose that's one way of saying, to some extent, what the work's about. Ordinarily, in the art history books, they say that my work is very Platonic and very ideal and all that, which to me is a lot of nonsense, since that is the opposite of my philosophical tendency. And so, when a work is very definite and looks Platonic to, say, Rosalind Krauss, I'm simply being definite in a very local way, and that implies that, while I can be definite, there can be a lot of chance elsewhere.[4] I can't deal directly with chance as, for example, Jackson Pollock or John Chamberlain do, because my temperament as an artist isn't suited to making a lot of random things right in front of me. But I think that the work implies beyond itself that it's a relatively chaotic and random world; it just happens to be that I want to order my own particular part of it. It's not an overwhelming ordering, as you have in the old rationalist philosophy. Color and the pieces are meant to have a certain amount of chance. Even if they were extremely controlled, as I'm trying not to do, it's still pretty unpredictable when you put two of them together, and especially if you put two or three together in different proportions or areas. It's hard to tell what it's going to look like, and that's even in the most controlled way. I like it if it's less controlled. I don't mind "taking a chance" on the whole thing. I think, as a general statement, art always has serious philosophical purposes, and this relationship of chance or not chance or how much ordering or not and all that is a view of the world that ordinarily the best art has to have, one way or another.

MA   If we take one of your zinc and plexiglass works and consider the space, in terms of years, between that kind of conception and these new aluminum pieces you're doing at the moment, how have you seen the development of your work between those two points?

DJ   Well, not so much; it's mostly change. I don't have a great idea of my own development. I didn't intend to — and I never intended to – push for some sort of progress or development, because I think that takes care of itself. You get older and have a different view of things, and when you're around a long time, the work develops and you think of different possibilities, and it's not something that has to be pushed, really, because I think it's a very natural activity. So I never had this built-in sense of progress that some artists are supposed to have in the history books, whether they have them or not. Mostly, I consider it just change. I have lots of older pieces; I like them perfectly well. They were done by me, not knowing a lot of what I know now, and with different attitudes about different things. But it's hard to view them as progress. When I first did the three-dimensional pieces, I considered them as opening up a lot of possibilities, and they did, and that's still what's going on.

I don't think there's sufficient communication from generation to generation anymore, and I think that's a necessity for art, and that the best artists should be teaching the students. The best artists mostly don't want to do this, because it's not economically good for them, and the schools aren't set up for that arrangement. So primarily, the students learn from artists who are not very good, or from teachers who are not artists at all. More and more they learn from magazines, too, which is a total disaster. I read recently some long article about where younger people were reacting to my work, but not from seeing it – and certainly not from knowing me – but from reading about it in the damn magazines, which are always wrong. So they're reacting to something that's a total artificial history. And then where do we wind up? I mean, it's one falsehood piled upon another one. They have to find out what the artist really thinks the works mean, and they can only learn that from the artist. It's not a matter of transmitting information; it's just not that kind of activity.

This conversation was sourced from an audio recording. The recording is in the *Audio Arts* archive, Tate, London.

First published: Michael Archer, "Donald Judd," *Audio Arts* 8, no. 2–3, 1987, tape 2; reprinted: "Donald Judd Interviewed by Michael Archer," in *Speaking of Art: Four Decades of Art in Conversation*, ed. William Furlong (London: Phaidon, 2010), 84–88.

1   Lehni AG, based in Dübendorf, Switzerland, was the first fabricator of Judd's painted aluminum works and metal furniture. See Judd's "On Furniture" (1986) in *Donald Judd Writings*, 453.

2   As Judd wrote in 1993, "Red and black together are so familiar that they almost form a new unity." See Judd's "Some Aspects of Color in General and Red and Black in Particular" (1993) in *Donald Judd Writings*, 832–58.

3   Ludwig Sander (1906–1975) was an American artist known for his colorful hard-edge paintings.

4   Rosalind E. Krauss (1941–) is an American art critic, theorist, and professor. Krauss was an associate editor of *Artforum* from 1971 to 1974 and is an editor of *October*, which she cofounded in 1976. "Allusion and Illusion in Donald Judd" was one of Krauss's first essays published in *Artforum* in May 1966.

"Interview with Donald Judd"
Article by Paul Taylor for *Flash Art*
September–October 1986

This interview was conducted just prior to the opening of *Donald Judd* at Paula Cooper Gallery, New York (October 4–November 1, 1986), but was not published until the following May. *Donald Judd* was Judd's first solo exhibition at Paula Cooper Gallery, although he had participated in a number of group shows at the gallery, beginning with *Benefit for the Student Mobilization Committee to End the War in Vietnam* (October 22–31, 1968).

One of the historical fictions that sustained minimal art was surely that of artistic progress – that art was going anywhere – anywhere, that is, but in circles. Its content, fundamentally, was the inscription of a historical consciousness onto an apparently neutral and idealistic circumstance: the encounter of a viewer with an object. Now, except for the firsthand accounts that we call art criticism, what remains of those days is just the viewers and the objects. The historical consciousness has disappeared like ice blocks in boiling water.

Since then we have become used to the gentle rocking motion of the art world. Haim Steinbach is the typical '80s version of a minimalist. There is nothing truly minimal about his art, of course, but he effectively "quotes" minimalism as a style and displays it in all its original gawkiness, dumbness, and razzamatazz – just as the "mature" work of Gilbert & George is more and more this decade's answer to Judy Chicago's, their recent photomurals *The Dinner Party* for meat eaters. The circular motion of the art world in the '80s has become a spectacle more interesting than its effects, and as captivating as the art of the past.

Donald Judd – earlier a prolific writer on art – has attempted an explanation of the current state of affairs. Writing of the art market and the corrupted expectations of the art audience, he mapped what appears to me as a fallacious economic fallacy onto the historicist one. The market might have replaced a particular reading of history as the motor of contemporary art, but such an observation falls far short of an explanation of the changes in art since the '60s. As the following interview shows, Judd even now finds it difficult to speak engagingly of his own art. Those terms – formal descriptions, arid environmental "contextualizations," historical validations – now simply fail to stir one's imagination.

Donald Judd spends most of his time in Texas, where he is at work on establishing the Chinati Foundation, following a legal debacle with the Dia foundation.[1] He seems happily ignorant of the contemporary art scene – including the so-called neominimalists, who outnumber the old minimalists a hundred to one. It was during a visit to New York, just prior to last year's exhibition at Paula Cooper Gallery, that I spoke to Donald Judd and was struck by his obstinance – and his isolation.

DJ   [Donald Judd] I don't have anything against *Flash Art*. I just don't read it. Art magazines have never been very good. It's a big generalization, but at this point I'm willing to make it. I think that art magazines are next to being irrelevant to the work that's being done. There's almost no discussion in them about art. *Artforum* was better in the '60s. It wasn't fabulous. It got a little better there for a short time, then it quickly went downhill. Art magazines don't even report what's happening. They aren't generally even correct factually. They're very much tied to the business, to the galleries.

PT   [Paul Taylor] Do you think that young artists are being written about too much?

DJ   I don't remember that when I was younger it was ever any different. There was very little written about the first show that I had at the Green Gallery [see images 2, 3].[2] And somehow that's switched from being almost ignored to being a famous show. Who knows what happened in the middle? I don't think that art criticism is taken – either by its practitioners or by other people – as a sufficiently serious activity, and as usual with anything, there's not enough money. People have to be paid well so they have enough time to do things. When I did all those reviews it was important to me economically, but I think I got about $120 a month. It was a valuable part-time job, but a good article would take at least a month to do. And you can't live in New York on less than $2,000 a month. It means you'd have to get a minimum of $2,000 for the article, and at the magazines no one is going to pay that.

But when commerce takes over and the whole structure takes over, it undermines the real art. Then forms of art develop that are commercially viable but are hardly art anymore, which also happens to music and architecture. I think a lot of the sloshy painting almost makes a new category where no rules – rules in the sense of thought – apply. They shrug and say, "Well, it's painting, it has to exist in its own category," and that's always a way of canceling out thought and critical judgment. Like, you're not supposed to say anything against musical comedy. People like musical comedy. You can say that musical comedy is junk, which I think it is pretty much, and if you put it up against good music, it's bad, that's all. That's legitimate to do.

PT   You are attaching a moral value to the state of art now. You are using the words "good" and "bad" a lot –

DJ   Yes, I'm rather free with them.

PT   What you think is bad, another might think is good.

DJ   I think it's bad if the idea of investment becomes too strong. To some extent that's all right because it's more or less going to happen, but when it becomes the main thing, it undermines the real nature of art. The commerce has to be the by-product of real activity.

PT   The corporations' infiltration of taste is a favorite subject of discussion now. Do you think the intelligent artist nowadays critiques that situation, the way, say, Hans Haacke does, or do you just battle on?

DJ   The way I differ from his is that I don't want it in my work. I think it undermines the work to deal with it directly as something within the work in a very literal fashion, as Hans Haacke does. I think the points are fine, and to do good work you have to be aware of what the society's like. The fundamental thing is to resist.

PT   How do you resist?

DJ   I write. You object, you try to control the shows and what happens to the work. Object and fight back, I have fights galore.

PT   We'll get around to that, but in the art object that you

make, is there a trace of this new context for art that is becoming so overpowering?

DJ   I am in favor of doing things directly. The art has to be
      done as a whole and literal things of almost any kind un-
      dermine the fundamental strength, the meaning of it. To
      me, Haacke's work is literature and not very good art. As
      art it's not interesting. I'm sympathetic with the points
      that are being made. I object very much when my work
      is said to not be political, because my feelings about the
      social system are in there somewhere. The idea is to have
      it all in there together – you can't pull it out.

PT   I remember reading an interview that you and Frank Stella
      gave in the early '60s in which you made the claims that
      European art was finished, that it was about the interrela-
      tionships of parts within a painting or sculpture, and that
      American art wasn't.[3] Do you now think that that com-
      ment was incredibly chauvinistic?

DJ   No, not necessarily, I don't think so. First of all, you have
      to remember it's 1964 and there was almost no good Eu-
      ropean art. Usually when I'm writing against European art
      I'm talking about the traditional art and not the so-called
      modern art, which I consider a transition into something
      new which everybody's doing, or should do. So generally,
      I was jumping on things that I considered old-fashioned
      and dead in European art. As a critic I used to receive
      Cimaise for some reason.[4] That magazine was unbeliev-
      ably chauvinistic; it was outrageous. I remember an arti-
      cle where they said that Pollock's work came from Wols;
      it's ridiculous. Wols is a much inferior artist to Pollock.
      The prevailing artists in France were [Alfred] Manessier,
      for example, and [Pierre] Soulages. A lot of it was slight.
      The whole tradition of the nature of European art – more
      or less the realistic tradition – is finished. I'm actually not
      against Europe. I'm in Switzerland a lot; I work with a fac-
      tory in Switzerland.[5] I will probably have a studio there.[6]

PT   Apart from those things, I still wonder about the idea of American art as somehow more rationalist; that European art is about the interrelationship of parts whereas American art did away with all that.

DJ   Well, it's not even all American art. For example, Rauschenberg – I will include him under the label of European art because he's very much the old-fashioned sort of artist with this particular interrelationship of parts. He's just a blown-up Schwitters. Schwitters is a lot better, in fact.

PT   Is this tendency you characterized as "American" still going on?

DJ   I think it's the major development and it's the way to make something brand-new that doesn't have anything to do with the tradition of art, but right now with a lot of the painting and sculpture there is a movement backward, and most of what is going on now I consider very traditional and old-fashioned.

PT   What is going on now that is not traditional and old-fashioned?

DJ   People like me, that's about it.

PT   You don't think that artists like yourself might have been an exception or aberration or temporary phenomenon? Maybe you were kidding yourselves that history was going in a particular direction –

DJ   In the first place I don't count too much on history, but that just as you make social generalizations you're bound to make historical generalizations. Of course, you should be very wary of them. I can't imagine that a lot of this stuff that I've seen a lot of my life and that is revived again is anything but dead.

PT   Is the idea that art is evolving and going someplace a perversion of some Judeo-Christian and Marxist notion of history?

DJ   I think that art has to change, which is not necessarily progress. "Change" is the bigger word.

PT   Yes, well, it's changed again.

DJ   I'm very much against those grand schemes of history –
       Christianity or Marxism or any grand scheme – because
       I don't see much sign of it. But things one way or another
       do change, and I think that art has to be new, just as peo-
       ple are new. Going backward is not change.

PT   It doesn't look like what was going on before.

DJ   It does too. It looks like what I saw all around me in art
       school. All these things I see in the galleries are the hack
       art by the GIs who didn't want to do anything in the Art
       Students League.

PT   You suggested in one of your recent essays that there was
       a complicity between the market and neoexpressionism.[7]
       Is there something intrinsically reactionary about expres-
       sionistic forms of art that assimilates it so well into the
       market?

DJ   I think that because it is old-fashioned the public likes
       it better, they're more likely to buy it. It's easier to sell.
       [Leo] Castelli and a lot of dealers are willing to undercut
       the market – to sell it a little cheaper. This is a standard
       mercantile activity. And it's what they're doing with the
       so-called neoexpressionist painting. Instead of them pay-
       ing, say, $60,000 or $70,000 for, say, a [James] Rosenquist
       painting – I think he's a good artist – they can sell [Julian]
       Schnabel or somebody for $40,000 or $50,000. The pub-
       lic likes it, and it's probably easier for them to take. Then
       you can undercut Schnabel too until finally the quality is
       shot completely and you have to start over.

PT   At what point will we start over?

DJ   When the public totally disbelieves that there's anything
       to it. People aren't going to quit making art, so good art
       will crop up somewhere else. In another area or simply
       with another group of people.

PT   I wonder whether we're already at a heightened stage of
       disbelief. In your writings there's a prejudice about neo-

expressionism and its success in the art market, and an implied superiority of previous art movements like minimalism. But in the case of the present neominimalism in painting in New York, the market can be shown to be just as involved. Obviously there's nothing intrinsically good or bad about any of these art forms.

DJ   Actually, I don't know anything about this. It's something I've heard about only very recently. I'm usually pretty wary of work that's related to mine. And I'm not for going backward. The thing is to do something new. I would assume that the taste for this new work comes out of the same ignorance that the liking for neoexpressionism does.

PT   In *House & Garden* you wrote that "nothing existing now, despite the growth of activity in museums and so-called public art, is sufficiently close to the interests of the best art."[8] What is in the interests of the best art?

DJ   First of all, that it gets made. I and the people I know mostly poke along. I live off smaller pieces, which is fine, but I want to do larger pieces. You don't live forever, so there's a little reason to hurry. Secondly, that it is placed in good situations, and thirdly, that it gets taken care of, and the critics and the museums are not doing that. Things have to be installed well and taken care of not in an environment that's made by some hack architect.

PT   In what ways is your work different now from twenty years ago?

DJ   There's a greater variety and certain ideas are clearer. There are certainly more larger pieces. Basically, it's the same work. One reason the new work developed was because I wanted to use more color [image 68; see also image 66]. In some ways these are more drastically spatial.

PT   What kind of painting do you think could be interesting now?

DJ   I wrote against painting as a whole form and naturally I was writing about it as it was at the time. I think I said it was dead, and that's quoted now and again. Maybe I was too right. I think it really is dead, and it's a shame. I believe you can take things into different contexts where you don't have the flat canvas against the wall and do something else with it. The big question is the integrity of the flat thing on the flat wall, and whether you can do something new with that without doing plain old paintings. I have some strong opinions about it all.

PT They give rise to what become a series of complaints in your two-part essay that was published in *Art in America* and *Art Monthly*.[9] Now you're talking about expanding on those essays.

DJ Yes, I think it's a lousy world and I hope I write the book.

First published: Paul Taylor, "Interview with Donald Judd," *Flash Art*, May 1987, 35–37.

1   For more on the Chinati Foundation's early relationship with Dia, see Judd's "Statement for the Chinati Foundation/La Fundación Chinati" (1987) in *Donald Judd Writings*, 484–89.

2   *Don Judd*, Green Gallery, New York, December 17, 1963–January 11, 1964. This exhibition was Judd's first solo show to include works in three dimensions. Reviews of the exhibition include Brian O'Doherty, "Recent Openings," *The New York Times*, December 21, 1963, 20; Michael Fried, "New York Letter," *Art International*, February 15, 1964, 25–26; G. R. Swenson, "Reviews and Previews: New Names This Month," *ARTnews*, February 1964, 20; Sidney Tillim, "The New Avant-Garde," *Arts Magazine*, February 1964, 20–21; Lucy R. Lippard, "New York," *Artforum*, March 1964, 18–19; and Hilton Kramer, "Art Centers: New York, the Season Surveyed," *Art in America*, June 1964, 112.

3   See "New Nihilism or New Art?" (1964) in this volume, 28–58.

4   *Cimaise* was a French review of contemporary art; it was published from 1953 to 2009.

5   Lehni AG, based in Dübendorf, Switzerland, was the first fabricator of Judd's painted aluminum works and metal furniture. See Judd's "On Furniture" (1986) in *Donald Judd Writings*, 453.

6   Judd refers here to Eichholteren.

7   See Judd's "A Long Discussion Not About Master-Pieces But Why There
        Are So Few of Them: Part I" (1983) and "A Long Discussion Not About
        Master-Pieces But Why There Are So Few of Them: Part II" (1984) in
        Donald Judd Writings, 352–76 and 378–97, respectively. "Part I" was first
        published in *Art in America*, September 1984, 9–19; "Part II" was first pub-
        lished in *Art in America*, October 1984, 9–15.
8   See Judd's "Marfa, Texas" (1985) in *Donald Judd Writings*, 430.
9   Judd, "A Long Discussion Not About Master-Pieces But Why There Are So
        Few of Them: Part I" and "A Long Discussion Not About Master-Pieces
        But Why There Are So Few of Them: Part II."

"Donald Judd's Little Logic"
Interview with Catherine Millet for *Artpress*
April 1987

Conducted by Catherine Millet, the founder and editor of *Artpress*, during Judd's
exhibition *Repères: Judd*, at Galerie Maeght Lelong, Paris (April 8–May 16, 1987),
this interview was published in November of the same year in French.

 Repères was Judd's first solo exhibition at Galerie Maeght Lelong. Included in
its catalogue was a large excerpt from Judd's essay "Art and Architecture" (1983),
in which he wrote: "My work has the appearance it has, wrongly called 'objective'
and 'impersonal,' because my first and largest interest is in my relation to the natural world, all of it, all the way out. This interest includes my existence, a keen interest, the existence of everything, and the space and time that is created by the
existing things. Art emulates this creation or definition by also creating, on a small
scale, space and time."

CM   [Catherine Millet] It strikes me that several sculptors of your generation, such as Tony Smith, Sol LeWitt, and yourself, worked as painters before becoming sculptors.

DJ   [Donald Judd] In my case, yes, it's true. I can't speak for the others.

CM   Does your sculptural work find its origin in painting? And does painting's tendency toward the picture still characterize your work today?

DJ   I think the origin of my work does lie in painting. My work doesn't arise from sculpture; it comes out of the paintings of Pollock, Newman, Rothko.

CM   That's a paradox.

DJ   Painting was more advanced than sculpture. For me, sculpture is a really old-fashioned thing. The only sculptor I've thought a lot about and admired is David Smith.

CM   Does that mean that sculpture has helped to resolve certain problems that existed in painting?

DJ   My work did away with these problems. These questions that arose from painting were eliminated by what is called "sculpture" and by what I myself don't call "sculpture." I don't know what you call "sculpture"; for me, it refers to carving, which is not what I do.

CM   Has the way in which Frank Stella evolved, adding more and more volume to paintings, helped to resolve these sorts of problems?

DJ   Frank is a friend, and it's a bit delicate talking about him. First of all, he transforms painting into bas-relief, which is still an old-fashioned approach. And although it may not be my choice, what the others do is their right. I think that [John] Chamberlain, for example, is more radical. You have to pay attention when someone talks about "problems," because problems in art are not like problems in science; their definition isn't as precise. To speak of my own situation, I thought that the problems of painting, in the vast sense of the word, couldn't be resolved, and I was tired of fighting against them. And then, for me, three-dimensionality simply revealed itself to be more interesting. I quickly got rid of what I couldn't resolve. Changing categories, moving toward sculpture, and turning away from painting: many artists have made this switch and produced work that's worse in my opinion, and I get a little sad about it, because I liked what they were up to before. If painting has a totality, and it likely does, it resides in flatness, which totally contradicts Michelangelo and totally agrees with the Greeks. And if we can do anything, it's keep the work very flat, make it even flatter, by approaching flatness – of course – by way of color. For example, mural painting is very interesting. It's existed for a long time, and it offers a lot of possibilities. As for three-dimensional work, it should be three-dimensional. In other words, you take the two categories and you push them as far as possible. Which leaves Frank in the middle of nowhere.

CM   What do you think of painters like Brice Marden or Robert Mangold?

DJ   They're two artists I respect.

CM   In any case, they work on a flat two-dimensional surface.

DJ   In both cases, I think their work should be even more flat, have more to do with the surface. Maybe Bob Ryman is more in the direction I'm thinking. Anyway, they're two good artists.

CM   Would you agree if I said that your old sculptures used more illusionism than the more recent ones, given your use of certain materials such as galvanized steel, plexiglass?

DJ   No, I'm not interested in the word "illusion," nor in "illusionism." That all goes back to illusionism in painting, and that illusionism is very different than what I'm capable of. For me, the materials are the materials. Certain ones are shinier than others. I'm interested in surfaces; plexiglass, for example, has a depth to it. For me, the reflection and depth of plexiglass don't produce illusionism in the traditional sense. If you'd like, you could use another word – "new illusionism," perhaps – but there's no intentional illusionism going on here.

CM   Even so, I have the impression that your use of these materials optically changes the volume.

DJ   The color and material change the volume, sure. But it isn't necessarily illusion. When you draw a square, it has a shape; when you color it in, its proportions change. That isn't necessarily illusion.

CM   Does this relationship between volume and color play a similar role in your recent work?

DJ   No. It's a bit complicated, because they have many colors. I find these pieces very three-dimensional, but as their constituent parts are rather narrow, the colors don't change them as much as in the wooden pieces. There's a certain limit to what color can alter in a volume.

CM   But what made you feel the need to use more color?

DJ   Maybe it's the fact that I'm a painter. Or that I just really love color. I consider metal a color, but metal only exists in a few colors: silver, aluminum, gold copper, red copper, et cetera. So the only way to achieve numerous colors is to use plexiglass or paint. And I wanted to use a lot of colors.

CM   Are these mural pieces, being long and narrow, conceived like your prior work, with an arbitrary system behind the dimensions of every part?

DJ   Why "arbitrary"? It isn't arbitrary. I decide.

CM   Yes, but isn't it a subjective arrangement?

DJ   Well, all art is subjective. It is a system, but it isn't arbitrary, because I decided it. For these pieces, which were all produced in Switzerland, and the first of which is only three years old, the color and the dimensions of the elements – which are always the same, either ninety centimeters or sixty centimeters – are, on the whole, relatively vague compared to those of certain older works.[1] One of

the big problems posed by color is that I don't want to
fall back into my old conventions. The first pieces inherently rang false because I reused the colors I had liked in
the first paintings and which in my opinion are awfully
conventional. It's really hard to place colors so they don't
form a combination or association. For me, all these arrangements aren't related to anything else, which I think
is just fantastic. But it's hard to do.

CM   I read in some old interviews that you were trying to avoid
what was once called composition.

DJ   You know, I haven't thought about that for years. For these
pieces, I spent a lot of time on the plans, on paper [see image 67], but they all have a logical basis; I don't think things
out in terms of composition. When you see a color below,
it isn't necessarily related to the color above. They aren't,
in any event, associated in the fabrication process of one
piece. I'm very meticulous about the logic of my pieces.
But you should only consider logic up to a certain point,
because, after all, all the interesting stuff is something else.
Having said this, logic is very important.

CM   Does the distribution of color follow a logic?

DJ   Yes, but you have to consider the basic problem. Logic
isn't necessarily so logical. We use it exactly how we feel
like using it. My hope is that things are logical in some
way. Eventually, that can lead to skepticism, but my feeling
is that I should continue in that direction. I try to make
pieces that are as logical as possible. And that ends up being my own little logic.

CM   Donald Judd's little logic!

DJ   *Ce n'est pas la logique du monde. C'est ma logique à moi.*[2]

CM   The other question I wanted to ask you about these pieces
is about the screws, which are very apparent, while, for
example, in the pieces in wood or plexiglass, you can't see
the joints at all. I find that this highlights the aspect of the
work as object.

DJ   It's not really a change for me, and I don't know if it high-
     lights the aspect of the work as object. I've thought a lot
     about it, and it's the only possible way to assemble the pan-
     els. We can't weld it, because it distorts the metal. Glue is
     the only other possibility, but I didn't want to use it; it cre-
     ates too much material, it has too much structure. Screws
     seemed the simplest to me. And having the panels screwed
     to each other also shows that it's made of metal.

CM   Does it also allow us to see there are different thicknesses,
     volumes, from the fact that there are three boxes super-
     imposed on each other?

DJ   Sure, maybe that allows me to better grasp the depth. If
     color can modify the depth, the screws allow us to main-
     tain it. An inch is always an inch.

CM   What determines the height at which you hang your mu-
     ral works?

DJ   There is a piece on the wall that, for the first time, has two
     parts. The lower part is at a height of fifty inches, so one
     can see the bottom and so, when one sees it, it doesn't flat-
     ten out. As for the format of the upper part, it's completely
     different: the space runs vertically.

CM   Do you work interchangeably between metal, plexiglass,
     and wood to make these volumes, or are certain forms
     better adapted to certain materials?

DJ   Volumes and materials are fairly connected. From the start,
     I try to think of my pieces in the material I'm going to use
     to make them. In some ways I work freely, but in general,
     when I think of a piece, I also think of the material. For
     example, the plywood piece could very well be made in
     another material, but the piece in metal couldn't be made
     in any other.

CM   For me, wood seems to be a banal material, whereas
     painted metal and plexiglass are much more sensual.

DJ   You may find it ordinary, but for me it's pretty hard to get
     my hands on. Either they don't have any, or they don't

make it, et cetera. Anyway, for me, wood and plexiglass are materials on the same level.

CM   Do the wooden pieces not have a more abstract quality than the pieces that use metal or plexiglass?

DJ   I wouldn't use the word "abstract." I don't see how one thing could be more abstract than any other. In general, I'm interested in making a thing in itself, not something abstract. Something else.

CM   It seems to me that in the wooden pieces – and pardon me if this isn't any ordinary wood – one is more likely to be drawn more toward the volume or the design of the piece than in the works that make use of color, from which we can imagine other things.

DJ   Most of the time, you know, you can't even think of the difference between the materials. I don't like to distinguish between them. It's just that I tend to see some parts as shinier than others.

CM   I'd like to talk now a bit more generally, particularly with regard to your articles in *Art in America*.[3] You were quite tough on the new figurative painters. The question I'd like to ask you is the following: often, these painters of the new generation dismiss the type of art you practice as meaningless, devoid of content. How do you respond to that?

DJ   I wasn't tough; I could do worse. It's only their point of view. Mine is that I certainly do not make meaningless art, which would be a contradiction. Nobody thinks of himself as making meaningless art. They look at my work and see what's missing – and according to them, there are a lot of things missing. On my end, I look at their work and I see what's missing. The critique could be mutual. For me, there's very little meaning in the work of Sandro Chia or David Salle, and the worst painter I can think of, [Georg] Baselitz, makes work that for me makes no sense. I'm fundamentally against reactionary art and think art should occupy the present and not necessarily move forward, because I don't believe in progress, but simply in change.

To content oneself with playing with what happened in the past is really easy. And it's almost like a politics; it's reactionary.

CM   You could say that this generation reintroduced a certain narrative content into art. How would you define the content of abstraction?

DJ   I think that this narrative content shouldn't be in painting but in literature, which is its origin. Telling stories is a form of falsification of the world. Stories can be so ambiguous that basing an entire art on them is dubious.

Like I was just saying, I try to make something that can exist in itself, like how a lot of things exist in themselves, such as, for example, the things we take pictures of. It's unnecessary to always conceive in reference to something else. Sure, there are references to what we think or feel, or at least to what I think and feel, but not to the world as it is. I love the world as it is. And it's perfectly fine that way. The best we can do is leave it as it is.

CM   Does this mean that you stand by what you were calling "specific objects" in your earlier writings?[4]

DJ   Not entirely. I was talking then as an art critic. That article I wrote on "specific objects" was a report on what was happening in New York, but it wasn't in any sense a manifesto.

CM   But the words remain.

DJ   Everything you write always sticks around – more and more so, in fact – as a sort of manifesto, which is wrong. I was far from writing that sort of thing, or from writing about my own work. The article was extremely general on what was going on in New York in that moment. It wasn't anything else. Of course, there were a few of my own ideas, but they had nothing to do with Mondrian or Malevich.

I don't write on my own work in particular. It takes a long time to figure out how the world works and to be

able to write a manifesto. I find that, for example, Malevich, or Mondrian, or the other artists of the first part
of the century were much more sophisticated than the
Americans and, later, no doubt, after the war, the Europeans. They grew up faster and were able to write manifestos. Now it takes more time to learn, because we're all
thrown deeper into society. It's really hard to slowly learn
to see the relationship between things, particularly in art,
in architecture, in these kinds of domains.

CM Just now, when we mentioned Brice Marden, Robert
Mangold, and Robert Ryman, I also had in mind some
interviews with them that we recently published. They
were asked about the content of their art, and what struck
me was that one could feel in their answers something on
the order of a metaphysical aspiration. I'd like to know
your opinion on that.

DJ Basically, I'm an absolute empiricist, coldhearted, not religious, not metaphysical.

CM But there is often this temptation with abstraction.

DJ I disagree. I never felt it philosophically, not when I was an
art student, not before. Fundamentally, I think my work –
and the mission of art, in large part – is connected to nature and life.

I don't think you have to practice art on religious or
metaphysical terrains, because they're both false in terms
of representation. But the question of the extension of
time in relation to life, which is very short, is completely
evident, and these elemental things occupy an important
place in art. Before all else, the greatest problem is imagining a person in himself, in the world, as this strange body,
this little space in the big space, and the same for imagining a span of time so great in relation to this life, which is
so short, and then to see everyone's reaction to that.

CM In the first article you published in *Art in America*, you give
a definition of art's role in society: art is an activity that

takes place in the margins and offers resistance to politics, to commerce, to everything that constitutes social life.

DJ   It's really a complicated problem. It's also different for someone who comes from the United States, where art has always existed much more on the periphery than it has here in Europe. Despite all the problems you may have – I was in the Soviet Union in January, and this country is very much a part of Europe – the attention paid to art is greater. Maybe it's paid in the wrong way sometimes, but the artist is held in higher esteem. Art is considered a more or less normal activity. In the United States, when I made it out to Texas, this wasn't the case. No one bothered with such silly things, so I am a part of an extreme periphery and have encountered a very hard society there, and the only way to work has been, practically, to ignore it. Thankfully, in Europe, everyone feels more concerned. Which is good; things should be more coherent everywhere. In its many forms, art is definitely a marginal activity in the United States. It's also very hard for me to imagine art as having any function in society, though maybe we can be a bit more nuanced. Maybe art has a small influence on the negative things in society; maybe it renders the people a bit more conscious. It could even – though here I'm being frighteningly optimistic and surely exaggerating – have a bit of an influence against the nuclear war, which could save us all, who knows? In general, I tend to think that art has no effect on society. However, in some places it does. I'm often in Switzerland, and there's an attitude toward construction that keeps urbanization from becoming a disaster, as it is in the United States. Some places, though, do show an interest in what artists and writers think. Actually, having just returned from the Soviet Union, it bothers me just thinking about it. Reagan and his government don't care at all about artists and writers. So we have no impact. But here [Europe], to a certain extent, the artists do have an impact. That's why there are dissidents in the Soviet Union. The government does terrible things to them, but in a way, this means it takes them seriously.

CM But isn't today's problem that art, even the art we call avant-garde, is completely hijacked by economic and political matters?

DJ It's true. I don't know the exact definition of the avant-garde, but I think that under democracy, as under other systems, institutions and commerce try to take hold of artists. And an artist must fight. We must fight for the integrity of what we do. Or simply not do it. But it's better to fight. Doing nothing, that might just be death. Artists should learn to defend their own territory, because they're really crushed by galleries. Here, the sellers offer at least a check and a show, and to a certain extent, they take care of practical problems, but with other galleries and museums it's really appalling. And of course, as the institutions represent the nation, their task is easy, and it lets them put themselves first, but I find them dangerous, more than anything else.

CM You mean that artists should be careful about how they engage with galleries and institutions, not only because of the quality of their work, but also because of their own position in society?

DJ Yes. Artists should quite simply demand that their work be shown in such and such a way, installed in such and such a way, because that's part of the nature of their work. I will soon have a series of museum shows, and I try to assure myself that my work will be shown how it should be, and not simply tossed up on the walls. Presentation is the most elemental thing there is. But taken to a certain point, it can almost take on a political implication. Either you control it, or you stay out. I try to do my own installations, which isn't always possible in museums. Nobody, and certainly not the legal or financial systems, wants to recognize the fact that art is an activity in itself, and that that's all it is. It's not an educational investment. In Texas, I just read some required document of financial declaration for a foundation down there, and my lawyer has to claim whether or not my work is performed to educational ends.[5] Even though it's art, and that's really all it is, and that's why it's there. Art for art's sake is out of bounds, or at least seems to create problems in the financial system. If you don't sell, they call it a hobby. It's not an established activity at all. You have to insist on these things. I think that the existence of art as art is ultimately – or rather, fundamentally – a social function. Because it's something that exists in itself.

Translated from the French by Kit Schluter.

First published: Catherine Millet, "La petite logique de Donald Judd," *Artpress*, November 1987, 4–10.

1   Lehni AG, based in Dübendorf, Switzerland, was the first fabricator of Judd's painted aluminum works and metal furniture. See Judd's "On Furniture" (1986) in *Donald Judd Writings*, 453.
2   Translates from the French as "That's not the world's logic. That's my very own logic."
3   See Judd's "A Long Discussion Not About Master-Pieces But Why There Are So Few of Them: Part I" (1983) and "A Long Discussion Not About Master-Pieces But Why There Are So Few of Them: Part II" (1984) in *Donald Judd Writings*, 352–76 and 378–97, respectively. "Part I" was first published in *Art in America*, September 1984, 9–19; "Part II" was first published in *Art in America*, October 1984, 9–15.
4   See Judd's "Specific Objects" (1964) in *Donald Judd Writings*, 134–45.
5   Judd refers here to the Chinati Foundation; see Judd's "Statement for the Chinati Foundation/La Fundación Chinati" (1987) in *Donald Judd Writings*, 484–89.

Interview with Paul Cabon
Spring 1987

This interview was conducted at the hotel Relais Christine in Paris. Paul Cabon and Judd first met a few days before the opening of *Repères: Judd*, at Galerie Maeght Lelong, Paris (April 8–May 16, 1987); Cabon assisted Judd with the installation of this exhibition, as well as with the installation of subsequent exhibitions of Judd's work.

P C [Paul Cabon] A lot of your metal work can only be made within an industrial context. So what kind of place is your own studio? How do you use it for metal? Is it to work, to show your pieces? To sum up: what are the functions of your studio, within your work?

D J [Donald Judd] Well, it has changed quite a few times. I had a loft on Nineteenth Street and Fourth Avenue in New York twenty years ago that was actually a working studio where I made the pieces myself, mostly out of wood. Before that, it was a painting studio; I painted paintings there and then I made the first wooden pieces there. So that was very much a workplace, not for exhibition at all. It was very messy, full of tools, junk, and work that was in the way. The last few years of the time I had that place, I started having work made by a sheet metal factory, and slowly the studio became much neater.[1] I had a lot of cacti in it, and I mostly sat around making sketches. So it was certainly not for exhibition, but the basic studio simply became a place to draw and to make sketches and think, and all the work was done in a small factory nearby. Pieces were put up to look at and think about – for me but not really for other people to look at. This was on 53 East Nineteenth Street.

Then I got the building, 101 Spring Street. It's a five-story building and has two basements. I only allowed one floor – the third floor – to be the real studio. I didn't allow too much for a real working studio, where things would actually get made; it was mostly to put up the pieces to look at and for me to sit and think. So the third floor was not a studio in a normal sense of a workplace. The other floors were to put the work up and look at the work, other people's and my work. That scheme has continued pretty much since. In Texas I have a studio, but that's mostly the same thing: pieces are put up to look at, and I sit around and think about them; the drawings are there and you can refer to them.[2] And the same in Switzerland:[3] it's still a small place, but it is for thinking, working on a table on sketches and drawings, rather than making pieces, since all pieces have been made in the factory.[4]

But even when you do that – make large pieces in a factory – you still need a space or a floor, I think, to work on drawings and prints, and which tends to get a little bit like storage for taken-down pieces; it tends to get messy. So I think I went a little too far in Spring Street in not having a more or less normal studio. In the place in Switzerland, if it's okay, if it doesn't fall through, I think I would like to have an actual shop, perhaps where plywood pieces are made, so the guy could come from New York, live there, and make the plywood pieces.[5] I kind of miss that activity. The place in New York was never really perfect – but in theory, it was a little too perfect. In Texas, the studio is pretty good [image 69], but it is still not so much a place to work and hang things up and take them down and kind of make a mess, and it probably should be more so. So basically, I have three studios – and more, in fact – but mostly, my work is done by me carrying a bunch of papers around and sitting around and thinking. So it could be anywhere.

PC Just like Einstein's laboratory was, as he said, in his pen –

DJ That he carried, yes, instead of a briefcase.

PC What kind of relationship do you have with the people who make the pieces for you? Especially if you want to slightly modify a metal piece – how do you cope with that?

DJ It has been a lot of different factories and different people, and all of that is a different situation with each one. Lately it has been very troublesome, but it has always been somewhat troublesome. It's not very simple to get things made well. I sketch out the idea in a very loose way to the extent of what I need for myself, and then I go to the factory. Then the factory translates the idea into an engineering drawing with the requirements necessary for the worker to know what he's doing. The first step is usually that the factory says that it can or cannot be made – more that it's too expensive or isn't. Then the piece on paper is modified somewhat: if it's too expensive, you either give it up or try to make it less expensive. If there is something technically wrong, you try to retain the idea and make the piece a little different so that it's corrected. For example, if I make a simple tubular piece, the first step is whether the top is going to sag or not. Elementary things like that. I can figure out the proportions just as nicely as I want, but if the top sags, that's the end of it. So they say, "It's got to be thicker," or, "It doesn't matter how thick you make it, it's still going to sag" – things like that. Usually big discussions are involved – how the sheets are fit together; whatever they are made of, concrete, metal, or plywood; where the screws go – and that can take a lot of time. There is a great deal of talking involved, and usually a great deal of trouble, and every time I go to a new factory, they say, "Oh, it's easy, we do this all the time, it looks like a box! Sure!" And then they make the first one – and the first one, well, it isn't good enough. That's what they're doing all the time. You tell them to make it again; if they're cooperative, actually after five or six tries, they make one that's fairly good. Perhaps, after that, they can get better and better, or they get mad and they won't do it anymore, or usually they raise the price as they find out that it's not so easy, and sometimes – as recently in Switzerland, with the concrete pieces and the plywood work done – it just collapses, they don't cooperate, and then nothing gets done.

You have to go to the right factory for the right material. A sheet metal factory is only a sheet metal factory. They don't put things together like this coffee table: they fold things. That's ordinarily just one kind of factory. The other kind of metal factory is where you have plates put together; the colored pieces in the show come from a sheet metal factory, and the aluminum quarter-inch pieces are from a factory that only does work like that, in Switzerland. So you can't ask the factory to do very strange things. They don't understand.

PC   You were just saying "the right factory for the right material." But even when you have that, do the people of the factory have always the same ideas that you have about the material?

DJ   Usually you have to get them to revise their idea of what they are doing. When I first went to Bernstein in New York, they made kitchen sinks out of stainless steel fairly well, and they made ventilating ducts, where the air goes through the building, out of galvanized iron.[6] The kitchen sinks were too expensive for me! The galvanized iron was a very nice material for me – but everybody handled it roughly because ordinarily nobody saw ventilating ducts. The big problem was to train them to make the ventilating ducts as well as you can make ventilating ducts and be careful with the seams, to be very neat about it all. They had a lot of trouble understanding that… it took a couple of years. They want to go ahead and do it the way they've always done it. What I am doing is upgrading a very ordinary technique in this case. If one makes stainless-steel pieces, then they are used to doing a better job.

In the case of plywood pieces: one man now makes them all – Peter Ballantine in New York. But at one point, I made two in Zürich, and the carpenters did a terrible job. If you had asked them to do a table, they would have done a beautiful job, but plywood to them was junk. That was what you made forms with for casting concrete – it disappeared in the building, so you never saw it. These were very simple pieces, but you couldn't even get them to take the drill and run it in to make the hole and bring the bit back out again without ripping every hunk out of the side of the piece. These were the simple boxes, five by five, with the colored bottoms. In fact, they never learned, and finally Peter remade them a few years later. That was because they had in mind that plywood was a cheap material, and there wasn't any reason to be careful.

PC   So the worker's state of mind depends on the material he uses and the way it's usually used.

DJ   It's very difficult, but sometimes it fits. The pieces made out of these plates of aluminum in the exhibition, like the one that was made in Switzerland, were difficult, because I wanted them made very well, and the company in Connecticut didn't make them well enough. But it's easier to get those pieces done well than, say, galvanized iron pieces or sheet metal pieces. Basically, except for real mass reproduction — making drawers for cabinets or something; making cabinets — sheet metal work is a little sloppy because it's used for all sorts of practical things like ventilating ducts: you never see it, or people think you don't see it; they don't care. So they are not used to being careful at all. They know that something like this is supposed to be fairly well made. These attitudes are hard to deal with.

It's very difficult. You were asking if the people working with metal were more precise than the people working with wood. With the person doing the plywood pieces — Peter Ballantine in New York — it's an absolutely personal arrangement. He's not a factory at all: he's one person, and basically that's what Peter does for a living. He does some other things — he does very careful work. He doesn't do furniture; he does mainly my work plus a little bit of art for other people that involves woodwork. He is a very different carpenter from, say, Jim Cooper, who makes the furniture, wooden furniture of mine and for other people. Jim makes very well-made, technically sophisticated, carpenter-like furniture. It's a totally different thing. I wouldn't allow Peter to use fancy joints or anything; it all has to be jointed in a very straightforward way. So Peter's whole way of working – which is more or less according to what I want – is extremely different. He has to put boxes together, just one side against the other side. That's that. I don't want a lot of fancy joints, like zigzags, at the corners.

PC   It seems to me that the relationship you have with this man is close to the one a traditional sculptor working with bronze or casting might have had with his foundryman?

DJ   Yes, it is. It's very particular, and in fact, I would have a hard time, I think, getting somebody else to do what Peter does if he didn't want to do it. Ordinarily, if it works out with the factories, it's pretty particular too – that's if they work out, and so many don't work out. Most of them don't work out. But ordinarily, if they do work out, they have difficulty understanding what I want, which doesn't make life any smoother.

There is basically one [person] at the Bernstein factory, the first one I used in New York – the work is done by one man, José Otero [image 70].[7] I don't like the owner of the factory; we had a big fight about pieces years ago, so I tend not to go there. José basically makes pieces which are like older ones. He knows how to make them well, how I originally want them, and they continue to get done in that way, and that all depends on José Otero. Bernstein himself could never do it. It's just this one guy, and that's kind of lucky.

PC   To come back a bit to the question of your studio: when you were speaking of your studios, of what you were doing in them, it made me think about some studios of architects, because in France, some architecture studios have the same way of working – they do plans, and they go and ask someone to make a small model. In fact, it has got nothing to do with your work, but with the relationships with the people who work with the architects. Do you think it's wrong to compare your studio with the architect's?

DJ   No, it's rather like it – not only that, but usually my studio functions as an architectural studio. Anyway, I am interested in all that.

PC   I wanted also to ask you whether you agreed or not with what Franz Meyer said about the materials you used more often in your work after 1965, such as steel, plywood, and concrete, which are supposed to be materials more "puritan" than the ones you were using before, as he says in this text.[8] What do you think of that?

DJ   No, I disagree, really. Not only that – I get accused of being poor, puritan, or too dry, or too pure, and then on the other hand, I get accused of being too sensuous, or too luscious, and using too much color. So what does it mean? It's all extreme. I am very interested in the materials as materials, for themselves, for the quality they have, and retaining that quality, not losing it. Like, you don't know what this table is made of; I don't like this sort of thing. This could be anything. You don't know about it by the time you get through with it. It could be cast in plastic. It's probably *plastique*.

PC   In general, what makes you go from one material to another – for example, from aluminum to plywood?

DJ   I didn't give up materials, I just add more different ones. So it just grows. I think that the basic thing is often simply because I like the material, the quality of the material, as it is, I start thinking of what I could do with it. A lot of the materials were selected – the metal, the galvanized iron, for example, and plywood, too, before the galvanized iron – for their lightness and ability to define a volume without being massive. Then I could make a fairly large thing that was still light. I wanted to get away from the idea of weight and mass; I was more interested in volume. So plywood is good for that – and then I realized I could make a nice big box out of galvanized iron. It was thinner, and I liked the zinc on it, the surface, a lot, and it made an even bigger and lighter volume. And it's really thin.

P C So if you don't give up materials, it's like a physical or mathematical theory – the old one can exist within the new one, like Einstein's theory includes Newton's theory.

D J Yes. Actually, the first piece that I used metal on is literally like that [see image 1]. I gave it to Frank Stella – and actually, it would be great to have it back again. It stuck out from the wall. It was made of plywood, and it seemed to me too heavy for what it was; it is just a simple box with a little trough. It's in the early part of the Canadian catalogue of the National Gallery of Canada.[9] It looked too heavy, and I went to the Bernstein factory in New York for a piece of metal – one single piece of galvanized iron that I drilled thousands of holes all over. It took a long time, because it couldn't be made at once; the whole surface couldn't be manufactured, Bernstein said, because a whole factory should be set to make a million of them. So I had that plywood box stuck out of the wall covered with galvanized iron by this factory. And I said, "Okay, here is this wooden box, simply put a layer of galvanized iron over the whole thing," and then, after they did that, we talked about it a lot, and weeks went by. But what if it doesn't have the wood? Do the same like this, make the metal a little heavier – and they did one without any wood inside. But the first one literally has the wood inside and the metal outside.

P C You were speaking of the fact that it would have been necessary to build a factory to make the metal part with the holes. Have you ever thought of building a special factory to make your pieces?

D J See, this one sheet that I got of galvanized iron that has a thousand holes in it – that's a perforated metal. It's a simple process, in fact. But you have to have a whole factory to run an enormous amount of material for them to set up a machine to do it. They are not going to just do one sheet for you. They'll do one sheet if you pay $100,000.

So a lot of all these problems are involved in the question of mass production, and in a way, when I go to the factory, I'm kind of turning the whole thing upside down. I like the quality of the mass production, but I want them to do one or two, and that just makes a mess. Or in the anodizing of the aluminum to get color: most anodizers – that's used a lot here in France – just do thousands of parts, all blue cups or all blue spoons, military parts. They do millions of them, and they don't want to be bothered to empty a tank and fill a tank and go through the whole process for just one piece – to them, it's six or seven boxes – and if they do finally kind of agree to it, they charge an enormous amount of money. Then, if you don't like it, you don't have any leverage, because they don't want to do it anyway, and you can't complain. Anodizing was one of the worst.

PC That might be one of the reasons why you don't use color in anodizing.

DJ Well, I do sometimes, but it's very difficult to get the color. They don't want to do it. For example, the company in Switzerland that made some of the new pieces – it's an enormous company, but they don't do colored anodizing.[10] They just do the plain ones.

PC What does this company usually do?

DJ I am not too sure –

PC The first time I saw your work, which was at the museum of Saint-Étienne, I wondered what you might think of early modern Russian sculptors like [Katarzyna] Kobro and [Vladimir] Tatlin, who was one of the pioneers in his modern way of using metal in sculpture.

DJ It didn't have much effect on me because I didn't know much about it, and it's somewhat a different history of what you would think, because when you look at books one after the other – as I said a lot of times, my work comes out of painting, and I didn't pay much attention to sculpture. I mostly considered it simply old-fashioned.

This includes David Smith. I liked it, but I thought it was rather old-fashioned.

I didn't pay too much attention to Tatlin because of the composition, which I was against and not interested in. So the fact that he used metal or formed things was not particularly important to me. Also, I didn't know so much about the constructivists at this time. I know more about them and I admire them more now.

PC   It was my first subjective impression.

DJ   A person can look at David Smith's work, especially those stainless-steel boxes, and say that I was influenced by them, but the fact is that it just wasn't so.[11] It's just an area I didn't think about. It was just an accident, almost.

PC   It's like in "Specific Objects" when you say: "The use of three dimensions is an obvious alternative. It opens to anything. Many of the reasons for this use are negative points against painting and sculpture, and since both are common sources, the negative reasons are those nearest commonage."[12]

DJ   You pay attention to certain things and not others for some strange reasons. I always paid a lot of attention to Matisse and Léger and Mondrian while I was making paintings; you know, I was aware of that. Going way back, early on, when I was making paintings, I took some elements out of those people to some extent, and I knew I was doing that, and I also knew that I didn't understand them very well, which was the reason for stopping and doing something else. And then the Americans in New York became more important to me, since I was there. I saw Jackson Pollock's work, and then some Rothkos, and so forth. So basically, I was thinking in terms of painting for a long time.

PC   Can you say that you are still thinking in terms of painting?

DJ   No, but it's not sculpture either, I don't think. I am interested in three-dimensional work, and of course that is, I suppose, sculpture. I don't like to use the word "sculpture," because it's carving to me; mostly to me it means compositional elements, and I don't like it. But I think that the basic nature of it is that it's, I hope, very three-dimensional. That's what I am really interested in. And I am really totally disinterested in painting – doing it myself.

PC   So three-dimensional aspects of reality seem to be very important to you. Is it true to say that you pay the same attention to very humble objects like tools, furniture, or other things? I remember when we went together to this hardware store in Paris, you were interested in this box wrench which is manufactured over here out of a hexahedral tube. And if I remember, you liked the way it was possible to realize, just in seeing it, how it was simply made by a machine.

DJ   Oh, the fold – the crimp. Yes, I like this kind of thing.

PC   Similarly, what about if it was possible for you to work with a machine – maybe a numerically commanded machine – which could shape the material you chose just as simply and as precisely as a computerized synthesizer does with sounds? Just like some computers can be used very simply, although they are technologically complex, providing you believe this famous advertisement saying: "If you know how to point at something with your finger, you will know how to use our computer, which is a very friendly machine."[13] Would you be interested in working in such a direction?

DJ   Well, we saw one in Switzerland, in the concrete factory that did such a bad job for us. The machine occupies the full room, to make very awful concrete tiles, fiberglass, and concrete panels for buildings – very bad designs, and the things were very complicated. It runs all over the room, goes on in different places.

PC   Like in Charlie Chaplin's movie *Modern Times*?

DJ   And it was a very expensive machine to make horrible

panels that look like old rocks! Actually, it's a bad version of trying to make a stone wall out of plastic. I am not interested in this.

PC   But there might be another way of using this machine?

DJ   Oh, yes; I am sure they can make very nice panels of wood out of concrete.

PC   Have you ever worked with complex machines in a factory?

DJ   Yes, but usually it's just too complicated to get a factory to cooperate. I can make pieces with that machine, but you would have to make an awful lot of them, and you can't, because it is probably very expensive just to turn the machine on. So they are not going to do it for five pieces. Perhaps you could do it like etchings, hundreds of them. You know, if they would cooperate, I could do something with it, because it molds rectangles, so certainly one could think of something. That's always been kind of interesting, but it's just so difficult that I never get into it.

There are several things that I have never done but I like as processes. Stamping is one. If you stamp a metal ball, it's just like this [*places one hand against the other*]. You can make a mold, and it will do anything. It will stamp any shape you want. It's pretty expensive – that's the main reason why I haven't done that. But, you know, that's great, because you see just how it was done, and it's done like that [*repeats gesture*]. So that's full of nice possibilities. And casting, of course, which turns out to be very expensive too. One thing I have always especially liked here – I think it's particular to France – is the use of corrugation in a lot of cars and a lot of factories. France developed corrugation more than other countries, such as in the little Citroën car, the Deux Chevaux.[14] I like the way some panels are made: they are just stamped. That's great to me, and it's a very French industrial design; I think it's very nice. If you look at other countries, they don't do that so much. The thing that is most characteristic in the department stores of the United States is corrugated iron roofs. That's all. They have always done that, but they don't use it for anything else. It's used for roofs – well, now sometimes for siding, but they use it more like a material, while here it's used more as the structural shape itself. The car doesn't have a shingle roof, it has a roof as doors; it isn't made of parts. In the United States, they will use it like shingling.

So that's why I liked those tools in the hardware store, because of this plastic quality, and this use of the machine to do it. It's a movement that the machine can make, and it's very un-American. As I said to you in the shop, I don't think they would think of that crimp; they would put a plastic handle on it! The differences between industrial designs are not very investigated, I think. But it's an interesting subject. The English have a certain quality in their own [industrial designs] too.

PC   Yes, it's very interesting to see the different ways of thinking, what a machine can do.

DJ   Yes, it's curious.

PC   And where do you think it comes from?

DJ   Perhaps for some historical reasons. There is an interesting essay by the Japanese novelist Jun'ichirō Tanizaki – he's from earlier in the century – called *In Praise of Shadows*.[15] It's just a speculation about what industrial design would have been like in general, and in Japan, if the industrial revolution had occurred in Japan first, and what things the Japanese would have stressed. Mostly he goes on a lot about – he makes the inside of a bowl, a soup bowl, black, because you make these things deep in shadow; that's one thing I remember. So he stressed things like that. He talks about lacquered bowls, dishes. Obviously, these things come out of preindustrial attitudes and then into the industrial attitudes. It's kind of a nice modern subject. I have a Land Rover that I've had for a long time; the English have a lot of plain constructions. They were using plain surfaces for hundreds of years. I mean, if you look at a lot of the old furniture, and the coloring, or the paneling, there's a lot of very plain and simple surfaces.

PC   Much simpler than over here.

DJ   Yes, this is real. It's getting very general and dangerous, but I think there is a certain tendency here to use plastic shapes. Most of the buildings in Paris are more plastic – more deeply baroque, in a way – than certainly in England or Japan. It's kind of interesting. Why do people like these things? It's curious.

PC   Sometimes when I see this kind of difference between England and France, I think of what Nietzsche says in *Birth of Tragedy* about the Apollonian and Dionysian character of art.

DJ   Now we are really generalizing. Okay, I'll think about that.

PC   To come back closer to your work, is it nonsense to say that your work is more Apollonian than Dionysian?

DJ   Yes, I think my tendencies are more in that direction. I am not so Dionysian.

PC   Apollonian, but not puritan.

DJ   No, I think there is a big difference.

PC   Thank you very much.

This conversation was sourced from an archival transcript in the Judd Foundation Archives, Marfa, Texas. Though the transcript is dated simply to 1987, the editors have dated the conversation to spring of that year, based on the circumstances under which Judd and Cabon met.

1   Judd worked with Bernstein Brothers Sheet Metal Specialties, Inc. from late 1963 until the end of his life. Although they moved to Long Island City by the end of 1964, their shop was originally located in Manhattan, at 191 Third Avenue.

2   Judd used the room that is now the north library at La Mansana de Chinati/ The Block as a studio until 1990, when he purchased a former Safeway grocery store on Oak Street in Marfa, Texas, and converted it into his art studio.

3   Judd refers here to Eichholteren.

4   Lehni AG, based in Dübendorf, Switzerland, was the first fabricator of Judd's painted aluminum works and metal furniture. See Judd's "On Furniture" (1986) in *Donald Judd Writings*, 453.

5   From 1971 to the end of Judd's life, Peter Ballantine was the primary fabricator of Judd's works in plywood.

6   Around 1970, Judd designed a pair of elliptical stainless-steel sinks for the fifth-floor dressing rooms at 101 Spring Street. Bernstein Brothers fabricated the sinks, which are still installed today in their original location.

7   José Otero was the fabricator of Judd's work at Bernstein Brothers, Inc.

8   Franz Meyer, "La nouvelle sculpture des années soixante," in *Qu'est ce que la sculpture moderne?*, exh. cat. (Paris: Centre Georges Pompidou, 1986).

9   Brydon Smith, ed., *Donald Judd: Catalogue Raisonné of Paintings, Objects, and Wood-Blocks 1960–1974*, exh. cat. (Ottawa: National Gallery of Canada, 1975), 56, 115.

10 Judd refers here to Menziken AG, located in the canton of Aargau, Switzerland. Menziken was a fabricator of Judd's work in anodized aluminum from 1986 until his death in 1994.

11 Judd likely refers here to Smith's *Cubi* series (1961–65) or his work *Five Units Equal* (1956); for more on the latter piece, see "Interview with Lucy R. Lippard and William C. Agee" (1968) in this volume, 304.

12 See Judd's "Specific Objects" (1964) in *Donald Judd Writings*, 135.

13 In the 1980s, Xerox advertised its model 820 desktop computer as "a very friendly machine."

14 The Citroën Deux Chevaux, or 2CV, was a popular economy car manufactured from 1948 to 1990. It employed innovative engineering and simple metal bodywork (included a corrugated bonnet, until the 1960s) to create a sturdy but lightweight vehicle.

15 Jun'ichirō Tanizaki, *In Praise of Shadows*, trans. Thomas J. Harper and Edward G. Seidensticker (Sedgwick, ME: Leete's Island Books, 1977). Judd included this book in his library in Marfa, Texas.

"A Change in a Degree That Is Valid for Good Art"
Interview with Markus Brüderlin for *Kunstforum International*
November 1987

This conversation was conducted in Vienna in November 1987, while Judd was working on a site-specific work for the back of the Vienna Secession, and published the following summer. As Judd wrote in the essay "Sezession" (1989), the work was based on "an architectural use of my old idea, present in a piece in Münster, in Adelaide, Connecticut, Missouri and in the Mansana in Texas, which also is a form of architecture, of parallel walls, one level and one parallel with the slope of the land." A site model of this unrealized work can be seen in Judd's Architecture Office in Marfa, Texas.

Born in Missouri, USA, in 1928, Donald Judd is regarded as one of the most important representatives of American minimal art and has repeatedly emerged as an active critic. His polemic diatribes of 1984 against the American art market[1] are increasingly seen as pleas for the aesthetic self-assertion and the moral conscience in the interest of a "sensible" discourse about art.[2] Since the beginnings of the 1970s, he has been working on a large installation in Marfa, a provincial backwater in southwest Texas, which is supposed to house installations of his own works as well as works by [John] Chamberlain, Flavin, and others. The Chinati Foundation is an unusual public museum project comprising fifteen buildings so far and an area of one and a half square kilometers. Based on its intentions, it is comparable with the Hallen für Neue Kunst of the Crex Collection in Schaffhausen or parts of the Saatchi Collection in London – but of a very American magnitude. Recently, a larger project has also come into existence, consisting of the involvement of urban space. The American designed a comprehensive sculpture for the Vienna Secession, heavily encroached by traffic, which is already secured financially.[3] Markus Brüderlin spoke with Donald Judd during his stay in Vienna in November 1987.

MB   [Markus Brüderlin] During your retrospective last summer in the Kunsthalle Düsseldorf, a large colorful painting from the '60s hung right at the entrance, basically as a visual prologue.[4] It's a painting of an astonishing currentness, especially if compared to works by John Armleder that were exhibited at the same time, a floor above, in the Kunstverein für die Rheinlande und Westfalen. How do you view those works retrospectively today, and how do you assess them within your overall body of work?

DJ   [Donald Judd] Those paintings originated about twenty-five years ago. I think that there is a relationship to my work today, but they do not have an actual meaning. They are simply old paintings, and I see in them approaches for later developments. But they don't have any influence on what I create today.

MB   The starting point for most so-called minimal artists in the beginning of the '60s was American painting of the '50s, from hard-edge to minimal art, "opting out of painting," et cetera, yes? Even Carl Andre let himself be inspired by Frank Stella's stripe paintings in his serially structured wood sculptures.

DJ   The good painters from back then were those who learned from Pollock, Rothko, Newman, and [Clyfford] Still and who admired them. They had created a starting point for thought, and what followed after them hasn't been that good. Carl Andre, however, was never a painter; about Sol LeWitt I am not so sure. In general, I would like to declare that there are no "minimal artists." Nobody likes the label "minimal art." Almost none of these artists knew each other. In my case, I felt the impetus and intrinsic need to create something new. I was looking for something that would go further, because the possibilities that painting offered were too limited. In order to develop something new, I had to leave painting.

      I saw that the first three-dimensional works had already resolved various formal questions, whereas in painting you can show something nice, something interesting in one work, but already the next painting will contradict it. And working like that just isn't pleasant.

MB   Especially the wall pieces carry obvious remnants of panel painting in them. Simply put, aren't these works paintings that are functioning in space?

DJ   No, they are definitely three-dimensional. It was difficult to get away from painting; the first three-dimensional works were simply freestanding and on the floor. It took me a few years to realize that I could hang something on the wall, provided it was obvious how far the work was extending away from the wall and in which relationship it was to the surrounding space.

MB   How do you view the relationship between Mondrian's concept of neoplasticism and your understanding of space and area?

DJ   I've always known Mondrian's works and liked them. The old paintings of mine carry a distant resemblance – only very general, however, and rather subconsciously. To me, Mondrian's paintings were always ambiguous. They were either very flat or very spatial, and what I learned from that is that this was something I didn't want. The problem with a painting is that it either wants to force its way into the space or recede; it wants to move somewhere. It's almost impossible to produce a completely flat painting. If someone would achieve that, I would actually welcome it. But it's always changing: either the image recedes into the distance or it's very close. In this context, I never saw my works as paintings; they are more closely related to being projections in front of the wall. They establish a proper relationship to the wall without projecting entirely from the wall area, like Frank Stella does, and developing into reliefs. It also has to do with mathematics, meaning that it could actually be calculated.

MB   The works radiate a strict, formal logic. You are actually opposed to the term "rational art." Isn't that a contradiction?

DJ   I don't see it like that. I don't follow a strict schema. It is a broad spectrum of different works. I am not at all interested in rational schematism; I am opposed to classifications of "rational," "emotional," and so on.

MB   Today one is tempted to regard the paint or the material not simply as a neutral medium, but in fact recognize sensuous, even expressive values in the materials that you are explicitly choosing.

DJ   Plywood has a very special quality that somebody else maybe doesn't even recognize. But it isn't expressive; it doesn't reveal emotions. Or is the surface on this table expressive?

MB   Not the surface, but perhaps what covers it – the veneer,

its utilitarian aspect? What I mean is that very strong illusionistic qualities arise by painting the base surfaces of
the plywood floor boxes, or the plexiglass facings in the
wall pieces.

DJ There are many different kinds of illusionism; I spoke
about one kind in connection with Mondrian. It's a basic problem in painting. It's the reflections with metal and
plexiglass that I am using. In the painted plywood boxes,
the paint is reflected on the sides, and that is very much
intended. I don't really see it as illusionism. If that's what
you want to call it, that's also okay, but it's an illusionism of
a different kind. But what I'm opposed to is an illusionism where one puts a sign on the wall. This inevitably refers to figurative painting.

MB The primary shapes used clearly give away the desire for
clarity and lucidity. Contemplating your installations,
however, there are repeated moments of irritation.

DJ What do you mean by "irritation"? Toward the audience?
I'm not interested in that at all, and I also don't agree with
Duchamp. One cannot have a reaction toward the audience. There are a lot of people out there one doesn't know
at all. It's best not to embark on that at all.

MB Is restricting yourself to primary forms somewhat of an
act of reduction?

DJ Again, I have a different opinion about that also. It's an old
question. All new works of art probably look reductive,
but that doesn't mean that they really are. People don't see
what's new; they only perceive what's missing as reductive.
I wouldn't use this word in regard to my work.

MB Your essay "Specific Objects" was published in 1965.[5] In it,
you described for the first time and analyzed the various
experiments of fellow artists – for example, Stella, Flavin,
Chamberlain, Oldenburg, et cetera – who were following
a similar direction. You called their work "objects." How
much were they objects, and how much were they sculp-

tures? I mean, Duchamp was already using the term "object" in a very different way.

DJ   I have no idea what Duchamp was thinking. But this article was commissioned: it was a report, and not a manifesto, as some people think. It was simply a description of the situation back then, and "Specific Objects" was the best title that I could think of. I refer to my own works as "three-dimensional" and not as "sculpture." That's something very general and has nothing to do with Duchamp. I also don't know much about him.

MB   His work exists at the beginning of an entirely different tradition of modernism, one that deals specifically with reality and everyday life – and which we might consider pop art a continuation of?

DJ   I'm really not much interested in the question of what reality looks like. Things around us exist whether we want it or not. They have or don't have a certain quality. I'm much more interested in creating something new, something that can exist without me and that has a life of its own. The only thing that I find interesting about Duchamp, contrary to what many think, is that there exists an interesting aesthetic quality in his work, even in the objects that he chose. Thereby they have a certain similarity with his paintings. The snow shovel, for example, possesses some degree of acuteness that also exists in his paintings.[6] Other than that, I believe that Duchamp is overrated. I think he's a good average artist.

MB   The so-called newness of the art in the early '60s was to be understood in the sense of a break with painting, et cetera. How do you view your own development today? Compared to Robert Morris and Frank Stella, your works show a certain constancy.

DJ   Sure, a lot has changed in Stella and Morris. I like Stella's earlier paintings, but now I have the feeling that he doesn't really know what he's doing. I'm risking that I'll offend him. And concerning Morris, I am convinced he doesn't know what he is doing. I can say that publicly.

MB   And the change in your work?

DJ   I believe that my work has changed to a degree that is valid for good art. I cannot comprehend when an artist, young or old, changes radically. To me, that means that he didn't know what he was doing in the first place. Frank was right in the beginning, but he didn't understand that he was right.

MB   There's a strange dynamic in Stella between systematic works in series, within which everything looks pretty much the same, and breaks from this continuity.

DJ   I purposely don't work in groups and series and exhaust all logical possibilities, because some of them aren't good, or are redundant. But who hasn't produced works that don't belong together? Ad Reinhardt made many good works, even if the black paintings all look the same or similar from the outside. To me, they aren't alike, and I am convinced that Reinhardt also saw them like that.

MB   The relationship of change and continuity is largely a question of degree?

DJ   I believe that quite a lot has changed in my work, but most don't recognize it because my work isn't easily available. One thing I never did was force a change and then worry about it. As long as it stays interesting for me, it could actually stop changing altogether. In general, I don't believe that there is a whole lot of progress and change in anyone's lifetime. This also corresponds with my understanding of history.

MB   One project that you have been pursuing continuously is establishing the Chinati Foundation in far West Texas. What comprises the basic idea of this collection or museum?

DJ   This is something entirely new. Others have tried it as well – for example, the Saatchi Collection in London, and they got this idea from me. In the '60s, they came to me in New York at Spring Street and listened to my thoughts.

M B   According to you, the project is "one of the largest visi-
       ble installations of contemporary art in the world."[7] Is it
       also some type of museum?

D J   In a certain sense, it is diametrically opposed to the idea
       of a museum. We refer to it as a foundation, but that term
       is also not very exciting. It's a museum in the sense that
       works are housed there permanently and they are exhib-
       ited in a way that I deem appropriate. Several large-scale
       works are shown there permanently; one group of works
       has been made specifically for the site. Then we also placed
       works by John Chamberlain in a large building,[8] and for
       the works by Dan Flavin, which are to come, we are con-
       structing a new building, because it's difficult to install the
       works appropriately in the existing buildings.[9]

M B   How did this foundation come into being, and why in
       Marfa, of all places, down there at the Mexican border?

D J   I first spent the summer there in 1971.[10] In 1973, '74, I bought
       three buildings – including the land around them – and
       started to install my own works. I've been living there
       since 1975, and then in 1979, the [Dia] foundation was
       added, which purchased the majority of Fort [D. A.] Rus-
       sell, where the Chinati Foundation is located. We had a
       huge clash regarding the foundation, and now I am also
       overseeing this part.

M B   The Dia foundation was involved in this, wasn't it?[11]

D J   Yes. As far as the current management of the foundation is
       concerned, it comprises myself and five other administra-
       tors. The money is going to last another three years; then
       we will have to come up with more. So we need the sup-
       port of companies, the state of Texas, et cetera. In short,
       any sum is welcome.

M B   How far are you yourself financially involved in the
       foundation?

D J   I own property there, but this is separate from the foun-
       dation. The money that I make I use for my own projects,

but I think that I might have to inject some money into the foundation, should funds run low.

MB   In an essay on the idea of the Chinati Foundation, you wrote, "Somewhere a portion of contemporary art has to exist as an example of what art and its contents were meant to be. Somewhere, just as the platinum-iridium meter guarantees the tape measure, a strict measure must exist for the art of this time and place. Otherwise art is only show and monkey business."[12] Are you referring to the foundation, or art in general?

DJ   Art in general; this was written when only half of the project in Texas had been realized. I believe that the works of all good artists should be housed permanently somewhere. But I don't want all works here in Texas where I am. Somewhere Ad Reinhardt's works should be installed so they don't get damaged. I just can't comprehend how you can gain an appreciation for the work of Reinhardt, Newman, [Josef] Albers, or any artist when their work is scattered all over.

MB   So Chinati is a pantheon of the standard of values?

DJ   It certainly establishes standards of value, but only in reference to the installation of particular works – let's say, mine or Dan Flavin's. In the best sense, they exist as controls against amateurish installations.

MB   Your motivation for the Chinati project also stems from your uneasiness about the art business today – its hustle and randomness. Is it different from the '60s?

DJ   The uneasiness doesn't originate from today. What I am doing today I already did back in New York when I bought the building in 1968.[13] My installations in Texas go back to 1971, '72, and were already an expression of uneasiness about the situation of the galleries and museums back then. The current business situation is of course different, but not fundamentally.

MB   Looking at these huge hangar-like halls installed with several dozen similar, aligned, big steel boxes [see image 61], one has the impression of a monument – a lonely monument?

DJ   No, I really don't like the word "monument." I do not want to create monuments. "Permanence" and "endurance" are better terms. The idea of a monument is just floating around, yet I do not like any form of monuments, be it for presidents, kings, or whatever.

MB   Doesn't the location – the desert – also have a further-reaching influence on the aura and significance of the foundation? Jean Baudrillard, a European, once said that American culture is the heiress of the desert.[14]

DJ   I think that's a vast exaggeration. My art has its roots in New York, because that's where the good artists were. So it really doesn't have anything to do with West Texas, although I like the region very much. If deserts would produce art, North Africa would be bustling with art – or the Gobi Desert.

MB   The postwar art dynamics were more or less shaped by a transatlantic cultural ping-pong: up until the '70s, an American dominance ruled, until Europe awakened more and more during the '80s, and recently there has been a strong, young New York scene coming forward again. What is your opinion on the principal differences between the European and American ideas of and sensibilities for art?

DJ   I believe these differences are slowly eroding. There is no hint in the works of Richard Long that those couldn't have originated in America, as far as I can see. Carl Andre, on the other hand, could equally well be European.

MB   But it's hard to imagine that Europeans could have created anything so pure and pragmatic in the '60s – or that they would have wanted to, for that matter – as what was being made in America.

DJ   It is obvious that Europe had almost entirely been destroyed. Ten years after the war, there were still people who were completely old-fashioned – [Pierre] Soulages, for example; the French put him on par with Jackson Pollock, which was pretty annoying. The reason for this was that many had emigrated to America, many had died, or they simply remained part of the old generation.

MB   So there are distinct differences?

DJ   The opposites aren't that extreme, and it takes two in order to have differences. Europe was willing to accept the cultural imperialism. America and Russia had won the war, and the culture of the winner is always very attractive. That's why it got so popular. America also had all the money; the bills were paid here. But America is actually just a semideveloped European colony.

MB   Many Americans see Europe as an elegant version of the third world, though!

DJ   That's true to a certain extent. Americans are somewhat ignorant regarding Europe. They don't know, for example, that Europe is a lot wealthier and has a higher standard of living. At the moment, America is in a truly miserable position: there is great poverty which doesn't exist here in Europe. The poverty that is present in Europe, e.g., in Sicily, is of a different kind – it's a poverty in the traditional sense, whereas in America, being poor means a complete marginalization and disenfranchisement. If you look at any arbitrary Swiss village, my god, it's the most amazing one in comparison to Marfa, Texas. Why are they so poor there? Because they are so foolish – and then there is also the US government. I believe Europe is wealthier in other respects as well, but we can't discuss everything here.

MB   All right. In closing, I would like to talk about your memorable criticism in the magazine *Art in America* in 1984. Those were two polemics against the art business in America, kind of a sweeping blow that didn't spare anyone involved: the galleries, the museums, the critics, even the artists. What were some of the reactions that followed?

DJ   This article was read by many people. There were a lot of reactions; I only got to hear the bad ones. But some people also told me that they liked it. The article was translated into many languages – it's even available in Catalan.

MB   It was published during a time when there was a considerable emphasis on painting. Did you feel your work was being neglected because of that?

DJ   No, not at all. In reality, nothing had changed. Painting as well as the fashion of the day were always dominating. I was with Leo Castelli [Gallery] in New York for a long time,[15] and the dominant people at that time there were also Lichtenstein, Jasper Johns, and so on. Any three-dimensional works, the gallery neglected. So that's nothing new. Every three, four years, Leo Castelli tried to find a new Jasper Johns. He never found him, but while he was looking, he neglected everyone else.

MB   Would you repeat the criticism today, in 1988?

DJ   Yes, I am actually doing that. I write regularly. What I wrote in 1984 was tame in comparison to some of the other articles. I am currently in the process of organizing the many writings.[16] I would have also needed more time to be more specific in the article you are referring to.

MB   It conveys a bit of a melancholy spirit, almost as if the development of art had come to a halt.

DJ   No, I didn't want to express that there is an end to the development, because that is not what I believe. It is always possible to do something new and unusual. I'm against defeatism, and I think that one needs to create. I'm simply of the opinion that the circumstances are bad.

Translated from the German by Susanne Maurer.

First published: Markus Brüderlin, "Veränderung in einem für gute Kunst gültigen Maß," *Kunstforum International*, June–July 1988, 111–21.

1   See Judd's "A Long Discussion Not About Master-Pieces But Why There Are So Few of Them: Part I" (1983) and "A Long Discussion Not About Master-Pieces But Why There Are So Few of Them: Part II" (1984) in *Donald Judd Writings*, 352–76 and 378–97, respectively. "Part I" was first published in *Art in America*, September 1984, 9–19; "Part II" was first published in *Art in America*, October 1984, 9–15.

2   Original note: "Compare Hans Ulrich Reck, 'On the End of Indifference,' *Kunstforum International*, September/October 1986, 68."

3   In the 1980s, Judd created a work to be sited behind the Vienna Secession, an 1898 Jugendstil building created as a showcase for the artists of the Secession movement and today a contemporary art museum. This unrealized work involved the construction of concrete walls in a triangular shape that would have defined a grass slope and allowed for walking and sitting. See Judd's "Sezession" (1989) in *Donald Judd: Architektur*, 117–19.

4   *Donald Judd: Sculptures 1965–1987*, Stedelijk Van Abbemuseum, Eindhoven, The Netherlands, April 26–June 2, 1987; Städtische Kunsthalle, Düsseldorf, June 27–August 9, 1987; ARC/Musée d'Art Moderne de la Ville de Paris, December 8, 1987–February 7, 1988; Fundació Joan Miró, Barcelona, February 25–April 24, 1988; Castello di Rivoli, Turin, June 4–September 30, 1988.

5   See Judd's "Specific Objects" (1964) in *Donald Judd Writings*, 134–45.

6   Judd refers here to Duchamp's *In Advance of the Broken Arm* (1915), a ready-made consisting of a snow shovel with "from Marcel Duchamp 1915" painted on the handle. At 101 Spring Street, Judd installed an authorized replica of the lost original produced by Galleria Schwarz, Milan, in 1964.

7   See Judd's "Statement for the Chinati Foundation/La Fundación Chinati" (1987) in *Donald Judd Writings*, 485.

8   Judd refers here to the Chamberlain Building.

9   Flavin's large-scale work in colored fluorescent light for six buildings (former barracks at Fort D. A. Russell) at the Chinati Foundation was initiated in the early 1980s. Flavin finalized his design in 1996, and the installation was completed and opened to the public in 2000. See Marianne Stockebrand, ed., *Chinati: The Vision of Donald Judd* (Marfa, TX: The Chinati Foundation; New Haven, CT: Yale University Press, 2010), 224–47.

10   In the fall and winter of 1971, Judd rented a small house in Marfa, Texas, spending his first summer there in 1972. See Judd's "Casa Lujan and La Catorcena" (1989) in *Donald Judd: Architektur*, 26–30.

11   Original note: "The Dia foundation, one of the largest private sponsors of contemporary art, also offered artists of the 1960s (minimal art, et cetera) the opportunity to experiment with types of works that due to their large scale were not shown in museums (e.g., John Chamberlain works and two rooms for Walter De Maria [*Broken Kilometer* and *Earth Room*] in New York). In 1985, the financing of such projects was drastically reduced. Leading this was the Chinati project, which had been supported by the Dia foundation since 1979. Donald Judd threatened the Chinati Foundation with a lawsuit, as he believed it was breaking contract. In its May–June 1985 issue, *Kunstforum International* printed a translation of a corresponding article that ran in *The New York Times* in February 1985, together with commentary by Franz Dahlem." After a settlement with Dia in 1986, the Chinati Foundation was realized by Judd and opened to the public that same year. For more on the Chinati Foundation's early relationship with Dia, see Judd's "Statement for the Chinati Foundation/La Fundación Chinati" (1987) in *Donald Judd Writings*, 484–89.

12   Judd, "Statement for the Chinati Foundation/La Fundación Chinati," 486.

13   Judd refers here to 101 Spring Street.

14   "American culture is heir to the deserts, but the deserts here are not part of a Nature defined by contrast with the town." Jean Baudrillard, *America*, trans. Chris Turner (New York: Verso, 1988), 63.

15   Judd's first show at the Leo Castelli Gallery was a group exhibition in December 1965. His last show was a solo exhibition in 1984.

16   Judd refers here to *Donald Judd: Complete Writings 1975–1986*, which was published in 1987.

Interview with Alexandra Munroe and Reiko Tomii
December 8, 1988

In October 1959, Judd favorably reviewed Yayoi Kusama's first solo show in the United States, at the Brata Gallery, New York (*Yayoi Kusama*, October 9–29, 1959). This was his second month as an art critic for *ARTnews*. The review begins: "Yayoi Kusama is an original painter. The five white, very large paintings in this show are strong, advanced in concept, and realized."

In this interview with art historians Alexandra Munroe and Reiko Tomii – conducted at 101 Spring Street as part of their research for *Yayoi Kusama: A Retrospective*, at the Center for International Contemporary Arts, New York (September 27, 1989–January 31, 1990) – Judd describes his first meeting with Kusama at her studio, saying, "I thought the paintings were terrific, and I wrote that all down…. They were the best paintings put out, or at least the best paintings that were new in any way. Aside from Newman and Rothko, people older."

Judd and Kusama became neighbors in 1960, living and working on different floors of a building at 53 East Nineteenth Street until Judd moved to 101 Spring Street in 1969. The two remained lifelong friends. In February 1978, Judd visited Kusama while in Japan for the exhibition *The Sculpture of Donald Judd*, at Galerie Watari, Tokyo (February 22–March 22, 1978).

AM   [Alexandra Munroe] Why don't you start with how you met her [Yayoi Kusama] – were you living in the same building?

DJ   [Donald Judd] I was living in a little apartment – an expensive little apartment; I had to take it on an emergency basis. It was on about Eighty-Fifth Street.[1] That's where I first had the big white painting.[2] I met her because I reviewed the Brata show, and I guess they told me to go to her studio or something.[3]

AM   What kind of gallery was the Brata Gallery at that time?

DJ   It was a small Tenth Street gallery.[4] And it was an artist cooperative, I think; it wasn't a regular gallery, I'm pretty sure. I believe it was run by two brothers who were painters who did framing, named [John and Nicholas] Krushenick.[5] One of them is fairly well known as a painter. And then I think they made frames and everything at the gallery. As far as I know, they had the four paintings in there; I'm just trying to figure out why I went to the studio. Anyway, obviously the magazine sent me there.

AM   That was *ARTnews*?

DJ   Yeah.

AM   And what did you think?

DJ   Oh, I thought the paintings were terrific, and I wrote that all down. Obviously, I met her and I talked to her. I mean, Yayoi could say things, but I realized after a while, a year or two, that she really didn't understand very much in English.

RT   [Reiko Tomii] Oh, really?

DJ   Later on, she learned a lot more English. But I think at first, she didn't. I overestimated it.

AM   You realized that you were not being understood. [*Laughter*] How did you react to her work?

DJ   She was very serious. As I said in the review, they were some of the best – they were the best paintings put out, or at least the best paintings that were new in any way. Aside from Newman and Rothko, people older.

AM   And you still feel that in retrospect?

DJ   Yes. She's an extremely, an extremely good painter.

AM   She's now beginning to paint more. She has a whole new series of paintings that are quite beautiful. Also net, but more translucent.

RT   Some of them are organic – some of them are like a sponge that's kind of moldy.

AM   And then a net one, too, that's more translucent and very beautiful.

   How do you place her work at that time – in retrospect, is it very individual? Where do you think it comes from?

DJ   I know where it comes from. It comes from Yayoi. [*Laughter*] Most of the paintings by people younger than the original artists or painters were very second rate, and it was not new at all. I felt that what she was doing was something new and, as people say, "advanced," if you want to call it that. If you compare it to almost anybody at that point, it's newer and more original, if you strike out Pollock, Newman, Rothko, Reinhardt, et cetera. The only person you could kind of find that might be a little bit close, and that was for a brief time, was Frank Stella. But actually, I think she's somewhat more original than Frank, and also, she clearly has more durability than Frank.

AM   We won't quote you. We'd like to, but we won't.

DJ   I don't care.

AM   Well, in that case, we might.

DJ   So, in a way, they're some of the best paintings done in '59. They are the best paintings, perhaps. I'd have to go back and sit and think about '59.

AM   What do you think they're about?

DJ   Well, you know what she says. It's hard to say what they're about; people ask me that question, too, and it's too complicated. You know what she says about obsessiveness … clearly, they are pretty obsessive. Anyway, you can never say what art is about.

AM   I know. Of course, as art historians, we have this desperate –

DJ   You can go all around these things, but you know, one of the jobs of the art is to be so complex that you can't say what it's about.

AM   I know.

Do you think that there were other artists at that time or later, related to her or not related to her, who shared this kind of obsessiveness? Or do you think it was her own individual –

DJ   I think it was very much her.

AM   I think so, too.

DJ   Obviously, she learned from Pollock and from the New York situation, with the big scale and wholeness and all that.

RT   I think that it's the general trend to learn from Pollock and the New York School; it seems that Kusama followed that path. Do you think she was aware of what [art] happened before?

DJ   Yes, very much so.

RT   Did you discuss this?

DJ   Yes, to some extent. She saw the place I lived in on Eighty-Fifth Street. And, let's see, she was living with an architect named George Matsuda; I visited them, and then she moved with George to a place on Nineteenth Street and Fourth Avenue.[6]

AM   I haven't heard of him. He's Japanese American?

DJ   Yes. She's probably trying to bury George [*laughter*]; they didn't get along too well. Anyway, they moved to the third floor of a four-story building on Fourth Avenue and Nineteenth Street. Then the fourth floor became vacant, and she told me about it, so I could have a real loft. Before that, I lived in a cold-water flat,[7] which was miserable, and the [Eighty-Fifth Street] apartment, which was miserable in its own way. So I got the loft, and I lived there for ten years or more because of her. She was a neighbor; she and George lived downstairs.

AM   That's great. Now, who else was living in that building? I
      know later she was living in a building with Larry Rivers.

DJ   That was later.

AM   This was '59?

DJ   Well, this was the '60s – I don't know, slightly later than '59.

RT   Sometime in the early '60s.

AM   We're going to get this chronology straight when we're in
      Japan. I'm determined.

DJ   Yeah, I don't know what year I moved there.

AM   Were you living there, or was this a studio for you?

DJ   I lived and worked there on the top floor. They were on
      the next floor. The second floor was a tailoring business,
      and the ground floor was a woolen business. So there were
      only two tenants.

AM   I'm sorry, the ground floor was what?

DJ   A woolen business. And they were not too fond of heat-
      ing the building, which was their job.

AM   What kind of memories do you have of interacting with
      her? You were great friends, from what I understand.

DJ   I saw a lot of her. We were neighbors, too, so it was easy
      to see a lot of her. Sometimes George would be gone
      or something, and sometimes she would come up and
      sit around my apartment and talk, or I'd go down there
      and we'd talk. So obviously I saw a lot of her. She worked
      very hard; she worked obsessively. She'd work nonstop,
      and then she'd kind of go to pieces for a while. She'd
      work right through the night and everything, as far as I
      could tell.

RT   So you witnessed how she developed from one piece to
      another?

DJ   Most paintings were done in one shot. I couldn't under-
      stand how she could do that, but she would start in a cor-
      ner and then go across. On the forty-foot painting, you
      could tell that it was probably rolled up, and she would
      start it at one edge and then go across.

AM   "In one shot" – meaning at one time? For forty-eight hours, she would do nothing but paint?

DJ   Seemed to be, yeah. I wasn't there all the time.

AM   That's a performance in itself.

DJ   I went to sleep upstairs. [*Laughter*]

RT   But that's the impression you got from the way she worked.

DJ   I doubt if many of her paintings were done stop-and-start. They were probably done straight through. Sometimes I'd go down there and there'd be a whole new painting. And I remember I helped her stuff the phallic things; it was days on end of stuffing. I had a lot to do with it. I helped get the rowboat through the streets originally.[8] We pushed the rowboat through the streets on dollies.

AM   Where did you find the rowboat?

DJ   I can't remember where we got it.

AM   That must have been her first boat.

DJ   Yes. We got it somewhere in the neighborhood, and we had to get it back, and I think another painter who lived in the adjacent building helped. We pushed it home on dollies. I don't know where it was from.

AM   She told me this wonderful story in Japan this time – that she was so poor that she couldn't afford paint, so all she could afford was the garbage on the streets, and that's what inspired her to start stuffing upholstery and couches. I'm sure there is more to it than that, but how did you find her finding things?

DJ   I don't know where she got the couches. They would just turn up sometimes.

AM   But they were all junk?

DJ   Yeah, pretty much. Those things you can find on the street. And old chairs. But somebody must have given her the rowboat, though, because as far as I know, it was a complete rowboat.

AM   Who else did she get to work for her?

DJ   I suppose George did some too, but I don't know. George didn't like to do things like that. I don't know, there were other people who helped. It took a while. And that wasn't the only piece.

A M   Was it socks then, or was she sewing?[9]

D J   She sewed them.

A M   Did she have a machine, or did she do it by hand?

D J   I think so, I think she had a machine – it was a lot of it.

A M   Did she talk about her work much?

D J   Yes. She talked a lot about her work, but not about what it meant, especially. She talked about her life, so I know lots of stories. There's too much to tell you, because I really know her well, though I haven't seen her in ten years. She was fairly paranoid about the New York art situation; I thought it was paranoid at the time. I mean, it's always a lousy situation, but –

R T   Could it be because she was Japanese?

D J   Yeah, because she was Japanese and a woman. I think one problem was that she was also very ambitious and wanted to become rich and famous, which wasn't exactly one of my interests for myself. So I was a little critical of that. But she was, for example, mad at Warhol because of the repeated images, because she had felt that she had done it first.

A M   What did you learn from her?

D J   A lot. She was a very serious artist. She really worked hard – but so did I. But she was ahead of me in terms of developing her work and her paintings. She paid more attention or understood more thoroughly what had to be done about the paintings that Pollock, Newman, Rothko, and [Clyfford] Still had done.

A M   What do you mean by that?

D J   How to deal with this still relatively new situation. So to some extent, she was kind of a model for me. Being in close range like that – it was very nice. She was very jealous of any kind of competition, though. I did, fairly early on, a little painting on glass that has chicken wire in it [image 71] – [the kind] that you just get out of a door, so I picked it up someplace – and she was very upset, because she had planned to use chicken wire sometime. It's not that I saw her using chicken wire; it's that she had it in mind to do it someday. So she was very upset, because here someone had already used chicken wire.

A M   She was very sophisticated. This is one thing one gets from her now meeting her. But people who knew her then also say, and you say, that she was very ambitious, and she had a very professional sense of what an artist is that now is very common but then was less common, possibly.

D J   Most people now don't have her sense of what that really means. She had a career side that I didn't agree with, because I didn't really have that so much. She was concerned about her reputation and her so-called career. Plenty of people are concerned with that now, but she was also concerned with making the art and did make the art. She really did a tremendous amount of work.

Another time when she was mad at me, I was doing paintings in Liquitex and water [image 72], and I had to do them flat on the floor. I was above her, but it was a pretty thick floor, so I wasn't too concerned about it running through, but it did run through to her painting. She was legitimately pretty mad. She wanted to throw the painting out. She started to step on it or kick it or something, but I had to stop her. Another time, when they were fighting about who was to get the loft when they parted – and who was to stay and who was to go – she and George had a big fight, and he started throwing paintings down the stairwell, which I stopped.

A M   God, you were really important.

D J   Yes. It was really horrifying. The guy was throwing them out the door and down the stairs.

A M   Can you tell us a little bit more about what it felt like in

New York at that time? What was going on? What were people's concerns?

DJ   It was a lot smaller. And it was a very lively time, compared to what happened afterward, which nobody expected to have it turn –

[*Break in recording*]

DJ   See, when I was writing criticism, I really knew everything that was being done in the art world for a while.

AM   How long did you write criticism for *ARTnews*?

DJ   Well, *ARTnews* was very short because I quit. It was only two or three months, but I wrote for *Arts Magazine* for, who knows – three or four years, five years. I'd stop and I'd start.[10] So for a while I really did know everything. It's enough to know it once; you don't have to know each painting. And when you consider all the shows that occurred, it's pretty fabulous. After that, in a way, I didn't have as much to do in New York as I did before. I was inclined not to get to know people and inclined to be alone. But with the reviewing and the fact that it's a city where you ran into people, and you start to get to know quite a few people, it's hard not to see people. I used to meet – just in the same building, going to get the Sunday *New York Times* on a Saturday night, it probably happened three or four times, you'd run into Ad Reinhardt, who usually didn't want to talk either, but he always wanted to talk in the cold, for a half an hour [*laughter*], on the street corner. I never went to his house, but he lived nearby, somewhat.

AM   So you're saying that artists, in a way, were more isolated unto themselves?

DJ   Both. They were pretty isolated. The younger people were more isolated than the older ones. I think people my age were comparatively solitary. Some people – Oldenburg and others – knew each other to some extent, but mostly didn't make a group in any direction.

A M   You don't feel part of a group?

D J   No. And I certainly wasn't then. While Newman and Pollock and everybody had the "artist group," they made an effort to meet; I think they would hang out with each other, too.[11] Some artists did that, perhaps Claes and some of the people he knew – but I never sat around with anybody. In fact, Yayoi was the only person I ever sat around with. So I never was in such a situation in New York, and my highest level of social activity – which was very infrequent – was actually in Los Angeles, where I met all of those people, because I used to stay with Larry [Bell]. That was the only sitting around.

I think Yayoi knew quite a few people … I'm trying to think.

A M   You seem so different, though. You must have been a wonderful combination. I can see that you would be very calming for her. It's a beautiful combination; I can see the dynamic.

D J   Maybe she's calmer now, and I'm the more manic. [*Laughter*]

A M   No, she's not calmer. [*Laughter*] You might be more manic, but she's definitely not calmer. She's very beautiful and very poignant and very intense.

D J   She's a pretty smart person.

A M   She is very smart.

D J   What she was saying when she showed us around Tokyo in '77 when I was there – what she had to say about the town, the architecture, the society – was all very smart. After a while, when she picked up her English, we talked quite a bit.

A M   But you haven't really kept in touch much?

D J   I'm bad with letters, as I said. Yayoi sends me catalogues now and then from exhibitions.

R T   Do you recall when she moved out of the loft building? The mid-'60s?

D J   I think it's earlier. She wasn't there too long after I got married. Maybe mid-'60s, because that was '64. She could have been there another year, which would make it '65. And Oldenburg came down, because Claes was still with Patty Oldenburg. I remember going there for a party, and also Yayoi's place, too, at a different time, I guess. That could be figured out.

   As you see, I have this foundation in Texas, and it's very lonesome out there.[12] One of the ideas I've had is to show Yayoi's work and make a document. It's not an enormous space.

This discussion was sourced from an audio recording. Due to the discussion's length and focus on Yayoi Kusama, only excerpts are included here. The original audio-cassettes are in the Collection of the Center for International Contemporary Arts, New York, Historical Music Recordings Collection, Fine Arts Library, The University of Texas at Austin.

1   Judd refers here to 326 East Eighty-Fifth Street.

2   Over the course of his life, Judd owned at least seven works by Kusama: two *Infinity Net* paintings (one six by ten feet, the other approximately two and half by four feet), at least two dresses, a large floor sculpture, a box work, and a small red sculpture that he installed in his library at La Mansana de Chinati/The Block in Marfa, Texas.

3   See Judd's review of *Yayoi Kusama* (1959) in *Donald Judd: Complete Writings 1959–1975*, 2.

4   In the 1950s and 1960s, many cooperative and artist-run galleries opened and operated in New York's East Village. The majority of these galleries were located on Tenth Street, whose name became shorthand for the larger scene.

5   In 1957, brothers John and Nicholas Krushenick opened a framing shop on Tenth Street; it shortly thereafter became the Brata Gallery.

6   Judd refers here to 53 East Nineteenth Street.

7   Judd refers here to 302 and 304 East Twenty-Seventh Street.

8   Kusama's first environmental installation, *Aggregation: One Thousand Boats Show*, Gertrude Stein Gallery, New York, December 17, 1963–January 11, 1964, included a rowboat covered in white phallic sculptures.

9   Kusama created her "accumulations" by sewing sock-like forms and stuffing them with cotton.

10   Judd began writing reviews in 1959, first for *ARTnews*, from September to November of that year. In December, he was hired by Hilton Kramer to review exhibitions for *Arts Magazine*; he continued to write for the magazine, with only a few interruptions, until March 1965.

11   Judd refers here to the Club, a meeting group of New York artists whose membership included many abstract expressionists. From 1948 until the mid-1950s, in a loft at 39 East Eighth Street, the Club hosted weekly discussions and lectures on art, metaphysics, psychology, philosophy, and other topics of shared interest.

12   Judd refers here to the Chinati Foundation; see Judd's "Statement for the Chinati Foundation/La Fundación Chinati" (1987) in *Donald Judd Writings*, 484–89.

"Donald Judd: An Interview with John Griffiths"
For *Art & Design*
May–June 1989

In addition to this interview, which was conducted on the occasion of the exhibition *Donald Judd*, at the Waddington Galleries, London (May 22–June 17, 1989),
the 1989 issue of *Art & Design* included an edited version of Judd's essay "Ausstellungsleitungsstreit" (1989).

"Ausstellungsleitungsstreit" was originally written for the catalogue accompanying the exhibition *Bilderstreit*, at the Museum Ludwig, Cologne (April 8–
June 28, 1989), by request of the show's curators, Siegfried Gohr and Johannes
Gachnang. In an addendum to "Ausstellungsleitungsstreit," Judd noted, "This essay was written for the exhibition *Bilderstreit*, Cologne, 1989, to be published in
the catalogue but was not used." Instead, it appeared in German in the April–May
1989 issue of *Kunstforum* and in English in the volume *Bilanz einer Debatte* (*Result of
a Debate*), compiled by the *Bilderstreit* curators and published later that same year.

In "Ausstellungsleitungsstreit," one of his many statements against large museum exhibitions, Judd wrote: "Very large exhibitions such as *Bilderstreit* are not
beneficial either to art and artists or to the public.... The large exhibitions enforce
the very strong attitude among museum personnel, those assembling large collections, and some dealers, especially in New York City where many of the post–
World War II commercial attitudes began, that the serious effort to make art by
many artists is just a 'scene,' one thing after another, one 'style' after another. The
point of an exhibition is usually to establish a kind of work on the 'scene.' To this
end everything is used and debased."

JG   [John Griffiths] Mr. Judd, in the last two hours I have been looking at your recent works and talking to a number of interested persons: critics, historians, curators, and gallery owners. I thought it would be of value to ask you to comment on some of the points raised when the objects were, so to speak, immediate to us.

I was chatting just now with Ronald Alley, who was Keeper of the Tate Gallery's Modern Collection at the time when your work in copper there was acquired.[1] We were studying your Waddington exhibit number nine in Cor-ten and purple plexiglass [image 73], and we both used the term "sculptor." But of course Mr. Alley, in his catalogue of the Tate's collection, "officially" classifies you as a sculptor.[2] Are you a sculptor?

DJ   [Donald Judd] It depends. That's a matter of definition. I don't use the word because, literally, it's not sculpting. I think the work is three-dimensional, and then it's sculpture if you think of sculpture as all work that's three-dimensional.

JG   But what word would you use if you needed a word to refer to it as a whole?

DJ   Then I'd say it was sculpture.

JG   Are you "an artist"?

DJ   Oh yes. And sculpture's very much a part of me — fabrication.

JG   You're a fabricator, then, but you're not a maker of myths, are you?

DJ   No. No myths. Just a fabricator.

JG   Do your works exist apart from your works? Are they merely the evidence of concepts? When you're out of the room, how do they exist for you?

DJ   I agree with Bishop Berkeley.[3] But yes. I think of them by now as works spread all over the world — at least, the industrialized world. And they exist inasmuch as I'm aware of them. And since I've seen a lot of other people's work, they will exist after I'm dead. Yes, like that, they exist.

JG   Someone said: "There are very beautiful objects in the sense that I might say a masterpiece of Georgian furniture is very beautiful." And someone commented: "Yes, I agree, and, except for pieces like the 150-by-70-by-150-centimeter galvanized iron object, and therefore the problem of size, I can see any of these going into a very beautiful Georgian room with Georgian furniture. Any one of Judd's pieces would be an object eminently suitable for such a room." Does that way of looking at them appeal to you? Do you agree?

DJ   That's fine by me, because I like beautiful old things. I have a certain amount of old furniture myself and it's strange, in New York on the fifth floor, though it's not Georgian but a bit later; the design is Directoire but it's Italian. I have a bench from about 1800, and that bench in its own way is about the only piece of furniture in a room with an Oldenburg, two pieces of mine, and a [John] Chamberlain, and it's just fine. They all work together perfectly well. The building is 1870, so the room is 1870. Yes, it's just fine.

JG   What does that mean, that they "work together"?

DJ   It means basically that visually there's no conflict. It means a nice space you like to be in winter.

JG   So you don't object to people defining a work of yours as a beautiful object in a particular context?

DJ   I think it's art, but it can also be a beautiful object.

JG   What is art as distinct from a beautiful object, with special reference to your work?

DJ   Well, as a piece of furniture … a piece of furniture can be a beautiful object. A beautiful chair or a carpet: I got a beautiful Chi'en Mung Chinese carpet the other day. It's fabulous, it's been used: that's a beautiful object. The category of beautiful object can include art and furniture.

JG   Someone might pay the same sum for one of your works as for another beautiful object from another century which is described as "art." You don't object to the inclusion of

one of your works as one among a number of beautiful
"art objects" from past and present?

D J No, but it's important that you call it art. That distinction
is important.

J G How does your art now differ from early Judd?

D J That point seems to come up quite a bit now. I haven't
thought about it a whole lot. When I started to make the
work that I considered my own, in a way that was that. It
would work the way it was according to whatever things
I was interested in. That's I think what has happened. So
the work does change. But I don't have a strong sense of —
call it development, and I don't have any great pressure to
do work. I don't have any great pressure to change, or to
do something new. I'm just quite happy with it in the first
place. So it's going to take its course. You know, you get
older, and you've got things to think about and the world
and lots of things, and that takes a natural course.

J G Is there then a conceptual connection between your maturing experience, as this or that thing happens to you,
and these particular works?

D J Sure there is. Yes.

J G Something you can conceptualize?

D J Yes, you have different assumptions. You're in a different
context. You have different assumptions about how long
you've lived and about how much longer you're going to
have to live and all that. It's kind of a drastic thing you
have to deal with, and that changes you a bit. I don't think
it necessarily changes my work a great deal, but it does
change it. There's also the fact that I never really expected
to have any money to do anything and the possibilities
now are greater than I ever imagined, because there's a lot
more money to do bigger pieces and greater variety.

J G Has there been any qualitative change, in texture say? Is
that more important? Someone just now warned a friend
not to touch one of your pieces, however lightly, because

delicacy of texture, the surface bloom almost, was now so important a part of the whole.

DJ   Well, the pieces are meant to be looked at, they are not made to be touched. But if you have the pieces yourself, in your own living space, yes, though it depends what pieces – well, the present pieces are pretty tough. But if there's a whole bunch of people it becomes impossible. It's a question of quantity.

JG   Someone said, for instance, that you've added more color, a lot more color, in the last ten years. Is there some ascertainable change of that nature?

DJ   Yes, the plexiglass; in one they're all red and so on. I don't think the color's changed a whole lot, though I'm very interested in the color, and I'd like to take it off into a certain area that I think is new to me. I'd like to take it further. It's just a beginning. We had trouble with the factory and that stopped it. I would like to use the bright colors more. Theoretically, I would consider the gray a color. The aluminum or Cor-ten is as much a color as anything else; to me it's all color. I had a conflict between bright color and the nature of the material. I liked the material a great deal, and perhaps color would have to be applied, and that's always been a certain conflict. Anodizing is one possibility.

JG   But it's a problem of fabrication and not, so to speak, an existential choice. It just happens.

DJ   Developing the color, you mean? It's an old interest which I realize is very important to me. It's an old problem. Somehow, I have to find a way to get at it, and at this point I don't know how to get at it. The small pieces, I think, are fine and I learned a lot from them, but the parts are small, and somehow, I have to learn how to make bigger printed parts and I don't quite know how to do that. Painting the metal was a problem.

JG   What sort of location do you conceive for your bigger

DJ   There's a lot of different categories. Ordinarily, no. The big piece in the corner was supposed to go into a large show in Germany, but I pulled it out of the show.[4] It's a long story.[5]

JG   You can't give me a précis?

DJ   I made an agreement with the organizer that if the catalogue would include a statement by me against large shows and their implications, we would make a piece and lend it to the show. When they got the text, they wanted to edit it, and then they didn't want to print it. So I pulled the piece out and told them not to have any other work of mine in the show. There is work in the show, but it's over my objections.

JG   You're not usually thought of as an artist who makes Beuysian gestures.

DJ   I've had lots of fights for the sake of the art, but they've been more private than this one. This one's not so much a fight as that I think that big shows are really bad for art.

JG   Why?

DJ   Because they give the public a very strange idea about art, and in this case, as was obvious from the press releases, the show was very slanted. It was all to support [Georg] Baselitz and such people.

JG   Do you see yourself as part of the history of modernism?

DJ   I know that people keep using the word "modernism." I'm not too sure what that means.

JG   It doesn't mean anything to you?

DJ   A whole lot ... well, what does it mean? Clem Greenberg and all those people? Actually, I'm mystified by it. Are the New York School and a few other people later "modernism"?

JG   Robert Hughes on TV told me the Eiffel Tower was modernism.[6] Do you see yourself as part of a history starting with the Eiffel Tower? It's a piece of metal, a construct, and people call it art.

DJ   Sounds like talk to me. You can always say it's the end of something else and the beginning of something else.

JG   Do you conceive of yourself historically?

DJ   In that my work developed in a certain context, in the context of painters in New York whose work I liked a great deal, and then Barnett Newman. Always, somehow, I've been on the wrong side of almost everything, and for some strange reason I was on the wrong side of Clement Greenberg and all those people. I'm thrown in with them when in fact they were hitting me over the head at the time. You have to talk about how things happen but it's very hard to make a really coherent history. Now no one's going around predicting anything because they don't have the faintest idea what's going to happen next. They don't know how to run a government, so five years from now…?

JG   You're in your own history, the history of your own art?

DJ   Yes. I think it's good work; that's one thing. It's important work; but that's a social statement. And social evaluations I take with a certain amount of salt, with skepticism.

JG   Nevertheless, you say it.

DJ   I have to judge it from my side.

JG   In spite of the Greenbergs.

DJ   Criticism hasn't been too great. But actually, Greenberg isn't one of the worst people. I'm not even particularly mad at the Greenbergs. Actually, they made a very narrow situation out of a very big situation. I think simplification and reduction to a few categories is very bad. I think you have to argue that there is a certain kind of change – there's better change and worse change. In the United States right now, for example, it's changing for the worse. And it wasn't good in the first place. Reagan. Bush. To be ever more drastic, it got worse after the war.

JG   Has this anything to do with art?

DJ   No. There's this preposterous book which connects the course of American art after World War II with America winning the war.[7] That's really preposterous. I really object to that.

JG   It is odd. But there is another book which follows up the story that in the Cold War period the CIA promoted a certain number of avant-garde artists abroad.

DJ   It's totally false. The CIA had its fingers in almost everything. I think the United States government knows very well that the artists are in opposition to it. Most public exhibitions are not of the best art. The first Russian show was Andrew Wyeth.[8] Just this shlock artist. One of the first institutional shows I was in was an exhibition in 1965 in São Paulo.[9] Stella and so on – about seven artists. Barnett was the only artist who actually went [to São Paulo], and he was sitting next to the ambassador and his wife, and she knew he was one of the artists. She said: "Why did they send your work down here and all these other guys when they could have sent Andrew Wyeth?"[10]

JG   Would you expect to see a Judd in a Gorbachev-invited show?

DJ   Maybe if Gorbachev did the show, but not if the Americans had anything to do with it. The United States is in the Brezhnev era. It's really poor, it's in bad shape.

JG   Do you think that in Russia they would be able to confront your work appropriately, after Wyeth?

DJ   Yes, but not with a mass show like *Bilderstreit*. That's a con. I'd like to have my own small show maybe. Or maybe with Richard Long.

JG   You find Long sympathetic?

DJ   A very good artist. He's probably the best. He's a real international artist. An important one.

JG   Like you?

DJ   A very different artist.

JG   Is there any other British artist you would put in the in-
      ternational class?
DJ   I don't think so. He's the best European artist. He's a far
      better artist than [Francis] Bacon or Henry Moore. His
      work is more genuine.
JG   More conceptual?
DJ   I'm not interested in things that don't exist. I'm interested
      in things actually being done. Of course, thinking goes
      into that. But it's not aside from that. I'm interested in the
      work, the thing that actually exists. What can you know
      about Michelangelo? What you really know is the art you
      see. That is the basic situation for an artist.

First published: John Griffiths, "Donald Judd: An Interview with John Griffiths,"
Art & Design, no. 7/8, 1989, 46–49.

1   In 1973, the Tate purchased a round-front progression in copper.
2   Ronald Alley, ed., *Catalogue of the Tate Gallery's Collection of Modern Art,
      Other Than Works by British Artists* (London: Tate Gallery, 1981).
3   Bishop George Berkeley (1685–1753) was an Anglo-Irish empiricist philos-
      opher who advanced a theory he called immaterialism. Judd included four
      books by Berkeley in his library in Marfa, Texas. Judd refers here, tongue
      in cheek, to Berkeley's idea that what he sees cannot exist without him.
4   Judd refers here to the exhibition *Bilderstreit*.
5   See Judd's "Ausstellungsleitungsstreit" (1989) in *Donald Judd Writings*,
      558–83.
6   Robert Hughes (1938–2012) was an Australian-born art critic and televi-
      sion documentarian. From 1970 until 2001, he was the chief art critic for
      Time magazine; his eight-episode 1980 television series on the develop-
      ment of modernism, *The Shock of the New*, was highly popular.
7   Judd refers here to Serge Guilbaut, *How New York Stole the Idea of Modern
      Art: Abstract Expressionism, Freedom, and the Cold War*, trans. Arthur Gold-
      hammer (Chicago: University of Chicago Press, 1983). Judd included four
      copies of this book in his library in Marfa, Texas.
8   In 1987, *An American Vision: Three Generations of Wyeth Art*, featuring work
      by N.C., Andrew, and James Wyeth, toured the Soviet Union. It was the
      first exhibition of American paintings to appear in the USSR since its
      formation.

9   VIII Bienal de São Paulo, Ibirapuera Park, São Paulo, September 4–
        November 28, 1965; National Collection of Fine Arts, Smithsonian Insti-
        tution, Washington, DC, January 27–March 6, 1966. This iteration of the
        Bienal de São Paulo also included works by Billy Al Bengston, Robert Ir-
        win, Barnett Newman, Larry Poons, and Frank Stella.
10   For another recounting of this anecdote, see Judd's "Imperialism, Nation-
        alism, and Regionalism" (1975) in *Donald Judd Writings*, 268–82.

"A Small Kind of Order"
Interview with David Batchelor for *Artscribe International*
May–June 1989

This interview was likely conducted in London on the occasion of the exhibition *Donald Judd*, at the Waddington Galleries, London (May 22–June 17, 1989). Included in this show were two works in Cor-ten steel, both of which were made in Marfa, Texas, at El Taller Chihuahuanese, a "small factory," as Judd referred to it, that he established in 1988 for the fabrication of his Cor-ten artworks.

DB   [David Batchelor] Your work of the late '60s has been represented as a critical response to certain features of abstract
      expressionism, its metaphysics, its claims to authenticity,
      the expressive surface, and so forth –

DJ   [Donald Judd] – which is absolutely not true. I knew Barnett Newman as a friend, and although I didn't know the
      others, my work has developed from theirs. My admiration
      for their work is perfectly straightforward. Of course, there
      are differences, but there are also many correspondences –
      philosophically and in other ways. My only reaction against
      anything was simply that their work was being debased by
      a number of artists. But this has more to do with de Kooning and a true expressionist style.

DB   What were these philosophical correspondences you
      mentioned?

DJ   In the case of Pollock, it has to do with what he called
      the complete omnipresence of chance. But I don't think
      his work, or Newman's, was expressionist in an ordinary
      sense. My work does not stand as a reaction to theirs. I'm
      simply attempting to do something that's my own, just as
      they did something that was their own.

DB   But your essay "Specific Objects" is nevertheless structured upon a set of oppositions.[1] You indicated a set of
      negative terms – "composition," in particular – which you
      saw it as necessary to escape.

DJ   I was given that essay as a job in 1964. It was not a manifesto. But there was only one side of abstract expressionism which has the kind of composition I objected to, that
      of [Franz] Kline and de Kooning, essentially. Their work
      was based upon the whole European tradition of composition, which has a certain philosophical attitude, a certain
      idea of experience. It's deeply buried in representation. I
      think those ideas are exhausted, and I have no interest in
      that kind of thing anymore. Which, by the way, doesn't
      make me anti-European. I admire European art a great

deal; I just don't see why it should be done over again, and badly. It's more a question of finding an equivalent to what they did and doing it for yourself. I always liked Matisse's work, and Léger's, but I realize I'm never going to understand those strange shapes that Matisse made. So the only way to make an effort to be as good as Matisse is to invent what I want to do, just as he invented what he wanted to do. And the same goes for Pollock; I can't take anything from his work.

DB   So what did act as a resource for your work of the '60s? What kind of antecedent work was usable?

DJ   Pollock and [Clyfford] Still and Newman and Rothko.

DB   What exactly was wrong with compositional, European-type art?

DJ   I think there's nothing wrong with Piero della Francesca, as it stands. I just can't use it.

DB   Against what you regarded as typifying European-type art you did posit an alternative set of technical procedures. At least, you identified with work which emphasized "singleness" or "wholeness" over relation between parts. And you claimed this work as anti-illusionistic, without allusion or anthropomorphism. Is that right?

DJ   Yes. But I wasn't really so interested in being anti anything. As I keep saying, I wanted to do something of my own. In any case, there were already examples of European artists whose work was not European in the old sense, like Yves Klein. His work was completely new.

DB   But where does the sense of something being "new" or "your own" come from if not out of some critical relationship with what has gone before?

DJ   It seems to me that's what quite a few artists in the past have done. There is a Sung dynasty painter, Mi Fei. I'm not as interested in the whole social context of his work as in the actual work you can see. That's a fairly traditional statement.

DB   I'm still troubled by the idea that it is possible for a work
      of art not to allude, or refer, or represent. I accept that
      you can more or less get away from representing a three-
      dimensional object on a two-dimensional surface. But is
      it not the case that simply by virtue of a work of art be-
      ing made from certain materials rather than others, of it
      being put together in one way rather than another, it is
      bound to refer to or imply a realm of associated things?

DJ   No. Again, Newman's and Pollock's thinking is appropriate
      here. You want to make something which is a new thing
      itself. Which means it doesn't allude to something else; it
      is something itself. People may come along and read cer-
      tain things into it, but perhaps that is their fault. I saw the
      Malevich show recently, which, incidentally, I thought was
      pretty much slanted in favor of his representational work.[2]
      I have trouble seeing what is interesting in this represen-
      tational work; for me the subject matter just acts as a kind
      of noise that gets in the way of the more interesting for-
      mal side of the work. I think something like the reverse
      happens to me: people find the abstractness the noise, so
      they look for something to put into it.

DB   Your work has a machine-tooled appearance. What is
      at stake in this, in the elimination of more traditional
      handling?

DJ   I don't like the quality of craft. I want my work to be well
      made, but not in that sense. There's a certain preciousness
      if a work is made too conspicuously well by hand. I don't
      want handwork to show at all.

DB   Why not?

DJ   Because it relates to the manipulation of painting and
      sculpture. Put crudely, the representational tradition has
      to do with looking at the world and representing the ob-
      jects you see. A certain reality is ascribed to those objects,
      which is anthropomorphism. Again, this is too simple, but
      what you feel about those objects also becomes part of the

painting. And in a way, it's always more to do with feeling than thinking, which serves to maintain a division I
don't like. I don't think that particular view of things is
real anymore. That's not the only kind of immediacy art
can have. I like the materials I use a great deal as materials,
and as far as I'm concerned, it doesn't go anywhere else.
Sheet aluminum is sheet aluminum, that's it.

DB   The repetition of more or less standardized elements is also
a feature of much of your work, as well as [Carl] Andre's.
What is the significance of this?

DJ   I can't speak for Carl, whose work I like a great deal, but
for me it's a small kind of order which I can deal with.

DB   Isn't your use of industrial materials, of machine-tooled
appearances, and of repeated standardized elements a way
of referring to a world of industrial production, to some
conception of *modernité*?

DJ   No. In a very general sense, the way the work is made
makes it look relatively new. But that's so general I'm not
sure how important it is. Certainly, if I carved the pieces
out of wood, they might look rather old-fashioned; in that
sense my things look quite modern, I guess. I like industrial things; I think they are mostly better than consumer
goods, but again, it's not a major interest of mine. And the
techniques I use are fairly routine. I'm certainly against
romanticizing the industrial. I hate the Centre Pompidou,
for example. It's pure romanticism, a kitsch view of industry and technology.

DB   In one way or another, all of the works in this show are
based on the format of a box with its front missing.[3] One
effect of this open format is that it avoids the "hollowness"
which for [Michael] Fried was one of the problems with
"literalist," three-dimensional work.[4] Is that important?

DJ   One of the things I figured out in my earliest three-
dimensional work was that I wanted to avoid any sensation of weight. This goes back to the business of represen-

tation. I think that most of the European tradition of art represented weight, if it was at all serious. I felt this reference to weight carried with it the problem of handiwork. I've always liked artists whose work has a kind of lightness – Cézanne, Matisse, and, to go a bit further back, Pierre Puget.[5] I wouldn't make a plain cube, like Tony Smith did – it's bound to seem heavy. Nor would I paint anything black, because black is not clear in space; it conceals more than it makes evident.

DB Some of your work is painted in a range of very bright colors. I take it you don't mix them yourself?

DJ They are all standard, numbered colors. Most of them come from Europe because it's hard to get good pure colors in the States.

DB The Cor-ten steel pieces in the current show are rather evenly and cleanly rusted [see image 73]. They have a kind of patina.

DJ Cor-ten produces a superficial rust which then stabilizes, supposedly. It's a kind of self-anodizing process – the rust acts as a layer of protection against the weather. It looks a little soft at the moment; it will toughen up after a while. The person who, I think, first made use of this was Richard Serra. But whereas we sandblasted these pieces to speed the process up a bit, he doesn't do that, so it takes years before the scale comes off. I particularly like his piece in the city of London, in spite of the site.[6] His *Tilted Arc* in downtown Manhattan has been taken away by the United States government.[7] The case was tried in their own court, which, like many things, is contrary to their claimed virtues. They found against him, and they took it away.

DB You said in an essay from 1973, "Somehow it is implied in good work that the artist wouldn't support the present oligarchy and the present war."[8] I take it you were referring to the Nixon administration and the war in Vietnam. Can you elaborate?

DJ   It's complicated. It is almost the definition of art that it is a totality, a whole. Which makes it very peculiar: it's both very personal and it's everything you know about the entire universe. So the span is terrific, and the problem every artist has is how to get everything together which doesn't easily go together. And temperament is one of the biggest mysteries, because you don't really know what's there. I think what you find in life has a lot to do with what you reject, what attitudes you disagree with. There are qualities in the work which would not agree with the fascist attitudes which a lot of architecture and some art has. I think when some people see the work, they can see that it lives in a certain area of acceptance and nonacceptance, but I think it is bad for art when it's overtly political – or overtly scientific or technical, for that matter. It becomes lopsided. With art you have to deal with all these things and not get overinvolved with one or another. In general, I think the future of art lies in stressing phenomena more, but you can also make too much of that.

DB   How does what you say here square with what you wrote earlier, namely that you "prefer art that isn't associated with anything"?[9]

DJ   I don't think they are contradictory. I think the attitudes are in the work, it's not to do with association; as I keep saying, the art is something itself – it's not about referring to anything. Barnett Newman said: "We've got to make something out of ourselves that is its own self."[10] I don't disagree with that. Therefore, you can't have something which refers to all sorts of things. I don't want to represent anything whatsoever. Why not just go ahead and make something new?

DB   But what about the fairly uncontroversial philosophical point that seeing is theory-laden: we don't just see the materials you put together, we see it first of all *as* art, and in relation to a whole range of other things we call art?

DJ   I intend it to be seen as art, there's no question about that.
     And within some general definition, I want to make art
     in a perfectly traditional way. I would like it if someone
     a couple of hundred years from now could see a piece
     somewhere, in a situation which is not a gallery or a mu-
     seum, and realize it is still somehow art.

DB   Doesn't this go against your rather more nominalist state-
     ment of a few years ago that "if someone says his work is
     art, it's art"?[11]

DJ   I took that position because I think the question of whether
     something is or is not art is best left alone; it's somewhat
     personal and it doesn't get you anywhere. The question is
     whether it is good art or bad art.

DB   On the issue of art and political engagement, you kept
     your distance from the Art Workers' Coalition [AWC], and
     were duly castigated by them, weren't you?[12]

DJ   That was always a little mysterious. But it was less the AWC
     than [Joseph] Kosuth and *The Fox*, I think.[13] I went to a
     couple of AWC meetings, but they were quickly taken
     over by [John] Perreault and by [Gregory] Battcock. The
     second meeting consisted of those guys talking and being
     very self-important without anything constructive being
     done or planned. I went to some more meetings later and
     they quickly became dominated by people who were not
     artists or who simply claimed to be artists, and they broke
     down into just talk.

DB   You had no particular political disagreement with the
     AWC?

DJ   Not really. I said something about their striking at MOMA;
     not that I was against it, it just seemed a little trivial. I think
     that these institutions should be taken on, but I said that
     picketing and striking should be reserved for more dan-
     gerous institutions, like the United States government.
     One of the big problems is that artists have lost whatever
     limited control of these institutions they once may have

had. Artists are supporting an enormous structure with a great deal of money and millions of bureaucrats, and most of these artists make very little money themselves. It's ridiculous.

DB   Is that one of the reasons you set up the Chinati Foundation, your own museum? To wrest control from these institutions?

DJ   Yes. But it was also about trying to get an installation done right. I don't think there are many things in the world that art can be used for. I don't mind a certain amount of it, but art shouldn't all be turned into education, into a public use. That's against the nature of the activity.

DB   During the late '60s and early '70s, weren't you involved in some political activities? Citizens for Local Democracy and some anti-Vietnam publications?[14]

DJ   Yes. I'm more interested in general politics. The problem in the United States is the lack of political activity across the board, as citizens. But I think it's also necessary to act in relation to your own professional activity, both to take on the museums and so on and also to object, say, to what the government is doing in Nicaragua. Artists should organize around Nicaragua, just as dentists should.

DB   Also, during the '60s and early '70s, you and a number of your contemporaries – Andre, [Robert] Morris, Smithson, and so on – produced quantities of textual material. How do you account for that occurrence?

DJ   I don't know. For me writing reviews was a part-time job, and I'd always liked writing. But I don't know why that bunch of people – who didn't necessarily know one another – were all writing around that time. I'm sorry now I stopped writing just when I should have continued. It left the field to Smithson and Morris. Perhaps it wasn't so unusual: several artists have written quite a bit – Matisse, for example.

DB   Nevertheless, the distinction between those who make

pictures and those who write about them is a thoroughly institutionalized one in our culture. And around the time we are talking about, those separations, among others, were disputed, at least temporarily.

DJ   I think it was very good, although I can't claim I was doing it intentionally then. I think the more you can handle without coming apart the better, which is to do with why I'm involved with architecture and furniture. I really admire people like [Theo] van Doesburg and Malevich. That's the way things should be.

DB   Do you regard the lack of such diversity in the way [Walter] Gropius and Van Doesburg did, as a symptom of academicism and social fragmentation?

DJ   It is academic, and it is a sign of an enormous decadence in society. It's very bad politically, and I think it's exactly what central governments want: to keep everybody in their cells. The United States has the worst form of this disease. The effect of this fragmentation is that you can't talk to architects or designers or historians. It eliminates the possibility of following through the implications of art or anything.

DB   It has become conventional to divide up the work of the '60s into three mutually exclusive categories, minimalism, post-painterly abstraction, and pop. What's wrong with this?

DJ   I've said it a million times before. There was no such thing as minimalism; it was not a group. My work was already my work before I met Robert Morris, who I think is a really bad artist. All his work is derived from somebody else's: Serra's, mine, always somebody else's. It's also so diverse that it's contradictory. I think Smithson was just a sophomore: what appears to be intellectual is really just kids' stuff. I think the early work was weak; even the photographs of the *Spiral Jetty* look weak. I was interested in Flavin, who I met quite early on. I met Andre a little later, but he hadn't shown his work. [Sol] LeWitt came along sometime after, and I wasn't keen on his early work, although it developed later. There really was no group.

DB   But you did identify with some of the painters associated with [Clement] Greenberg and Fried?

DJ   Yes, my connections were in those directions. I never understood what Greenberg and Fried were complaining about; I never understood why there was such antagonism. I never understood why they supported Anthony Caro, whose work I consider antithetical to that of [Morris] Louis and [Kenneth] Noland. But as far as the art goes, certainly the connections are with Louis and Noland. I think their work has wholeness. Of Noland's work I like the concentric circles best – I don't think they are incompatible with Pollock's perceptions. Louis's work is probably more unusual. Certainly, he did many more things than Noland which were really new. The work is a single thing, a thing in itself, a whole. These are fairly fundamental attitudes which I learned, and I haven't changed my mind about them.

This conversation was sourced from the published interview. A digital recording of the original audio cassette is in the Judd Foundation Archives, Marfa, Texas.

First published: David Batchelor, "A Small Kind of Order," *Artscribe International*, November–December 1989, 62–67.

1   See Judd's "Specific Objects" (1964) in *Donald Judd Writings*, 134–45.
2   *Kazimir Malevich: 1878–1935*, Stedelijk Museum, Amsterdam, March 5–May 29, 1989.
3   *Donald Judd* primarily included wall works, both single and multi-unit. In many instances, the front or top of the work is completely open, or divided into sections with part of the top or front of the piece remaining visible.
4   See Michael Fried, "Art and Objecthood," *Artforum*, June 1967, 12–23. This essay focused on the work of Judd and Robert Morris.
5   In 1959, Judd wrote an essay on Pierre Puget for a course on baroque sculpture with professor Meyer Schapiro while a graduate student at Columbia University. See Judd's "Puget" (1959) in *Donald Judd Writings*, 54–61.

6   Richard Serra, *Fulcrum* (1987), Broadgate, London.

7   Serra's *Tilted Arc* (1981) was installed at Manhattan's Foley Federal Plaza
        in 1981. After acrimonious public debate and a drawn-out federal lawsuit,
        the sculpture was removed in 1989.

8   See Judd's "Letter to Irving Sandler" (1973) in *Donald Judd Writings*, 236.

9   See Judd's "Complaints: Part I" (1969) in *Donald Judd Writings*, 201.

10   In a 1948 article for *The Tiger's Eye*, an art and literary magazine, New-
        man wrote, "Instead of making *cathedrals* out of Christ, man, or 'life,' we
        are making [them] out of ourselves, out of our own feelings." Newman,
        "The Sublime Is Now," in *Barnett Newman: Selected Writings and Interviews*,
        ed. John P. O'Neill (New York: Knopf, 1990), 173.

11   See Judd's "Statement" (1966) in *Donald Judd Writings*, 179.

12   For further commentary from Judd on the Art Workers' Coalition, see
        Judd's "The Artist and Politics: A Symposium" (1970) in *Donald Judd Writ-
        ings*, 214–19.

13   *The Fox*, founded by Sarah Charlesworth and Joseph Kosuth in 1975, was
        a conceptual art magazine. The second issue included a critical piece on
        Judd and minimalism; see Karl Beveridge and Ian Burn, "Don Judd," *The
        Fox*, no. 2, 1975, 129–42.

14   Citizens for Local Democracy, a civic organization formed to promote the
        principle of local self-government, was founded by H. R. Shapiro in New
        York in the 1960s; it operated until sometime in the 1970s. Judd became
        an advisory member of Citizens for Local Democracy in the late 1960s
        and wrote for its publication, *Newspaper (of Lower Manhattan Township)*.

"Back to Clarity: Interview with Donald Judd"
With Jochen Poetter and Rosemarie E. Pahlke for the
exhibition catalogue *Donald Judd*
August 7, 1989

Held at the Staatliche Kunsthalle Baden-Baden in Germany, this conversation between Judd and art historians Jochen Poetter and Rosemarie E. Pahlke was conducted
in conjunction with the venue's exhibition *Donald Judd* (August 27–October 15,
1989). In an essay for the show's catalogue, "Hermetic and Open – Precision and
Beauty: Donald Judd at the Kunsthalle Baden-Baden," Poetter wrote, "Consideration, care and precision are hallmarks of his [Judd's] thinking and his work."

JP   [Jochen Poetter] From the first sketches and technical drawings, we can see that even during the process of planning and creation of the works, there is already complete transparency and clarity. Is the discouragement of false speculations and hidden secrets in this preparatory phase already part of the work and its conception?

DJ   [Donald Judd] It seems to me that regardless of the kind of art, clarity is one of the fundamental factors. And so confusion is simply confusion; it isn't a kind of art. Stuart Davis, in a book that I do not have right now, says almost the same thing, for example, in 1940: "Confusion is simply confusion and clarity is fundamental to art."[1]

JP   Would you accept for the works exhibited in the Kunsthalle Baden-Baden [image 74] the description "variations on a theme," as, for instance, in the music of Bach?[2]

DJ   I'm not so sure, because it can be taken different ways. I don't mind the comparison with Bach, of course, but they are definitely not variations. They are totally distinct works. The group they make is by accident, because there is that much room in the Kunsthalle. Ordinarily we would have only made one or two of them. So I intend to break them up. They are not at all a group. I have made things that are a group, but they do not make a work as a whole. In Texas I tried to keep the pieces together, but they are still separate works [see image 61].[3] It depends on what the theme is; it can be very narrow, or it can be very broad, or it can simply be a large generic category. You could say, well, of [Jean-Baptiste-Siméon] Chardin that the still lifes could be a theme. That means a very broad theme.

JP   In our case, the number of variations is limited.

DJ   No. There are probably, as I said the other day, as many as two or three hundred, as many as five hundred possibilities. Because with all the colors and different thicknesses of metal, there is probably no end to the possibilities. The color is more or less infinite. The thickness and the divisions are not infinite, but the number is very large. So the chances are that if you tried to think it out logically, you'd wind up with several hundred.

JP And still you had to decide on twelve variations within the system.

DJ But I never tried to think of the total system. I only thought of twelve, that's all. Because that's what we needed for the space. It's not that I started with all the possibilities and picked twelve; I just started at one spot. The colors came from colors in small pieces that I've been doing.

JP How much has the specific architecture of the Kunsthalle Baden–Baden influenced your choice of twelve possibilities?

DJ Moderately. It's not a very definite installation. But it was also, I think I said a year ago, derived from the show I had in Bern in the Kunsthalle, with the plywood pieces which filled all the rooms [image 75].⁴ They could be seen throughout the rooms, but they fit the rooms very definitely – their size was determined by the rooms, and this certainly is not the case here. But you can see the pieces through the rooms. And in that way, it pulls the space together.

JP There is then no speculative element, calculated for its effect, in the working out of this particular conception?

DJ As I keep saying, as I've said a million times, I have no interest whatsoever in the public. There is no way you can know the public, and therefore you cannot think about it. It's not derogatory or anything, it's simply that all those people are totally unknown and there is nothing to think about.

JP Can one say that basically, the interior proportions of the Kunsthalle were taken into consideration when you were determining the dimension and proportion of the pieces, but that the exact structure is more strongly related to the individual work of art?

DJ   Yes. The particularity is very far from that of the Kunsthalle in Bern. It only comes down to the fact that the pieces are all the same size and that you can see them in the rooms; there is the obvious number of four to the big room, two to a small room – the obvious number to a room.

JP   Is there an element of surprise when you now see the finished works, which previously existed only in your imagination?

DJ   Yes, sure. It's always a big surprise. There is always a big gap between what I think they are going to look like and what they actually look like. And in fact, I can never really imagine what they will look like.

JP   The element of surprise implies acceptance of imponderabilia. Do you with your sketches in a way merely provide the initial impulse for the work, letting it then develop on its own?

DJ   My basic interest is in the actual work of art or architecture. Of course, things start as "ideas," which are not ideas in a very cut-and-dried way. They are not very fixed ideas. But I'm always interested in works that can actually be built, and I'm not very much interested in those that cannot. I do a lot of sketches of things that will never be built, by accident or money or whatever, but I am really interested in the ones that will get built. And that's to me the only reality. The actual works are very different from what I can imagine. I can't imagine what they will actually be like.

JP   Would you accept for your art the definition "open hermetic"?

DJ   Yes. Open enclosed. "Hermetic" is okay.

JP   Would you agree that in this field of tension there is a point where art exists?

DJ   That's one of the aspects. I think there are a lot of aspects, but that's one of them.

JP   How does this openness relate to Reinhardt's postulate, "Art is art. Everything else is everything else"?[5]

DJ   No. We're very different artists, but I think a great deal of his paintings. He's a very good artist. But I think Reinhardt's work has – "hermetic" is a more precise word than "enclosed" – has a more hermetic quality than mine. You could say that mine has a contradiction, maybe, in the closed and the openness, or a tension, but I think his is definitely on the somewhat hermetic side. This is not a criticism, it is just a comment.

JP   In the catalogue of the exhibition in Münster,[6] you wrote about proportions, and in the faculty of perception you saw an approach that uses the totality of things: the unity of thinking and feeling.[7]

DJ   I think that's also back to clarity. That also even precedes clarity as one of the fundamental things that makes things art. Art's a totality. To be a totality it has to be clear – and there isn't any other way but to make it a totality. That's one of its basic natures. So it's not about subdividing things or analyzing things, or, "This is A, and that's B, and that's C," and so forth. It's about putting all these things together in a clear way when perhaps they don't even fit together very well. But you have to put them together.

JP   The open character of your works allows the surrounding architecture to be absorbed and thus become part of them. Do you think that this is equally valid for society and the individual person?

DJ   Who knows … It suits me. I don't know what it does to the society. Just what I said before: I, myself, obviously have political and social opinions and I think almost everything somehow goes into the work. It would be different if I thought otherwise. But I don't think you can make any direct interpretations, say that the work somehow makes a definite political statement that you could translate into words. It's not meant to be translated into words, and it's not meant to be opened to the society or closed to the society or anything.

JP   Will the works remain essentially the same when they are installed in a different place?

DJ   Yes. I will probably keep two of these pieces.[8] We'll have to build a building, probably build a separate freestanding building just for the two pieces, for some use, function, since I think we should be able to use the space on the ranch.[9] The chances are very few people will ever see them again – exactly the same pieces as they are here.[10]

JP   True, they are the same pieces, but will they be identical, once they have absorbed a different environment?

DJ   Yes, but that's not so important. So in that way, they are the same pieces no matter where they are. They are the same pieces when I am dead. See, I do not agree with Bishop Berkeley about the trees. He is an English philosopher who speculated that maybe when no one was around, the trees – he was, despite being a bishop, a radical skeptic – that maybe when no one was around, the trees in the forest didn't exist.[11]

JP   And what do you think?

DJ   I think the trees in the forest are still there.

JP   But could not the particular surroundings effect a change?

DJ   Sure, but that's a certain amount of accident, which, as I said, I don't think is so important. Of course, the light will be different in West Texas and they will look a bit different, but I don't think that's so important. They will still be the same pieces.

JP   Do you, within the framework of your idea of art, deliberately work against handed-down traditions, and are you aiming for a new consciousness?

DJ   I'm not interested in anything opposite. In the first place, you couldn't really do something opposite because you're talking about the whole past, and I'm only one person. And also, I'm not interested in reactions against anything; I do not want to go with anything or, on the contrary, react against anything. It's rather large in the society and I

think the main thing is to find something new for yourself, which seems to be a point that's lost nowadays, but
it's fundamental. We are living in a very different time
and situation than a hundred or two hundred years ago.
But I don't think that's the main reason. I can't help having something to do with the past. I have a short life, you
pick up things, but the main reason for trying to do something new – and I mean "new," not opposite, not sideways,
not near geometric, not anything – and as new as you can
do, is that it's the only thing that you are going to do well
and understand well. And you have to invent it: if you use
forms that are from somebody else, you are not going to
understand them, you are not going to equal that work,
and you'll always be behind. I used Matisse earlier; I like
Matisse's and Léger's paintings. I like both of them a great
deal. Matisse, of course, is fabulous, and Mondrian. I realized a long time ago when I was painting that I was never
going to understand the strange shapes that Matisse liked.
You know, back of that is Matisse's mind, and he likes these
peculiar things that I absolutely don't understand and will
never understand. And therefore, if you follow that, if you
use what he's thought about, you're going forever to be
second rate. So the only way you can be equal to Matisse
is to invent as much as Matisse invented. I think that's all
pretty obvious, but there are people now saying that you
can't invent anything. Some guy, I think it was in a Tate
Gallery brochure, and I think the person was an artist, said
that, of course, we can't invent anything now, it's all been
invented. Those statements are ridiculous – to be second
rate for fifty years, or else third rate, fourth rate … Barnett
Newman and Jackson Pollock and others arrived at something that they thought out and that was natural to them,
so I'm going to arrive at something that I've thought out,
that's clear and natural to me. And that's the only way that
you can be on the same level with them. So there is no

way to use the past. It's totally cut off, even if you want to: people try and you can see that it's doomed.

JP   Certainly this was also a basic motive of the Dadaists, who, however, in addition, also denied all meaning. How does the question of meaning apply to your work?

DJ   But it depends on how you're — that's a very loaded word. That depends on how you mean it. To make art at all — see, I get in a pickle on this. Go back to what you said before. I'm strongly against any division of thought and feeling, which I think is a completely wrong division. So when you start dividing it up and talking about it, then I don't know how to deal with it. I've written this somewhere — I think it's in the Yale lecture — I think it's much exaggerated in its use and rather dangerous in its use.[12] We don't have, basically, contrary to what everybody says, we don't have nonsensical, irrational feelings. The feelings are, ordinarily, fairly practical matters. Society may not agree with them, or there may be other circumstances, but ordinarily they're pretty practical and they are based upon thinking; thinking is based upon feeling, it's all one. The feeling is a shortcut; you can't sit around here spending five minutes trying to figure out how to stand up — the feeling gets you off the ground fast. It's a functioning thing. So I'm against that division. Socially, art is very much on the periphery, so you can't say it makes sense that way; it's not scientific, so it isn't practical in that sense. I think in some ultimate social way — I didn't think this until the last five or ten years — I think maybe it does have some helpful, very broad, very general, and small, too, social effect. I think it could moderate the nonsense a bit. I think it's fairly dim, but there is something there.

JP   As a visitor in Marfa, especially in your living area, one strongly experiences the feelings of clarity, calmness, and peace. The word "peace" is also included in your writings on the subject of proportion.[13] Is there a direct relationship between work and life?

DJ   Of course, my life.

JP   Yes, but one senses this also in general.

DJ   Well, we're not so different. In one way, people are not so
      different – in one way, they are very different, but in other
      ways, they are not so different, and my assumption always
      was that what makes sense to me might make sense to
      someone else. And as I keep saying, I didn't really worry
      about that very much. I think Carl Andre said somewhat
      the same thing: he makes it for himself – it's not a direct
      quote – and he also assumes people are not so different. I
      would hope that they are not even so different that, just
      as we can understand very strange art from the past, such
      as the Phoenicians or the Greeks, that comes now un-
      der the classification of strange, or the Mayans – if we
      can make sense, as art, out of Mayan work, maybe they
      will be able to make sense out of ours, who knows, if it's
      around.

JP   The interaction of simplicity and wholeness is the crucial
      experience when one is confronted with your work.

DJ   Yes, I think that's fundamental to art. Art is certainly about
      the existence of whoever is doing it and, by implication,
      about the existence of other people. And, of course, the
      existence and the circumstances a person exists in, those
      circumstances are overwhelmingly the whole universe.
      You are not just living in Baden-Baden; you are living in
      a bigger situation of a few million light-years. So that's a
      factor. Everything is infinite in all directions. We are liv-
      ing in a very short time and a very small space in a very
      big situation. Basically, we are living in a little point and
      everything is infinite in all directions. You have to think
      about it. I don't think people think about it much.

JP   The attempt to imitate and intensify the effects of nature
      through the means of art as creativity, especially at the end
      of the nineteenth century, is a fundamental contradiction
      to your idea of art.

DJ   Yes, I'm pretty much against that. Nature is just fine. The
      best thing to do is leave it alone, stop chopping it down.
JP   In Marfa, I had this experience in front of your large con-
      crete works [see image 60]. They do not injure nature and
      the landscape, as they follow their own laws which do not
      differ from the basic conditions of nature.
DJ   To quote other people, Barnett Newman said that he was
      trying to make something that was a thing in itself, that is
      not a copy of something else.[14] Stuart Davis said that one
      of the points of art was to make it as different as possible
      from its surroundings.[15] I like nature a great deal. It seems
      just fine; I don't see any reason to copy it at all.
JP   Is your art beautiful?
DJ   Yes, I think so. No one else has to think so.
JP   Has "beauty" the same meaning as "aesthetics"?
DJ   I tend not to think about aesthetics. "Aesthetic" doesn't
      mean so much as an adjective. Aesthetics as a subject is a
      noun. That's a subject that applies, too. You can say it's aes-
      thetic. It's art, therefore it's aesthetic.
JP   Beauty and aesthetics are different concepts in German.
      The latter may be compared to the art nouveau move-
      ment in Germany or the aesthetic movement in England.
      Aesthetics, for us, sometimes has an ambiguous or even
      opposite meaning.
DJ   Well, in English, too. That's why it's not so much in use. In
      fact, it's not quite a good word anymore. But I think that's
      because of the quality of [Dante Gabriel] Rossetti and
      [Edward] Burne-Jones. That's probably because they had
      a somewhat otherworldly quality. To me it's rather pre-
      cious; it's not like Courbet, who is very straightforward.
      So we ordinarily say, "Well, it's aesthetic," or the people are
      aesthetes. You don't say Courbet is an aesthete. His paint-
      ing is too direct, the subject matter is too ordinary. So in
      that case I hope I am not with Burne-Jones and Rossetti.
JP   A different characteristic depends on the specific intention:

when creating beautiful things to please, one is an aesthete in the sense of Rossetti or Burne-Jones.

DJ   Maybe they were trying too hard. I have a category of things, an aesthetic category, of how the word "intention" or the use of intention works. They were trying too hard, or it was too intentional, while Cézanne or Courbet are – which is one reason they are much better artists – are much more natural, much more at home.

JP   This again refers to those places of mysteries which are, as affectation, included in bad art, instead of emphasizing clarity: to show what is really there to see.

DJ   Actually, I think that is one problem with those people. I think, for example, that William Morris is terrific.[16] And the things of William Morris that are best are architecture or patterns or furniture. When he starts to design too carefully, or sometimes to write – but sometimes the writing is pretty good, too – it doesn't hold together as well as it should. I don't sympathize much with medievalizing. But when you come to Rossetti and Burne-Jones and so forth, that already shows a breakdown in art and divisions between art, architecture, and design. Something has already gone a little sour. While in France, with Cézanne and Courbet and Manet, it's still very much down-to-earth.

JP   What do you think of the endeavors of the Bauhaus in this context?

DJ   I think it's admirable. I think it's just fine that they did that. Probably we believe we can't do it, which is probably exactly right. So we can't work in such a fundamental way and do such a thing. Naturally the industrial civilization we're in thought at the beginning that things were a lot simpler than they've turned out to be. And therefore, all of these grand schemes are the schemes of people between a dying religion and a new civilization. And naturally, they tried to apply very grand ideas to the situation: communism, capitalism. All of these schemes are very broad and they don't really work out. They [the Bauhaus] were trying to do that, also. They are a lot better than those other two because they didn't cause any wars. I think the contribution of the Bauhaus was terrific, very useful, and while it was destroyed, I think it has had a big influence in Europe in terms of raising the level of design. Things in Europe look a lot better than they do in the United States. Even though it has been debased to be commercial, to make factories, it enters into design and things don't look so bad. I think it had a much bigger influence maybe than people think. And I don't think you can blame them for attempting a grand scheme. It was not an aggressive scheme.

JP   Richard Wagner did exactly the opposite when he tried to bring the arts together: a large orchestra, more quantity than quality. And Hitler indeed succeeded during the Third Reich in realizing the Gesamtkunstwerk by completely eliminating the difference between idea and reality.

DJ   Very bad uses of it, but not Wagner's fault. The United States government has strong tendencies in that direction. It's not alien at all; I know it very well. What they build has strong – even now – strong fascist qualities, so it's not new. Museums, government buildings, and everything. Fascist architecture is simply architecture that's almost meaningless and tries to show power – but basically just meaningless.

JP   That's the same question of proportions again.

DJ   Yes, no proportion. The forms mean next to nothing.

JP   Here, this is also valid in architecture since the '50s. So-called beauty as "art" is being applied and does not result from the functional relationship.

DJ   Because they don't think about the materials, and because all the materials of this architecture … forms and everything are about something else, status or who knows what, and not about what you are actually looking at.

REP   [Rosemarie E. Pahlke] While we were talking about your
      biography and that you are living in Marfa, you said that
      it is not Marfa but Ayala de Chinati.

DJ   I seceded from Marfa; I got mad at them.

REP   So in a way, you have your own country.

DJ   I'm retreating into Mexico. [John] Chamberlain once
      said, "Oh, this is really Mexico; it's just an accident [that
      it's part of the United States]." You know, it was sort of an
      accident. Nobody knew where it was when they made
      the border. They just picked the river. And of course, the
      United States conquered that part of Mexico anyway. So
      in a way, it should be Mexico. But the Mexican govern-
      ment is just as difficult as the United States government,
      so it wouldn't be any improvement. I'm for secession, but
      I don't think I'll ever manage it.

REP   What does "secession" mean?

DJ   Leaving totally. You declare your own state. I would love it.
      Like Liechtenstein. No, I don't want to build in the town
      anymore, and it makes sense to use the ranch. Basically,
      I'm slowly moving to the ranch. Among other things, the
      town is very noisy, and then they are disagreeable. And
      anyway, the place I have there is too small and the ranch
      is very big, and so I moved down there. That changes the
      address, the voting address, but it's the same county.

REP   What about color in your work?

DJ   I don't like plain plywood or plain concrete or plain metal
      to be considered without color. So to me, they are col-
      ored. But I also know that at least it's not bright color, it's
      not red and blue. So it is a pretty big span. But it's best to
      consider everything as color. On the outside the pieces
      are gray; that's pretty easy, gray.

JP   But here the characteristics of the material are indeed
      stronger than with the mere application of color.

DJ   Everything is anodized aluminum; so is the gray. You know
      that it's not just an applied color. And the plexiglass is

plexiglass. Those are materials, but it's a big problem to be able to use bright colors and not destroy the nature of the materials. And when I make the sheet metal pieces that are painted, of course they are painted. There is no question about them being painted. And I'm a little sorry about it, but it's the only way I can use a big variety of colors. The only way to help the situation somewhat is to be perfectly obvious that it's painted sheet metal.

JP   The elements necessary for the construction of the pieces – for instance, screws – can only be seen on the outside. This permits the conclusion that the interior space was intentionally reserved for the free interplay of form and color.

DJ   Yes, I think the less screws the better in this case. But it also has to do with the construction. That's the way they are held together. Now, if we made them to be whole and not taken apart – it would be very difficult – you might be able to put them together without anything showing. But with the anodizing you can't weld. It doesn't take the anodizing well. And then if you weld – we have this problem with the round piece we are trying to make – if you weld, you don't get a sharp edge, you get a welded edge, so that's no good. And if you put it on the outside, it involves a lot of grinding and handwork that I don't want.

JP   The visibility of the constructional elements also establishes the credibility of the work.

DJ   You can't really hide it, and I don't have any great, in this case, desire to do it.

REP   Can we talk about something that doesn't really belong to this discussion, but something that is very interesting for the German audience? You wrote this article entitled "Ausstellungsleitungsstreit" and everybody read it in *Kunstforum*.[17] And then, on the other hand, there were some [of your] pieces in the same *Bilderstreit* exhibition.[18] That's difficult for the people to understand.

DJ   That's a dirty trick. When they were sent the article, the agreement was that they would publish the article in their catalogue and I would make and lend a very large piece, which actually was shown in May at the Waddington Galleries in London.[19] When they said they wanted to edit the article, and started to stall and fool around with the article, I pulled the large piece out of the show. That happened in February, at the same time when it became clear they weren't going to print the article. And foreseeing that they would borrow pieces, we sent a fax or a telegram to [Siegfried] Gohr and [Johannes] Gachnang saying that no pieces whatsoever were to be in the show.[20] They put pieces in anyway. When I began to know which pieces were in, we sent further messages. I think we got one pulled out by some owner, I can't remember – oh, [Charles] Saatchi, whom I don't like, but they did take the piece they'd lent out. Three more stayed in. They were badly put together, badly installed. And so those pieces were in the show, totally despite my objection. And I understand [Anselm] Kiefer had the same problem.

REP   I think Ellie [Meyer] told me it was a piece from the Museum Ludwig.[21]

DJ   Well, yes, they kept their own piece, the piece they own and that they've always installed badly. They left that in.

REP   And the other one [was loaned] by Heiner Friedrich, perhaps, I don't know.[22]

DJ   No, I don't think so. I think it was someone, maybe a collector down here. But the large plywood piece, I believe, was from the Stedelijk. We sent a letter to them telling them to pull it out. I don't know what answer Ellie got. But I definitely objected to the pieces being in the show. The problem for the artist is that you have no legal standing on that, as you don't on a lot of things. You can complain and everything, but if you get a lawyer, you don't have any ground. They won't do anything.

JP   This conflict arises easily as soon as your work is being exhibited in public.

DJ   Oh, people install it so badly, and they are so careless. Museums and owners often don't even pay any attention to the spaces between the parts or anything about it. I heard there was one that did belong to Heiner Friedrich in Documenta a few years ago.[23] It has small parts that subdivide a room; Thordis Moeller[24] had run them in a row around a corner, something totally wrong, with no connection whatsoever to the piece. She made up her own piece. [Giuseppe] Panza[25] does that all the time; he just makes them up. Flavin has the same complaint. In that case, legally you could do something, I think. But legal fights are not positive.

REP   There was something curious in the Prospect exhibition in Frankfurt…[26]

DJ   I'm not crazy about any of these shows. I was sorry that there was a piece in Prospect, but that planning preceded the *Bilderstreit* situation. We're committed – Ellie and I being "we" in this case – I'm committed to putting a piece in Harald Szeemann's show.[27] This promise goes back a ways too. After that, I'm not going to do this with large exhibitions. But what they'll do is borrow from other people.

JP   And so you have no influence.

DJ   Yes, but anyway, it won't be my fault.

JP   How do you feel about the influence your work has on other artists, and do you have the ambition to be a teacher?

DJ   It's fine. Naturally, I like it to have an impact. I'm not interested at all in followers or any such things, but of course a person likes for other artists to be interested in his work. I'm not trying to teach. As I said, I don't know the audience, so I'm not trying to teach anything. Teaching is teaching, art is art. I'm not against teaching, teaching as teaching. As I said before, the art is a whole thing in itself. It's not a medium for something else, so it's not teaching.

It's not a moral thing, it's not an ethical thing, it's not a scientific thing; it's art. It's not about something else; it's about itself and its own qualities.

JP Maybe your idea of teaching is more in conformity with Josef Albers's principles and whose *Interaction of Color* is a work of art and not a compendium for artists.[28]

DJ I'm very interested in teaching. Teaching art is very difficult. But I think it's pretty well proven by now that teaching styles and techniques is useless. I taught a little at the level of colleges and universities, not much, but mostly I taught kids.[29] I didn't know what to teach. I decided to go along with what the people wanted to do and tried to add to it; I did that spontaneously. After a while, I realized that's exactly the right thing to do: see where they want to go and then supplement that and add to their information, and then that leads further. Perhaps that should be for all students. A big mistake is to consider someone who should be a young artist as a student. Because a young artist, a person who intends really to be an artist, is right away after what he wants. They are artists from the very beginning. It's a big mistake to treat them as students. Therefore, you deal with them as artists and try to provide whatever information they need, art history or whatever, that makes them more capable of thinking. If they need to know how to weld, teach them welding. If there is a crazy one who wants to know how to draw, teach them drawing. That's all. You can't apply a program to them because somebody is going to be bored stiff because they have to learn about color and they don't like color. You can't teach irrelevant or dead information.

I was reading a while back an autobiography by Werner Heisenberg.[30] He knew what he was doing when he was twenty years old or so; he made serious contributions at twenty-two or twenty-three. And so it occurred to me that he never thought he was a student or that his professors, also scientists, never really considered him a student, because he was already doing something. By considering all the graduate students as students in almost any activity, it is throwing away a great deal of work and information. To be a graduate student, you are busy until thirty, so they are throwing all of that away. Also, I'm on the Board of Visitors of the McDonald Observatory.[31] Two astronomers in their late twenties have already done serious work. They are working on the Whole Earth Telescope, where they watch a particular star; as the earth turns, they pass it to the next telescope, so it's always in sight. Therefore, they can watch very small variations, and by that they can determine what happens, of course, but also distance. There are about nine telescopes around the earth. Like everything serious in the United States, they don't have any money. As the star goes out of sight, say in Ireland, they pass it on to Hungary – I don't know where they are. The star is constantly under surveillance. The two astronomers are already serious grown-up scientists with maybe six years of contributions, they've already received awards; they're not kids. You can take that idea of education and apply it to almost everything.

REP   You are on the board?

DJ   It's called the Board of Visitors of McDonald Observatory. It's mostly people who should try to raise money or help out. It's not that you tell anybody what to do.

REP   It's for scientific research?

DJ   Yes, it's an observatory, to watch the stars. They are building a new telescope called the SST, a spectroscopic telescope.[32] The idea is brand-new. They couldn't get enough money to build a regular one with a lens, so they are building this one for $6 million. They've devised a totally new way to build it, with eighty-three, I think, one-meter lenses. They were going to have a lens seven meters across cast in one piece; well, they couldn't get the $45 million necessary for that. So they devised a new one. It does less, but on the other hand, it's infinitely cheaper to cast one-meter discs. It's easier to maintain.

JP   The purpose is to observe one star?

DJ   Yes, one star, but also clusters, nebulae, and galaxies. But mostly it's not visual observations; it's analyzing light. The visual observation doesn't mean so much anymore. Radio telescopes and spectroscopic telescopes are more important. They [the observatory] just had their fiftieth anniversary in Marfa last week; I just came from there. As an instance of what is wrong with the United States government, one of the new stealth bombers costs $530 million. But, for the anniversary, with Marianne [Stockebrand]'s help, we got a large banner from the *Bürgermeister* of Weil der Stadt, where Johannes Kepler was born.[33] It turned out that the banner was spectacular, with a big black eagle. It even has "SPQR" for Rome and is red, yellow, and black; it's gorgeous, very big.[34] I gave it to the director of the observatory. He is going to hang it either at The University of Texas at Austin or at the observatory.

These people are hardly students. They start right out and are doing something. Their professor puts them to work; they are not learning something for ten years, waiting to go to work. They're already working. I think we should just get rid of the whole category of student; that's my radical solution for the educational system. The other one is, like presidents and prime ministers, people should not teach too long. There should be a limit, ten years perhaps. I think they go to pieces. Also, that's the equivalent to being a student; then you're just a teacher because you're not doing accumulative work. Also, I think that would be true of what we call high school students. The teachers are too dead; high school in the United States is terrible. My son has never gotten over it. My daughter could see further ahead, but he could not see beyond the misery of it.

JP   Another question: what do you think about the term "abstraction"?

DJ   Yes, that's another issue. That's important because "geometry" and "abstraction" are being used to put certain things – my work, for one – into a category when it was never meant to be a category. It is not a category for Mondrian, it is definitely not a category for Barnett Newman or Rothko. Robert Irwin, for example, was subjected to this at an architectural meeting we went to in California.[35] By making work a style, you make it small and something that can be dismissed as irrelevant, when, in fact, from my point of view, the work is something new. The geometry suits me – I would never have imagined that I would have done such a thing, but I can get what I want with the geometry. I think the main issue, as I said before, is to do something new, something that is the person's own work, not old-fashioned junk.

JP   And that does not mean abstraction.

DJ   Yes. In the first place, none of the people I just mentioned wants to be called abstract, because basically they want to say that the work is something in itself. As far as being new, I don't think there is anything contradictory, say philosophically, fundamentally, between my work and Claes Oldenburg's. Naturally I have an affinity with Flavin and Carl Andre; you can see that. Or Michael Asher's empty room where the sound was reduced.[36] To me that's not a contradiction; that's doing something new. All I ask is for art to go somewhere, be something new. After that, we will worry about whether there are fundamental philosophical contradictions or not. The big contradictions are between the old-fashioned work and my work and other people's which is new. Recently I've objected a lot – it's worse than "minimal art" – against being pushed into the little category of "geometric abstraction." There are a lot of differences among everyone which are ignored.

JP   In art, words are the first step to misunderstandings, and
      "abstraction" is one of these dangerous words.

DJ   "Abstraction" is actually a bad word; it should be dropped.
      Almost no one is really abstract. The cubists, [Lyonel]
      Feininger was abstract, but otherwise –

JP   Is it objectivity you are aiming for, less in the sense of truth
      but rather of logical rightness?

DJ   It's another reality, or a new reality. I was reading Stuart
      Davis; he said that a painting is as much a reality as the
      subject matter it's taken from.[37]

JP   In a similar way, one can have the same experience with
      these colored aluminum pieces as one has with Josef Al-
      bers's *Interaction of Color*. Especially when the sun is shining
      brightly through the skylights, one can observe a glowing
      column of color rising out of the cases. Is this inherent
      quality of light and color a deliberately calculated effect?

DJ   I only planned on one; the blue one I knew about [see
      image 74].[38] I knew the blue would do that. But I didn't
      think about the others in that way. So that's pretty; it's free,
      like light.

JP   Are you interested in painting as well?

DJ   As I've said, I've absolutely no interest in making paintings.
      Someone wanted me to do big woodcuts, but I wouldn't
      do that either. There are some old ones that are a little big-
      ger than the new ones – they never were printed – which
      we're going to print, but otherwise I will not go larger.
      Oil on canvas and something on a plane that's parallel to
      the wall … I don't think, say, painting on metal, as [Rob-
      ert] Ryman has done, is better. So that's not a solution ei-
      ther. Obviously, someone is going to come along and do
      something drastically different on the wall, because having
      something flat on the wall is a nice thing. One thing that
      has more life and is more interesting, but I don't think I'll
      do it, is simple wall painting. That's a somewhat more in-
      teresting possibility. I'm not inclined to do it but I can see

that somebody else might do it, paint directly like fresco on the wall. If you used a very different type of surface that is far from oil paint, it would never be connected to traditional painting.

JP   In the case of your woodcuts, there is yet a certain plastic element noticeable, due to the hard pressure on soft material.

DJ   I think it's a little contradictory for me to do prints, but I like doing them. And also I can learn something from them. The new prints are related to these pieces. You don't know them, but there are reliefs that Chamberlain did in '64 – reliefs, but they are also very much paintings. They're on masonite.[39] So they are something new in the way of painting. That's an idea of what might be done. Yves Klein's paintings are pretty new because they're flat shapes, and the surface is new.

JP   You are not using any material that has a long tradition in art and possesses a specific aura, as, for instance, oil on canvas or bronze.

DJ   No, you can't deal with the aura. No. And the oil paint is hopeless – there is a connotation in the canvas and in the oil which you cannot get rid of.

JP   We were already talking about monumentalism and power as an expression of architecture. Can art be "unguilty"?

DJ   Now, certainly, art should be "unguilty." It should be new and perhaps seem rather ordinary. I suspect a lot of older art at the very beginning looked that way too, and now it looks so important to us. After a while, it acquires such a terrific social impact that it's hard to look at the art. With Barnett Newman, it's still just what it was, it's Barnett Newman, but probably by now for a lot of people it looks terrifically important. I knew Barney and can see around that, so it doesn't bother me much. Ordinarily these things look pretty plain and not important. I think a lot of people want instant importance; they want the importance of several decades instantly, when what you really want to do is to get rid of it.

The chances are, for example, that when Giovanni Bellini painted his first Madonna, because it was more naturalistic, it looked less important than a Madonna of the generation before. So the people used to the old Madonna thought, "This looks just like everyone." It probably didn't look important. Of course, it looks important to us because we are taught its history. I imagine a lot of work looked unimportant at first. A lot of Chinese work looks very casual; we see it now with a history.

JP   Something I noticed already when looking at the schematic sketches for your Baden-Baden pieces – you avoid using the perspective as an illusionary, illustrative means of presentation.

DJ   Yes, I don't care about perspective. I didn't learn it at school. It would probably be very hard for me to do it.

JP   But it's very difficult to see, let's just say, the things as plain as they are.

DJ   Of course, all good work has many different meanings, and so you can't say it has no meaning. You have to find the real ones and you have to forget the false ones. For a lot of people, contemporary art, twentieth-century art, can quickly seem so important as an image on the wall that they can't see what it really looks like. And I think general education and museums encourage this fake importance rather than telling people to forget it when they look at the work.

I think an individual work of art should be just as autonomous as, say, the Bellini. One work of art, say, by Josef Albers a few hundred years from now should be just as strong and clear as the Bellini, the Madonna. In that way there is no difference.

JP   Therefore, one can understand the pieces in this exhibition even if one does not know what Donald Judd has done previously?

DJ   Or even one by itself.

JP   The knowledge one needs, for instance, for the compre-
      hension of a symbolist painting of the nineteenth century
      is not a necessary condition here?

DJ   Naturally, seeing more of a person's work and knowing
      about what they think, their life, is interesting and use-
      ful. But I don't know much about Bellini. It's a good idea,
      but I don't think it's necessary. I know much more about
      some parts of the past than about others. I have a pretty
      good idea what Dürer did, but I don't have a good idea of
      what Giovanni Bellini did.

JP   Do you believe that there is something like a development
      in your work?

DJ   It's more of a change than a development. Naturally, I've
      been doing this for quite a while, and I get older, and so
      it does change. But the work was meant to change. That's
      one reason I liked the first pieces. They had a lot of im-
      plications, and they change without painting light all the
      time. I think you have to work hard, sometimes there has
      to be trouble, but basically if you're going to work for fifty
      years you have to enjoy it. Therefore, you can't have a daily
      struggle. Of course, you worry, but basically you have to
      like it. It became pretty tiresome when I had to fight with
      every painting.

JP   Getting back to proportions again: you do not like the
      elaborate systems for calculating proportions, as, for in-
      stance, the golden section?

DJ   Yes, it seems unnecessarily elaborated. Someone enjoyed
      figuring it out a little too much for its own sake. It doesn't
      do more than 1:2, 2:3, 3:4. These work perfectly well;
      I can never remember the formula for the golden sec-
      tion, but it comes pretty close to 2:3. It's only changing a
      normal proportion a little. The most abstruse one that I
      like, which is pretty easy, is that of Alberti's Sant'Andrea
      in Mantua, 5:6. But 5:6 is just off square. So it's pretty

obvious too. The proportions that Palladio uses, numbers in the teens — unless proportions are near 2:3 or 1:2, you can't see them. What is 11:13 — I don't know whether that's Palladio — what is 11:13 … 5:6, maybe.[40] Well, I can't write about everything.

The situation in art in the United States is worse than the situation in Europe. I'm writing about the situation in New York a little, because I want to get it done, and New York is pretty much the United States, unfortunately. Of course, the more general thing is that the United States is declining and, because of the Cold War and other policies, is in very bad shape economically. And they don't seem to know it, and of course most Europeans don't go there, so they don't know it either. The fact is it's becoming at least a second-world country by now — approaching the third world. It's really getting poor, and it shows through the homeless, and through the run-down cities, and run-down streets and highways. It made a big economy out of winning the war and then it pursued a military economy for forty years, so it's ruined everything. Gore Vidal says that two-thirds of the budget is military. It's impoverishing the people and it's becoming more repressive. They have new laws against drugs that will annihilate the Bill of Rights, civil rights. If they find a little bit of marijuana in your car, the local police department can seize the car as its own property, or your house. A fisherman off of Alaska had his ship seized because his nephew had a little marijuana, just for cigarettes, in his pocket. They kept the ship all summer. He had to go to court to get it back. He lost the whole season. This was a year ago. These are fundamental rights that have always existed and that are now gone. My theory is — because I think this is what Nixon was up to, one reason he was kicked out, but now they are not kicked out anymore — is that, and especially now because the United States no longer has the

Cold War, they are building up the War on Drugs; that's the new big war. And they need a war; you know, it's not that they need a war against the Soviet Union, they need a war against the American people. When you lose your reason for one war and for being, you've got to find a new one. And the new one is the War on Drugs. They can now do things that they could not do before in the history of the United States.

JP   That will become a civil war?

DJ   It's possible. The American people are very passive, I don't know if they will ever say no to anything.

JP   I think the struggle for life in America is much harder than it is here.

DJ   Sure is; it's getting worse.

JP   No Social Security as we have.

DJ   There is Social Security; I mean just simple things. I've never seen so many people – at one point there was hardly anyone; earlier there were some – but I've never seen so many people on the streets homeless in New York as there are now. New York is a mess. I dimly remember the Depression in the '30s, but I didn't know New York then. New York is like Calcutta is supposed to be. The democracy is a joke. Only 50 percent of the people voted. And capitalism is a joke. The banks were foolish enough to lend Mexico $54 billion, which Mexico can't pay back. These are the great businessmen. The Russians should not copy American capitalism. The United States is committing suicide, and most Americans don't seem to be aware of it; they can look around and see the situation, but they don't. The election was the flattest election ever in history: no argument, no discussion, no issues, nothing. There is no concern even through elementary self-interest. You would think one guy would say, "Look out, look, you're really getting poor. The money you take home doesn't last, you can't get a new TV." They don't say this to each other.

I hope the Russians stay away from futures in the stock market and corporate takeovers…They shouldn't do that for a while, if ever.

JP   In Germany this is not very different. The apolitical basic attitude goes so far that people do not want to hear the truth, and politicians make use of this fact. But I believe that slowly things are happening, that a new awareness is growing.

DJ   It takes two. Naturally, you can explain the leaders, so-called, and the politicians, but it takes a lot of passive people to allow them to be there. That's why they're there.

JP   For this reason, it is so very important to teach people to see (and recognize) what they actually see. But they are being programmed otherwise; they are easily manipulated.

DJ   No, and they won't go to any trouble to find out. In Russia, you can be a dissident; you can't even be a dissident in the United States. You're just a crackpot, just a silly person. If you say that it's a lousy government, it spent so much money on the military for forty years, and it's a waste of money, that's just nonsense: you know no one is going to listen. You don't necessarily get in trouble right away, as you might in Russia a few years ago, but neither are you taken seriously.

JP   So in this sense, there is some political content in your work, anyhow?

DJ   I have definite political opinions and, to some extent, they are more developed than some other people's, and some other artists', too. That's got to be in there, I guess.

REP   Did you ever travel to Eastern countries?

DJ   I've been to Russia, yes, twice. To Estonia and then to Leningrad – that was a few years ago; about two years, a year and a half ago, I went with my two children for three weeks to Moscow, Leningrad, and the old towns: Suzdal, Yaroslavl, Novgorod, and so on. But other than that, I haven't been to the Eastern countries. It's very interesting. It was extremely cold, −46 degrees Celsius, for a few days in Suzdal.

I'm very interested in Russia. While I was in the army, the US Army, for a year and a half [see image 19][41] – World War II had only been over a year – they gave the soldiers all sorts of books, paperbacks. This was the beginning of educational paperbacks in the United States. The books were usually just dumped in a corner in an empty barrack, so I used to take them. I traveled with a pretty good library. One of the books was a history of Russia by Bernard Pares; I probably read it three times.[42] There wasn't much to do. And I was very interested in it, I like reading history. So I knew Russian history pretty well at eighteen. And also, there was a lot of Russian literature – Chekhov, Turgenev, Tolstoy.

REP   Didn't you also go to Korea?

DJ   Yes, I was a year in Korea, but that was between wars. I'm ready to go to Russia again anytime, it's just fitting it in and maybe somebody to go with.

JP   You have often talked about the Russian constructivists. What is your opinion on Malevich and his radical solution of the *Black Square*?

DJ   The whole thing is very amazing. I'm still amazed at the *Black Square*; I don't know how he thought of it. That's a case where it's very hard to see – the paintings, the *Black Square* and the *Red Square* that was in Vienna – I think I can see them for themselves, but it's very hard to see around their historical and social standing. If I had one myself, maybe, and lived with it for a year, it would become normal. But when you see the paintings in museums and in public, they are historical. It's extremely difficult to forget. The *Red Square* in Vienna at the exhibition *Kunst und Revolution* was pretty nice.[43]

First published: Jochen Poetter, "Back to Clarity: Interview with Donald Judd," in *Donald Judd*, exh. cat. (Stuttgart: Cantz, 1989), 65–104 (in English and German).

1   The quotation in fact reads, "The secret of art is order, and order means absence of confusion, and this means relaxation, and 'take it easy.'" See "A Selection of Davis Quotations," in Karen Wilkin, *Stuart Davis* (New York: Abbeville Press, 1987), 36. Judd included this book as well as three others on Davis's work in his library in Marfa, Texas.

2   The exhibition included twelve large works for the floor in anodized aluminum, all with the same dimensions, from 1989, and two series of ten woodcuts from 1988.

3   Though Judd's 100 untitled works in mill aluminum all have the same exterior dimensions, each has a unique interior.

4   *Donald Judd: Skulpturen*, Kunsthalle Bern, April 14–May 30, 1976. This exhibition included five room-sized works in plywood made specifically for the Kunsthalle Bern.

5   This postulate was first published in a manifesto-like text by Reinhardt that ran in *It Is*, a New York–based publication, in the spring of 1958. See Reinhardt, "25 Lines of Words on Art: Statement," in *Art-as-Art: The Selected Writings of Ad Reinhardt*, ed. Barbara Rose (New York: Viking Press, 1975), 51. Judd included this book in his library in Marfa, Texas.

6   *Donald Judd: Architektur*, Westfälischer Kunstverein, Münster, Germany, April 16–June 4, 1989. The eponymous catalogue for this exhibition republished the 1983 article by Judd; see note 7.

7   See Judd's "A Long Discussion Not About Master-Pieces But Why There Are So Few of Them: Part I" (1983) in *Donald Judd Writings*, 352–76. This article has more than one part: see also Judd's "A Long Discussion Not About Master-Pieces But Why There Are So Few of Them: Part II" (1984) in *Donald Judd Writings*, 378–97. "Part I" was first published in *Art in America*, September 1984, 9–19; "Part II" was first published in *Art in America*, October 1984, 9–15.

8   Judd installed two of the large floor works from the Baden-Baden exhibition in the Print Building.

9   Judd refers here to Las Casas. The freestanding building was never built.

10 The exhibition *Donald Judd*, David Zwirner, New York, May 6–June 25, 2011, included nine of the twelve works that were installed in the original exhibition at the Staatliche Kunsthalle Baden-Baden.

11 Bishop George Berkeley (1685–1753) was an Anglo-Irish empiricist philosopher who advanced a theory he called immaterialism. Judd included four books by Berkeley in his library in Marfa, Texas.

12 "I've always considered the distinction between thought and feeling as at the least exaggerated; this is a small description that has been raised to a central fact of human nature.... I've always blamed it on the mind and body distinction of the Christians since it's handy for mysticism and their kind of belief." See Judd's "Art and Architecture" (1983) in *Donald Judd Writings*, 344.

13   "Proportion is very important to us, both in our minds and lives and as objectified visually, since it is thought and feeling undivided, since it is unity and harmony, easy or difficult, and often peace and quiet. Proportion is specific and identifiable in art and architecture and creates our space and time." Ibid., 347–48.

14   In a 1948 article for *The Tiger's Eye*, an art and literary magazine, Newman wrote, "Instead of making *cathedrals* out of Christ, man, or 'life,' we are making [them] out of ourselves, out of our own feelings." Newman, "The Sublime Is Now," in *Barnett Newman: Selected Writings and Interviews*, ed. John P. O'Neill (New York: Knopf, 1990), 173.

15   "In Art things do not get stronger as they get bigger – they get stronger as they get different from their environment." See "A Selection of Davis Quotations," 36.

16   Judd included over three dozen books on or by William Morris in his library in Marfa, Texas.

17   See Judd's "Ausstellungsleitungsstreit" (1989) in *Donald Judd Writings*, 558–83.

18   *Bilderstreit*, Museum Ludwig, Cologne, April 8–June 28, 1989.

19   *Donald Judd*, Waddington Galleries, London, May 22–June 17, 1989.

20   Siegfried Gohr (1949–), a German art historian and curator, and Johannes Gachnang (1939–2005), a Swiss artist and curator, organized *Bilderstreit*, along with Walter Nikkels.

21   Ellie Meyer worked as a studio assistant to Judd from 1983 to 1991.

22   Heiner Friedrich (1938–) is a German art dealer. Along with Philippa de Menil and Helen Winkler, he cofounded Dia Art Foundation in 1974.

23   Documenta 7, Kassel, Germany, June 19–September 28, 1982.

24   Thordis Moeller is a German art collector and a former director of Galerie Heiner Friedrich's Cologne and New York locations.

25   Giuseppe Panza di Biumo (1923–2010) was a prominent Italian collector of modern art. See Judd's "Una stanza per Panza" (1990) in *Donald Judd Writings*, 630–99.

26   Prospect 89, Frankfurter Kunstverein, Frankfurt, March 21–May 21, 1989.

27   Harald Szeemann (1933–2005) was a highly influential Swiss curator and art historian. Included in the Szeemann-curated exhibition *Einleuchten: Will, Vorstel un Simul in HH*, Deichtorhallen Hamburg, Germany, November 11, 1989–February 18, 1990, was a small stack in stainless steel with transparent green acrylic sheets.

28   Josef Albers, *Interaction of Color* (New Haven, CT: Yale University Press, 1963). Judd included this book in his library in Marfa, Texas.

29   During the 1950s and early 1960s, Judd held a variety of part-time teaching positions at youth-oriented institutions in New York. Though he primarily taught art, he also instructed courses in world history and woodshop.

30   Werner Heisenberg (1901–1976) was a German physicist and philoso-
      pher known for his contributions to quantum mechanics, for which he
      was awarded a 1932 Nobel Prize. Judd refers here to Heisenberg's *Physics
      and Beyond: Encounters and Conversations*, trans. Arnold J. Pomerans (New
      York: Harper & Row, 1971). Judd included this book, as well as three oth-
      ers by Heisenberg, in his library in Marfa, Texas.

31   Judd refers here to the McDonald Observatory, part of The University
      of Texas at Austin, located in the Davis Mountains of West Texas. He be-
      came a member of the observatory's Board of Visitors in 1989.

32   The Spectroscopic Survey Telescope (SST) at the McDonald Observa-
      tory, known as the Hobby-Eberly Telescope (HET), was built in 1997.

33   Marianne Stockebrand is a German art historian and curator. She was the
      director of the Kölnischer Kunstverein from 1990 to 1994 and the direc-
      tor of the Chinati Foundation from 1994 to 2010.

34   An eagle and "SPQR" appear on the Weil der Stadt coat of arms, whose
      main colors are red, yellow, and black.

35   Twice yearly, the Frederick R. Weisman Art Foundation conducted work-
      shops related to contemporary art. Judd participated in the workshop "The
      Relationship between Art and Architecture," held January 21–22, 1989, in
      Santa Monica, California. The workshops were recorded, transcribed, and
      published. See *The Relationship between Art and Architecture: Summary of a
      Workshop, 21–22 January 1989* (Los Angeles: The Frederick R. Weisman Art
      Foundation, 1990).

36   Judd likely refers here to Asher's installation *Untitled* (1969) from the group
      exhibition *Spaces*, The Museum of Modern Art, New York, December 30,
      1969–March 1, 1970.

37   "The picture is just as real as the subject that inspired it." See "A Selection
      of Davis Quotations," 37.

38   Two works in the Baden-Baden exhibition included blue acrylic sheets
      on their bottoms.

39   From 1963 to 1965, Chamberlain made a series of paintings on twelve-
      by-twelve-inch pieces of masonite on which he built up dozens of layers
      of auto lacquer, creating a relief effect. See Diane Waldman, *John Cham-
      berlain: A Retrospective Exhibition*, exh. cat. (New York: Solomon R. Gug-
      genheim Museum, 1971), 9, 73, 74. However, it is possible that Judd is in-
      stead referring to works such as Chamberlain's *Conrad* (1964), which has
      more definitive elements of relief, though it is on formica, not masonite.
      See Waldman, *John Chamberlain*, 72.

40   In their writings on architecture, both Alberti and Palladio follow Vitru-
      vius in giving 5:6 and 11:13 as ratios to follow for the proper diminution
      of column diameter.

41   Judd enlisted in the United States Army on June 28, 1946, and was assigned
      to the Corps of Engineers in Korea. He was honorably discharged on No-
      vember 20, 1947.

42   Bernard Pares, *A History of Russia* (New York: Alfred A. Knopf, 1927). Judd
      included the 1944 edition of this book, published by the United States
      Armed Forces Institute, in his library in Marfa, Texas.

43   *Kunst und Revolution: Russische und sowjetische Kunst 1910–1932*, Öster-
      reichisches Museum für angewandte Kunst, Vienna, March 11–May 5, 1988.

"Discussion with Donald Judd"
Seminar discussion with Angeli Janhsen (moderator)
and students from the Ruhr-Universität Bochum from
the exhibition catalogue *Donald Judd*
February 1, 1990

On February 1, 1990, Judd participated in a seminar series titled "Gespräche mit Künstlern" ("Talking to Artists"), organized by Angeli Janhsen at the Ruhr-Universität Bochum, Germany. The seminar session with Judd was attended by approximately thirty students. Previous seminars in the series had hosted artists Ulrich Erben, Monika Huber, Raimer Jochims, François Morellet, David Rabinowitch, Erich Reusch, and Richard Serra.

Judd later asked Janhsen for a record of the discussion so that it could be included in the exhibition catalogue for *Donald Judd* at the Kunstverein St. Gallen, Switzerland (April 21–July 29, 1990). The record, which is reproduced here, was prepared by Michael Vignold, one of the seminar participants. Other participants include Gerd Blum, Georg Imdahl, Mathia Löbke, Dagmar Schmidt, Mathias Schwartz-Clauss, and Rafael von Uslar.

A J   [Angeli Janhsen] For art historians in Bochum you are a kind of a myth; I think generations of students have studied your work and discussed it with Max Imdahl, and I have to admit that we have often discussed it as "minimal art" – if it is useful or not, we will see – but we have discussed it that way.[1] I have to say also that art historians from Bochum are known to be less interested in categories of art; on the contrary, we are more interested in special artists, special kinds of art, special works. And so, I hope we will not make traditional art history out of you, but understand more of your work. Thank you for coming. I have to say to the audience that this seminar session will be a little different: we won't have a lecture, but a discussion, a discussion without slides, as far as possible.

D J   [Donald Judd] If everyone wants slides we can show them. I am very tired of my slide shows, it's incredibly boring to me; I always say the same thing. The condition for this is that everybody has to ask questions, because basically it's a lot more interesting for me if you do. I have written quite a bit, mostly about social and art things, not so much about my work. It doesn't make sense for me to write a lecture because you can read.

A J   As we have discussed your work as "minimal art," perhaps you could tell us in the beginning why you don't like this denomination, or what you think about it?

D J   I hate it, of course, and I've said that and written that many times. There are lots of reasons for disliking it. One of the least, to begin with, is that it was simply a derogatory publicity label. There were other labels like "A B C," all of them derogatory.[2] The main objection is that it makes a group out of something that was not a group, out of several people who were definitely not a group. This is a simplification. It is false art history. I objected when they did that to Pollock, Newman, and Rothko: all of them knew each other, but were very independent people. Just as "abstract expressionism" was a label and not a group, neither is "pop art" or so-called minimal art. Basically, it is a destructive political technique, malicious and also just an easy way to write about art. It's *Time* magazine stuff. Not Robert Hughes, though.[3]

AJ   One has to ask for special qualities of each work of art and of each artist?

DJ   Yes. The artists wanted that and expected that; no one expected to wind up in a category with a lot of other people, and they resent that a good deal. Before the term "minimal art" came along, I disliked "abstract expressionism," "action painting," even "New York School," which is fairly harmless, because it's just geographical. But all that is quite unfair and very much a simplification of what was going on. The reality of it is that as a label "minimal art" changed a great deal. Originally it meant three, four people, now it means half the world; there's been a great development in how many people are part of this. Somehow Frank Stella has become the father of it all, although originally not part of it, since his wife was the one applying "ABC" to us,[4] so it's all turned around again and Frank is the father, while of course Frank has totally reneged on any such thing as simple art or even good art; that whole elaboration is not useful at all. The original people did not necessarily know each other; their work developed at different times. You can tell me who you think the original people are, but usually it's me, Carl Andre, Dan Flavin, and Robert Morris. Or it started as Flavin, me, and Morris, then Carl, who showed a little bit later, was added. And so the list slowly grew. These people were the original "group" of so-called minimal artists. They didn't know each other in most cases. The only person I really knew was Dan Flavin. Flavin and I have certain things in common, but we also have wide and different things not in common. We are friends, but couldn't be more divergent. Certain elements – the repetition, the use of geometry, and obviously rather simple schemes – are in common, but you can also say that that is in common with Barnett Newman. I didn't know Morris until I met him after I reviewed a group show he was in.[5] Morris is claimed to be a part of "minimal art"; there were really only two such works in the group show at Gordon's [the Gordon Gallery]. And the gray pieces that were in his one-man show at the Green Gallery[6] were basically like the work he had at Gordon's, Duchampian-Dada sort of work. They weren't meant to be three-dimensional work in itself. They were named – one was called *Cloud*, one *Window*, one *Column*. They were all Duchampian things, like the bucket in which the water was constantly flowing.[7] In accordance, there was the *Box with the Sound of Its Own Making*. I didn't know of Morris before this and of course there was no exchange of thought or context or anything.

AJ   Was it a [useful] kind of climate to do work like yours?

DJ   No, not at all. Doing anything geometric was nearly unknown. It was a totally alien thing to do. At one point there was no work, hardly any work at all, of people who did somewhat geometric work, because the loose side or conventional side of abstract expressionism, such as de Kooning, [Franz] Kline, and Guston, was the most popular side. Very quickly it became an academy with hundreds of artists doing it. That was the dominant judgment in New York in the late '50s. There was no real public in New York for Pollock and Newman, Rothko, and [Clyfford] Still. So there was actually a serious bias that hurt them in the most ordinary ways, such as no sales, no money. They had almost no public, and didn't quite know how to deal with it anyway. Newman and Reinhardt – Newman did not like Reinhardt, so they are not a group either – were very much outsiders. Their painting was not taken seriously by the general public in New York. Anything geometric was very alien and there was a tremendous bias against the previous geometry. This comes from the thinking of Pollock, [Arshile] Gorky, and Rothko; their great interest was in surrealism and generally loose painting and psychology rather than in work like that of Mondrian. Among a lot of artists, Mondrian and anyone connected with straight lines were complete enemies. And when Newman's work, which had been somewhat loose, became more geometric – though it is never very tightly painted – the peripheral public turned against him. When Reinhardt's painting, which had always been loose, became more and more geometric and then nearly unified into one area, these aspects were absolutely verboten.

No one paid much attention to their work. I am sympathetic to them, though they are not particularly predecessors of mine. Reinhardt's work to me is very strange and, in its way, a little bit old-fashioned; I knew Newman and I was very fond of him and liked his work a great deal, but I was interested in something newer than I thought painting was.

A J   What does geometry mean to you? There's a lot of geometry in your work. What does it mean? Has it the same meaning as it has had for artists in the Renaissance, for example?

D J   No, it has a very different meaning. I think that they clearly considered it as part of the structure of the world; my new use, which is relatively simpleminded, is simply as I would use materials; there's no difference to me. It's just fine: you have gray aluminum, you like it and do something with it. And if proportion is available, you can use it like that.

A J   But there is all this tradition of geometry, isn't there?

D J   Yes, but I am not very sympathetic to it. If Palladio made himself happy doing abstruse calculations, that's fine, the result is fine, but I don't think that proportions are very difficult. You can't see very complicated proportions: you know this room is a little off square, that's all you know. To take the mathematics back to some fundamental thing in the universe is a complete fallacy. It is the same fallacy as trying to paint flowers or something. I don't think I know anything about what flowers are like, and neither do I know much about the structure of the universe. My use of arithmetic is for my own personal use as an artist. It does what I want, just like the color or the material or anything else.

AJ It is a thing given to you?

DJ Yes.

AJ It is given in a cultural way, not in a natural way.

DJ Yes, but I am not responsible for the culture.

AJ So you take out of culture, out of nature, or out of everywhere what you want for your work?

DJ Yes. I am after some particular quality. I don't like the division of thought and feeling — I don't deal with that problem — but I'm after one thing, one whole thing, which is the work of art; that quality of the whole, which is a complicated matter and comes from particular materials, from particular arrangements and proportions of things on the wall, of a row of things. It's not that somehow arithmetic is disclosing anything. Even in science, mathematics is basically descriptive. It's not any longer thought of as the basis for the structure of the world: it is thought of as a description which is incredibly useful and can't be done in any other way. But it's no longer some secret that we're trying to find.

  I would never have thought that I would use geometry or straight lines. Like everybody else in New York, I was totally against it and thought that it was very alien. I always liked Mondrian a great deal. But this is true of everybody who really made a quality that was strong, and I was afraid of using anything like that at all. It's the same as with Jackson Pollock: we can't think that Jackson Pollock is structural; everything was so particular to Jackson Pollock. That was one reason, too, that he didn't become the person to be imitated in New York, as de Kooning did, because there is not anything anybody can do with Jackson Pollock. Also, they didn't understand what was really interesting about his work and good about his work. It's a lot easier to follow the side de Kooning is linked with, it's easier for people to understand. To be complete on that: geometry was always coupled with the clear, primary colors of Mondrian, so it was hard to think of a geometry that was not allied to those colors. The de Stijl tradition was so strong that in a way it excluded geometry – it was restricted to work like Mondrian's. And unlike now, the Russian artists such as Malevich were not very well known in New York, so it was hard to be influenced by them.

Slowly I became very much against the naturalistic quality of the curves and the serpentine lines, and, slowly, I straightened them all out. I liked the result better than before, so I got rid of all the referential things [image 76]. The geometry did what I wanted and still does. Spheres are also very good; spheres are incredibly expensive to make, but they are just fine no matter of economy. So circles are okay; they are just expensive, that's all.

AJ   We've seen your circles in Münster [see image 57].

DJ   Yes, there are not many for that reason.

AJ   But you don't think that a circle or a proportion, for example, in itself is meaningful? It's just a form you've found and used?

DJ   It's meaningful only in the context of the whole work. I make a work of art out of it just as anyone for the last couple of thousand years has done. There are a lot of different reasons for doing art, but much is the same.

The circles taken as part of the whole work of art, the circles or the square or whatever, is meaningful, but re-

ferring to the circle somewhere else or the square somewhere else is meaningless. I am not interested in the history of the circle, the cultural situation of the circle, the
archetype of the circle.

AJ That might be the same with proportion, because someone could say that a proportion like 2:4, 4:8, 8:16, referring to solids, and 16:8, 8:4, 4:2, referring to the space between the solids, is a progression, which could show some
kind of time or infinity, but that's not what you mean?

DJ No, not so much. Time is interesting; it's a factor in the
work of course, but it wouldn't be that literal. It is more
visual; it's to lock the two directions together.[8]

AJ There is no kind of philosophy?

DJ Lots of philosophy. But you can't take things out of the art
and separate them. I hope there's plenty of philosophy.

I think the work in a very general way has to do with
time, it's very much about time, but to take a progression
like that as an example of time is too literal. For example,
there is one so-called progression – these are not titles,
they are just a way of reference – there was one that I simply found in a book. I don't know anything about arithmetic – the book was very dense – but I could see that it
was a very nice idea. It is the piece which is twenty-one
feet long and almost evenly divided; the Whitney Museum had the old one [see image 26].

The main virtue of progressions is that they allow a
certain variation without getting involved in composition;
there's a scheme. The one in the book was $1 - \frac{1}{2} + \frac{1}{3} -
\frac{1}{4} + \frac{1}{5} \ldots$, it's an inverse natural number series. It goes to
infinity without ever going below a half, so that it's very
even running along the room, and of course, at length,
you wouldn't see any change at all. But I could see that it
would do what I wanted.

One more thing about "minimal art": it was definitely
not a group. If you follow the chronology of what was

done then, and this is what an art historian should do in a different time, it was very much against the whole situation in New York to have a group. It wasn't like people to do that. People of my age were even less inclined to do it than the people of Barnett Newman's age. They at least met with one another and had the artists' club.[9] They met once a month and discussed things. At the point in which I was developing my work in New York, lots of people didn't know each other.

AJ   You don't like art historians?

DJ   I like a couple. I studied art history at Columbia, so I had firsthand experience.[10]

DS   [Dagmar Schmidt] Does mathematical order in your work have the function of establishing a kind of security in perception?

DJ   No.

DS   Because order makes sense anyway, one could rely on a firm order when involved in the varying experience of the work of art?

DJ   Well, I haven't thought of it that way. I've always been fairly uninterested in security. I have a lot of elements in the work, and perhaps what the order does most conspicuously is to make a relatively pragmatic order, saying that this is the way something is, here and now, which I don't think is security, rather that it's given and it happens in the present. This is here, you can't say it isn't here. It has some of that nature. Sometimes the color is fairly pragmatic and definite; a lot of times it's not. The same with the surface – the metal is often shiny and hard to pin down. But I think the order makes it perfectly clear that it's one of the reasons for all of that. I guess it's obvious that it isn't a big order, it's only a small order. If anyone wants to make a big order, he should think of something better. This is very simple – four things in a row.

GB   [Gerd Blum] The fact that your work is so very simple to understand – for example, just five cubes – in my opinion is not a fact of security, but, on the contrary, a kind of irritation. If you look very shortly and just recognize five cubes of a certain size –

DJ   I'm not so fond of odd numbers. Four cubes or six. Threes and fives are doubtful. So are two. Earlier these were hierarchical.

GB   You have just four cubes, and *basta*. But all those things which you see – for example, that the space between the cubes is very dense – these are all facts you can't understand. You can't understand why you are fascinated, why you are looking at four cubes. There's a difference between the things you can define in understanding and the things you see or experience. And I think this is the great irritation.

DJ   It's okay. It's not meant to be anything to anybody else, but that's another point. I'm not thinking about the public, so it's not meant to have any effect on anybody, because that is an unknown matter.

The space between the units, the boxes, or whatever they are is very important, of course. Originally that was done by eye, but it turns out to be one quarter of the distance. If you make it too far apart, it becomes just a space between the boxes, so you've got to make some equivalence between the volume of the boxes or the enclosed space and the open space.

GB   One can think four cubes, five cubes, six cubes, seven cubes, and so on, but that is not possible in visual experience. What is possible in visual experience is only four cubes with a specific space in between.

DJ   It's good. You find things that are interesting to you and do what you want to do, which hopefully hasn't interested anyone before. I don't think anybody has really considered these matters before. To me they are quite important. That's what the nature of present art is – who would think that somebody would be interested in stripes down the canvas, like Barnett Newman? That's a situation he made for himself, which turns out to be interesting for other people.

The four units in a row cannot have any other space in between them. The first one I did was thirty-four inches, which is less than a meter, with a seven-inch gap. And then I did some that were forty inches, which is almost exactly a meter, and the gap was ten inches, which is about twenty-five centimeters. This [gap] was one-fourth [of a meter], which is strange. But I did it pragmatically at first, just to see how it looked. I had no interest then in proportion. I don't know how I lost it before I did it. Proportions were obviously very good in architecture, and very useful.

RVU   [Rafael von Uslar] As you've said, you don't develop your work for a public. But I think in the moment you develop more than a concept – you work on sculpture so that you automatically address something or someone outside. And in that moment, you work for a public, though a limited public – it's comparable to *The Lightning Field* by Walter De Maria – but at the same time you do have an addressee, and then it's clear that you are working not only for your own and for your own spaces in New York and Texas, but also for a worldwide audience. How can you say, then, "Well, I do have this audience, I do have this public and decide to live on that as an artist, but I am not working for it"?

DJ   Originally, and even now, I assume there's no way to know anything about the public and there's no way to think about the public; there's no way to think of art as communication. In fact, if you thought about it even a little bit as communication, it would be a big problem in the way. Thinking of art as communication is too simple and makes a big rock that's right in the road which you can't get around. Of course, originally, in New York, when I was developing the work, there wasn't any public, so you couldn't think of a general public, and it was academic, whether you wanted to think about it or not. Naturally I thought everyone would like other artists to look at their work, but that did not mean that they had to see the same things or agree. It would be very far-fetched to think that Newman or Pollock or anyone was making work for the public or even trying to communicate directly. I know it's a funny attitude, but the fact is, you don't know the public. You simply don't know what this vast number of people – maybe Gorbachev does, that's his job – really think; there's nothing to think with. If it makes sense to me, if I like it, maybe it'll make sense to someone else and they will like it; that's all you have to work with. Communication is a totally alien aspect of visual art, I think.

RVU Maybe it's an educational aspect, because you've started writing and you put a great number of demands on how work should be presented and treated. I would like to mention your idea of the individual museum in this context. I think this is a way of communication; it's in any case a way of self-referential thinking.

DJ Yes, that part can be communication, but the work of art itself cannot be. I don't think an artist would think about that in that way. They have to think about what they are after. If they start to consider what Joe is going to think tomorrow morning, it's impossible. Writing is obviously communication, that's one reason I do it, or did it, and stopped when I shouldn't have stopped. It is a little lesson, too, that even though you write for yourself, you are still writing words of communication, so that's fundamental. The way art is fundamental is otherwise – that is, not being so directly. If you assume that there is something to the art for other people and that it is out in the world, it should be installed well and taken care of, all of which of course is a social matter. I am very keen on protecting the integrity of the single work of art and not letting it become part of communication and, certainly, education. All museums claim that their real role is to educate the public, but it's hard to know what they are really teaching. Fundamentally, at this point, art is not made to fortify the society, to fortify individuals, to be religious, to be political, to be all the different things that it's been over the centuries. Basically, it's one person's view and not the view of the rest of the world, which can be more or less peculiar or not peculiar. So, it's a funny thing: we are making art as individuals, and of course it does reflect being in the society, that that is in the existing universe, and yet – it's not part of it. It's not part like true religious art would have been part of religion in the Middle Ages.

MSC   [Mathias Schwartz-Clauss] Is your art of a philosophical concept and enclosed in itself, or is the progress of your work influenced by experiences you have in your life besides being an artist?

DJ   Naturally it's influenced by lots of things besides being an artist. Most things that I'm concerned about are in there. It does involve a philosophy. Clear ideas about the work go with clear work. When I did the first three-dimensional pieces, I thought everything became fairly clear. One of the things I liked about them was not only what they looked like here and now, but that they could develop and change without any great fundamental change in attitude. There are also a lot of things you don't know in yourself that you have to recognize and that become qualities in the work, which is a very mysterious thing for all artists to deal with.

MSC   So we can say the connecting factor of your different works at least is your life and not a certain idea or philosophy?

DJ   It is a certain philosophy.

MSC   Which is life itself?

DJ   Yes, of course.

GI   [Georg Imdahl] Would you say that there's just one true
     meaning in your work the onlooker must come to, or
     would you say that different meanings by different peo-
     ple looking at your work are okay?

DJ   Well, some meanings I would be able to say right away are
     not there, or that they're wrong, but I think people are
     going to see different things in the work. And some of
     those hopefully will be original – I would have thought
     of them and they would be true. I think there would be
     some diversity of experience in looking at the work. But
     I can think of certain interpretations that will be com-
     pletely wrong.

DS   Do you want to make the observer understand something,
     or to make him just look at the work?

DJ   That's the division between thought and feeling. You have
     to do it all at once. You have to look and understand, both.
     In looking, you understand; it's more than you can de-
     scribe. You look and think, and look and think, until it
     makes sense, becomes interesting.

DS   Do you want to say that the way of doing something, for
     example, doing art, is the aim, that the way is the aim and
     that it doesn't matter really if people say your work is just
     nice and decorative, or if they consider it more deeply and
     intellectually?

DJ   No, that's not quite right, because if it's wrong, I object. If
     they tell me it's decorative, I'll tell them they are wrong.
     But the opportunity doesn't come along very often, be-
     cause people don't come to tell me it's decorative. One
     conspicuous misinterpretation, for example, is the idea of
     order: most writers in the United States have always said
     that it's Platonic in some way and involved in some great
     scheme of order. If I know about that and talk to the per-
     son, that's certainly wrong. That's a view of the work and
     a misinterpretation of the work.

A J   If there's no message in your work we have to disclose, is a work of yours – I've read it somewhere – an instrument for seeing? Is that right?

D J   No, it's isolating one aspect. All works of art involve seeing. They are not hammers and nails, they are not instruments. Again, that involves doing something with the audience that I don't know about.

A J   Your work is not didactic?

D J   No. I think anything in the work that has an element of didacticism is really objectionable; it's part of the communication problem. I've had work of other artists, only two cases, where I thought there was a didactic quality. I have always liked Cy Twombly's work, but I use this as an example: I had a drawing whereby he transferred Leonardo da Vinci's waves, circular, swirling drawings, and then did his own scribbles in between. The drawing had the quality of saying Cy Twombly's scribbles are like Leonardo's waves. And I couldn't get over it. I got rid of it, because I really objected to Cy's trying to teach me that his scribbles are like Leonardo's waves. That's didactic, which is not at all usual in Cy Twombly's work, almost never, but it just happened to be in this case, or I saw it that way. So therefore, when you see a whole exhibition in a museum that's didactic, that's multiplying the mess, of course you object. And you often have museum shows where they want you to proceed chronologically, which is didactic, or by materials, or by color, or almost anything you can think of. I try to make the shows natural, and to make the work go together as well as it can, to avoid doing anything like that.

M L   [Mathia Löbke] What does color mean to you?

D J   Color is very important; I think I don't know enough about it yet. To transfer this to everybody else, I don't think artists know enough about it yet. I think color is still fairly new, despite a couple of thousand years, four thousand since the flood. Some people have used color in a new way in their work and developed it, like Josef Albers, but I think there's still a lot more to be done with color. I'm trying to figure it out, trying to do more. The color I use tends to be monochromatic or just two colors. That was the reason for doing the sheet metal pieces on the wall [see image 68]. I tried to do something more with the colors, but I got stuck with the structure of those. I like the structure, but the structure, especially in bright colors, involves colors being offset; I don't want the same colors next to each other. So the offsetting bothers me, as it has always bothered me, because it's a traditional, compositional device. I would like to get away from offsetting. Also, I didn't allow enough divergence in the color, where it is bigger and smaller. I think that slowly, maybe with the large pieces in Baden-Baden, I know more about it.[11] I am also thinking of making large pieces with sheet metal.

The color of Albers and Matisse is a big lesson, of course. There's a lot of good color, but I think it can go further. Of course, it's not very usual for a person making three-dimensional work to be interested in color, but I've always thought that it was vital. I also think that materials are colored – they are not gray or whatever, they are not just neutral; it's gray as a color. That's why the first pieces were bright red and not colorless.

MV   [Michael Vignold] Very often you use color which comes as an effect from the material.

DJ   Yes, I like the color to be in the material.

MV   What is the relation between the color in the material and the color painted on?

DJ   Painted color is second choice. I like the plexiglass because the color is in the plexiglass, right in the material. Of course, metal or plywood are a certain color, but you don't have big areas of bright color that are in the material except the plexiglass. Painting the aluminum, the sheet of aluminum, is something of a compromise; it makes it obvious. It's painted sheet aluminum dealt with by the bending process as sheet metal. I would have preferred it if originally it had color, but it didn't. So the best solution seemed to be to make it obvious – that is, painted sheet metal just like an automobile. There's nothing mysterious about it or underneath it – if you scratch it, it's aluminum. But if possible, I prefer the color to be in the material. Anodized aluminum, even though it's a surface too, is a little better to me, because at least a little layer of it is color in the material. If I can ever have red pieces of stainless steel, I will love it. That will be perfect.

GB   I've read a text of yours, a very precise description of a painting by Barnett Newman titled *Shining Forth (To George)*.[12] You've shown that its formal structure is very complex: the surface is behind the stripes, but in the stripes, and so on. Then you stop your formal analysis and quote Newman saying: "We are making art of ourselves, out of our own feelings."[13] If I am looking at a work of Newman, I can see all those formal facts as you described them, but deeper, there's a kind of precise emotion. The titles are connected with these emotions: for example, *Midnight Blue*, or *Jericho*. You can see the title without knowing the title. I think Newman did his painting to evoke a special emotion. When you are doing a work of art, is there a certain feeling or a certain kind of idea before you choose, for example, four cubes?

DJ   Not quite; this is why you make art. You can't find it any other way. You have some idea of what you want, but you don't quite know what you want. When you find what you think you want, or what you are looking for, you don't really know that, because it's very new, and of course you didn't plan it at any time. As I said, I don't like the division of thought and feeling, so I can't say I'm looking for a feeling. I use the word "quality" to get away from using a division of those two. I have some idea of the quality I am after, but it's actually making the work of art that makes that clear. I'm sure Barney was surprised, too, when he saw the painting. He thought about it for a long time, and he did it in one day in a little studio in Carnegie Hill in one shot, with his monocle, because he couldn't find his glasses.[14] Because the studio was from here to the wall, he was face-to-face with the painting. His wife told me that he thought about it even for several months. But no one is going to know until a work actually exists, which is one reason to make art.

One reason I described the painting so carefully is because I don't think people look at art very carefully. My experience with art history at Columbia was that art historians never look at paintings.

In this particular case, as I said, I knew Newman, and I met him to show him the article before I sent it to the magazine. I did not want to get into a lot of speculation, philosophizing about what he meant. It's a real construction to talk about what an artist really means. I have hardly ever done that. It's a real speculation that you have to build. You have to build a philosophical framework to say, "This means this, this has this attitude, that attitude is in the work." It's very important to analyze the appearance, and to also enjoy analyzing the formal means: in this case, it's so beautiful formally. Though the formal side is important, it is by itself meaningless. That's again another jackass division of form and content. That's like saying it's an instrument of thinking or something – you separate it out. The whole form and content discussion in art is ridiculous.

MV As three-dimensional work, your work is closely connected with space, of course. What kind of space are you thinking about – when you do your work, do you have any special idea of space? Is space an empty container before you put some of your work in?

DJ   I have to start from the beginning philosophically, which is very dangerous: space doesn't exist; time doesn't exist either. So you have to make them exist. We know space and time because things occur in them, are in it or happen in it. They are made by positions, events. When you make a work of art, you are making space or further architecture. You are definitely making a space. We have space here in this room, but this is a weak, nondescript, neutral space. If we reorganize the room, it could become real space, perhaps. You can have different degrees. It can be very general or it can be very particular, but a definite fact is: you are making space. One reason I didn't like to make paintings but like three-dimensional work so much is because I like space a great deal. I spent a lot of time sitting around waiting for classes to begin at Columbia – there was a gap between art school and the university[15] – and I realized that the space underneath the desk was a lot more interesting than what was happening down in the art school. It always looked very good under there. That's my particular interest in space. Carl Andre, for example, is interested in mass, difference in masses and materials. I like Carl's work a great deal, but mass to me is extremely strange. I had to deal with the idea of mass because it's usual in traditional painting; I had to get away from that, because almost all painting represents a certain weight, represents a certain mass. I realized I wasn't that interested in weight and mass. I like volume. For that reason, I like [John] Chamberlain's sculpture.

US   [Unknown speaker] I've read that you don't like to talk about the content of a work. You wouldn't like to call the generated, created space which is established by your work "content"?

DJ   It's destroying what should be together, and it's destructive in the work of art. The artist is trying to make a totality. It's a bad idea for the artist to demolish that totality.

That's the main reason, I think, why artists don't want to talk about their work: they put it all together, and it's sort of perverse to sit at a table and take it apart again. It's a legitimate activity, or it should be, when an art critic does it. To discuss it, they have to demolish it; in thinking about it, you reduce it. It's perhaps necessary to do that.

AJ   If you put some cubes on the wall here, would they change the room?

DJ   Yes.

AJ   In which way?

DJ   They would make a very definite space. The room is a general space; it's not very particular in its quality. You can do things in art or architecture with a room which make it much more particular, much more defined. It's okay for what it is, but it's very general. You wouldn't really call it architecture. David Rabinowitch's room is architecture, a highly defined room.[16] It's defined because the space is constructed, the space is made. That's why you don't have good architecture. They don't make real spaces. The space is not thought out; nothing is defining the space.

AJ   But your work would be an addition to the existing space?

DJ   In this case, yes.

AJ   Is it possible to do works of other artists together with yours, or would it change the room in another way?

DJ   It will change the room, but probably it wouldn't make it as definite a space because I would have to avoid being too definite with my work in order to not overrule other people's work. If you had several artists here, the most important thing is that all the work goes well together and that the room itself as a whole is not destroyed, because then the work looks bad anyway.

AJ   Your work is not an installation in that sense which tends to change the room?

DJ   It can. I've a lot of different kinds of work; some can virtually make a room.

AJ   But it's okay in the museum, too, if there are other works?

DJ   Yes, but it's a difference in particularity. Also, three-dimensional work and painting don't go together well, because the relationship to the wall is so different.

AJ   You made paintings, reliefs, three-dimensional works, and architecture and furniture.

DJ   Yes, but I'm still making three-dimensional works.

AJ   You do not deal with painting?

DJ   No, I've no interest in it. However, I've made prints, which are flat, but they are small. The only painting that might be interesting is wall painting.

AJ   That would be a kind of architecture?

DJ   Yes. I painted some rooms once, but they're destroyed now.[17] It is a kind of architecture. I ran a band of color along the floor and around, which made very different rooms. Just outlined the walls. In a very simple way you have a much more definite room than before.

AJ   If you show your work together with works by other artists – for example in a museum – where is the limit between the work of Donald Judd and the work of another artist? Isn't it a new totality?

DJ   Yes, I think the room should be a new totality in a way. In saying this, I'm arguing a little bit against my complete defense of the integrity of art, because I'm arguing for something else and the art being used a little bit for the sake of the whole room, but on the other hand, the art is not going to look very good if the whole room doesn't look good, too. The whole installation, the whole room has to come first and look good, and if you have too many pieces, or if the different kinds of work really conflict, something has to go. Otherwise the work is going to look bad, so you really haven't lost anything. I've written: installation is enormously important.[18] Therefore, of course, the architecture should be better than it usually is, so you don't have to fight with it all the time.

You can always make another room with different works. You know that I have a building in New York and spaces in Texas.[19] I spent an enormous amount of time pushing the art around, for years taking things out, whether it's all mine or mixed with others – just one room would continue for years. And the selection concerns me a great deal. One floor in the building in New York has two pieces of mine, a piece of Chamberlain's, a piece of Oldenburg's, and a big piece of Flavin's. I think it all goes together somehow, but it took many years. I had a painting by Bob Irwin where the Oldenburg now is that never worked there. It should be alone. So the work by Oldenburg, which is fine in itself, thus had the useful side of having solved the problem of working well with the other pieces. But anyway, installation is extremely important. Ordinarily in museums it's not done well, and so far, I've come across very few museum curators, directors, and gallery people who take it seriously and could do it well. It can be done. One person – I haven't seen enough – is Brydon Smith from the National Gallery of Canada.[20] Brydon made a room look very good with beautiful pieces. And a dealer I do like a great deal in New York, Richard Bellamy, did very nice installations at the Green Gallery in the '60s: many shows looked good.[21] Two people have and thirty haven't.

A J   You've written and said many times that you are interested in the things that are there. Some things are really there, but others aren't; so art is a kind of utopia?

D J   No, art is not a kind of utopia, because it really exists. It's not utopia. Perhaps it's the other stuff that is utopian. People don't pay enough attention to what is there. I don't know what has happened to the pragmatic, empirical attitude of paying attention to what is here and now; it's basic to science. It should be basic to art, too.

First published: Angeli Janhsen, "Discussion with Donald Judd," in *Donald Judd*, exh. cat. (St. Gallen, Switzerland: Kunstverein St. Gallen, 1990), 39–56 (in English and German).

1   Max Imdahl (1925–1988) was a German art historian. He taught at the Ruhr-Universität in Bochum from 1965 until his death in 1988.

2   Judd refers here to terminology used by Barbara Rose in her article "ABC Art," *Art in America*, October–November 1965, 57–69, which was one of the first essays devoted to defining minimalism as a style.

3   Robert Hughes (1938–2012) was an Australian-born art critic and television documentarian. From 1970 until 2001, he was the chief art critic for *Time* magazine; his eight-episode 1980 television series on the development of modernism, *The Shock of the New*, was highly popular.

4   Frank Stella and Barbara Rose were married from 1961 to 1969.

5   *Boxing Match*, Gordon Gallery, New York, February 27–March 24, 1963. See Judd's review of *Boxing Match* (1963) in *Donald Judd: Complete Writings 1959–1975*, 90.

6   *Robert Morris: Sculpture (part one)*, Green Gallery, New York, December 16, 1964–January 9, 1965.

7   Robert Morris, *Fountain* (1963), Museum für Moderne Kunst, Frankfurt am Main.

8   The published version of this discussion reads, "it's to look the two directions together." The editors have changed "look" to "lock," as they believe this is more likely the correct word.

9   Judd refers here to the Club, a meeting group of New York artists whose membership included many abstract expressionists. From 1948 until the mid-1950s, in a loft at 39 East Eighth Street, the Club hosted weekly discussions and lectures on art, metaphysics, psychology, philosophy, and other topics of shared interest.

10   Judd received his BS in philosophy from Columbia University, cum laude, in 1953. He began graduate work in art history at Columbia in fall 1957 and completed his coursework in fall 1961; no degree was conferred because he did not complete the requirements.

11   *Donald Judd*, Staatliche Kunsthalle Baden-Baden, Germany, August 27–October 15, 1989. This exhibition included twelve large works for the floor in anodized aluminum. For more on this exhibition and the works under discussion, see "Back to Clarity: Interview with Donald Judd" (1989) in this volume, 662–93.

12   See Judd's "Barnett Newman" (1964) in *Donald Judd Writings*, 152–59.

13   In a 1948 article for *The Tiger's Eye*, an art and literary magazine, Newman wrote, "Instead of making *cathedrals* out of Christ, man, or 'life,' we are making [them] out of ourselves, out of our own feelings." Newman, "The Sublime Is Now," in *Barnett Newman: Selected Writings and Interviews*, ed. John P. O'Neill (New York: Knopf, 1990), 173.

14   Carnegie Hill is a neighborhood within Manhattan's Upper East Side.

15   Judd attended the Art Students League, in New York, during the day from
      1948 to 1953, while also working toward an undergraduate degree at night
      at Columbia University.

16   David Rabinowitch, *Tyndale Sculpture (for Bud Powell and Coleman Hawkins)*
      (1986–88), Situation Kunst (für Max Imdahl), Bochum, Germany.

17   The painted rooms were in Casa Lujan, Marfa, Texas. Judd lived with his
      family in Casa Lujan, a four-room house in the Sal Si Puedes neighbor-
      hood east of Marfa, before and during the move into the Block. See Judd's
      "Casa Lujan and La Catorcena" (1989) in *Donald Judd: Architektur*, 26–30.

18   See Judd's "On Installation" (1982) in *Donald Judd Writings*, 308–15.

19   Judd refers here to 101 Spring Street and La Mansana de Chinati/The
      Block.

20   Brydon Smith (1938–) is a Canadian art historian and curator. In 1967, he
      became curator of contemporary art at the National Gallery of Canada,
      Ottawa, where he curated Judd's first retrospective: *Donald Judd*, May 24–
      July 6, 1975. Smith, along with Dudley Del Balso and Roberta Smith, also
      produced the catalogue raisonné of Judd's work published on the occa-
      sion of the exhibition. See Brydon Smith, ed., *Donald Judd: Catalogue Rai-
      sonné of Paintings, Objects, and Wood-Blocks 1960–1974*, exh. cat. (Ottawa: Na-
      tional Gallery of Canada, 1975).

21   Richard Bellamy (1927–1998) was the founder and director of Green
      Gallery, New York.

Interview with Claudia Jolles
April 5, 1990

In 1986, Judd began work on the renovation of Eichholteren, a former hotel located on Lake Lucerne near Küssnacht am Rigi, Switzerland. Judd used this property as a home and studio beginning in 1987, and it is here that this conversation with art historian Claudia Jolles took place. Jolles is the sister of Adrian Jolles, a Swiss architect with whom Judd worked on a number of projects in Europe, including the renovation of Eichholteren.

Additionally, in July 1990, Judd established another studio in Europe, in a former brewery in Cologne. He called this studio Hafenstrasse, for the road on which it was located.

C J   [Claudia Jolles] You usually choose very remote spots for your work, in contrast to Richard Serra, who said that his sculptures work best in active urban centers; they need the public.

D J   [Donald Judd] I am absolutely in disagreement with that attitude. I like Richard's work a great deal, but as I said many times, I am not interested in the public. My work is not private, it is not public; it is just my work.

C J   But still it is always scaled to human size.

D J   That is because I happen to be human size. I am not interested in any kind of a reaction, for or against the public. I will do exactly the same work in the middle of the city as down at the ranch where very few people would ever see it. I am interested in good spaces. I am not interested in fighting bad spaces. So I have done very few so-called public pieces, or commissioned works. If I do them, I would do them in good circumstances, not in bad circumstances.

C J   So if the public opposed your work – as, for example, in the case of the *Tilted Arc* – would you withdraw your work?[1]

D J   There was an agreement for *Tilted Arc* to be permanent. I defend him [Serra] thoroughly. This is also my problem with [Heiner] Friedrich[2] and Giuseppe Panza[3] and so forth. In that case, I am absolutely on Richard's side. I wouldn't have put it there in the first place, but given his thinking, and the fact that it is there, it should stay there.

C J   But if, for example, a factory would commission a piece from you and the workers wouldn't like it, what would you do?

D J   If this happened before the work was installed there and within the factory, I would forget about it, I wouldn't insist on it.

C J   Does the fact that Marfa is so far away mean that this kind of total vision, of Gesamtkunstwerk, can't be realized in the midst of a social environment?

DJ   That is the actual fact. The work is in Texas because I live there; this is an accident. It is not a choice to be remote, but the fact is that you can't do anything very large and serious in the middle of society. Not in America, not in Europe, not anywhere. And I am against fighting. I don't think the work should develop in a hostile situation.

CJ   Your work is often built up on a system of variation. But it's never very obvious whether this system follows a precise rule. Do the existing possibilities stand for all the other unrealized ones?

DJ   I just do the possibilities which are the most interesting. I don't want to realize a comprehensive sequence of all the possible solutions, because usually just some of them are good. Usually I can think of many more possibilities than I can afford to build.

CJ   Do you ever change the works when they come from the fabricator?

DJ   No, you can't. Once they are made, they are made.

CJ   Do your metal pieces come all finished from the factory, or do you get them in parts and put them together yourself?

DJ   The parts have a specific determination. The whole piece is made by the factory from the beginning to the end. It is not that I juggle with colors afterward. They are joined more carefully than that.

CJ   And how was it with the earlier pieces of lacquered metal?

DJ   The older ones I painted, but it is not good for you. I hated to do it. If I can give it to somebody else to do it … Also, in the factory, they are set up so that they don't have to breathe in the vapors.

CJ   Do you work with assistants?

DJ   The factories are the assistants. There are quite a few different enterprises and people doing the work. We have a small factory now in West Texas.[4] Peter Ballantine in New York makes the plywood pieces.[5] Menziken is the factory

here in Switzerland that does the anodized plate aluminum;[6] they made all the pieces for Baden-Baden.[7]

CJ   So the works in Baden-Baden were not site specific?

DJ   No. I knew the space ahead of time, so I chose the works
in relation to the museum space. There is a range of pieces
which are very particular and can never be moved and pieces
more general which are going to look well in any room that
is big enough and isn't specifically bad architecture.

CJ   If you make pieces of this size, do you first make a model
to try them out?

DJ   No, usually not. Models usually don't do me much good.

CJ   I thought it must be fun?

DJ   No, I hate models, and they don't provide any information.

CJ   In a text about Kazimir Malevich, you wrote that time and
space are made by events and positions.[8] How do your objects define time and space? Does it have something to do
with perception, as with Serra's works, which you have to
walk around, or does the seriality refer to a certain rhyth-
mical flow of time?

DJ   Not intentionally. I don't differ with Richard on what you
just said. I think that pretty much this work defines the
space, as architecture does, too. And if you don't have a
very clearly thought-out space, in some way it is less space.

CJ   Your wall pieces seem to deal with space in a very American way. It is not a space that rises from the ground but
airspace that can be measured and sold to a skyscraper-
building company.

DJ   Well, this hasn't anything to do with it. This is really more
recent than these pieces of mine. It is only during the last
ten years that this has become a big racket. Skyscrapers
are just silly.

CJ   Walter Gropius once said that art, architecture, furniture,
and crafts can be placed in a hierarchical order.

DJ   That is a big subject. There is a little bit of truth to what he
says, except that I don't like the hierarchy between all these

things. I think the hierarchy is possibly more in their definition, in their individuality. The art is this strange thing that one person is interested in. It is found to be in some way more particular because it is useless. The qualities of architecture tend to be more general and therefore can't be that peculiar. This is where to place it; it is not a criticism or to make a hierarchy. Generally, people don't appreciate the importance of crafts. Pots can have a lot of particularity, or they can be more general, like dishes. That is kind of open.

CJ   What do you think about this discussion of whether furniture and art have the same intensity?

DJ   Furniture is furniture, it is not art. It is made to sit in, it is not made just to look at. I object to that whole category of art furniture.

CJ   So your furniture can be manipulated by the user? For example, could he put a cushion on it?

DJ   Sure, it is real furniture. I know other people who think it is uncomfortable, but I think it is just fine.

CJ   Robert Mangold once said that the perception of a piece of art must be very quick, at one glance. You build houses so that one can live with your pieces. Do you want them to have a kind of meditative quality?

DJ   I don't agree with the speed of visual perception. I think that ordinarily, art takes time, and if something is worth looking at, you want to look at it again and again. I think basically all art is meditative.

CJ   In the East, reality is poor and shabby. Personal fantasies and dreams seem much more reliable than the visible world. A pragmatic attitude as in minimal art seems unthinkable in the East.

DJ   Everything is poor and shabby in New York and West Texas, too.

CJ   But the perfection that you require in your work couldn't even be done in Moscow.

DJ   It is very difficult to achieve in New York, too. In fact, this
      is about the best New York can do. The level of factories
      is pretty low. I am almost sure that there is no factory east
      of the Mississippi that can do as good a job as Menziken.
      That is one reason why I am doing it there. So much for
      the perfection of the United States. I don't consider the
      pieces perfect; I just don't think of them in that way. They
      should be well made, because if they are badly made, it
      is obtrusive, that's all. Being well made is just eliminating
      troubles and things to be distracted by. So perfection is
      not exactly what my idea is.

CJ   But there are no mistakes.

DJ   There are a lot of mistakes, but we are trying to get rid of
      them. Actually, the works are not handmade by me, but
      they are surprisingly handmade by the factory. One of the
      big problems is to keep the handwork out of it, or to keep
      it down. I don't like the quality of handwork. I don't want
      the pieces to look as if someone worked on the edge.

CJ   Why not?

DJ   Because it goes against what I am after in terms of the art.
      There is a whole philosophy. I am not interested in the
      surface of this wooden table, for example; I don't want to
      imitate the edge, fooling around to get it to look worn.
      It is just fine the way it is — just leave it alone. I don't
      want the work to look as if some sculptor had handled
      it, was carving the edges. I don't like that kind of art be-
      cause back there is a big philosophy, a big tradition, with
      which I don't agree. So I don't want it to shimmer through
      even halfway. It is a whole important position that I don't
      agree with. I don't want a little bit of Michelangelo stick-
      ing along the edge somewhere. He is just fine; leave him
      alone, too. Some people are interested in what the world
      looks like and have done pretty good things. Claes Olden-
      burg is a pretty radical artist. But I think either the world
      is natural and it is fine and you just leave it alone, or if it is

man-made – as things go now – it is bad and you better leave it alone. I don't see any reason to play around with it. I would rather do something new, as a complete alternative, as far as the man-made side is concerned.

CJ   Are there artistic ideas which you didn't realize because they were done before?

DJ   Not really. I wouldn't worry about it if someone did do it. For example, I held off using Cor-ten for a while because Richard Serra started using it. I don't know when I thought about it in relation to when he started – it doesn't matter. The surface seemed rather soft to me, so I didn't use it, and anyway it was beyond my money at that time. Then he started working with it and I thought, "Well, that kind of takes care of that; I shouldn't use it." But after a while I thought, "That is ridiculous. If I use it, I use it." I started to make pieces. The surface turned out not to be so soft. Barnett Newman used it, too; he probably was the first one.

CJ   For the *Broken Obelisk*.

DJ   Yes, or the *Zim Zum*. Mostly it turns out not to be much of an issue. I remember earlier times when I was a little bothered when people started doing things on the land, because I had this in mind. But then it turned out they were not doing great things, so it didn't matter. Except for the destruction of the land.

This conversation was sourced from an archival transcript in the Judd Foundation Archives, Marfa, Texas.

1   Richard Serra's *Tilted Arc* (1981) was installed at Manhattan's Foley Federal Plaza in 1981. After acrimonious public debate and a drawn-out federal lawsuit, the sculpture was removed in 1989.
2   Heiner Friedrich (1938–) is a German art dealer. Along with Philippa de Menil and Helen Winkler, he cofounded Dia Art Foundation in 1974.
3   Giuseppe Panza di Biumo (1923–2010) was a prominent Italian collector of modern art. See Judd's "Una stanza per Panza" (1990) in *Donald Judd Writings*, 630–99.

4   From 1988 until 1994, Judd operated El Taller Chihuahuense, a studio for
     the production of his Cor-ten steel artworks, out of a former ice factory
     in Marfa, Texas. The building is now part of the Chinati Foundation and
     is used for special exhibitions and artist-in-residence studio space, among
     other activities hosted by the foundation.

5   From 1971 to the end of Judd's life, Peter Ballantine was the primary fab-
     ricator of Judd's works in plywood.

6   Menziken AG, located in the canton of Aargau, Switzerland, was a fabri-
     cator of Judd's work in anodized aluminum from 1986 until Judd's death
     in 1994.

7   For more on Judd's Baden-Baden works, see "Back to Clarity: Interview
     with Donald Judd" (1989) in this volume, 662–93.

8   "Time and space don't exist; they are made by events and positions. Time
     and space can be made and don't have to be found like stars in the sky or
     rocks on a hillside." See Judd's "Russian Art in Regard to Myself" (1981)
     in *Donald Judd Writings*, 298.

Interview with Kerry Freeman
1990

This interview was conducted for *Detour*, which was founded in Dallas in 1987; a shortened and edited version of it was published in the magazine's October 1990 issue, under the title "The Book, the Beliefs, His Life & His Architecture." "The Book" refers to *Donald Judd: Architektur*, which was published on the occasion of an exhibition by the same name held at the Westfälischer Kunstverein, Münster, Germany (April 16–June 4, 1989). In *Donald Judd: Architektur*, Judd wrote about his realized and unrealized architectural projects.

Not long before this interview was published, *Donald Judd*, Judd's 1988 retrospective exhibition at the Whitney Museum of American Art, New York (October 20–December 31, 1988), traveled to the Dallas Museum of Art (February 12–April 19, 1989).

KF   [Kerry Freeman] I haven't seen any of the buildings that you have recently purchased in town [Marfa, Texas]. I would very much like to see them.

DJ   [Donald Judd] Well, I try to reach some kind of balance between here and the ranch.[1] I want to move my library and studio into one big building [on the ranch].

KF   Is that in the plans you have in the book?[2] I noticed that you have some expansion plans for the ranch.[3]

DJ   Yeah, there are little things, but the ranch is growing a mile a minute, at least a mile a month [*laughs*], and so actually in one year the situation has changed a great deal. It's not a little ranch. The trick is how to make it all liveable and useful.

KF   Do you have more than one ranch?

DJ   In a sense that the two parts do not join. So far, it's maybe seventy square miles. We don't know, I haven't counted lately.

KF   I guess I'll begin by asking you about how you feel about the state of architecture today?

DJ   I think it's very bad, and I say that in various things that I write. I think one of my standard ways of saying it is there has been no architecture since Louis Kahn died.[4]

KF   When I first read that I was taken aback by it, and I felt for the most part you were correct in saying that, for various reasons, but there are also some other architects living –

DJ   Obviously there are people I don't know about, so I figured out a better way to say it in an article, published in Germany: all the people that we know of as international architects are no good.[5] That's more accurate. Of course, that's what is wrong; you do not know the other people. I know of people who are decent architects, but they don't have big reputations; all the people we know of are bad.

KF   Yeah, I agree. In many cases that seems too true unfortunately, especially with the postmodern architects of the late '70s and '80s.

DJ   Yeah, I mean them, any people that you might know of,
      that I might know of – [Michael] Graves, Cesar Pelli, Hans
      Hollein, the whole list. They're really bad!

KF   What do you think of [Peter] Eisenman?

DJ   He's terrible. He's an idiot, I know him. Absolute idiot.
      You can put it in the article, too. I've known him for a long
      time, and we were on a panel together along with some
      other people in Santa Monica a year ago or something.[6]

KF   I have found that a lot of artists are really ignorant concern-
      ing the basic nature, schools of thought, movements, or
      what's going on in general with contemporary architecture.

DJ   They are. They are really not interested. Not only today,
      but earlier. There is no interest, or, I do not know, they
      see it as something separate from their own activity, and
      so they don't judge it in the same way.

KF   Well, a lot of people feel that it is not a valid art form, as
      well.

DJ   Certainly it's art. Cesar Pelli gave a big fuss at the con-
      ference about – he felt that the artists were saying it's
      not art. Of course it's art. It's just that all arts are different
      media.

KF   I wanted to get your response. You think it's art, but do
      you think it is as valid as painting or sculpture?

DJ   Sure.

KF   You have talked about architecture involving utility, and I
      just wondered –

DJ   Yeah, but that to me is really important. It's really serious
      and a nice thing. Utility does not bring it down at all; in
      fact, it elevates it a little bit. My general distinction is that –
      this applies to now, not, say, five hundred years ago – if
      you're making art, the art by definition is one person's ac-
      tivity, and therefore, it can be quite peculiar. It doesn't have
      to really do anything. You can make the funniest thing you
      can think of to put on a wall. There is no function or any-
      thing to worry about, and therefore the art can be more

unusual or more particular in the quality that it has, and ordinarily, to some extent, the architecture is generalized by the necessity to function well, and if it doesn't function well, it's ridiculous to call it architecture. It has to function well. On the other hand, obviously a great building is the same as a great painting. There is no reason in arguing about it. I certainly don't want to be in the position of running it down. I like it a lot; that's why I am doing more. It's why I interfere in somebody else's profession. I am not willing to leave that profession for them to decide.

Art is one thing – right away you have a function and right away that is somewhat public, even though that is your own function or whatever. Architecture can't ignore the function; therefore it can't ignore the public. I don't know – as far as the art goes – I don't know the public. There is no way for me to make art for West Texas or East Germany. I think if I built a building in East Germany, I would be very serious about it, getting into the circumstances, the material that's possible there, the labor situation – so right away, it's a more sociable activity than art. Art is a little bit crazier, which is to not run-down architecture. I think it's a bad idea for architecture to be crazy.

KF   I agree; for instance, Eisenman – he wants architecture to be chaotic.

DJ   He wants to be an artist. He talks like that. It's silly, and as an artist, he is an old-fashion derivative artist. He is a bad artist!

KF   Do you feel your work to be the only one with merit?

DJ   No, that's too general. It's valid for me. I have to make work that I believe in. That does not bother me at all, that they may disagree with someone else's work. I don't want to make universal art that is valid. I have to make the one I believe in.

KF   Do you theoretically feel that painting can be used as a means of expression for the contemporary artist?

DJ   It's up to someone to make painting valid. It's not up to
       me, because I don't really think about it. And also, it's the
       definition of painting – it's something up against a wall,
       something that has to be hung. If you can get around the
       conventionalities of it, fine, it's just there are very few
       good painters. Anyway, you got one right up the road,
       Agnes Martin, who by far is probably the best painter in
       the world, in New Mexico. She is great, a terrific painter,
       and that is painting on canvas.

KF   You still work in prints.

DJ   Yeah, I like the prints. It doesn't quite hang together, so
       you can't question me too tightly on that. I don't really
       want to do paintings. I like prints a lot, and you know, it's
       not that flat things against a wall are going to disappear,
       so it's up to somebody to kind of move the whole defini-
       tion around somehow and do something new. It just isn't
       going to be me.

KF   One of the things I find really extraordinary about your
       work – the architecture, the sculpture, the furniture, even
       your lifestyle – is that there is this great sense of honesty
       about it all.

DJ   It seems to me that art and architecture have to be that
       way. It's very much an artist's and architect's job to question.

KF   In *What Will Be Has Always Been*, Kahn mentions that a
       number of times – that it's up to the artist to question ev-
       erything, and within questioning, things will open up and
       reveal a larger structure, order, nature. He talks about the
       "ugly" and the "unmeasurable" that questioning reveals.[7]

DJ   You have to question yourself. It's a very material thing. I
       do art all the time – in fact, we are building all the time –
       and you have to say, "Look, okay, you are just doing this.
       It was the easy way out. You did it before. That was nice,
       it's great. Are you going to do it again because you know
       how to do it?" I say to myself, "Wait a minute and stop
       and think."

KF   After reading some of your essays, I've noticed that you don't use or feel comfortable with the word "order" or with the concept of the sublime. But through questioning, don't you open yourself up to some kind of order? That order is never a finite situation; it's always evolving outward. Through your search, to use some sort of analogy, you come to a miniscule point, look at the point, walk through it, and another unfathomable volume is revealed. It's not the classical notion of order, with a hierarchy or what have you.

DJ   I very much don't think so. I think it's pretty obvious from a philosophical base that we don't live in a determined situation. Society is a bit of a joke as a fixed order. You look out at the physical world — we really don't know very much.

KF   So you disagree with the concept of a fixed order, but not entirely with some type of order, I guess?

DJ   My own personal feeling is there is some kind of order, and actually it is a big problem in my work. I thought Jackson Pollock was terrific, but Pollock's work or John Chamberlain's work is real chaos. So that doesn't fit my mind very well. So I really figured out that I had to get orderly circumstances that did not imply anything bigger. It's my orderly circumstances. You know, just as you might want a room — which I can never achieve — want the room to be neat. I mean, it doesn't seem to be so neat. So what's next?

KF   I like your ideas about symmetry — the idea of not deviating from symmetry unless it's absolutely necessary.

DJ   That's a little strong, but I think I hold to it. I was reading [Eugène-Emmanuel] Viollet-le-Duc's *Lectures on Architecture*; it was the other way around.[8] He was upset because you had a tight school situation, and everybody wanted to do symmetrical building. You were brought into the neoclassical tradition. So he was arguing against symmetry, and that was interesting, so I've been thinking about that. I began to think that maybe what I said there on the subject was pretty strong, but I think it holds up. Viollet-le-Duc had a situation where everything had to be rigid and symmetrical. He walked into a tradition like that. So what we have is a situation where everything has to be asymmetrical and cockeyed.

KF   I don't think the idea of a symmetrical situation could apply to painting or sculpture, but somehow it makes perfect sense as a principle for architecture.

DJ   No, I'm speaking about architecture. Symmetry in art you don't necessarily have to worry about.

KF   The haphazardness of buildings by Frank Gehry seem so superficial and affected.

DJ   Just terrible buildings.

KF   It seems that he's determined to be a sculptor and not an architect.

DJ   He does. I know him to some extent, and he says proudly to me, "Oh, I was so influenced by your work," and all that stuff. I mean [*throws hands in the air*], there is no way, except he uses galvanized steel.

KF   He is probably referring to his use of industrial materials, which is the only similarity I can detect.

DJ   Well, I like architecture a lot, and I just realized after years and years that part of each day I was building something or fixing something up. I realized that a lot of thought went into it. The building in New York[9] – I've worked really hard on it, and I wouldn't dare think of selling it. I don't like New York, but now it [the building] is very valuable, and so forth, and very dangerous, and so forth and so on. Right now I am in the process of restoring it.

KF   One of the repetitive features you seem to have used is the placement of a bed in each building.

DJ   You have to be able to feel that you are able to live and work in the same circumstances. So in a way, I don't understand a place where you just go to see art. I understand somebody living in contemporary art. But really going to a museum, I don't like that. I think it should be around you – it's not enough to go look at something and come home. You have to go there, take a nap, have a drink, and so on. You know, day after day.

KF   That's one of the things I really enjoyed while staying at the foundation.[10] To be able to wake up and see a building or art when you step out of the door.

DJ   It takes time; things aren't made to be understood just like that. You walk into some building, maybe in Florence or somewhere … Of course, they are great buildings, but it's so important to be able to go there a lot.

KF   Do you feel confident with your role as an architect?

DJ   Yeah.

KF   So you feel really strongly about your architectural work.

DJ   Yeah, I actually think I know what I'm doing. I don't have any technical training as such, but as far as actually designing the buildings here –

KF   Well, I think the Artillery Sheds are great buildings, very beautiful, which I think comes about due to the fact that you made the pieces for the building, and you renovated the building drastically to complement the pieces. It is incredible how it works so well.

DJ   The ends are supposed to be open.

KF   I was going to ask you about that, because that was the only part of each building that I felt to be unresolved.

DJ   No, what's unresolved there is money. Within the curve it's supposed to be glass.

KF   Is it going to be mullioned off?

DJ   Yeah, big simple windows like down below, so the whole end will be glass. Actually, it looks fine if you tear the metal out.

KF   The space is huge up there. It's almost the same size as the volume below.

DJ   The space is enormous.

KF   Do you plan on using it?

DJ   I don't know. Having the space is an accident. The roof is tar and to put a hard floor on it could be very expensive. The thing is to use gravel, maybe, and put some art on the gravel. I don't know.

KF   As I was walking within the groupings of the concrete pieces outside [see image 60], I noticed that the spacing between each group was the same as between the two Artillery Sheds. I didn't know if that was a determining factor for the concrete pieces or what?

DJ   It wasn't intentional. Did you measure it?

KF   I walked it and measured by my steps, but it turned out exactly the same. Do you consider there to be a relationship between the concrete pieces and the sheds?

DJ   Just in a very general way, in that you look and see them, or look back from the pieces and see the two sheds. If there is a measurement there, I didn't know it. It could be. The fifteen just fits into what is flat.

KF   Yeah, there is a small knoll at the end. It also follows the street. Is that intentional?

DJ   The highway. It's not exactly paralleled to the highway; the main thing was to get it on that piece of land in a natural way. It's exactly north–south.

KF   What do you consider to be the difference between architecture and engineering? You've stated that there were a greater number of better-designed engineered buildings than architecturally designed buildings. [11]

DJ   Basically, in this century, last century too, we have more good buildings built by engineers than by architects. Engineers don't feel they are obliged to really think about artistic concerns. They can say, "Okay, this works best." The architect will never say that.

KF   Exactly, but I also agree with your statement that a great work of architecture is more important than a superior work of engineering, simply because architecture, when it's done correctly, is much more powerful and it's such a complex entity on many levels; it deals with a huge and significant array of concerns.

DJ   Yes, I think so, ultimately. For Kahn, the engineering was important. That's where I come into trouble. Kahn, for instance, knew a lot more about engineering. He dealt with very sophisticated engineering principles – those long spans at the Kimbell [Art Museum].

KF   Yes, but he didn't come up with those spans; his engineer did.

DJ   Yeah, sure, but he knew enough to look for – or the Richards Medical Research Laboratories, there's a lot of engineering in that.

KF   Could you comment on your views about not constructing new buildings but using existing ones? It's really interesting.

DJ   I believe that labor, thought, and material should not be wasted. The idea of tearing down buildings all the time is incredibly wasteful. It's also a certain affront to the past and the people who built them. It makes more sense to just – in fact, economically, it should be a little over the hill, a little bit more money spent, perhaps, to save the buildings, to use them. Ordinarily, the buildings produce a lot of things that new ones don't, if you fix them up. I'm basically against destruction. It is a shame to tear down buildings. Someone had to make it. It represents a certain wealth and that wealth is being destroyed, only to do it over in a worse way, so it's better to save them.

KF   But you are building several new buildings on the edge of the fort.[12] It seems to conflict with your position.

DJ   Well, that's a different situation. Firstly, we are building there because all the barracks are being reserved for the Dan Flavin installations.[13] Secondly, there were existing foundations there, so it isn't really building on new land.

KF   Well, the idea seems plausible for buildings like the Artillery Sheds or the barracks. They are basically fairly good buildings to begin with.

DJ   They weren't good buildings. The buildings don't have to be that good. It's better to save them. I lived in Dallas as a kid, went to Spence Junior High School, and Dallas was a better-looking city in the late '40s than it is now.

KF   Why do you say that?

DJ   Because the buildings were better. Nicer buildings.

KF   When I was at breakfast this morning at the Thunderbird restaurant, two older guys were having a cup of coffee, and their conversation focused on you as an employer – how you had hired a lot people recently and boosted the economy with tourists and visitors, which brought in revenue to the businesses in the community. I would imagine that you do help out the economy a great deal here.

DJ   Yeah, for a long time. For years now. One of the best statements was by the president of the bank, at least fifteen years ago or something, that he was glad I came, because Marfa needed a second business.

KF   You and the government, I guess.

DJ   No, the first one being the cattle business. He wasn't thinking about the government. Actually, the government is the biggest business – the Border Patrol.

KF   Are the buildings that you purchased recently separate from the Chinati Foundation, or are they your own?[14]

DJ   Yeah, they are mine. So you have to maintain a big distinction between me and the foundation.

KF   Yeah, at times I was a little confused about what was the foundation's and what was your own personal property.

DJ   Basically, the fort is the foundation and anything beyond that is mine. Except the Chamberlain Building; it's part of the foundation.

KF   The Artillery Sheds and a lot of the unrealized designs are very Kahnian in nature. Is he a big influence on you?

D J I don't know about that, but I like Kahn's work a lot. As I said, he is really the last serious architect.

K F The last question involves the controversy over whether there is or isn't political implication in your work.

D J Always.

K F Could you elaborate?

D J I don't think that any work, by anybody, ever, was without social implications. I really object when people, museums, whatever want to take it out of context: "Oh, look at this, it's abstract art, it's meaningless." That's why it's art; in it are all my opinions, what I know about the nature of the universe, the society, so forth. It's not separate from those things.

K F So it's inherent in the way you think about the work.

D J You put the art together to be a totality. So somewhere in there are political, social attitudes.

K F Well, I made a sort of pilgrimage in coming down here; it's a long way from North Texas. I guess that's part of the effect. If you want to see the Giottos, you go to Padua, and if you want to see the Judds, you go to Marfa, right?

D J Sure.

This conversation was sourced from a transcript, as well as from the published interview. The archival transcript is in the Judd Foundation Archives, Marfa, Texas.

First published (excerpt): Kerry Freeman, "The Book, the Beliefs, His Life & His Architecture," *Detour*, October 1990, 26–29.

1   Judd refers here to Las Casas.
2   Freeman refers here to *Donald Judd: Architektur*, which had been published the previous year.
3   See Judd's drawings of both planned and completed additions to his ranches in *Donald Judd: Architektur*, 56–63.
4   Louis Kahn died in 1974.
5   See Judd's "Ausstellungsleitungsstreit" (1989) in *Donald Judd Writings*, 558–83.

6   Twice yearly, the Frederick R. Weisman Art Foundation conducted work-
        shops related to contemporary art. Judd participated in the workshop "The
        Relationship between Art and Architecture," held January 21–22, 1989, in
        Santa Monica, California. The workshops were recorded, transcribed, and
        published. See *The Relationship between Art and Architecture: Summary of a
        Workshop, 21–22 January 1989* (Los Angeles: The Frederick R. Weisman Art
        Foundation, 1990).

7   Richard Saul Wurman, ed., *What Will Be Always Has Been: The Words of
        Louis I. Kahn* (New York: Rizzoli, 1986). Judd included this book, as well
        as many other books concerning Kahn, in his library in Marfa, Texas.

8   Eugène-Emmanuel Viollet-le-Duc, *Lectures on Architecture* (1872), trans.
        Benjamin Bucknall, 2 vols. (New York: Dover, 1987). Judd included both
        volumes of this work in his library in Marfa, Texas.

9   Judd refers here to 101 Spring Street.

10   Freeman refers here to the Chinati Foundation.

11   See Judd's review of *Twentieth Century Engineering* (1964) in *Donald Judd
        Writings*, 146–50.

12   Judd designed ten concrete buildings in which he planned to permanently
        install work made for the Chinati Foundation (located on the site of the
        former Fort D. A. Russell). These buildings were to be constructed on a
        grid on the southwestern side of the grounds of the Chinati Foundation.
        Construction began on two of the ten buildings, but the project was not
        completed at the time of Judd's death. See Judd's "Concrete Buildings"
        (1989) in *Donald Judd: Architektur*, 88–89.

13   Dan Flavin's large-scale work in colored fluorescent light for six buildings
        (former barracks at Fort D. A. Russell) at the Chinati Foundation was ini-
        tiated in the early 1980s. Flavin finalized his design in 1996, and the in-
        stallation was completed and opened to the public in 2000. See Marianne
        Stockebrand, ed., *Chinati: The Vision of Donald Judd* (Marfa, TX: The Chi-
        nati Foundation; New Haven, CT: Yale University Press, 2010), 224–47.

14   Judd Foundation was conceived by Judd in 1977 to maintain and preserve
        his permanently installed living and working spaces, archives, and librar-
        ies in New York and Marfa, Texas. See Judd's "Judd Foundation" (1977)
        in *Donald Judd Writings*, 284–86. In 1978, Judd and Dia Art Foundation
        entered into a partnership over Judd's "Marfa project." After a separation
        with Dia in 1986, the "Marfa project" was realized by Judd as the Chinati
        Foundation, established to preserve permanent large-scale installations by
        a select group of artists; it opened to the public in 1986. See Judd's "State-
        ment for the Chinati Foundation/La Fundación Chinati" (1987) in *Don-
        ald Judd Writings*, 484–89.

"War Destroys Culture"
Interview with Ólafur Gíslason for *Þjóðviljinn*
January 20, 1991

Þjóðviljinn was an Icelandic daily newspaper founded in 1936. It was aligned with
the Communist Party of Iceland and its successors, the People's Unity Party and
the People's Alliance Party. The paper ceased publication in 1992.

Judd wrote the following introduction for this interview, but it was not published: "This interview was made in Reykjavík for the newspaper 'The Will of the
Nation' *Þjóðviljinn*, on the twentieth of January 1991, just after the Americans began bombing Iraq. Hekla erupted at the same time and was shown on Icelandic
television in bright orange and black. CNN's logo and its pictures of the new war
were also orange and black. These and their explanations by military maniacs were
triumphantly continuous. Gíslason made notes in Icelandic of what I said in English and then for my benefit translated it back into English, so that it is somewhat
bumpy. I have not changed it much because of when it was done and because of
that I include it as it is. This interview adds objections to those which I gave against
the war, just before the war, in the catalogue of my exhibition of architecture at
the Museum für angewandte Kunst in Vienna. There should be a long third part
because the Americans will do it again."

In the penultimate sentence, Judd refers to his essay "Nie Wieder Krieg" (1991),
which translates from the German as "No More War," which he published in
Donald Judd: Architektur, the exhibition catalogue for his show of the same name
at the Österreichisches Museum für angewandte Kunst, Vienna (February 14–
April 8, 1991).

DJ   [Donald Judd] War destroys everything. It not only destroys human lives and property in Iraq, it also destroys culture. It also destroys the work I am doing in Texas.

OG   [Ólafur Gíslason] [*Written*] These are the words of Donald Judd, the American artist, on a private visit to Iceland. It was his fourth visit to Iceland, whose saga literature from the thirteenth century aroused his interest in the country. Donald Judd, an outstanding name in twentieth-century American art, did not want to discuss his own work as he met with an Icelandic journalist. The war was on his mind, the destructive force of war, which is contrary to the constructive and creative work he has dedicated himself to as an artist. And he was asked, "Why is the United States at war?"

DJ   Ever since late in the '30s, when the US was preparing for World War II, the US economy has been a military economy, where military spending has had an absolute priority. No civilization can stand such a policy in the long run. A military economy is a fake economy built on waste. It doesn't confront the economic or cultural problems of society. On the contrary, it takes resources from culture and all life and dissipates them into the military. It works against culture, and all those who support war are enemies of culture.

OG   Do you mean that the US government is against culture?

DJ   Yes, they are, and they have been for a long time. First Nixon, then Reagan, then Bush. They have been pressing against culture in many ways. The military economy has caused the rapid decline of the United States, both economically and culturally. As far as I and other creative artists are concerned, we now see the collapse of the art market. There is no more money for culture because war has absolute priority. This is also the case in other branches of the arts and in science which is not involved in the military complex. In the West, especially in the US, we have witnessed a rising wave of the totalitarian right-wing. They like to call themselves conservatives, but they are in fact very destructive. This wave of the totalitarian right-wing attitude is reflected in our culture. We can, for example, see it in architecture. The totalitarian right-wing wants its own architecture, as all dictators have always wanted it. Maybe it is not conscious, but you can notice striking parallels between the fascist architecture of the '20s and '30s and the architecture of the last decade. The so-called postmodernism is the architecture of those forces and of the fake economy which is the military economy. It is based on cheap, superficial, and meaningless art, such as that which has dominated the art scene in New York in the last two decades. They say the financial deficit of the government doesn't matter. They say the cost of war doesn't matter. But the truth is that in the US, the general decay is apparent wherever you go. Also in the little town of Marfa in Texas, where I live, buildings and construction have not been maintained, and even the streets and the roads are squalid. Still they have sent half a million soldiers to Saudi Arabia.

OG   You had an exhibit in the Soviet Union last year.[1] I suppose you have seen an even worse state of degradation there?

DJ   Yes, they have the same problem, the military economy. They do not know how to get rid of this parasitic military and bureaucratic complex; Gorbachev himself said that it was the military economy that was ruining the Soviet Union. Now we are witnessing exactly the same thing in the US. They are falling back to the Cold War. They have sent their military to the Baltic republics. It seems that neither the US nor the USSR could stand the end of the Cold War. They didn't know what to do with the military apparatus. The US first invaded Panama, but it was a minor war and not sufficient for them. Then they tried to find their enemy in the so-called drug war in Latin America, but it didn't satisfy them either. They desperately needed an enemy of the right size. A very similar thing is now happening in the Soviet Union, and it is a very dangerous development. Because just as the US is taking advantage of the weakness of the Soviets in the Gulf War, so the Soviets are taking advantage of the Gulf War in their military intervention in the Baltic.

We can see that the US has minimized the extremely dangerous situation in the Baltics, even though these countries are far more important to Europe, both because they have a bigger population than Kuwait and because they stand closer to Europe culturally. And their independence is a crucial precedent. They also seem to overlook the fact that the Soviet Union still has about 350,000 soldiers in East Germany. How independent is East Germany with 350,000 Soviet soldiers within its borders? How independent are they if the Soviets change their mind and decide not to leave East Germany? Is it possible that the unification of Germany was only a paper unification? Everybody should see that this is an extremely dangerous situation.

OG   Could you explain how this situation affects the culture of these countries?

DJ   It is no coincidence that there is hardly any significant culture in the Soviet Union. It has been deliberately suffocated by the totalitarian militarism to the extent that all cultural life in the Soviet Union is now in ruins. The United States is heading the same way. Both the Reagan and Bush administrations have put severe pressure on culture. The latest example is the condition the government has set up for the official state grants to artists. They are obliged to sign documents where they promise to repay the grant if they happen to be convicted for pornographic or obscene acts or performances. I am not sure if antipatriotism is included in these acts, but that is sure to come. The military economy is a fake economy that overlooks the real problems of society and practices superficiality in all fields. We can see it in the architecture of postmodernism, where superficiality is dominating, and the war itself is superficial beyond all means. Instead of solving the problems, you make war. When the Vietnam War was going on, the government was forced to explain its policy because of the public protest. But Bush didn't feel that he needed to explain why he went to war. He just did it and sent all these soldiers to the gulf. James Baker, the secretary of state, came closer to the point when he said that the war was necessary to "save jobs." Those are the jobs in the military industry and the whole destructive industrial complex that it involves. The American soldiers are mercenaries, so the government doesn't care, because half of their salaries are being paid by the Saudis. But I heard that the military has ordered eighty thousand coffins for the war, and the television is now reporting that they are producing body bags in the US day and night. While this is going on, we have crises in the arts. A year or two ago, I had over forty people employed, executing my works in the US. Now they are less than twenty. The money goes from the culture to the war.

OG   What effects do you think this war will have on the relationship between the Muslim world and the West?

DJ   It is evident that all Muslims will become filled with hatred toward the US, and this will turn into a kind of religious war between Christians and Muslims. They should have learned something from the experience of the Russians in Afghanistan. They got their lesson there. But I think the West should be more concerned about the danger that is now building up in the Baltics and the Soviet Union. It is far more serious than what happened in Kuwait. A year ago, the US citizen didn't know where on earth Kuwait was. I am not so informed about Islam, but

I know that if the Iraqi people were "a white and Christian nation," as they say in Texas, then the US government wouldn't have behaved as it did. It is evident that their attitude is racist; they only behave like that toward Asians and Muslims. It is also evident that the overwhelming majority of the US soldiers are of poor black and poor white origin. It is the same pattern as happened after the Civil War in the United States, when the former black slaves were used as soldiers under white command to kill Indians.

OG You could say that the military economy has had such devastating consequences for the US. But isn't Europe under the same pressure?

DJ No, there is a big difference. The Europeans don't waste so much money on the military machine. The European nations are better organized, and they are also better off economically. Here in Europe the governments are not as strong and the governments can't allow themselves to do what they do in the US. The worst European government in this field is the French one, which has wasted so much money on armaments. But I know Europe somewhat, as I have my own studios in two European countries, Switzerland and Germany, and I know that Europeans have a greater respect for art than you find in the United States.[2] In Europe you also have more freedom. Freedom is essential for the arts, and it is not sufficient that it is enjoyed by the elite. It has to penetrate the whole society. If people do not have freedom, art will die as everything else. I consider that Europe is now facing a great danger. If the military economy is now driving both the US and the Soviet Union back to the Cold War, then Europe will be caught in between. And if the Russians stop withdrawing their troops from Eastern Europe, the danger is evident.

OG Does this situation affect your way of creating art?

DJ No, it does not affect my way of working directly, but indirectly. It is very depressing to face the war news every day. I just hate the war. But the effect of the military economy on art is evident in the general state of the arts in the US, which has been degenerating for the past two decades. We are heading for the same thing that happened in the Soviet Union, where art has been ruined by force.

OG   Do you believe that artists or people working in the cultural field should organize themselves somehow to oppose the war?

DJ   Yes, all organized demonstrations are important. The only thing that affects the US government is the people's demonstrations on the streets. Voting is just a joke in the US. I have participated in that joke, but everybody knows that it is not meant to change anything. It was bad that no one said anything in August, when the troops were sent to the gulf. Then protests could have had some effect. All those who hate to live with war should go into the streets and protest the war.

This conversation was sourced from an archival English transcript with handwritten corrections by Judd in the Judd Foundation Archives, Marfa, Texas.

First published: Ólafur Gíslason, "Stríðið Tortímir Menningunni," *Þjóðviljinn*, January 25, 1991, 10–11.

1   Soviet Cultural Foundation, Moscow, August 15–September 11, 1990.
2   Judd refers here to Eichholteren and Hafenstrasse.

"Interview with Donald Judd"
With Angeli Janhsen-Vukićević for *Nike*
January 26, 1991

Conducted for the magazine *Nike* at Hafenstrasse, Judd's studio in Cologne, this was
Angeli Janhsen-Vukićević's second interview with Judd; in 1990, Janhsen-Vukićević
had organized a seminar discussion with the artist (see "Discussion with Donald
Judd" [1990] in this volume, 694–717).

Judd participated in multiple exhibitions in Germany in 1991, including a solo
presentation at Galerie Rolf Ricke, Cologne (January 11–February 26, 1991), that
featured wall pieces in aluminum and plywood.

AJV [Angeli Janhsen-Vukićević] There is a difference between
     the works of Mondrian, for example, which are illusion-
     istic in a certain sense, because color always is illusionistic,
     and three-dimensional works like yours, which are not il-
     lusionistic. I think it would be necessary to distinguish that
     kind of concrete art where the viewer feels as if he were
     somewhere, where he has an illusion, and that kind of con-
     crete art where the viewer feels that he is just right here.

DJ   [Donald Judd] Well, obviously that has developed in this
     century. The paintings of Pollock and Newman are meant
     to be things in themselves, which is a kind of reality and
     concrete. It is just the same idea – a thing in itself.

AJV But isn't there a difference between Newman's kind of
     concreteness and yours? The space you experience stand-
     ing in front of a painting of Newman's is illusionistic.

DJ   Oh, I think this is part of the general historical change.
     And as you go along, different artists in this century – they
     all began working representationally and you have a de-
     velopment into work that is so-called concrete. There
     is a transition, and I would hope that my work is more
     concrete – if we use that word – than Newman's. This is
     why I am not doing paintings.

AJV Because that illusionism is a problem of painters, and not
     one of sculptors?

DJ   He and Pollock went as far as you can go and I couldn't
     think of any way to take it any further.

AJV Maybe wall painting?

DJ   Maybe wall painting. It is the only painting that is inter-
     esting – not for me, but for someone else. It is not being
     developed. I am interested in a thing in itself and that de-
     velopment of the concrete and in a work of art as a thing
     in itself. That, naturally, was the part of art that Newman
     was interested in – he said so.[1]

AJV There is a contrast between the first concrete artists at the
     beginning of this century like Kandinsky, Mondrian, or

Malevich and the later ones. The first ones had a utopia, they wanted to reach a distinct point – that utopia.

DJ   That's definitely not my way. It must be the opposite.

AJV   Is yours the opposite way – to have a point, and then go further?

DJ   It is decidedly not my way of working, which is very much me personally. But the bigger side of it is that we can't believe it anymore. We know that the arts don't have any effect on the society. So it's a pessimistic situation.

AJV   Do you really think that?

DJ   Yes, look at the present, a superficial war. There is no reason to believe it does anything. You can't see it. So there is no way to believe for anyone who looks around that art is going to change anything very much. So you don't have that underpinning, it doesn't connect to any ideal world, you can't think it.

AJV   But isn't it an ideal in itself when you say you are interested in the thing itself, in the things that are there? We are not naturally interested in the thing itself or the things that are there – we do not even notice things. So perhaps that is another kind of utopia, a modest utopia?

DJ   Yes, it is a certain ideal, it is obviously an ideal, which is to pay more attention to things as they are. And to pay more attention to the present. To talk about the future does no good, and in fact it has turned out to be dangerous, because then it enforces the big political systems and causes trouble. But naturally – there is a good way of paying attention to the present, and there is the bad way of some idiot business people making a dollar and not thinking of anything else. So what they do is live from day to day, hand to mouth, and not even note a bigger ideal. There is little thought about the future, which should be essential.

AJV   Yes, that could be very dangerous to think just of oneself and the things one can really reach, that are really there. That could be a solipsistic position, couldn't it?

DJ   Yes.

AJV   You don't see this danger for you, for your work?

DJ   No, because paying attention leads to larger concerns.
      Some good ideas go wrong because they are taken to their
      extremes. And so you can take an idea like paying atten-
      tion to the present of course – all people who won't look
      around and pay attention to the situation are looking in
      a small way at their situation and not in a larger way. Ob-
      viously in the present situation with the war, people are
      not even acting because they are self-interested. The pub-
      lic is not, people in general are not, the government is not,
      other governments are not. They are not even obeying
      self-interest, they are following some little thing. So that
      is not what I mean.

AJV   But there is a relation. If everyone says that he can't reach
      all that and that he can't influence, then no one will do
      anything.

DJ   A large point should be this: you should admit that you
      can't influence anything, and then do it anyway. The po-
      sition is finally that art has no effect on the society, it is al-
      most completely meaningless to almost everyone in the
      society, and who knows what it means in the long run,
      in centuries. And there is the fact that you don't live very
      long anyway – and then take all that and do the art any-
      way. So you have to put these two things together. There
      is a completely hopeless side. Face it and do it anyway.
      Same with politics. I'm absolutely against people who do
      nothing. That is one reason why we have the present war.
      I know very well that I'm nothing in the United States
      as a citizen. I'm just there to get money from to pay for
      the war, like everybody else. That's all we are. And the
      only thing I can think of is to write and hope someday
      for change. That's all you can do. These things have to be
      done. You can't get carried away about change. It won't
      do any good. You only fool yourself. So it is cheerful to be

here in Cologne, Germany, now, where there is opposition to the war, and not in the United States, where there is almost none. I went to a demonstration in New York. It would have had much more effect earlier. They should have had it right away in August in the United States. It was clear what Bush was planning.

AJV   So you think that making art is something that doesn't concern the daily politics and can't concern it, also that it can't influence quickly because it hasn't that kind of pragmatism? But art must have an influence at least on the people who deal with art, who want to know art. Doesn't it change their lives at least a little bit?

DJ   Probably. Hopefully. But I think it is really a little. Art isn't meant to have a direct influence. Social meanings, political meanings are there, but not directly.

AJV   But in a situation like this with the war, one asks oneself if there is the time to wait for a slow change and to hope that someone will learn something and do something in ten or twenty years. I don't know when.

DJ   There is no time to wait, but also, people are not going to change. When you watch now, you see that people accept things conventionally. This whole business of the war is absolutely standard. It all happened before. And it looks like nothing. Somebody says "patriot" and everyone jumps up. And no one says, "A patriot for what? What does it mean?" They don't ask any questions.

AJV   So you think your public doesn't notice anything? Anything about politics, about Iraq, about themselves?

DJ   Probably not. Maybe a handful.

AJV   That might be a difference between us and people at the beginning of this century?

DJ   They thought we could do something, and I just don't see that we can do anything. All those people were destroyed by their central governments. That happens now to everyone.

AJV   But you continue to do something.

DJ   You have an absolute contradiction and you have to live
      with it. I continue because I like art. For me, it's life. And
      I think that's really the only source of art. But I can't give
      up searching for reasons. It's nice to feel that there is a fu-
      ture. But you never see it happen.

AJV   So this is an activity step by step by step, and you can't see
      where it leads to?

DJ   I don't see, or even think, after all this time, that the art of
      the past and the architecture of the past help anything. It's
      a lot of time, a lot of great work. In this society it doesn't
      have any influence. So why should I think that my work
      can have any influence? I don't see that Michelangelo turns
      anyone from the courses they run. Why should mine?

AJV   But there is a claim in your work. You say that people
      should be interested in the things which are there. That is
      a kind of ideal.

DJ   Yes. But my idea of things that are there is different from
      the idea of the first concrete artists.

First published: Angeli Janhsen-Vukićević, "Interview with Donald Judd," *Nike*,
no. 38, 1991, 6–7 (in English and German).

I   In 1950, Newman stated: "Perhaps we are arriving at a new state of paint-
      ing where the thing has to be seen for itself." Newman, "Remarks at Art-
      ists' Sessions at Studio 35," in *Barnett Newman: Selected Writings and Inter-
      views*, ed. John P. O'Neill (New York: Knopf, 1990), 241.

"Art, War, and Money: Art Hero Donald Judd on
the Powerlessness of Art and the Power of the Powerful"
Interview with Georg Schöllhammer for *Der Standard*
February 9–10, 1991

This conversation with Austrian curator and writer Georg Schöllhammer for *Der Standard* was conducted in conjunction with the exhibition *Donald Judd:Architektur*, at the Österreichisches Museum für angewandte Kunst, Vienna (February 14–April 8, 1991).

In addition to drawings and furniture, Judd also included three antiwar posters in this exhibition. One of the posters features a black-and-white diptych with white text on one side and black text on the other reading, "Klein heisser Krieg / Klein kalter Krieg," which translates from the German as "Small Hot War / Small Cold War." The second poster is a black-and-white photograph of graffiti on a wall in Madrid reading, "Sadam [*sic*] es malo, Bush es peor," which translates from the Spanish as "Saddam is bad, Bush is worse." For the third poster, Judd placed text in English and Russian on the bottom of a color photograph of a cemetery in Saint Petersburg (then Leningrad) that read, "Piskaryovskoye Memorial Cemetery, Leningrad. 500,000 people who died in the siege are buried here. What is to be done?" Judd refers here to "What Is to Be Done? Burning Questions of Our Movement," a political pamphlet written by Vladimir Lenin in 1901 and published in 1902.

GS   [Georg Schöllhammer] The text that you wrote for the
exhibition catalogue[1] for your show in Vienna deals exclusively with war. Does anyone who is talking about art
today in fact have to speak about war?

DJ   [Donald Judd] Yes. No civilization can survive the politics conducted by the major powers today. It's policy dominated by a defense economy. After the end of the Cold
War, a hot war had to come.

GS   Isn't that somewhat of a simplified analysis of the real trig-
ger factors of this war? Don't you think you are relating
the downturn in the art market too closely?

DJ   No. War economy is a pretense economy. And contemporary art is mostly pretense art.

GS   So what you are indicating is that the American economy
of the '80s has valued the commerce of information and
payments higher than the one of goods; that it was in some
sense a symbolic one. Your work attempts something like
the logic of the form, an intrinsic logic of design, placing
the product back into the foreground. It is moral.

DJ   I hope so. It is an attempt of the small form against the big.
Any centrality, any central government destroys thought,
freedom. Slowly everything begins to freeze. Everything
collapses. Except small democratic systems.

GS   But especially in the USA, there are a number of such independent, small, democratically organized worlds, e.g.,
your artist colony in Marfa.

DJ   Yes, but I also had to let half of my people go because of
the war. This year I will only sell half as much as I did last
year. Now I have only twenty people working for me; last
year there were still forty. The money just goes toward
the war.

GS   But until recently, the money went toward the art; the
market was booming.

DJ   It was only symbolic, anyway. This also concerns sciences.
For example, I am a member of a committee of proponents

that supports a big observatory in Texas.[2] It has become increasingly difficult to come up with funds. Everything that would be needed for the next ten years costs as much as one assault chopper.

GS   So your work is also deep research?

DJ   This implies that it is often referred to as political. Structures only exist on the surface now; people nowadays are only thinking superficially. And they don't notice. It is the result of this pretense economy that art and architecture only disagree on the surface as well. A lot, almost everything, that happened in architecture during the '80s has been phony. Just look at Austria – Hans Hollein and the Guggenheim New York are planning such a negation and falsification: a giant hole in the ground.[3]

GS   Doesn't the illusion exist, on the other hand, that it is in museum spaces where society can find its reflection, away from the surface?

DJ   For the last twenty years, art in the US has been meaningless and hollow. This may be one of the reasons why stylizing museums has been so important. Art is ridiculous if its forms just exist for their own sake and ignore their function. Perhaps that is why architects believe that they have no moral function. Museums have turned into an exaggerated, distorted, empty expression of their architects, most of which are in fact incapable of expression.

GS   You are exhibiting your architecture here in Vienna. What separates it from what you are criticizing?

DJ   Artists and architects have authority over what they are doing, but this authority isn't actual power. Nevertheless, art and architecture are two different things. When I make a piece of furniture, a simple grammar of forms is important to me, just as in my objects. But art in a chair doesn't mean that it looks like a work of art but rather that it is well constructed, functional, and that it possesses the right proportions.

GS   Still, your furniture looks like works of art and not objects for use.

DJ   A good chair is a good chair.[4] General forms started to slowly emerge out of the given actuality of my work, and these aren't deductions anymore. I can make a chair or a building today and I don't deduce forms from my artwork for it.

GS   Your style still remains in the foreground, however.

DJ   No. For some time now, the fakes are outnumbering the authentic work. In this sense, postmodern architecture is similar to fascist architecture. It's based on cheap solutions and superficiality. War is also a falsification. It also covers up the problems of the American society and distracts it from the real crisis. Panama was over too quickly to accomplish this, and the drug war in Colombia wasn't efficient enough; everything was too vague.

GS   Again you are speaking about war.

DJ   This has ramifications for art as well. In the '50s and '60s, minimalism formally and structurally attempted to work against this dilemma by redefining the relationship of the spectator with the work. In this regard it was highly political. American art of the '80s only occurred on the surface, however, and it only existed in decals of reality. Its proximity to the media stripped it of all directness, of its consistency, of its content. It's a problem of society. Just like the USSR, the USA has proven that large bureaucratic systems cannot produce any worthwhile art of substance because it understands art merely as a function of its dominant information structures: in the USSR this is the apparatus, in the USA it's the media. One of the latest examples is the executive order of the Bush government which requires all artists who are receiving government aid to repay those funds if their art is pornographic.

GS   Isn't war also pornographic?

DJ   What is fatal about the multilateral justification of this war

is that the only arguments used are moralistic, or even religious. But the only industry that remains functional in
America is the defense economy.

Translated from the German by Susanne Maurer.

First published: Georg Schöllhammer, "Die Kunst, der Krieg und das Geld: Kunst-
Heros Donald Judd über die Ohnmacht der Kunst und die Macht der Mächtigen,"
Der Standard, February 9–10, 1991, 11.

1   See Judd's "Nie Wieder Krieg" (1991) in *Donald Judd Writings*, 722–31. As
Schöllhammer indicates, this text first appeared in *Donald Judd: Architektur*,
exh. cat. (Vienna: Österreichisches Museum für angewandte Kunst, 1991).
2   Judd refers here to the McDonald Observatory, part of The University
of Texas at Austin, located in the Davis Mountains of West Texas. He became a member of the observatory's Board of Visitors in 1989.
3   In 1989, architect Hans Hollein won an international competition to design a museum in Salzburg, Austria, with a proposal for a subterranean
building. The Guggenheim pursued the possibility of constructing Hollein's design as the Guggenheim Museum Salzburg. Neither the building
nor the partnership was realized.
4   "A good chair is a good chair" is a direct quotation from Judd's "On Furniture" (1986) in *Donald Judd Writings*, 451.

"Donald Judd"
Interview with Ariane Müller for *Artfan*
March 1991

This interview with Judd was the first that artist Ariane Müller conducted for *Artfan*, an art fanzine that was produced and published in Vienna between 1991 and 1995 by Müller and the artist Linda Bilda. Also included in this issue was an interview with the Austrian artist Gerwald Rockenschaub. The conversation between Müller and Judd was conducted at the Österreichisches Museum für angewandte Kunst, Vienna, during the exhibition *Donald Judd: Architektur* (February 14–April 8, 1991) and published in the May 1991 issue of *Artfan*.

A M   [Ariane Müller] Do you live in exactly the places you want
        to live in?

D J   [Donald Judd] Pretty much. I live in a very beautiful part
        of the world, in West Texas. It's very empty. It's rather high
        in altitude. It's a very nice place. Very few people, which
        helps.

A M   And the houses? The views inside?

D J   The houses are mostly buildings that already existed, which
        I fixed up or changed, but we tried to make new buildings
        also. What you see here [in the Museum für angewandte
        Kunst] is pretty much what I see all day; these are places
        where I live, so here it's not very much like Texas. I have a
        building in New York, but I'm not there very much.[1] I like
        what I have done to it. But New York is not very pleasant
        to live in.

A M   And America – is it pleasant to live in?

D J   No, it's not. It's even worse. America doesn't mean much.
        America is a disaster right now. I like the land where I live
        in Texas.

A M   The things, they are so expensive, even as they look –

D J   Plain – "plain" is the word.
            We tried to keep the costs down, but there is a cer-
        tain limit to how far you can keep it; we tried to keep the
        prices low on the metal furniture. It's meant to be cheap,
        but it's still around $2,000. The person who makes it has
        to get something, I have to get something, the distributor
        has to get something.

A M   I've seen an exhibition of yours in Barcelona,[2] and there,
        for the first time, it didn't look so American, perhaps be-
        cause of the light there and the sight outside, but I don't
        know if you had been there.

D J   Yes, I have been there, except I don't know what "Amer-
        ican" means?

A M   I mean the difference between the mess outside and the
        cleanliness inside. Like, New York is such a dirty place.

DJ   It's horrible.

AM   And then you live in these clean, white, open spaces.

DJ   This shows you the complete political breakdown. You don't have any kind of social or political organization that works; the contrast is a classic case of a failed society. People on the street, people cold, people hungry. It looks exactly as bad as it looks, and it's just as dangerous as it looks.

AM   But you live inside.

DJ   I live in buildings. I try to maintain the inside. It's an island in New York. New York is breaking down.

AM   But what are your feelings? I mean, you are laughing.

DJ   I'm against it, but I'm living right in it, therefore it's got its grim side and its comical side, but I'm against what the United States is doing – it gets worse and worse.

AM   But that's not the step to going into politics?

DJ   The US is too conventional, that's why you have Bush. I wouldn't get anywhere. And parties – there are only two parties, both parties are very conservative, there is not much difference. One is a little worse than the other. Both parties supported the Cold War for fifty years. So they are not going to have anything to do with anybody who disagrees with them.

AM   So the artists in America, they come together in spaces like this and talk?

DJ   Yes, but not too much, they are not sociable. Artists don't count very much in the US.

AM   But they earn money, and to earn money counts.

DJ   Yes, it counts. But to make your money as an artist means that it counts less. My money in the little town of [Marfa,] West Texas, which for the little town is important, is less important because of the way I make it. [To be an] artist is a strange thing.

AM   You support the town by taxes?

DJ   No, by hiring people. You can't support it by taxes because the government takes it away from them to Washington, to fight Iraq. You can't control your taxes. It's a lot of money taken away from me and everybody in town. So the way I put money into the town economy is by employing people and buying things.

A M   So you employ as many people as you can afford, or as many as you need?

D J   "Afford" is it — if I have money, it grows, and if I don't have money, it shrinks. We are mostly working on buildings, fixing up buildings, but I do have a shop there which has four people, but used to have five or six.[3] We still make business. Considering that the town has no factories — which is a problem, it's the only factory in town. It's a cattle town, but the cattle business, agriculture in general, goes down. It used to be rather rich as a cattle town in the '30s, '20s, and before, and for economic reasons it goes down and down.

A M   You feel at home in these aesthetic things?

D J   Yes, I don't like to look at a lot of ugly things, it's like listening to bad music. The music on the airplanes or something. It's really disagreeable to have to look at ugly things — stupid.

[*Question from* Volksstimme *reporter about what kind of music Judd likes*]

D J   I like piping.

A M   Do you have any Scottish ancestors? You are also wearing plaid.

D J   I like it, it's pretty. All Anglos in the United States have a little Scottish. It's widely spread.

A M   Because they were so poor. Do you come from a poor family?

D J   Middle class, middle-middle.

A M   And then you went to art school?

D J   Yes.[4]

A M   Do your works look different in Texas?

D J   Texas has a tremendous light because of the altitude. Most of Texas is low, but this part is fifteen hundred meters [above sea level].

A M   Then you can run faster.

D J   Less wind resistance.

A M   How long are you staying in Vienna?

D J   Until Friday night.

A M   Did you meet any Viennese artists?

D J   Not so much. I know them from earlier trips.

A M   Whom?

D J   Franz Graf; he is not here today, he went somewhere. But I don't know what is being done here.

A M   How much do you look around? You are always here for such a short time.

D J   I went to the openings last night. That's because I know [Ilya] Kabakov.

A M   But you didn't go to the party, sort of your party, too?

D J   No, there were too many people, but to know what is happening in Vienna you have to be here for some time.

A M   And in America, how much do you look around?

D J   Not so much. I'm interested a great deal, but I don't think the levels of it are very high. In New York there are so many bad shows that you wouldn't.

A M   And in Texas?

D J   There are a few artists in Dallas, but the next artist is a thousand kilometers from the place where I live.

[*Question from* Volksstimme *reporter about American roots*]

D J   I don't think it means too much. It's a different situation coming from a land that was rather empty a while ago, but it's usually exaggerated. I don't think it means too much. The level of European culture that got to the United States, if it was good, as in the case of Thomas

Jefferson, never lasted too long, and anyway most of it never got there, so I think the level of civilization is pretty low.

And the exports are military culture and hamburgers – not much art came – and I think the Europeans in general don't estimate the American painting that was done. And American painting never had anything to do with the government; it was against the government.[5] So whatever culture got exported was rock and roll, hamburgers, McDonald's, and that stuff.

[*Question from* Volksstimme *reporter about whether Judd considers himself a political artist, and if he considers himself a political person, shouldn't he get involved in the current political situation*]

DJ   You should get involved. I'm perfectly pessimistic about what anyone can do, but if nobody wants to do it, nothing is going to change. I don't think art does anything, and nobody pays attention to art, nobody pays any attention to any kind of opposition, to any changes, so I think it's a very pessimistic situation. But obviously the only answer is that people have to try to change it, and I think it's something everyone should naturally spend a lot of time on. People have to make a living, but I think they also have to spend perhaps a third of their time dealing with other people, which is what it is. Politics have been taken away from them by the central [government] but they have to get them back. First they take the money away, then they take the politics away.

AM   How did you come to work with metal?

DJ   I like the surface and the idea that it can be made somewhere else. I don't like the handwork.

AM   No? You never painted?

DJ   I did, but I didn't want to do it anymore. I want the quality of it done by a factory.

A M   You make sketches and then you say, "That's blue, that's yellow"?

D J   We use color charts, R A L – this is a European color chart – we use the numbers.[6]

        I could make a lot of art. Making art is to be sure you are not making art to make a living; you have to keep it clear, to make the art to make art, not to turn the art into a way to make money.

A M   You are not making art to make your own living circumstances?

D J   No, not primarily, that comes afterward. That's distinct from the work.

A M   But when you say being an artist counts less in America, then you make your living circumstances when you decide to be an artist in choosing a socially weak position.

D J   Yes, in a way, you choose the weak position.

A M   What are you going to look at until Friday?

D J   Now we are going to the [Museum für] angewandte Kunst storeroom; tomorrow morning we go to the Albertina to look at drawings by Dürer. Wittgenstein's house.[7] I saw it before but I want to see it another time.

A M   You are already drinking white wine?

D J   Yes.

A M   But it's before noon.

D J   It's twelve thirty.

First published: Ariane Müller, "Donald Judd," *Artfan*, May 1991, n.p.

1   Judd refers here to 101 Spring Street.
2   *Donald Judd: Sculptures 1965–1987*, Stedelijk Van Abbemuseum, Eindhoven, The Netherlands, April 26–June 2, 1987; Städtische Kunsthalle, Düsseldorf, June 27–August 9, 1987; A R C /Musée d'Art Moderne de la Ville de Paris, December 8, 1987–February 7, 1988; Fundació Joan Miró, Barcelona, February 25–April 24, 1988; Castello di Rivoli, Turin, June 4–September 30, 1988.

3   From 1988 until 1994, Judd operated El Taller Chihuahuense, a studio for
     the production of his Cor-ten steel artworks, out of a former ice factory
     in Marfa, Texas. The building is now part of the Chinati Foundation and
     is used for special exhibitions and artist-in-residence studio space, among
     other activities hosted by the foundation.

4   Judd attended the Art Students League, in New York, during the day from
     1948 to 1953, while also working toward an undergraduate degree at night
     at Columbia University. He received his BS in philosophy from Colum-
     bia, cum laude, in 1953.

5   Judd refers here to a thesis recently popularized by French art historian
     Serge Guilbaut, who proposed that abstract expressionism was put to ideo-
     logical use by the postwar US government – and that its success as a move-
     ment was indebted to that use. See Guilbaut, *How New York Stole the Idea
     of Modern Art: Abstract Expressionism, Freedom, and the Cold War*, trans. Ar-
     thur Goldhammer (Chicago: University of Chicago Press, 1983). Judd in-
     cluded four copies of this book in his library in Marfa, Texas.

6   Judd used the RAL industrial color standard system to select the colors of
     his multicolored works.

7   From 1926 to 1928, Ludwig Wittgenstein, in partnership with architect
     Paul Engelmann, designed an exactingly precise townhouse for his older
     sister Margaret, going so far as to fashion custom door knobs and win-
     dow latches for the building. The only structure designed by the philos-
     opher, the Wittgenstein House today houses the cultural department of
     the Bulgarian embassy in Vienna.

"Donald Judd: Artist"
Interview with Fietta Jarque for *El País*
May 22, 1991

Published in *El País*, a Spanish-language daily newspaper based in Madrid, this conversation was conducted on the occasion of the exhibition *Donald Judd* at Galería Theospacio, Madrid (May 22–July 1991). Judd's work had been presented in group exhibitions in Spain since 1981, but this was his first solo show in the country.

Judd's essay "On Installation" (1982) was included in the show's catalogue. As Judd wrote, "The installation and context for the art being done now is poor and unsuitable. The correction is a permanent installation of a good portion of the work of each of the best artists." He echoes this observation in this conversation for *El País*, stating, "The majority of the art we see today isn't exhibited in appropriate situations, but in situations that are designed to separate it from society."

D J   [Donald Judd] Art should be everywhere, it doesn't have to be isolated. And it doesn't only have to serve a decorative function. It's not made so it can be installed in an office building. Art should be exhibited in the manner in which it was conceived, in an architecture suitable to it. The majority of the art we see today isn't exhibited in appropriate situations, but in situations that are designed to separate it from society – basically, according to an idea that is contrary to the idea of the art itself. There is a real conflict between the attitudes of architecture and exhibition and the ideas of most of the artists of this century. Nothing could be more out of context than what is on view now at The Museum of Modern Art in New York. It's like asking a revolutionary to join a conservative government. It's a total opposition. Of course, it's the art that suffers because it can't disassociate itself from the architecture.

People in museums and the galleries want conservative art. Over the last twenty years in New York, there hasn't been a single place where you could see the best contemporary art. There are very few good young artists; I couldn't name more than five. The situation for art is worse now than it was in 1940. The superiority of the art in New York is a myth. The public wants a conservative art and that's what they're sold. And there's a lot of people whose living relies on it. Most of what passes for art in New York is a form of commerce. It has stopped being a nexus.

In New York, people think a new style should appear every two or three years. But it isn't that way. There aren't so many artists. They don't all die at thirty, at the height of their careers. In reality, it's an activity that takes a couple decades before you reach a certain level, before you get somewhere. The important thing is that people should be able to know what the best art is of their own generation, and that of the past. I think now it's essential for artists to travel. Because making art requires a deep knowledge of your field, like science does. You have to really know what you want to do and what you are doing. Like it or not, you can't learn about art in the magazines. You have to travel. All artists should know what's happening internationally. But it's not about accumulation, it's about establishing the right criteria. I've just returned from Korea, and I've seen things that I think everyone should see.

Translated from the Spanish by Tim Johnson.

First published: Fietta Jarque, "Donald Judd: Artista," *El País*, May 22, 1991, n.p.

"Treat Art as Art Only: Discussion with Donald Judd"
Interview with Seungduk Kim for *Space*
June 1991

In June 1991, Judd spent several days in Seoul during his exhibition at the city's Inkong Gallery (May 6–June 30, 1991). On this occasion, curator Seungduk Kim interviewed Judd at the gallery for the monthly magazine *Space*, published by the Korean architecture and design firm Space Group. This was Judd's first solo exhibition in Korea; a catalogue for the show was planned and prepared but not realized.

Judd was in Seoul and its nearby surroundings for the majority of 1947, while in the United States Army Corps of Engineers.

S K   [Seungduk Kim] Could you tell us about the exhibition in Inkong Gallery? Did you have any specific ideas about the space of the Inkong Gallery for the selection of your works?

D J   [Donald Judd] The space was bigger than I expected, because once I had a show in Japan, and the space was really small. I knew about the space a little bit. If I had not known the space, I would not have sent two large Cor-ten steel pieces.

S K   What would be the ideal space in which to present your works? Is there any space in which you prefer to show your works?

D J   Yes, the space is very important. If I were designing a gallery it would be very simple, even simpler than the Inkong Gallery. But the Inkong Gallery is fairly simple compared to most other galleries. Of course, one of the greatest virtues is that it's on the ground floor. Otherwise, we would not have brought the large Cor-ten pieces.

S K   I would like to ask about the installation since it is an important part of your work. When I saw the exhibition at the Whitney in 1990, the *New Sculpture* show,[1] I felt somehow some works were presented out of context. I guess sometimes artists can direct how the works should be installed if the artists are alive. However, it is often the case that artists cannot direct the installation. In that case, if the museums try to do the installation for later generations, how could it be done? Could it be presented close to the artist's spirit? Or could the artist write all the instructions as a part of how the work should be installed?

D J   It is going to be very difficult. Who knows what the later generations would be like? In fact, for the present generation, especially at the Whitney Museum and especially in New York, museums are totally uninterested in how the artists want the installations. They think, the curators of the museums – for example, The Museum of Modern Art, the Whitney Museum, and the Guggenheim Museum – that they are better than the artists in terms of how to install art. They are uninterested in knowing how the artists want the installation. So it is always a fight, a fight that artists tend to lose. I think as far as New York goes, the installations of almost all of the artists have seriously damaged the understanding of their work. Starting with Jackson Pollock, Barnett Newman, and Mark Rothko, the whole idea of the architecture of installation is completely opposite to the ideas involved in the art. So in a way, there is a war against the art. This goes for architecture, too. It is very hard to see how it could be better in the future.

My solution is to try to do it myself now, at least some of the work. And then people can see how I want it to be done. They can follow that. It is an attitude [of the museums], it's a serious attitude that basically causes the destruction of the art as it is. But it's also – I don't care so much about the public – but also it is against the public interest because the public is taught to see the art in a way that is wrong.

SK   Do you consider museums to play an important educational role?

DJ   It is a destructive educational role. There are museums which are beneficial, especially in Europe. But a lot of exhibitions, especially big exhibitions with lots of art and artists, I think, are very destructive. Partly the present museum has grown up from an older museum, which was really a completely different idea, which was to collect for somebody's palace, so it comes out of a dilettante, good or bad situation, and a very different situation. The present museums, I think, almost just happened. It doesn't seem to me there is really much thought involved, and they become a cultural symbol. And it really has nothing to do with art. It is just a symbol, a very expensive symbol for cities all over the world. No one thinks about what art is like or how it should be shown, or whether it should even be collected or accumulated for the spot. So there is the old premise and new situation that do not go together. There is no reason to bring and to concentrate the art in one spot, to bring so much of it together. And possibly, that is true, as we saw in Gyeongju, possibly that is true for the older art, too.[2] Why should it all be piled together in The Metropolitan Museum of Art in New York? I think it would be better if it was all back home in some place. It even distorts old art, and certainly distorts contemporary art, to put it all together.

And a lot of contemporary artists don't like each other's work. I mean, there is a real difference. This is covered by the fact that the public sees it all in one museum and it does not have real differences to them. It just looks different. That is called individuality without any depth. There is no context. It just looks like what the museums want — peculiar people each doing their own thing as they say. And this "doing your own thing" is, by definition, doing your own thing, and therefore there is no philosophical conflict or meaning. It becomes pointless.

SK   But in reality, it is hard to really go around the world to see artworks.

DJ   That's not true. In the first place, the contemporary art that does wind up in museums is fairly small in comparison to what was done. And if it were spread around, it would be everywhere. That is not difficult. It is nice, for example, in Switzerland, or in the Alsace in France, because sometimes little museums have two or three pieces by [Jean] Arp and other people. That is nice because he is from the area. To me it is much better to go to some little museum and there are a few pieces by Arp, Max Bill, and people who lived there.

SK   When the Guggenheim Museum spread its collections to annex museums, rather than keeping them all in one museum, do you think it improved the situation?

DJ   No, what they are doing in a way is worse. It's because of
      the way they are operating — they are involved with cor-
      porations, a cigarette company. I don't know, are they in-
      volved with Philip Morris?[3] I can't remember. Anyway,
      they don't disperse it in a real way; they disperse it in a
      corporate way. So you have a Guggenheim headquarters,
      and then you have little offices all around. That is not the
      way to do anything.

SK   But then there is a problem in getting support. Without
      these financial sources, it is very hard to maintain support
      for the art.

DJ   I think you do not take money. That is the only solution to
      that. You don't ask those people for money and you do not
      take their money. That is the only way to deal with that.
      The art is not made to support a corporation or a govern-
      ment; therefore you don't take their money. I would not
      take money from the United States government, because
      they're too awful to take money from. And so, the Whit-
      ney should not take money from the cigarette company —
      it may be oil.

SK   Then what could be the source to support the art?

DJ   They get it the best they can from individuals. If you take
      it from slick corporations, you are going to get a slick sit-
      uation and a museum system. And eventually, as is happen-
      ing now, you are going to have a slick art for a slick situ-
      ation. And then you don't have anything. So it doesn't do
      any good. The people who run corporations, who are on
      the boards of museums and all that, have a very ignorant
      and superficial idea of art and architecture. They want all
      the junk that they ordinarily build for their corporations
      or business headquarters. They want the same things they
      are used to switched over to the museums, which is one
      reason you have such bad museum architecture. It just
      does not get you anywhere. There is a lot of money in
      the world, but it ruins the art; it is useless money. So you

have to leave it alone. It happens over and over again; it is always a catastrophe for everybody.

SK   Could you tell us about your museum or foundation in Marfa, Texas?[4]

DJ   It is not a museum, and the word "foundation" is for legal reasons and because there is no other word I can think of. At this point the situation is a lot larger than the foundation itself. Partly it is a natural situation, but obviously it is not a natural situation, because a great deal of art has been put down in a small town that has never been interested in art and is not interested in art. So that of course is arbitrary. I came along and I started putting it there, that's all. So it's not that the people want it or are interested in it. That would be true anywhere. But I tried to install it in a fairly natural way. It's spread around town and it's not in one spot. I am very concerned about the architecture and the placement of the work. The idea is to treat the art as art only. If you are in a scientific enterprise, what you are doing is just what you are doing. That is why the museums fail. They do not treat the art as art. It's always something else. It's a whole array of other things, education being the first one. Art is not education. It is crazy to educate people about art by destroying the art. It is a hopeless situation. Marfa is about installing art, about making the art and installing it properly. So the art is the main thing and the only thing.

　　　People can come and they cannot come. That takes its course. It is open to the public, and actually, people do come. But I am not out to educate anybody. It is to treat as much art as I can deal with, my own and other people's, in the way I think it should be treated. In my case, I am the expert on my own art; as to other people's, I do my best, but that can probably alter their work a little bit too. But at least it's something that is being done here and now: it's done in the present and will last some time.

The chief artist – actually, there's a lot of work by John Chamberlain, it's more work of Chamberlain's than exists anywhere in the world.[5] We tried to do that with Dan Flavin but it collapsed; we tried to do that with some other artists.[6]

And the best thing, of course, is if the artist is working there, does something, and decides where it goes, and that's it. Claes Oldenburg is doing that and making a big piece outdoors.[7] It's his idea and he saw the place which he wanted. And the whole thing – he volunteered, and it was completely his idea as to what he wants to do, so that is very good. And it all happened much more naturally. The place won't be a sculpture park, it won't be a museum; it will be liveable to some extent, which is important. It will have a lot of variety.

SK   Museums have been playing the role of conditioning people to look at art a certain way. When you say art should be treated as art only, you are offering a new way to look at art. Does this not also involve education?

DJ   Unavoidably – we can learn. I am not saying that there is no education, but I am saying it's not for education. The minute we start to use art for other things, it goes wrong, because we have a strange situation where the art is done by individuals with their own concerns. Art is not done for institutions, for an aristocracy, for government, nor for religion. There is a big conflict. People of all sorts, without thinking too much, recognize, yes, the artist is an individual and so forth. But a lot of people, especially museums, and institutions, really do not want that. They would like to have, as I said, their own art. That will never happen, because it cannot be good enough. Philip Morris is never going to have its own art, no matter what. Or, for example, Mobil oil. They will never have good art. Or the United States government. So when you show the work in museums, you are putting it in an institutional situation for an institutional purpose, and this whole thing does not hang together. So it would be a lot better if the individual artists had their own small museums or little museums everywhere, or the whole thing dispersed through the society.

SK   How it can be realized is another question.

DJ   Change of attitude, of course. All attitudes are only attitudes. They can be changed. You have to destroy the idea of the museum and start over, get people to put their money into smaller and more serious things. Which is a difference in attitude and which can happen. All the Buddhist temples that we've been looking at are because people will put their money in one particular spot to make something.

That is all serious and in a different time. New York should have had a museum, a whole museum for Barnett Newman's work, Jackson Pollock's work – separate museums.

If you go to New York you see almost nothing of the work by the artists who were there. It is a joke. You cannot imagine how many paintings were made there. Now those works are dispersed. They are all over the world. So there is no way to get a good idea of Barnett Newman's work, or Jackson Pollock's, without an enormous amount of traveling. That defeats the whole idea that it is better for the public for it to be in one spot. Because that destroys the information. If you want to have a good idea of Jackson Pollock's work, you'd have to travel all over the world. You'd have to go to Australia, Japan – I mean, it's crazy.

SK   Do you believe that people from a postindustrial society would need to acquire a new sense of beauty? In other words, do you believe that the beauty from the technological form has been misunderstood or not been accepted in the right way by the majority of contemporary people?

DJ   What do you mean by "postindustrial"? Our time is

postindustrial? This is almost preindustrial. It's a different version of history. This is the very beginning of the industrial period, and the period will be more or less forever. It's obviously a beginning. That is why life is such a mess. It is a big catastrophe. It is very fast, very new.

So it is not post-anything. It is almost pre-everything. I hope that there will be a different sense of beauty in due time. But one of the problems, of course, is that everybody lets industrial techniques and building destroy the world and their own environment. The factory owner does not care where he is building a factory or what it is like, what he does with the waste products and so forth. He does not want that in his house. In his house he wants fake additional stuff.

Naturally, because that is the way I work, I like it – I am not against industrial construction. It should be treated in a more intelligent way. I like the industrial process and what can be done. People tend not to regard my work as art because of the way it is done. There has been a lot of animosity toward the work.

SK So you feel that it will require some time for people to appreciate the aesthetic of our industrial period and industrial environment.

DJ I think it will take a very long time, unfortunately, maybe since almost everybody's idea of aesthetics is nostalgic. Maybe only when all the industry is totally blown up by nuclear bombs will it then become romantic. And people will think that it is nice. Then they will collect little bits and pieces as souvenirs.

And the industrial product does have an aesthetic. You can't just say it is nothing. In a way, almost all consumer products are like that. So in a way, the machines that are really made to work, not consumer machines, machines that really have to work properly, are the only ones that are good-looking. Most airplanes are nice-looking, maybe painted badly, but they are seldom ugly. Most cars are ugly because they do not have to work very well.

SK   People often say that art is another way of doing philosophy, that art is a way of expressing particular ideas. Do you consider that the artwork, in an autonomous way, should not interfere with the contemporary philosophical world?

DJ   Art has to have a philosophical basis. Any good art has a fairly well-thought-out philosophy, but it is not a philosophy itself, because it is a physical thing. You look at it. It's a different way of experiencing things. For the most part I consider philosophy in the past, probably now, in a way, as a form of literature. So to me philosophy is just another form of art. Unlike science, which is fairly real — and that is not to be derogatory. But it [philosophy] is another way of making an art. There are certain attitudes in philosophy underlying visual art. I have attitudes that don't agree with other people's attitudes. So it is very important. I object very much when people say that art has no meaning. I make art as a totality.

SK   People sometimes say that art's major point is to express a philosophical idea, not respecting the visual elements of the art. It is intruding on what the philosopher is trying to do with words. In a way art has too much meaning and no meaning.

DJ   Art cannot have too much meaning. Art cannot have no meaning. It is impossible. The fact is anything you can see or anything human beings do has meaning. It's just that it can have a trashy or bad meaning, that's all. There is no way that you can get out of the fact that it has meaning. The table, this very superficial table, its superficiality itself is a meaning. You don't like it, but it is a meaning. It is never neutral. I think this is the way we act. When it's an ugly situation, it's ugly, that's all.

SK   What kind of relationships are there between your work and the idea of positive utopian thoughts?

DJ   I am so far from the utopia that I have never taken it seriously. I am interested in the things that can be done here
and now. I have never been interested in very hypothetical situations. I tend to get interested when it is real and
when something can be done. So I react when it is a bad
situation. I try to think about the future. I noticed that
other people, despite all of the propaganda for war and
everything, do a great deal of talking and planning in all
forms, but nobody has the faintest idea what is going to
happen five years from now. So to think about utopia, five
hundred years from now, seems silly. Also, the utopia that
you never live to see I am not very interested in. So I am
not intrinsically utopian or idealistic. My general thinking is somewhat empirical and I want to actually exist and
I want to be able to deal with it.

SK   What do you think about the US involvement with the
Gulf War? As an artist, as an intellectual, you must have
some opinion about it.

DJ   I think it was a major crime. I saw a sign on a wall in
Spain saying, "Saddam is bad, but Bush is worse" [image 77].
I think we got Hitler mixed up. Bush is the real Hitler.
The United States is the real Hitler. Saddam Hussein is a
small crook, very nasty and mean, and a stupid little crook,
but the Americans are the real Nazis and very dangerous.
Bombing Iraq was just a test. It can become far worse.
Taking back Kuwait and bombing Iraq was sort of Bush's
Sudetenland.

It was just a beginning of what the Americans want.
The Americans have failed as a society just like the Soviet Union, not yet quite as badly. They have failed. Capitalism is not winning, capitalism is losing. The United
States has failed and all it has is weapons. The only way it
can maintain its power is to have wars. It is a very dangerous situation. The Soviet Union can imitate the United
States and can start doing that too. All the Soviet Union

has is weapons. If they both start, it is going to be a terrible situation.

The United States is very jealous and very envious of Germany and Japan. All this stuff about getting Germany and Japan to send weapons and soldiers to Iraq is about getting them involved and breaking their economy. So then they will be like the United States, and they will be broke. It is very smart, I think, for both Germany and Japan to stay out of it, because it will, in addition to what it does to Iraq, which is unfair, ruin their economies and kill their soldiers.

The United States is out to cause a great deal of trouble. I think it has to be resisted by everyone; Europe is in the best position to resist. The idea of bombing – 80,000 sorties and 80,000 airplane trips – a country that is not as big as California is horrifying. Fifty or eighty billion dollars, when you do not have money for all sorts of things in the United States – they do not have money for the least little thing in New York. That is an incredible amount of money. They even said it didn't matter. So I think that it is a great crime. Really a crime.

SK Is there this kind of awareness among artists and intellectuals?

DJ I was in Europe at the time. Well, first I was in Texas, then I went to New York, and I was in a demonstration on the twentieth of October with my daughter. There were quite a few people. The newspapers stuck it way in the back. *The New York Times* put it in way back in the middle of the newspaper. So it did not have much effect on the government. Except they were afraid of demonstrations. It was all big enough. But there was no opposition within the government, no opposition from the so-called public. No opposition from the university people and the intellectuals.

Noam Chomsky complained about this. Intellectuals in the United States are not very important, but at least we should speak and try to do something. People in the United States had a whole autumn to try and stop this war. It was obvious on August 4 and 5 what Bush was up to. He was trying to set up the war. I think Saddam Hussein was set up. I think he was tricked into going into Kuwait, so there would be a war. Bush was concerned that the whole thing didn't get upset, that it could go along and the war could occur. That is mainly what he was involved in the whole fall. So there was a lot of time for intellectuals and groups in the US to raise a big opposition which would've disturbed all of that. But they didn't do that. Nobody said anything. Like a bunch of rabbits in front of a rattlesnake. They didn't make any objection, even little words. All the newspaper people, everything, TV, they did not say no at all. You could see that a lot of people were going to get killed and a lot of things destroyed if the war occurred.

It's all very predictable and nobody said no to it. You know, they talked about 139 or 179 American soldiers dead. And on American TV they never mention how many Iraqis are dead. I still don't know whether it was a hundred thousand or two hundred thousand. There is a big difference between that, one hundred thousand or two hundred thousand, and 137, 179, or whatever.

Bush killed those people.

Somebody in Switzerland said to me the other day, "Look how many people Saddam Hussein killed." For Christ's sake, Bush killed those people, a direct order, a very clean way.

So the people should not let the Americans do those things. The Americans are more dangerous than Saddam Hussein and any such person. There are plenty of Saddam Husseins in the world. There is also a great big powerful country with nowhere to go, and it's more dangerous.

SK   How would it be possible that the American public would not react to these situations?

DJ   The US is one of the most passive, undemocratic, zero societies in the world. If the Soviet Union is the most zero,
the US is only one or two points above zero. There are no
politics in the United States. You can see it from the last
election and the elections before that. It is absolutely dead
politics. The United States government has destroyed any
kind of political life, from the top to the bottom. To make
a central government, that's what you have to do. The purpose of the central government is to be a central government. People are slaves. That's the purpose of it. I don't
know how the Americans can wake up. They are finished,
unless they wake up, for a long time to come. It is partly
the whole nature of this century to have big heroes like
Stalin and Hitler.

People think that they can set up a constitution and
do so-and-so, and that's it. You don't have to do anything
more. But the fact is it's a daily fight. It's just one of the
fights that people have to have. If you are in a political
situation you are always going to fight. The Americans
think it was solved by the revolution, and so they wrote
the Constitution and the Bill of Rights. And the government wants them to think that way. So there is no political
life, no pressure against the government. The government
can do anything they like. Send the FBI and the CIA, take
all their money, anything they want. Naturally the central
government wants to promote this idea. They want to say,
"Everything comes from us, give us all the money, and we
will do everything, and you do what you are told."

It is the same old thing that started in Russia with Ivan
the Terrible. So it is not so different from the Soviet Union
and it's having the same economic results. I find it strange
that sometimes in Europe people seem to believe that the
United States is actually democratic.

The United States has no interest in democracy and
freedom. It is pathetic to see that the Chinese students put

up the Statue of Liberty.[8] To us that's really pathetic. It is really sad. Because the US is against liberty and freedom.

What I have to do as an artist in the United States, I have to do against and despite the United States government.

SK Could you give some advice to young artists in Asia who are studying art, especially contemporary art? Today we have dominant models coming from Europe and the United States. We are strongly influenced by the outside, but often it is taken without much context. What kind of advice could you give to those who do not have a chance to go out and experience outside art, and often get information about it through books?

DJ That is no good. The art has to be seen, and if that means there aren't that many artists in the world, artists must travel. It's not a mass movement. That's also why the museums are such failures. The main thing for young artists everywhere is to see the art of the people somewhat older than they are. The most important thing is to see all art, old art and everything. But it is absolutely necessary to be really familiar with the art of the generation, the two or three generations before you, because that's where your admiration for art comes from and the context for your own work. I think that art is art wherever it's developed.

It occurs in different places, many places all over the world. I think that it is very important to keep it in mind that it can occur anyplace. It is not limited to some big cities. Even if the artist has to travel to several different places … Now you have to live in several different places. But they really have to know the work. The best is to really know the older artists.

They don't have to follow them but to understand – maybe to go against them. You cannot understand them completely – that's why there has to be new art – but to understand enough to make something else. So that kind of information is sort of like a science, which means it is everywhere and you simply go where they're doing the most advanced work. Science is now everywhere. I have a small connection to an observatory.[9] Observatories are all over the world, and the astronomers are all over the world. You go wherever the best work is being done. You learn and understand. Then you can come back home for the rest of your life. But it can't be done without seeing a lot of work. The United States hardly made any first-rate art before the '40s and '50s, so it had a great inferiority complex. The artists were interested in the fact that good art can be made in the United States, first-rate art in New York. I remember that I was old enough to have a sense of that through the magazines. You can't feel that you are in a second-rate situation. The strange thing is that everybody, almost everybody as far as art goes, feels that they are in a backwater, except New York, when they really are in a backwater. They think that they are still important, when, in fact, they are no longer important. Some people in Vienna said, "We are way off in the East, where Vienna is not important, it's just a leftover capital," and so forth. Everybody feels that way, so it doesn't matter.

First published: Seungduk Kim, "Treat Art as Art Only: Discussion with Donald Judd," *Space: Arts, Architecture & Environment*, June 1991, 74–78.

1   *The New Sculpture 1965–75: Between Geometry and Gesture*, Whitney Museum of American Art, New York, February 20–June 3, 1990.
2   The city of Gyeongju, on the eastern coast of South Korea, is home to a number of major historical and cultural sites, most dating to the first millennium BCE.
3   Philip Morris, a longtime donor to the arts, has sponsored many exhibitions at the Guggenheim.
4   Kim refers here to the Chinati Foundation.
5   Judd refers here to the Chamberlain Building.

6   Flavin's large-scale work in colored fluorescent light for six buildings (for-
        mer barracks at Fort D. A. Russell) at the Chinati Foundation was initi-
        ated in the early 1980s. Flavin finalized his design in 1996, and the instal-
        lation was completed and opened to the public in 2000. See Marianne
        Stockebrand, ed., *Chinati: The Vision of Donald Judd* (Marfa, TX: The Chi-
        nati Foundation; New Haven, CT: Yale University Press, 2010), 224–47.
7   As a gift to the Chinati Foundation, Claes Oldenburg and Coosje van
        Bruggen created and installed *Monument to the Last Horse* (1991), their ver-
        sion of an equestrian sculpture, on the foundation's grounds. See Judd's
        "*Monument to the Last Horse*: Animo et Fide" (1992) in *Donald Judd Writ-
        ings*, 790–806.
8   Judd refers here to the Goddess of Democracy, a statue erected by dissi-
        dents during the 1989 Tiananmen Square protests. Though commenta-
        tors noted its likeness to the Statue of Liberty, people involved in the con-
        struction of the sculpture have rejected this reference.
9   Judd refers here to the McDonald Observatory, part of The University
        of Texas at Austin, located in the Davis Mountains of West Texas. He be-
        came a member of the observatory's Board of Visitors in 1989.

Interview with Klaus Stefan Leuschel
April 22, 1992

On the transcript from which this conversation was sourced, interviewer Klaus Stefan Leuschel made the following note: "The interview has been recorded in Eichholteren on Wednesday, 22nd April 1992, in Donald Judd's house at an old table; the interviewer having taken the occasion to seat himself on the only Judd chair in the living-room downstairs."

In 1992, on the recommendation of Dieter Schwarz, director of the Kunstmuseum Winterthur, Judd was selected to redesign the *Fischmädchenbrunnen*, or "fish maiden" fountain, on the Steinberggasse in Winterthur. Instead of replacing the existing fountain from 1938, Judd submitted a design for three additional fountains to be built in line with it. He used the elliptical shape of the original fountain as the basis for his new fountains in sandblasted concrete, each weighing twenty metric tons. Construction of the fountains did not begin until summer 1995, with the inauguration of the fountains occurring on June 14, 1997.

KSL [Klaus Stefan Leuschel] Some of your statements made last year [*laughs*] about the lousy museums, for me, have a similarity to statements Clyfford Still made. Clyfford Still, on the other hand, referred to a solitary position as an American artist. Could you accept such a term for yourself?

DJ [Donald Judd] No, I do not even want to be an American artist. But I would also question that about Clyfford Still. So I do not know about those quotes. I know about the situation in New York. He was very [prescient] about the museums and the whole situation there; I think he was absolutely right. I do not know what he said about being an American artist. I know that Jackson Pollock said he did not want to be an American artist.

KSL I think he said that to define an American art he needed to free himself from the whole European background.

DJ But being free from that tradition does not mean that you want to be – over here somewhere. The European tradition is a European tradition, it is a certain civilization, and other people from other places are not necessarily part of that civilization. That can explain, as far as art is concerned, why most of the artists in Europe are not part of the European tradition anyway. And that still struggles on. But that is not one of the major issues.

KSL Well, when we talk about your idea of art, is it possible to transfer that idea onto architecture and design?

DJ I was always interested in architecture, and, naturally, in all visible things. And as I wrote somewhere about the furniture: I tried to make furniture deliberately, twenty or thirty years ago.[1] And, to simplify, taking art over here and overworking it and calling it furniture was a disaster. Then I really stayed away from it for a while. I think the distinction between the two has to be kept very clear. It is going to have a connection, if one person does it, through the use of certain forms. But I never think from the art to the architecture. It is absolutely guaranteed to be bad, and it does not work vice versa, either. So there is really a separation between the two. To me it only seems natural [to make both]; some people can switch between two languages easily, maybe.

KSL   So is it difficult for you to explain why you started to design furniture?

DJ   No, that is easy, because it relates to a time in my life. I brought my kids to West Texas, where it was impossible to buy any furniture that we wanted there. Basically you could only find a few old things. So I started making it, first for the children: a bed, a desk, a shelf. It was made very simply, because I was not very good at carpentry. So I went to the lumberyard. I figured it all out and then told them, "So many boards this long, so many boards that long," and so forth. That is how it all started; I just had to put it together. That is the beginning of the desk. Then we made chairs for around the table, which – as you see – we have not done here[2] yet, so that just developed like something for myself –

KSL   Like a basic need?

DJ   – and for many years we have not bothered trying to sell it. So finally, we published it and tried to sell it ourselves. But you cannot take the forms from art and put them directly into architecture. And I think the attempt to do so is why we have so much bad architecture. They are thinking they are making 3-D sculptures, but it is a horrible idea.

KSL   That brings me to what you said about architects in your Viennese catalogue.[3] You mentioned the Mies van der Rohe furniture, which is looked at as being extremely functional; you related to that tradition in your first catalogue on furniture, where you said that furniture has to be functional.[4] As there are lots of struggles in the field of design that relate to that question, what does that word mean to you?

DJ   Well, "functional" means to me what it means. Basically,

I am all for the Bauhaus, so this is an exception. But the problem of some of the Bauhaus pieces is that functionality becomes a form of decoration. I do not, for example, like very much the Breuer chair.[5]

KSL   That is the one that resembles the military chair?

DJ   Yes, the one with the leather straps. I had one for a long time. It is now in storage, because it is super functional in appearance but in effect is not as functional as the old-fashioned nineteenth-century military portable chair, or safari chair, which is where it really comes from.

KSL   A very good example!

DJ   That is its source, and also that of the little Le Corbusier chair.[6] That's a kind of function as decoration. I do not think that this is the case with Mies van der Rohe's furniture.

KSL   And the choice of materials? The Bauhaus had a kind of dogmatic preference for certain new materials that had not been used for furniture before.

DJ   That is a nice idea. I do not think that it is necessarily dogmatic, either. First you should think about the idea, and then what materials are possible. I think that that led them to use the plumber pipes and so on.

KSL   Coming back to the situation when you moved to Texas, would you have experimented much more if you had had more money? Would you have used, I do not know, for example, carbon fiber or whatever for furniture?

DJ   Sure. Well, what I do is technically pretty simple. It is made by factories, but there is nothing chic about it. And of course, you could make cheaper and lighter furniture by using stamping and molded metals or, presumably, plastic.

KSL   From a formal point of view, your chairs seem to have a familiarity with chairs by, say, Robert Wilson[7] or Peter Wigglesworth.[8]

DJ   Naturally I just saw Peter Wigglesworth's chairs at Formatera.[9] Yes, there is a little resemblance, but of course I did not know his work. I hardly know about Robert Wilson's. I saw a couple of his productions a long time ago in Boston and I think they are just ridiculous and I have no interest. And I am highly against, as you might guess, furniture as art. It is kind of silly, so I did not really like or agree with Scott Burton, for example.[10] It is nothing I would do. I would not even like to have it for myself.

KSL   But these aspects of function, nonartistic values, et cetera, make it difficult for me to understand why you have so many modular forms in your work?

DJ   I'll tell you: I tend to think like that. Once I start to think about one particular thing, I am thinking of twenty of it. So that is the price of thinking. As this wall has recently been finished, I am thinking of a piece for here. And once I start, it produces immediately half a dozen pieces. I can't help it. Probably not all of them are as good as one or the other; they all are not equally good. So it is just obvious: you make a chair, you make a stool. That was it, at least with the metal furniture: easy, quick. The chair you are sitting on has a different, particular story. The metal furniture was done here in Dübendorf and it was all made up very quickly.[11] It was a nice situation. I could do the drawings and three days later you could see the piece, which was extremely unusual for me. The wooden chairs were first made in Texas but are now made in Yorkshire.[12] The metal furniture is based on fifty by fifty centimeters, which is a bit too big for a chair. The wooden chair is a completely different story, with stretchers, crossbars, and proportions.

KSL   Does time mean something to you?

DJ   I have lots of faith in time! [*Laughs*] I think my work has a lot to do with time, and it's over the course of time that I can tell if I really like something. For instance, the divisions in these chairs [frame chairs] were really difficult, but now I really like them and I know they're right. Originally the spacing between the bars was 37.5 [centimeters], but the bottom bar didn't look right, so I had to have it moved up to make them look equal. That now is an architectural problem.

KSL You have used in your writing the pair "simple" and "complex" to make clear that "complicated" is not the opposite of "simple." I somehow have the impression that everything is complicated.

DJ Well, pretty much put stuff on the table and it is complicated. Take it away, and it is not complicated.

KSL Do you want to make it simple?

DJ I think as far as art and architecture are concerned, they have to be relatively simple for us to understand, because primarily you understand them at once, or at least the initial interest is there at once. You understand it in a different way over a period of time, but I don't think in the same way as in the beginning.

KSL Well, I know your furniture fairly well, but know little of your artwork – in particular, I have not yet been to Marfa – and everything seems to be very simple, very reduced. But does that mean, as the computer people put it, "what you see is what you get"?

DJ Yes.

KSL But isn't there a complexity behind it?

DJ Yes, but don't you see art and architecture basically all at once? And naturally, in both cases, the work can be larger and complicated. So it does not necessarily matter whether the work of art is complicated or the people make complicated work. There is an artist in New York who makes very complicated work; I think that it is his way of thinking. It is a certain requirement of his thought, and a certain requirement of mine is to make simple things. And also, the painters I was interested in earlier made notably simple work, too. Behind this simplicity, the complexity is the same. Ultimately a painting by Barnett Newman is just as complex as –

KSL   For your house in New York, you used an ellipse.[13] This is by itself a very complex form.

DJ   It is, especially if you try to do it.

KSL   You never used this form in your artwork?

DJ   No. The sink was for practical matters, because you bend over when you wash your face. So it had a certain practicality, although it was within a very narrow space. The main reason is that in art the ellipse costs a lot. But circles are just fine. So that is also art and money. I am doing fountains in Winterthur now [image 78], which seem, as it looks now, as if they will be built. Those are ellipses, but the ellipse follows an existing fountain which is an ellipse. The ellipse looks very nice.

KSL   For your wooden furniture, what wood do you use? I come to that as I just read in the newspapers that the Japanese Pavilion in Seville is made of tropical wood.[14] Also, you stated in your text on the museum buildings that, although not being too familiar with the architecture of Tadao Ando, you might exclude him from the terrible.

DJ   Since I wrote that, I saw buildings in Osaka. The little church, which is one of the early buildings, is pretty nice.[15] Actually, I like his use of concrete. Basically, his work is pretty simple and of course I am sympathetic to that. But sometimes things are not completely thought out and perhaps do not have a very good reason. Some things I like – I am not against the church. But I think it should be thought out more carefully. It is a very small, narrow lot. In particular, the entrance – I am not sure whether the angle was necessary. You should have a reason for this kind of solution in architecture, one that is part of its function. Thin. So if you make a cute shape, it is just a cute shape – that is all. I thought the building was nice; it is very plain, and the concrete work was very nice. It could be worked out further and more carefully. And I saw a brand-new, huge factory building in Osaka, whose name I cannot remember either. It has some nice areas, but it has also a lot of complicated aspects of usual architecture, which I do not like at all. It has an enormous lobby, which I do not see as necessary. Things like that. It is easy to hate [Hans] Hollein or people like that. But Ando is a little unnerving for me, because he is using some of the proportions, the simplicity, and devices like the quartering of the windows that I use. So maybe I think the details are a little off; a kind of rattlesnake, you know. Complexity going wrong – I am used to that, but simplicity going wrong is like the world upside down.

KSL   Is Marfa somehow a utopian model?

DJ   No, it is perfectly real, and it is perfectly as disgusting as the rest of the world. The landscape is beautiful, the people's treatment of the landscape is pretty bad, and the people are pretty apathetic, like all of the United States. And the sheriff, named [Rick] Thompson, was sheriff for nineteen years. He just got caught with 2,400 pounds of cocaine at the border and is going to jail.[16] So it is pretty sticky. It is not utopia.

This conversation was sourced from an archival transcript in the Judd Foundation Archives, Marfa, Texas.

1   See Judd's "On Furniture" (1986) in *Donald Judd Writings*, 450–53.
2   Judd refers here to Eichholteren.
3   *Donald Judd: Architektur*, exh. cat. (Vienna: Österreichisches Museum für angewandte Kunst, 1991).
4   *Donald Judd: Möbel Furniture*, exh. cat. (Zürich: Arche Verlag AG, 1985).
5   Judd refers here to Breuer's Wassily chair, which Breuer designed in 1925 and 1926, while he was the head of the Bauhaus's cabinet workshop.
6   Judd refers here to Le Corbusier's Basculant chair, designed in 1927.
7   Robert Wilson (1941–) is an American experimental stage director, playwright, and furniture designer.
8   Peter Wigglesworth (1945–) is an English furniture and lighting designer.
9   Formatera was a furniture business in Zürich which had a showroom that sold Judd furniture as well as furniture by Wigglesworth.

10   Scott Burton (1939–1989) was an American sculptor and performance artist; he both designed furniture as such and made sculptural works that functioned as furniture.

11   Lehni AG, based in Dübendorf, Switzerland, was the first fabricator of Judd's painted aluminum works and metal furniture. See Judd's "On Furniture" (1986) in *Donald Judd Writings*, 453.

12   Judd worked with a number of fabricators to produce his furniture in wood, including Design Workshop in Yorkshire, England.

13   In the 1970s, Judd designed a pair of elliptical stainless-steel sinks for the fifth-floor dressing rooms at 101 Spring Street. Bernstein Brothers fabricated the sinks.

14   Leuschel refers here to Tadao Ando's Japan Pavilion, built for the 1992 Universal Exposition of Seville.

15   Judd refers here to Ando's 1989 Church of the Light, in Ibaraki, a suburb of Osaka.

16   Rick Thompson of Marfa, Presidio County's sheriff from 1973 to 1991, was indicted and later convicted on federal felony drug charges while seeking his fifth term in office. He was found guilty of smuggling more than a ton of cocaine from Mexico into Texas. See Judd's "Letter to the Attorney General of the State of Texas" (18 December 1991) in *Donald Judd Writings*, 717–20.

Interview with Chris Felver
For the film *Donald Judd's Marfa, Texas*
June 3, 1992

Filmed on Judd's sixty-fourth birthday in Marfa, Texas, Chris Felver's *Donald Judd's Marfa, Texas*, released in 1995, includes a conversation with Judd intermixed with footage of his private living and working spaces in New York and Marfa, as well as footage of the Chinati Foundation. Critic John Yau provided commentary for the film.

In his essay "Ayala de Chinati" (1989), Judd described a ranch that had been cut up into many parcels, writing, "Within a real view of the world and the universe this violence would be a sin – there are no words since there are no ethics that correspond to the present known nature of the world. I've never built anything on new land." In this interview, Judd reiterates his position while describing the siting of his fifteen untitled works in concrete at the Chinati Foundation, stating, "They're laid out on a level part of the land. It's land that was already torn up and used. I've been trying to allow it to grow back for more than ten years."

In 1992, the same year that *Donald Judd's Marfa, Texas* was filmed, Judd joined Alert Citizens for Environmental Safety, an El Paso–based activist organization fighting a proposed nuclear waste dump in Sierra Blanca, Texas, about one and a half hours from Marfa.

   [Donald Judd] Originally, I just wanted a place in the Southwest for the summertime. And I became interested in having some art, and that made it impossible to do anything in Baja California, which I had gone to [for] several summers [images 79, 80].[1] I figured the Americans wouldn't let me out, the Mexicans wouldn't let it [art] in, and the Americans wouldn't let it back in again, and so on – or me, either. So once there started to be some art there, it was uncertain.

So when I first came here, I came here with a truckload of art. But it was originally just a place for the summertime. It just developed. I gave up on, forgot the idea of having the place just for the summer after a couple of years and, after acquiring the large warehouses [the east and west buildings at La Mansana de Chinati/The Block], started to make permanent installations. And of course, I brought more and more work down here. It wasn't something that occurred all at one time, as an idea, and it's come and gone with a lot of different circumstances and, of course, with money. I'm very interested in not destroying the buildings, if they have any good qualities at all as they were built originally. Usually the buildings have been drastically damaged. Also, sometimes the buildings aren't really very interesting, or I have particular purposes for a part of the building. In some cases, very different things have been done inside the buildings, but again, sort of as a parallel to the attitude toward science, I don't think anything should be done in the buildings that goes against what they were or their original nature. So I think there should be a greater respect for the past, the buildings, and all things than there generally is.

Those two buildings were artillery sheds, which means they were for trucks and half-tracks and probably a little cannon for the army, and they were in very bad shape. The sides that are now glass had garage doors that worked like an ordinary suburban garage door; those were all broken, and [it was] very confusing on the ceiling. We tore all those out and I designed the new windows. At the time of designing the new windows, I also figured out the works that go in there. It is individual work – it could be somewhere else, but it was made to go in those buildings, and made to always be there.

The aluminum pieces: there's a hundred of them [see image 61]. They were figured out in a relatively short time. The idea with the concrete pieces [see image 60] was to do them one by one and think about them from one to the second, then the third one, and so on, but the construction was very difficult. We did the first one by itself, but then after that it was two or three at a time; and then the situation with the Dia foundation was very disagreeable, and that interfered a lot.[2] So basically, they were done in groups, like the aluminum pieces. But I wanted to do them in a more slow and experimental way. They're laid out on a level part of the land. It's land that was already torn up and used; I've been trying to allow it to grow back for more than ten years. As you know, they're a stretch of one kilometer on the only part of the field, really, that's level, and they're directly north and south. I think it's rather obvious that the work should – I don't call it "sculpture," incidentally – that the work should sit on the floor or sit on the ground, and that any other arrangement is the same as putting a picture in a frame. So to me it was logical to put the work directly on the floor, in contrast to all previous three-dimensional work, or sculpture, so-called, which had been on pedestals – which really comes back to putting the figure on a pedestal. So just as the picture in the frame is obsolete, the figure on the pedestal is obsolete.

I wouldn't be able to run around the world having exhibitions in very strange spaces if I didn't have a situation that was permanent, where the work looked normal and right to me. So this is my tradeoff. I lose a lot of pieces because they have to be sold; it's very important to me to maintain a balance between what I can keep and what I have to sell. And if you sell it, it always ends up in bad circumstances, so it's important to have some of it in proper circumstances, which can only be here – and then the building in New York, too.[3] It's a building from 1870, actually a cast-iron building, and it has that quality. What I've done to the inside, I think, doesn't violate the nature of the building.

I think that the art that's done now should be installed more or less as the artist wants, or in what I consider normal circumstances, which could be abnormal for the public, but normal for the artist, and should remain that way – and that things should not be constantly moved around and made into some sort of entertainment business. I don't think art is show business, and it's not commerce. When it's produced – generally, when it's around someone's studio – it's in a very different situation than when it's in a museum or a gallery, and the attitude and the architecture of museums and galleries are very different from the original attitude of the work. In a way, it's a falsification of the work. If you put paintings by Pollock, or Rothko, or Barnett Newman into The Museum of Modern Art, which is a relatively moderne, fascist building, you put them in a fascist context. That's bound to change people's attitude toward the art and make it look different.

Generally, expensive art is in expensive, chic circumstances; it's a falsification. The society is basically not interested in art. And most people who are artists do that because they like the work; they like to do that [make art]. Art has an integrity of its own and a purpose of its own, and it's not to serve the society. That's been tried now in the Soviet Union and lots of places, and it doesn't work. The only role I can think of, in a very general way, for the artist is that it [art] tends to shake up the society a little bit just by its existence, in which case it helps undermine the general political stagnation and, perhaps by providing a little freedom, supports science, which requires freedom. If the artist isn't free, you won't have any art. If Jesse Helms runs it, you're not going to have any art.[4] There's no such thing as public art, because if you're making public art, you're making a monument for George Bush or something.

Art, at this time, is done by individuals; it's not done by institutions or for institutions. Therefore, the same art, whether it occurs in private or in public, is the same art, done by one artist. It's a big mistake to make two categories; I think it's been very destructive to have made those two categories.

You have to make new art all the time, because it has to be the individual's own art. There's no way to revive old forms or to rework old forms, because the artist is never going to understand them well enough to do first-rate work. So if you want to rework Matisse, you'll just be a bad Matisse, that's all. There's nothing to be gained by that. So in order to do work comparable to Matisse, for example, you have to invent as much as Matisse did.

Architecture and art are not the same thing. Naturally, it's very important in the architecture that there is a function, where to violate the function is simply to be ridiculous. That's one of the reasons why architects are so fond of museums: they don't think there's a function. The art isn't anything to them. Therefore, they can make very strange shapes and be the artists themselves. This produces a very awful Disneyland situation. To see a form that does nothing whatsoever, like Peter Eisenman's stairs going up and ending in midair, or columns that don't do anything, or spaces that don't work or don't do anything, or are strange shapes, is simply ridiculous.[5] I think good architecture, and in fact almost the definition of architecture, is that there has to be both an inside and outside to a building, to a space. If the inside is not evident, you can't have a really good building; if you were really strict about it, perhaps you couldn't even call it architecture. And I've written before that, say, the skyscrapers in Dallas or Houston are not really buildings and they're not really architecture.[6] They're basically just large toys in the landscape.

It has to work visually first, spatially. What I originally did pretty much turns out to be simple proportions in the long run. All the first things were trial and error. They turned out to be very close to 1:2 or 2:3, 3:4, but I wouldn't – if you had told me to start from the beginning with 1:2, 3:4, and so on, I would've been very suspicious and skeptical about it. So it's only the other way around that it seems valid. I tended to be skeptical of the great emphasis placed upon proportion in traditional architecture, but it turns out to be valid, I think. In contrast to, say, the complicated proportions of Palladio, the proportions that I use – and the proportions I think that you can understand – are relatively simple proportions. Basically, it's being able to understand something that defines space, whether it's a building or whether it's a three-dimensional work of art. We understand symmetry easiest, and our general tendency is to look at things that way and, especially if it's architecture, to be able to comprehend it pretty quickly – just so you don't get lost in it, for example. [*Laughs*] Symmetry, of course, can seem a restriction to people, and it's very nice to have some good reasons for not doing it. As far as architecture goes, the landscape or existing buildings, which have to be dealt with, are a good reason for breaking the symmetry. The art has to have a certain flexibility. While it can be very symmetrical, you have to have possibilities for it not to be symmetrical.

I'm absolutely against the division of thought and feeling, or mind and body, form and content in art – that whole big area. Therefore, rational and irrational are not sensible positions to me. I think it's a false division in philosophy that's fairly destructive. It's a division that somebody made a few thousand years ago which still is around, and it's one of the major ways to talk about art. It causes a lot of trouble and provides no information and should simply be forgotten.

Both three-dimensional art – painting is a somewhat ambiguous situation – and architecture make space. You could say they define space, but that assumes that space existed prior to the definition, which is debatable. By making lines or points or planes in space, you actually make the space. The thing that a person likes most about three-dimensional art or architecture is the created space. That's the main given aspect of it – basically, it's that and the color.

Furniture is furniture. The color is not so particular to the furniture as it is to the art. And the fact is that there are some horrible colors, but mainly, most artificial colors are just fine. There's a whole European RAL book of colors, and all of them are fine.[7] They come and you spray them on. There's a couple of ugly ones, but even that you should question. In regard to both the color and the material, these are things that I consider primarily given; they already exist in the world, and I'm interested in using them as they are, and in their nature as they are.

Philosophically, it's probably very dangerous to say that time and space don't exist. You'd have to really read a lot, I think, and work on that. But there is no space in itself, as a something that continues throughout everywhere, and there is no time that goes on and on and on and on and is something all by itself. Neither one of those are things are all by themselves, like ether. They're made by something happening in them, in the case of time, or by something existing in them, in the case of space. So those are the things that continue, or do something. But the time and space in themselves are just the way we feel about the whole situation. We have a sense of time because we live a certain length of time. It's functional, just like the way you don't trip over the chair, either, but that doesn't mean it's true scientifically.

I hope the foundation won't be destroyed.[8] I think everything is against the existence of the foundation. I basically take the institutions as enemies of the existence of art and doing anything in a normal, natural way; the problem is that the foundation not be seized by the museums or by some public institution. And the foundation will have more and more works of art by other people. Also, I'd like to point out that the foundation and I are not the same thing: the foundation is a public institution, unfortunately, and at this point the foundation is a lot smaller than my own private activities and buildings. Eventually, there will be two foundations side by side – the Chinati Foundation and one using my name[9] – all of which is to remain and be permanent.

CF   [Chris Felver] If you had a wish on any subject on this day, what would it be?

DJ   I'd like a few million dollars to do what I want to do. [*Laughs*]

CF   And what would you do?

DJ   Same thing I'm doing right now and have been doing. Should I specify how many millions maybe, just to be safe? [*Laughs*]

This conversation was sourced from the film *Donald Judd's Marfa, Texas*. It was transcribed in the order that the edited conversation was presented in the film.

First published: *Donald Judd's Marfa, Texas*, directed by Chris Felver (published by the director, 1995), digital video, 25 min.

1   Judd refers here to Rancho El Porvenir, in the canyon of Arroyo Grande, Baja California, on which nothing was ever built. See Judd's "Arroyo Grande" (1989) in *Donald Judd: Architektur*, 22–25.

2   In 1978, Judd and Dia Art Foundation entered into a partnership over Judd's "Marfa project." After a separation with Dia in 1986, the "Marfa project" was realized by Judd as the Chinati Foundation, established to preserve permanent large-scale installations by a select group of artists; it opened to the public in 1986. See Judd's "Statement for the Chinati Foundation/La Fundación Chinati" (1987) in *Donald Judd Writings*, 484–89.

3   Judd refers here to 101 Spring Street.

4   Jesse Helms (1921–2008) was an American conservative politician and a senator from North Carolina from 1973 to 2003, particularly known for his leading role in the censorship wars of the late 1980s and early 1990s. He repeatedly fought to forbid the National Endowment for the Arts from awarding grants to artists whose work he considered "obscene."

5   Judd likely refers here to Eisenman's House VI, completed in 1975 in Cornwall, Connecticut, which features all of these elements.

6   See Judd's "A Long Discussion Not About Master-Pieces But Why There Are So Few of Them: Part I" (1983) and "Fine Art and Commercial Architecture" (1992) in *Donald Judd Writings*, 352–76 and 778–89, respectively. The former article has more than one part: see also Judd's "A Long Discussion Not About Master-Pieces But Why There Are So Few of Them: Part II" (1984) in *Donald Judd Writings*, 378–97. "Part I" was first published in *Art in America*, September 1984, 9–19; "Part II" was first published in *Art in America*, October 1984, 9–15.

7   Judd used the RAL industrial color standard system to select the colors of his multicolored works.

8   Judd refers here to the Chinati Foundation.

9   Judd refers here to the Judd Foundation, conceived by Judd in 1977 to maintain and preserve his permanently installed living and working spaces, archives, and libraries in New York and Marfa, Texas. See Judd's "Judd Foundation" (1977) in *Donald Judd Writings*, 284–86.

Interview with Gunnar Jóhannes Árnason,
Ingólfur Arnarsson, and Pétur Arason
July 1992

Judd exhibited his works for the first time in Iceland at The Living Art Museum in
1988, during the biannual Reykjavík Arts Festival, in the show *Donald Judd, Richard Long, Kristján Guðmundsson* (June 4–19, 1988), curated by Pétur Arason. In the
summer of 1992, he also had an exhibition in the Slunkariki gallery in Ísafjörður,
in the Westfjords of Iceland. Judd had first traveled to Iceland in the early 1980s.

This interview was conducted in Reykjavík in July 1992. An abridged version
was published in November 1992 in *Myndvagl*, a school paper made by the students of the Icelandic College of Art and Crafts, Reykjavík.

The transcript from which this interview was sourced makes no distinction
between the three interviewers, and as no known audio recording of the interview exists, the editors have used the generic "interviewer" to apply to Árnason,
Arnarsson, and Arason.

I [Interviewer] Let's say there is such a creature as the "ideal viewer"; how should he react to your works, what should he look for in them?

DJ [Donald Judd] I realized long ago that you can't be thinking of the viewer. There are too many people in the world, too many very different people. Anyway, when I started out on my career in the States, I was very isolated, I had no viewers. Until my 1963 show [see images 2, 3], there was literally no one who knew of my art.[1]

I But if you look at it from your own point of view, you might say that a work is finished only when it has been perceived. Only then can it be said to have been brought to a conclusion.

DJ I can see that, but others do not necessarily see things my way. It's a question of how you look. Of course, there are certain things that everyone should be able to notice: the size of an object, its placement on a wall, and so on. I assume that if a work is explained to me, that if it makes sense to me, it may also make sense to others.

I Should the viewer be wondering what Donald Judd is thinking in a particular work, or why he is doing things this way and not in another way? Does it matter?

DJ The viewer may think what he likes. Given the enormous number of people in the world, what's the point of pondering what others are thinking? This is one way of looking at it. The other thing to remember is that the United States is a fairly barbaric society, so that one has no way of knowing what people there are thinking, if at all.

When I started out, there was no common ground. The artists that I was thinking about were nowhere near. I knew hardly any artists. To make a work with one eye on what others might possibly be thinking is simply too vast an undertaking, too vague, too complicated.

I It must be disappointing when critics misunderstand your works entirely.

DJ   Critics – what's now written about art is horrible, almost worthless, and this has been going on for a number of years. Present-day criticism is amazingly unimaginative. People pick up the wrong ideas from each other and perpetuate them endlessly. There is no serious thought involved to begin with. I didn't realize how serious the situation was, so I didn't try to counter it. I should have. But you can't put an end to this ceaseless chatter about "minimalism" and all the rest. The superficiality is astounding. These things go round and round, and before you know it, they have been published.

I   But surely some writers are more perceptive than others?

DJ   Some writers are better than others, but most of their writing is abysmal. The state of criticism is so low that I don't really want to think about it. It achieves nothing. It would be nice if there was someone out there with the ability to write something worth thinking about, but there isn't. Everything comes out as simplistic or downright wrong. Even when a show is criticized favorably, it means nothing.

I   Are the criteria you apply to your works equally applicable to other art forms – architecture, for instance? Are your works based on some kind of "common aesthetic"? Are you aiming for such an aesthetic?

DJ   I tend to think so. Of course, I work from a common bank of ideas, based on certain consistent aesthetic beliefs, but I try not to air these beliefs publicly. I have difficulty in speaking about what I am doing. It's easier for me to write it down. But I haven't done what Ad Reinhardt did, which was to make a list of dos and don'ts.[2] It's not a bad idea to do so, but I haven't done it.

     I certainly believe in the common ground between art and architecture. But, as I have stated a thousand times, the two should be kept separate. Blurring the distinctions between the two only confuses architects.

I   That brings to mind the photographs we've seen of your
    place in Marfa, Texas. They show brick walls, mazes, an
    arena, and so forth. Do you regard these edifices as works
    of art?

DJ That's a difficult question, for I differentiate in principle
    between art and architecture. These buildings are a con-
    tinuation of the artworks, sure, but they are also architec-
    tural creations, so that in this particular case the question
    is left open. They are somewhere in between, especially
    the ones without a roof; they are really of no proper "use."
    I changed the Arena a bit, which made a great difference,
    since I was able to create a space which has always pleased
    me. I haven't put any artworks in that building; I like it as
    it is.

I   Do you consider your artworks in any way as archetypes
    for other designed or crafted objects?

DJ Everything is a model for something else. "Archetype" is
    a dangerous term. When you have a good work of art, it
    becomes the archetype for a "good work of art." There are
    no such models in architecture. But one shouldn't con-
    sciously aim to create models, to use art to control or in-
    doctrinate. Pedagogic art is bad art.

I   What do you think of Walter Gropius's assertion that
    we should stop thinking about art and start thinking
    about architecture, that if we start there, art will follow
    naturally?

DJ It won't happen. I don't think he could have cared much
    about art, saying that. Art is a very special discipline, a fact
    all too many people don't seem to appreciate. I have been
    opposing people who think of art as unimportant, who
    don't think of it as a real discipline, for a very long time.
    True artists are very rare; there aren't six million of them,
    it only seems so. People think of us as being freer than
    architects, and I think they are right; we are allowed all
    kinds of crazy stunts. Unlike architects, we don't need to

think of the usefulness and the context of our creations. We can take the Perlan as an example, or the national library building in Reykjavík, which is just as bad – and I'm not saying that the architectural situation is any worse in Iceland than it is elsewhere, it's pretty bad everywhere – the fact remains that the Perlan represents the attempt of an architect to create a work of art, while blatantly disregarding the fact that it dominates a cityscape completely and destroys the existing harmony between the local landscape and architecture.[3] In architecture, you have to take all these things into account. It's okay for artists to aim for fantastic effects, but an architect shouldn't be thinking in those terms.

I   Do you have ambitions to design both a house and its interior?

DJ   I've come close to doing that. The interior of my house in Switzerland is more or less my own [images 81, 82].[4] But I don't necessarily want to design all of these things myself. I like having furniture and works of art by other people around me. In my house in Switzerland there is mainly furniture by Alvar Aalto, but not that many works of art. But my house on Spring Street, in New York, is mostly my own creation. I don't keep many works of mine there, mostly works by other artists.

I   Are there any architects who have inspired you?

DJ   Mostly older architects. Louis Kahn is the youngest of them. I recently saw buildings by the Japanese architect Tadao Ando; one could say a lot about him, criticizing him is a big task. It's not architecture of the first order. It does give you something to think about, though not much. When it comes to past architecture, I confess a fondness for Frank Lloyd Wright and Mies van der Rohe.

I   What about older architecture? The Renaissance period, for instance?

DJ   I taught myself to appreciate the architecture of Brunelleschi and Alberti. I was interested in their buildings before I had a chance to see them. I still appreciate them. I also like traditional Japanese architecture. When it comes to modern Japanese architecture, Tadao Ando is the best; the rest is pretty horrible. The affluent part of Osaka looks like Perlan. If this is the future, we should all be worried. When every plot in Reykjavík has been built on, when you won't be able to see either land or water, it will look exactly like Osaka.

I   We'd like to talk about the materials you use. When you pick a particular material, are you aware of its meaning, its associations?

DJ   It's best to ignore these things.

I   Is it possible to do that?

DJ   Why not? When you start worrying about what others might be thinking, or how they would interpret something you are doing, you're on the wrong track. You mustn't let others turn perfectly good material into something unacceptable, just because they have used it badly. You mustn't rule it out. I can't stand formica panels myself, but someone else might be able to do something with them. Everyone wants to stay clear of bronze or marble, because these materials carry such heavy cultural connotations. When you say that something is "symbolic" it really means that it has become meaningless, a mere question of definition. Bronze is a fine material, not as fragile as many others. I don't know if marble has become too "dangerous." Certain precious materials are probably difficult to work with. I avoid marble, but I think one ought to forget all about material's associations. If you didn't, it would be like being dictated to by the tourist trade. That mustn't happen. Marble comes with certain built-in clichés; we have been conditioned to regard it as costly, inherently noble, historical, and so on, which is how tourists think. It's best to forget all about that.

I   We'd like to ask you about color. It says somewhere that you picked the colors for some of your works from a color chart for Harley-Davidson motorcycles.[5]

DJ   I have always used premixed colors. They are chosen, not mixed. I was only interested in the varnish because it was semitransparent. You could see the galvanized metal under the varnish, and these were the choices I had. But I didn't care about the motorcycles themselves, and in any case, I didn't use the colors like the motorcycle people did, because they start by sealing the surface, covering it up. I like materials because of their inherent qualities, not because of the layers of "meaning" that they have acquired. They are what they are.

I   Where you use wood for your sculptures, you invariably use plywood, not the "finer" type of wood that furniture makers do.

DJ   Peter [Ballantine] is trained to use plywood.[6] He is a great carpenter; he can put together things by dovetail jointing and so on. But we use plywood on purpose. [Giuseppe] Panza, who puts together works of mine by himself, uses a fine northern Italian plywood with a veneer.[7] But I use plywood where all the layers are identical. European plywood is usually knotted.

      I think technique can be an obstacle of sorts. That's also true of works made from galvanized steel; it's possible to do an even more meticulous job of them. You could weld the steel plates together so neatly that you wouldn't see any joints or screws. I don't want technique to take over. The same goes for architecture. I don't want the works to look "well made."

I   But you also like things to be "well made."

DJ   Of course. Some of the furniture that I've designed, especially the massive pieces, are "well made," in the traditional sense; they have dovetail joints, which adjust to changes in temperature and so forth. You can do this with massive wood, but not with plywood. My plywood chairs are put together with ordinary wood glue and screws.

I   But you don't think art ought to be "well made."

DJ   Everyone has his own objective. A work of art wouldn't be very good if the artist's technique was the first thing you worried about. My wood furniture is put together very well, but it doesn't look well crafted. Things ought to be well made. If they aren't, they also bother you. I expect there is a middle course here. When I started on my three-dimensional pieces, I didn't want carpentry, so the workmanship is rough; I sort of threw them together. But then I found that their roughness was in the way. I didn't always hit the nails on the head, there were cracks and abrasions, so in the end I tried to stay clear of that kind of thing.

I   Have you given much thought to art education?

DJ   I've given it some thought, yes. I think artists have an unusual education. But I have to think this through. The problem is that you really can't teach anything to anybody; that's what my experience tells me. I'm not alone in thinking this. At the same time there is obviously so much that needs to be taught, because one is always coming across people, in museums and galleries, who know next to nothing, and one wishes someone would give them an education. There is a very widespread lack of education.

Firstly, all art students should passionately want to become artists. Otherwise I don't see how a real artist can cope with the other 90 percent who never turn into artists. How can you adjust to that? So if you take into account the 10 percent who really want to become artists, then you have to treat them as artists from the very beginning, because they are doing the same kind of thing as the "professionals," only more rudimentary. They are trying to work out what they want to do. The teacher has to present points of view and furnish information, especially about history. You also have to take art history out of the hands of the art historians. It is also important that art students get first-class artists to teach them, not just ordinary teachers, and these artists are obliged to communicate their knowledge to others. The role of the teacher is to give students what they need in order to develop their own work. It serves no purpose to teach them skills which they have no need for. Once it was the fashion to teach everyone to weld, because everyone wanted to be like David Smith. But there were people who had no need for welding. If someone really wants to learn how to draw the figure, someone ought to teach that to them, though I myself am not keen on the idea. It's the same as with welding; it shouldn't be a part of a general course, but be taught privately, when a student feels the need for it.

You always need to point out context, to make students aware of earlier artists, especially students of architecture, who think that forms have no meaning and no history, so that when you get one of them putting together two disparate ideas – ideas that originally belonged to two very different artists, to whom they were desperately important – you should point out to him that he is dealing with two contrasting philosophical viewpoints.

I   Art schools often work from a basic educational model, a combination of nineteenth-century academic values and Bauhaus ideals, which consists of certain "classic" subjects, subjects which everyone is supposed to benefit from.

DJ   I was very much against learning something that I really didn't want to learn. But you make mistakes. I didn't want to study [Josef] Albers's theories on colors. No one tried to teach me his or anybody else's color theories, but also, I felt I had no use for them. I do think color is a much-neglected subject in art education, even today. Color is the study of the future. Maybe a course on colors could go back to the very beginning of things.

I You mentioned the importance of models. Students tend to get hold of a model and stick to it. Do you think that's a problem?

DJ Yes, I do. But it's something you can't avoid. Everyone idolizes someone. I think it's one of the reasons why people become artists. You have to realize how other people do things, how far you can take something, what you should stay clear of. Everyone has a positive role model. I think that art education should tackle the process of becoming an artist. You should look upon this process as something constructive, not as a boring preliminary to the "real" task of being an artist. The same is true of other subjects — in physics, for instance. Some physics students are doing things that are so remarkable that no one realizes that they are just students. But if students only want to learn about art, that's a different thing altogether and has to be handled differently. If they only want to know about what's happening in the arts, the teaching should be restructured. It's bad to have a studio full of people who don't intend to become artists. I attended classes in the Art Students League, a dreadful school, but it was the only one available.[8] It was just after World War II and two-thirds of the students were ex-soldiers on the GI Bill. There were also a lot of housewives there. In each class there were perhaps four students who were serious about becoming artists.

I Art schools usually cater both to art and the crafts, textiles and ceramics, for instance. Should all these disciplines be taught within the same institution, or should the crafts be kept separate?

DJ I think you should classify the crafts with the arts. It depends on their usefulness, though. Best thing is to leave out the "crafts" bit, just talk of "arts." Nevertheless, the so-called crafts are very much looked down on in the United States and Europe. The situation is very different in Japan or Korea. Good ceramics hardly exist in the Western world. Our clay bowls or jars are useless and most of our "artistic" ceramics are horrible creations.

I   Young artists in the Western hemisphere have recently shown an interest in faraway cultures. Do you think that any art that originates outside the mainstream of Western modernism has any chance of being recognized internationally?

DJ   I am now working on a series of articles on art and internationalism, which is a vast subject and a very important one.[9] It's fine if people develop a serious interest in the art of other cultures, the art of the past, or what's commonly called folk art. The things I encountered in Korea when I was there in 1947 [see image 19] have now been placed in museums or specially designed museum villages.[10] It's a peculiar situation, if you think of it in terms of its thousand-year-old history. Looking at Seoul, you realize that the Koreans don't seem to have learned anything from their traditional architecture. The Japanese have learned nothing from their old architecture, either. People should know about these things and be prepared to learn from them.

Nationalism is of course a very sensitive subject. To start with, you have to differentiate absolutely between art and politics. No culture can create an art that serves only its nationalistic sentiments or some political purpose. It cannot be done, it's too farfetched. Art is too international. It would be like developing a provincial tradition in science; it's out of the question.

You can have an advanced internationalism, as in astronomy, which bypasses the whole idea of nationhood, or you can have an internationalism in architecture, which means that people build the same kind of houses, whether they live in Reykjavík, Seoul, or Russia. This is the reverse side of the internationalist coin. No attempt is made to utilize the materials that are indigenous to each place, no account is taken of localized knowledge and traditions. I've noticed a lot of sand and gravel in Iceland, yet no one puts this black building material to use. No one seems to have learned anything from Guðjón Samúelsson's fine buildings.[11]

I   Does this also apply to art?

DJ   Art has more freedom, it doesn't need to respect local circumstances. Art is essentially more international than architecture. Internationalism is dangerous because it can become so trivial. Large international units, such as multinational corporations, are dangerous. Provincialism is also dreary, and large chunks of localized nationalism, such as you get in the United States, is terrifying.

I   This is the fifth time you've come to Iceland. What is the attraction?

DJ   The first time I came because of the Icelandic sagas, bringing my two children with me.[12] I think it was 1981.

I   What was it about the sagas that attracted you?

DJ   They are about the only thing that exists from this period. They describe an even earlier period and a way of life so lucidly. They are about people rather than religion. If they'd been about myths, I wouldn't have been interested. Gods are so boring.

Then I came back in 1988 to show in The Living Art Museum with Richard Long and Kristján Guðmundsson. Originally, I thought of settling in Iceland. I was looking for a piece of land, but when I arrived in Iceland it was already too late; my place in Texas had become a reality. I was a few years too late. I would have been an outsider here, but for that matter, I'm an outsider in Texas, too, so it's the same difference. I was scared of the language; it would have been hard for me to learn Icelandic. But I expect I would have done things exactly the same way that I did in Texas, if I'd arrived earlier. I wanted to escape the United States, because it was becoming unbearable there.

Translated from the Icelandic by Aðalsteinn Ingólfsson.

This discussion was sourced from an archival English transcript in the Judd Foundation Archives, Marfa, Texas. The interview was originally conducted in English; subsequently, Gunnar Jóhannes Árnason edited and translated the text into Icelandic, and his finished version was then retranslated into English by Aðalsteinn Ingólfsson in order to share it with Judd.

First published (excerpt): Gunnar Jóhannes Árnason, Ingólfur Arnarsson, and Pétur Arason, "Donald Judd," *Myndvagl*, November 1992, n.p.

1   *Don Judd*, Green Gallery, New York, December 17, 1963–January 11, 1964. This exhibition was Judd's first solo show to include works in three dimensions.

2   Judd refers here to Reinhardt's 1957 *ARTnews* article "Twelve Rules for a New Academy," which includes multiple lists of dos and don'ts. See Reinhardt, "Twelve Rules for a New Academy," in *Art-as-Art: The Selected Writings of Ad Reinhardt*, ed. Barbara Rose (New York: Viking Press, 1975), 203–7. Judd included this book in his library in Marfa, Texas.

3   Perlan ("Pearl" in English), Reykjavík, is a 1991 building designed by Ingimundur Sveinsson. It is composed of a glass dome atop six tanks that serve as the city's water reservoir.

4   Judd refers here to Eichholteren.

5   Judd used Harley-Davidson hi-fi blue lacquer on a 1964 wall-mounted work [see image 9].

6   From 1971 to the end of Judd's life, Peter Ballantine was the primary fabricator of Judd's works in plywood.

7   Giuseppe Panza di Biumo (1923–2010) was a prominent Italian collector of modern art. See Judd's "Una stanza per Panza" (1990) in *Donald Judd Writings*, 630–99.

8   Judd attended the Art Students League, in New York, during the day from 1948 to 1953, while also working toward an undergraduate degree at night at Columbia University.

9   See Judd's "Art and Internationalism" (1992) in *Donald Judd Writings*, 766–77.

10   Judd enlisted in the United States Army on June 28, 1946, and was assigned to the Corps of Engineers in Korea. He was honorably discharged on November 20, 1947.

11   Guðjón Samúelsson (1887–1950) was a state architect of Iceland and the first Icelander to be formally educated in architecture. His designs include the main building of the University of Iceland, the National Theatre of Iceland, and the iconic Hallgrímskirkja church.

12   Judd included dozens of books of Icelandic sagas in his library in Marfa, Texas.

"Interview with Donald Judd"
With Katharina Winnekes for *Kunst und Kirche*
December 14, 1992

Kunst und Kirche (*Art and Church*) is a quarterly ecumenical art magazine that explores religious and philosophical ideas within art and architecture. Katharina Winnekes, an editor at the magazine, visited Judd in Cologne and Marfa, Texas. According to Winnekes, the issue of *Kunst und Kirche* in which this article appears, titled "Raumerfahrung" ("Spatial Experience"), explored approaches to "assembling examples of rooms with different purposes and thinking about their different qualities and qualitative implications that may carry beyond their functional purpose."

In 1987, Judd wrote about St. Isaac's Cathedral in Saint Petersburg, and the following year he wrote about Santa Maria del Mar in Barcelona, which he describes in this conversation as having proportions that are "absolutely complete."

K W   [Katharina Winnekes] In Marfa, Texas, you are working
as an architect, as a sculptor, as a curator, as a writer, and as
a rancher. In a way, I think you are working on a utopian
scheme. What is the aim of all of your different efforts?

D J   [Donald Judd] It's a very complicated question. I believe
it's not utopian, it's real. I don't think utopia will come.
At least not for thousands of years. The chances are that it
will never come.

K W   Are you thinking of social structures or different contexts?

D J   In all ways – in regard to what I can do. And I can do my
own work. That's the clearest category. Also architecture
a little bit, since I'm not a trained architect. Mostly I'm
dealing with old buildings. I can write a little bit. You can't
alter the society, but you can try to be perfectly critical of
the society. And I have some ideas about what is wrong
with it. I'm absolutely pessimistic about having any effect
on it or changing it. But in a little way, I can make a better example in a small place like the country in West Texas.

K W   In spite of your basically pessimistic attitude, you take the
chance to change something?

D J   Yes, I'm very pessimistic, but I also think that it's absolutely
necessary to do what you can. I'm very much against be-
ing pessimistic and doing nothing. You know, between the
wars and the depressions and all the troubles, you can't be
optimistic about things. But I also really object to the people who sit around complacently being lazy and not being interested. Certainly it won't change if you don't do
anything. And there will be no example for later.

K W   What is your personal view of architecture concerning intention and function?

D J   I think that the particular function of a train station, a
warehouse, or somebody's kitchen is very important. But
I think I probably have a different idea of what is an agreeable space than that of most architects and most people.

K W   Can you describe this idea of a liveable space?

D J   The easiest thing is to say that it is larger. Most spaces to me are too small. Of course, that has to do with economics. But it's really just a matter of attitude. I think it's very important to have a connection with the outside and that the inside and the outside are not separate from each other. But the most important thing is to make spaces that are well proportioned, that feel good, and are dignified.

K W   What does it mean, "well proportioned"? Are you thinking of the golden section?

D J   My idea of proportion is simpler than that, although it's rather complicated to explain. My first work was developed by looking. Then I figured out that many things were very close to even proportions. And slowly I made proportions even. I think what you see are just the simple ones, 1:2 and 2:3 and 3:4, not Palladio's elaborate proportions but Alberti's simple ones, as in the cathedral in Mantua.[1] An example of that is one of Frank Lloyd Wright's cheap houses. I was once asked to dinner, and the minute I went in, I felt that it was dignified. It wasn't big, it was rather small. But the spaces were good. The main quality is dignity, which is in very short supply in our days.

K W   When you talk about dignity, I just think of church spaces.

D J   Some spaces in churches are good. There is a cathedral in Barcelona called the Santa Maria del Mar.[2] The proportions are absolutely complete. The chapels and the nave and the vertical section and the whole thing – I think it's on a module of two and a half times one thing. It is completely worked out. When I first went there I felt that there was something good about it. I thought it must be the proportions. Then I bought a book that had simple plans, and I started to analyze it all. And it all worked out as an absolute scheme.

K W   There is some architecture which we perceive and make use of repugnantly. I'm thinking of fascist architecture, particularly.

D J   This may be because of the lack of a style or because of
      the lack of proportion. This is one of my definitions of
      fascist architecture. They don't know what they are do-
      ing. In addition, they want to show power, usually derived
      from earlier power. Like the new museums in Bonn.[3] I
      think what is especially aggressive in that is the lack of pro-
      portion and the lack of real space. Franco could not have
      made good architecture. I think there is a direct connec-
      tion with politics. It has to do with belief; people make
      space. Because space is nothing – it's a philosophical mat-
      ter. In a way, by making the space, they also make dignity,
      which is very much of value to people.

K W   Let's talk about sculpture. Would you say you are a sculptor?

D J   No, it means carving to me.

K W   So how would you say …

D J   I never had a word. "Fabricator" sounds like lying, so that's
      not good. "Sculptor" means carving, so that seems very
      inappropriate. It also means going in from the outside, to
      reach a core inside. I never had a word; I don't know. There
      is no word, really.

K W   What is your aim in making these objects you "fabricate"?

D J   The same as any art. That's a big question. I don't have it
      handy. I think, like all art, at perhaps any time, it's a to-
      tality of experience, the artist in regard to the world, to
      the universe, to society, and to very personal matters, all
      things at once. I think it's the all things at once without
      any regard for function. The architects can't and shouldn't
      do that; they should pay attention to function. There is a
      difference between art and architecture. The capacity of
      art to deal with your whole experience is the main defi-
      nition and the most important.

K W   Is art without function?

D J   Yes, I think it's pretty much without function. It usually
      doesn't keep the rain off. The worst thing to talk about is
      whether it has a social function. As we have no effect upon

the society, we are bound to think that it has no function in the society. I think art has a certain correspondence to freedom and that it might help to maintain freedom a little. Not much, but a little. It might be good for science or whatever is going on that's progressive at the time to have something a little divergent. We might be a little guarantee of freedom, which would be nice to think. It's perhaps being too optimistic.

KW   When we were in Marfa and visited the rooms and the houses, the predominant view was that everything was very straight and rather empty. And everything fits this straightness and this clarity. Is this impression connected with your definition of clarity?

DJ   Yes, sure. I'm very careful about the spaces, and I have thought about all of them a great deal. Also, I know everything can be an example. And everything is meant to stay that way: I want the spaces to be clear. But that doesn't mean necessarily a greater clarity or an abstract clarity. My clarity is just one person's clarity.

KW   Do you think that spaces have an effect on people?

DJ   Yes, I think so, but actually don't know. Yes: I think if there were good architecture throughout the world, everybody would be a lot happier. I think that people don't know the effect that bad spaces can have upon them. And I don't think they appreciate good spaces. And if you had really good architecture throughout the world, as, for instance, the traditional Japanese architecture was, I think unavoidably everybody would be a lot more cheerful.

KW   How would you describe your ideal room or house?

DJ   The Japanese houses in general – a strong relation between the inside and outside. I know about climate and heat and so on, but it's also a question of attitude again. I think all buildings should at least have balconies – that would be a big achievement – and there should be more access to the outside. Instead they go the other way, and all new apartment buildings in Japan and Korea ignore the old architecture. They are indoor boxes, like in Russia. It doesn't have to do with the climate. It's just a certain style.

KW   Have you ever thought about religious space and what it should look like?

DJ   In this we probably disagree. To me, all spaces in a fundamental way should be religious, because if you use the world "dignity," you are talking about religion and about spirituality. So I don't think it should be or it needs to be a distinct type of space. If you have a really well-developed space like the Santa Maria del Mar or the Cappella Pazzi, it seems to me that that is spiritual or religious. That doesn't mean that I agree on god and that philosophy.

KW   For whom do you make art and other things?

DJ   Art for me. I have to regard the art as only for myself, except that I know it will last. But I can't think of it publicly. I'm perfectly willing in regard to architecture or anything practical to think about it in relation to others, what they might want or need.

First published: Katharina Winnekes, "Interview mit Donald Judd," *Kunst und Kirche*, February 1993, 134–37 (in English and German).

1   Judd refers here to the Basilica of Sant'Andrea, in Mantua, Italy, which Alberti designed just before his death in 1472. Parts of the building's proportional system are based on the ratio 5:6.

2   "When I first saw Santa Maria del Mar, perhaps two years ago, I wondered why it was so fine, since it's plain, both in nature and because it was gutted in 1936. And then I realized that its proportions were very good, though now I don't remember in what way." See Judd's note from 20 February 1988 in *Donald Judd Writings*, 499.

3   Judd refers here to the Kunstmuseum Bonn (designed by Axel Schultes) and the Bundeskunsthalle (designed by Gustav Peichl), both completed in 1992 in Bonn, Germany. That same year, Judd wrote that "Gustav Peichl's new Bundeskunsthalle in Bonn, very general and bland, big and sightless, as in the 1930s, is in style fascist, neofascist." Judd, "Fine Art and Commercial Architecture" (1992) in *Donald Judd Writings*, 780.

"Donald Judd"
Interview from the book *Inside the Studio*
March 30, 1993

From 1981 until the mid-2000s, the New York–based arts organization Independent Curators International hosted "New York Studio Events," an annual spring benefit program consisting of ticketed visits to artists' studios. Conducted at 101 Spring Street as part of the 1993 edition of "New York Studio Events," this conversation was edited from an audio recording and included in *Inside the Studio: Two Decades of Talks with Artists in New York*, a 2004 collection that presents excerpts from nearly seventy artist talks held as part of the program. Audience members asked Judd questions throughout the studio visit; these were elided in the published conversation.

DJ   [Donald Judd] I've had this building for a long time, it's hardly ever had so many people in it.[1] This floor has had exhibitions by myself and by other artists. Ordinarily this is sort of a casual studio, things coming in and going out. The upper floors are partly studio, partly living, so it's a studio and a living space, but I also consider it sort of the last gasp of the situation in New York with Jackson Pollock, Barnett Newman, Mark Rothko, and all those people, and then of my own generation. The whole building is intended to stay exactly the way it is forever. When you see what's happening to the SoHo area, and what they're doing to the buildings, this building I think is important as an example of something serious done in its own time. So it's intended to be this way. The building was built in 1870 – the architect was Nicholas Whyte – so it's a little bit earlier than most of the buildings down here. It's also the only one [in New York] by Nicholas Whyte.

I have a number of architecture projects in Europe. I take it for granted by now that I've settled in as an artist, but the architecture is relatively new, and is becoming very serious, with a wide scope. I'm the coarchitect on the new part of the railroad station in Basel [image 83],[2] I'll probably build an archive and office for a new museum in Austria [image 84],[3] and so on. The railroad station, of course, comes with a developed architectural firm; they have forty people full time on this, plus there's a whole other firm. I worked on the building I have in Switzerland with a young architect there, so he did a lot of the work on the spot and in relationship to the carpenters and plumbers.[4] In Texas, a lot of people have their hands in it.[5] So the architecture's a serious enterprise, the writing is a serious enterprise, and so, of course, is the art. The architecture came about in a very natural way, very early on. Furniture to me is part of architecture, and the furniture I've made came about partly in relation to the installation of the art, partly because there was no way to buy anything I wanted to have. I made the first pieces for myself in Texas, because there was nothing whatsoever to buy, and it slowly developed in a very normal way. There's a lot of different kinds of furniture now: metal furniture, very well-made wooden furniture, well-made but cheaper plywood furniture. I don't like anybody else's furniture now, but I do have a lot of [Gerrit] Rietveld furniture and Mies van der Rohe furniture and [Marcel] Breuer and [Josef] Hoffmann.

History's constantly warped by various people; I thought Ad Reinhardt and Barney Newman were a little excessive in worrying about history, but if you've been around a while you do see bizarre histories, and then you get irritated. Actually, I was almost the first person to use color in so-called sculpture. John Chamberlain is prior in some way, and there are various connections that could be worked out, but I assumed my work would have color. I never thought otherwise, because I was a painter; I had no training in chopping marble or wood or anything, and always thought that was probably a horrifying thing to do. I think color is very important, and it's been very important to a lot of artists. It's a very, very big aspect of twentieth-century art, one of the biggest developments, though it's ordinarily not thought about very much.

So color has always been very important to me – my work began colored. And it's not that these works don't have color, it's that they're just one color. As far as being sensuous, to me that's dividing something, taking one aspect. Philosophically I'm very much against the division of thought and feeling, and to use an adjective like "sensuous" is to me already splitting it up. As far as being sensuous in an ordinary way, that's just fine. That always is. But the early ones had lots of color and they still do.

I've said this one million times and I hope the recording is working to hear me say it one million and one: "minimalism" was a derogatory term that someone coined. Barbara Rose gave "ABC" a try, and that was derogatory.[6] The "primary structures" term was not meant to be derogatory, but it was very misleading: there is no such style and there was no such group.[7] It's very easy to find out there wasn't a group. I hardly knew Robert Morris; I met him in March or April maybe of '63. I had a show at the end of that year [see images 2, 3], so I didn't have anything to do with Morris's work.[8] Also, his work comes out of Duchamp. I knew Dan Flavin for about a year prior to that and I didn't know him well. And there was no discussion. There was no group. Sol LeWitt is many years later. Carl Andre I met because he was a friend of Frank Stella's, but he told me on the street, walking along, that he carved things out of wood, and at that point he was also flirting with my then wife, and I stopped listening to Carl. Three or four years passed before I had any idea what he was doing, when he finally had an exhibition.

That's the so-called original minimal. Since then, half the world has become minimal, but that's just more publicity. Now Stella's considered a minimal artist, and so are a whole bunch of painters – so in no way was it a group. These people didn't know each other. The idea of a minimalist movement is a very careless falsification of the history. At any time, you're going to have certain correspondences between the best artists, which is ignored, too. People don't talk about that, and that's a legitimate thing to write about; you can say there are certain things in common between me and Claes Oldenburg, say. But I naturally feel I'm an independent artist, and I don't like suddenly disappearing into some group that I consider to be nonsense.

To make more pieces, we have to sell pieces. I would like to keep everything except for the fact that in my case, if you think about one piece, you've thought about a dozen, and it would become preposterous to keep all of them. So there is a natural overflow, but basically, except that we need the money, I'd prefer that these works were in Texas. Well, the art business is not so good now, and the happy thing about that is you get to keep more pieces. So I have a lot. I have almost all the first reliefs, almost all the paintings. Almost all of the first three-dimensional pieces are in Texas because no one was interested in buying them. And I'm, as usual, worried about the rent and such things, but now we have them and they're permanently installed in Texas.

Being an empiricist, I'm a little down on ideals. I never understood perfection, and I'm still trying to figure out what "pure" means – they jumped on Ad Reinhardt for being "pure," and I've never understood what "pure" was. I think it's a very strange word. It's something that needs to be traced. Elaine de Kooning wrote an article against Reinhardt calling him "Mr. Pure," and I don't know – is she "Ms. Impure"?[9] People are very free with the word and I don't really quite know what it means. I suppose it comes out of Plato.

I probably have a pretty definite philosophy and I take philosophical ideas, political ideas, social ideas perfectly seriously. And as you can see, for thirty or forty years, the ideas in my work haven't changed too much. And that's what I intended in the first place. I wanted something that would develop naturally without being forced, and it changes on its own or as I go along. I don't expect a great contradiction at some point. There won't be a big revelation and I go to Rome and meet the pope.

First published: "Donald Judd," in Judith Olch Richards, ed., *Inside the Studio: Two Decades of Talks with Artists in New York* (New York: Independent Curators International, 2004), 118–21.

1   Judd refers here to 101 Spring Street.

2   Judd refers here to the Peter Merian Haus in Basel, next to the Bahnhof Basel SSB (the city's central train station). Judd worked in collaboration with Zwimpfer Partner Architekten to design the façade of the building, an alternating matte and transparent glass exterior. The building was completed in 2000.

3   In 1991, Judd was approached to design the administrative building of the Kunsthaus Bregenz in Bregenz, Austria. Judd produced drawings for the building in 1992, but due to his death in 1994, Peter Zumthor, lead architect for the Kunsthaus Bregenz, realized the building according to his own design in 1997.

4   Judd refers here to Eichholteren and to the Swiss architect Adrian Jolles, whom Judd hired to work on a number of projects, including Eichholteren, the administrative building of the Kunsthaus Bregenz, and a group of three fountains Judd designed for the city of Winterthur, Switzerland.

5   Judd refers here to his architectural work at Judd Foundation and the Chinati Foundation in Marfa, Texas.

6   Judd refers here to terminology used by Barbara Rose in her article "ABC Art," *Art in America*, October–November 1965, 57–69, which was one of the first essays devoted to defining minimalism as a style.

7   *Primary Structures* was the name of an influential exhibition of so-called minimalist art that included work by Judd: *Primary Structures: Younger American and British Sculptors*, Jewish Museum, New York, April 27–June 12, 1966. For a symposium on this exhibition, see "The New Sculpture" (1966) in this volume, 90–102.

8   *Don Judd*, Green Gallery, New York, December 17, 1963–January 11, 1964. This exhibition was Judd's first solo show to include works in three dimensions.

9   Elaine de Kooning, "Pure Paints a Picture," *ARTnews*, Summer 1957, 57, 86–87.

Interview with Hans Keller
For the television program *Roerend Goed*
Summer 1993

This conversation with Judd was filmed and conducted by Dutch filmmaker Hans Keller in Marfa, Texas, for the weekly Dutch television talk show *Roerend Goed*, which focused on art and culture. The episode in which the interview appeared also featured a conversation between the host of *Roerend Goed*, Hanneke Groenteman, and art historian and curator Rudi Fuchs, who was a friend of Judd's and part of the team that traveled to Marfa to make the episode.

The episode featuring this interview aired a few days before Judd was awarded the Sikkens Prize in Amsterdam, at the end of November 1993. The Sikkens Prize is awarded once every few years to individuals or institutions that are considered to have made a special contribution to the field of color. For the occasion of the award presentation, Judd wrote the essay "Some Aspects of Color in General and Red and Black in Particular" (1993), which was subsequently published as a small book.

HK   [Hans Keller] Mr. Judd, it seems to me to be a very radi-
      cal choice to settle here in what you could say is the mid-
      dle of nowhere, West Texas.

DJ   [Donald Judd] To me, it's not the middle of nowhere; as I
      said, it's the center of the world, and it's basically because
      I like the land and I like to be here. A rancher once said to
      someone who once criticized his piece of land which was
      very barren – you know, asked him why he had it – he said
      he had it and he liked it because it held the world together.
      If you took it away, the world would fall apart, all the way
      down to China. So this is part of the world, and there are
      economic reasons for being here. The state of Texas has
      no income tax. We hope it will never have an income tax.
      The buildings are relatively cheap to buy. The land is rel-
      atively cheap to buy. And therefore, you can have more
      space to install works of art. But one main reason is that
      art is something in itself, which seems to be an idea that
      most people do not realize and acknowledge, especially
      including the art professionals. And since it's a thing in it-
      self and has its own integrity, has its own necessity for in-
      stallation, it can occur anywhere. And it's important that
      it be well done and that its installation be well done, and
      that can happen anywhere where that's possible. That's the
      primary thing for the integrity of the art. It's way down
      the line as to the education of the public, which the mu-
      seums make the first thing. That's a big difference between
      me and the ordinary museums.

      You wouldn't be able to do this [in New York]; no
      one in New York wanted such a thing. It could have been
      possible with Barnett Newman's work, Jackson Pollock's
      work. There is no such thing in New York. No one would
      want it, no one would finance it. So this is financed by me.
      The art world in New York is terrible and has been terri-
      ble for a long time. It's a very superficial, nonserious situ-
      ation, and my general attitude is that New York sold out

Barnett Newman, Jackson Pollock, Mark Rothko, everyone, and they have been selling out everyone ever since. I am very much against the museums and the critics and the business in New York.

I want to create, as I said in a lecture in Austin the other day, in a way I want to create what I conceive to be a normal situation. Rudi [Fuchs][1] likes to call it utopian, but to me, I want to make a real and normal situation, which means that it's not outside of the social activity, it's not outside the fighting and the disagreeableness, and it's not above it or below it or anywhere else, and it's not outside of politics. Because we have all the fights here: we're fighting against nuclear waste; we're fighting against the city of El Paso, who wants to take all of the water away to El Paso; so we have all these normal fights. And unlike a lot of strange ideas about art being involved with the public, here's a great deal of art all over town without making the town look precious or silly or strange or anything. The people look at it or they don't look at it. But it's quite visible, and it's involved in saving the buildings, it's involved in making the art visible. I want it in all ways normal, and in that way a real civilization, instead of a fractured non-civilization, which is basically what the United States is.

So I consider this a serious, complete endeavor, like, for example – comparable in a little way, not in a big way – to the McDonald Observatory nearby.[2] The McDonald Observatory is here because the air is clear and the sky is clear. It's absolutely serious as an observatory which does not work for the government.

I've been here twenty, a little over twenty years, and also, I have a building in New York, which is the same thing, but it's only one building.[3] It takes a long time and a lot of chance and accident in acquiring the buildings. The money comes and the money goes. There are different circumstances all the time; my attitudes toward it change.

The town is a normal place, which means it is both good
and bad, like New York City, like Küssnacht am Rigi in
Switzerland.[4]

HK   It's not paradise.

DJ   It's not paradise. So there are a lot of fights, and we fire a
lot of people, and there's all the normal troubles. And it's —
for a number of different reasons, long-range reasons and
short-range reasons — financially, it's going downhill. The
cattle business is basically not a great business in West Texas
anymore, as you can tell by how the town used to be in
the '20s and '30s. And generally, the whole world is against
agriculture anyway; it's a long-range tendency.

HK   When did you discover this place?

DJ   I first came here in November '71 looking for empty land
that would pretty much stay empty in the southwest of
the United States, because I like the land and I like to be
near Mexico. My ranch borders on the Rio Grande.

HK   And it was a former army camp?

DJ   The Chinati Foundation occupies a former army fort
named Fort D. A. Russell.

This conversation was sourced from a video recording; the *Roerend Goed* episode
includes most of the interview, but elides the interviewer's questions and rearranges
the chronology. The original video recording is in the archives of The Netherlands Institute for Sound and Vision, Hilversum.

First published (excerpt): *Roerend Goed*, directed by Hans Keller (Hilversum, The
Netherlands: VPRO, 1993), aired November 23, 1993, 50 min. (in English and Dutch).

1   Rudi Fuchs (1942–) is a Dutch art historian and curator and was a friend
of Judd's. In 1975, Fuchs became director of the Van Abbemuseum, Eindhoven; between 1987 and 1993, he was director of the Gemeentemuseum
Den Haag, The Hague, a position he vacated to become director of the
Stedelijk Museum, Amsterdam.

2   Judd refers here to the McDonald Observatory, part of The University
of Texas at Austin, located in the Davis Mountains of West Texas. He became a member of the observatory's Board of Visitors in 1989.

3   Judd refers here to 101 Spring Street.

4   Küssnacht am Rigi is the village where Eichholteren is located.

"Donald Judd: Great Art through Simple Means"
Interview with Lars Morell for *Skala*
August 30, 1993

Skala, published from 1985 to 1994, was a Nordic magazine based in Copenhagen dedicated to architecture and art. Historian of ideas Lars Morell spoke with Judd in Cologne for this interview.

In 1993, Judd was given the Stankowski Award, which allowed for the organization of the traveling exhibition *Kunst + Design: Donald Judd*, which began at the Museum Wiesbaden, Germany (December 12, 1993–March 6, 1994), and traveled to the Kunstsammlungen Chemnitz, Germany (June 19–July 31, 1994); Badisches Landesmuseum Karlsruhe, Germany (August 2–November 20, 1994); Museum of Modern Art, Oxford (January 15–March 26, 1995); and the Kunsthallen Brandts Klædefabrik, Odense, Denmark (June 30–October 1, 1995).

L M   [Lars Morell] As a young man, you served in the U S Army in Korea in 1946 and 1947 [see image 19], and that was your first practical experience in construction.[1]

D J   [Donald Judd] When I arrived in Korea, I was assigned to the engineers. I was in the U S Army, but I worked with Korean workers digging ditches and getting rock from the rock quarry with a construction company building a boiler plant. We were attached to Kimpo Air Base, which is now Kimpo airport. The main thing was that I was virtually on my own because I was the only American soldier overseeing these things.

L M   Then you went home and had a choice between becoming an architect or an artist.

D J   I was only eighteen out in Korea, with a year and a half to think about what I wanted to do. Primarily, I wanted to be an artist, but I thought about being an architect. The main reason why I didn't become an architect was that I didn't think I could deal with the business aspect of being an architect.

L M   Then you became a painter, and one of your sources for inspiration in the 1940s was Stuart Davis.

D J   In the 1940s, before Pollock, Newman, Rothko, and [Clyfford] Still and the others became well known, the best American artist very probably was Stuart Davis. Stuart Davis was influenced by Léger, he was in Paris, but I think he was very much his own, too. Stuart Davis's work is a transition from representational to abstract works.

L M   What did you find important in American painting during the 1950s? There came a break with the European tradition.

D J   To some extent, but it also came out of not the European tradition, but the modern European tradition, which I think is better at this point to call international. If you consider the time after Cézanne, everybody is transitional. Cézanne was the last real European painter. After that,

I think it is better to consider everything international. Matisse is not so much a French artist – everybody is from someplace – he is an international artist. I very much object to the big European/American division. I think it is a real case of ignorance. I don't like nationalism. I like local politics, but I don't like nationalism.

L M   What is the difference?

D J   Everybody has to deal with their local situation and how they make a living and what happens, and that is perfectly legitimate, but I don't think you have to say it is the most important place in the world. I am not going to work for the United States, but I feel committed to Presidio County in West Texas because I feel it is my obligation politically to deal with some particular place, to try to make it better, to contribute to the community.

L M   Why did you drop paintings and reliefs and begin to make objects around 1962?

D J   The first three-dimensional works were done in 1962, I think.[2] I could not get what I wanted in paintings. I was very much interested in large, broad areas of color, which make the whole rectangle of the painting, and of course that is related to Newman, Pollock, and Rothko, so that the whole painting is one thing. If you want a painting with six or seven lines, the minute you put the lines on the big area, there are two things: you have the lines and the big area. The split between having two things instead of one bothered me a great deal. I didn't like the one thing being on top of the other. So when I made the first three-dimensional pieces, there were large areas of surface and color and the edges very naturally made the lines. The object is one thing. It comes together much better.

L M   Why don't you like the category of minimalism?

D J   Because it is an ignorant label by a reporter. It does not come from an artist; it comes from magazine writing. It implies that there was a group, but there was no group, and if anybody would bother looking at the chronology, it would be obvious that people did this at different times. Some people invented and some people followed, and I don't like being thrown together with followers.

LM   But isn't it true that you are seeking some sort of simple expression?

DJ   Not if the expression is complicated. There may be simple means but a complex expression. The expression is not different from any other art, but the means are relatively simple, which has a lot to do with the simplicity of my way of thinking. I don't really like little complicated things. I can understand that other artists like them, but for myself I don't like that. That is not a big philosophical difference; that is just a personal difference.

LM   You wrote an article in 1964 entitled "Specific Objects."[3] Is that your manifesto?

DJ   No, that was a report on the situation in New York. A magazine wanted me to write it, and that was the purpose of it. It was supposed to be a simple descriptive report, so it is definitely not a manifesto. Writing manifestos would have been pretty strange to me at that point.

LM   Why?

DJ   Because I would have been reluctant to put my intentions into words. A part of the definition of art is making a totality; if you have to write down what it means, you are smashing the totality that you just made yourself. So that is very uneasy.

LM   Some people say that artworks in the early 1960s became very open and infinite and that totality and wholeness were lost.

DJ   I think it was increased and developed. Certainly it is a major aspect of my work to increase this totality.

LM   An autonomous totality.

DJ   I think "totality" is enough. "Autonomous" is another word.

LM   How can one see when a work of art is a totality, totally based on itself?

DJ   It doesn't mean that it is totally based on itself. It means that it is one thing in itself. I think most of the work had a greater wholeness than work had had previously, when it was interested in parts. I mean, all art has a certain totality, but there are different degrees.

LM   You made a rebellion against European composition. Some of your keywords were "singleness" and "wholeness."

DJ   Yes, the European tradition that I was talking about in regard to composition is mainly the old representational tradition. That is why it is better to make a break between Cézanne and Matisse and Mondrian.

LM   Do you feel connected with artists like Léger, Matisse, and Mondrian?

DJ   Yes, sure, everybody learned from those artists.

LM   What happened, why did this break after Cézanne come?

DJ   It is a new civilization now, an industrial civilization. We don't have the civilization they had three hundred years ago, we don't have the same philosophy. Religion is still a bad influence, but it is gone. We have a very different population, a larger population, and a very different way of living. It is a complete transition from agricultural societies and it is basically an international civilization, and therefore it is obvious that we should have a different art.

LM   Some people use the categories modernism, late modernism, and postmodernism. What do you think about it?

DJ   Basically, I think it is silly. I don't think these things say anything. As I said, the big change in a way is pretty simple. It is from an agricultural society to an industrial society. Most of the changes and the difficulties are in that transition. I think the agricultural society is to be protected at this point, since now things are going too far the other way. There should be protection of the land and of the farming and that side of everything. That is the big transition. Within that are a lot of the problems, so I think little subdivisions are not so hopeful.

LM   Talking about agriculture and the land, artworks like yours deal with very formal problems, but now we discover that an artist like you, whom we thought worked with purely formal problems, has a lot of attitudes toward ecology, toward the local community, and toward history.

DJ   I think those attitudes are in the work and that is part of the totality. I think that art is mainly its own means and is mostly interested in the color and the shapes. If you look at old art, you are not much interested, say, in Jesus on the cross or Mary at the bottom, you are really interested in how good the painting is, but you can't say that the artist didn't take the subject seriously. The artist had to take it seriously. One bit of evidence that it was taken seriously is the development of the form. But the form and the colors and everything that is visible is the art. Within that, it carried certain attitudes. I think if it is good art, it is probably not bland fascist architecture, say.

LM   In your writings from the last ten years, you often use the expression "fascism in architecture." What do you actually mean by that?

DJ   Here I refer to all the public buildings from the 1920s and 1930s, not only in Europe, but also in the United States, which I hated as a kid. That is basically fascist architecture, and one element of it was that it was meant to be powerful. An even more important side is that they were without thought and were undeveloped, and so, power with no brains. This is exactly what the two museums in Bonn are like now.[4] They are absolutely fascist buildings, built last year. They take forms from everywhere – a staircase from Egypt, a roof from Le Corbusier, et cetera. I think behind it is the following attitude: "We are not going to make architecture that serves a function, we are not going to make architecture that has anything to do with the people, we are going to make architecture that expresses an institution." But the institution doesn't have the brains to build a good building.

LM   But in what way are they bad? Bad proportions?

DJ   No proportions!

LM   What characterizes a good building?

DJ   Again, a certain wholeness, consistency, coherence, attention to the function, attention to what the building is supposed to be for, consideration for the people who work in the building or use it. The two museums in Bonn are not built for art, not built for the audience, not built for anybody.

LM   Since 1968, you have restored a lot of buildings. You started in 1968 with 101 Spring Street in New York. It cannot be an accident that a person like you, who loves the right angle, bought a house on a corner.

DJ   It's not a complete accident. It was an accident that I bought it, but when I saw the building, I thought that it was really good. The strange thing is that the building where I had a studio at the same time was also on a corner and had a glass section on the corner.[5]

LM   You didn't change much at 101 Spring Street.

DJ   Of course, I didn't change the façade. The building had been very damaged inside. It was built in 1870, but there were no moldings and nothing left, so I didn't want to put it back the way it was; we did not even know the way it was. I also wanted to be able to do something, so I did what I could do to make it my building in a way that was consistent with the building. I didn't want to cut it up with a lot of divisions, so I just used one function for each floor, five floors above, two below ground. The main changes are the floors and the ceilings. On the fourth floor there is a wooden floor and a wooden ceiling that make two identical, parallel planes. I did that in Eichholteren in Switzerland, too; there I restored a hotel from 1943 [see images 81, 82].

The ceilings were very low, so I used the same idea in the building there.

LM   In 1971, you moved to Marfa, in southwest Texas, and in 1975, you officially became a Texan. What are you actually doing in Marfa?

DJ   Storing a great deal of art, fixing up a lot of buildings, to some extent making new buildings. It is a very large situation, partly in the town, partly in the county, partly on a ranch I have in the county. There is a great deal of art by myself and others.

LM   In the town, at Mansana de Chinati, you placed a wall around the block.

DJ   I did that to define it and make a whole, because it is between the highway and the railroad tracks, so it is a busy part of town. It is still not very quiet. A part of the land was level and is still level; the other part had a slight slope already, and so I increased the slope, which was also for getting the water away. The outer wall is level at the top and between the two buildings there is an inner wall which slopes to follow the land, which also slopes.

LM   Two concentric walls, where the outer is level and the inner follows the ground. That is again a very simple solution. You fence the block with the wall, you collect the rainwater, you have pergolas for the shade. It is like the mythological paradise garden, which is fenced and contains the source of the trees.

DJ   And it has a vegetable garden, it has two dogs, it has a bunch of chickens; it is very nice. And a big library.

LM   When you restore a building, you say that you transform it into architecture.

DJ   If I can.

LM   What does that mean?

DJ   What you said: if it is possible. Sometimes there is a terrible building. Sometimes a building has some natural virtues and then you can turn it into real architecture.

At the Chinati Foundation at the old Fort D. A. Russell, I think I made real architecture out of two artillery sheds and the building we call the Arena. The Arena is actually quite simple. We fixed up the building and made the floor, which was in a way done very casually; it was done on the spur of the moment. The two Artillery Sheds, however, were long range and deliberate. They took more time.

LM   You put a round roof on top of the Artillery Sheds –

DJ   And made the windows [see image 61].

LM   You work a lot with a grid for the floor and the windows.

DJ   I like these things. It is obvious that I like symmetry, I like repetition, and I take these as the first situation, the given situation, and therefore not to have these requires some reason. I think that is natural; that is what you think about when you look. If you can't make it symmetrical, as in the case of the slope inside the Mansana, then you have to have a good reason for not making it symmetrical. Sometimes saving old buildings and building in a city gives you a good reason, and you don't want everything to be symmetrical. In a great deal of present architecture that is known, there is a lot of asymmetry for no reason – like Frank Gehry's work, where everything is going every which way for no reason at all.

LM   When you came to Marfa, you began to make furniture for yourself and your children. Meanwhile, a lot of different kinds of furniture have come into being, and many are for sale. One of your sources for inspiration is the furniture from the 1920s, but you never used chrome steel tubes like [Ludwig] Mies [van der Rohe] or [Marcel] Breuer.

DJ   It seems too far away; it is too alien to me. I have no idea what I could do with them. Mies van der Rohe's furniture, I think, is more elegant than mine. It certainly is a different way of thinking.

LM   You are always working with boxes that are open on one

side. Are you experimenting with some sort of philosophy of the box?

DJ   No, it is not so definite. As I keep saying, I am perfectly
interested in circles. Circles are fine. I am interested in a
very simple geometry, but it is not so much about geometry, it is about what it can do for the qualities I want. As
I have written for a long time, in the world there are only
two possibilities: either something rather chaotic taken
from nature or something that is geometric.

LM   Why don't you like Italian furniture?

DJ   It is because I don't like things where the design is im-
posed from the outside and where the function is ignored
and an object is meant to show status and prestige, to show
how up to date the people are, or to be symbolic. I think
almost all furniture is meant to show that.

LM   For the past ten years, you have been a sharp critic of the
American society, of the suburbs and the postmodern skyscrapers. What is all this about?

DJ   When I was a young man, interested in becoming an artist
and thinking about architecture, there was a certain level
in the world, because, though Mies van der Rohe couldn't
do much in Europe, at the end of his life he did do quite
a bit in the United States. I don't think that can happen
now. I think this is part of the change from an agricultural to an industrial society and the growth in the population. There are too many people. Society cannot educate them, and of course some of these ignorant people
come up and have money and positions, but they don't
know anything. They no longer have respect for the architects, and the architects have no resistance. They give
in and do whatever they are told to do.

LM   You refer to the postmodern architects?

DJ   They are just commercial architects. There is nothing left
of their integrity. Somebody told me the other day that a
client said to [Robert] Venturi, "Oh, I think there should

be a window there," and Venturi said, "Okay, I'll put a window there." The person said that he would really have had a much higher regard for Venturi had Venturi said no. Frank Lloyd Wright must have been tough with his clients; we have stories. Mies van der Rohe had to concede a little at the back of the building in New York, but he obviously had an idea what the Seagram Building should be like, and he really fought for it. So it is two sides: one side gives in, the architects give in completely; the clients don't know anything and have no regard for the architects. The art situation is the same.

LM   What can we do, then?

DJ   Fight back, write and talk and fight back, not make trashy buildings and not make trashy art.

This conversation was sourced from an archival transcript with handwritten corrections by Judd in the Judd Foundation Archives, Marfa, Texas.

First published: Lars Morell, "Donald Judd: Great Art through Simple Means," *Skala*, no. 29, 1993, 40–46 (in English and Danish).

1   Judd enlisted in the United States Army on June 28, 1946, and was assigned to the Corps of Engineers in Korea. He was honorably discharged on November 20, 1947.

2   Judd's first relief dates to 1961.

3   See Judd's "Specific Objects" (1964) in *Donald Judd Writings*, 134–45.

4   Judd refers here to the Kunstmuseum Bonn (designed by Axel Schultes) and the Bundeskunsthalle (designed by Gustav Peichl), both completed in 1992 in Bonn, Germany. That same year, Judd wrote that "Gustav Peichl's new Bundeskunsthalle in Bonn, very general and bland, big and sightless, as in the 1930s, is in style fascist, neofascist." Judd, "Fine Art and Commercial Architecture" (1992) in *Donald Judd Writings*, 780.

5   Judd refers here to 53 East Nineteenth Street.

Interview with Regina Wyrwoll
For the television documentary *Bauhaus, Texas*
October 4–5, 1993

This interview with art historian and filmmaker Regina Wyrwoll was conducted
on October 4 and 5, 1993, at Judd's Architecture Office and his library at La Mansana de Chinati/The Block in Marfa, Texas. It was organized in conjunction with
the filming of *Bauhaus, Texas: The American Artist Donald Judd*, an hour-long documentary for German television produced by the Goethe-Institut in Munich,
which was completed in 1994.

R W   [Regina Wyrwoll] I'm very curious: when you give a lecture to students, what do you tell them about architecture? What is the main aspect you emphasize?

D J   [Donald Judd] That's a very general question, and I always have a lot of trouble with general questions.

R W   How did you find your way into architecture?

D J   I was always interested in architecture. I was interested as a child and thought about it and made sketches, which I no longer have. To some extent, when I was in the army in Korea, which was 1947 without a war, I thought of being an architect [see image 19].[1] But I had already, in a way, fundamentally decided to be an artist. And being an artist is primary. But I'm thoroughly interested in architecture. I've been doing it for myself for twenty, thirty, forty years, and happily it's possible now to do it in cooperation with other people.

R W   Where was your first architectural project? Was it here in Marfa?

D J   It was the building in New York.[2] But all the spaces I lived in in New York I reworked for myself – to live in and for my work and for other people's work. I've always had a lot of work by other artists.

R W   Wherever I could see your architecture, I noticed certain materials you use and certain kinds of structures you consider when you rework an existing building.

D J   Well, a lot of architects over the past thousands of years have thought the materials were very important, and I think the materials are very important – absolutely fundamental. One of the main criticisms of present architecture would be that the architects are not interested in the materials as materials, as they're used in the construction. No matter how complex or advanced the construction is, you're still using materials, and that use should be clear. It should be clear that they're materials. So in some mysterious way, they even manage to make plastic look fake when plastic is already fake. Plastic can be made to look like plastic and therefore relatively real. But almost everything they touch looks fake. For example, the museum by James Stirling in Stuttgart, it's got a veneer of rock, but it still looks fake.[3]

RW   Is architecture for you an artistic manifestation?

DJ   Yes. I think it has to be. I think it always is.

RW   But you make a very clear distinction between architecture, furniture, and art.

DJ   Yeah, but that doesn't mean that the furniture or the architecture isn't artistic. "Artistic" is an adjective. I think it's important to have good furniture and good architecture, and especially now, when the buildings built by the architects I'm criticizing are very derivative of art, that it's very important to maintain the distinction between art and architecture. Art is done in a very different way and for a different purpose — very much the purpose of the individual. The architect cannot go against the purpose of the people who use the building, the function of the building. Architecture can be quite individual and ultimately very creative, but it cannot be in opposition to the function of the building. You just get a hunk of junk, like [Hans] Hollein's buildings.

RW   Why are the rooms you create so wide with so few things inside?

DJ   Partly it's my judgment — of what I like and how I think things should be. But ultimately, as a general statement, I find it very strange to want to live in a very crowded and dense space. I don't think it's very real for human beings. I think it has a lot to do with social status and symbols. It's very much like the overcrowded Victorian rooms, and a great deal about consumption and showing that consumption.

RW   You have a certain vision about architecture in Marfa — the architecture you are building, rebuilding, or restoring here. What kind of a vision do you have for a city like Marfa?

DJ   Whatever I do here, and in general anyplace, has to fit into the situation. I reworked the building in New York, the interior; it's a building from 1870. What I did would not have occurred in 1870, but it doesn't go against the quality of the building. Marfa is a small town built centrally – they probably stopped building in the 1930s because the cattle business went downhill. So it's a small town with a certain style of architecture. I don't think a new, strange building, even if it were good, should be built. I don't think I should put a large contemporary piece of sculpture, for example, out in front of the Chamberlain Building. I wouldn't commission John Chamberlain to put a big piece of his in front of that building because I think it would collide with the nature of the town. It also would be somewhat offensive to some of the people in the town. In some ways they deserve to be offended, but I don't think you should go out of your way to do it. It's basically a cattle town of a certain period and you don't want it to become a cattle-town museum. It's a dying town, but it shouldn't be dead – it should be maintained as a live cattle town. It doesn't hurt to add in some buildings that do other things. I don't think this office, which is on the main corner, is a great contradiction to the town and to the main street.[4] We sandblasted the façade and we fixed up the windows and this space, and it's now more like it was than it has been for thirty years. The only thing different is that it has unusual furniture inside, but that's all inside and kind of quiet. So nothing is very extravagant as to what shows on the street.

RW   What is very astonishing for a visitor like me is seeing the Chinati Foundation and the barracks – buildings where soldiers used to live are now filled with art.

DJ   Yes, well, that's a big improvement.

RW   Were you afraid that this would collide with the old mission of Fort D. A. Russell? Now you have this foundation that has become a meeting point for people and for presenting art in a very quiet way.

DJ   The fort was long gone when I got it. It had been empty for decades, ever since just after World War II. And it had been severely damaged, the roofs had been taken off, et cetera. I was in the army myself, as I said, and I don't like living in barracks. It doesn't have much meaning to me as an army installation. It's a little boring in terms of architecture, but that's the nature of the army. But otherwise, it's not such a great contradiction.

RW   Isn't it a contradiction that soldiers' barracks are now museum spaces or exhibition halls?

DJ   Hmm, I don't know. The world's full of old buildings, and there's no use for them. In this case, the buildings didn't have to be saved, but often buildings should be saved, and the installation of art is one of the useful ways to do that. Europe's full of old buildings that could be used that way.

RW   You will design the Bahnhof in Basel [see image 83].[5] I think this will be your first building in Europe.

DJ   Yes. It's in cooperation with a firm in Basel, mainly Hans Zwimpfer. The excavation for the railroad tracks begins in early '94, and that will take a long time, so it'll be a year or two before any construction starts. Possibly the little building in Bregenz will start before then [see image 84].[6] So it depends on which one is first.

RW   What are some of your principles when you accept such a task, inside a town like Basel? Do you follow the same principles you've already described — looking at the surroundings, the function of the building?

DJ   Yeah, very much. But this is a new building in Basel, obviously, next to the existing Bahnhof. The surroundings are not unusual, it's not in an older part of town. It's over the railroad tracks, so nothing much is being destroyed. The height of the building is restricted already, but it would make sense not to make it higher. You have two or three taller buildings, which are very unfortunate, nearby, which should be chopped in half. So the considerations for what's around it were not so great. I didn't have to worry too much about that. If you worked in the older part of Basel, there'd be many more concerns.

R W   What kind of materials will you use? Concrete?

D J   Well, Zwimpfer worked out a scheme in which the columns are steel, and large concrete panels are set down upon the columns, containing all the wiring and piping and everything, in a so-called sandwich, and those are somehow dropped into place. The floor and the ceiling are exactly the same, concrete and very plain, without – this is all his idea – light switches and sprinkler systems and all the usual stuff. The ceilings, which are a little bit my doing, will be higher than usual, because I don't like low ceilings. The present scheme now is that the exterior will mostly be glass. It's an alternating scheme, between the taller parts and areas that serve as courtyards. The taller parts will be a gray glass that you cannot see through, and the parts in between, the courtyards, or the *Höfe*, will be clear glass and will actually be courtyards. So it'll be alternating between middling dark glass that you can't see through and clear glass that encloses the courtyard. It'll be a new use of glass, I think.

R W   You have developed a certain style of windows and doors for your architecture [see image 65]. Did you invent, for example, the ones we see in the Arena? Did you develop these while designing your house? Was it all one process?

D J   I had used that same idea for the library at La Mansana. The doors that swivel were invented for that space, not for the Arena. It was a good idea, so I made them over. The gates, I guess, in a way were invented for the Arena. I also used the swiveling doors and windows in the Chamberlain Building.

RW   Don, this project, the Mansana, how did it develop?

DJ   It was originally two warehouses that had been airplane
      hangars that were moved by the US Army in the '30s from
      an old airfield out where the golf course is now. The two
      large buildings were the main attraction for buying the
      area. Then there was a small building that we call the two-
      story building. These were very exposed to the highway
      on one side and the railroad tracks on the other, and to
      the feed mill.[7] In fact, it was so exposed people used to cut
      through between the buildings. It was an obvious thing –
      to put the wall around the whole area [see image 63]. But
      it took years to complete. The adobes were made from
      the land right here. I don't think I figured out the whole
      scheme right at the beginning but enclosed the walls ac-
      cording to the lower part of the windows on the high-
      est corner, which is the southeast corner. I don't know if
      I had the idea of the slope at that time. I don't think so. It
      was a very undetermined piece of land, with a slight slope
      or sag and a level area that originally had lots of trash. It
      was also open to the arroyo, which made it susceptible to
      a certain amount of vandalism. I thought about the whole
      problem of the level area and the part with the slight slope,
      and then I realized it had something to do with the piece
      that I made that's now in Saint Louis, from 1970 [see im-
      age 64]. The outer part of that piece – the edge of it is level
      with the horizon, and the inner part slopes with the land,
      parallel to the slope of the land. So in a way it's the same
      idea as here. I increased the slope and made the level part
      more level, sharply dividing the two. This also was good
      for drainage – being flat near the arroyo, it tended to flood.
      And that enclosed part, the sloped area with the wall par-
      allel to the slope of the land, somehow makes a large work
      of art – it's about the only combination I have that's both
      art and architecture; it's hard to say just what it is.

RW   Did you add the plants and trees?

D J   Yes. Only the elm tree over by the greenhouse was here. The cottonwoods I placed, the plum trees, the pool of water…

R W   And you designed the pergola under the vine, and the swimming pool?

D J   Yes.

R W   Is it a pool?

D J   Yeah, it has steps at one end.

R W   Do you ever go in?

D J   Yeah, sure – it's a swimming pool. They're filling it up now, I think. If you want to swim tomorrow afternoon, it'll be full.

R W   Thank you.

How did you decide to make one part into a library, and the other for living?

D J   The main consideration was to install works of art in the east building, which has two big rooms. This building [the west building] has one big room, next to us. That was the main reason for buying the place, and my first consideration. The library's always been a big problem because, no matter what the situation, there are always more books. And this part was too narrow for any other use, but seemed to be good for the library. When the library became too big, I bought the building in town for the Art Studio and put the other part of the library into the old studio space [see image 69]. That happened some time later. But this library's pretty old in terms of the place.

R W   It is your personal library.

D J   Yeah. Who else?

R W   I wanted to know if other people come and use it – students, for example.

D J   No, no. I'm fanatic about it. Never. It's absolutely my library.

R W   How did you develop it?

D J   Well, no plan. It goes back, of course, to buying books long ago, as a student.

R W   We are sitting, as you said, in the European library.

D J   Yeah, I divided the library – this part is now all of the countries of Europe before 1900. Everything after 1900 is international and therefore next door, plus Asia and Mexico.

R W   It is art and cultural history?

D J   Well, it's about everything. It has a great deal of literature and history, art and architecture, philosophy. But there's not much of a plan. Some of the books are really nice, but I'm not a real collector of old books.

R W   You are a collector of art, and of what else?

D J   Pretty much a collector of art, as far as collectors go.

R W   And furniture.

D J   Yeah. It's a big collection. Real estate.

R W   What do you think of art critics today? Was there a time when art critics played a more important role? In the '60s, when you wrote about your colleagues – this was a time when it seemed very important.[8] I have the impression now that art writing is not that important for art.

D J   Well, first, it's not at all important now, and actually, it was not important in the '60s either. In the United States it's always been a very meager activity. But I don't think it's ever been a very important activity; I don't think there's really that much in Europe either, in terms of art criticism.

R W   I have the impression that good art criticism comes out of describing, very thoroughly, the piece of art, the material, and its dimensions.

D J   Yeah, that's important, but also the philosophy behind it. These things are basically not done. I don't think many people are interested in art, and therefore they don't want to read descriptions of it. I don't believe they really think the art means anything; therefore they're not too interested in the philosophy behind it, or even the sociology behind it.

R W   Is there a clear relationship between philosophy and art?

DJ   Sure. All art has to be based upon a philosophical attitude. It's not possible without that.

RW   Right now, we have a lot of very well-known French philosophers being discussed. Do you think they have any influence on art?

DJ   I doubt if they've had any influence on art. But I don't know. You would have to know more about the situation in France.

RW   This is a discussion we're having in Germany and in Europe now. People are asking for more philosophical help to define the world and to gain a deeper knowledge of art. But I think it's been absolutely lacking in criticism.

DJ   As you know, I studied philosophy, I majored in philosophy and took it as basic information – it was always very important to me.[9] And there are certain general principles, which are not very sophisticated philosophically, that I take for granted.

RW   Is there any contemporary philosopher you feel is important, that you accept, that you try to gain a knowledge of or dialogue with?

DJ   Well, I'm interested, but I don't know enough about the contemporary situation. I do think it's a necessary and valuable activity and not at all obsolete. I don't agree that it's over with; it'll never be over with because society changes and the knowledge of the world in general changes. Philosophy continues to deal with that. I don't think I know enough about any of the contemporary philosophers for them to be that important to me. I like [Noam] Chomsky in terms of politics, but that's not philosophy, I guess.[10]

RW   You also collect books on science, you said.

DJ   Well, yeah. There are all kinds of science. But again, I don't know that much about it. I'm on the Board of Visitors of McDonald Observatory here, and so I have more to do with astronomy than anything else.[11] This is a very interesting

place to be for astronomers, and, maybe not today, but ordinarily it has very clear skies.

RW You're very concerned about contemporary art, and you
collect young artists. How do you find them?

DJ I think I have an absolutely perfect eye. Which means a
mind behind the eye.

RW So is it by chance that you, for example, met Roni Horn?

DJ Yeah, there's always a little bit of chance. Well, not quite
chance. I saw an exhibition of her drawings around ten
years ago, at Galerie Lelong in New York. I liked the drawings, and I bought a couple. Then I went there one day
and by chance she was there. And so on. That's not exactly an accident. So I got to know Roni, and then I saw
another show where she had three-dimensional work. By
now I've seen a lot of her shows. I saw the really beautiful exhibition in Winterthur of the drawings.[12] So that's
pretty deliberate. Of course, you're not going to meet everybody who's somewhat young or middle-aged or anything. In terms of numbers, the art situation is very big.
In terms of quality, it's very small. But it's not so easy to
meet everybody or know everything.

RW Yes, but sometimes it's very hard to find the quality.

DJ It's not so hard if you really know what you're doing. See,
this is very obvious to me. The discrepancy between high
quality and thought and the lack of it is very obvious. For
example, at the [Kölnischer] Kunstverein two years ago,
there was the exhibition of Michael Scholz.[13] Well, I had
no trouble seeing that that was really good work. I don't
even know him. I only know of him because of that exhibition. It doesn't come from anywhere else. It's because
I can see that he's really thinking and really trying to do
something. He's not just reworking old stuff. And then
the problem is that most people, including art dealers and
museum people, really don't know what they're looking
at, and of course, that's a contradiction.

R W   How could one teach them to see again?

D J   The first step is that they should be a little more modest
       about it and look more carefully. I think they tend to be
       very arrogant and would much rather go by gossip rather
       than really thinking and looking. What I'm concerned
       about with the art situation is that the people who I think
       are good – and this includes Roni, who is, as things go,
       pretty successful – but she and all of us don't have enough
       money to do the work we want to do. And I don't see
       how on earth a person who does installations, or what-
       ever label you put on it, like Scholz, how on earth he will
       ever get the money to do what he wants to do. That's the
       big problem for the artists and the art and the society in
       general.

R W   We have quite a developed system of helping young art-
       ists in Germany. Do you think it's sufficient?

D J   I don't think it works. It doesn't seem to get to anybody
       who's any good.

R W   Why doesn't it work?

D J   I don't think anybody has any judgment, or they won't ex-
       ercise the judgment. Everything is supposed to stay in a
       middle ground and everyone's afraid to make a decision,
       and art doesn't work like that. There are only a handful of
       people who are really good and who really should be sup-
       ported. The US government gives a little bit of money to
       maybe a hundred and fifty people each year. It isn't any-
       thing. Doesn't do anything. There's no choice, no decision,
       and they give most of the money, anyway, to institutions. I
       would say that art in Germany is being starved down. It all
       goes to buildings like those awful buildings in Bonn and
       never to the artists.[14] Awful buildings in Frankfurt, too.[15]

R W   Do you have an idea of how this system of supporting
       young artists who are doing quality work could be devel-
       oped in a way that functions?

D J   I think it's a really difficult problem. The really difficult philosophical contradiction is that any good art is not art for the society. It's not there to reflect the society. It's not there to represent an institution. And ordinarily, it's somewhat against or totally against the society. But you still have to ask the society somehow to support it; the market can't do it, won't do it, because they're always fifty years behind. So the market's insufficient. Therefore, the society has to be willing, in one form or another, to produce money for a subversive activity. And it has to have the freedom and tolerance to do that. It has to do that for radical science, too, otherwise they're not going to have it. If they don't have it, they're not going to have a civilization. Or maybe they don't have the civilization already.

RW   Then you must be absolutely against the idea somebody recently told me, that art is a consensus in society – that there must be a consensus in a certain society that art is art of a certain quality.

DJ   I don't think that can happen now. At this point, the society's too diverse, and you're talking about an international society made up of civilizations and several civilizations in transition, so there's no way you can get a consensus. And you have an enormous population that doesn't know anything, who could probably only agree maybe on Mickey Mouse and orange juice. So you'll never get a consensus, and if you wait for a consensus, you'll never have any art. And you won't even get a small consensus. As I said, the quality is the creation of the artist. It's up to the artist to raise it as high as possible and develop what they're interested in as much as possible. That's the artist's job. Someone else can come along and see that. As I claimed, I don't have any trouble seeing that. To me it's much more obvious than it is to other people.

RW   One of the collectors I know, a museum collector, told me, "Art becomes art when it is collected."

DJ   Well, of course, that's a complete perversion. That's obviously nonsense – it cannot be possible. Art is art made by the artist and developed by the artist, and quality is made by the artist. There's no way art can be determined by collecting it. You could say that milk bottles are art because everybody collects them – Coke bottles, whatever. So there are a number of perversions like that. [Achille Bonito] Oliva in Italy is along that line of thinking, too.[16] Because they see nothing in the visual art, they don't understand anything about it; they think it's made by its social circumstances, and it's very far from being made by its social circumstances. Scientific knowledge has a great deal more to do with art than the state of the society, which is more in transition, more accidental. To say that art is made by the collectors is a complete failure of museum judgment, and it's an indication of what's wrong. If art is made by the collectors, why don't they go ahead and do it, and then, you know, go away?

RW You fought a very special case against one of your biggest collectors, [Giuseppe] Panza di Biumo from Varese.[17]

DJ Yes.

RW Why did you dare to do it? This was absolutely unique in art history.

DJ Well, I'm very concerned about my work, and the original arrangements with the man were very dubious, made through the Castelli Gallery. The whole situation was very dubious, and the finances, to say it again, were dubious. The main thing was that Panza went ahead and made work himself, my work, without my seeing it, which is contrary to all agreements and contrary to all common sense. I'm very much concerned with the integrity of my work and the installation of my work, and I felt I had to fight that, which I did by writing, rather than with the law.

RW Did it have any effect on your market, on the selling of your works?

DJ No. At that time, the art business was very good, and it

didn't change. The art business now is bad and my money is down along with everyone else's, but I don't think it – I don't care. The work has to be dealt with honestly, and I don't care what the results are from fighting Panza.

RW At the Chinati Foundation, you are running a kind of museum yourself – for example the Chamberlain Building, as well as your own installations [see images 60, 61]. What are your principles for presenting art?

DJ I think it should be installed much more carefully and thoughtfully than is usually done, and I think that there's so much work that some of it should be permanent, and it should be in enough quantity that you understand what the person is thinking. It also should be in a much less pretentious and more natural circumstance than museums usually are. Museums have become very elaborate and very artificial, and with certain attitudes that I think are against the attitudes of the artists. I think no artist, living or dead, ever, would want his work in the two buildings in Bonn. They're absolutely contrary to the art. There couldn't be a greater contradiction. And so there has to be something better somewhere. So I'm trying to do that. The only thing I know of that's somewhat better, very good in some ways – there's an artist involved I don't like so much, and that's a criticism – is the [Museum] Insel Hombroich.[18] Basically that seems to be a good effort in Europe. Panza was just a real estate dealer. It wasn't a serious effort in installation or showing a collection. There are things in storage here, but I don't want things in storage. Everything should be in the spaces and be here for people to come and see, permanently. There's nothing left, for example, in New York that has anything of the quality or naturalness of the art situation of thirty or forty years ago, except my building. It's a complete island. Even as architecture it's an island, because all the buildings around it, even though the façades are there, the insides have

been turned into what look like Upper East Side apartments. It's a perversion to show paintings by Pollock and
Newman and Rothko in slick places like The Museum
of Modern Art. They're too far from the conditions that
the paintings were first painted in or shown in. They're
totally different parts of the society.

R W   If you could design a museum or think about a museum
in Europe, let's say mostly state funded, would you prefer to have a stable installation that wouldn't change? And
besides that, to organize special exhibitions?

D J   Yeah, that was the original intent here, not to have exhibitions, but it happened rather naturally and mostly because
I quickly made a nice space for them. It works very well
to have a lot of work that doesn't change, that's permanent, and then each year to have either a temporary exhibition or an addition to the collection. This scheme seems
to be working very well and very naturally and quietly
and much more seriously than any museum – and much
more cheaply.[19]

R W   If a museum keeps collecting more and more and keeps
growing, you're either going to need more space or be
able to sell pieces.

D J   You should have more space. I'm against selling anything.
I think if you buy it, you should keep it. And that's true
of big museums, too. They should just have more space.
And it doesn't have to be next to the original building. It
could be in another part of the city. Anywhere. The obvious solution here and in Europe is to use old buildings,
old factory buildings, of which there are plenty. They are
often very nice and don't need so much work to fix up.

R W   The presentation of your own collections here – you chose
every piece and you personally placed it?

D J   Yes, and not only just like that; a great deal of time and
thought went into the process. The front room of the east
building at La Mansana probably took two years. That's

why I don't think it should be changed. It's just too much work.

R W   Yesterday I went through a very personal museum, a mixture of centuries, of styles, of things. Do you think it will stay like this, or is it an installation you will change?

D J   It will never change. Again, it's too much work and too much thought. It's like making another work of art. If the individual works are short stories, those buildings are the novels, and they're just too much effort. And I'm very careful about what goes next to what and the space each thing has and the contradictions between the civilizations and lots of other considerations.

R W   Do you think that artists would be good museum directors?

D J   For installation, yes, if they're interested. A lot of artists are not interested. I take installation very seriously and I'm good at it. I've done almost every show I've ever had. I don't think other people are that interested.

R W   How do you see yourself here in Marfa, in West Texas, the balance between the way you are, your survival, how you make a living, while providing work to a lot of people? And the art here – is it a "total art" project? How would you describe Marfa yourself?

D J   In a way, it's totally an art project, or art and architecture. Naturally, everything here is financed by the art market, by selling my work. A little bit now, happily, by architecture. So it just comes from money that I can make one way or the other. The furniture brings in some money. When there's no money coming, we save a little by eating our own steers, but otherwise no money comes from West Texas. All the money is coming in from around the world. It's mainly about making the art and then installing the art, both mine and other people's. And of course it's what I want to do. It's what I like to do. It's not wildly altruistic.

R W   You are writing an essay now. Are you planning to write other books?

DJ   Yeah. I don't write anything very long – they're all essays.
      And as you probably know, the new book, *Book One*,
      comes out soon.[20]
RW   Now you are writing an essay about color.
DJ   Yeah. For the Sikkens award.[21]
RW   You started writing after you studied philosophy and be-
      came an art critic, but you started as a painter.
DJ   Yeah, but I went to art school while I was studying philos-
      ophy.[22] I went to art school full time and Columbia Uni-
      versity in the evenings and in the summer.
RW   What kind of role does color play in your work?
DJ   Color is one of three or four major aspects of my work. I
      think color is probably the most important aspect of art in
      this century. It's the one that's strongest in keeping the art
      from turning backward. Everybody wants to turn it back-
      ward, and I think the color is the toughest in resistance.
RW   Why?
DJ   Well, color's color – it's very hard to pervert it and make it
      weak. It's a very strong force in this century. And I think,
      basically, it's something new – for thousands of years.
RW   But the old Greeks painted their sculptures.
DJ   Yeah. Other people, too. It's not that there wasn't any color,
      but I think so far in this century it's been developed more
      than it's ever been. But I think it has a long way to go. Well,
      it's pretty developed – but I think that in another two or
      three hundred years it'll be highly developed.
RW   Would you ever go back to painting?
DJ   No, I have no ideas. A few for wall painting, maybe, but
      really no ideas or interest in canvas and easel painting. Not
      for a long time.
RW   You are going to start a little Marfa enterprise concern-
      ing textiles?
DJ   Well, yeah. Some of the names painted on the office
      window are projections of possibilities. This town and this
      county need some small businesses. Their main business

is cattle, and that's just fine, but the economics of it go steadily downward, for various reasons — it's a complicated situation. Cattle should be supported, and, as a business, they should be more particular about the cattle in this area, which was once famous for the Highlands, so-called Highland Herefords, the brown and white cattle. But it's not enough. As you see, the town is going downhill rather quickly. Basically, they're against anything changing. They're against me — they're against all little businesses. Somebody twenty years ago wanted [to build] a shoe factory; they [the town] didn't want it. They have the same attitude toward the observatory that they have toward me. The observatory brings a lot of people to this area, plus it's a major scientific effort. They need a diverse economy. It's just normal common sense. You need two or three factories. We have the one little factory for the art, but you need two or three very different factories, not large, not polluting. And you need a really good hotel and a restaurant, also really good, so people have a reason to come. You need a source for the beef and whatever, vegetables — everything that can be grown here. You need to put it together and build it back up economically. The town, as I said, only has two thousand people right now — it's not that many. The county perhaps has five thousand. And I don't want it to grow — I think a lot of people don't want it to grow, because it would change a great deal. But obviously what you want is a decent education, decent housing, and a decent standard of living for all of the people. It's an enormous county, and they should be able to make that money from five thousand people. I think they're basically very uneducated and very passive and, as I said earlier, I think there's a small group of old Anglos who don't want anything to happen. And it'll just die if they succeed in that.

RW   So you interfere socially and politically?

DJ   Yeah, and I want to — I intend to. I think it's everybody's obligation to do that. It's my obligation. I'm a resident here, and I vote from the ranch, so I'm a resident not of the town but of the county. I feel it's my job to be a citizen somewhere. And it's my job to interfere, it's my job to try to make it better, and the same goes for everyone else. Especially since I travel a lot and I'm involved in a lot of other places, it would be very easy for me to slide over, complain about the United States, which I do, and slide over the whole situation and be international and make more money. If I didn't bring it back here, I would probably have a lot more money. But I think that would be wrong. So I want to make it clear that I'm trying to work with this community and with this county and with the United States too, which means mostly fighting them.

R W   As somebody who creates businesses, do you want to have a concentration, or do you prefer to have a lot of small businesses working together?

D J   I think the town should have very different businesses. There should be me, but there should be others – the area raises cattle; therefore, why not make shoes? Why not kill the cattle here, sell the meat at a higher price, keep the leather, and make shoes? I mean, I don't want to do this, but I think somebody should do it. I would like to start a produce company – we already have the legal side of it done, La Junta de los Rios – and sell produce, sell bottled water, the local tequila called sotol, and whatever else can be made here.[23]

R W   Do you think such small businesses have a chance against the big concentration of economies?

D J   I think they take a beating and everything's against them. In the United States there are constantly less and less, and it hasn't changed with Clinton – with Bush it dropped rapidly, with the Iraqi-American war. Little businesses went down. During the last three years it's dropped enormously. But I think it would be a much better society with more small businesses. Therefore, they should fight back, and they should organize politically and defend themselves. Basically, I'm a small businessman – we have a few employees, but we have to fight to make and keep money for those employees. We're pretty loyal to them; I don't like to fire them. I think it's very good for the environment and the economy, everything. Whatever can be produced in a particular area should be produced there, instead of shipped all the way around the world. A lot of my best examples are in Switzerland, because I've been there a lot. I spent a summer in Malans, near Chur, and we were just across the street from the *Milchzentrum*.[24] Every morning and evening the farmers would bring in their milk, and a lot of that milk, maybe half, went out – that's a guess – to Chur, or wherever, so that brings in money. But a lot of it is made into cheese, or they come with the milk bottles; it's used by the town. That means money that's not spent elsewhere. And there are other products too – the wine, of course, which is famous. So they build a real economy where they don't lose a lot of the money.

One other thing about the conflict between the small businesses and the corporations is that the small businesses in their own communities can produce a better product and better food than the corporations can. People have fallen for the supermarkets and the corporations when, in fact, everything can be done better right here. The milk here in Marfa comes from San Angelo. There used to be dairies here, but the government made it too difficult. The people don't believe in it – they don't believe in having gardens. This was a little town full of gardens. Everybody had windmills. All of that's gone. It's not fashionable. They would rather buy expensive, bad food from the supermarket. And as far as food goes, the corporations really don't produce very good food, and it's very expensive. The money's taken away from the community. All the food here is imported; you could be on an island. If it has to come in, the money goes away. And that's very foolish – including beef, which is grown right here and nobody here eats it; they buy it in the supermarket. There are many other things that could be made in cities or small towns. Almost anything we have. A little country like Switzerland should make automobiles. Why do they bring automobiles from Germany? Doesn't make sense. I think they make trucks, perhaps.

RW   Weapons.

DJ   Do the Swiss make weapons, too? I know there are a lot of them flying around.

RW   Do weapons play a role in your personal life?

DJ   Well, I have weapons, but that's because you need them here. Is that what you're asking? I'm very much against weapons, and I'm against the United States producing them in such quantities. Basically, I consider this a military state, as some other people do. I'm very much against the weapons business – the United States and France, all countries cause a lot of trouble by selling weapons, and they turn it into a big business. I think it's the equivalent of the slave trade of the 1800s, and it's horrifying.

RW   Let's talk briefly about politics.

DJ   This is politics.

RW   Yes. This is politics – it's true. We have now a crisis in Russia, and you're getting ready to open now a permanent installation by Ilya Kabakov.[25] This is something like a striking coincidence.

DJ   Well, it's a coincidence because we didn't plan Yeltsin fighting Congress.

RW   Why did you invite Kabakov?

DJ   I didn't actually invite him. He came down as a friend, and then he proposed this project – it was his idea. And naturally, I thought it was great. But I didn't ask him – he's not paid for it, and I don't like to ask people for things. I'm very much against artists not being paid for their work. We didn't have the money to do it. We would have never been able to. Claes Oldenburg and Coosje van Bruggen built their piece without being paid.[26] And to me that's just good luck and friendliness on the part of artists, which is rare.

R W   We have now a conflict in Somalia – again, U S troops are going to be involved in a conflict far away. As far as I remember, your show in Vienna was held during the Gulf War.[27]

D J   Yeah, it was horrible. I call it the Iraqi-American war because all of the United States' fake wars have been Mexican-American, Spanish-American – these are all pure aggression.[28] So I think "Iraqi-American" is just fine. I can't remember whether the show had opened. It's the only absolutely scheduled war in history, which is pretty perverse. I'm not sure when it started in relation to the show.

R W   But why do American presidents, even Clinton, get involved so quickly in such wars? What is the reason?

D J   As I said, it's a military state. Other people – Gore Vidal, Noam Chomsky – say this; I didn't invent it. But I came to the conclusion all by myself. The United States is very seriously a military state, verging on totalitarianism of its own kind. Clinton's job, Bush's job, is to ensure the military budget does not decline. When the Iraqi-American war was scheduled, when they went into Kuwait, which I think was a setup between Bush and Hussein, the budget was to be cut by about 2 percent, and that disappeared in a flash. Only 2 percent. Now Clinton has it scheduled to go down from, I'm not sure the figure, something like $297 billion to around $270 billion over the next five years. This is a pretty small reduction, and it doesn't change the military economy. The reason for the war against Iraq, and for Somalia – one reason was to provide an excuse to keep the military at that level. And now there will be little wars everywhere, and they have to deal with it. The question is whether they will keep it at a level where they can deal with two Iraqi wars at once or one and a half. It's absurd.

Clinton was nominated to protect the military and protect the way things are, but he was also elected by the people for economic change. The people don't understand that much about the military, so that's the reason he bumbles around and is a total contradiction – on the one hand, he's elected for something; on the other, he's put there to do the opposite. His job is to defend the military. And he does. It doesn't change. And so Somalia is also good for that. It's a little dangerous, because it's a very vague situation. The other big reason, of course, and this pertains to Kuwait too, is that Conoco and other American oil companies bought very expensive leases from the previous Somalian government. They've got millions of dollars invested with the previous government. So now their leases are worthless because that government's not there. The Americans are there to reestablish a government and protect the right to go in and get oil.

RW   Do you think that the things going on in Russia now, this change, poses a political or military threat to the world?

DJ   If they get into a real, old-fashioned Russian civil war, I don't know, yeah. Even if they get into a war like Yugoslavia, it'll be on such a big scale that it would probably be a threat. It would certainly be a horrible thing.

RW   But the US seems to be a very peaceful country.

DJ   But that's because they take it to everybody else. The US had an enormous war in the Civil War, not much more than a hundred years ago. Six hundred and twenty thousand people died – soldiers. So that was a very violent – the bloodiest [American] war in history, up to that time. But most Americans have totally forgotten the Civil War. And they're not afraid of war because they have no experience. World War II had no effect – it was just a game. The Russians are very afraid of it. Have you been to Russia?

World War II is very present. They're seriously afraid of it. Which, of course, is good.

RW   But do you have any idea what one can do, what American citizens can do to fight such ideas?

DJ   They have to organize politically. I think he's probably not so great, but one thing [Ross] Perot would have caused is the breakup of the two political parties. The two political parties are a complete pair, controlling everything, and they need to be destroyed. You need to have more political parties. See, we're not as free as you are in Germany – you can't start a party here. You can't have a little thing like you had in Hamburg, how the Green Party came up a little, and then you have some people seated in Parliament. That can't happen here. There's no way. Clinton went through this enormous process to be nominated. You could have several million people who have no representative in Congress.

RW   So would you suggest to split the US into different countries, like Texas seceding on its own?

DJ   I think it'd be a good idea. I think the United States is too large to govern or to run. It would be better if it were a number of smaller countries, which would still be very big. Because I don't think it works. Russia's too big, too. Happily, it got smaller. But we have absolutely no say in anything here.

RW   Is there any kind of place or role you would give to the arts in such a process as educating society?

DJ   Well, the problem with supporting the arts, especially here – I mean, Germany's a real federal situation and not nearly as large a country. But it's absolutely dangerous to have the United States government have anything to do with art. Support has existed now for twenty or thirty years, but it's done nothing. In fact, the situation's worse. It goes mostly to standard institutions, it doesn't go to artists, it doesn't go to good artists, and there's no result – there's always attempts at political control. And so I don't think anything as large as the US government should be involved. The money has to come from the society, and the society has to be tolerant of this expenditure. Otherwise you don't have any art. And you don't have a certain freedom that goes with the art. And if you don't have the freedom, maybe you don't have science, and so on. You can see over the course of history that things are different at certain times. In the 1700s there was a lot of fighting – before that there was the Thirty Years' War in Germany, the Civil War in England. There was a lot of trouble, but evidently, with the development of science, there was a certain looseness in the society that permitted that, and it's also, not by coincidence, a very good century for art. I think if society doesn't have a certain looseness and freedom you're not going to have any continuation of scientific knowledge. And so the art helps in that way. Naturally, I'm also interested in defending art for itself.

R W   In this century, there were a lot of art movements that perhaps had an influence on you while you were developing your own work – de Stijl, Bauhaus, maybe this idea of the Gesamtkunstwerk, a very German expression.

D J   Yes, it's a nice word. I like it. I knew of the Bauhaus and of de Stijl, and the Russian constructivists, of course, but other than the beginning work, which has some influence from Matisse and Mondrian and Léger, my work is basically developed from the paintings of Barnett Newman, Jackson Pollock, and Mark Rothko – none in a direct way, but more as a context. And the Bauhaus and the rest all seem, which is a function of age, very remote in time to me – so very long ago and very far away. I'm much more knowledgeable and interested in them now than I was thirty or forty years ago. There was also not so much to see in New York. A little bit in The Museum of Modern Art, but not much. So my interest in all of those groups is very roundabout. The Russians were very obscure at that point — well, they existed, there were paintings in The Museum of Modern Art, but not much was known about them; there was no book. Camilla Gray's book came out later.[29]

R W   While you developed your art, what kind of discussions among the intellectuals of New York were going on?

D J   I have no idea. The situation in New York and, I think, in the whole United States was very much split into groups. I didn't know any of the painters in New York; I knew their work, but I made a point of not knowing them because I didn't want to be too involved in it before I was ready to be involved in it. I only got to know Barnett Newman in 1964, not earlier. I never met Jackson Pollock, and basically I never sat around talking with anyone. The literary situation in New York seemed to me rather backward. I didn't know much about people like Hannah Arendt; I knew of her, that she wrote about social matters.[30] My main intellectual connection was to Columbia University and American and English philosophy. I majored in philosophy; therefore, that was the context, and Columbia, at that point, was very empirical in its philosophy, and that suited me fine — that was a very happy arrangement. And afterward, with a lapse of years, I studied in the art history department at Columbia.[31] The art historians were, on the whole, rather limited. The person there that was most interesting by far, and the only one perhaps you could really call an intellectual, was Meyer Schapiro.[32] I had a course with him, American Painting 1940–1950, in 1959, probably. So he knew Barney, Reinhardt, everyone — Pollock — and he was interested in their work. Of course, he's a very good historian in his own right, with very nice books that are printed in German, on Romanesque art; nice-looking books. But it was very difficult to know writers or people in other fields. It's a little bit easier in Europe.

RW   You started as a painter and you gave up painting com-
     pletely. Why?

DJ   Well, the easiest answer is, I couldn't get what I wanted
     with painting. The problems that it presented were not
     possible to be solved.

RW   So you started to work on volumes, on a geometrical basis.

DJ   Yeah.

RW   Here in Marfa, we see different kinds of works, aluminum,
     anodized aluminum elements in series you have in the
     two big buildings [see image 61].

DJ   Yeah. They're not anodized, they're straight from the
     mill, which was even more difficult to do. So they're not
     touched, they're just cut.

RW   This is, for sure, one of your masterpieces.

DJ   Sure. It's a hundred pieces – I think it's a hundred. You're
     looking for things, for different aspects of how you think.
     But you're not really solving problems the way a scien-
     tist would solve problems. The pieces are obviously very
     spatial and very much about volume and the inside and
     the outside and how it's divided. It would be very easy to
     make another hundred, all quite different.

RW   You also use wood.

DJ   Plywood.

RW   Why do you insist on one material that has one structure
     and one color?

DJ   Well, first, because I like the material, and I don't like it to be
     confused with other materials. I don't like to hide the ma-
     terial. Work tends to become decorative, for both architec-
     ture and art, when you start combining different materials.
     Adolf Loos knew this, because he made it decorative. So if
     you start having different materials combined – metal with
     stone and so forth – it can be nice, but it is basically decora-
     tive. I feel they're too far apart in qualities. It's better to stick
     pretty much with one material. But I don't always do that –
     the one over there is green plexiglass and Cor-ten steel.

RW   I wanted to ask: when did color come back?

DJ   The color was there from the beginning.

RW   It never went out of your work?

DJ   No. I was used to being a painter. Part of the things that I thought about involved color; part of the problems I couldn't solve in the painting involved color. And it never even occurred to me not to have color. So in a way, mine is the first three-dimensional work with color. You can find exceptions, in [Jean] Arp's or Schwitters's reliefs, and so forth. Or you can say that Brancusi used color with the brass, which is color, too — but basically it's the first work with color. Chamberlain used color to some extent.

RW   Why did you choose Chamberlain for the building next door?

DJ   I liked his work, and he was relatively neglected for a long time. Myself, Chamberlain, Dan Flavin, and Robert Morris, whose work I don't like — there are probably some others that you don't even know — we were used by the Castelli Gallery as avant-garde decoration. I think I was better at surviving, but Chamberlain was very poor for a long time, decades. I thought he needed some support and that his work should be available to be seen.

RW   When we think that your work extended from sculpture, from volume in sculpture, and now to even new and greater dimensions in Marfa, I want to come back to the idea of the Gesamtkunstwerk. Do you find any relationship to this notion, or do you reject this expression completely for what you call your artistic work here in Marfa?

DJ   Well, I don't think you can think of it as a "total" artwork. My understanding of the definition of "Gesamtkunstwerk" is a theatrical situation where you have several elements: the set, the dancing, theater. I'm not interested in mixing it all up; I'm more interested in separating the activities, which is one reason for the separate studios.[33] One of the things that is wrong now with architecture is the casual mixing up of everything. I certainly don't want to make the town into a total work of art, and the town isn't going to agree to be made into a total work of art, and I don't think they should. Basically, back to Meyer Schapiro and normal matters, I think the art should be in a normal situation. It shouldn't be presented, as [José] Ortega y Gasset says, in a shopwindow.[34] It's not jewelry. Even jewelry shouldn't be presented that way. It should be mixed in with all sorts of normal activities. Art today is totally packaged, and that denies it a lot of its value and intention. In a way, it's a negation of the art, because it doesn't have any natural effect upon anyone. Everybody thinks, "Oh, it's very far from our concerns; it's something you do on Sunday with the family," or whatever. It's an intentional negation by a commercial, market-driven capitalist society. Almost done on purpose. You see it packaged everywhere. It was too natural to have a lot of little *Kunstvereins* in Germany and small museums; therefore, they had to make two big monstrosities in Bonn so it could be properly packaged. Same with The Museum of Modern Art in New York. There's no art around New York; it's all in three museums – four if you count the Metropolitan.

R W Do you think that art is still in the studios in New York?

D J Well, there aren't so many good artists, but there are some, yes. But there are fewer good artists in New York than there were in 1945.

R W What is the reason for that?

D J I think it's the debasement of the art situation by the ignorance of the museum people, of the critics, of the dealers, of everyone. If there's no thought about it and everyone wants to just sell it or play with it, then the better artists are driven away.

R W I would like to talk with you about music, because at your big parties or openings, very often there's Joe Brady, the bagpipe major.[35] Is this the music you like the most or would make, personally?

DJ   Well, I tried to make a little music in relationship to some dances by Trisha Brown, which I'll talk about in a minute. I really don't know anything about music. Naturally, I went along with everyone else and I liked Bach and Mozart and other people, but classical Scottish music is very great music – on the same level as those people – and it's relatively unknown. Unfortunately, it's often mixed in with tourist Scottish schmaltz, so people tend not to listen to it seriously. Basically, the pieces are called piobaireachd; I like the small tunes and everything, but what I really liked was the piobaireachd. I think it's great music; it has ideas in it that I like. I'm not very interested in tunes and stories and beginnings and endings and conversations anyway, and in music, certainly. The pipe music doesn't have that.

RW   But you live in a country where the blues were invented.

DJ   Blues are fine. There's a lot that's nice. A person like Lead Belly is a great musician – amazing. And a lot of the old bluegrass was great. Of course, I object to it being debased into country music. I do have records.

RW   What kind of music should I put into this film besides Joe Brady's bagpipe music?

DJ   Well, maybe we can make a little bit. But Joe has to play some of the piobaireachds; he knows which ones I like. That's easy to do. It was very difficult for me to get started with music. I was helped a little bit, or a lot, by a composer in New York named Peter Zummo,[36] who has perfectly clear ideas of his own. He put away his ideas to help me with mine, which was very nice. He was working with Trisha Brown.[37] What I needed were sounds – I just wanted sounds. I didn't want them to be associated – I didn't even want them to be from instruments, I didn't want them to be natural; I just wanted a lot of sounds. And then a great range of volume, of density, of all the possibilities, and then I wanted to be able to cut it up into parts where you hear one, then one stops, and you hear the other with lots of subdivisions. There were even sketches somewhere for all of this [image 85]. We tried it a bit, but Trisha Brown wasn't very cooperative. It's an idea. It doesn't mean it'll amount to anything. But I think music is something of a failure in this century compared to visual art and architecture. Something drastic should be done about it. There needs to be a really new music.

RW   People like Philip Glass don't really interest you?

DJ   It's too old-fashioned. Unlike visual art, most of that is just the dying end of the European tradition in music, and it's been decades and decades now, so it's very dying.

RW   In the show in Vienna, you rebuilt a stage set [image 86], and I was told you had developed it for some kind of a ballet, a dance.[38]

DJ   Yeah, this was based on an original request of Trisha Brown's. She wanted a set — and then she changed her mind — she wanted a set that could go up in a *Platz* or piazza around Europe; it could go up in the middle of the square for two days, and then be taken down. It was for a dance, but it became too much to do for the money they had. The set in Vienna was made specifically for the exhibition and its steel welded together, so it doesn't actually work. All the parts were originally meant to move up and down. And, of course, it should be made out of aluminum; it probably would have to have a special extruded frame. It would take quite a bit of mechanism. But it could be done; then it could travel all over — it could go on a tractor-trailer and it could go all over the country.

RW   So are you still interested in the piece?

DJ   Oh, yeah — it's beautiful. It's on the poster that Rutger [Fuchs] is designing.[39] It's something that should be made to work. And it would be just like a circus tent: it would go up in three or four hours, you would be able to bring the panels all the way to the ground, dividing the ground space into halves and fourths, and the upper spaces all which ways. The originating idea, which goes all the way back to watching Yvonne Rainer, back thirty years, was that the set would actually influence the choreography. If you don't want to embrace the proscenium stage, then why go along with the circumstances – this was a little bit of a Gesamtkunstwerk, actually – why go along with the circumstances where the dancers have no reaction to the set, the set has no effect upon them? With the set I made, you would suddenly have a very shallow space for people on one side and a very deep space with people on the other side, and all sorts of different circumstances; dancers would have to deal with that. Or the players in a play.

RW   Is this the only work you did for the stage?

DJ   I did two things for Trisha Brown. One where the choreography was almost finished, so what I did was almost a backdrop, and it was very quiet.[40] But they still perform that piece. And then this one, which was supposed to have more to do with the dancers, but in her judgment, it had too much to do with the dancers. She didn't really want to cooperate, despite what she said.

RW   That happens from time to time.

DJ   When I'm really interested in something and think about it and worry about it for a certain length of time, then I think I should do something about it. Architecture is a very permanent interest. Writing was always pretty natural to me, and I like to do it if I'm pushed a little bit. Usually I need a little pushing. It comes from being critical of what is being done. There is some good choreography. There's work by Trisha Brown that's very new – mostly older work – very new and nice, and, of course, Yvonne Rainer and others.

RW   But let's come back to you as an artist. When did you have your first exhibition as a sculptor?

DJ   At the Green Gallery in 1963 [see images 2, 3].[41]

RW   When did you come in contact with Leo Castelli?

DJ   Green Gallery closed, and I believe I went to Castelli in '66. I'm pretty sure I had the exhibition there in '66.[42] Probably went into the gallery in 1965.

RW   Was it through the connections and the knowledge of Castelli that you first came to Europe?

DJ   Partly, but partly not. A lot of art dealers wanted worldwide control. Castelli and Ileana Sonnabend together were certainly interested in that. Ileana really wanted to control everything in Europe for her artists. I had a show at her gallery.[43] But about the same time — I think she was mad about it, but I didn't even think to ask her — I had a show with [Rudolf] Zwirner in Cologne.[44] Anyway, we never got along afterward.

RW   But you also had a show very early with [Galerie] Heiner Friedrich.[45]

DJ   Well, that's quite a bit later, if you really compare dates. Those shows were in the late '60s, 1970, maybe. I think I had already had my first show in Eindhoven at the Van Abbemuseum; I think the first one was 1970.[46]

RW   You worked together with the Dia Art Foundation. Was it your idea to collaborate with them, or did they come to you?

DJ   They definitely came to me. I had shown in Heiner Friedrich's[47] gallery in Cologne.[48] I didn't especially dislike him, but I did not especially like him either, or trust him. They came to me. I would never have gone to them. I was already here, and had been here for some time.

RW   But then they made this a Dia project.

DJ   Only Fort D. A. Russell — my situation was already pretty large. I first came to Marfa in November 1971, spent the summer, and came back down in the winter. I bought the Block in '73, '74 maybe; it was in two parts. The connection with Heiner Friedrich began in '78, '79. So that was much later, as things go.

R W   Can you describe the way you worked together, and how or why it finally broke?

D J   I was suspicious of Heiner Friedrich and his colleague Thordis Moeller[49] when they proposed this. Of course, it was handy for me to be here, because it was more or less home – I was getting divorced and my kids were to stay here, so it was convenient for something to be happening here. When they made their proposal, I said I wanted a contract, and we made a contract saying that I would be totally in charge of everything, that everything would be permanent – nothing could be taken away later. He told me at that meeting – it was in the building they had in downtown New York – that he had a grand scheme whereby he would make the projects, make the installations, make the artists famous, and then Thordis would sell a lot of the work in Europe. But Thordis was not so smart, so I thought, "That'll never happen." But of course they did try it, and I imagine they're still doing it. It was all rather shady. I was very afraid that they would try to take the art from the projects, the installations, and then possibly put it on the market. This was just a suspicion, because I never gave them a chance to do that. But I think that's what they intended. Therefore I had the contract, and the contract said "in perpetuity," which is forever. The contract was absolutely clear – it was drawn up by my friend John Jerome of Milbank, Tweed in New York, and it saved the day.[50] They couldn't fight it. I think the whole thing was meant to be commercial. I think if they had gotten this place, they would have sold the aluminum pieces. That's probably what they're now doing with Dan Flavin.[51]

R W   When did you separate?

D J   It was really drawn out. The contract was over by the end of '84, and we'd already been fighting for a long time. I threatened to sue them, and then Dominique de Menil, with the new board, kicked Heiner out. But they all turned out to be absolute rats as well and lied about everything. They threw Bob Whitman out of his building and were incredibly ruthless.[52] Both groups were ruthless. When I realized they had no intention of maintaining the projects and the artworks, which is in the contract, and that they might close everything down and possibly try to sell it, I said, "Let's go ahead and sue them." That was the end of '85. That evidently scared them, and they settled.

R W How did you find the strength to be so independent?

D J I don't think the work should be mistreated. I don't think anyone's work should be mistreated. And visual art is an activity in itself; it's not meant to make Heiner Friedrich rich or make Panza feel good or to advance the career of some museum curator. All of these uses are against the art, and it obviously needs a strong defense. I did not intend to let them ruin my work. There was the agreement that this was to be permanent; it was meant to be taken care of. I wouldn't let them, or anyone else, for that matter, destroy it. Otherwise, you're not going to have anything. Unfortunately, most of the other artists involved did not do that. Dan Flavin could easily have defended his small project, it was all that he was left with on Long Island, and he lost that to them.[53] The whole enterprise was very much about property. They still have a lot of real estate. The bulk of the money went to real estate, to the Twombly paintings, to the Warhol paintings, and not to the projects.

R W Let's come back to your career again. When did your success start?

D J It hasn't started yet. I'm waiting.

R W You worked as an artist in New York for a long time without having money, without having success. When did this change? When did the public interest in your work begin?

D J In a strange way, there's not so much public interest. It's only half a joke that there's no success. I've been on the outside of almost any group or art activity that you can think of. As I said, the Castelli Gallery treated me and the other people I mentioned just as decoration. We were meant to be the radicals, while the real money went to Jasper Johns, Rauschenberg, and Roy Lichtenstein for relatively conservative paintings. It was good to have some radicals, because it's a selling point, but it wasn't so good for our work. It's easy to see if you look in the old magazines: there was no critical support. In some ways, I was well known, and in some ways, I still am well known, but I don't quite know how or why. There's absolutely no writing, hardly any – there's a nice article[54] by Robert Hughes[55] from 1970 in *Time* magazine, but there's almost no writing that says anything.

RW You helped describe your own position in art by writing and publishing. You're famous now. Do you think people fear you because you remain something of a secret? Maybe they don't understand you?

DJ I think partly I'm a secret; partly people are a little afraid of me. They probably don't want to think too hard about the work – it doesn't fit into any of their rather simple categories. There are so many reviews where they clearly don't know what to say. So it's a funny combination of being well known but also rather invisible.

RW But now you are well known, even in Japan.

DJ Yes, well, Japan didn't buy a damn thing – we had to pay for both museum shows.[56] So that's another kind of invisibility. When it costs us money to make the shows, it's a lot of extra work. One museum, Shizuoka, was supposed to buy a piece; it was an agreement that wouldn't have cost them much. And they didn't even do that. So basically, we financed two big museum shows. I'm mad at Japan. I don't know what it means. You can be in lots of magazine articles, but there's still a lack of money and lots of dirty tricks.

RW How do you support all of your activities?

DJ Well, things have dwindled considerably. Once George

Bush started, the art market went downhill fast. There were a lot of sales over three years – maybe the art business went a little crazy. Since everyone else was selling a lot, I benefited, but it went sharply down. My main connection now, of course, is with the Pace Gallery.

RW   Why did you change to Pace?

DJ   Two things. I like Paula Cooper, but Paula clearly did not understand that the art market was going to pieces at the speed it was, and she was not going to do anything about it. Perhaps she didn't have the money. And also, which is too bad, I don't really like any of her artists except Carl Andre. So in a way, it's not a very good gallery.

RW   But now at Pace you are together, for example, with the painter Georg Baselitz.

DJ   What can I do about some of these people? [Julian] Schnabel, too. All I can say is that at least there's a majority in the Pace Gallery.

RW   Do you still think that it is important for an artist to have one main gallery?

DJ   No. My general philosophy, and this is the same intention as in my politics, would be to have a lot of galleries all over the world. But the art business is too small and too primitive and the dealers really will not pay attention to where they are and build up that kind of situation; instead they run around and sell to each other and try to create their own little international market – that defeats the local gallery. I would like to have at least two galleries in France and two in Germany and so forth. But it all winds up in the same bucket and doesn't do any good.

RW   Many of your pieces are in European collections. The Amsterdam show at the Stedelijk, Rudi Fuchs[57] told me, is all from public collections – eight rooms filled with your art.[58]

DJ   Eight rooms?

RW   Eight rooms, he told me.

DJ   God, it grew.

RW   Yeah, it's big. Can you name one museum with your work that you like?

DJ   The museum I've liked best is Rudi's old museum, the Van Abbemuseum in Eindhoven. The architecture is clear and simple and it's very flexible. For that reason, you can do a lot with it. It's not so large, but it's large enough, and I dealt with it three times with three very different shows.[59] The first show was under Jan Leering. I don't have a clear idea of the collection; I've never seen it together. They have several pieces of mine. The show in Baden-Baden in the Kunsthalle also looked good.[60] Of course, they don't have a collection, which is okay, too, but older spaces are easier to work with. [The Kunstverein] St. Gallen was pretty nice to deal with.[61] I guess they have a collection, but it's in the early stages, I believe. At least there are some places where the director or the curator is serious, and where the building is a place you can make a decent show in. Basically you can't say that of the United States; the Whitney is horrible to have exhibitions in.

RW   Is there a private collector you think has a particularly good collection?

DJ   A lot of people have a lot of art, but that doesn't necessarily make good collections. If you have a hundred works of art and fifty of them are trash, that's not very good judgment. And almost all collectors tend to collect across the board, which I think is naive and certainly not what I do. They think it's all one scene and that you should have a little bit of everything, and I think that's a big mistake. There are people who have smaller collections that are nice. But the really enormous collections, unless you try to install them in a really good way, seem to me pointless. Or a collection that is in a basement somewhere is pointless.

RW   Or in the bank. What is the role of the banks in the art market? For example, Chase Manhattan Bank started an art investment fund…

D J   Again, that's a use of art, and I think it would be better if
      art were not used for all these other purposes. I don't think
      Chase or anyone else, nearly, will know enough. Actually,
      they're not such great bankers – they lost a lot of money.
      They're not going to know enough to invest well. I assume
      if you buy stocks, you really should know what you're do-
      ing, but there's almost no one who knows. I think I can do
      it. You really have to know the good work, but you also
      have to be really patient. If I had had a little cash thirty
      years ago, I would have a fabulous collection. I told my
      friend John Jerome, "Just give me a couple hundred dollars
      every now and then and I'll really make an incredible col-
      lection for you," which I could've done. There were two
      sizes of [Josef] Albers's paintings – the smaller ones were
      $500, the bigger ones $1,000. Frank Stella bought a big
      painting by Ad Reinhardt for $1,000, and so on. I almost
      got a great big painting by Reinhardt for $25,000, later.
      So I think this is easy to do, but you really have to know
      how, and almost nobody knows. There's no art dealer I
      can think of whose judgment is really good enough. And
      if they don't know, who else is there? I mean, not some-
      body who works for Chase Manhattan.

R W   There's a newly created profession called "art consultant."

D J   I think this is adding bureaucracy to a situation, which is
      always bad.

R W   Yes, that's true. Okay, Don. Thank you very much.

This conversation was sourced from an audio recording. The original recording is
in the Chinati Foundation Archives, Marfa, Texas.

First published (excerpt): *Bauhaus, Texas: Donald Judd, ein amerikanischer Künstler*,
directed by Regina Wyrwoll (Munich: Goethe-Institut; Mainz, Germany: Zweites
Deutsches Fernsehen, 1994), aired 1994, 55 min. (in English and German); reprinted: "Donald Judd in Conversation with Regina Wyrwoll," Chinati Foundation newsletter 14, October 2009, 13–35 (in English and Spanish).

1   Judd enlisted in the United States Army on June 28, 1946, and was assigned
        to the Corps of Engineers in Korea. He was honorably discharged on No-
        vember 20, 1947.
2   Judd refers here to 101 Spring Street.
3   Judd refers here to the Neue Staatsgalerie, Stuttgart, a postmodern museum
        developed to complement the city's 1843 Staatsgalerie. It was designed by
        James Stirling in 1977 and completed in 1984.
4   Judd refers here to the Architecture Office.
5   Wyrwoll refers here to the Peter Merian Haus in Basel, next to the Bahn-
        hof Basel ssb (the city's central train station). Judd worked in collabora-
        tion with Zwimpfer Partner Architekten to design the façade of the build-
        ing, an alternating matte and transparent glass exterior. The building was
        completed in 2000.
6   In 1991, Judd was approached to design the administrative building of the
        Kunsthaus Bregenz in Bregenz, Austria. Judd produced drawings for the
        building in 1992, but due to his death in 1994, Peter Zumthor, lead archi-
        tect for the Kunsthaus Bregenz, realized the building according to his own
        design in 1997.
7   The Godbold feed mill, located across the street from La Mansana de
        Chinati/The Block, was constructed around 1963 and operated as a com-
        mercial livestock feed manufacturing facility until fall 2018.
8   Judd worked as a for-hire art critic, often reviewing over fifteen shows a
        month, from 1959 to 1965.
9   Judd received his bs in philosophy from Columbia University, cum laude,
        in 1953.
10   Judd included eleven books by Noam Chomsky in his library in Marfa,
        Texas.
11   Judd refers here to the McDonald Observatory, part of The University
        of Texas at Austin, located in the Davis Mountains of West Texas. He be-
        came a member of the observatory's Board of Visitors in 1989.
12   *Roni Horn: Rare Spellings, Selected Drawings 1985–1992*, Kunstmuseum Win-
        terthur, Switzerland, March 20–May 16, 1993.
13   *Michael Scholz*, Kölnischer Kunstverein, Cologne, March 17–April 14, 1991.
14   Judd refers here to the Kunstmuseum Bonn (designed by Axel Schultes)
        and the Bundeskunsthalle (designed by Gustav Peichl), both completed in
        1992 in Bonn, Germany. That same year, Judd wrote that "Gustav Peichl's
        new Bundeskunsthalle in Bonn, very general and bland, big and sightless,
        as in the 1930s, is in style fascist, neofascist." Judd, "Fine Art and Commer-
        cial Architecture" (1992) in *Donald Judd Writings*, 780.

15   Judd likely refers here to the recently completed Museum für Moderne Kunst, Frankfurt, designed by Hans Hollein. He wrote about this building, "The new museum by Hans Hollein in Frankfurt is highly fascist in its external appearance – I haven't been inside since animals tend to avoid pain. Hollein's museum is bland and cute." Judd, "Fine Art and Commercial Architecture" (1992) in *Donald Judd Writings*, 780.

16   Achille Bonito Oliva (1939–) is an Italian critic and art historian.

17   Giuseppe Panza di Biumo (1923–2010) was a prominent Italian collector of modern art. See Judd's "Una stanza per Panza" (1990) in *Donald Judd Writings*, 630–99.

18   Opened to the public in 1987, the Museum Insel Hombroich, located in Neuss, Germany, is both a park and a museum.

19   The temporary exhibition program at the Chinati Foundation began in 1987, with three exhibitions that year: Josef Albers, *Prints*; Barnett Newman, *Notes*; and Robert Tiemann, *Drawings*.

20   The publication of *Book One*, the intended first volume of a new edition of Judd's writings, was not realized due to Judd's death in February 1994.

21   On November 27, 1993, Judd was presented with the Sikkens Prize in Amsterdam. For the occasion of the award presentation, Judd wrote an essay; see "Some Aspects of Color in General and Red and Black in Particular" (1993), which was printed as a small book and later in *Donald Judd Writings*, 832–58.

22   Judd attended the Art Students League, in New York, during the day from 1948 to 1953, while also working toward an undergraduate degree at night at Columbia University. He received his BS in philosophy from Columbia, cum laude, in 1953.

23   In December 1989, Judd incorporated La Junta de los Rios for the purpose of promoting and distributing produce and goods from the Big Bend region of Texas.

24   Translates from the German as "milk center."

25   As a gift to the Chinati Foundation, Ilya Kabakov created and installed *School No. 6* (1993) on the foundation's grounds. The work occupies an entire former barrack that was subdivided into rooms and reminiscent of an abandoned schoolhouse from the former Soviet Union.

26   As a gift to the Chinati Foundation, Claes Oldenburg and Coosje van Bruggen created and installed *Monument to the Last Horse* (1991), their version of an equestrian sculpture, on the foundation's grounds. See Judd's "*Monument to the Last Horse*: Animo et Fide" (1992) in *Donald Judd Writings*, 790–806.

27   *Donald Judd: Architektur*, Österreichisches Museum für angewandte Kunst, Vienna, February 14–April 8, 1991.

28   See Judd's "Nie Wieder Krieg" (1991) in *Donald Judd Writings*, 722–31.

29   Camilla Gray, *The Great Experiment: Russian Art 1863–1922* (London: Thames & Hudson, 1962). Judd included the 1986 revised and expanded edition of this book, *The Russian Experiment in Art: 1863–1922*, in his library in Marfa, Texas.

30   Judd included eleven books by Hannah Arendt in his library in Marfa,
      Texas.

31   Judd began graduate work in art history at Columbia University in fall
      1957 and completed his coursework in fall 1961. No degree was conferred
      because he did not complete the requirements.

32   Judd studied with Meyer Schapiro (1904–1996) while a graduate student
      at Columbia University. Schapiro was an influential art critic, art histo-
      rian, and professor. Judd included nine books by Schapiro in his library in
      Marfa, Texas.

33   Judd worked out of a number of studio and office spaces, each which
      served a distinct purpose, including the Architecture Studio, the Art Studio,
      the Architecture Office, the Ranch Office, the Cobb House, the Whyte
      Building, and a studio at Las Casas, his largest ranch.

34   Judd refers here to a passage from José Ortega y Gasset's *Man and People*
      in which Ortega y Gasset likens modern society's approach to culture to
      a person standing in front of a jeweler's window, deciding whether or not
      to acquire a discrete object. See *Man and People*, trans. Willard R. Trask
      (New York: W. W. Norton, 1957), 31–32. Judd included this book in his li-
      brary in Marfa, Texas. Additionally, see Judd's "Statement for the Chinati
      Foundation/La Fundación Chinati" (1987) in *Donald Judd Writings*, 486–
      87, where Judd quotes this passage in its entirety.

35   Judd met Joe Brady, Sr., a bagpiper, in New York around 1970; over the
      years, Judd invited Joe Brady, Sr., and his son, Joe Brady, Jr., who is also a
      bagpiper, to participate in many events, openings, and celebrations.

36   Peter Zummo (1948–) is an American trombonist and composer.

37   Zummo and Judd worked together to create the sound concept for Tri-
      sha Brown's *Newark (Niweweorce)* (1987). Judd also designed the produc-
      tion's visual presentation and costumes.

38   In 1991, Judd took the set he had designed for Brown's *Newark (Niweweorce)*
      and developed it into a stationary piece for indoor display in the exhibi-
      tion *Donald Judd: Architektur*, Österreichisches Museum für angewandte
      Kunst, Vienna, February 14–April 8, 1991. In 1996, it was moved to Vienna's
      Stadtpark, where it is permanently installed outdoors.

39   Rutger Fuchs (1970–), the son of art historian and curator Rudi Fuchs,
      is a Dutch designer.

40   Judd's first stage collaboration with Trisha Brown was for *Son of Gone
      Fishin'* (1981). Judd designed the visual presentation and the set; he also
      provided the idea for the costumes, which were based on the color scheme
      of his set design.

41   *Don Judd*, Green Gallery, New York, December 17, 1963–January 11,
      1964. This exhibition was Judd's first solo show to include works in three
      dimensions.

42   *Don Judd*, Leo Castelli Gallery, New York, February 5–March 2, 1966.

43   *Don Judd: Structures*, Galerie Ileana Sonnabend, Paris, May 6–29, 1969.

44   *Don Judd*, Galerie Rudolf Zwirner, Cologne, June 4–30, 1969.

45   *Zeichnungen und Graphik von Don Judd*, Galerie Heiner Friedrich, Munich, January 15–26, 1971.

46   *Don Judd*, Stedelijk Van Abbemuseum, Eindhoven, The Netherlands, January 16–March 1, 1970.

47   Heiner Friedrich (1938–) is a German art dealer. Along with Philippa de Menil and Helen Winkler, he cofounded Dia Art Foundation in 1974.

48   Galerie Heiner Friedrich had locations in Munich, Cologne, and New York; Judd had solo exhibitions at all three locations in the 1970s, showing work at the Cologne gallery at least three times during this period.

49   Thordis Moeller is a German art collector and a former director of Galerie Heiner Friedrich's Cologne and New York locations.

50   John J. Jerome (1933–) was Judd's lawyer and longtime friend. The name of his firm was Milbank, Tweed, Hadley & McCloy, now Milbank LLP.

51   In 1983, Dan Flavin established a permanent installation of nine of his works in a renovated firehouse in Bridgehampton, New York. Known as the Dan Flavin Art Institute, the building and installation are part of Dia Art Foundation.

52   Judd refers here to 512 West Nineteenth Street, a Dia-owned building in New York, which the foundation had been loaning to artist Robert Whitman to use as a performance space. In 1985, as part of a swath of austerity measures, Dia put the building up for sale. It was rented to and then purchased by The Kitchen, which continues to operate there today.

53   In the 1980s, Dia purchased a building in Garrison, New York (north of Manhattan, along the Hudson River), with plans to permanently install work by Flavin there; this project was abandoned in 1985 due to financial concerns. However, the Dan Flavin Art Institute, established by Dia and the artist in Bridgehampton, Long Island, in 1983, still exists and continues to be stewarded by Dia.

54   Robert Hughes, "Exquisite Minimalist," *Time*, May 24, 1971, 68, 69, 71.

55   Robert Hughes (1938–2012) was an Australian-born art critic and television documentarian. From 1970 until 2001, he was the chief art critic for *Time* magazine; his eight-episode 1980 television series on the development of modernism, *The Shock of the New*, was highly popular.

56   *Donald Judd*, Gallery Yamaguchi, Osaka, January 20–February 22, 1992; Shizuoka Prefectural Museum of Art, Shizuoka, Japan, June 13–July 26, 1992; Kitakyushu Municipal Museum of Art, Kitakyushu, Japan, May 1–30, 1993.

57   Rudi Fuchs (1942–) is a Dutch art historian and curator and was a friend of Judd's. In 1975, Fuchs became director of the Van Abbemuseum, Eindhoven; between 1987 and 1993, he was director of the Gemeentemuseum Den Haag, The Hague, a position he vacated to become director of the Stedelijk Museum, Amsterdam.

58   *Donald Judd: Werken uit Nederlandse openbare collecties en een Belgische privé verzameling t.g.v. de Sikkensprijs 1993*, Stedelijk Museum, Amsterdam, November 28, 1993–January 23, 1994.

59   Judd's three solo exhibitions at the Stedelijk Van Abbemuseum, Eindhoven, The Netherlands, were *Don Judd*, January 16–March 1, 1970; *Donald Judd*, April 26–June 2, 1979; and *Donald Judd: Sculptures 1965–1987*, April 26–June 2, 1987.

60   *Donald Judd*, Staatliche Kunsthalle Baden-Baden, Germany, August 27–October 15, 1989.

61   *Donald Judd*, Kunstverein St. Gallen, Switzerland, April 21–July 29, 1990.

Interview with Joshua Homnick and Rainer Judd
October 10, 1993

This conversation with Rainer Judd, the artist's daughter, and her friend the film-maker Joshua Homnick took place around the kitchen table of the Porter House in Marfa, Texas. Homnick filmed the conversation. In the early 1990s, Judd purchased this house with the intention of creating a space specially dedicated to writing. It was built by the family of the writer Katherine Anne Porter.

JH [Joshua Homnick] My question is related to something
    you said earlier that I'm really interested in hearing more
    about it. You were saying how it's stupid to think that suc-
    cess and money mean anything, so I wanted to hear about
    what does mean something.

DJ [Donald Judd] The people – everybody – which is per-
    haps one reason you have a society. Everybody believes in
    the society to an extent that I find bizarre. The society is
    a hierarchy, which is very strong, despite all the nonsense
    about democracy. I think that it's a very local and little
    view of the society and of history. The little society they
    believe in will be a very different society in twenty years
    than it was fifty or one hundred years ago.

RJ [Rainer Judd] What do you think there should be a be-
    lief in? Don't you think there should be a belief in some-
    thing?

DJ Perhaps you can do without beliefs in things you can't
    believe in.

RJ What do you think there is that somebody can believe in?

DJ Perhaps you can't have a big generalization to believe
    in. Maybe it can't be simple anymore – maybe it's too
    simple-minded to make a big belief. It doesn't hold. You
    can't believe in a big societal order now, as in commu-
    nism, or whatever capitalism is, which is sort of a joke.
    But you have a certain knowledge about the universe be-
    yond the earth and a lot of bits and pieces. So what else
    is there? One reason you have the religions is it's widely
    simple-minded. But you don't want to promote that kind
    of stuff. Certainly now it's dangerous for everybody to
    have a bunch of people who are simple-minded. I don't
    think you can make such a simple and general belief as
    they used to. Which I think is fine. How can you believe
    in the future? The future is up there, probably, and nobody
    knows much about it. There is so much that is unknown,
    you can probably just carve it on the table. So why claim

that it's more? I think we operate pretty much on the little beliefs, and we should recognize them for what they are. The fact is, people, more or less historically, will use what's here or there or so forth for their little beliefs, and that's a big mess. It causes big excuses for little wars – big little wars and whatnot.

JH   And for you personally, would you be able to put your finger on some of these little beliefs?

DJ   Yeah, you don't want your kids to get chopped up in the garbage disposal and things like that. These things are serious. People ordinarily construct their beliefs on small things, but they want to claim that it's the whole world. Justice Holmes said in the '20s or '30s that he liked champagne, but that he saw absolutely no reason why the cosmos should like champagne.[1]

JH   So these are the little things that drive you day to day?

DJ   You have to think that most of it is fairly little and shouldn't be blown up to defend some mass war against somebody else doing the same thing. Or to justify the society. Use the whole universe all the way up to justify the US government.

JH   What happens when you are gone?

DJ   It's just a joke. In the short run, I have a standing in the history of art and so forth. Most people are not very interested in the history of art anyway. And in the long run, a thousand years maybe, who knows if they will even know much about Michelangelo. Michelangelo at this point is not so long ago, so who knows how durable all that is. It's a new situation. And in ten or twenty thousand years, people's brains might be so different that they couldn't possibly see what Michelangelo was interested in.

JH   I'd be interested to know what you believe metaphysically will happen to you personally when you die?

DJ   Bones on the land. Bones and rocks.

RJ   Worms and bugs.

DJ   Yeah, worms, they go pretty fast, too. Around here, even bones tend to not last very long. I don't believe in any sort of continuation of actuality at all.

RJ What about the idea that your spirit or your soul is continued on through your art?

DJ The art exists. It's not metaphysical: there's the art, and something exists, and other people later figure it out as best they can. They are not going to understand all of it, either. Everybody thinks they understand Rembrandt and all that, but most of what Rembrandt was thinking about is probably beyond imagining. Do you know we are all second-hand anyway, as an astronomical fact? The earth is not a product of the sun, it's just debris, and this debris is from the other suns that have collapsed. The sun hasn't gotten to the point of producing iron or carbon or anything. We are all made of other suns, long gone. So, think about that.

RJ Yeah. So this is really all there is: the sky, the ground, the glass, the bread, the people and all their strange little psychological reflections. There is no other world, there's just this world. And then there's that world, the scientific world —

DJ Well, there's worlds up there, we just don't know anything yet. The other stars. I haven't read Carl Sagan's book, the one on the cosmos, or no, the one on other worlds.[2] There has to be other worlds and other civilizations. Apparently, we will never get there and never know it.

RJ People ask me if you are at all spiritual, and all I remember is once we were in a Barney Newman show, and I understood that Barney Newman had these little spiritual interests and that you were really good friends with Barney Newman, but I didn't know anything about what Barney was interested in.

DJ Barney had a certain amount of philosophical language that is rather grand, but basically, it's this is here and now.

RJ Barney is here and now. Have you had any wanderings into nonhere-and-now thoughts?

DJ   I'm afraid it's a here-and-now situation. Or afraid or not afraid. It's pretty clear that nothing at all lasts forever. So why should people be so upset about it?

RJ   Ilya and Emilia [Kabakov] were talking about how most of their installations concern their idea that nothing lasts forever and that the end is soon.

DJ   Yeah, probably. We're sitting on land now that was probably a million years ago a hundred feet higher.

JH   Or totally submerged in water.

DJ   That's a couple of hundred million years ago.

This discussion was sourced from video footage filmed by Joshua Homnick and a 1997 transcript in the Judd Foundation Archives, Marfa, Texas.

1   The source of this quotation is not in fact Oliver Wendell Holmes, Jr., the Supreme Court justice, but his father, the popular American author Oliver Wendell Holmes, Sr. Holmes wrote, "I find [champagne] by far the best borne of all drinks containing alcohol. I do not suppose my experience can be the foundation of a universal rule." *The Writings of Oliver Wendell Holmes*, vol. 4, *Over the Teacups* (Cambridge: Riverside Press; Boston: Houghton, Mifflin, 1892), 184.

2   Judd included three books by Carl Sagan in his library in Marfa, Texas: *Cosmos* (New York: Random House, 1983); *The Dragons of Eden: Speculations on the Evolution of Human Intelligence* (New York: Random House, 1977); and *Intelligent Life in the Universe* (San Francisco: Holden-Day, 1966), cowritten by I. S. Shklovskii. Sagan's *Other Worlds* was published by Bantam Books in 1975.

Images

Unless otherwise noted,
all works are by Donald Judd.

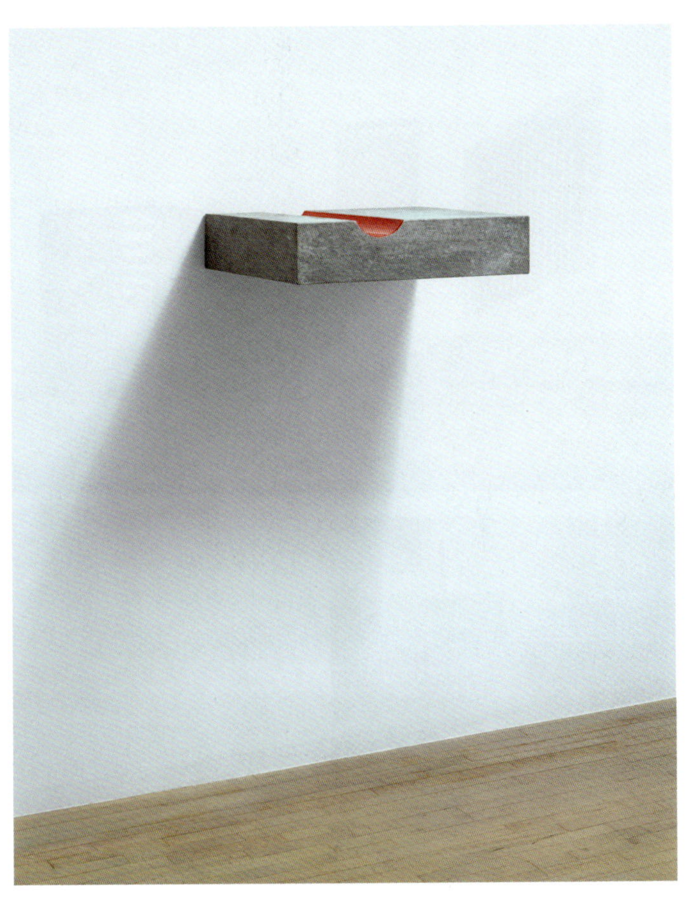

I
Untitled, 1964
Red enamel on galvanized iron
over wood
6 × 27 × 24 inches
15.2 × 68.6 × 61 cm

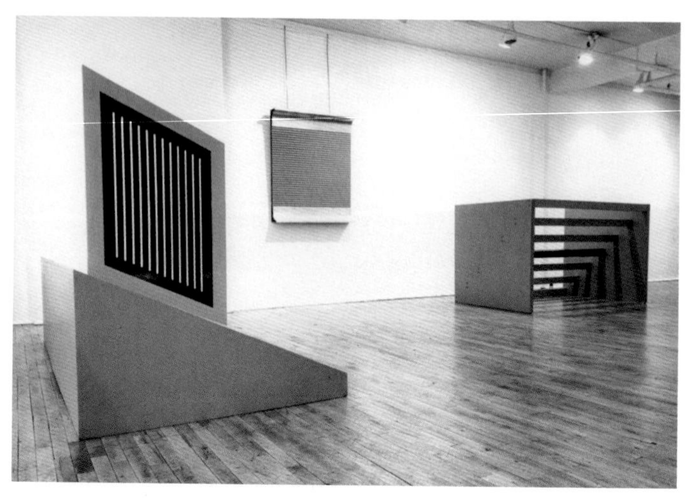

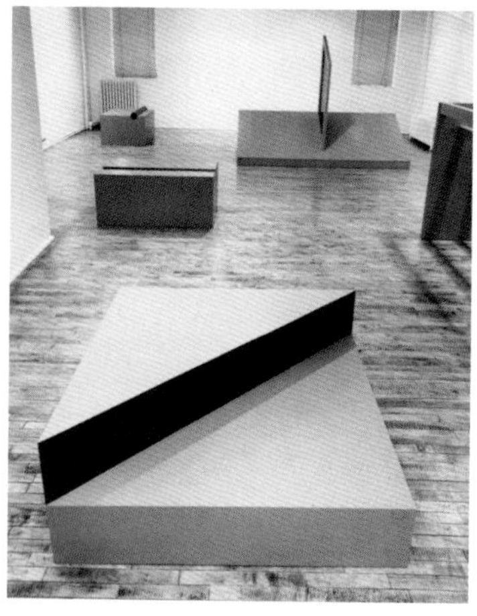

2 and 3
Installation views of *Don Judd*,
Green Gallery, New York,
December 17, 1963–January 11, 1964

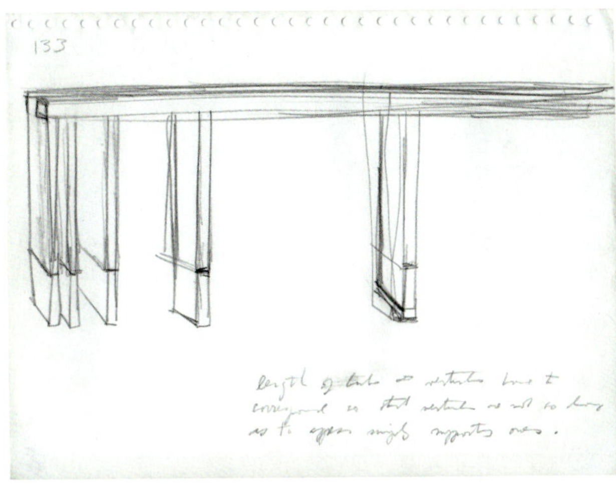

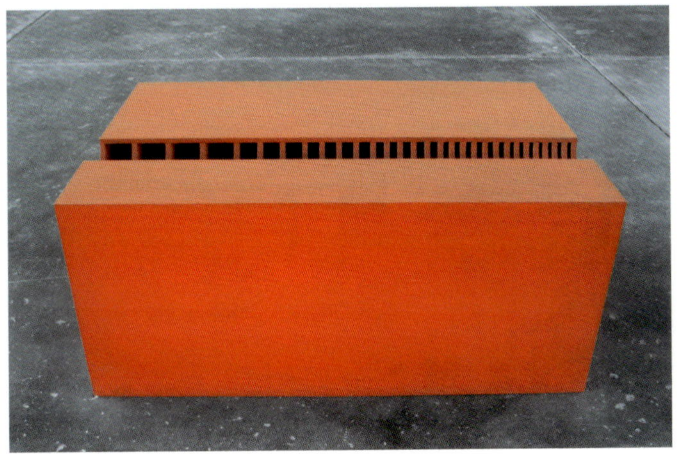

<table>
<tr><td>

4
Drawing from sketchbook,
c. 1963
Pencil on paper
8 ½ × 11 inches
21.6 × 27.9 cm

</td><td>

5
Untitled, 1963
Cadmium red light oil
on plywood
19 ½ × 45 × 30 ½ inches
49.5 × 114.3 × 77.5 cm

</td></tr>
</table>

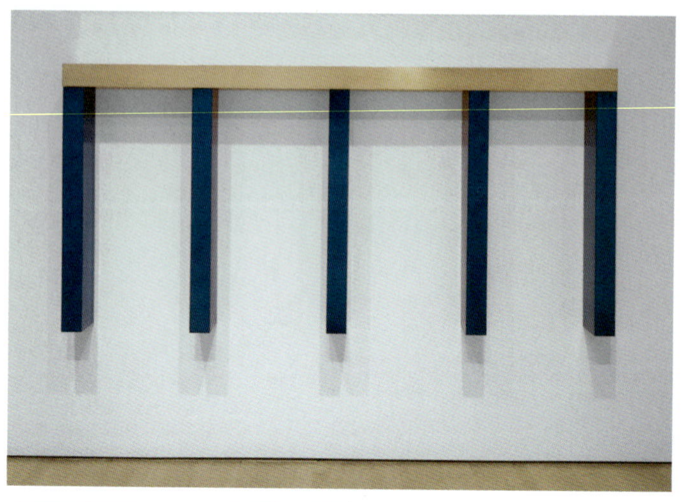

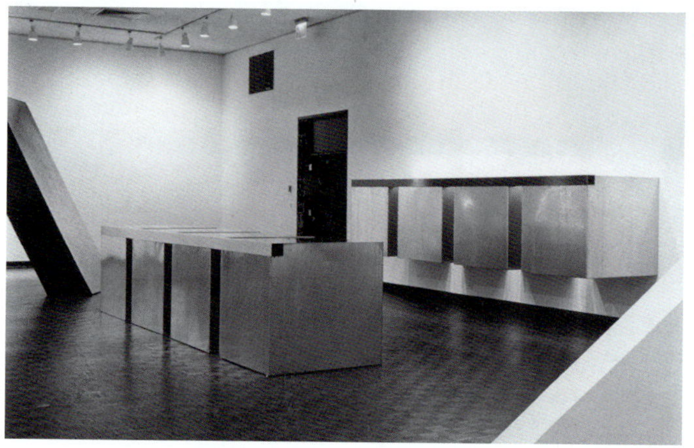

6
Untitled, 1964
Brass and blue lacquer on
galvanized iron
40 ½ × 84 × 6 ¾ inches
102.9 × 213.4 × 17.2 cm

7
Installation view of *Primary
Structures: Younger American and
British Sculptors*, Jewish
Museum, New York, April 27–
June 12, 1966

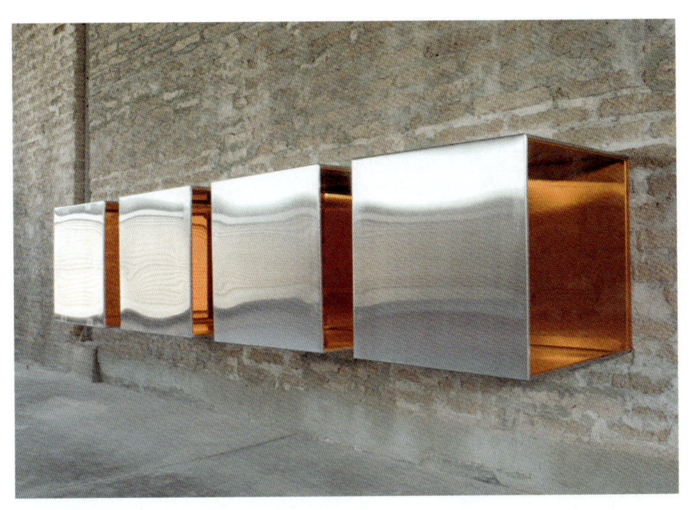

8
Untitled, 1966
Stainless steel and amber
acrylic sheets
4 units, each: 34 × 34 × 34 inches
86.4 × 86.4 × 86.4 cm

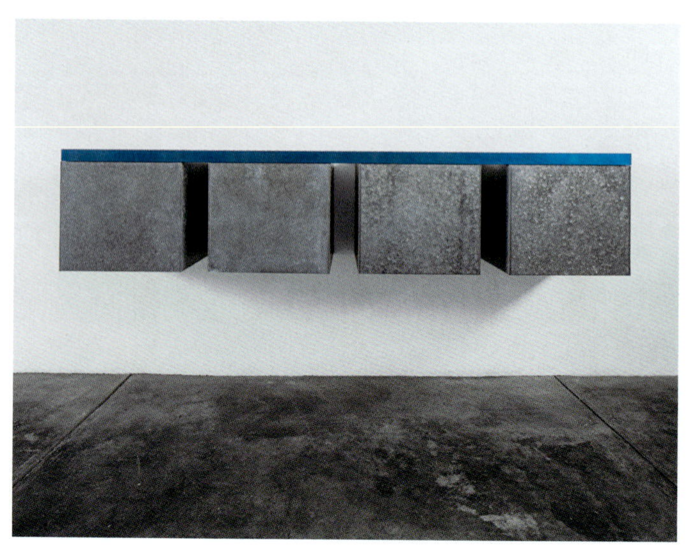

9
To Susan Buckwalter, 1964
Galvanized iron and blue lacquer
on aluminum
30 × 141 × 30 inches
76.2 × 358.1 × 76.2 cm

Note: This work shares similar
dimensions and materials to the one
discussed on 152–53 and 350–51.
The work in reference is from 1966.

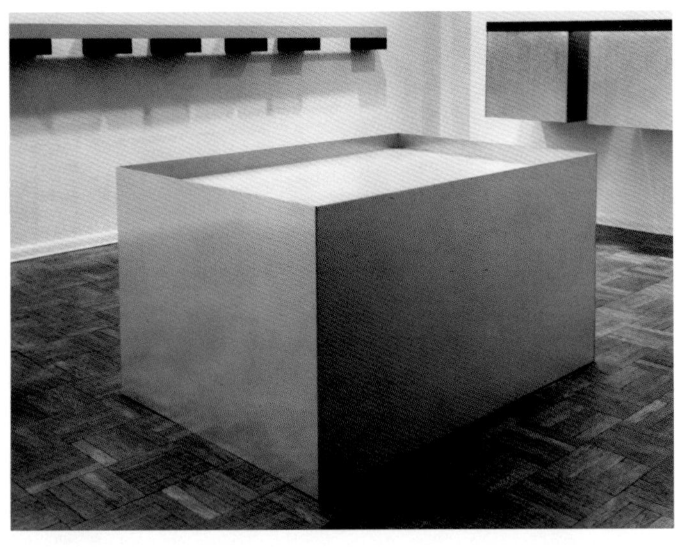

10
Installation view of *Don Judd*,
Leo Castelli Gallery, New York,
February 5–March 2, 1966

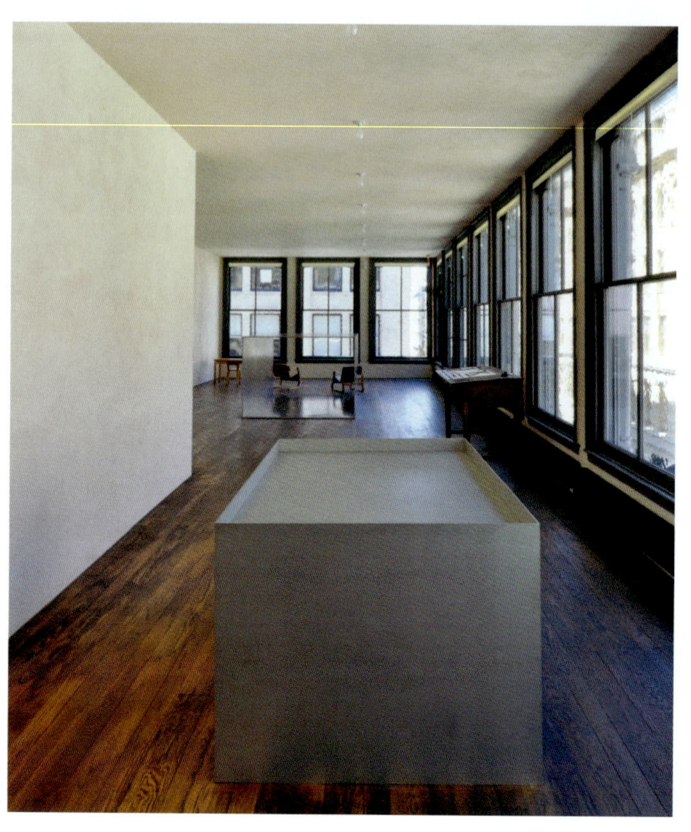

11
Untitled, 1966
Clear anodized aluminum
40 × 72 × 51 inches
101.6 × 182.9 × 129.5 cm
Installed on the third floor
of 101 Spring Street,
Judd Foundation, New York

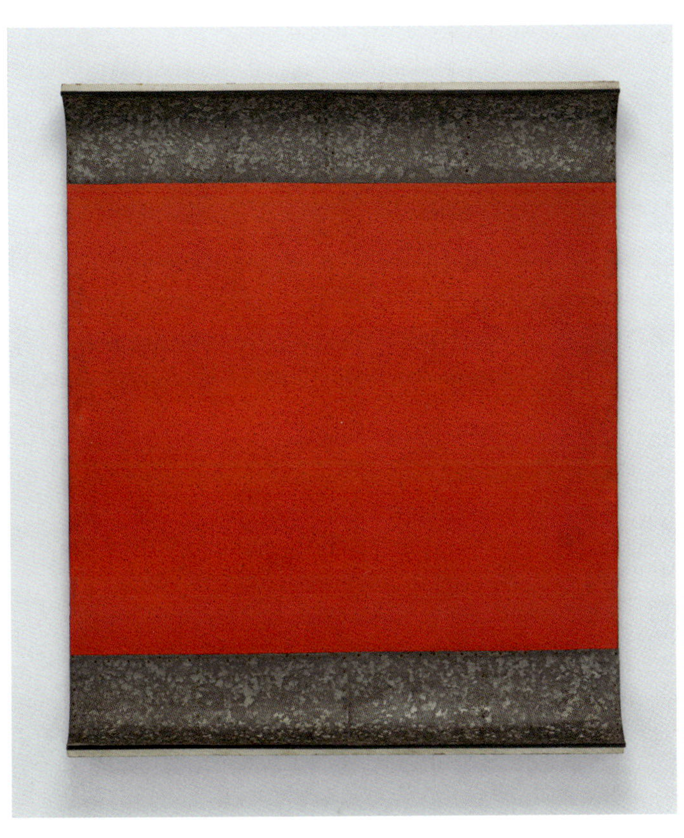

12
Untitled, 1962
Cadmium red light oil and sand,
black and white oil and galvanized
iron on wood
52 × 43 × 5 inches
132.1 × 109.2 × 12.7 cm

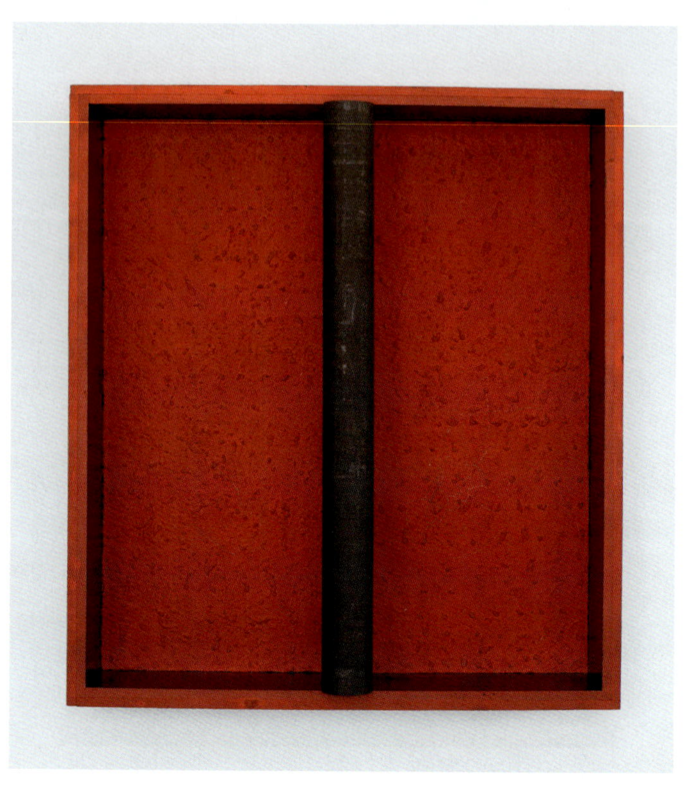

13
Untitled, 1962
Cadmium red light oil, black
enamel, wax, and sand on canvas
and wood with asphalt pipe
50 ½ × 45 × 9 ⅝ inches
128.3 × 114.3 × 24.5 cm

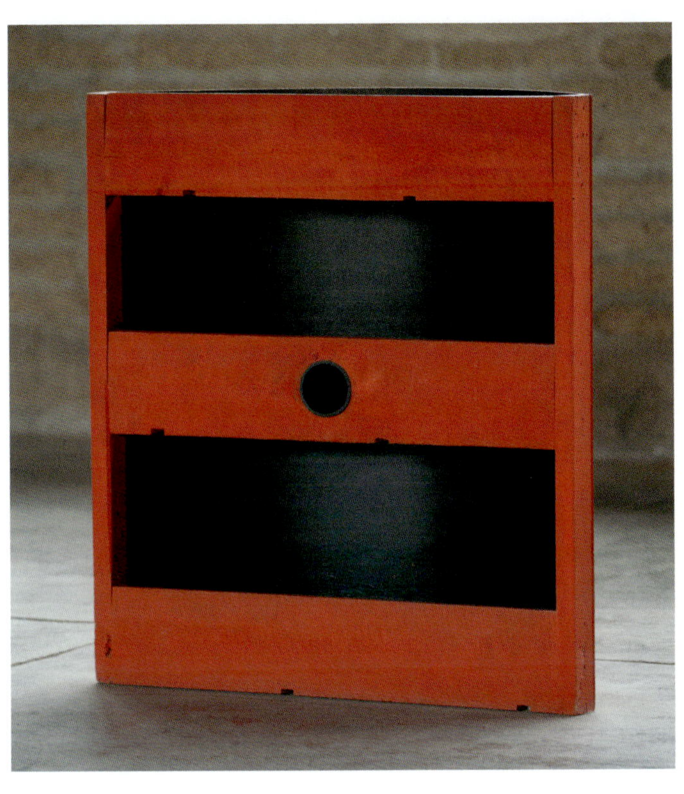

14
Untitled, 1962
Cadmium red light oil and black
enamel on wood and fiberboard
with asphalt pipe
44 ¼ × 40 ⅜ × 13 ¾ inches
112.4 × 102.6 × 34.9 cm

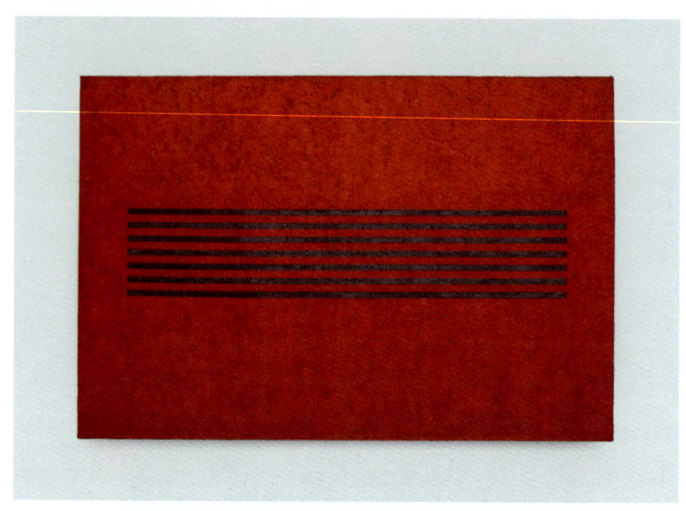

15
Untitled, 1962
Oil and wax on canvas
69 × 101 ¾ inches
175.3 × 258.5 cm

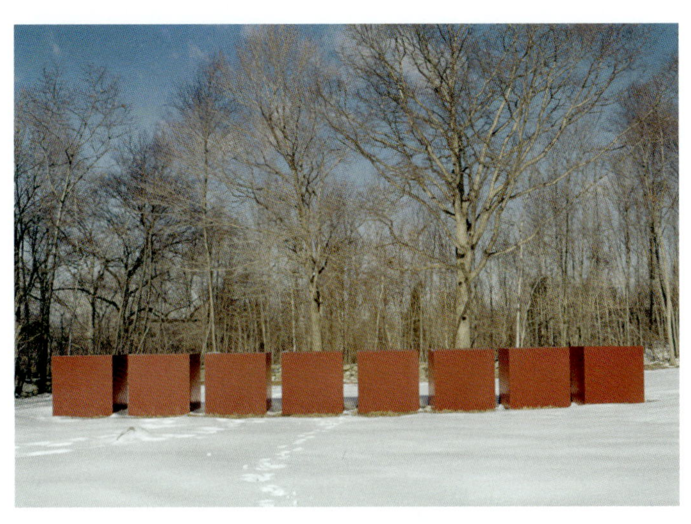

16
Untitled, 1967
Burnt sienna enamel on
cold-rolled steel
8 units, each: 48 × 48 × 48 inches
121.9 × 121.9 × 121.9 cm

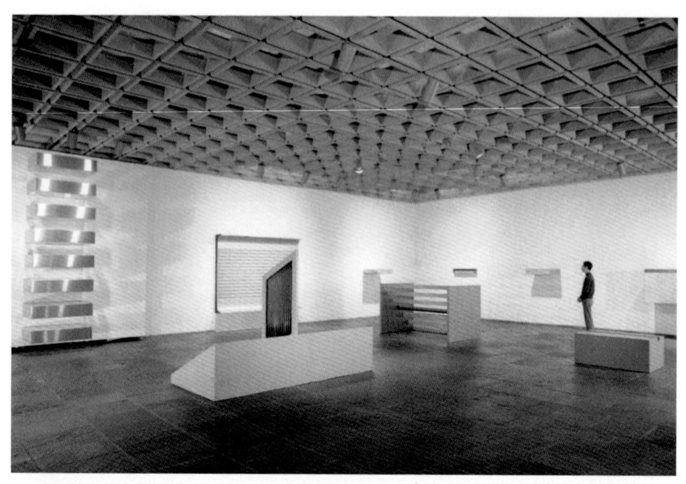

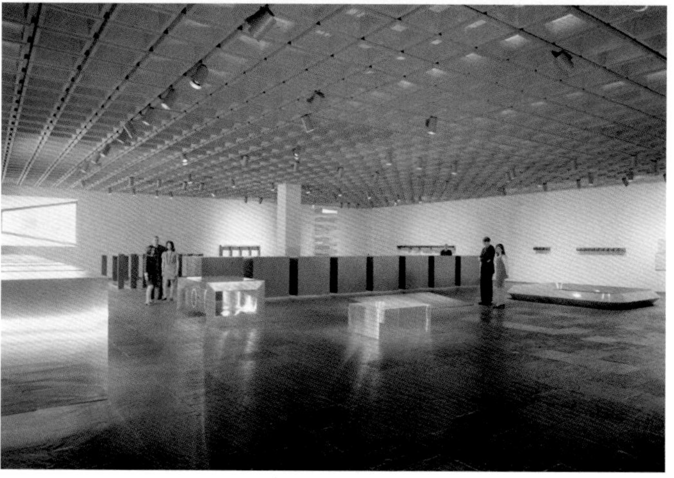

17 and 18
Installation views of *Don Judd*,
Whitney Museum of American Art,
New York, February 27–March 24,
1968, extended through April 14

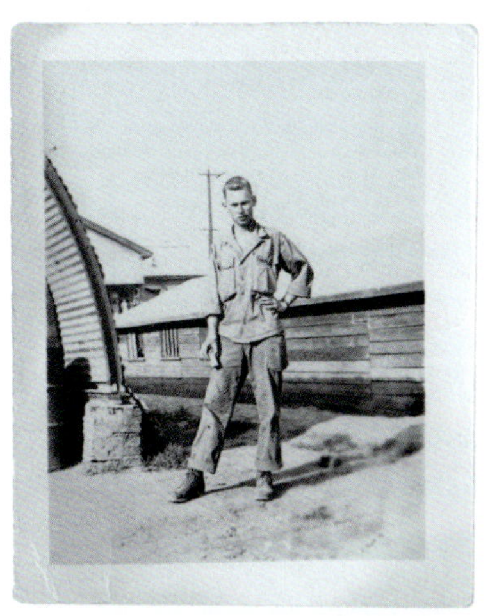

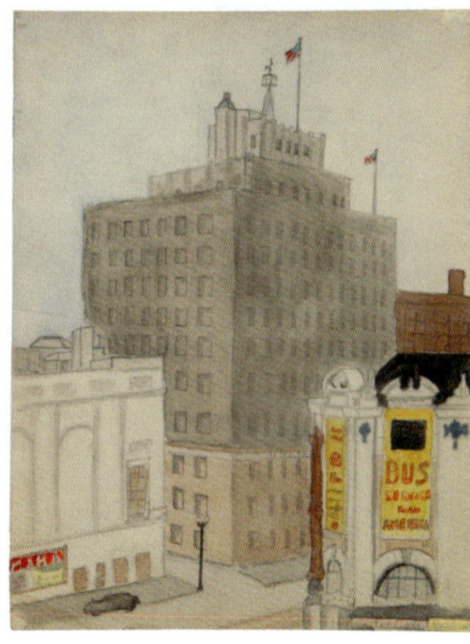

19
Donald Judd in Gimpo,
Korea, 1947

20
Untitled, 1939
Watercolor and pencil on paper
11 ¾ × 8 ¾ inches
29.8 × 22.2 cm

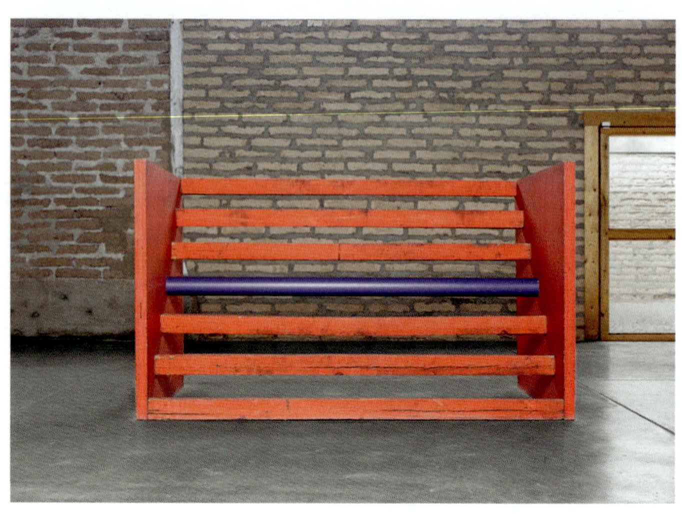

21
Untitled, 1963
Cadmium red light oil on wood
and purple enamel on aluminum
48 × 81 ½ × 48 inches
121.9 × 207 × 121.9 cm

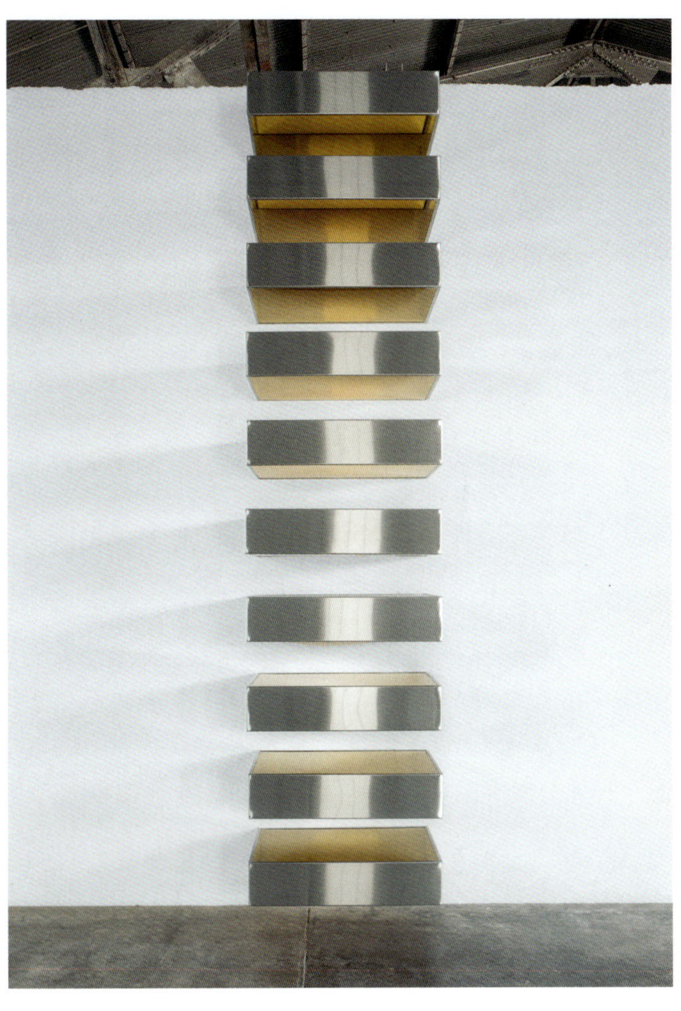

22
Untitled, 1968
Stainless steel and yellow acrylic sheets
10 units, each: 9 × 40 × 31 inches
22.9 × 101.6 × 78.7 cm

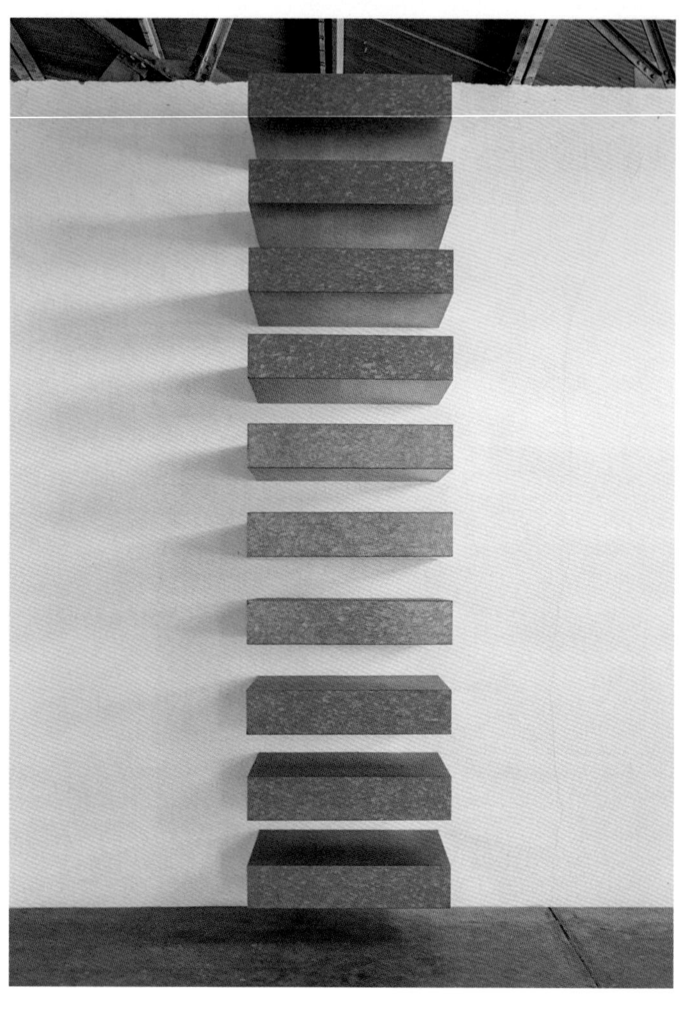

23
Untitled, 1966
Galvanized iron
10 units, each: 9 × 40 × 31 inches
22.9 × 101.6 × 78.7 cm

Note: This work shares similar
dimensions and materials to the one
discussed on 230. The work in
reference comprises eight units, not
ten as pictured here.

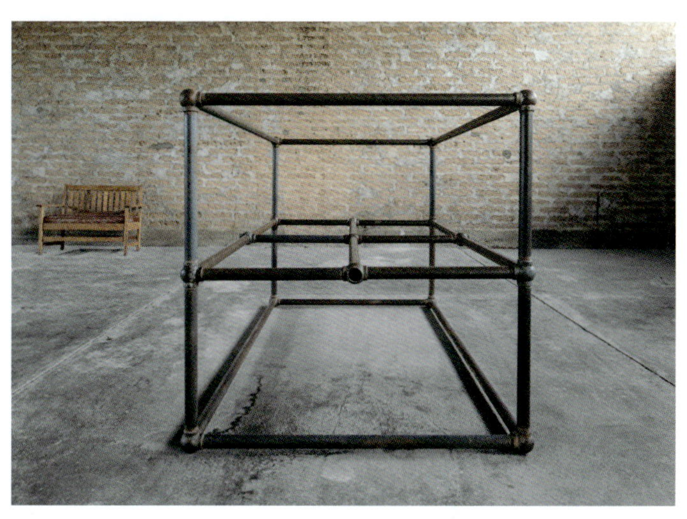

24
To Dave Shackman, 1964
Iron pipe and fittings
54 ¾ × 88 × 54 ¾ inches
139.1 × 223.5 × 139.1 cm
Installed in the south room of
the west building of La Mansana
de Chinati/The Block, Judd
Foundation, Marfa, Texas

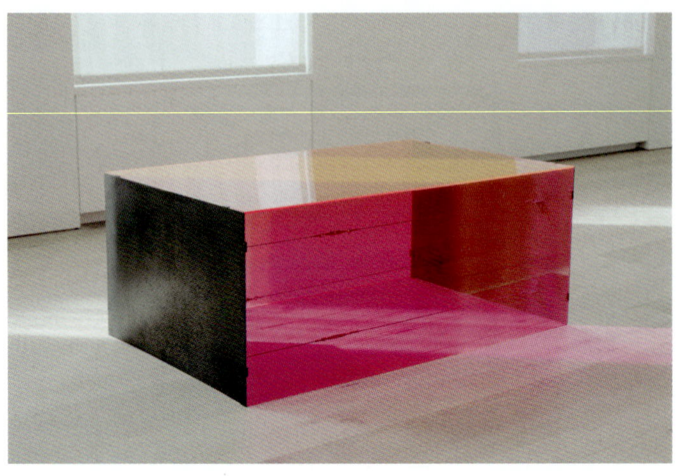

25
Untitled, 1970
Hot-rolled steel and red
fluorescent acrylic sheets
20 × 48 × 31 inches
50.8 × 121.9 × 78.7 cm

Note: This work shares similar
dimensions and materials to the ones
discussed on 237, 350, and 357.

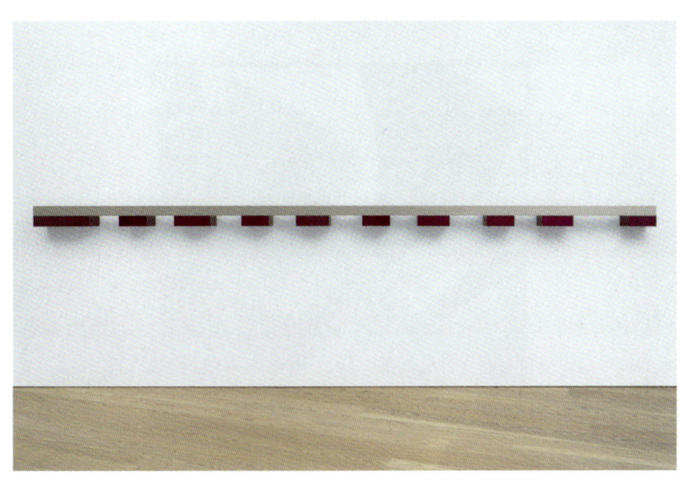

26
Untitled, 1966
Aluminum and purple lacquer
on aluminum
8 ¼ × 253 × 8 ¼ inches
21 × 642.6 × 21 cm

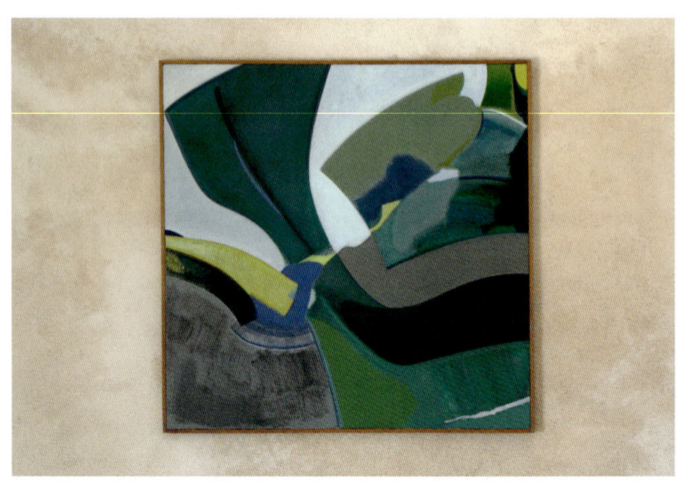

27
Untitled, 1958
Oil on canvas
36 × 36 inches
91.4 × 91.4 cm

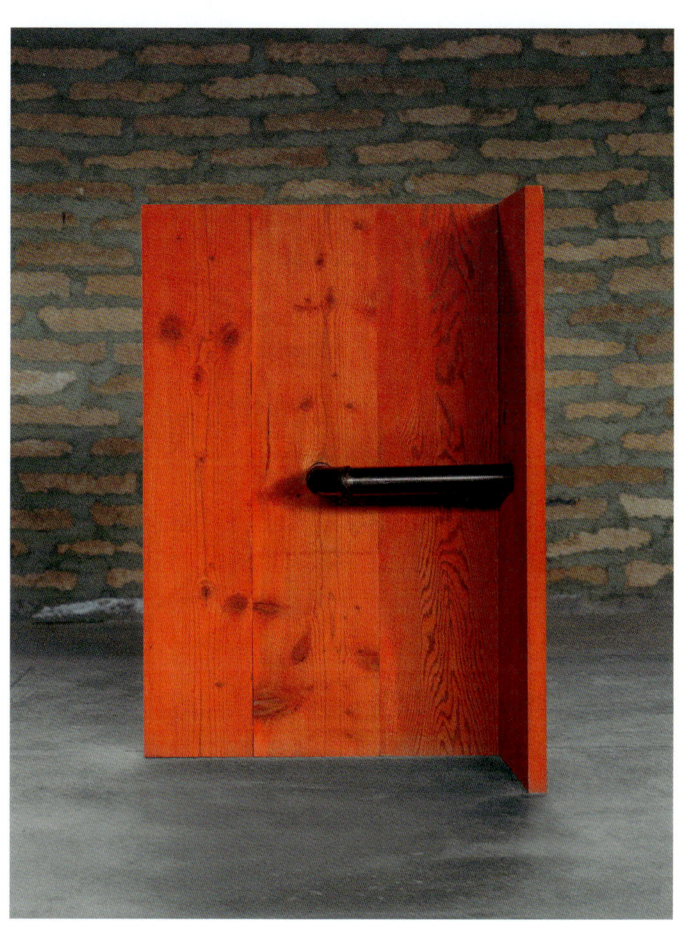

28
Untitled, 1962
Cadmium red light oil on wood
with black enameled metal pipe
48 × 32 ½ × 21 ¼ inches
121.9 × 82.6 × 54 cm

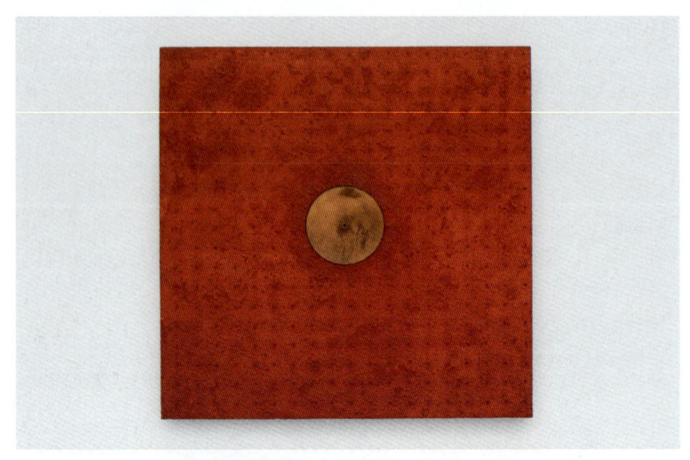

29
Untitled, 1962
Oil on acrylic and sand on
fiberboard with copper
48 × 48 × 4 inches
121.9 × 121.9 × 10.2 cm

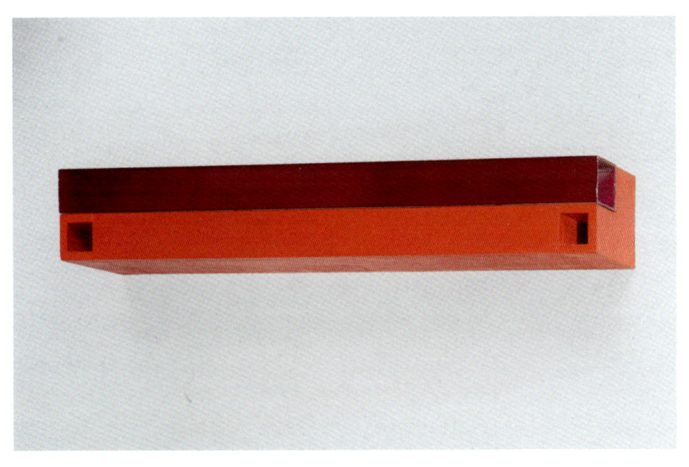

30
Untitled, 1963
Purple lacquer on aluminum and
cadmium red light oil on wood
5 ⅛ × 32 ⅝ × 5 ⅛ inches
13 × 82.9 × 13 cm

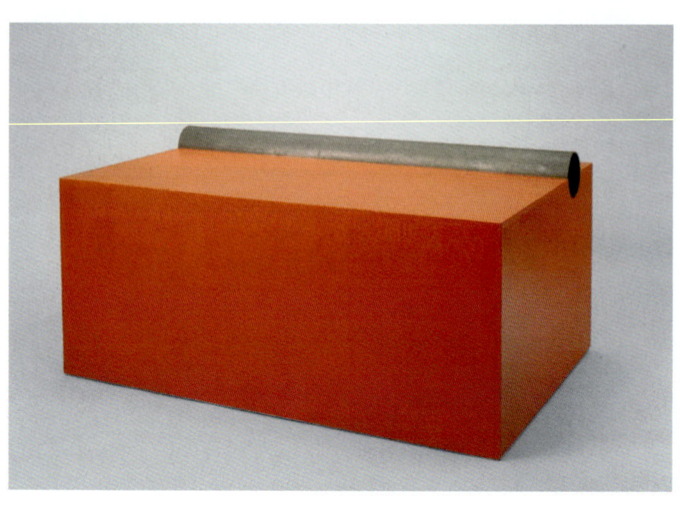

31
Untitled, 1963
Cadmium red light oil on wood
with iron pipe
22 ⅛ × 45 ⅜ × 30 ½ inches
56.2 × 115.3 × 77.5 cm

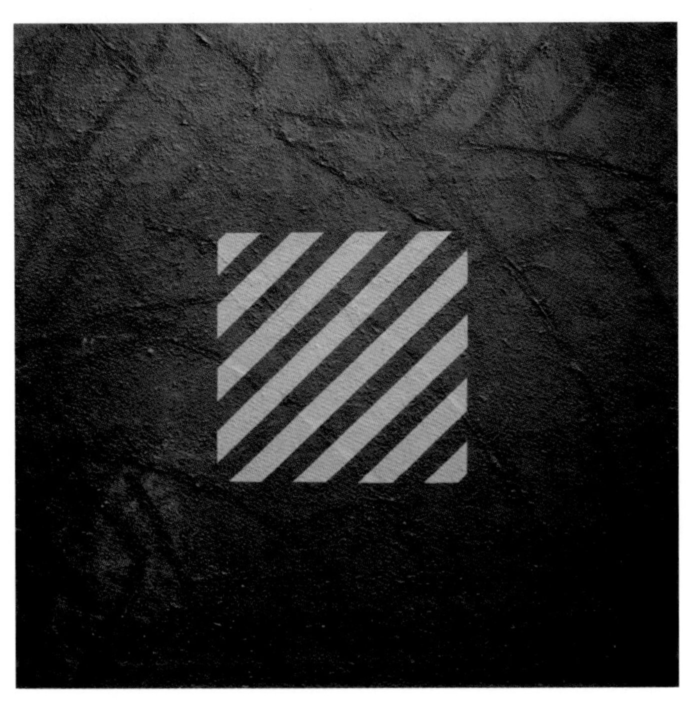

32
Untitled, 1961
Oil, wax, and sand on canvas
45 ¼ × 45 ¼ inches
114.9 × 114.9 cm

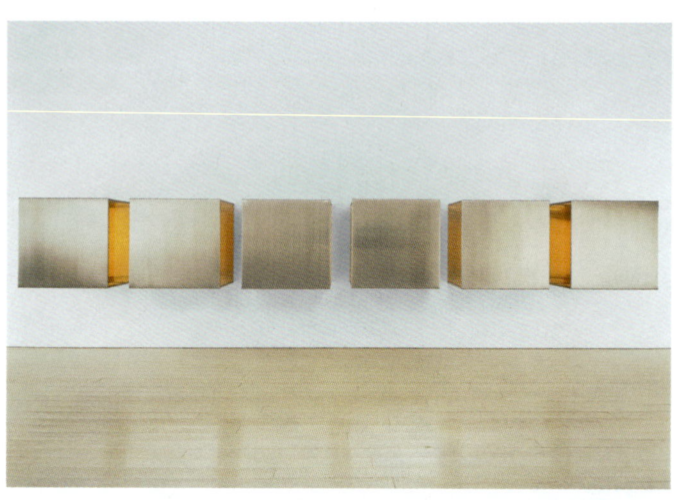

33
Untitled, 1967
Stainless steel and yellow acrylic sheets
6 units, each: 34 × 34 × 34 inches
86.4 × 86.4 × 86.4 cm

34
Untitled, 1963
Black enamel on aluminum and
raw sienna enamel and galvanized
iron on wood
52 × 42 ⅛ × 5 ⅞ inches
132.1 × 107 × 14.9 cm

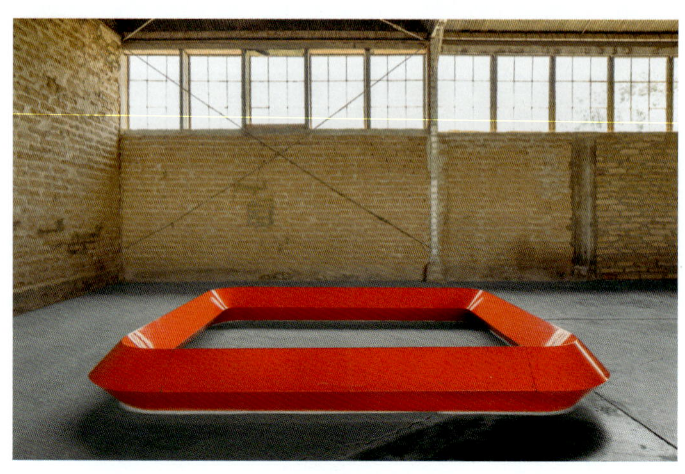

35
Untitled, 1965
Cadmium red light enamel
on cold-rolled steel
15 ⅝ × 138 × 117 inches
39.7 × 350.5 × 297.2 cm
Installed in the south room of
the west building of La Mansana
de Chinati/The Block, Judd
Foundation, Marfa, Texas

Note: This work shares similar
dimensions and materials to the one
discussed on 349–50. The work in
reference is from 1964.

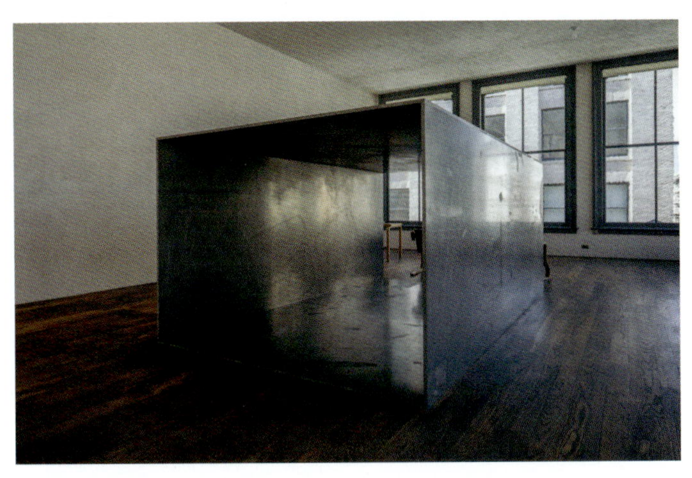

36
Untitled, 1969
Aluminum
60 × 144 × 84 inches
152.4 × 365.8 × 213.4 cm
Installed on the third floor
of 101 Spring Street,
Judd Foundation, New York

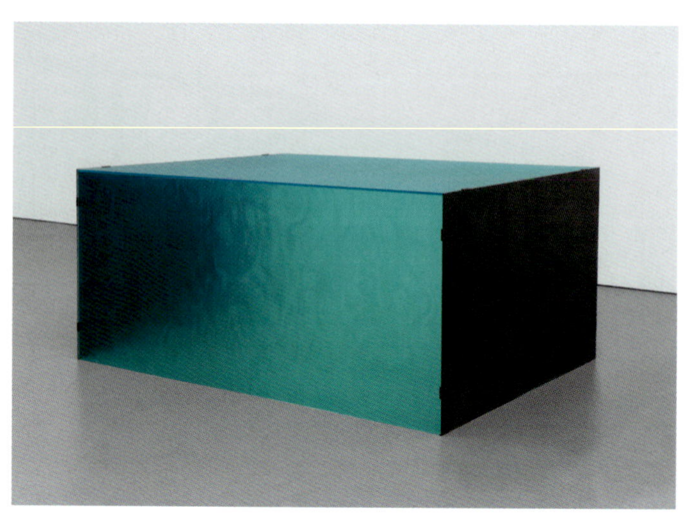

37
Untitled, 1964
Hot-rolled steel and turquoise
pebble acrylic sheets
20 × 44 ¼ × 30 ½ inches
50.8 × 112.4 × 77.5 cm

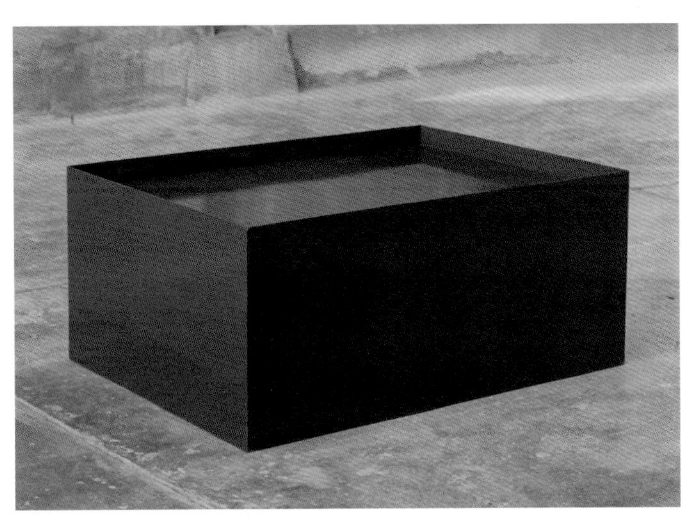

38
Untitled, 1965
Brown enamel on hot-rolled steel
22 × 50 × 37 inches
55.9 × 127 × 94 cm

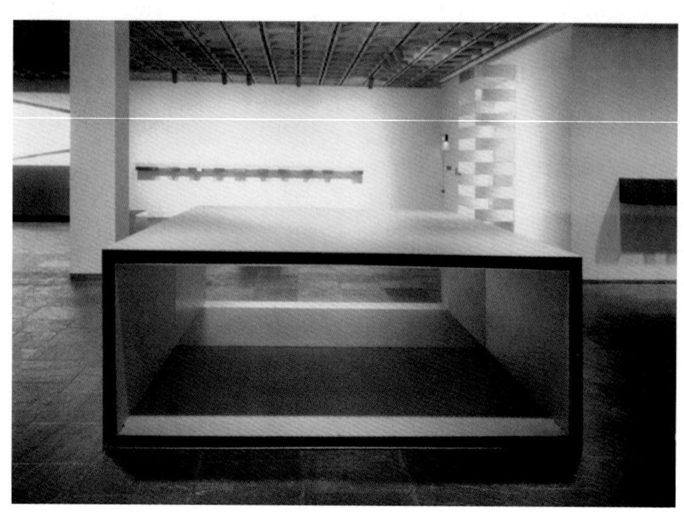

39
Untitled, 1968
Clear anodized aluminum
48 × 120 × 120 inches
121.9 × 304.8 × 304.8 cm

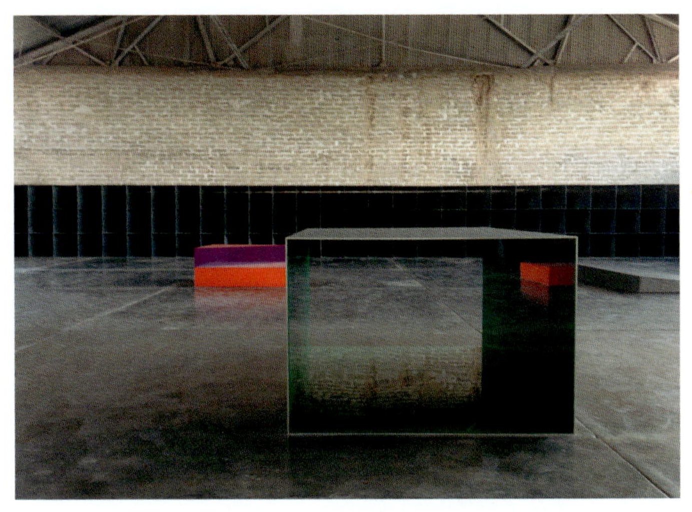

40
Untitled, 1969
Clear anodized aluminum
and green acrylic sheets
33 × 68 × 48 inches
83.8 × 172.7 × 121.9 cm
Installed in the south room of
the east building of La Mansana
de Chinati/The Block, Judd
Foundation, Marfa, Texas

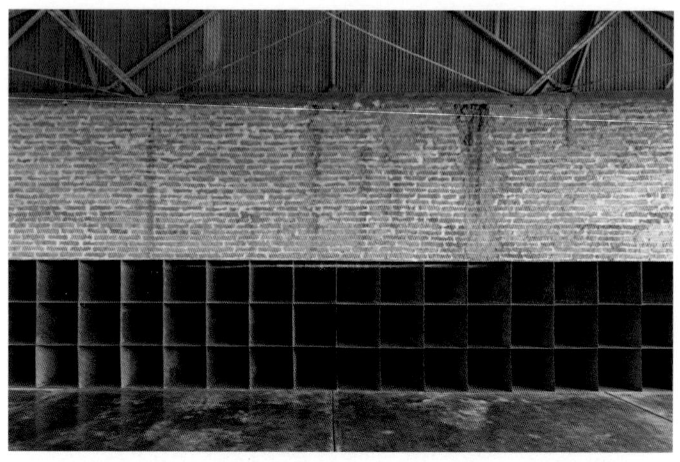

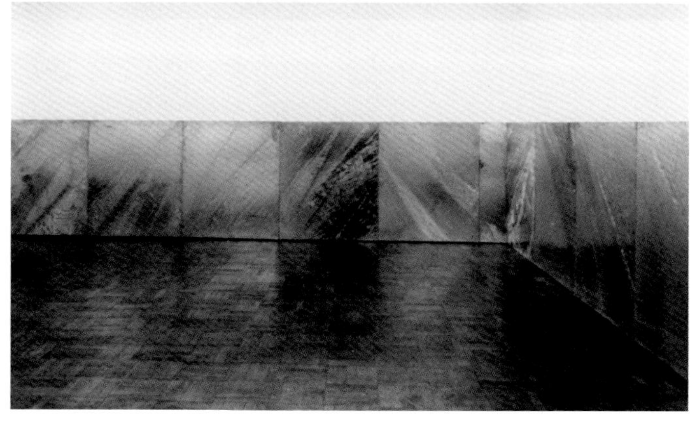

41
Untitled, 1969
Galvanized iron
108 units, each: 21 × 21 × 120 inches
53.3 × 53.3 × 304.8 cm

42
Untitled, 1970
Hot-dipped galvanized iron
60 × 289 × 269 inches
152.4 × 734.1 × 683.3 cm

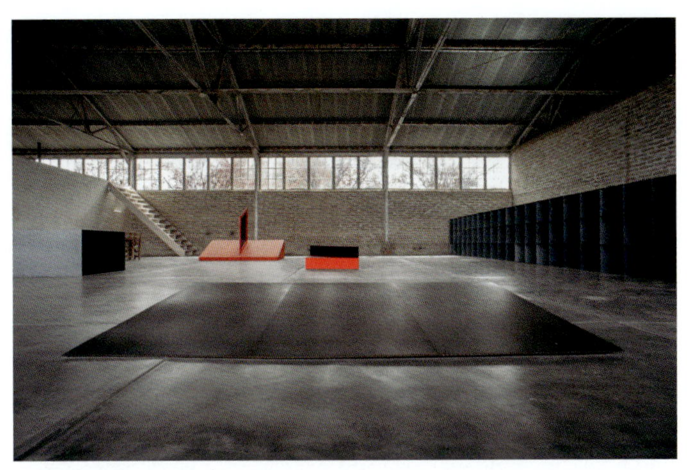

43
Untitled, 1968
Perforated 12-gauge cold-rolled steel
8 × 120 × 66 inches
20.3 × 304.8 × 167.6 cm
Installed in the south room of
the east building of La Mansana
de Chinati/The Block, Judd
Foundation, Marfa, Texas

Note: This work shares similar
dimensions and materials to the one
discussed on 359–60. The work in
reference is from 1966.

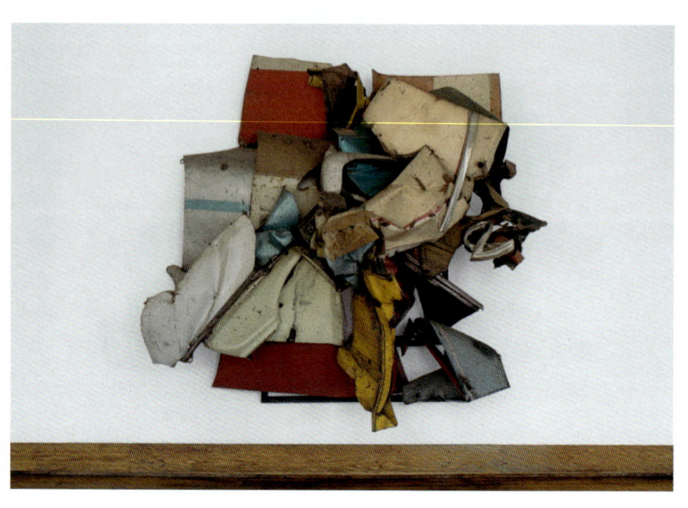

44
John Chamberlain
Mr. Press, 1961
Automobile parts with paint
and fabric
106 × 96 ½ × 45 inches
269.2 × 245.1 × 114.3 cm

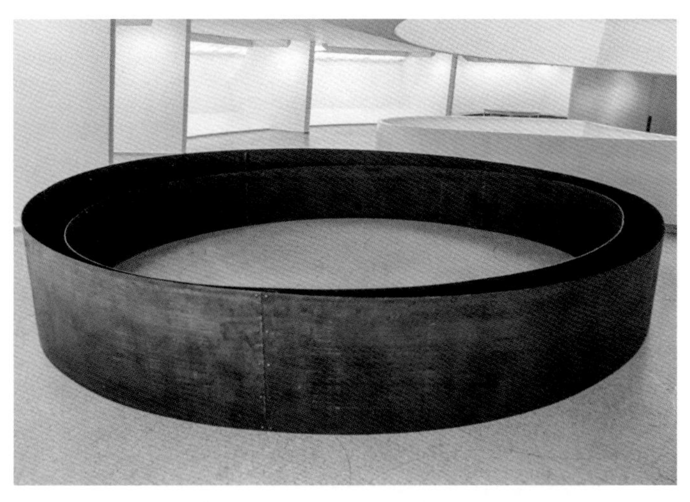

45
Untitled, 1971
Hot-rolled steel
Outer circle: 24 to 32 ¼ inches ×
180 (diameter) inches
61 to 81.9 cm × 457.2 cm
Inner circle: 24 ×
161 ½ (diameter) inches
61 × 410.2 cm

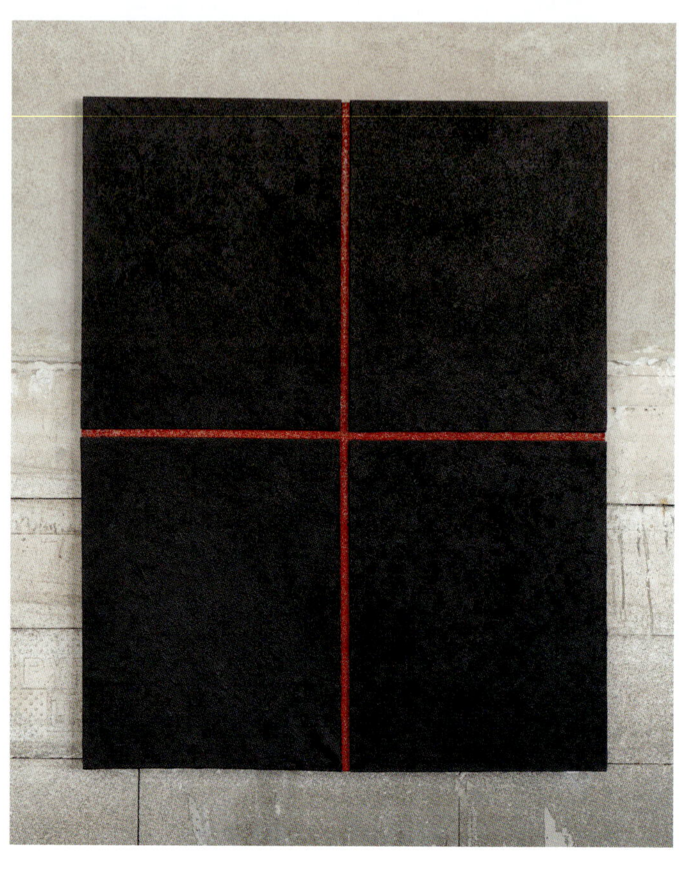

46
Untitled, 1961
Oil, wax, and sand on canvas
and wood
62 ⅛ × 48 ⅞ × 1 ¾ inches
157.8 × 124.2 × 4.4 cm

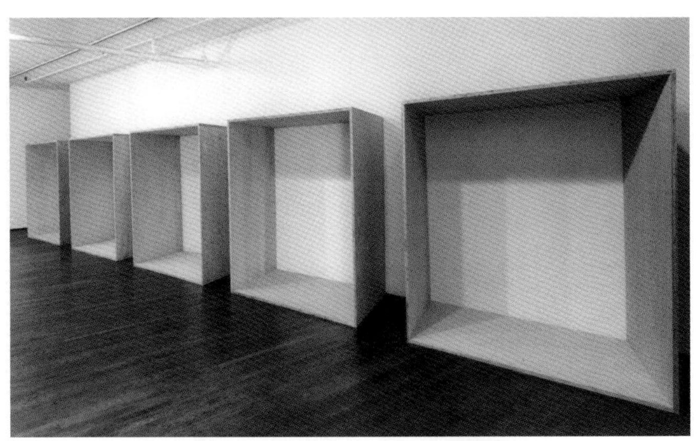

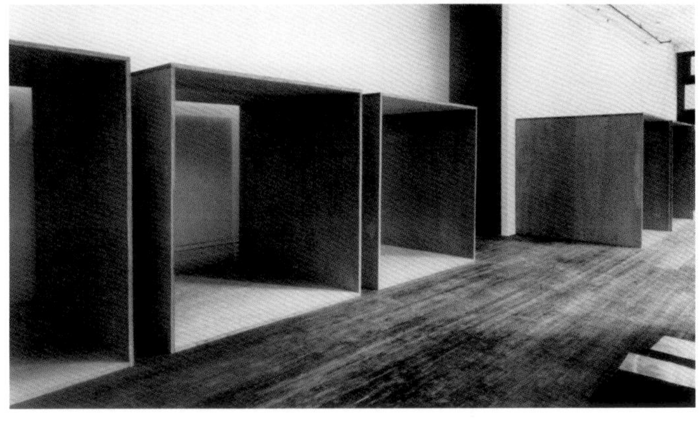

47
Untitled, 1972
Plywood
5 units, each: 72 × 94 ¾ × 41 inches
182.9 × 240.7 × 104.1 cm

48
Untitled, 1974
Plywood
7 units, each: 77 × 77 × 77 inches
195.6 × 195.6 × 195.6 cm
Installed on the ground floor of
101 Spring Street, Judd Foundation,
New York, April 1974

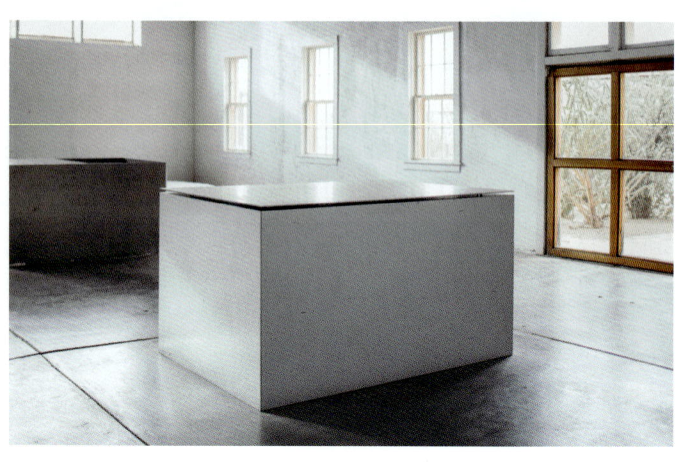

49
Untitled, 1967
Clear anodized aluminum
41 × 51 × 72 inches
104.1 × 129.5 × 182.9 cm
Installed in the north room of
the east building of La Mansana
de Chinati/The Block, Judd
Foundation, Marfa, Texas

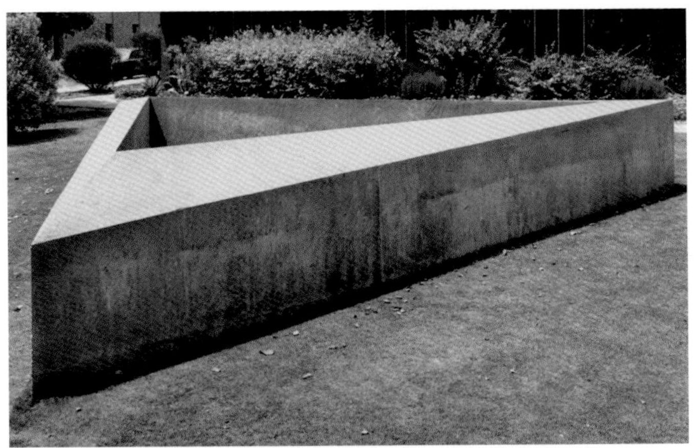

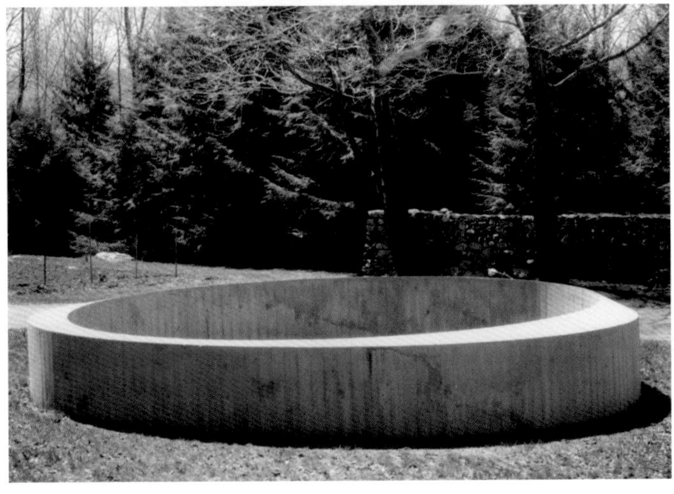

50
Untitled, 1974
Concrete
3 sides, each: 36 to 50 inches ×
300 × 18 inches
91.4 to 127 cm × 762 × 45.7 cm

51
Untitled, 1971
Concrete
36 to 48 inches × 300 (exterior
diameter) × 18 inches
91.4 to 121.9 cm × 762 × 45.7 cm

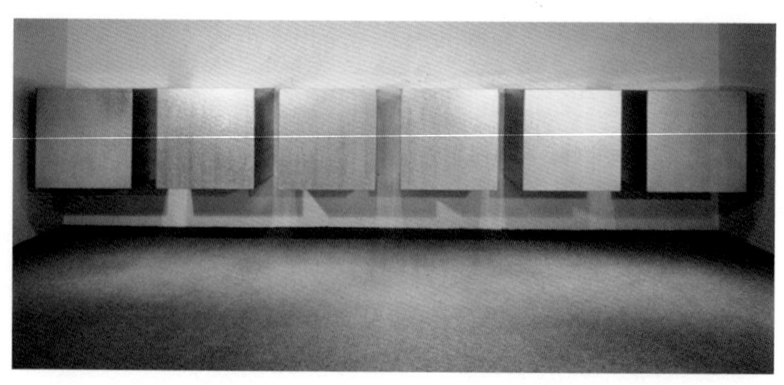

52
Untitled, 1966
Galvanized iron
6 or 8 units, each: 40 × 40 × 40 inches
101.6 × 101.6 × 101.6 cm

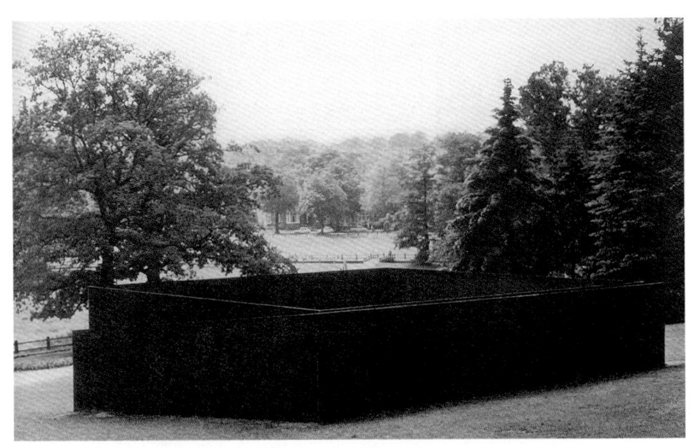

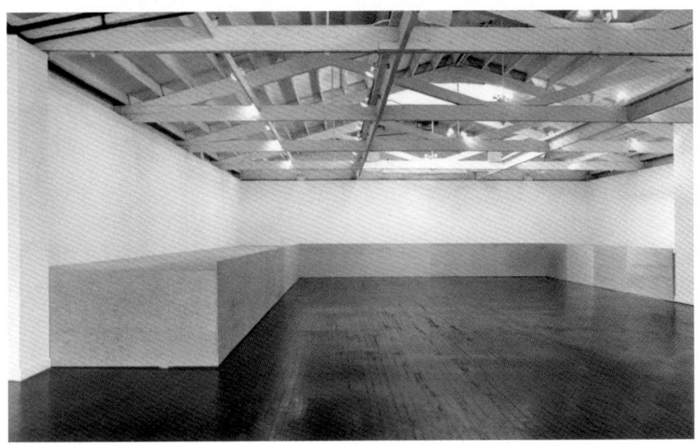

53
Untitled, 1971
Cold-rolled steel
Outer rectangle: 59 × 295 ¼ ×
295 ¼ inches
149.9 × 749.9 × 749.9 cm
Inner rectangle: 59 to 89 ½ inches ×
275 ½ × 275 ½ inches
149.9 to 227.3 cm × 699.8 × 699.8 cm

54
Untitled, 1974
Plywood
Approximately: 48 × 96 × 1200 inches
121.9 × 243.8 × 3048 cm
Temporary installation at Portland
Center for the Visual Arts, Oregon,
November 2–December 1, 1974

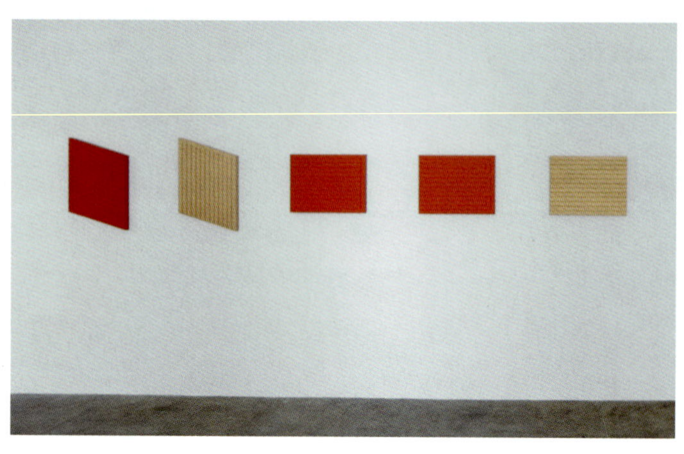

55
Installation view of *Donald Judd:
Selected Works from the Judd
Foundation*, Christie's, New York,
May 9–10, 2006

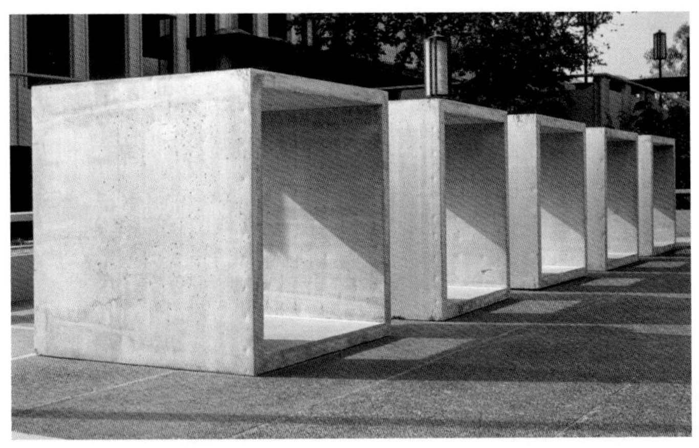

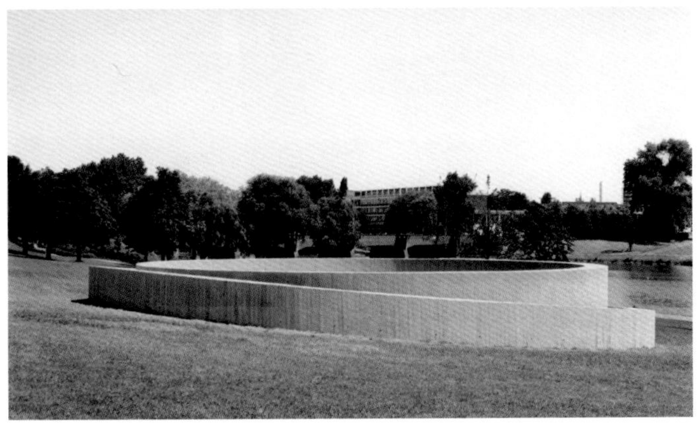

56
Untitled, 1977
Concrete
5 units, each: 84 × 84 × 89 inches
213.4 × 213.4 × 226.1 cm

57
Untitled, 1977
Concrete
Outer circle: 35 ½ × 590 ½
(diameter) × 23 ⅝ inches
90 × 1500 × 60 cm
Inner circle: 35 ½ to 47 ¼ inches ×
496 (diameter) × 23 ⅝ inches
90 to 120 cm × 1260 × 60 cm

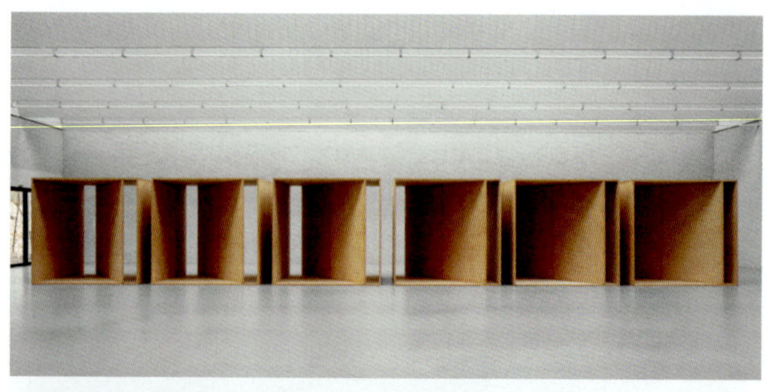

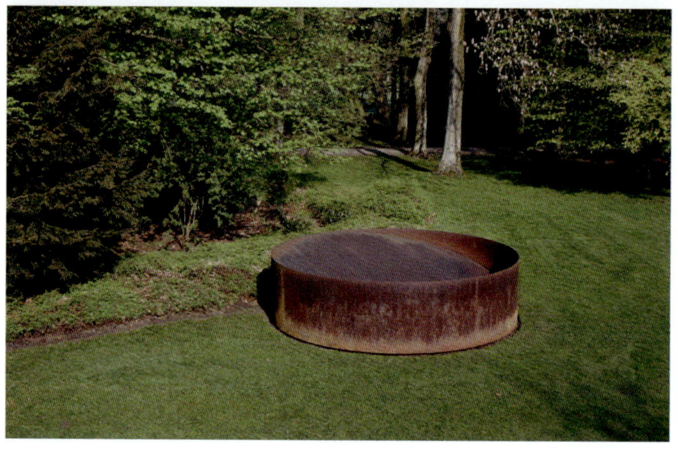

58
Untitled, 1977
Pressed wood
6 units, each: 96 × 96 × 96 inches
243.8 × 243.8 × 243.8 cm

59
Untitled, 1977
Cor-ten steel
47 ½ × 179 ½ (diameter) inches
120 × 455.9 cm

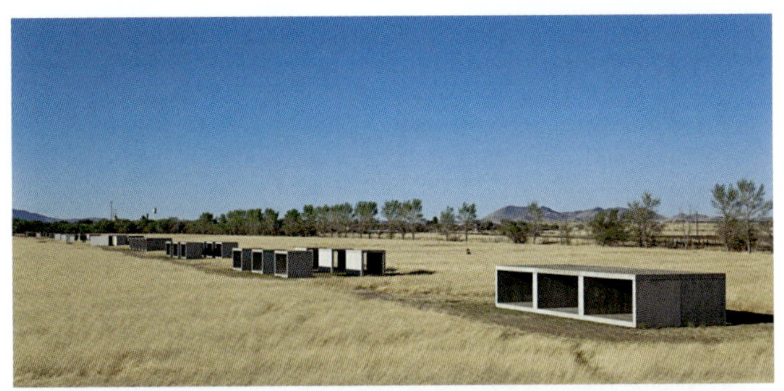

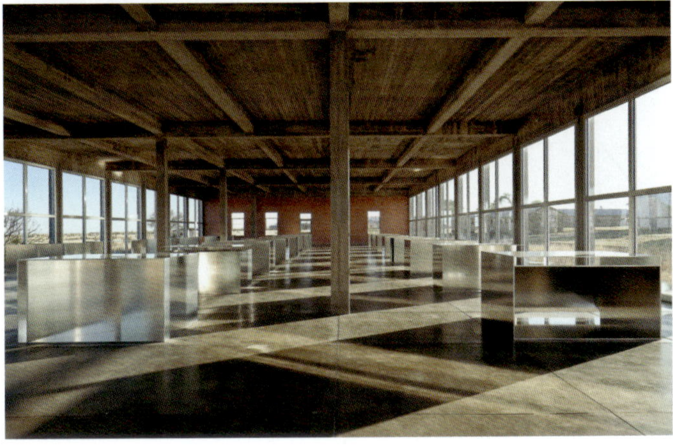

60
15 untitled works in concrete,
1980–84
Concrete
2 to 6 units per work, each unit:
98⅜ × 98⅜ × 196¹³⁄₁₆ inches
250 × 250 × 500 cm
Installed at The Chinati Foundation,
Marfa, Texas

61
100 untitled works in mill
aluminum, 1982–86
Mill aluminum
100 units, each: 41 × 51 × 72 inches
104.1 × 129.5 × 182.9 cm
Installed in the Artillery Sheds,
The Chinati Foundation,
Marfa, Texas

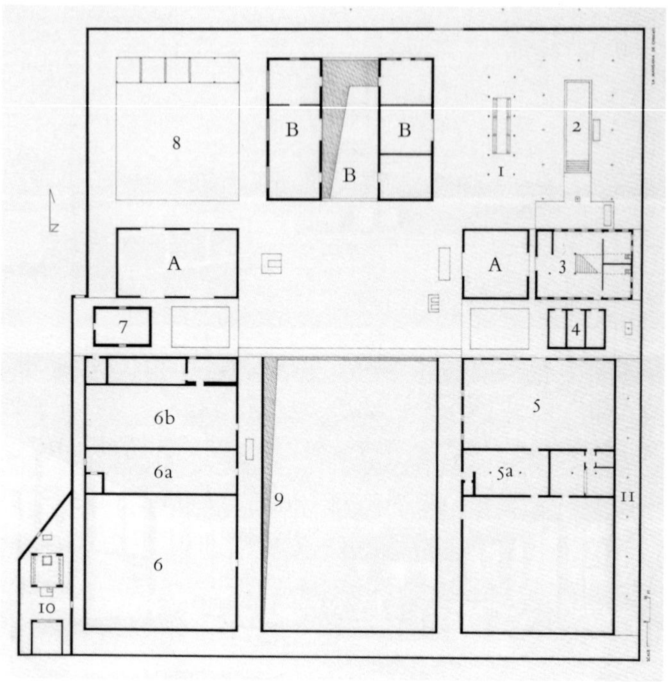

62
Schematic plan of La Mansana
de Chinati/The Block,
Judd Foundation, Marfa, Texas
Based on plan drawing by
Claude Armstrong and Donna
Cohen, 1987

Existing structures
1. Pergola; 2. Pool; 3. Two-story
building; 4. Bathrooms/utility;
5. East building; 5a. Bedroom;
6. West building; 6a. Library;
6b. Studio; 7. Office; 8. Garden/
chicken coop; 9. Tilted adobe wall;
10. Winter garden; 11. Plum tree yard

Proposed structures by Donald Judd
A. Concrete and steel buildings;
B. Adobe buildings

954

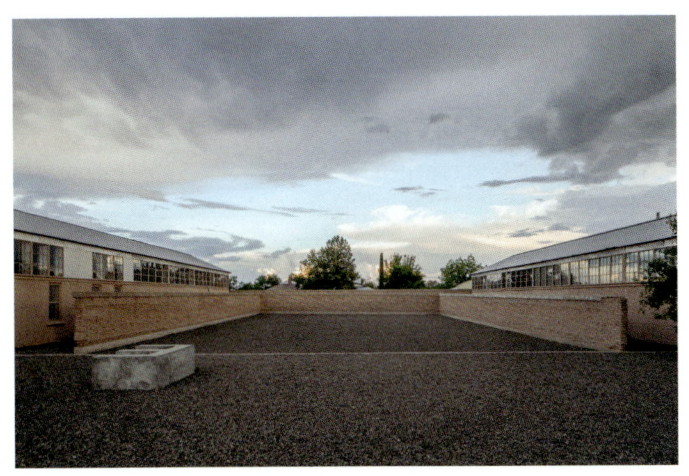

63
Untitled, 1977
Adobe bricks and cement
Outer wall: 108 to 120 inches × 3160 × 3160 inches (12 inches thick)
274.3 to 304.8 cm × 8026.4 × 8026.4 cm (30.5 cm thick)
Inner wall: 96 × 864 × 1440 inches (12 inches thick)
243.8 × 2194.6 × 3657.6 cm (30.5 cm thick)
La Mansana de Chinati/The Block, Judd Foundation, Marfa, Texas

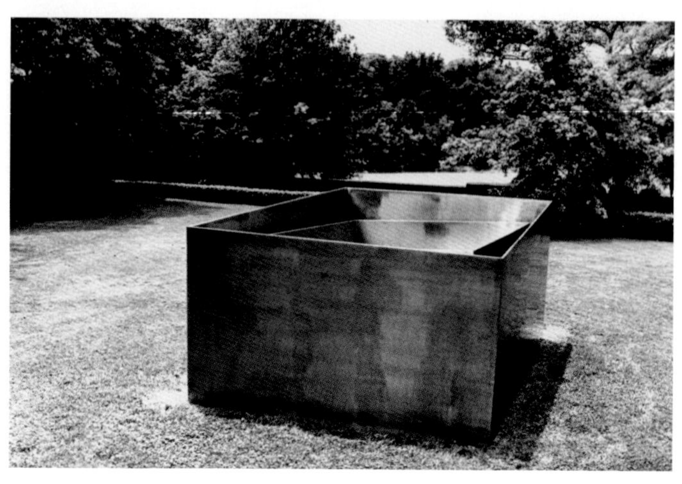

64
Untitled, 1971
Stainless steel
Outer rectangle: 54 ½ to 68 ½ inches ×
97 ½ × 145 ½ inches
138.4 to 174 cm × 247.7 × 369.6 cm
Inner rectangle: 54 × 81 × 129 inches
137.2 × 205.7 × 327.7 cm

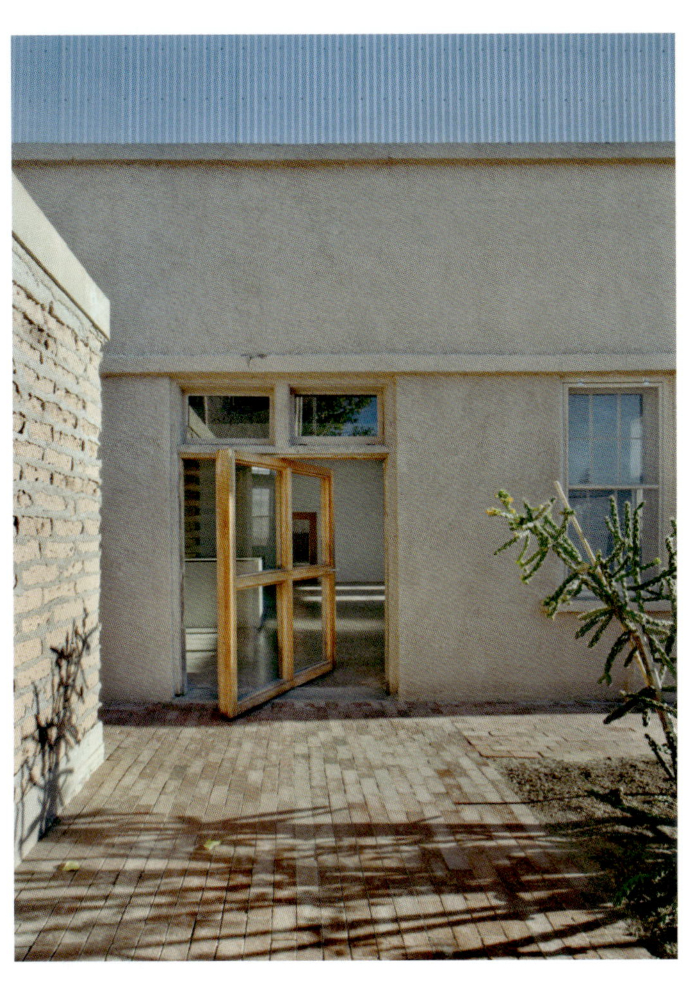

65
Entrance to the north room
of the east building, La Mansana
de Chinati/The Block, Judd
Foundation, Marfa, Texas

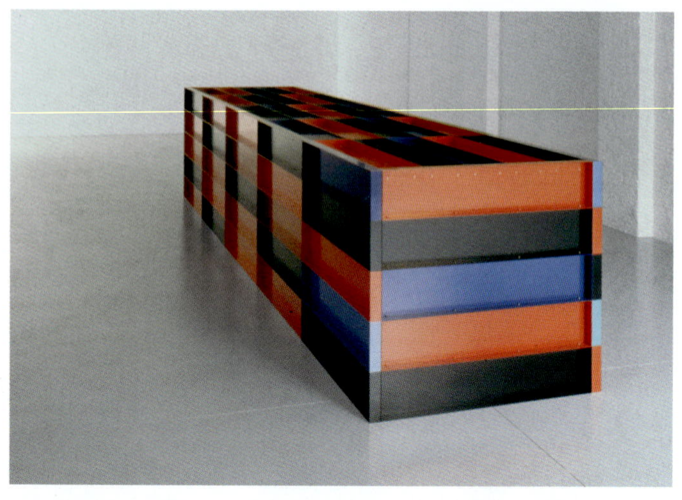

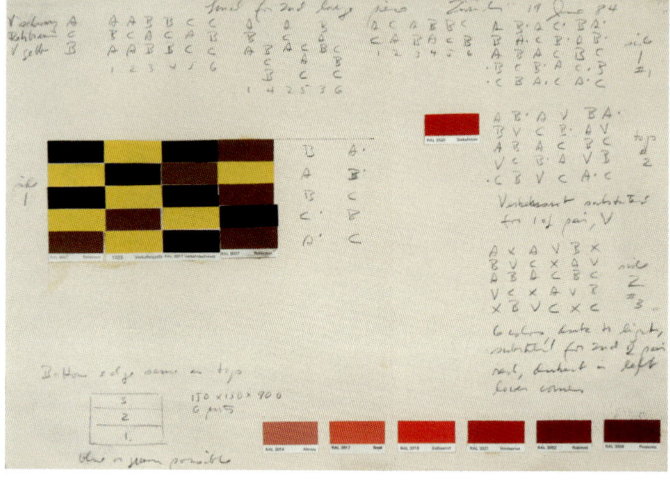

66
Untitled, 1984
Painted aluminum
59 × 295 ⅜ × 59 inches
150 × 750 × 150 cm

67
Drawing for untitled, 1984
Color samples from RAL
color chart

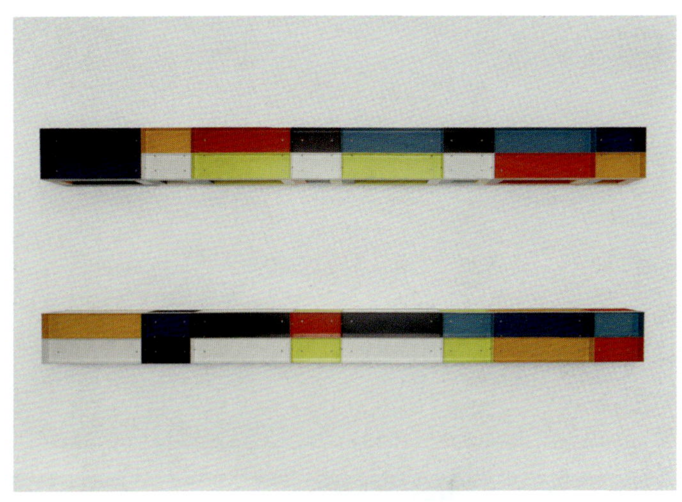

68
Untitled, 1987
Painted aluminum
2 units, each: 11 ¾ × 141 ¹¹⁄₁₆ ×
11 ¾ inches
30 × 360 × 30 cm

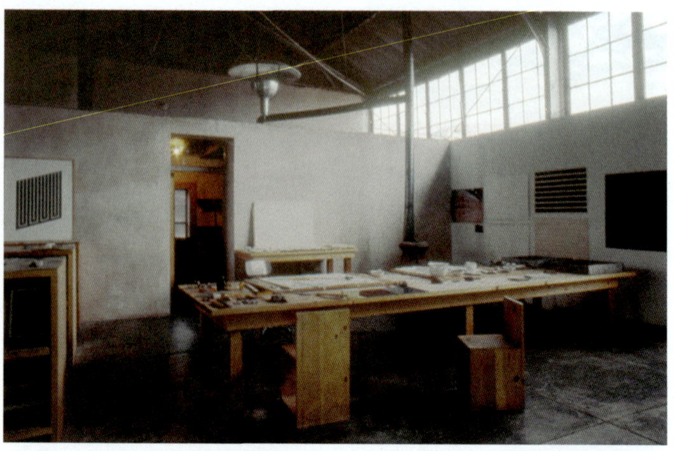

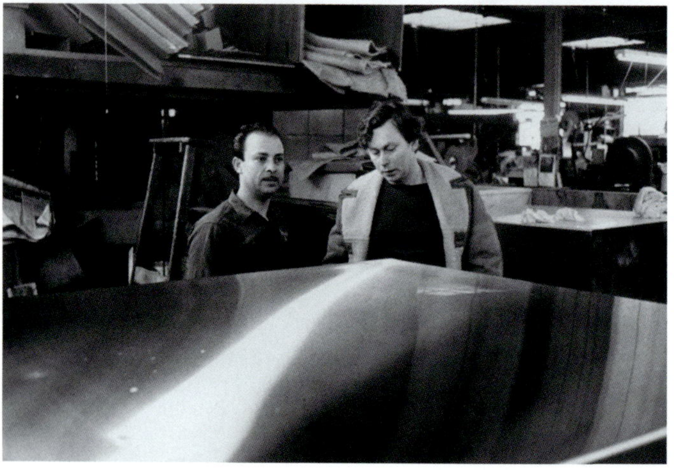

69
Original studio at La Mansana
de Chinati/The Block, now the
north library, Judd Foundation,
Marfa, Texas

70
José Otero and Donald Judd
at Bernstein Brothers, Inc.,
New York, 1968

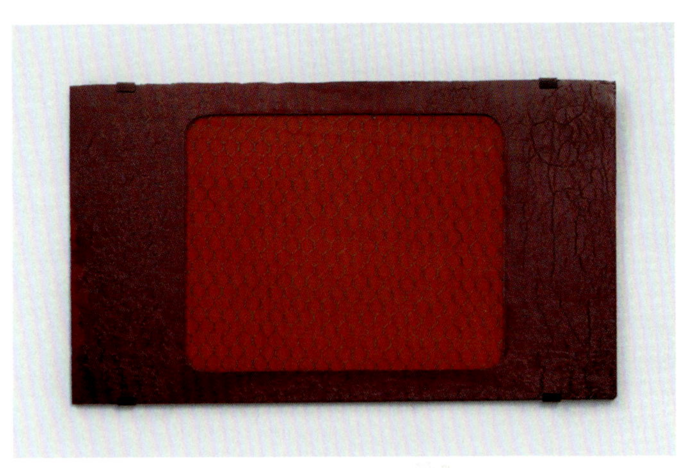

71
Untitled, 1961
Maroon enamel on recto and
cadmium red light oil on
verso of wire-enforced glass
18 × 31 × ½ inches
45.7 × 78.7 × 1.3 cm

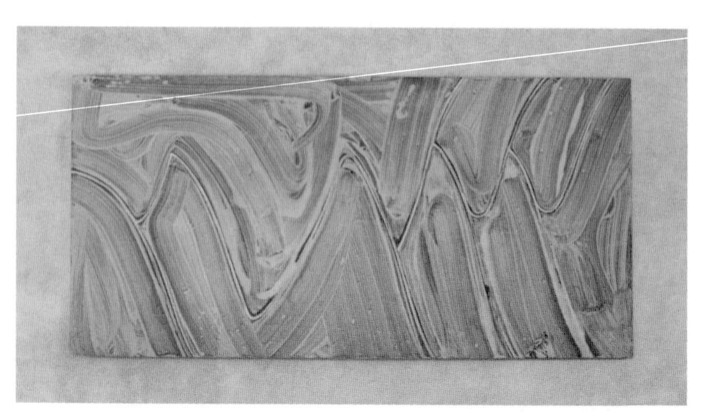

72
Untitled, 1960
Acrylic on fiberboard
48 × 96 inches
121.9 × 243.8 cm

73
Untitled, 1986
Cor-ten steel and purple acrylic sheet
$39\,^{5}/_{16} \times 39\,^{5}/_{16} \times 19\,^{5}/_{8}$ inches
100 × 100 × 50 cm

Note: This work shares similar
dimensions and materials to the one
discussed on 641 and 655. The work
in reference is from 1989.

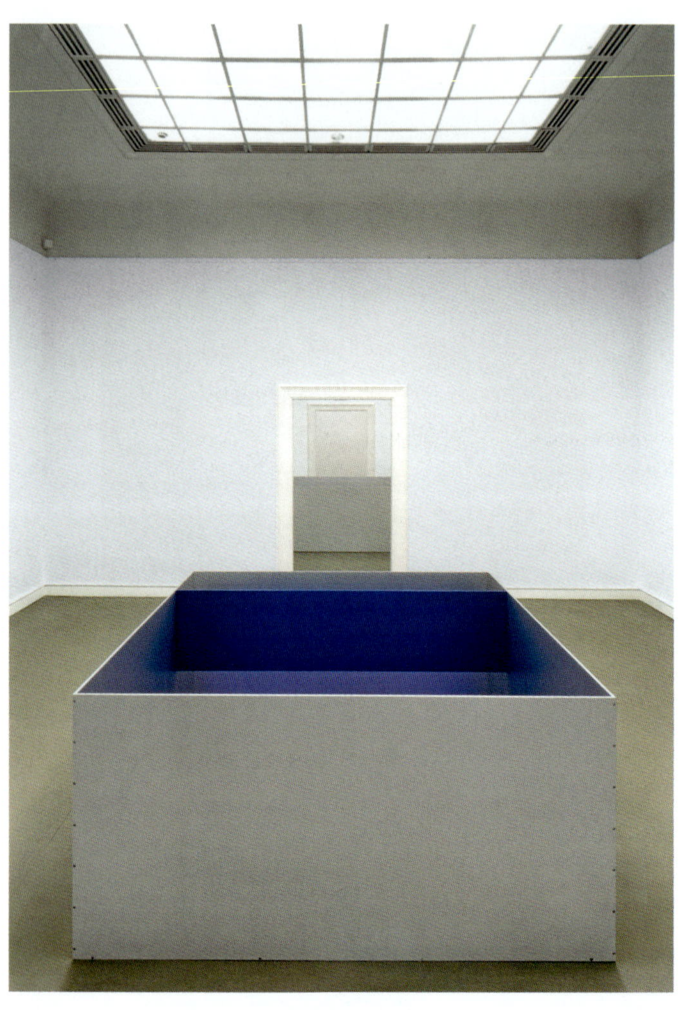

74
Installation view of
Donald Judd, Staatliche Kunsthalle
Baden-Baden, Germany,
August 27–October 15, 1989

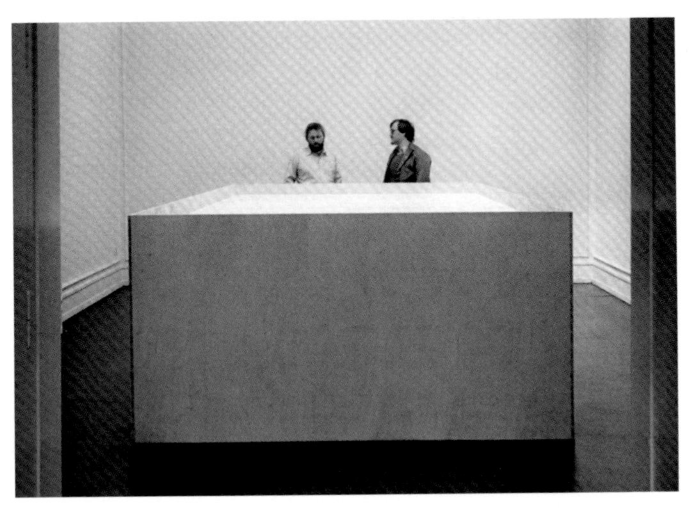

75
Donald Judd and Johannes
Gachnang at *Donald Judd: Skulpturen*,
Kunsthalle Bern, Switzerland,
April 14–May 30, 1976

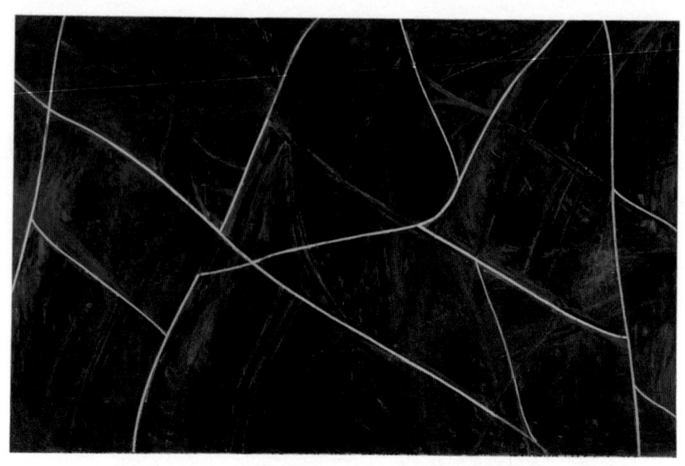

76
Untitled, 1960
Oil on canvas
67 ¾ × 103 inches
172.1 × 261.6 cm

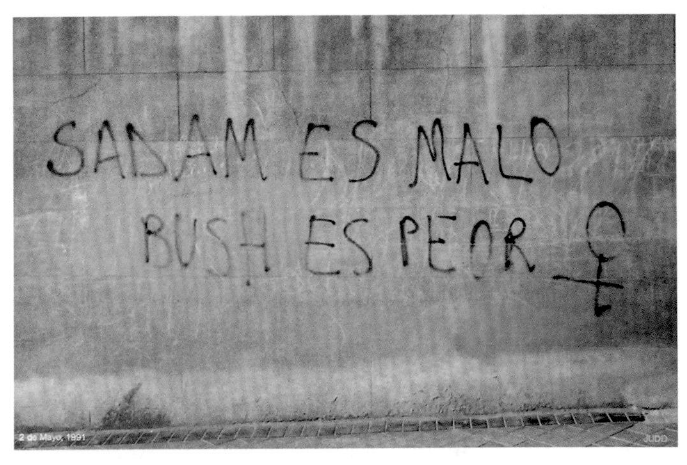

77
Sadam es malo, Bush es peor, 1991
Poster for show at Galería
Theospacio, Madrid
17 × 25 inches
43.2 × 63.5 cm

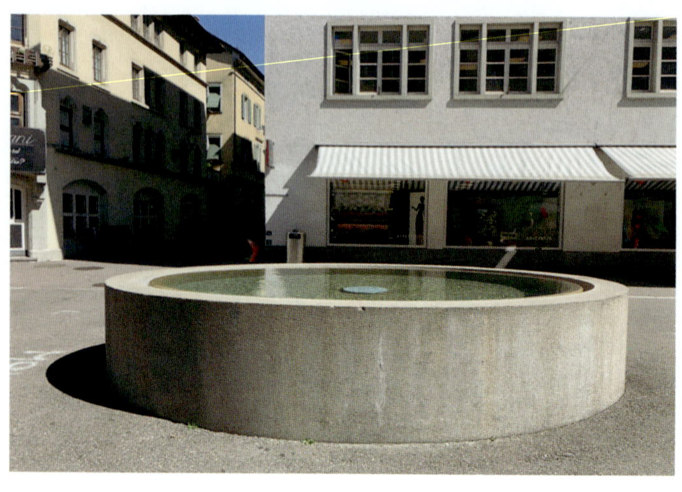

78
3 elliptical fountains in concrete,
Steinberggasse, Winterthur,
Switzerland, 1992–97

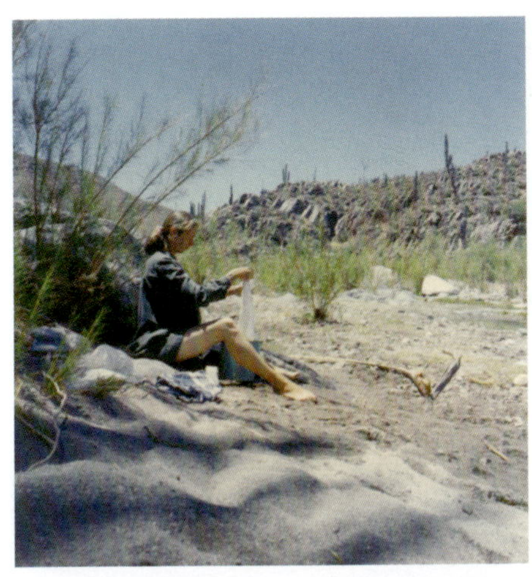

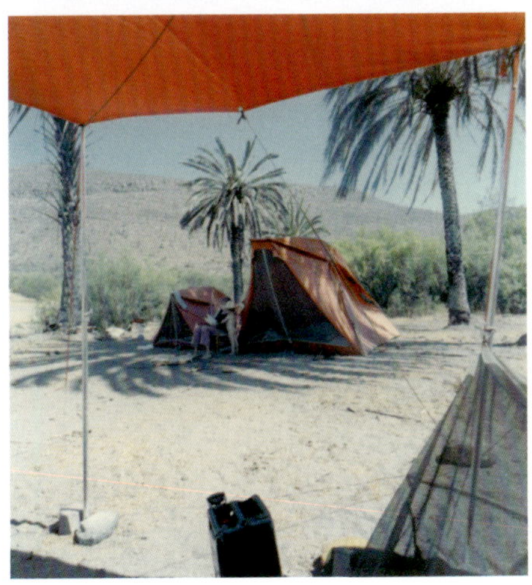

79
Julie Finch Judd in Baja California,
Mexico, June 1970

80
Julie Finch Judd and Flavin Judd
in Baja California, Mexico,
June 1970

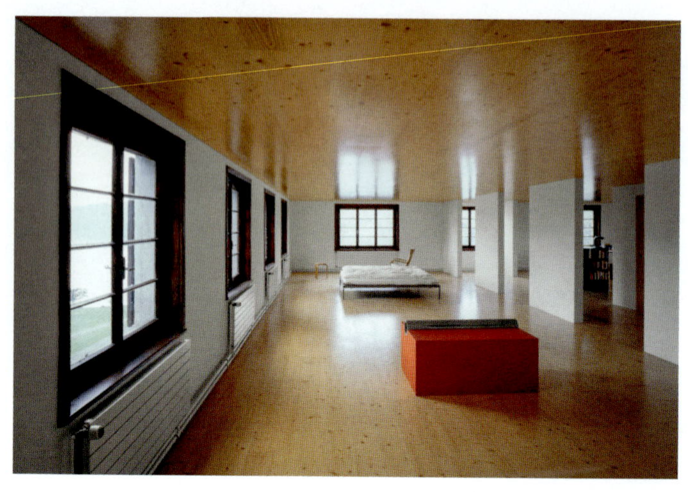

81
Interior, Eichholteren,
second floor, Küssnacht am Rigi,
Switzerland, 1991

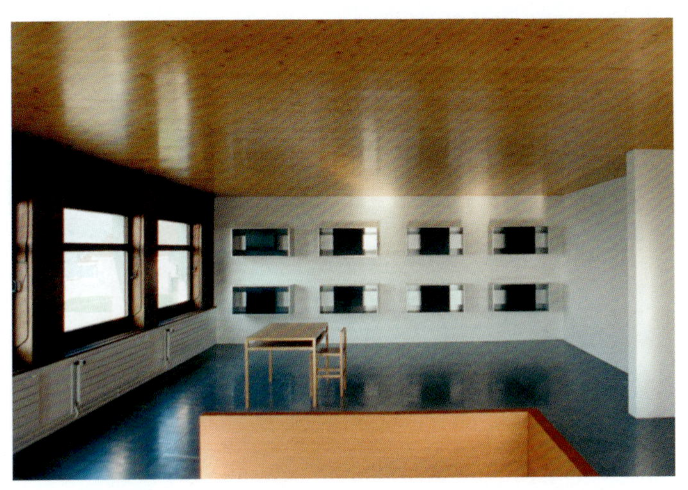

82
Interior, Eichholteren,
ground floor, Küssnacht am Rigi,
Switzerland, c. 1993

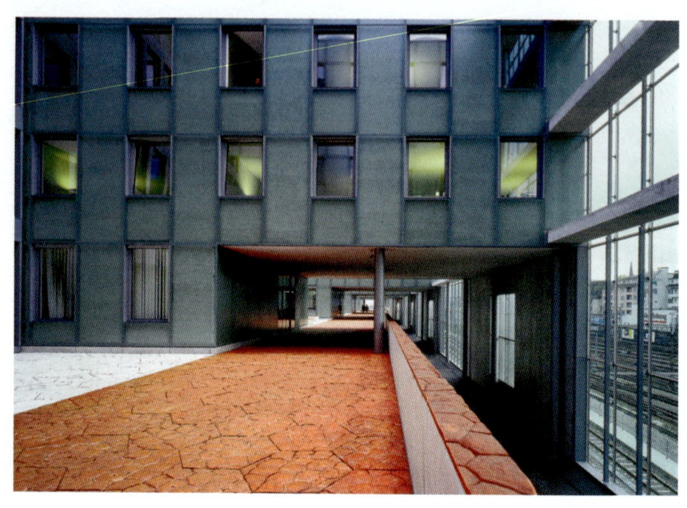

83
Exterior, Peter Merian Haus,
Basel, Switzerland

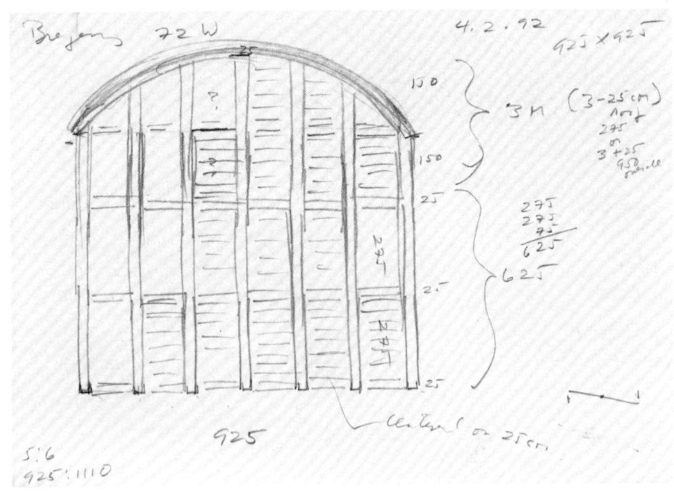

84
Drawing for the administrative
building of the Kunsthaus Bregenz,
4.2.92, 1992
Pencil on paper
8 ¼ × 11 ¾ inches
21 × 29.9 cm

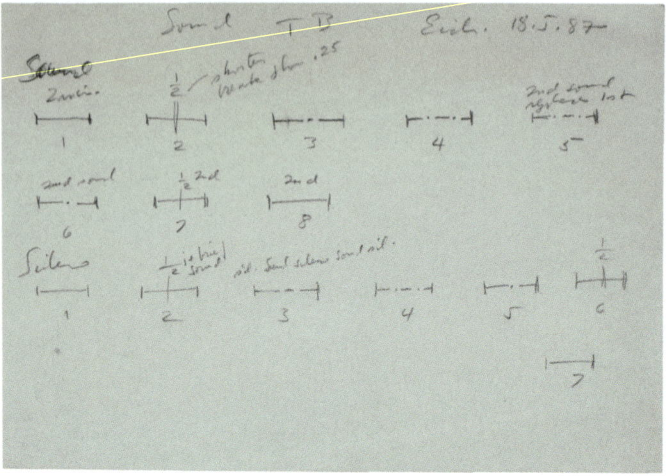

85
Drawing for sound for
Trisha Brown, May 18, 1987
Pencil on paper
9 ⅜ × 13 ⅜ inches
23.8 × 34 cm

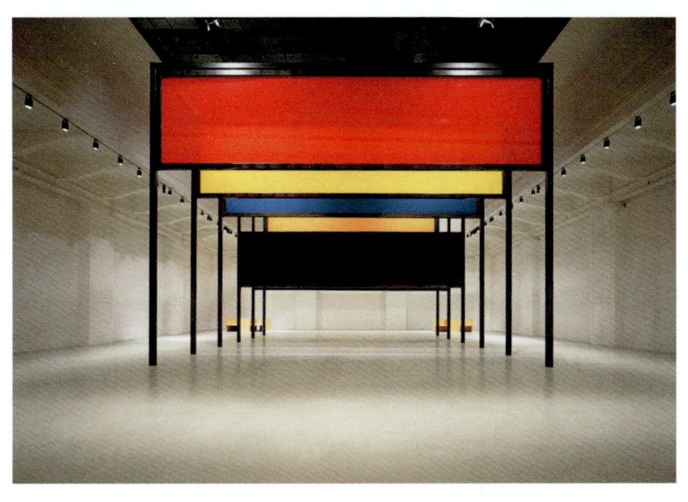

86
Installation view of *Stage set* (1991)
in *Donald Judd: Architektur,*
Österreichisches Museum
für angewandte Kunst, Vienna,
February 14–April 8, 1991

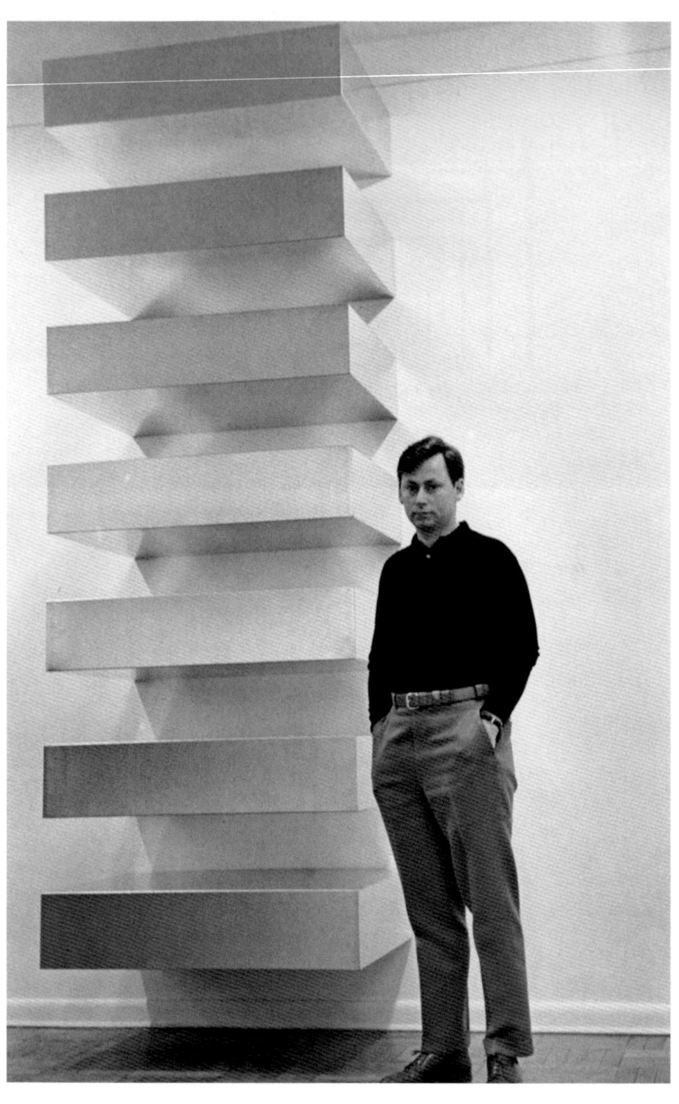

Donald Judd at *Don Judd*,
Leo Castelli Gallery, New York,
February 5–March 2, 1966

Index

Names of people, artworks, books, articles, exhibitions, magazines, newspapers, institutions, and major events have been indexed. Page references in <u>underline</u> indicate participation in an interview or panel discussion; page references in *italics* indicate an image. Notes are indicated by the format 835n4.

3 elliptical fountains in concrete 790, 796, 835n4, *968*

7 for 67: Works by Contemporary American Sculptors (exhibition, 1967, City Art Museum of St. Louis) 196

9 Evenings: Theatre and Engineering 307, 317n115

9th Street (exhibition, 1951, New York) 224, 308n6

15 untitled works in concrete 532, 622–23, 734, 800, 802, 866, *953*

53 East Nineteenth Street (New York) 21, 206, 213, 214, 423, 496, 599; Glueck, Grace, interview at 212; and Kusama, Yayoi 628, 631, 635, 638; Lippard, Lucy R., and William C. Agee, interview at 216

100 untitled works in mill aluminum 532n6, 663, 690n3, 802, 866, 879, *953*

101 Spring Street (Judd Foundation, New York) 23, *26–27*, 318, 423, 483, 599, 600, 732, 796, 803, 831, 855; in *American Art in the 1960s* (film) 394; art collection 28, 485, 497, 715, 814; Chamberlain, John, work at 485, 715; Flavin, Dan, work at 28, 485, 715; *Furniture by Donald Judd* (1984) 537, 538n2; Gifford, J. Nebraska, and M. B. Shestack, interview at 482; Irwin, Robert (Bob), work at 715; Kusama, Yayoi, *Infinity Net* series at 497; Lichtenstein, Roy, work at 485; in *Masters of Modern Sculpture Part III: The New World* (film) 476; "New York Studio Events" (Independent Curators International), interview at 830; Newman, Barnett, work at 485; Oldenburg, Claes, work at 485, 715; Reinhardt, Ad, work at 485; remodeling 846, 855; Stankiewicz, Richard, interview at 422; Stella, Frank, work at 28; Tuchman, Phyllis, interview at 490; Untitled, 1966 (Clear anodized aluminum) *912*; Untitled, 1969 (Aluminum) *935*; Untitled, 1974 (Plywood, 7 units) 500, *945*; Wesley, John, work at 485; and Whyte, Nicholas 487

302/304 East Twenty-Seventh Street (New York) 21, 225, 484

326 East Eighty-Fifth Street (New York) 21, 631

VIII Bienal de São Paulo (1965) 82, 311n34, 354–55, 647

A

Aalto, Alvar 814

Abrams, Ruth 253

Agee, William C. 213, <u>216–317</u>; "Unit, Series, Site: A Judd Lexicon" 498

Agostini, Peter 247

Albers, Josef 133, 381, 505–6, 691n28, 818, 891; *Homage to the Square* series 504; *Interaction of Color* 505, 678, 682; Lohse, Richard Paul, influence on 242; *Prints* (1987, Chinati Foundation) 893n19; *Variant/Adobe* series 504

Alberti, Leon Battista 685, 692n40, 814–15, 826

Albright-Knox Art Gallery (Buffalo) 303

Alert Citizens for Environmental Safety 800

Allen-Stevenson School (New York) 256

Alley, Ronald 641

American Art '85: A View from the Whitney (TV documentary) 556

American Art in the 1960s (film) 394

Gallery) 537, 538n2; *Donald Judd*
(1986, Paula Cooper Gallery) 576;
Donald Judd (1986, Waddington
Galleries) 568; *Donald Judd* (1988,
Whitney Museum of American
Art) 726; *Donald Judd* (1989, Dallas
Museum of Art) 726; *Donald Judd*
(1989, Staatliche Kunsthalle
Baden-Baden) 25, 662–65, 690n2,
690n10, 721, 890, *964*; *Donald Judd*
(1989, Waddington Galleries) 640,
641, 650, 660n3, 676; *Donald Judd*
(1990, Kunstverein St. Gallen) 694,
890; *Donald Judd* (1991, Galería
Theospacio) 768, *967*; *Donald Judd*
(1991, Galerie Rolf Ricke) 748;
Donald Judd (1991, Inkong Gallery)
772, 773; *Donald Judd* (1992–93,
Shizuoka Prefectural Museum of
Art) 888; *Donald Judd* (1992–93,
various locations, Japan) 888;
Donald Judd (2011, David Zwirner)
690n10; *Donald Judd: Architectural
Drawings and Furniture* (1984–85,
Max Protetch) 537, 538n3; *Donald
Judd: Architektur* (1989, West-
fälischer Kunstverein) 511, 543,
666; *Donald Judd: Architektur* (1991,
Österreichisches Museum für
angewandte Kunst) 740, 754, 756,
760, 792, 883, *975*; *Donald Judd: Für
Josef Albers* (1977, Moderne Galerie
Bottrop) 504, 505, 511, 516–17;
Donald Judd: Painted Wall Sculptures
(1984, Margo Leavin Gallery)
534, 535, 537; *Donald Judd, Richard
Long, Kristján Guðmundsson* (1988,
The Living Art Museum) 810, 821;
Donald Judd: Sculptures 1965–1987
(1987–88, various European
locations) 615, 626n4, 761; *Donald
Judd: Selected Works from the Judd
Foundation* (2006, Christie's)
950; *Donald Judd: Skulpturen* (1976,
Kunsthalle Bern) 487, 510, 664,
690n4, *965*; *Donald Judd Visiting
Artist* (1966, Dartmouth College)
441, 463; *Donald Judd: Werken* […]
(1993–94, Stedelijk Museum,
Amsterdam) 889–90; *Donald Judd:
Zeichnungen/Drawings 1956–1976*
(1976, Kunstmuseum Basel) 487,
490; *Einleuchten: Will, Vorstel un
Simul in HH* (1989–90, Deichtorhallen Hamburg) 677, 691n27; *Four
Americans* (1955, Panoras Gallery)
493, 501n9; *Furniture by Donald Judd*
(1984, 101 Spring Street) 537,
538n2; *Judd* (1974, Portland Center
for the Visual Arts) 458–61, 465,
949; *Kunst + Design: Donald Judd*
(1993–95, various European
locations) 840; *Mid-Season Salon*
(1956–57, Camino Gallery) 253–
54; *The New Sculpture 1965–75:
Between Geometry and Gesture* (1990,
Whitney Museum of American
Art) 773; *New York Painting and
Sculpture: 1940–1970* (1969–70, The
Metropolitan Museum of Art) 352,
416, 446; *Primary Structures: Younger
American and British Sculptors* (1966,
Jewish Museum) 90, 91, 93–94,
100–101, 346–47, *908*; *Repères: Judd*
(1987, Galerie Maeght Lelong)
586; *Richard Serra – Don Judd* (1972,
Leo Castelli Gallery) 412–13;
The Sculpture of Donald Judd (1978,
Galerie Watari) 628; Slunkariki
gallery (1992, Ísafjörður) 810; *Some
Recent American Art* (1974, Adelaide/
New York) 438, 446–47; *Zeichnun-
gen und Graphik von Don Judd*
(1971, Galerie Heiner Friedrich,
Munich) 885

Judd, Donald: works: 3 elliptical
fountains in concrete 796, 835n4,
968; 15 untitled works in concrete
532, 622–63, 734, 800, 802, 866, *953*;
100 untitled works in mill aluminum 532n6, 663, 690n3, 802, 866,
879, *953*; Drawing for sound for

Morris, William 672, 691n16
Muchnic, Suzanne 534–38
Müller, Ariane 760–67
Munich (Germany) 885
Munroe, Alexandra 628–39
Münster (Germany) 511, 543, 666, *951*
Murray, Robert (Bob) 558
Museum Abteiberg (Mönchenglad-
    bach, Germany) 459
Museum für Moderne Kunst
    (Frankfurt) 863, 893n15
Museum Insel Hombroich (Neuss,
    Germany) 866, 893n18
Museum Ludwig (Cologne), *Bilderstreit*
    (1989) 640, 645, 675–76, 691n19
Museum of Modern Art, The (New
    York) 260–61, 445, 455n1, 562, 769,
    803; *Barnett Newman* (1971–72)
    362; *Claes Oldenburg* (1969) 446;
    Frank Stella (1970) 446; *The New
    American Painting* (1959) 284,
    311n36; *Sixteen Americans* (1959–
    60) 316n103, 336n4, 494–95,
    502n12; *Twentieth Century Engineer-
    ing* (1964) 318
Myndvagl (school paper) 810

N
National Arts Club (New York) 252
National Endowment for the Arts 558
National Gallery of Canada (Ottawa)
    562, 606, 715, 717n20; *Donald
    Judd* (1975) 462, 494, 498
Nauman, Bruce 460
Nelson-Atkins Museum of Art
    (Kansas City) 217, 218, 404–5
Netherlands, The: Park Sonsbeek 543,
    949; Stedelijk Van Abbemuseum
    (Eindhoven) 562, 839n1, 885, 890,
    896n59
Neue Staatsgalerie (Stuttgart,
    Germany) 852, 892n3
Neuss (Germany) 866, 893n18
Nevelson, Louise 75, 96
Nevelson, Mike 75–76
"New Aesthetic, A" (symposium) 231

"New Nihilism or New Art?" (radio
    program) 28
"New Sculpture, The" (symposium) 90
New Work: Part I (exhibition, 1963,
    Green Gallery) 28
New York 408, 411, 444–45, 450, 513,
    634, 636, 686, 761–62, 769, 837–38;
    302/304 East Twenty-Seventh Street
    21, 225, 484; 326 East Eighty-Fifth
    Street 21, 631; Allen-Stevenson
    School 256; Art Students League
    66, 79n2, 220–21, 222–24, 322,
    450, 493, 819; Betty Parsons Gallery
    251, 252, 311n38; Brata Gallery 497,
    502n18, 628, 629; Brooklyn Insti-
    tute of Arts and Sciences 336n1;
    Byron Gallery 69, 79n4; Camino
    Gallery 253–54, 311n45, 493; Cedar
    Street Tavern 301, 493; Charles
    Egan Gallery 223; Christie's *950*;
    Christodora House 225, 309n8;
    Club, the (artists' group) 637,
    639n11; Columbia University 66,
    79n2, 221, 256, 264; David Zwirner
    690n10; Downtown Gallery 80n9;
    Emmerich Gallery 269, 314n74;
    Fischbach Gallery 289, 316n100;
    Galerie Lelong 862; Gertrude
    Stein Gallery 632, 638n8; Gordon
    Gallery 276, 315n86, 315n87, 697;
    Hansa Gallery 315n79; Hunter
    College 378, 385n7; Knoedler &
    Company 367, 369n8; Kootz
    Gallery 255, 312n47; Kornblee
    Gallery 413, 420n20; Marlborough-
    Gerson Gallery 42; Max Protetch
    537, 538n3; National Arts Club 252;
    Nippon (restaurant) 487, 488n9;
    Pace Gallery 889; Panoras Gallery
    253–54, 265–66, 493, 501n9; Park
    Place Gallery 92, 102n1, 332; Police
    Athletic League 505, 529; School
    of Visual Arts 450; SoHo 406, 444,
    483, 486, 529; Tanager Gallery
    258–59, 311n44; Tenth Street 253,
    311n44, 395, 406, 629; Tibor de Nagy

Police Athletic League (New York)
505, 529

Pollock, Jackson 67, 70–71, 301, 473,
700, 731, 779; *The Deep* 251; *Gray
Ocean* 252; *Jackson Pollock* (1964,
Marlborough-Gerson Gallery) 42;
Judd, influence on 223, 250, 478,
507, 508, 651, 652; and Kusama,
Yayoi 631; and Newman, Barnett
76; and Reinhardt, Ad 267–68;
technique 37–38, 97, 111, 160–61,
323, 383–84, 403; and Whitney
Museum of American Art 567n11;
and Wols (Alfred Otto Wolfgang
Schulze) 580

Poons, Larry 37, 46, 83, 104–41, 161,
162, 171–72, 183n10, 222, 239–41,
242

Porter, Fairfield 283, 284

Porter House (Judd Foundation,
Marfa, Texas) 24, 898

Portland Center for the Visual Arts
(PCVA, Oregon), *Judd* (1974)
458–61, 465, *949*

Poussin, Nicolas 47, 189, 218

*Primary Structures: Younger American and
British Sculptors* (exhibition, 1966,
Jewish Museum) 90, 91, 93–94,
100–101, 346–47, *908*

Print Building (Judd Foundation,
Marfa, Texas) 24–25, 667, 690n8

Progressive Architecture (magazine) 540

Prospect 89, Frankfurter Kunstverein
(Germany) 677

Puget, Pierre 655, 660n5

Q
Quick, May 520

R
Rabinowitch, David 484; *Tyndale
Sculpture (for Bud Powell and
Coleman Hawkins)* 713

Rainer, Yvonne 884

Ranch Office (Judd Foundation,
Marfa, Texas) 24, 894n33

Rasmussen, Waldo 439, 455n1

Rauh, Emily 196–211

Rauschenberg, Robert 104–41, 274,
538, 581; *Oracle* 105, 141n1

Reinhardt, Ad 76, 246, 252, 261–62,
264, 282–84, 535, 636, 697–98, 832;
"25 Lines of Words on Art: Statement" 665–66, 690n5; and Albers,
Josef 506; black paintings 620; in
Judd's collection 485; and Pollock,
Jackson 267–68; "Pure Paints a
Picture" (Elaine de Kooning) 55,
834; and Stella, Frank 891; and
Truitt, Anne 267; "Twelve Rules
for a New Academy" 812

Rembrandt van Rijn 218

Resnick, Milton 42, 49–50, 563

Reykjavík (Iceland) 815

Rice, Dan 374

Richmond Professional Institute
(Virginia) 364–65, 369n3

Ricke, Rolf 417

Rietveld, Gerrit 832

Rivers, Larry (Yitzroch Loiza Gross-
berg) 373–74, 632

Roerend Goed (TV program) 836

Rohe, Ludwig Mies van der. *See* Mies
van der Rohe, Ludwig

Rose, Barbara 90–102, 102n2, 104–41,
148–84, 256, 394–420, 476, 696;
"ABC Art" 148, 833; "A New
Aesthetic" (symposium) 231

Rosenberg, Harold 407

Rosenblum, Robert (Bob) 52, 54,
58n21

Rosenquist, James 295, 582

Rossetti, Dante Gabriel 671–72

Rothko, Mark 68, 143, 284; and
Matisse, Henri 474; and Newman,
Barnett 366; and Panza di Biumo,
Giuseppe 460

Rowan, Robert 356

Rubens, Peter Paul 184n19; *Daniel in
the Lions' Den* 178–79

Ruhr-Universität Bochum
(Germany) 694

Russia 595, 647, 648n8, 688–89,
742–43, 744, 746, 829, 875–76
Ryman, Robert (Bob) 248, 298, 300,
312n61, 588, 594, 682

S
Saatchi, Charles 676
Saatchi Collection (London) 615
Sadam es malo, Bush es peor 782, 967
Saddam Hussein 782, 784
Sagan, Carl 901, 902n2
Salle, David 592
Salzburg (Austria) 756, 757n3
Samaras, Lucas 73, 203, 208, 211n1,
273; *Untitled (Floorpiece)* 347
Samúelsson, Guðjón 820–21, 822n11
Sandback, Fred 269, 484
Santa Maria del Mar (Barcelona) 824,
826
São Paulo, VIII Bienal de (1965) 82,
311n34, 354–55, 647
Schaffhausen (Switzerland) 615
Schapiro, Meyer 54, 58n23, 104, 177,
184n15, 256, 283–84, 312n50, 362,
878
Schematic plan of La Mansana de
Chinati/The Block (Marfa, Texas)
540, *954*
Schnabel, Julian 537, 582
Schöllhammer, Georg 754–58
Scholz, Michael 862, 863
School of Visual Arts (New York) 450
Schultes, Axel 827n3, 829n3, 845
Schulze, Alfred Otto Wolfgang (Wols)
580
Schwitters, Kurt 581
Segal, George 497
Serra, Richard 403, 465, 484, 558, 721,
724; *Fulcrum* 655; *Richard Serra –
Don Judd* (1972, Leo Castelli
Gallery) 412–13; *Tilted Arc* 557,
566n2, 655, 719
*7 for 67: Works by Contemporary Ameri-
can Sculptors* (exhibition, 1967,
City Art Museum of St. Louis) 196
Shestack, M. B. 482–88

Shizuoka Prefectural Museum of
Art (Japan), *Donald Judd* (1992–93)
888
Sidney Janis Gallery (New York):
*The Classic Spirit in 20th Century
Art* (1964) 29, 31, 32, 36, 47, 49,
56n1; *Eleven Abstract Expressionist
Painters* (1963) 365, 368n6; *An
Exhibition of New Work by Claes
Oldenburg* (1967) 184n11; *Jackson
Pollock* (1958) 251; *New Paintings by
Mark Rothko* (1955) 253; *Recent
Work by Claes Oldenburg* (1966)
184n11; *Shining Forth (To George)*
(Newman) 365
Siegel, Jeanne 362–68
Sikkens Prize 836, 869
Skala (magazine) 840
Slunkariki gallery (Ísafjörður,
Iceland) 810
Smith, Brydon 715, 717n20; *Donald
Judd: Catalogue Raisonné of Paintings,
Objects, and Wood-Blocks 1960–1974*
494
Smith, David 96, 97, 98, 157, 163–64,
190, 228, 261, 345, 403; *17 h's*
245–46, 310n30, 311n31; *Agricola*
sculptures 371, 372; *Cubi* series 150,
608; *Five Units Equal* 304, 317n111,
608; *Hudson River Landscape* 210,
495; Oldenburg, Claes, compared
to 286; *Tanktotem* 304, 317n112
Smith, Leon 253, 493
Smith, Tony 236, 243–44, 266, 275–
76, 655; *The Elevens Are Up* 173–74,
184n12, 332–33; *Free Ride* 361n5
Smithson, Robert 235, 236, 237,
309n18; *Spiral Jetty* 659
Smithsonian Institution 64
Snyders, Frans 179, 184n19
SoHo (New York) 406, 444, 483, 486,
529
Solomon R. Guggenheim Museum
(New York) 445, 484, 562, 756,
757n3, 775–76; Guggenheim
International Exhibition (1971)

Wittgenstein, Ludwig 766, 767n7
Wittkower, Rudolf 499–500,
    502n23
Wolpe, Stefan 374
Wols (Alfred Otto Wolfgang Schulze)
    580
Wright, Frank Lloyd 551, 814, 826,
    850
Wyeth, Andrew 647, 648n8; *Christina's
    World* 191
Wyrwoll, Regina 852–96

Y
Yale School of Art and Architecture
    283, 315n88
Yvaral (Jean-Pierre Vasarely) 32,
    57n9

Z
Zummo, Peter 882–83, 894n36,
    894n37
Zumthor, Peter 835n2
Zürich (Switzerland) 487, 793
Zwimpfer Partner Architekten 831,
    835n2, 856, 857

Interview Participants

William C. Agee is an American art historian, writer, museum director, curator, and educator. He curated the 1968 exhibition *Don Judd* at the Whitney Museum of American Art, New York.

Pétur Arason is an Icelandic collector and curator. He founded the exhibition space Safn, in Berlin and Reykjavík, with the artist Ragna Róbertsdóttir.

Michael Archer is a British critic and writer on modern and contemporary art.

Ingólfur Arnarsson is an Icelandic artist. He was invited by Donald Judd to the Chinati Foundation in 1992 as a resident artist, where he prepared an exhibition that later became part of the foundation's permanent collection.

Gunnar Jóhannes Árnason is an Icelandic art critic and philosopher who has written extensively about Icelandic art and art history.

Friedrich Teja Bach is a German art historian.

Jo Baer is an American painter living and working in Amsterdam. Her work has been the subject of numerous monographic exhibitions at national and international venues.

Elizabeth C. Baker is an American art writer and editor. She was the editor in chief of *Art in America* from 1974 until 2008.

Darby Bannard was an American abstract painter and a leading figure in the development of color field painting in the late 1950s.

David Batchelor is a Scottish artist and writer.

Michael Blackwood is an American independent documentary filmmaker. Since 1959, he has produced and directed over 150 films.

Markus Brüderlin was a Swiss curator, art historian, museum director, and writer.

Paul Cabon is a French professor of art history and design theory. He was previously the director of the Fonds régional d'art contemporain in Normandy, France.

John Chamberlain was an American sculptor. The Chamberlain Building at the Chinati Foundation includes twenty-two of his works in painted and chromium-plated steel installed by Chamberlain and Donald Judd; it opened in spring 1983 as the foundation's first publicly accessible, permanent installation.

Russell Connor is an American painter and museum educator.

John Coplans was a British artist, art writer, curator, and museum director. He was on the founding editorial staff of *Artforum*.

Mark di Suvero is an American artist whose architectural-scale, interactive sculptures have been exhibited throughout the world.

Beth Fagan covered the Portland art scene for over thirty years. She began working at *The Oregonian* as an art editor in 1964.

John Fekner is an American multidisciplinary artist. He received his BFA from the New York Institute of Technology in 1972.

Chris Felver is an American filmmaker and photographer.

Dan Flavin was an American artist known for his work with fluorescent lights. His large-scale work in colored fluorescent light for six buildings at the Chinati Foundation was initiated in the early 1980s, although the final plans were not completed until 1996. The permanent work was inaugurated in October 2000.

Kerry Freeman founded Dallas's N.NO.0 Gallery in 1989, which exhibited the work of Aldo Rossi and David Lynch, among others, before closing in 1991. He held an internship at the Chinati Foundation in 1994.

J. (Jessie) Nebraska Gifford is an American artist and member of the International Society of Copier Artists. Gifford married M.B. Shestack in 1965.

Shelley Gilbert-Allison was the editor of the *Marfa Independent* and *The Big Bend Sentinel*.

Ólafur Gíslason is an Icelandic artist. He has exhibited widely in Iceland and Europe.

Bruce Glaser was the director of several art galleries in New York. He conducted radio interviews with emerging and prominent artists in the 1960s.

Grace Glueck is an American arts journalist. She wrote and edited for *The New York Times* from the 1960s until the early 2010s.

Amy Goldin was an American art critic and painter. She attended the Art Students League, New York, and Black Mountain College, North Carolina.

John Griffiths was a British illustrator and printmaker.

Joshua Homnick is an American filmmaker and creative consultant based in Los Angeles.

Bruce Duff Hooton was an American art critic and editor. In 1975, he founded the monthly newspaper *Art/World*.

Angeli Janhsen is a German art historian. She studied with Max Imdahl at the Kunstgeschichtliches Institut of the Ruhr-Universität Bochum, Germany.

Fietta Jarque is a Spanish journalist and writer. She began writing for *El País* in 1984 and was later the editor and art critic of the newspaper's culture section.

Claudia Jolles is a Swiss curator, writer, and editor.

Hans Keller is a Dutch journalist, screenwriter, director, producer, and documentary filmmaker. He began working for VPRO in 1969.

Seungduk Kim is a Korean curator. In 2000, she joined Le Consortium (now the Consortium Museum), a contemporary art center in Dijon, France, where she is now codirector.

Kasper König is a German museum director and curator. He cofounded Skulptur Projekte Münster in 1977.

Jean-Claude Lebensztejn is a French art historian, critic, and honorary professor at the Université Paris 1 Panthéon-Sorbonne.

Klaus Stefan Leuschel is a German writer on architecture and design.

Lucy R. Lippard is an American writer, activist, curator, cofounder of various activist artists groups (including Heresies, Printed Matter, and PAD/D), and the author of twenty-four books on contemporary art and cultural studies.

Kynaston McShine was a Trinidadian museum curator and director, first at the Jewish Museum, New York, where he curated the influential 1966 exhibition *Primary Structures: Younger American and British Sculptors*, and then, from 1968 to 2008, at The Museum of Modern Art, New York.

Ed Mieczkowski was an American painter and a founding member of the American art group Anonima, which was active from 1960 to 1971.

Catherine Millet is a French writer, art critic, curator, and the founder and editor of *Artpress*.

Lars Morell is a Danish historian of ideas, specializing in art of the 1960s.

Suzanne Muchnic is an American art writer and a longtime contributor to the *Los Angeles Times*.

Ariane Müller is an Austrian artist, writer, and publisher. With Linda Bilda, she copublished *Artfan*, a Vienna-based art fanzine, between 1991 and 1995.

Alexandra Munroe is an American curator, Asia scholar, and author. She guest-curated *Yayoi Kusama: A Retrospective* for the Center for International Contemporary Arts, New York, the center's 1989 inaugural exhibition.

Ian North is a New Zealand curator, visual artist, and art writer. He is emeritus curator at the Art Gallery of South Australia, Adelaide.

Rosemarie E. Pahlke is a German art historian.

Charles Parkhurst was an American curator, museum director, and administrator.

Jochen Poetter is a German art historian, curator, and museum director.

Larry Poons is an American artist. He taught at the Art Students League, New York, from 1966 to 1970 and returned to teach at the league in 1997.

May Tupper Quick was an American artist and teacher known for her work in batik. She lived for fifty-five years in Marfa, Texas.

Emily Rauh (later Emily Rauh Pulitzer) is an American curator and collector. She was a curator at the Saint Louis Art Museum from 1964 to 1973 and founded the Pulitzer Arts Foundation, Saint Louis, in 2001.

Robert Rauschenberg was an American artist who worked in painting, sculpture, photography, printmaking, and performance. In 1964, he became the first American to win the Grand Prize at the Venice Biennale.

Barbara Rose is an American art historian, critic, and curator. She was educated at Smith College, Northampton, Massachusetts; the Université Paris-Sorbonne; and Columbia University, New York, where, while obtaining a PhD in art history, she met Donald Judd, who was working toward a master's in the same subject.

Georg Schöllhammer is an Austrian curator, writer, and editor. He was one of the founders and the editor in chief of the quarterly Vienna-based art magazine *Springerin*.

M.B. (Melvin Bernard) Shestack was an American editor, author, filmmaker, and television producer. Shestack married J. Nebraska Gifford in 1965.

Jeanne Siegel was an American art historian, critic, and editor. She was the chair of the fine arts and art history departments at the School of Visual Arts, New York, from 1976 to 2005.

Richard Stankiewicz was an American sculptor who worked primarily in scrap metal.

Frank Stella is an American artist. Early in his career, his work was included in a number of significant exhibitions that defined postwar modern art.

Paul Taylor was an Australian art critic, curator, editor, and publisher. In 1981, he founded the contemporary art journal *Art & Text*.

Reiko Tomii is a Japanese independent art historian. She was senior research associate at the Center for International Contemporary Arts, New York, from 1988 to 1992, and conducted biographical and bibliographic research for *Yayoi Kusama: A Retrospective*, the center's 1989 inaugural exhibition.

Ernest Trova was an American painter and sculptor, known for his *Falling Man* series. He was born in Saint Louis, where he lived and worked throughout his life.

Phyllis Tuchman is an American art critic and historian. She writes for *ARTnews*, *Artforum*, and *The New York Times*.

Pilar Viladas is a writer and editor in the fields of design and architecture. She was a design editor at *The New York Times* from 1997 to 2013.

Diane Waldman is an American curator and writer. She was previously deputy director and senior curator of the Solomon R. Guggenheim Museum, New York.

Margot Willett (later Willett-Getsinger) received a PhD in education from the University of Massachusetts at Amherst. Her doctoral dissertation focused on community arts development in rural communities.

Katharina Winnekes is a German art historian and editor. She was previously an editor at *Kunst und Kirche*.

Regina Wyrwoll is a German art historian, filmmaker, and writer. She has worked internationally as a media producer for the Goethe-Institut.

Collection and Photography Credits

Pages 26–27:
Gianfranco Verna and Donald Judd
at 101 Spring Street, second floor,
Judd Foundation, New York, 1984.
Photo: Doris Lehni Quarella
© Antonio Monaci

Image 1:
Collection of Jill and Peter Kraus

Image 2:
Photo courtesy Paula Cooper
Gallery, New York

Image 3:
Photo courtesy Paula Cooper
Gallery, New York

Image 4:
Judd Foundation.
Photo © Judd Foundation

Image 5:
Judd Foundation.
Photo © Judd Foundation

Image 6:
National Gallery of Canada,
Ottawa. Purchased 1974

Image 7:
Photo: The Jewish Museum,
New York/Art Resource, NY

Image 8:
Judd Foundation.
Photo © Judd Foundation

Image 9:
Judd Foundation.
Photo © Judd Foundation

Image 10:
Photo courtesy Castelli Gallery,
New York

Image 11:
Judd Foundation.
Photo: Alex Marks
© Judd Foundation

Image 12:
Private collection.
Photo © 2019 Christie's Images
Limited

Image 13:
Judd Foundation.
Photo © Judd Foundation

Image 14:
Judd Foundation.
Photo © Judd Foundation

Image 15:
Judd Foundation.
Photo © Judd Foundation

Image 16:
Photo courtesy Judd Foundation

Image 17:
Photo: Geoffrey Clements,
courtesy Whitney Museum of
American Art, New York

Image 18:
Photo: Geoffrey Clements,
courtesy Whitney Museum of
American Art, New York

Image 19:
Photo © Judd Foundation

Image 20:
Judd Foundation.
Photo © Judd Foundation

Image 21:
Judd Foundation.
Photo © Judd Foundation

Image 22:
Judd Foundation.
Photo © Judd Foundation

Image 23:
Judd Foundation.
Photo © Judd Foundation

Image 24:
Judd Foundation.
Photo: Alex Marks
© Judd Foundation

Image 25:
Private collection.
Photo: Tim Nighswander/
Imaging4Art, courtesy Judd
Foundation and David Zwirner

Image 26:
Whitney Museum of American
Art, New York. Purchase, with
funds from the Howard and Jean
Lipman Foundation, Inc.
Photo: Ron Amstutz, courtesy
Whitney Museum of American
Art, New York

Image 27:
Judd Foundation.
Photo © Judd Foundation

Image 28:
Judd Foundation.
Photo © Judd Foundation

Image 29:
Judd Foundation.
Photo © Judd Foundation

Image 30:
Collection Martin Z. Margulies

Image 31:
Hirshhorn Museum and Sculpture
Garden, Smithsonian Institution,
Washington, DC. Joseph H. Hirshhorn
Purchase Fund, 1991.
Photo: Lee Stalsworth

Image 32:
Judd Foundation.
Photo © Judd Foundation

Image 33:
Private collection

Image 34:
Collection Pinault.
Photo: Tom Powel Imaging

Image 35:
Judd Foundation.
Photo: Alex Marks
© Judd Foundation

Image 36:
Judd Foundation.
Photo: Alex Marks
© Judd Foundation

Image 37:
Private collection, Chicago.
Photo: Tim Nighswander/
Imaging4Art, courtesy Judd
Foundation and David Zwirner

Image 38:
Judd Foundation.
Photo © Judd Foundation

Image 39:
Photo courtesy Whitney Museum
of American Art, New York

Image 40:
Judd Foundation.
Photo: Alex Marks
© Judd Foundation

Image 41:
Judd Foundation.
Photo © Judd Foundation

Image 42:
Photo courtesy Judd Foundation

Image 43:
Judd Foundation.
Photo: Alex Marks
© Judd Foundation

Image 44:
Judd Foundation.
Photo © Judd Foundation.
Art © 2019 Fairweather &
Fairweather LTD/Artists Rights
Society (ARS), New York

Image 45:
Solomon R. Guggenheim Museum,
New York. Purchased with aid of
funds from the National Endowment
for the Arts in Washington, DC,
a Federal Agency; matching funds
contributed by The Louis and Bessie
Adler Foundation, Inc., Seymour
M. Klein, President.
Photo: Paul Katz © SRGF, NY

Image 46:
Judd Foundation.
Photo © Judd Foundation

Image 47:
Photo © Judd Foundation

Image 48:
Photo © Judd Foundation

Image 49:
Judd Foundation.
Photo: Alex Marks
© Judd Foundation

Image 50:
Art Gallery of South Australia,
Adelaide. South Australian Govern-
ment Grant in association with
Marshall & Brougham Pty Ltd 1974.
Photo courtesy Judd Foundation

Image 51:
Collection of the Philip Johnson
Glass House, National Trust for
Historic Preservation, New Canaan,
Connecticut.
Photo: Eric Pollitzer, courtesy
The Glass House, New Canaan,
Connecticut

Image 52:
Photo courtesy Judd Foundation

Image 53:
Photo courtesy Judd Foundation

Image 54:
Photo courtesy Judd Foundation

Image 55:
Photo © 2019 Christie's Images
Limited

Image 56:
Los Angeles County Museum of Art.
Purchased with funds provided by
the Modern and Contemporary
Art Council and Robert H. Halff.
Digital Image © 2019 Museum
Associates/LACMA. Licensed by Art
Resource, NY

Image 57:
City of Münster.
Photo courtesy Judd Foundation

Image 58:
Collection Kröller-Müller Museum,
Otterlo, The Netherlands

Image 59:
Josef Albers Museum Quadrat
Bottrop.
Photo: Werner J. Hannappel
© Artists Rights Society (ARS),
New York/VG Bild-Kunst, Bonn

Image 60:
Permanent collection of the
Chinati Foundation, Marfa, Texas.
Photo: Douglas Tuck, courtesy the
Chinati Foundation, Marfa, Texas

Image 61:
Permanent collection of the
Chinati Foundation, Marfa, Texas.
Photo: Douglas Tuck, courtesy the
Chinati Foundation, Marfa, Texas

Image 62:
Judd Foundation.
Photo © Judd Foundation

Image 63:
Judd Foundation.
Photo: Alex Marks
© Judd Foundation

Image 64:
Private collection.
Photo courtesy Judd Foundation

Image 65:
Photo © Elizabeth Felicella, courtesy
Judd Foundation

Image 66:
Herbert Foundation, Ghent.
Photo: Philippe De Gobert

Image 67:
Judd Foundation.
Photo © Judd Foundation

Image 68:
Private collection.
Photo: Michel Nguyen, courtesy
Galerie Lelong, Paris

Image 69:
Judd Foundation.
Photo © Judd Foundation

Image 70:
Photo © Elizabeth Baker, courtesy
Judd Foundation

Image 71:
Judd Foundation.
Photo © Judd Foundation

Image 72:
Judd Foundation.
Photo © Judd Foundation

Image 73:
Private collection.
Photo courtesy Paula Cooper
Gallery, New York

Image 74:
Photo: Philipp Schönborn,
courtesy Staatliche Kunsthalle
Baden-Baden, Germany

Image 75:
Photo: Albert Winkler, courtesy
Judd Foundation

Image 76:
Judd Foundation.
Photo: Silvia Ros, courtesy
ICA Miami

Image 77:
Photo © Judd Foundation

Image 78:
Photo © Judd Foundation

Image 79:
Photo: Donald Judd
© Judd Foundation

Image 80:
Photo: Donald Judd
© Judd Foundation

Image 81:
Photo © FBM Studio

Image 82:
Photo © Adrian Jolles

Image 83:
Photo: Margherita Spiluttini
© Architekturzentrum Wien

Image 84:
Judd Foundation.
Photo © Judd Foundation

Image 85:
Judd Foundation.
Photo © Judd Foundation

Image 86:
Photo © Gerald Zugmann/
MAK – Austrian Museum of
Applied Arts/Contemporary Art

Page 976:
Photo: Fred W. McDarrah/
Premium Archive/Getty Images

Text Credits

Judd Foundation Board and Staff

Donald Judd Interviews

Copublished by

Judd Foundation
101 Spring Street
New York, New York 10012
+1 212 219 2747
104 South Highland Avenue
Marfa, Texas 79843
+1 432 729 4406
juddfoundation.org

David Zwirner Books
529 West 20th Street, 2nd Floor
New York, New York 10011
+1 212 727 2070
davidzwirnerbooks.com

Editors:
Flavin Judd, Caitlin Murray
Project Manager:
Anne Wehr
Project Assistant:
Elizabeth Koehler
Copy Editor:
Clare Fentress
Proofreader:
Anna Drozda
Image Research:
Caitlin Murray
Indexer:
Tanya Izzard

Design:
Flavin Judd, Michael Dyer/Remake
Production Manager:
Jules Thomson
Color Separations:
VeronaLibri, Verona
Printing:
VeronaLibri, Verona

Typeface:
Monotype Bembo
Paper:
Fedrigoni Arcoset, 70 gsm;
GardaMatt Art, 90 gsm

Distributed in the United States
and Canada by
Simon & Schuster, Inc.
1230 Avenue of the Americas
New York, New York 10020
simonandschuster.com

Distributed outside the United States
and Canada by
Thames & Hudson, Ltd.
181A High Holborn
London WC1V 7QX
thamesandhudson.com

ISBN 978-1-64423-016-9
LCCN 2019909644

Printed in Italy